W9-BNR-215

HOW TO DEVELOP YOUR OWN DRAFTING AND REVISING PROCESSES BY:

- Maintaining engagement with your problem (pp. 3–21, 23–27, 417–26)
- Using a variety of exploration techniques (pp. 22–39; Writing Projects chapters)
- Reducing writer's block by lowering expectations for drafts (Chapter 17)
- Following revision practices of experienced writers (pp. 418–27)
- Identifying readers and revising with their needs in mind (pp. 429–32; Chapter 18)
- Editing for gracefulness, clarity, and correctness (pp. 422, 424; Handbooks 1–6)

HOW TO WORK PRODUCTIVELY IN GROUPS BY:

- Viewing writing as "joining a conversation" (pp. 6–7, 509–10)
- Listening to the views of your classmates (pp. 510–14)
- Working together to brainstorm and solve problems (pp. 517–18)
- Collaborating through electronic media (pp. 588–602)
- Becoming an effective peer reviewer (pp. 517–18; Guidelines for Peer Reviewers in the Writing Projects chapters)
- Using peer feedback to stimulate revision of your drafts (pp. 429–32, 517–18)

HOW TO BECOME AN EFFECTIVE RESEARCHER BY:

- Unlocking resources of libraries (pp. 527–35)
- Finding resources in your community (pp. 535–38)
- Using the Internet and World Wide Web (pp. 602–06)
- Incorporating sources into your writing through summary, paraphrase, and quotation (pp. 110–15, 138, 540–54)
- Avoiding plagiarism (pp. 552–54)
- Citing and documenting your sources (pp. 554–87)

HOW TO PERFORM WELL IN EVALUATIVE SETTINGS BY:

- Writing effective essay exams (Chapter 24)
- Writing reflective self-evaluations (Chapter 25)

HOW TO EDIT YOUR PROSE FOR CORRECTNESS AND GRACE BY:

- Improving your editing process (pp. 653–55)
- Avoiding comma splices, run-ons, and fragments (Handbook 3)
- Editing for Standard English usage (Handbook 4)
- Editing for style (Handbook 5)
- Editing for punctuation and mechanics (Handbook 6)

Second Edition

The
Allyn and Bacon
Guide to Writing

John D. Ramage
Arizona State University

John C. Bean
Seattle University

ALLYN AND BACON

Boston

London

Toronto

Sydney

Tokyo

Singapore

Vice President: Eben W. Ludlow
Editorial Assistant: Grace Trudo
Executive Marketing Manager: Lisa Kimball
Editorial-Production Administrator: Susan Brown
Editorial-Production Service: Matrix Productions
Text Designer: Glenna Collett
Composition Buyer: Linda Cox
Manufacturing Buyer: Suzanne Lareau
Cover Administrator: Linda Knowles

Copyright © 2000, 1997 by Allyn & Bacon
A Pearson Education Company
160 Gould Street
Needham Heights, MA 02494
Internet: www.abacon.com

All rights reserved. No part of the material protected by this copyright notice
may be reproduced or utilized in any form or by any means, electronic or
mechanical, including photocopying, recording, or by any information
storage and retrieval system, without written permission from the copyright holder.

Library-of-Congress Cataloging-in-Publication Data
Ramage, John D.
    The Allyn and Bacon guide to writing / John D. Ramage, John C.
Bean. — 2nd ed.
        p.   cm.
    Includes index.
    ISBN 0-205-29791-9
    1. English language—Rhetoric—Handbooks, manuals, etc.   2. English
language—Grammar Handbooks, manuals, etc.   3. Report writing
Handbooks, manuals, etc. 4. College readers.   I. Bean, John C.
II. Title.
PE1408.R18   1999b
808'.0427—dc21   99-22480
                                                                                    CIP

Printed in the United States of America
10 9 8 7 6 5   03 02 01 00

Acknowledgments:
    Page 3.   Rodney Kilcup, "A Modest Proposal for Reluctant Writers," *Newsletter of the Pacific North-west Writing Consortium* 2, no. 3 (September 1982): 5.
    Page 4.   Stephen D. Brookfield, *Developing Critical Thinkers: Challenging Adults to Explore Alternative Ways of Thinking and Acting* (San Francisco: Jossey-Bass, 1987): 5.
    Page 5.   Andrea Lunsford and Lisa Ede, *Singular Texts/Plural Authors: Perspective on Collaborative Writing.* (Carbondale and Edwardsville, IL: Southern Illinois University Press, 1992): 21, 45–48.

Acknowledgments continue on page 726, which constitutes a continuation of the copyright page.

Brief Contents

p   α   r   t   **T   H   R   E   E**

A Guide to Composing and Revising   415

p   α   r   t   **F   O   U   R**

A Guide to Research   521

p   α   r   t   **F   I   V   E**

A Guide to Special Writing Occasions   609

p a r t **S I X**

A Guide to Editing 641

W R I T I N G   P R O J E C T S

Brief Projects

Major Projects

Contents

p α r t

T W O *Writing Projects* 77

Writing to Learn

c h a p t e r **5** *Seeing Rhetorically: The Writer as Observer* 79

Writing to Express

Writing to Explore

Writing to Inform

Writing to Analyze

chapter **13**   *Investigating Questions About Cause and Consequence*   288

Writing to Persuade

chapter **14**   *Writing a Classical Argument*   316

p   a   r   t

THREE   *A Guide To Composing and Revising*   415

chapter **23** *Electronic Writing and Research* 588

part

FIVE *A Guide to Special Writing Occasions* 609

chapter **24** *Essay Examinations: Writing Polished Prose
in a Hurry* 611

chapter **25**   *Writing a Reflective Self-Evaluation*   628

p a r t

S I X   *A Guide to Editing*   641

Handbook **1**   *Improving Your Editing Skills*   643

Handbook **2** *Understanding Sentence Structure* 650

Handbook **3** *Punctuating Boundaries of Sentences, Clauses,
and Phrases* 664

Handbook **4**   *Editing for Standard English Usage*   674

Handbook **5**   *Editing for Style*   690

Abbreviations 723

Manuscript Form 724

Thematic Contents

The Allyn and Bacon Guide to Writing, second edition, contains 58 readings—38 by professional writers and 20 by students. These readings can be clustered thematically in the following ways:

Nature and Ecology

Issues of Race and Class

Perceptions of Gender

Educational Choices

Thinking Scientifically

Popular Culture and Advertising

Identity and Values

Social Problems and Public Choices

Preface

Gratified by the success of the first edition of *The Allyn and Bacon Guide to Writing,* we have attempted in this second edition to retain the text's original strengths while making judicious changes aimed at enhancing clarity, comprehensiveness, and usefulness in the classroom.

In creating *The Allyn and Bacon Guide to Writing,* we set for ourselves three major goals. First we wanted to create a comprehensive rhetoric that integrated up-to-date composition theory with pedagogical research in critical thinking, inquiry, and assignment design. Second, we wanted our book to be a pleasure for teachers to use in the classroom. The book had to be intellectually stimulating for teachers, be easily adaptable to a wide range of course designs and curricular goals, and guide students toward idea-rich essays that teachers would enjoy reading. Finally, and most important, we wanted the book to be valuable to students. By rooting writing in a student's engagement with an intellectually interesting problem or question, we hoped to prepare students for academic tasks across the curriculum.

Enthusiastic responses from users of the first edition show that we achieved these goals. The book, in either the regular or brief edition, has been adopted at a wide range of two- and four-year institutions. From all quarters, instructors have praised the book's success in linking practical classroom activities to a sound theoretical base, forming the structure for a coherent, intellectually stimulating course.

◩ DISTINCTIVE FEATURES OF THE TEXT

The second edition retains the following distinctive features that characterized the first edition:

- An emphasis on problem posing, critical thinking, and inquiry
- An emphasis on writing as a rhetorical act in which writers pose both subject-matter questions about content and rhetorical questions about purpose, audience, and genre
- The concept of a continuum from closed to open forms of writing in which the writer's choice of form is always a function of the rhetorical situation
- Concentration on academic/professional writing balanced with personal and narrative forms

- Carefully designed, class-tested writing projects that engage students with interesting and significant problems and guide them through the writing processes used by experts
- An emphasis on exploratory writing, talking, and collaborative learning through frequent For Writing and Discussion exercises that promote inquiry and complex thinking
- Copious professional and student readings throughout the text chosen to stimulate inquiry and discussion and to illustrate a range of rhetorical strategies and structures
- A flexible organizational structure that facilitates different emphases, course structures, and course lengths
- Thorough treatment of rhetorical concerns in Part One (question asking, inquiry, aims, relation of closed and open forms to the writer's purpose, audience, genre) and of compositional concerns in Part Three (composing processes, peer review sessions, revising and editing strategies for both closed- and open-form prose, use of groups)
- Student-tested Guidelines for Peer Reviewers at the conclusion of each chapter in Part Two

▨ WHAT'S NEW IN THE SECOND EDITION?

While retaining the distinctive features of the first edition, we have added new features that increase the flexibility, breadth, and classroom usefulness of the text.

- *Twenty new professional readings (out of thirty-eight total) chosen for high student interest and for a range of styles and genres.* For example, Chapter 6, "Reading Rhetorically," contains an academic article on teenage tattooing by a psychiatrist, an essay on racism and legal writing by attorney Patricia J. Williams, and an article from the *National Review* comparing the education systems of the United States and Japan. Later chapters include articles with similar variety—for example, one praising the sitcom *Roseanne* for its sensitivity to the working class; another analyzing sexism in *Sesame Street;* and still another examining the dilemma of a biracial young man having to indicate "race" on a questionnaire.
- *Nine new student essays (out of twenty total) on a variety of engaging topics.* Susan Meyers' causal analysis of anorexia in Chapter 13 illustrates a student research paper in APA style. Other new student essays include pieces on old-growth forests (Chapter 14), on the film *Picnic at Hanging Rock* (Chapter 15), and on the rhetorical use of statistics in an article about troubled teenagers (Chapter 11).
- *A new chapter (Chapter 24) on writing self-reflective evaluations.* This chapter teaches students strategies for doing self-reflective thinking and for writing reflective evaluations of drafts in progress or end-of-term self-evaluations to

accompany portfolios. Particularly useful in programs requiring portfolios, this chapter's ideas can be integrated into any course.

- *An effective new method of integrating instruction on revision into a course.* As part of our substantial reconceptualizing of Part Three, "A Guide to Composing and Revising," we have consolidated the materials on closed form prose into one chapter (Chapter 18), presenting nine short, self-contained lessons, each of which can be covered in one class session or assigned as one day's homework. These lessons can be covered sequentially or taught independently at appropriate moments throughout a writing course.
- *A new section on evaluating websites.* Used as an illustration of evaluation arguments in Chapter 15, this section can be assigned independently as a supplement to any research unit.

WHAT'S IMPROVED IN THE SECOND EDITION?

Besides adding new features, we have improved the second edition by making numerous smaller changes and revisions.

- General streamlining throughout the book with improved examples, more concise explanations, and clearer use of headings. Examples used to illustrate concepts now include an explanatory title and annotations to make ideas readily graspable and available for quick reference.
- An enriched discussion of style in Chapter 4, "Solving Rhetorical Problems: Purpose, Audience, and Genre," including creative imitation exercises to develop students' stylistic options at the sentence level.
- Extensive revision of Chapter 6, "Reading Rhetorically," with new readings, student examples, and a clearer, more unified writing assignment.
- A shortened, more interesting, and timelier discussion of numerical analysis in Chapter 11, including a revised writing assignment. The chapter's explanatory material now focuses on the distribution of wealth in the United States and includes an example student essay.
- A more focused treatment of analyzing a short story (Chapter 12) and the substitution of a Gabriel García Márquez story for the Maupassant. A new student essay on Alice Walker's "Everyday Use" lets students compare the analysis to the short story.
- An extensively revised treatment of argument (Chapter 14), including new professional and student readings. The revision includes more examples, sequences material more effectively, emphasizes argument as truth seeking rather than pro/con debate, and focuses more clearly and helpfully on argument as a rhetorical act.
- More hands-on explanations and exercises of evaluative writing (Chapter 15), including a new student essay evaluating an art film. Evaluation arguments are now illustrated by a stand-alone unit on evaluating web sites.

- Material on peer reviewing has been consolidated into Chapter 17 rather than divided into two chapters.
- The discussion of open-form writing (Chapter 19) has been shortened and reorganized; new annotated examples pragmatically package and illustrate the concepts for student use.
- Part Four on research writing includes updated explanations of MLA and APA documentation styles, with the latest guidelines for citing electronic sources.

◾ STRUCTURE OF *THE ALLYN AND BACON GUIDE TO WRITING*

Part One, "A Rhetoric for College Writers," provides a conceptual framework for the text by showing how writers pose problems, pursue them through exploratory writing and talking, and try to solve them as they compose and revise. Chapter 1 shows how writers grapple with both subject matter and rhetorical problems, introducing the concept of a continuum from closed to open forms of prose. Chapter 2 presents an array of techniques for exploring ideas and deepening inquiry, including strategies for making exploratory writing and talking a regular habit.

Chapters 3 and 4 together describe the kinds of problems that experienced writers try to solve as they compose. Chapter 3 explains how academic writers pose good questions, formulate a surprising thesis, and support that thesis through a hierarchical structure of points and particulars. Chapter 4 shifts from subject matter problems to rhetorical problems, demonstrating that decisions about content, structure, and style are controlled by a writer's purpose, intended audience, and genre.

Part Two, "Writing Projects," contains twelve self-contained assignment chapters arranged according to purposes for writing: to learn, to express, to explore, to inform, to analyze, and to persuade. Each chapter within this part has a consistent structure that guides students through the process of generating and exploring ideas, composing and drafting, and revising and editing. The heart of each chapter is a writing project designed to teach students new ways of seeing and thinking. The project is defined early in the chapter so that students will be pondering the problem it poses as they absorb the chapter's explanatory material. The exploratory exercises throughout each assignment chapter help students generate ideas for their essays while developing their skills at posing problems, delaying closure, speaking back to texts, valuing alternative points of view, and thinking dialectically. A set of Guidelines for Peer Reviewers concludes each chapter, showing students how to critique classmates' drafts and revise their own.

Part Three, "A Guide to Composing and Revising," focuses on nuts-and-bolts strategies for composing and revising along the continuum from closed to open forms. Its four self-contained chapters can be read in any sequence at the instructor's discretion.

Chapter 17 explains how experienced writers use multiple drafts to manage the complexities of writing and suggests ways that students can improve their own writing processes. It also includes instruction on how to conduct peer reviews. Chapter 18 presents nine brief lessons on composing and revising closed-form prose. Designed for easy integration into a course, each lesson can be covered easily in an hour or less. The lessons themselves—derived from reader expectation theory and studies of textual coherence—explain both the theory and practice of effective revision. In Chapter 19, the focus shifts from closed to open forms that play with conventions in various ways. Exploring major differences between open- and closed-form writing, the chapter offers advice on how to "open up" prose in appropriate rhetorical situations. Finally, Chapter 20 shows students how working in small groups can help them generate ideas, solve problems, and gather feedback for revision.

Part Four, "A Guide to Research," is an introduction to conducting research and incorporating sources into prose. Chapter 21 guides students through the process of posing and focusing a research problem and of unlocking the resources of libraries and one's community. Chapter 22 explains how to summarize, paraphrase, quote sources, and avoid plagiarism. The most recent MLA and APA formats for citing and documenting sources—including electronic media—are provided. Finally, Chapter 23 introduces students to a wealth of new online resources for writers. Introducing options available through the Internet and World Wide Web, it suggests ways to explore and develop ideas, work collaboratively, conduct research, and evaluate sources.

Part Five, "Writing for Special Occasions" covers essay examinations and reflective self-evaluations. Chapter 24, "A Guide to Writing Under Pressure," draws on research into the demands of timed writing, showing students how to plan and draft an exam essay by applying the principles of rhetorical assessment discussed throughout the text. Chapter 25, "Writing Self-Reflective Evaluations," is new to the second edition. Written by Alice Gillam, Director of Writing at the University of Wisconsin–Milwaukee, this chapter draws on research in reflective writing to teach students how to think metacognitively about their own composing processes and thus to produce helpful self-reflective evaluations of a draft in progress or an end-of-term portfolio.

Finally, Part Six, "A Guide to Editing," provides a brief review, with exercises, of the sentence-level skills students need to produce polished writing. The first chapter develops self-assessment skills and includes a series of brief write-to-learn microthemes aimed at helping students learn important grammatical and stylistic concepts. The second chapter reviews basic concepts of grammar and sentence structure. The third chapter explains fragments, comma splices, and run-ons within the context of the main punctuation rules for signaling phrases and clauses to readers. The fourth and fifth chapters address usage and style concerns, and the final chapter is devoted to punctuation and mechanics. Throughout the handbook, revision and editing symbols appear in the margin to indicate key points addressed in each section. A list of the page numbers on which these symbols appear is printed on the inside back cover of the text so that students can quickly locate help for specific problems.

STRATEGIES FOR USING *THE ALLYN AND BACON GUIDE TO WRITING*

The logic of the text's organizational structure makes it easy to design a syllabus. The overarching rhetorical concepts that students should know early in the course are developed in Part One, while explanations of compositional strategies and skills—which students will practice recursively throughout the course—are placed in Part Three. Students can work their way through assigned material in Part Three while engaged with writing projects from Part Two. Additional instructional material related to research and to special writing occasions are included in Parts Four and Five.

Although there are many ways to use *The Allyn and Bacon Guide to Writing,* the most typical course design has students read Chapters 1–4 (Part One) during the opening weeks. The brief, informal write-to-learn projects in these chapters engage students with the instructional material while allowing teachers to assess students' initial writing skills.

For the rest of the course, instructors typically assign writing project chapters from the array of options available in Part Two, Chapters 5–16. While students are engaged with the writing projects in these chapters, instructors can assign material from the compositional chapters in Part Three, or from the additional instructional materials in Parts Four and Five and the Handbook, selected and sequenced according to their own needs. (For suggestions on how to select and sequence materials from Parts Three, Four, and Five, see the sample syllabi in the *Instructor's Resource Manual.*) While students are working on a writing project, classroom discussion can alternate between issues related directly to the assignment (invention exercises, group brainstorming, peer review workshops) and those focusing on instructional matter from the rest of the text.

USING THE WRITING PROJECTS IN PART TWO

Because each of the twelve assignment chapters in Part Two is self-contained, instructors can select and organize the writing projects in the way that best fits their course goals and their students' needs. The projects in Chapters 5 and 6 introduce students to the rhetorical ways of observing and reading that underpin mature academic thinking, showing students how to analyze a text, pose questions about it, and understand and resist the text's rhetorical strategies.

Chapter 7 on autobiographical narrative is the text's primary "open-form" assignment. Introducing students to strategies of plot, character, and dramatic tension, the project often produces surprisingly sophisticated narratives. Some teachers like to give this assignment early in the course—on the grounds that personal writing should precede more academic forms. Others like to give it last—on the grounds that open-form writing is more complex and subtle than closed-form prose. We have found that either choice can work well.

Chapter 8's assignment, an exploratory essay, asks students to narrate their engagement with a problem and their attempts to resolve it. Teachers may want to pair this chapter with Part Four on research writing, using the exploratory essay as the first stage of a major research project. The two student essays in this chapter are in fact early explorations for finished projects that appear later in the text.

Chapter 9 on informative writing urges students to reach beyond straightforward reporting by employing a "surprising reversal" strategy aimed at altering the reader's initial assumptions about the topic. Surprising reversal is a powerful rhetorical move that can be used to enliven almost any kind of informative, analytical, or persuasive prose.

The four writing projects in the analysis section (Chapters 10–13) allow instructors to select among different kinds of phenomena for analysis: images in advertising (Chapter 10), numerical data (Chapter 11), a short story (Chapter 12), or causes/consequences (Chapter 13). These chapters teach the generic skills of close observation, close reading, and close attention to detail while offering specific guidance in the skills unique to each category of analysis.

The persuasion chapters (Chapters 14–16) teach key concepts of argumentation. Providing a strong introduction to both academic and civil argument, they combine accessible Toulmin and stasis approaches while emphasizing argument as truth seeking and consensus seeking rather than win/lose debate.

FLEXIBILITY OF *THE ALLYN AND BACON GUIDE TO WRITING*

Although *The Allyn and Bacon Guide to Writing* is a comprehensive rhetoric, we have consciously designed it to be highly teachable in a wide variety of courses and settings. The first edition has been used successfully in courses with different lengths and focuses and with students at all levels of preparation from developmental to advanced. In the second edition, we have focused even more consciously on making the text versatile and flexible.

Our goal has been to structure a text that offers instructors multiple possibilities for course design. To that end, *The Allyn and Bacon Guide to Writing* allows numerous options for selecting and sequencing chapters to suit courses with different writing emphases and student needs. Instructors may teach some chapters thoroughly, using all the class activities and exploratory writing as well as major writing projects while assigning others largely for students' preparation outside class. Some chapters may be taught in numerical sequence; others may be skipped or paired in a particular course. Our intent has been to give instructors appealing choices and to equip them with pedagogical material that has both depth and breadth.

◪ SUPPLEMENTS FOR *THE ALLYN AND BACON GUIDE TO WRITING*

The *Allyn and Bacon Guide to Writing* is supported by a variety of helpful supplements for instructors and students.

For instructors

- The *Instructor's Resource Manual* by Vicki Byard of Northeastern Illinois University offers detailed teaching suggestions to help both experienced and new instructors: practical teaching strategies for composition instructors in a question-and-answer format; suggested syllabi for courses of various lengths and emphases; chapter-by-chapter teaching suggestions; answers to handbook exercises; suggestions for using the text with non-native speakers; suggestions for using the text in an electronic classroom; transparency masters for class use; and annotated bibliographies.
- *The Allyn and Bacon Guide to Writing Website* enables instructors to access on-line writing activities and weblinks keyed to specific chapters; post and make changes to their syllabi; hold chat sessions with individual students or groups of students; and receive e-mail and essay assignments directly from students. *http://www.abacon.com/ramage*
- *An Introduction to Teaching Composition in an Electronic Environment,* developed by Eric Hoffman and Carol Scheidenhelm, both of Northern Illinois University, offers a wealth of computer-related classroom activities. It also provides detailed guidance for both experienced and inexperienced instructors who wish to make creative use of technology in a composition environment.
- *The Allyn and Bacon Sourcebook for College Writing Teachers,* second edition, compiled by James C. McDonald of the University of Southwestern Louisiana, provides instructors with a varied selection of readings written by composition and rhetoric scholars on both theoretical and practical subjects.
- *Teaching College Writing,* an invaluable instructor's resource guide developed by Maggy Smith of the University of Texas at El Paso, is available to adopters who wish to explore additional teaching tips and resources.

■ *CompSite Website* is an easily navigable and informative forum for instructors and students of composition. Instructors can learn and share teaching strategies with colleagues. New resources include material on writing across the curriculum, teaching tips for newer instructors, and advice on using technology in the composition classroom. *http://www.abacon.com/compsite*

For students

■ *The Allyn and Bacon Guide to Writing Website* presents chapter summaries; writing activities; the course syllabus; Web links keyed to specific text sections; and the ability to chat with and e-mail classmates and the instructor. *http://www.abacon.com/ramage*

■ *CompSite Website* offers resources and instructional material for students, including helpful information on using computers for writing, techniques for using the Internet for research, and a forum for exchanging papers and writing ideas. *http://www.abacon.com/compsite*

◢ ACKNOWLEDGMENTS

We wish at the outset to thank June Johnson Bube, John Bean's colleague at Seattle University, for collaborating with us on the second edition. An experienced composition teacher who used the first edition of *The Allyn and Bacon Guide to Writing* in a variety of settings and levels, June brought to our project both classroom savvy and an interest in composition theory. She joined us as a virtual co-author for the second edition. We wish also to thank Alice Gillam of the University of Wisconsin-Milwaukee, who wrote the new chapter on self-reflective evaluations (Chapter 25) and Virginia Chappell of Marquette University, who revised Chapter 12 on analyzing a short story. Dan Anderson, who wrote the chapter on electronic writing and research for the first edition, graciously agreed to revise it for this edition (Chapter 23). Finally, we wish to thank again Christy Friend, who wrote Chapter 24 on essay examinations.

Grateful acknowledgment and thanks again go to our editor, Eben Ludlow, vice-president of Allyn & Bacon, with whom we have worked productively over the last fifteen years. Eben deserves his reputation as one of today's premier editors.

To the many scholars and teachers who reviewed *The Allyn and Bacon Guide to Writing* in its many stages we give special thanks: June Johnson Bube, Seattle University; Sandra Carey, Lexington Community College; Virginia Chappell, Marquette University; Reg Gerlica, Henry Ford Community College; Alice M. Gillam, University of Wisconsin–Milwaukee; Loretta S. Gray, Central Washington University; Lorna J. Hallal, University of Central Florida; Chrisa Hotchkiss, Mendocino Community College; John Levine, California State University–Hayward; Mary

Sue MacNealy, University of Memphis; Robin A. Mosher, Kansas State University; and Alison Russell, Xavier University.

Most of all, however, we are indebted to the hundreds of students who, over the past quarter-century, have entered our classrooms and shared with us their enthusiasms, quandaries, and revelations as they strove to become better writers. They sustained our love of teaching and inspired us to write this book.

John C. Bean

John D. Ramage

A Rhetoric for College Writers

part O N E

c h a p t e r   1

Posing Problems
The Demands of College Writing

WHAT YOU WILL LEARN IN THIS CHAPTER

In this chapter we show you that writers are questioners and problem posers who focus on two kinds of problems:

- Subject-matter problems, in which they wrestle with the complexities of their topic
- Rhetorical problems, in which they must make decisions about content, organization, and style based on their purpose, audience, and genre

To illustrate subject matter problems, we present a case study of a beginning college writer. To illustrate rhetorical problems, we show you how the rules of writing vary along a continuum from closed to open prose.

> It seems to me, then, that the way to help people become better writers is not to tell them that they must first learn the rules of grammar, that they must develop a four-part outline, that they must consult the experts and collect all the useful information. These things may have their place. But none of them is as crucial as having a good, interesting question.
>
> —Rodney Kilcup, *Historian*

Our purpose in this introductory chapter is to help you see writers as questioners and problem posers—a view of writing that we believe will lead to your greatest growth as a college-level thinker and writer. In particular, we want you to think of writers as people who pose interesting questions or problems and struggle to work out answers or responses to them. As we will show in this chapter, writers pose two sorts of problems: *subject matter* problems (for example, What is the effect of caffeine on a spider's web-making ability? Should the homeless mentally ill be placed involuntarily in mental hospitals?) and *rhetorical* problems (for example, How much background do my readers need on caffeine research? What is my audience's current view about best treatment for the homeless mentally ill? What alternative solutions do I need to address? What form and style should I use?).

We don't mean to make this focus on problems sound scary. Indeed, humans pose and solve problems all the time and often take great pleasure in doing so. Psychologists who study critical and creative thinking see problem solving as a productive and positive activity. According to one psychologist, "Critical thinkers are actively engaged with life. . . . They appreciate creativity, they are innovators, and they exude a sense that life is full of possibilities."* By focusing first on the kinds of problems that writers pose and struggle with, we hope to increase your own engagement and pleasure in becoming a writer.

This chapter opens by showing you some good reasons for taking a writing course with particular emphasis on the relationship between writing and thinking. We then show how writers are engaged with subject matter questions that drive the writing process and bring writers into community with readers interested in the same questions. Since writers also face rhetorical questions, we provide an extended example—what we call the problem of choosing closed versus open forms. The chapter concludes with a brief writing assignment in which you can try your own hand at proposing a subject matter question.

▨ WHY TAKE A WRITING COURSE?

Before turning directly to the notion of writers as questioners and problem posers, let's ask why a writing course can be valuable for you.

For some people, being a writer is part of their identity, so much so that when asked, "What do you do?" they are apt to respond, "I'm a writer." Poets, novelists, script writers, journalists, technical writers, grant writers, self-help book authors, and so on see themselves as writers the way other people see themselves as chefs, realtors, bankers, or musicians. But many people who don't think of themselves primarily as writers nevertheless *use* writing—often frequently—throughout their careers. They are engineers writing proposals or project reports; attorneys writing legal briefs; nurses writing patient assessments; business executives writing financial analyses or management reports; concerned citizens writing letters to the editor about public affairs; college professors writing articles for scholarly journals.

In our view, all these kinds of writing are valuable and qualify their authors as writers. If you already identify yourself as a writer, then you won't need much external motivation for improving your writing. But if you have little interest in writing for its own sake and aspire instead to become a nurse, an engineer, a busi-

---

*Academic writers regularly document their sources. The standard method for documenting sources in student papers and in many professional scholarly articles is the MLA or APA citation system explained in Chapter 22. By convention, textbook authors usually cite their sources under an "Acknowledgments" section that begins on the copyright page. To find our source for this quotation (or for the quotation from Kilcup at the beginning of this chapter), see the copyright page at the front of the text; acknowledgments continue at the end of the text.

ness executive, a social worker, or a marine biologist, then you might question the benefits of taking a writing course.

What are these benefits? First of all, the skills you learn in this course will be directly transferable to your other college courses, where you will have to write papers in a wide variety of styles. Lower division (general education or core) courses often focus on general academic writing, while upper division courses in your major introduce you to the specialized writing and thinking of your chosen field. What college professors value are the kinds of questioning, analyzing, and arguing skills that this course will help you develop. You will emerge from this course as a better reader and thinker and a clearer and more persuasive writer able to meet the demands of different writing situations.

Effective writing skills are also essential for most professional careers. To measure the importance of writing to career success, researchers Andrea Lunsford and Lisa Ede recently surveyed randomly selected members of such professional organizations as the American Consulting Engineers Counsel, the American Institute of Chemists, the American Psychological Association, and the International City Management Association. They discovered that members of these organizations spent, on the average, 44 percent of their professional time doing writing, including, most commonly, letters, memos, short reports, instructional materials, and professional articles and essays.

Other things being equal, professionals who can write effectively advance further and faster than those who can't. In the workplace, the ability to identify and analyze problems, to propose solutions, and to argue persuasively to different constituencies is critical. Lunsford and Ede report numerous on-the-job situations where written communication skills are crucial. Here, for example, is how one of their respondents—an engineer working as a city planner—described his frustration at not being able to produce adequately persuasive documents:

> After I had been out of school a number of years practicing as a city planner, I had become concerned about why we could develop a good plan for a community and try to explain it to people and they wouldn't seem to understand it. They wouldn't support it for one reason or another. And time and time again we would see a good plan go down the drain because people didn't agree with it or for some reason didn't actively support it.

The city manager describes here a situation often encountered in professional life—the need not only to solve a problem but to sell one's solution to others. As he implies, those who can write clearly and persuasively contribute invaluably to the success of their organizations.

Besides the pragmatic benefits of college and career success, learning to write well can bring you the personal pleasure of a richer mental life. As we show throughout this text, writing is closely allied to thinking and to the innate satisfaction you take in exercising your curiosity, creativity, and problem-solving ability. Writing connects you to others and helps you discover and express ideas that you would otherwise never think or say. Unlike speaking, writing gives you time to think deep and long about an idea. Because you can revise writing, it lets you pursue a problem in stages, with each new draft reflecting a deeper, clearer, or more complex level of thought. In other words, writing isn't just a way to express thought; it is a way to do the thinking itself. The act of writing stimulates, challenges, and stretches your mental powers and, when you do it well, is profoundly satisfying.

▨ SUBJECT-MATTER PROBLEMS: THE STARTING POINT OF WRITING

Having made a connection between writing and thinking, we now move to the spirit of inquiry that drives the writing process. Thus far in your writing career, you may have imagined writing primarily as gathering and assembling information. Someone handed you a broad topic area (for example, contemporary urban America or Renaissance love poetry) or a narrower topic area (homelessness or Shakespeare's sonnets), and you collected and wrote information about that topic. In the process of writing your paper, you may have learned some interesting things about your subject matter. But if you approached your writing in this way, you weren't approximating the thinking processes of most experienced writers. Experienced writers usually see their subject matter in terms of questions or problems rather than broad or narrow topic areas. They typically enjoy posing questions and pursuing answers. They write to share their discoveries and insights with readers interested in the same problems.

Shared Problems Unite Writers and Readers

Everywhere we turn, we see writers and readers forming communities based on questions or problems of mutual interest. Perhaps nowhere are such communities more evident than in academe. Many college professors are engaged in research projects stimulated and driven by questions or problems. At a recent workshop for new faculty members, we asked participants to write a brief description of a question or problem that motivated them to write a seminar paper or article. Here is a sampling of their responses.

> **A Biochemistry Professor**   During periods of starvation, the human body makes physiological adaptations to preserve essential protein mass. Unfortunately, these adaptations don't work well during long-term starvation. After the body depletes its carbohydrate storage, it must shift to depleting protein in order to produce glucose. Eventually, this loss of functional protein leads to metabolic dysfunction and death. Interestingly, several animal species are capable of surviving for extensive periods without food and water while conserving protein and maintaining glucose levels. How do the bodies of these animals accomplish this feat? I wanted to investigate the metabolic functioning of these animals, which might lead to insights into the human situation.

> **A Nursing Professor**   Being a nurse who had worked with terminally ill or permanently unconscious patients, I saw doctors and nurses struggle with the

question of when to withdraw life-support systems. I wondered how philosophers and ethicists went about deciding these issues and how they thought physicians and other clinicians should make the decision to withdraw life support. I wanted to answer this question: What is the relationship between the way "experts" say we should solve complex ethical problems and the way it actually happens in a clinical context? So I chose to look at this problem by reading what philosophers said about this topic and then by interviewing physicians and nurses in long-term care facilities (nursing homes) in the United States and the Netherlands—asking them how they made decisions to withdraw life support from patients with no hope of recovery.

A Journalism Professor   Several years ago, I knocked on the wooden front door of the home of an elderly woman in Tucson, Arizona. Tears of grief rolled down her cheeks as she opened the door. The tears turned to anger when I explained that I was a reporter and wished to talk with her about her son's death in jail. Her face hardened. "What right do you have coming here?" I recall her saying. "Why are you bothering me?" Those questions have haunted me throughout my journalism career. Do journalists have the right to intrude on a person's grief? Can they exercise it any time they want? What values do journalists use to decide when to intrude and violate someone's privacy?

Of course these are not new college students speaking; these are college professors recalling problems that fueled a piece of professional writing. We share these problems with you to persuade you that most college professors value question asking and want you to be caught up, as they are, in the spirit of inquiry.

As you progress through your college career, you will find yourself increasingly engaged with questions. All around college campuses you'll find clusters of professors and students asking questions about all manner of curious things—questions about the reproductive cycles of worms and bugs, the surface structure of metals, the social significance of obscure poets, gender roles among the Kalahari Bushmen, the meaning of Balinese cockfighting, the effect of tax structure on economies, the rise of labor unions in agriculture, the role of prostitutes in medieval India, the properties of concrete, and almost anything else a human being might wonder about. A quick review of the magazine rack at any large grocery store reveals that similar communities have formed around everything from hot rods to model railroads, from computers to kayaks to cooking.

At the heart of all these communities of writers and readers is an interest in common questions and the hope for better or different answers. Writers write because they have something new or surprising or challenging to say in response to a question. Readers read because they share the writer's interest in the problem and want to deepen their understanding.

The Writer as Problematizer

Few writers discover their "answers" in a blinding flash. And even fewer writers produce a full-blown essay in a moment of inspiration. Professionals may require weeks, months, or years of thinking to produce a single piece of writing.

A new insight may start out as a vague sense of uncertainty, an awareness that you are beginning to see your subject (the metabolism of a starving animal, the decision to let a patient die, a grieving mother's anger at a journalist) differently from how others see it. You feel a gap between your view of a topic and your audience's view of the same topic and write to fill these gaps, to articulate your different view. Rarely, however, do writers know at the outset what they will write in the end. Instead, they clarify and refine their thoughts in the act of writing.

One of the most common causes of weak writing is the writer's tendency to reach closure too quickly. It's difficult, of course, to keep wrestling with a question. It's easier simply to ignore alternative views and material that doesn't fit and to grab hold of the first solution that comes to mind. What characterizes a successful writer is the ability to live with uncertainty and to acknowledge the insufficiency of an answer.

One term that describes serious writers is *problematizers;* that is, serious writers are not merely problem solvers, but problem posers, people who problematize their lives. We learned the term *problematize* from South American educator Paulo Freire, who discovered that adult literacy was best taught as a problem-solving activity tied to essential themes in his students' daily lives. Freire's method contrasts starkly with the traditional mode of teaching literacy, which Freire called the banking method. The goal of the banking method is to deposit knowledge in students' memory banks, rather than to teach students to discover or question or act.

The banking method encourages a passive attitude, not only toward learning, but also toward reality. Freire characterized students indoctrinated in such methods as "submerged in reality," unable to distinguish between the way things are and the way things might or should be. When people are taught to read and write by the banking method, they are likely to learn the word *water* by constantly repeating an irrelevant, self-evident sentence, such as "The water is in the well." Using Freire's method of teaching literacy, students might learn the word *water* by asking, "Is the water in our village dirty or clean?" and if the water is dirty, asking, "Why is the water dirty? Who is responsible?" The power of reading and writing lies in making discriminations, in unveiling alternative ways of seeing the world in which we live. By using language to problematize reality, Freire's students learned the meaning of written words because they recognized the power of those words.

Skilled writers, thus, are seekers after alternatives who look deliberately for questions, problems, puzzles, and contradictions. They realize that they can't write anything significant if they don't bring something new or challenging to the reader, something risky enough to spark disagreement or complex enough to be misunderstood. The surest way to improve your writing is to ground your essay in a question or problem that will motivate your thinking and help you establish a purposeful relationship with your audience. In the process, you'll have to live for a while with a sense of incompleteness, ambiguity, and uncertainty—the effects of engagement with any real problem.

Posing a Problem: A Case Study of a Beginning College Writer

So far we have talked about how professional writers pose problems. In this section we show you how student writer Mary Turla posed a problem for an argumentative paper requiring research.

At the start of her process, Mary's general topic area was mail-order brides. Her interest in this subject was sparked by a local newspaper story about an American man who gunned down his Filipina mail-order bride outside the courtroom where she was filing for divorce. Although Mary was immediately intrigued by the topic, she didn't initially have a focused question or problem. She began doing library research on the mail-order bride industry and discovered that 75 percent of mail-order brides come from the Philippines. Because Mary is a Filipina American, this statistic bothered her, and she began focusing on the image of Asian women created by the mail-order bride industry. Early in her process, she wrote the following entry in her journal:

Mary's Paper—Early Journal Entry

The mail-order bride industry may create & perpetuate the image of Asian women as commodities, vulnerable, uneducated, subservient; this image is applied to Asian American women or women of Asian descent. . . . Obviously, the mail-order bride is wrong—but what is the statement I want to make about it? Exploits/develops & creates negative image of Asian women. This image passes on to Asian American women. The image makes them sexual objects, "object" period—love as a commodity—exploitation industry—twists our culture— unrealistic expectations. What is the consequence?: domestic violence, unsatisfied partners, multimillion-dollar industry; subtle consequence: buying/selling people OK; Love/marriage a commodity.

This journal entry helped Mary see the more complex aspects of her subject— especially the connection of the mail-order bride industry to the image of Asian or Asian American women—but she was not yet able to define a central question or problem. Shortly after writing this journal entry, Mary discussed the topic with her classmates. After class, Mary wrote again in her journal.

Mary's Paper—Later Journal Entry

Class was great. We all had a chance to discuss our research so far and give others input on theirs. It was an extremely helpful exercise. A few helpful hints I got from the gang: 1) Define participants (men/women/business); 2) Are some "brides" there because they want to be? 3) *Find* a question! Most everyone (as far as I could tell) felt the mail-order bride industry was comparable to prostitution or trafficking of women. I have to ask: Is it? If it is, is it inherently so? Or, is it something about the mechanics of the industry now that justifies criticism? I could also sense an attitude—a mix of pity and contempt for the women involved.

Shortly thereafter, a conversation between Mary and her mother produced a focusing problem. After Mary complained about the evils of mail-order brides, her mother unexpectedly supported the practice. Women in the Philippines are desperately poor, her mother explained. Marrying a stranger, she said, may be the only way for some women to escape lives of abject poverty. Although Mary disliked the mail-order bride industry, her mother's response gave her pause. Perhaps being treated like a commodity might be a small price to pay for escaping near starvation and an early death.

Mary was now caught in a dilemma between her own gut-level desire to outlaw the mail-order bride industry and her realization that doing so would end many women's only hope of avoiding a life of poverty. She finally posed her problem this way: Should the mail-order bride industry be made illegal? She was no longer certain about her own answer to this question. Her goal was to make up her mind by learning as much as she could about the industry from the perspectives of the husband, the bride, and the industry itself. We return to Mary's story occasionally throughout this text. (You can read her final paper in Chapter 22, pp. 573–87; you can also read her earlier exploratory paper in Chapter 8, pp. 171–74.)

Types of Subject-Matter Questions

Academic researchers often conduct two kinds of research: applied research, in which they try to solve a practical problem in the real world, and pure research, in which they pursue knowledge for its own sake. We can call these two types of research questions *practical application questions* and *pure knowledge questions*, both of which examine what is true about the world. Frequently, writers also explore *values questions*, which focus not on what is true about the world but on how we should act in it. (Mary Turla's question about whether the mail-order bride industry should be made illegal is a values question.) A famous illustration of these kinds of questions involves the development of atomic power:

- **Pure-knowledge question:** Is it possible to split the atom?
- **Practical-application question:** How can we use our knowledge of splitting the atom to build an atomic bomb?
- **Values question:** Should scientists build an atomic bomb? Should the United States drop it on Hiroshima and Nagasaki?

FOR WRITING AND DISCUSSION

Almost any topic area will give rise to pure knowledge questions, practical application questions, and values questions. In this exercise we invite you to generate questions about the topic area "animals." We choose this topic because it is widely studied by university researchers across many disciplines (the metabolism of starvation is just one example; see p. 6) but also because almost everyone has had some experience with animals through owning a pet, observing a hornets' nest, wondering about dinosaurs, or questioning the ethics of stepping on ants.

1. Working in small groups, brainstorm a dozen or so good questions about animals. These should be questions that really puzzle at least

one person in your group and that no one else in your group can answer authoritatively. Try generating questions in each of our three categories, but don't worry if some questions don't fit neatly into a category. Here are some examples of questions about animals:

Pure knowledge questions

- Why did dinosaurs become extinct?
- Why does my dog always bark at people who wear hats but not at anyone else?
- Why does one of my goldfish always swim on its side rather than straight up like the other goldfish?

Practical application questions

- How can I best keep slugs out of my vegetable garden?
- What is the best way to teach a parakeet to talk?
- Can zoos be used to preserve endangered species?

Values questions

- Is saving the spotted owl worth the economic costs?
- Is it cruelty to animals to keep them in zoos?
- Should we tear down several dams on the Columbia River to restore salmon runs?

2. After each group has generated a dozen or more questions, try to reach consensus on your group's three "best" questions to share with the whole class. Be ready to explain to the class why you think some questions are better than others.

◪ RHETORICAL PROBLEMS: REACHING READERS EFFECTIVELY

As we suggested in the introduction, writers wrestle with two categories of problems—subject-matter problems and rhetorical problems. The previous section introduced you to subject-matter problems; we turn now to rhetorical problems.

In their final products, writers need to say something significant about their subjects to an audience, for a purpose, in an appropriate form and style. This network of questions related to audience, purpose, form, and style constitute rhetorical problems, and these problems often loom as large for writers as do the subject-matter problems that drive their writing in the first place. Indeed, rhetorical problems and subject-matter problems are so closely linked that writers can't address one without addressing the other. For example, the very questions you ask about your subject matter are influenced by your audience and purpose. Before you can decide what to say about content, you need to ask: Who am I writing for and why? What does my audience already know (and not know) about my topic? Will the question I pose already interest them, or do I have to hook their interest? What effect do I want my writing to have on that audience? How should I structure my essay and what tone and voice should I adopt?

In Chapter 4, we discuss extensively the rhetorical problems that writers must pose and solve. In this chapter we simply introduce you to one extended example of a rhetorical problem. From a student's point of view, we might call this "the problem of varying rules." From our perspective, we call it "the problem of choosing closed versus open forms."

◤ AN EXAMPLE OF A RHETORICAL PROBLEM: WHEN TO CHOOSE CLOSED VERSUS OPEN FORMS

In our experience, beginning college writers are often bothered by the ambiguity and slipperiness of rules governing writing. Many beginning writers wish that good writing followed consistent rules, such as "Never use 'I' in a formal paper" or "Start every paragraph with a topic sentence." The problem is that different kinds of writing follow different rules, leaving the writer with rhetorical choices rather than with hard and fast formulas for success. To develop this point, we begin by asking you to consider a problem about how writing might be classified.

Read the following short pieces of nonfiction prose. The first is a letter to the editor written by a professional civil engineer in response to a newspaper editorial arguing for the development of wind-generated electricity. The second piece is the opening page of an autobiographical essay by writer Minnie Bruce Pratt about her experiences as a white woman living in a predominantly black neighborhood. After reading the two samples carefully, proceed to the discussion questions that follow.

READINGS

DAVID ROCKWOOD
A LETTER TO THE EDITOR

Your editorial on November 16, "Get Bullish on Wind Power," is based on fantasy   1
rather than fact. There are several basic reasons why wind-generated power can in no way serve as a reasonable major alternative to other electrical energy supply alternatives for the Pacific Northwest power system.

2   First and foremost, wind power is unreliable. Electric power generation is evaluated not only on the amount of energy provided, but also on its ability to meet system peak load requirements on an hourly, daily, and weekly basis. In other words, an effective power system would have to provide enough electricity to meet peak demands in a situation when the wind energy would be unavailable—either in no wind situations or in severe blizzard conditions, which would shut down the wind generators. Because wind power cannot be relied on at times of peak needs, it would have to be backed up by other power generation resources at great expense and duplication of facilities.

3   Secondly, there are major unsolved problems involved in the design of wind generation facilities, particularly for those located in rugged mountain areas. Ice storms, in particular, can cause sudden dynamic problems for the rotating blades and mechanisms which could well result in breakdown or failure of the generators. Furthermore, the design of the facilities to meet the stresses imposed by high winds in these remote mountain regions, in the order of 125 miles per hour, would indeed escalate the costs.

4   Thirdly, the environmental impact of constructing wind generation facilities amounting to 28 percent of the region's electrical supply system (as proposed in your editorial) would be tremendous. The Northwest Electrical Power system presently has a capacity of about 37,000 megawatts of hydro power and 10,300 megawatts of thermal, for a total of about 48,000 megawatts. Meeting 28 percent of this capacity by wind power generators would, most optimistically, require about 13,400 wind towers, each with about 1,000 kilowatt (one megawatt) generating capacity. These towers, some 100 to 200 feet high, would have to be located in the mountains of Oregon and Washington. These would encompass hundreds of square miles of pristine mountain area, which, together with interconnecting transmission facilities, control works, and roads would indeed have major adverse environmental impacts on the region.

5   There are many other lesser problems of control and maintenance of such a system. Let it be said that, from my experience and knowledge as a professional engineer, the use of wind power as a major resource in the Pacific Northwest power system, is strictly a pipe dream.

MINNIE BRUCE PRATT
FROM "IDENTITY: SKIN BLOOD HEART"

1   I live in a part of Washington, D.C. that white suburbanites called "the jungle" during the uprising of the '60s—perhaps still do, for all I know. When I walk the two-and-a-half blocks to H St. NE, to stop in at the bank, to leave my boots off at the shoe-repair-and-lock shop, I am most usually the only white person in sight. I've seen two other whites, women, in the year I've lived here. (This does not count white folks in cars, passing through. In official language, H St., NE, is known as "The H Street Corridor," as in something to be passed through quickly, going from your place, on the way to elsewhere.)

2   When I walk three blocks in a slightly different direction, down Maryland Avenue, to go to my lover's house, I pass the yards of Black folks: the yard of the lady who keeps children, with its blue-and-red windmill, its roses-of-sharon; the yard of the man who delivers vegetables with its stacked slatted crates; the yard of the people next to the Righteous Branch Commandment Church-of-God (Seventh Day) with its tomatoes

in the summer, its collards in the fall. In the summer, folks sit out on their porches or steps or sidewalks; when I walk by, if I lift my head and look toward them and speak, "Hey," they may speak, say, "Hey" or "How you doing?" or perhaps just nod. In the spring, I was afraid to smile when I spoke, because that might be too familiar, but by the end of summer I had walked back and forth so often, I was familiar, so sometimes we shared comments about the mean weather.

I am comforted by any of these speakings for, to tell you the truth, they make me feel at home. I am living far from where I was born; it has been twenty years since I have lived in that place where folks, Black and white, spoke to each other when they met on the street or in the road. So when two Black men dispute country matters, calling across the corners of 8th St—"Hey, Roland, did you ever see a hog catch a rat?"—"I seen a hog catch a *snake*"—"How about a rat? Ever see one catch a *rat*?"—I am grateful to be living within sound of their voices, to hear a joking that reminds me, with a startled pain, of my father, putting on his tales for his friends, the white men gathered at the drugstore.

3

FOR WRITING AND DISCUSSION

Working in small groups or as a whole class, try to reach consensus on the following specific tasks:

1. What are the main differences between the two types of writing? If you are working in groups, help your recorder prepare a presentation describing the differences between Rockwood's writing and Pratt's writing.
2. Create a metaphor, simile, or analogy that best sums up your feelings about the most important differences between Rockwood's and Pratt's writing: "Rockwood's writing is like . . . , but Pratt's writing is like. . . ."
3. Explain why your metaphors are apt. How do your metaphors help clarify or illuminate the differences between the two pieces of writing?

Now that you have done some thinking on your own about the differences between these two examples, turn to our brief analysis.

Distinctions Between Closed and Open Forms of Writing

David Rockwood's letter and Minnie Pratt's excerpt are both examples of nonfiction prose. But as these examples illustrate, nonfiction prose can vary enormously in form and style. From the perspective of structure, we can place nonfiction prose along a continuum that goes from closed to open forms of writing (see Figure 1.1, on p. 15).

Of our two pieces of prose, Rockwood's letter illustrates tightly closed writing and falls at the far left end of the continuum. The elements that make this writing closed are the presence of an explicit thesis in the introduction (i.e., wind-generated power isn't a reasonable alternative energy source in the Pacific Northwest) and the writer's consistent development of that thesis throughout the body (i.e., "First and foremost, wind power is unreliable. . . . Secondly, there are

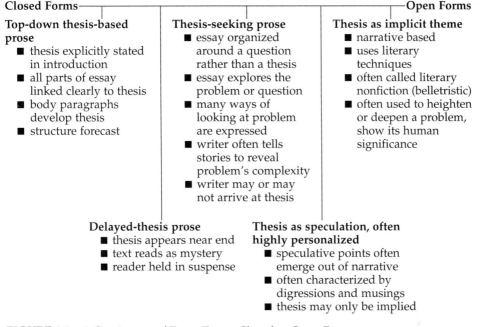

Closed Forms————————————————————————————————**Open Forms**

Top-down thesis-based prose
- thesis explicitly stated in introduction
- all parts of essay linked clearly to thesis
- body paragraphs develop thesis
- structure forecast

Thesis-seeking prose
- essay organized around a question rather than a thesis
- essay explores the problem or question
- many ways of looking at problem are expressed
- writer often tells stories to reveal problem's complexity
- writer may or may not arrive at thesis

Thesis as implicit theme
- narrative based
- uses literary techniques
- often called literary nonfiction (belletristic)
- often used to heighten or deepen a problem, show its human significance

Delayed-thesis prose
- thesis appears near end
- text reads as mystery
- reader held in suspense

Thesis as speculation, often highly personalized
- speculative points often emerge out of narrative
- often characterized by digressions and musings
- thesis may only be implied

FIGURE 1.1   A Continuum of Essay Types: Closed to Open Forms

major unsolved [design] problems. . . . Thirdly, . . ."). Once the thesis is stated, the reader knows the point of the essay and can predict its structure. The reader also knows that the writer's point won't change as the essay progresses. Because its structure is transparent and predictable, the success of closed-form prose rests entirely on its ideas, which must "surprise" readers by asserting something new, challenging, doubtful, or controversial. It aims to change the reader's view of the subject through the power of reason, logic, and evidence. Closed-form prose is what most college professors write when doing their own scholarly research, and it is what they most often expect of their students. It is also the most common kind of writing in professional and business contexts.

Pratt's writing falls at the far right of the closed-to-open continuum. It resists reduction to a single, summarizable thesis and leaves the reader in suspense about where it is going. Open-form essays are often organized chronologically; they tell a story rather than support an announced main point. This kind of writing is narrative based rather than thesis based. Narrative-based essays still have a focus, but the focus is more like the theme in a work of fiction than the thesis of an argument. Often the point of a narrative is implied rather than explicitly stated. Readers may argue over the point in the same way that they argue over the meaning of a film or novel.

As you can see from the continuum in Figure 1.1, essays can fall anywhere along the scale. Not all thesis-with-support writing has to be top down, stating its thesis explicitly in the introduction. In some cases writers choose to delay the thesis, creating a more exploratory, open-ended, "let's think through this together" feeling before finally stating the main point late in the essay. In some cases writers explore a problem without *ever* finding a satisfactory thesis, creating an essay that is thesis seeking rather than thesis supporting, an essay aimed at deepening the question, refusing to accept an easy answer. Such essays may replicate their author's process of exploring a problem and include digressions, speculations, conjectures, multiple perspectives, and occasional invitations to the reader to help solve the problem. When writers reach the far right-hand position on the continuum, they no longer state an explicit thesis. Instead, like novelists or short-story writers, they embed their points in plot, imagery, dialogue, and so forth, leaving their readers to *infer* a theme from the text.

Where to Place Your Writing Along the Continuum

Clearly, essays at opposite ends of this continuum operate in different ways and obey different rules. Because each position on the continuum has its appropriate uses, the writer's challenge is to determine which sort of writing is most appropriate for a given situation.

As you will see in later chapters, the kind of writing you choose depends on your purpose, your intended audience, and your genre (a genre is a recurring type of writing with established conventions, such as an academic article, a newspaper feature story, a grant proposal, an article for *Seventeen* or *Rolling Stone,* and so forth). Thus if you were writing an analytical paper for an academic audience, you would typically choose a closed-form structure and your finished product would include such elements as the following:

- an explicit thesis in the introduction
- forecasting of structure
- cohesive and unified paragraphs with topic sentences
- clear transitions between sentences and between parts
- no digressions

But if you were writing an autobiographical narrative about, say, what family means to you, you would probably move toward the open end of the continuum and violate one or more of these conventions (note how extensively Pratt violates them). It's not that open-form prose doesn't have rules; it's that the rules are different, just as the rules for jazz are different from the rules for a classical sonata.

For another perspective on how rules vary, consider two frequently encountered high school writing assignments: the five-paragraph theme and the "What I Did Last Summer" essay. The five-paragraph theme is a by-the-numbers way to teach closed-form, thesis-with-support writing. It emphasizes logical development, unity, and coherence. The five-paragraph structure may emerge naturally if you are writing an argument based on three supporting reasons—an introductory paragraph, three body paragraphs (one for each reason), and a concluding paragraph. Rockwood's letter is a real-world example of a five-paragraph essay, even though Rockwood certainly didn't have that format in mind when writing.

In contrast, the "What I Did Last Summer" assignment calls for a different sort of writing, probably an open-form structure closer to that of Pratt's piece. If you tried to write the "What I Did Last Summer" essay with the thesis-up-front rules of the five-paragraph essay, you would be hamstrung from the start; the summer essay calls not for an argument, but for a well-plotted, vivid story. Whether the writer chooses a closed-form or an open-form approach depends on the intended audience of the piece and the writer's purpose.

FOR WRITING AND DISCUSSION

Do you and your classmates most enjoy writing prose at the closed or more open end of the continuum? Prior to class discussion, work individually by recalling a favorite piece of writing that you have done in the past. Jot down a brief description of the kind of writing this was (a poem, a personal experience essay, a research paper, a newspaper story, a persuasive argument). Then, working in small groups or as a whole class, report one at a time on your favorite piece of writing and speculate where it falls on the continuum from closed to open forms. Are you at your best in closed-form writing that calls for an explicit thesis statement and logical support? Or are you at your best in more open and personal forms?

Is there a wide range of preferences in your class? If so, how do you account for this variance? If not, how do you account for the narrow range?

▨ CHAPTER SUMMARY

This chapter has introduced you to the notion of writers as questioners and problem posers who wrestle with both subject-matter and rhetorical problems. We have shown how writers start with questions or problems about their subject matter, rather than with topic areas, and how they take their time resolving the uncertainties raised by such questions. We saw that writers must ask questions about their rhetorical situation and make decisions about content, form, and style based on their understanding of their purpose, their audience, and their genre. We described how the rules governing writing vary as the writer moves along the continuum from closed to open forms.

The next chapter looks closely at how writers pose problems and pursue them in depth through behind-the-scenes exploratory writing and talking.

BRIEF WRITING PROJECT

We close out this chapter with a brief writing project aimed at helping you appreciate historian Rodney Kilcup's advice to writers: Begin with "a good, interesting question" (see the epigraph to this chapter, p. 3). As you will see later in this text, your brief essay will be similar in structure to the question-posing part of a typical academic introduction.

> Write a one-page (double-spaced) essay that poses a question about animals (or about some other topic provided by your instructor). Besides explaining your question clearly and providing needed background, you will need to help readers understand two things about it: (1) why the question is problematic—that is, what makes it a genuine question or problem; and (2) why the question is significant or worth pursuing—that is, what benefit will come from solving it. Your essay should not answer the question; your purpose is only to ask it.

This assignment builds on the For Writing and Discussion exercise on pages 10 and 11, which asked you to brainstorm questions about animals. For this assignment, choose a puzzling question about animals that interests you. Aim your essay at readers who are not familiar with your question. Your task is to make your question interesting to those readers. To hook their interest, you have to explain what your question is (often providing needed background) and then elaborate on the question by showing two things about it: why the question is problematic and why it is significant. To illustrate what we mean by these terms, we provide the following student essay as an example.

MELISSA DAVIS (STUDENT)
WHY DO SOME DOGS LIKE CATS WHILE OTHERS HATE THEM?

Background story introduces question

Whenever my dog sees a cat, he starts chasing it, barking and snapping his teeth. No matter how much I have tried to teach Sandy to like cats, he chases them ferociously on first sight. However, not all dogs are cat-haters. I often babysit a family that has a dog and two cats. When I let the dog, Willa, into the house, she goes straight towards the cats and starts playing with them. They nudge and cuddle with one another almost as if Willa were their mother. Willa never growls at the cats, but always treats them tenderly.

Statement of question

The contrast between Sandy and Willa makes me wonder why some dogs despise cats and will do any thing to hurt them while others mother them as if they were their own puppies. What causes dogs to react so differently to cats?

Contrasting theories show why question is problematic

One possible theory is genetic; maybe different breeds of dogs have different reactions to cats. My dog is a very small Chihuahua terrier, and Willa is a large chocolate lab. Maybe in this case the difference involves the sizes of the two breeds. Perhaps being small, a Chihuahua is more intimidated by cats while the Lab is so large that the cat is no threat to it.

Yet my friend's big German Shepherds chase and attack cats. Perhaps some breeds are genetically wired to hate cats while others aren't.

Another theory concerns the way dogs are first introduced to cats as puppies. I remember that in the past while visiting relatives Sandy stuck her nose under a bed when a cat reached out and scratched it, sending Sandy howling out of the room. Maybe this memory caused Sandy to hate all cats. In contrast, perhaps Willa was taught to play with cats when she was a puppy. Maybe some kind human being petted Willa and a kitten simultaneously so that cat and dog bonded. Under this theory, hating or liking cats would be a learned experience.

Solving this question might further our knowledge about genetics and the environment in accounting for animal behavior. It might help us discover something useful about the way animals can best be trained.

Suggests significance of question

In this essay, Melissa asks why some dogs hate cats while others don't. Melissa uses her own personal experience—the contrast between her dog Sandy and a neighbor's dog Willa—as background to explain the question clearly to readers. Since most people believe that dogs naturally hate cats, the case of the cat-loving Willa automatically makes her question problematic. (If dogs naturally hate cats, then how do you explain Willa?) She further shows its problematic nature by contrasting several possible theories, none of which is fully satisfactory. Finally she speculates on why this question is significant: Answering it might help us better understand the role of nature versus nurture in animal behavior and lead to better ways of training animals.

With this illustration as a starting point, let's look more closely at what we mean by a problematic and significant question.

Showing Why Your Question Is Problematic

A question is said to be problematic if it has no apparent answers or if the answers that come to a reader's mind can be shown to be unsatisfactory. A question whose answer can be looked up in an encyclopedia or can be completely answered by an expert is not problematic. Problematic questions imply either that the answer is not known or that it is not agreed upon by experts. In other words, problematic questions imply answers that have to be argued for, that have to be justified with reasons and evidence. Some strategies writers use to show that a question is problematic include the following:

- Show how your own (or previous researchers') attempts to solve the problem have failed. (If your problem were "How can I train my dog not to dig holes in the yard?" you could show how your various attempts to solve the problem all failed.)
- Show different ways that people have attempted to answer the question (different theories or hypotheses or competing explanations) and indicate how no one answer is fully adequate. (This is the strategy used by Melissa to show why her question about dogs hating cats is problematic.)

- If you pose a values question, summarize the competing positions on the issue. (For example, if the question concerns the value of saving the spotted owl, the writer can summarize opposing arguments.)
- Show why an expected or "easy" answer isn't satisfactory. (For example, you might show why "to keep itself clean" may not be a satisfactory answer to the question "Why do cats lick themselves?")
- Narrate your own attempts to think through the problem, revealing how none of your possible answers fully satisfied you. You might use the strategy "Part of me thinks this . . . ; but another part of me thinks this. . . ." or "I used to think . . . but now I think. . . ." (For example, if you ask "Is it ethical to eat meat?" you might describe your shifting positions on this issue and show why no single position satisfies you.)

Showing Why Your Question Is Significant

Often a question can be problematic without seeming significant to an audience. A reader might not know why one of your goldfish swims sideways rather than upright and yet not care about it. Thus writers often need to show why a problem is worth pursuing in order to keep the audience from saying "So what?" or "Who cares?" It is easy to show the significance of practical-application questions because their solution will solve real-world problems such as getting one's dog to stop digging holes in the yard, or, in the case of professional applied research, getting rid of acid rain, building a faster microchip, or finding a cure for AIDS. But when you pose a pure-knowledge question, the significance of finding an answer is harder to see. What professional scholars do is show how solving one knowledge question will help us understand another, larger knowledge question. For example, if you understand how Shakespeare uses dog imagery in his plays, you might understand better how he creates other imagery patterns or how his culture regarded the relationship between the human and animal world. Here are two typical ways that writers can show the significance of a problem:

- *Show how solving the problem will lead to practical, real-world benefits.* (For example, finding out what odors trigger the mating of certain insects might lead to an environmentally safe method of controlling their populations.)
- *Show how solving a pure-knowledge problem will help us solve a larger, more important knowledge problem.* (For example, if we understand how spiders "know" how to spin webs, we may be able to understand better how genetic encoding works.)

Planning Your Essay

A premise throughout this book is that a good finished product grows out of a rich exploratory process. We suggest that you talk through your proposed essay with a classmate, explaining your question and showing why it is problematic and significant. Make an informal outline or flowchart for the essay in which you plan out each of the required parts. Here are some examples of student plans that led to successful question-posing essays.

Example 1

I would like to question the ethics of interspecies transplants and show why it is not an easy question to answer.

Illustrate question with case of a man who had a transplant of a baboon heart.

Side One: Interspecies transplants are unethical. It is unethical to "play god" by taking the organs of one species and placing them in another.

Side Two: Interspecies transplants are ethical. They may save lives.

This is a significant problem because it causes us to ask deep questions about what we most value.

Example 2

What can we do about the raccoons that pester our home near Golden Gate Park in San Francisco?

Start by telling story of how horrible the raccoons are—raid our garbage, invade our yards during the day while children are playing, come in the house through the cat door and eat cats' food—most horrible they once ate our kittens.

Nothing seems to work.

Describe our attempts to solve problem: Tried various tricks to discourage raccoons—spraying the hose on them, getting better garbage cans, moving cat food, etc.

Our dilemma: Is it ethical to trap, poison them or otherwise kill them? Wildlife versus humans and domestic animals problem.

Significance: Getting rid of raccoons will increase our quality of life. Answer to ethical question will help us see when human needs should take priority over animals; when is it OK to harm animals? Are raccoons like rodents?

Example 3

Why do starlings change their ordinary behavior and start to swarm?

Describe the strange swarming behavior of starlings.

Show why this behavior is problematic by explaining that starlings don't usually act like this and that no other birds swarm the way starlings do. Explain that I have no theories why this behavior occurs or what triggers it.

This is significant because knowing this answer might tell us something about how the brains of birds have evolved.

Pursuing Problems

Exploratory Writing and Talking

WHAT YOU WILL LEARN IN THIS CHAPTER

In this chapter we show you how writers pursue problems through exploratory writing and talking. In particular, you will learn the following:

- The kind of thinking that college professors value—what one professor calls "wallowing in complexity"
- How each academic discipline is a field of inquiry and argument, not just a repository of facts and concepts to be learned
- How the thinking process of posing questions and proposing answers is reflected in the introductions of academic articles
- How to do exploratory writing and talking through freewriting, idea mapping, dialectic discussion, active reading and research, and other strategies
- How to deepen and complicate your thinking through the believing and doubting game

When Ofelya Bagdasaryan completed her first university exam in the United States, she was confident that she would earn a high grade. "I had studied hard, memorized the material and written it perfectly in the examination book," she recalled.

But Ofelya, 26, a recent immigrant from Armenia in the former Soviet Union, was in for a rude shock. When the exams were returned the following week, she discovered that the professor had given her a D. "But I repeated exactly what the textbook said," she told her teaching assistant. "Yes," he replied, "but you didn't tell us your [judgment of what the book said]."

—David Wallechinsky, *Journalist*

My professor said that I received a low grade on this essay because I just gave my opinion. Then she said that she didn't *care* what my *opinion* was; she wanted an *argument*."

—Student overheard in hallway

> "In management, people don't merely 'write papers,' they solve problems," said [business professor Kimbrough Sherman]. . . . He explained that he wanted to construct situations where students would have to "wallow in complexity" and work their way out, as managers must.
>
> —A. Kimbrough Sherman, *Management Professor*

In the previous chapter, we introduced you to the role of the writer as questioner and problem poser. In this chapter and the next, we narrow our focus primarily to academic writing, which most frequently means closed-form, thesis-based essays and articles. Mastering this kind of writing is necessary to your success in college and requires a behind-the-scenes ability to think deeply and rigorously about problems, pursuing them at length. In this chapter we show you how to use exploratory writing and talking to do this behind-the-scenes work. The strategies explained in this chapter will help you develop powerful thinking and studying habits for every discipline.

▨ WHAT DOES A PROFESSOR WANT?

It is important for you to understand the kind of thinking that most college professors look for in student writing. As the first two chapter-opening quotations indicate, many first-year college students are baffled by their professors' responses to their writing. Ofelya Bagdasaryan mistakenly thought her teachers wanted her to rehash her textbook. The second student thought her teacher wanted her to describe how she felt about a subject (opinion), not why someone else ought to feel the same way (argument). But as management professor A. Kimbrough Sherman explains in the third quotation, college instructors expect students to wrestle with problems by applying the concepts, data, and thought processes they learn in a course to new situations. As Sherman puts it, students must learn to "wallow in complexity" and work their way out.

Learning to Wallow in Complexity

Wallowing in complexity is not what most first-year college students aspire to do. (Certainly that wasn't what we, the authors of this text, had uppermost in our minds when we sailed off to college!) New college students tend to shut down their creative thinking processes too quickly and head straight for closure to a problem. Harvard psychologist William Perry, who has studied the intellectual development of college students, found that few of them become skilled wallowers in complexity until late in their college careers. According to Perry, most students come to college as "dualists," believing that all questions have right or wrong answers, that professors know the right answers, and that the student's job is to learn them. Of course, these beliefs are partially correct. First-year students who hope to become second-year students must indeed understand and memorize mounds of facts, data, definitions, and basic concepts.

But true intellectual growth requires the kind of problematizing we discussed in Chapter 1. It requires students to *do* something with their new knowledge, to apply it to new situations, to conduct the kinds of inquiry, research, analysis, and argument pursued by experts in each discipline. Instead of confronting only questions that have right answers, students need to confront what cognitive psychologists call *ill-structured problems.*

An ill-structured problem is one that may not have a single, correct answer. Often these problems require the thinker to operate in the absence of full and complete data. People face ill-structured problems every day in their personal lives: What should I major in? Should I continue to date person X? Should I take this job or keep looking? Likewise, many decisions in professional and public life are excruciatingly difficult precisely because they concern ill-structured problems that are unsolvable in any clear-cut and certain way: What should be done about homelessness? What public policies will best solve the problem of global warming or the national debt or the lack of affordable health care for our citizens?

Similarly, college professors pursue ill-structured problems in their professional writing. The kinds of problems vary from discipline to discipline, but they all require the writer to use reasons and evidence to support a tentative solution. Because your instructors want you to learn how to do the same kind of thinking, they often phrase essay exam questions or writing assignments as ill-structured problems. They are looking not for one right answer, but for well-supported arguments that acknowledge alternative views. A C paper and an A paper may even have the same "answer" (identical thesis statements), but the C writer may have waded only ankle deep into the mud of complexity, whereas the A writer wallowed in it and worked a way out.

What skills are required for successful wallowing? Specialists in critical thinking have identified the following:

1. The ability to pose problematic questions
2. The ability to analyze a problem in all its dimensions—to define its key terms, determine its causes, understand its history, appreciate its human dimension and its connection to one's own personal experience, and appreciate what makes it problematic or complex
3. The ability (and doggedness) to find, gather, and interpret facts, data, and other information relevant to the problem (often involving library or field research)
4. The ability to imagine alternative solutions to the problem, to see different ways in which the question might be answered and different perspectives for viewing it
5. The ability to analyze competing approaches and answers, to construct arguments for and against alternatives, and to choose the best solution in light of values, objectives, and other criteria that you determine and articulate
6. The ability to write an effective argument justifying your choice while acknowledging counterarguments

We discuss and develop these skills throughout this text.

In addition to these generic thinking abilities, critical thinking requires what psychologists call *domain-specific* skills. Each academic discipline has its own characteristic ways of approaching knowledge and its own specialized habits of mind. The questions asked by psychologists differ from those asked by historians or anthropologists; the evidence and assumptions used to support arguments in literary analysis differ from those in philosophy or sociology.

What all disciplines value, however, is the ability to manage complexity, and this skill marks the final stage of William Perry's developmental scheme. At an intermediate stage of development, after they have moved beyond dualism, students become what Perry calls "multiplists." At this stage students believe that since the experts disagree on many questions, all answers are equally valid. Professors want students merely to have an opinion and to state it strongly. A multiplist believes that a low grade on an essay indicates no more than that the teacher didn't like his or her opinion. Multiplists are often cynical about professors and grades; to them, college is a game of guessing what the teacher wants to hear. Students emerge into Perry's final stages—what he calls "relativism" and "commitment in relativism"— when they are able to take a position in the face of complexity and to justify that decision through reasons and evidence while weighing and acknowledging contrary reasons and counterevidence. The three quotations that open this chapter exemplify Perry's scheme: Whereas the first student sees her task as recalling right answers, the second sees it as forcefully expressing an opinion, and Professor Sherman articulates what is expected at Perry's last stages—wading into the messiness of complexity and working your way back to solid ground.

Seeing Each Academic Discipline as a Field of Inquiry and Argument

When you study a new discipline, you must learn not only the knowledge that scholars in that discipline have acquired over the years, but also the processes they used to discover that knowledge. It is useful to think of each academic discipline as a network of conversations in which participants exchange information, respond to each other's questions, and express agreements and disagreements. The scholarly articles and books that many of your instructors write (or would write if they could find the time) are formal, permanent contributions to an ongoing discussion carried on in print. By extension, your college's or university's library is a huge collection of conversations frozen in time. Each book or article represents a contribution to a conversation; each writer agreed with some of his or her predecessors and disagreed with others.

As each discipline evolves and changes, its central questions evolve also, creating a fascinating, dynamic conversation that defines the discipline. At any given moment, scholars are pursuing hundreds of cutting-edge questions in each discipline. Table 2.1 provides examples of questions that scholars have debated over the years as well as questions they are addressing today.

Of course, students can't immediately address the current, cutting-edge questions of most disciplines, particularly the sciences. But even novice science students

TABLE 2.1   Scholarly Questions in Different Disciplines

Field	Examples of Current Cutting-Edge Questions	Examples of Historical Controversies
Anatomy	What is the effect of a pregnant rat's alcohol ingestion on the development of fetal eye tissue?	In 1628, William Harvey produced a treatise arguing that the heart, through repeated contractions, caused blood to circulate through the body. His views were attacked by followers of the Greek physician Galen.
Literature	To what extent does the structure of a work of literature, for example, Conrad's *Heart of Darkness,* reflect the class and gender bias of the author?	In the 1920s a group of New Critics argued that the interpretation of a work of literature should be based on close examination of the work's imagery and form and that the intentions of the writer and the biases of the reader were not important. These views held sway in U.S. universities until the late 1960s, when they came increasingly under attack by deconstructionists and other postmoderns, who claimed that author intentions and reader bias were an important part of the work's meaning.
Linguistics	Do all the languages of the world descend from the same protolanguage or, in the evolution of humankind, did a variety of languages spring up independently around the globe?	Do humans learn language through behavior modification, as proposed by many learning theorists in the 1950s, or is there an innate language-learning center in the brain that is "hard wired" to learn a language, as proposed by Noam Chomsky?
Psychology	What are the underlying causes of gender identification? To what extent are differences between male and female behavior explainable by nature (genetics, body chemistry) versus nurture (social learning)?	In the early 1900s, under the influence of Sigmund Freud, psychoanalytic psychologists began explaining human behavior in terms of unconscious drives and mental processes that stemmed from repressed childhood experiences. Later, psychoanalysts were opposed by behaviorists, who rejected the notion of the unconscious and explained behavior as responses to environmental stimuli.

can examine historical controversies. Beginning physics students, for example, can wrestle with Archimedes' problem of how to measure the volume of a crown, or with other early problems concerning the mechanics of levers, pulleys, and inclined planes. In the humanities and social sciences, beginning students are often asked to study, explore, and debate some of the enduring questions that have puzzled generations of scholars.

- Is there a rational basis for belief in God?
- Why does Hamlet delay?
- Should Truman have dropped the atomic bomb on Hiroshima? On Nagasaki?
- What is the most just economic system?
- Do humans have free will?

As you study a discipline, you are learning how to enter its network of conversations. To do so, you have to build up a base of knowledge about the discipline, learn its terminology, observe its conversations, read its major works, see how it asks questions, learn its methods. To help you get a clearer sense of how written "conversation" works within a discipline—that is, how a writer poses a question and proposes an answer—the next section examines a typical introduction to an academic article.

How a Prototypical Introduction Poses a Question and Proposes an Answer

To illustrate the typical structure of an academic introduction, we will use as our prototype an article by theoretical physicist Evelyn Fox Keller originally published in 1974 in *Harvard Magazine*. (A *prototype* is the most typical or generic instance of class. Thus a prototype dog might be a medium-sized mutt but not a Great Dane or a toy poodle; a prototype bird might be a robin or a blackbird or a crow, but not a hummingbird, a pelican, or an ostrich.) Because *Harvard Magazine* is an alumni publication rather than a specialized science journal, Keller's influential article is free of heavy academic jargon, making it easy to see the question/ solution structure of a typical closed-form introduction.

Women in Science: An Analysis of a Social Problem

Are women's minds different from men's minds? In spite of the women's movement, the age-old debate centering around this question continues. We are surrounded by evidence of *de facto* differences between men's and women's intellects—in problems that interest them, in the ways they try to solve those problems, and in the professions they choose. Even though it has become fashionable to view such differences as environmental in origin, the temptation to seek an explanation in terms of innate differences remains a powerful one.

Perhaps the area in which this temptation is strongest is in science. Even those of us who would like to argue for intellectual equality are hard pressed to

Presentation of question

Shows why the question is problematic and significant

explain the extraordinarily meager representation of women in science, particularly in the upper echelons. Some would argue that the near absence of great women scientists demonstrates that women don't have the minds for true scientific creativity. While most of us would recognize the patent fallacies of this argument, it nevertheless causes us considerable discomfort. After all, the doors of the scientific establishment appear to have been open to women for some time now—shouldn't we begin to see more women excelling?

In the last fifty years the institutional barriers against women in science have been falling. During most of that time, the percentage of women scientists has declined, although recent years have begun to show an upswing. Of those women who do become scientists, few are represented in the higher academic ranks. In order to have a proper understanding of these data [the original article includes several tables showing the data], it is necessary to review the many influences that operate. I would like to argue that the convenient explanation that men's minds are intrinsically different from women's is not only unwarranted by the evidence, but in fact reflects a mythology that is in itself a major contribution to the phenomenon observed.

Presentation of thesis

This introduction, like most introductions to academic articles, includes the following prototypical features.

- *Focus on a clear question or problem to be investigated.*   In this case the question is stated explicitly: "Are women's minds different from men's minds?" In many introductions, the question is implied rather than stated directly.
- *Elaboration on the question, showing why it is both problematic and significant.*   In this case, Keller highlights competing explanations for the low number of famous women scientists: innate differences versus environment. The social significance of the problem is implied throughout.
- *The writer's tentative "answer" to this question (the essay's **thesis**), which must bring something new, surprising, or challenging to the audience.*   In closed-form articles, the thesis is stated explicitly, usually at the end of the introduction, following the expected sequence of question first and then the answer. Here Keller takes a strong stand in favor of environment over innate differences.
- *[optional] A forecasting statement previewing the content and shape of the rest of the article ("First I will discuss X, then Y, and finally Z").*   Keller's introduction doesn't forecast the structure of her article, but it clearly announces her two purposes: (1) to show that evidence does not support the intrinsic difference theory, and (2) to show that the intrinsic difference myth itself helps explain the paucity of women scientists.

Of course, the body of Keller's article has to present strong arguments to support her controversial thesis. What she presents is a shocking account of the social forces that hindered her professional development as a theoretical physicist: sexual favor seeking and harassment; "isolation, mockery, and suspicion"; "incessant prophecies of failure"; and the pressure to conform to conventional views about women. She concludes that preconceptions about gender roles "serve as strait jackets for men and women alike." Her article is often cited, favorably or unfavorably, by those on all sides of this debate, for the controversy between innate differences and environment in the formation of gender roles still rages today.

We have used Keller's article to show how academic writers—in posing a problem and proposing an answer—join an ongoing conversation. Many of the papers you will be asked to write in college will require you, in some way, to exhibit the same kind of thinking—to pose a problem; to assert a tentative, risky answer (your thesis); and to support it with reasons and evidence. One of the major aims of this book is to teach you how to do this kind of thinking and writing.

In the rest of this chapter we will explain the behind-the-scenes role of exploratory writing and talking. The neatness of Keller's introduction—its statement of a focused problem and its confidently asserted thesis—masks the messiness of the exploratory process that precedes the actual writing of an academic essay. Underneath the surface of finished academic papers is a long process of exploratory writing and talking—periods of intense thinking, reflecting, studying, researching, notebook or journal writing, and sharing. Through this process, the writer defines the question or problem and eventually works out an answer or response. Some of your professors may build opportunities for exploratory writing and talking directly into the course in the form of journals, in-class freewriting, collaborative group work, e-mail exchanges, class discussions and debates, and so forth. Other teachers will spend most of the class time lecturing and leave you on your own to explore ideas. The rest of this chapter presents strategies and techniques that many writers have found useful for exploring ideas.

▨ TECHNIQUES FOR EXPLORATORY WRITING AND TALKING

To use language for exploration, you need to imagine a friendly, nonjudgmental audience with whom you can share ideas in a risk-free environment. Perhaps you can imagine yourself as your audience, or, if you prefer, a friend or classmate. Your purpose is to get ideas down on paper to help you see what you are thinking. Exploratory writing jogs your memory, helps you connect disparate ideas, lets you put difficult concepts into your own words, and invites you to see the relevance of your studies to your own life. In this section we describe four useful techniques for exploratory writing and talking: freewriting, idea mapping, dialectic discussions, and active reading and research.

Freewriting

Freewriting, also sometimes called *nonstop writing* or *silent, sustained writing*, asks you to record your thinking directly. To freewrite, put pen to paper (or sit at your computer screen, perhaps turning *off* the monitor so that you can't even see what you are writing) and write rapidly, *nonstop,* for ten to fifteen minutes at a stretch. Don't worry about grammar, spelling, organization, transitions, or other features of edited writing. The object is to think of as many ideas as possible. Some freewriting looks like stream of consciousness. Some is more organized and focused, although it lacks the logical connections and development that would make it suitable for an audience of strangers.

Many freewriters find that their initial reservoir of ideas runs out in three to five minutes. If this happens, force yourself to keep your fingers moving. If you can't think of anything to say, write "Relax" over and over (or "This is stupid" or "I'm stuck") until new ideas emerge.

What do you write about? The answer varies according to your situation. Often you will freewrite in response to a question or problem posed by your instructor. Sometimes you will pose your own questions and use freewriting to explore possible answers or simply generate ideas. Since the authors are avid freewriters, we can use ourselves for illustration. We use freewriting for many purposes in our scholarly work. We freewrite when we are first becoming engaged with a problem. We often pose for ourselves trigger questions: "What really puzzles me about X?" "Why did I react so strongly to what person A said about X?" "How are my ideas about X different from A's?" We also freewrite extensively when doing scholarly reading. Although our notetaking systems differ, we both react strongly to articles or books we are reading and freewrite our own ideas about them into our notes. (See Chapter 6, in which we explain the process we use for "speaking back" to texts.) Finally, both of us freewrite when we get stuck in the process of writing a draft. If we come to a difficult section and find ourselves blocked, we turn away from the draft itself, find a sheet of scratch paper, and freewrite rapidly just to get the ideas flowing.

Many teachers assign freewriting in the form of journals, invention exercises for a formal essay, or in-class explorations. Mary Turla's journal entries, which you read in Chapter 1 (p. 9), are examples of freewriting. Here is another example of a student's freewrite in response to the prompt "What puzzles you about homelessness?"

> Let's see, what puzzles me about homelessness? Homeless homeless. Today on my way to work I passed a homeless guy who smiled at me and I smiled back though he smelled bad. What are the reasons he was out on the street? Perhaps an extraordinary string of bad luck. Perhaps he was pushed out onto the street. Not a background of work ethic, no place to go, no way to get someplace to live that could be afforded, alcoholism. To what extent do government assistance, social spending, etc, keep people off the street? What benefits could a person get that stops "the cycle"? How does welfare affect homelessness, drug abuse programs, family planning? To what extent does the individual have control over homelessness? This question of course goes to the depth of the question of how community affects the individual. Relax, relax. What about the signs that I see on the way to work posted on the windows of businesses that read, "please don't give to panhandlers it only promotes drug abuse etc" a cheap way of

getting homeless out of the way of business? Are homeless the natural end of unrestricted capitalism? What about the homeless people who are mentally ill? How can you maintain a living when haunted by paranoia? How do you decide if someone is mentally ill or just laughs at society? If one can't function obviously. How many mentally ill are out on the street? If you are mentally ill and have lost the connections to others who might take care of you I can see how you might end up on the street. What would it take to get treatment? To what extent can mentally ill be treated? When I see a homeless person I want to ask, How do you feel about the rest of society? When you see "us" walk by how do you think of us? Do you possibly care how we avoid you?

Note how this freewrite rambles, moving associatively from one topic or question to the next. Freewrites often have this kind of loose, associative structure. The value of such freewrites is that they help writers discover areas of interest or rudimentary beginnings of ideas. When you read back over one of your freewrites, try to find places that seem to you worth pursuing. Freewriters call these places hot spots, centers of interest, centers of gravity, or simply nuggets or seeds. The student who wrote the preceding freewrite discovered that he was particularly interested in the cluster of questions beginning "What about the homeless people who are mentally ill?" and he eventually wrote a research paper proposing a public policy for helping the mentally ill homeless. Because we think this technique is of great value to writers, we suggest that you use it to generate ideas for class discussions and essays.

Idea Mapping

Another good technique for exploring ideas is *idea mapping,* a more visual method than freewriting. To make an idea map, draw a circle in the center of the page and write down your broad topic area (or a triggering question or your thesis) inside the circle. Then record your ideas on branches and subbranches that extend out from the center circle. As long as you pursue one train of thought, keep recording your ideas on subbranches off the main branch. But as soon as that chain of ideas runs dry, go back and start a new branch.

Often your thoughts will jump back and forth between one branch and another. This technique will help you see them as part of an emerging design rather than as strings of unrelated ideas. Additionally, idea mapping establishes at an early stage a sense of hierarchy in your ideas. If you enter an idea on a subbranch, you can see that you are more fully developing a previous idea. If you return to the hub and start a new branch, you can see that you are beginning a new train of thought.

An idea map usually records more ideas than a freewrite, but the ideas are not as fully developed. Writers who practice both techniques report that they can vary the kinds of ideas they generate, depending on which technique they choose. Figure 2.1 (on p. 32) shows a student's idea map made while he was exploring issues related to the grading system.

FIGURE 2.1   Idea Map on Problems with the Grading System

Dialectic Discussion

Another effective way to explore the complexity of a topic is through face-to-face discussions with others, whether in class, over coffee in the student union, or late at night in bull sessions. Not all discussions are productive; some are too superficial and scattered, others too heated. Good ones are *dialectic*—participants with differing views on a topic try to understand each other and resolve their differences by examining contradictions in each person's position. The key to dialectic conversation is careful listening, made possible by an openness to each other's views. A dialectic discussion differs from a talk show shouting match or a pro–con debate in which proponents of opposing positions, their views set in stone, attempt to win the argument. In a dialectic discussion, participants assume that each position has strengths and weaknesses and that even the strongest position contains inconsistencies, which should be exposed and examined. When dialectic conversation works well, participants scrutinize their own positions more critically and deeply, and often alter their views. True dialectic conversation implies growth and change, not a hardening of positions. (For more discussion of how to work cooperatively with others through dialectic discussion, see Chapter 20 on working in groups.)

Active Reading and Research

If dialectic discussion engages you in live, face-to-face conversation with others, active reading and research engage you in conversation with others through reading. The key is to become an *active* reader who both listens to a piece of writing and speaks back to it through imaginative interaction with its author. Chapter 6 offers instruction on becoming an active reader, showing you how to read texts both with the grain and against the grain. In addition, Part Four, "A Guide to Research," describes in detail how to use an academic library as well as the Internet to find sources, how to use those sources to stimulate your own thinking, and how to incorporate them purposefully into your own writing.

When you pursue a question through active reading and research, you join the conversation of others who have contemplated and written about your problem. Not all college writing assignments require library or field research, but many do, and most of the rest can benefit by the process. The writing assignments in Part Two of this text involve varying degrees of research, depending on the assignments selected by your instructor and the problems you choose to pursue.

FOR WRITING AND DISCUSSION

The following exercise is a simulation game that asks you to try some of the exploratory writing and talking techniques we have discussed.

The Situation.   The city attorney of a large U.S. city* has proposed a "get-tough" policy on "vagrants and panhandlers" in the city's downtown shopping areas. It is time, says the city attorney, to stand up for the rights of ordinary citizens to enjoy their city. Supported by the mayor, the city attorney is ready to present his proposal to the city council, which will vote to pass or reject the proposal. The details of the proposal are outlined in the following newspaper article:

Proposed Law Calls for Fines, Arrests

Proposed public-conduct ordinances before the Seattle
City Council focus on repeated drinking in public, urinating

*The actual city is Seattle, Washington, but this proposal is similar to those being debated in many cities across the United States. For the purposes of this simulation game, assume that the city in question is any city close to your college or university where homelessness is a serious problem.

in public, sitting or lying on public streets, aggressive panhandling and public drug trafficking. Among their provisions:

- The second and any subsequent drinking-in-public offense becomes a criminal misdemeanor punishable by up to 90 days in jail, a $1,000 fine and up to one year of probation.

- The second and any subsequent offense of urinating or defecating in public becomes a criminal misdemeanor punishable by up to 90 days in jail, a $1,000 fine and up to one year of probation.

- The purchase, possession or consumption of alcohol by those between ages 18 and 21 becomes a criminal misdemeanor punishable by jail, fine and probation.

- Between 7 a.m. and 9 p.m., it would be unlawful to sit or lie on sidewalks in commercial areas, including Broadway, the University District, other neighborhoods and downtown.

- A tighter definition of "intimidation" would be created to make the present law against aggressive panhandling more effective in prosecution.

- Alleys where drug trafficking occurs could be closed for specific periods of the day or night, except for authorized use. Those who enter without permission could be arrested.

The Task.   In class, hold a simulated public hearing on this issue. Assign classmates to play the following roles: (1) a homeless person; (2) a downtown store owner; (3) a middle-class suburban home owner who used to shop downtown but hasn't done so for years because of all the "bums" lying on the streets; (4) an attorney from the American Civil Liberties Union who advocates for the civil rights of the homeless; (5) a college student who volunteers in a homeless shelter and knows many of the homeless by name; (6) a city council member supporting the proposal; (7) a city council member opposing it. Every class member should be assigned to one of these roles; later, all students assigned to a role will meet as a group to select the person to participate in the actual simulation.

The Procedure.   (1) Begin with five minutes of freewriting. Class members should explore their own personal reactions to this ordinance. (2) Class members should freewrite again, this time from the perspective of the character they have been assigned to play in the simulation. (3) Classmates should meet in groups according to assigned roles in the simulation, share freewrites, and make a group idea map exploring all the arguments that the group's assigned character might make. Group members can choose a person to play the role; those not chosen can play members of the city council. (4) Allow time for people playing the roles to develop their arguments fully and to exchange views. (5) After each participant has spoken, the remaining members of the class, acting as city council members, should sit in a circle and hold a dialectic discussion (listening carefully to each other rather than conducting a shouting match), trying to decide whether to accept or reject the city attorney's proposal. (6) Finally, the class should hold a vote to see whether the proposal is accepted or rejected.

◤ HOW TO MAKE EXPLORATORY WRITING AND TALKING WORK FOR YOU

All of the formal writing assignments in Part II of this text have built-in opportunities for exploratory writing and talking, but we hope you will use the techniques in this chapter for all of your college courses. In this final section of the chapter we will discuss some of the habits you can cultivate to make exploratory writing and talking a regular part of your intellectual life.

Make Marginal Notes on Readings

Experienced scholars often make extensive notes in the margins of books and articles. (If you don't own the book, you will need to write your notes in a journal or reading log.) In Chapter 6 we discuss this technique in detail, showing how critical readers regularly write two kinds of marginal notations: (1) *summarizing notes* that help them understand and recall the gist of the text, and (2) *responding notes* that help readers "speak back" to the text by agreeing or disagreeing, posing questions, drawing connections to other ideas, supplying new examples from their own experience, and so forth. See pages 108–23 for further elaboration of this method.

Keep a Journal or Learning Log

Another good exploratory strategy is to keep a *journal* or *learning log*. Many teachers assign journals in their courses and provide guidance about topics to explore. Most professional writers keep regular journals, since they know that ideas for formal pieces often take root in a journal as they record daily observations, play with ideas, and reflect thoughtfully upon the "stuff" of their lives. You can keep a journal or learning log for any of your courses by posing questions about course material and then writing out exploratory answers.

Discuss Your Ideas with E-Mail Correspondents

At a number of institutions, teachers use electronic mail (e-mail) to connect students with each other. The great advantage of e-mail is that it facilitates dialogue in a leisurely, nonthreatening atmosphere. You and classmates can share questions and insights, rehearse your understanding of course material, and try out new ideas. In many situations, the teacher can also enter the conversation, asking questions and stimulating further dialogue.

If your teacher doesn't set up an e-mail network for your course, you can set up your own by finding classmates with e-mail accounts. Sometimes, too, if you are doing research on a particular problem, you can find an international network of people interested in the same topic through an Internet Listserv, news group, or chat room (see Chapter 23).

Join Focused Study Groups

A focused study group, unlike a bull session, is a collection of individuals who voluntarily come together to study for a course. Many students do their best work by alternating between private and communal study. Focused study groups work best if members prepare for them in advance by creating lists of questions about course material and focusing first on comprehension. If parts of the material are confusing to everyone in your study group, then you can formulate questions to ask the teacher. Focused study groups also help you predict the kinds of critical thinking questions teachers are apt to ask on exams. When they function effectively, study groups can stimulate thinking about course material and send you back to private study with more confidence and an enhanced appreciation for complexity.

Participate Effectively in Class Discussions

Class discussion provides an excellent opportunity for exploratory talking. The key is learning to listen to classmates' ideas and to tie your own contributions to what others have said. Often students are so busy rehearsing what they want to say in a class discussion that they fail to listen carefully to other points of view, thus diminishing their sense of the topic's complexity. Because it is difficult to take class notes on a good discussion (ideas are flying everywhere, and you don't know what is important and what isn't), many students don't take notes in class but summarize what they got out of discussion as soon as class ends.

■ CHAPTER SUMMARY

In this chapter we looked at the kind of wallowing in complexity that professors expect from students and introduced techniques for exploratory writing and talking that will help you become fully engaged in an academic problem. We saw how an academic essay contributes to a conversation by posing a question and then offering a tentative and risky answer. We also saw how an academic essay is preceded by a long process of thinking, reflecting, studying, researching, and talking. The starting point for such an essay is exploratory writing and talking. We explained four strategies for exploring ideas—freewriting, idea mapping, dialectic conversation, and active reading and research—and then offered suggestions for making exploratory writing and talking a regular habit throughout your academic career.

BRIEF PROJECT

One of the best ways to dwell with a problem is to play what writing theorist Peter Elbow calls the "believing and doubting game." This game helps you appreciate the power of alternative arguments and points of view by urging you to formulate and explore alternative positions. To play the game, you imagine a possible answer to a problematic question and then systematically try first to believe that answer and then to doubt it.

Playing the Believing and Doubting Game

Play the believing and doubting game with two of the following assertions (or other assertions provided by your instructor). For one of the assertions, play the game by freewriting your believing and doubting responses (following the example on pages 38–39). For your second assertion, use the idea-mapping method. Label one side of your center circle "Believe" and the other side "Doubt." Spend approximately twenty minutes believing and doubting each assertion for a total of about forty minutes for the whole assignment.

1. State and federal governments should legalize hard drugs.
2. Grades are an effective means of motivating students to do their best work.
3. If I catch someone cheating on an exam or plagiarizing a paper, I should report that person to the instructor.
4. The city council should pass a get-tough policy on vagrants (see For Writing and Discussion, pp. 33–35).
5. In recent years advertising has made enormous gains in portraying women as strong, independent, and intelligent.
6. For grades 1 through 12, the school year should be extended to eleven months.
7. It is a good idea to make children take music lessons.
8. States should legalize marriage for gays and lesbians.
9. Cutting off welfare payments for single mothers will reduce teenage pregnancy.
10. Hate speech should be forbidden on college campuses.

When you play the believing side of this game, you try to become sympathetic to an idea or point of view. You listen carefully to it, opening yourself to the possibility that it is true. You try to appreciate why the idea has force for so many people; you try to accept it by discovering as many reasons as you can for believing it. It is easy to play the believing game with ideas you already believe in, but the game becomes more difficult, sometimes even frightening and dangerous, when you try believing ideas that seem untrue or disturbing.

The doubting game is the opposite of the believing game. It calls for you to be judgmental and critical, to find fault with an idea rather than to accept it. When you doubt a new idea, you try your best to falsify it, to find counterexamples that disprove it, to find flaws in its logic. Again, it is easy to play the doubting game with ideas you don't like, but it, too, can be threatening when you try to doubt ideas that are dear to your heart or central to your own worldview.

Student Example

Here is how one student played the believing and doubting game with the following assertion from professional writer Paul Theroux that emphasizing sports is harmful to boys.

> Just as high school basketball teaches you how to be a poor loser, the manly attitude towards sports seems to be little more than a recipe for creating bad marriages, social misfits, moral degenerates, sadists, latent rapists and just plain louts. I regard high school sports as a drug far worse than marijuana.

Believe

Although I am a woman I have a hard time believing this because I was a high school basketball player and believe high school sports are *very* important. But here goes. I will try to believe this statement even though I hate it. Let's see. It would seem that I wouldn't have much first-hand experience with how society turns boys into men. I do see though that Theroux is right about some major problems. Through my observations, I've seen many young boys go through humiliating experiences with sports that have left them scarred. For example, a 7-year-old boy, Matt, isn't very athletic and when kids in our neighborhood choose teams, they usually choose girls before they choose Matt. I wonder if he sees himself as a sissy and what this does to him? I have also experienced some first-hand adverse affects of society's methods of turning boys into men. In our family, my dad spent much of his time playing football, basketball, and baseball with my brother. I've loved sports since I was very young so I was eager to play. In order to play with them, I had to play like a boy. Being told you threw or played like a girl was the worst possible insult you could receive. The phrase, "be tough" was something I heard repeatedly while I was growing up. Whenever I got hurt, my dad would say, "Be tough." It didn't matter how badly I was hurt, I always heard the same message. Today, I think, I have a very, very difficult time opening up and letting people get to know me, because for so long I was taught to keep everything inside. Maybe sports does have some bad effects.

Doubt

I am glad I get to doubt this too because I have been really mad at all the sports bashing that has been going on in class. I think much of what Theroux says is just a crock. I know that the statement "sports builds character" is a cliché, but I really believe it. It seems to me that the people who lash out at sports clichés are those who never experienced these aspects of athletics and therefore don't understand them. No one can tell me that sports didn't contribute to some of my best and most meaningful friendships and growing experiences. I am convinced that I am a better person because through sports I have had to deal with failure, defeat, frustration, sacrificing individual desires for the benefit of the team, and so on. After my last high school basketball game when after many years of mind games, of hating my coach one minute and the next having deep respect for him, of big games lost on my mistakes, of hours spent alone in the gym, of wondering if the end justifies the means, my coach put his arm around me and told me he was proud. Everything, all the pain, frustration, anxiety, fear, and sacrifice of the past years seemed so worthwhile. You might try to tell me that this story is hackneyed and trite, but I won't listen because it is a part of me, and something you will never be able to damage or take away. I think athletes share a special bond. They know what it is like to go through the physical pain of practice time and again. They understand the wide variety of emotions felt (but rarely expressed). They also know what a big role the friendships of teammates and coaches play in an athlete's life.

We admire this writer a great deal—both for the passion with which she defends sports in her doubting section and for the courage of walking in a sports basher's shoes in the believing section. This exercise clearly engaged and stretched her thinking.

This brief writing assignment asks you to stretch your own thinking by choosing any two of the assigned assertions and practicing believing and doubting each in turn. Use freewriting to explore your first assertion. Spend ten minutes believing the assertion and ten minutes doubting it for a total of twenty minutes. Then choose a second assertion, but this time use idea mapping. Spend ten minutes entering reasons for believing the assertion and then ten minutes for doubting it (or move back and forth between believing and doubting, since an idea map gives you this flexibility), again for a total of twenty minutes. The total assignment should take forty minutes.

c h a p t e r 3

Solving Content Problems
Thesis and Support

WHAT YOU WILL LEARN IN THIS CHAPTER:

In this chapter you will learn the importance of drafting as a problem-solving process in which writers seek a surprising thesis and convincing support. In particular, you will learn the following:

- How to create a thesis statement aimed at changing your readers' view of the topic
- How to give your thesis tension
- How to support your thesis with a network of points and particulars

By seeing how points convert information to meaning, you will understand essential structural principles behind closed-form prose that will help you revise your drafts, write summaries, and move easily up and down the scale of abstraction.

> The commonsense, conventional understanding of writing is as follows. Writing is a two-step process. First you figure out your meaning, then you put it into language. . . . This idea of writing is backwards. . . . Meaning is not what you start out with but what you end up with.
>
> —Peter Elbow, *Writing Teacher and Theorist*

Chapter 2 explained how to use exploratory writing and talking to discover and develop ideas. This chapter and the next describe the kinds of problems that experienced writers try to solve as they move beyond exploratory writing and talking to produce a formal finished product. This chapter explains how writers of academic essays seek a final product that poses a good question, has a surprising thesis, and supports that thesis with strong arguments and convincing detail. Chapter 4 shifts from subject-matter problems to rhetorical problems and demonstrates that what writers say and how they say it are controlled by their purpose, intended audience, and genre. In these two chapters we temporarily separate subject-matter problems from rhetorical problems for the sake of instructional clarity. But, like the classic problem of the chicken and the egg, it is impossible to say which should or can be addressed first, subject-matter problems (What's my thesis? What's my supporting evidence?) or rhetorical problems (Who's my audience? What's my purpose?). Throughout the writing process, writers wrestle simultaneously and recursively with both subject-matter problems and rhetorical problems.

▨ DRAFTING AND REVISING AS A PROBLEM-SOLVING PROCESS

Beginning writers often don't appreciate the extent to which experienced writers struggle when they compose. Unlike beginning writers, who often think of revision as cleaning up errors in a rough draft, experienced writers use the writing process to "wallow in complexity." The more experienced the writer, the more likely that he or she will make large-scale, global revisions in a draft rather than local, sentence-level changes. Experienced writers, in fact, often dismantle their first constructions and start fresh. They build on what they learned the first time to create a more appropriate structure the second time around. Chapter 17 describes this writing process in more detail.

Our point in this chapter is that writers often need multiple drafts because early in the writing process they may be unsure of what they want to say or where their ideas are headed. As Peter Elbow puts it (in the epigraph for this chapter), "Meaning is not what you start out with but what you end up with." To appreciate Elbow's point, consider the following partial transcript of a writing center conference in which the student writer is responding to a political science assignment: Is U.S. involvement in Central America a case of imperialism?

> TUTOR: If I said, tell me whether or not this is imperialism, what's your first gut reaction?. . . .
>
> WRITER: There's very strong arguments for both. It's just all in how you define it.
>
> TUTOR: Okay, who's doing the defining?
>
> WRITER: Anybody. That's just it, there's no real clear definition. Over the time it's been distorted. I mean, before, imperialism used to be like the British who go in and take Hong Kong, set up their own little thing that's their own British government. That's true imperialism. But the definition's been expanded to include indirect control by other means, and what exactly that is, I guess you have to decide. So I don't know. I don't think we really have control in Central America, so that part of me says no that's not imperialism. But other parts of me say we really do control a lot of what is going on in Central America by the amount of dollars and where we put them. So in that essence, we do have imperialism. . . .
>
> TUTOR: So you're having a hard time making up your mind whether it is or isn't imperialism?

WRITER: Yes! The reason why I'm undecided is because I couldn't create a strong enough argument for either side. There's too many holes in each side. If I were to pick one side, somebody could blow me out of the water. . . .

This student writer is blocked because she thinks she has to make up her mind about her issue before she starts writing. The assigned problem requires her both to define imperialism and to argue whether U.S. activity in Central America meets the definition. What we admire about this student is that she is "wallowing in complexity," fully aware of the problem's difficulty and actively confronting alternative views. The best way for her to think through these complexities, we would argue, is to start doing exploratory writing—freewriting, idea mapping, or another of the strategies described in Chapter 2. This exploratory writing can then evolve into a first draft. Our point here is that the act of writing generates thought. The more she writes, the more she will clarify her own ideas. Her first drafts may have to be dismantled once she finally commits herself to a position. But the discarded drafts won't have been wasted; they will have helped her to manage the complexity of the assignment.

This writer needs to realize that her difficulty is a sign of strength. A good thesis statement is a risky one. Knowing that a skeptical reader might "blow you out of the water" motivates you to provide the best support possible for your thesis while acknowledging the power of opposing views. Perhaps this writer hopes that a miraculous insight will give her the "correct" solution, which she can then write out effortlessly. "In your dreams," we reply. Or perhaps she thinks that her present difficulty is a sign of her own inadequacy. To the contrary, her awareness of complexity and risk means that she is on the right track.

◨ TAKING RISKS: SEEKING A SURPRISING THESIS

As we have seen, most academic writing is thesis based. By *thesis based* we mean that the writer aims to support a main point or thesis statement, which is the writer's one-sentence summary answer to the problem or question that the paper addresses. The writer supports the thesis with reasons and evidence because he or she assumes that the audience will regard it skeptically and will test it against other possible answers. As the quotation from Peter Elbow implies, many writers do not formulate their final arguments until quite late in the writing process because they are constantly testing their ideas as they draft. The underlying motivation for multiple drafting is the search for a strong argument headed by a strong thesis.

But what makes a thesis strong? For one thing, a strong thesis always contains an element of uncertainty, risk, or challenge. A strong thesis implies a counter thesis. According to Elbow, a thesis has "got to stick its neck out, not just hedge or wander. [It is] something that can be quarreled with." Elbow's sticking-its-neck-out metaphor is a good one, but we prefer to say that a strong thesis *surprises* the reader with a new, unexpected, different, or challenging view of the writer's topic. In this section, we present two ways of creating a surprising thesis: (1) trying to change your reader's view of your subject and (2) giving your thesis tension.

Try to Change Your Reader's View of Your Subject

To change your reader's view of your subject, you must first imagine how the reader would view the subject *before* reading your essay. Then you can articulate how you aim to change that view. A useful exercise is to write out the "before" and "after" views of your imagined readers.

Before reading my essay, my readers think this way about my topic:

_____.

After reading my essay, my readers will think this different way about my

topic: _____.

You can change your reader's view of a subject in several ways.* First, you can enlarge it. Writing that enlarges a view is primarily informational; it provides new ideas and data to add to a reader's store of knowledge about the subject. For example, a research paper on wind-generated electricity might have the following thesis: "The technology for producing wind-generated electricity has improved remarkably in recent years." (Before reading my essay, the reader has only limited, out-of-date knowledge of wind-power technology; after reading my essay, the reader will have up-to-date knowledge.)

Second, you can clarify your reader's view of something that was previously fuzzy, tentative, or uncertain. Writing of this kind often explains, analyzes, or interprets. Engineers, for example, in comparing the environmental impact of dams versus wind towers might be uncertain how to calculate the environmental impact of dams when their costs (loss of fish runs, destruction of streams and natural habitats) are weighed against their benefits (flood control, irrigation, power generation). An economist might write an article that would clarify this problem. (Before reading my article, engineers and politicians will be uncertain how to measure the environmental costs of dams. After reading my article, these persons will have a clearer understanding of how to calculate these costs.)

Still another kind of change occurs when an essay actually restructures a reader's whole view of a subject. Such essays persuade readers to change their minds or make decisions. They can be threatening to a reader's identity because they shake up closely held beliefs and values. For example, in Chapter 1 we printed a letter to the editor written by a civil engineer who argued that "wind-generated power can in no way serve as a reasonable major alternative [to hydro, coal-fired, or nuclear power]." (Before reading my letter, the reader believes that

---

*Our discussion of how writing changes a reader's view of the world is indebted to Richard Young, Alton Becker, and Kenneth Pike, *Rhetoric: Discovery and Change* (New York: Harcourt Brace & Company, 1971).

wind-generated power is a solution to our energy crisis; after reading my letter, the reader will believe that wind-generated power is a pipe dream.) One person we know—a committed environmentalist with high hopes for wind energy—said that this letter persuaded him that large-scale harnessing of wind energy wouldn't work. He was visibly dismayed; the engineer's argument had knocked his view of wind energy off its props. (We aren't saying, of course, that the engineer is *correct*. We are saying only that his letter persuaded at least one of our acquaintances to change his mind about wind energy.)

Surprise, then, is the measure of change an essay brings about in a reader. (Of course, to bring about such change requires more than just a surprising thesis; the essay itself must persuade the reader that the thesis is sound as well as novel. In the last part of this chapter we talk about how writers support a thesis through a network of points and particulars.)

Give Your Thesis Tension

Another element of a surprising thesis is tension. By *tension* we mean the reader's sensation of being stretched from a familiar, unsurprising idea to a new, surprising one or of being twisted by two ideas pushing in opposing directions.

Theses that induce stretching are compelling because they continually give the reader something new to consider. Often the purpose of these essays is to inform, explain, or analyze. They are satisfying because they fill gaps in knowledge as they take the reader on a journey from old, familiar ground into new territory—stretching the reader, as it were, into a new place. Stretching theses teach readers something they didn't already know about a subject.

A thesis designed to twist a reader sets up an opposition between the writer's claims and various counterclaims. The reader is asked to choose among alternative ways of looking at a topic. Twisting theses argue for a particular view of the subject in the face of alternative or countering views.

One of the best ways to create tension in a thesis statement is to begin the statement with an *although* or *whereas* clause: "Whereas most people believe X, this essay asserts Y." The *whereas* or *although* clause summarizes the reader's "before" view of your topic or the counterclaim that your essay opposes; the main clause states the surprising view or position that your essay will support. You may choose to omit the *although* clause from your actual essay, but formulating it first will help you achieve focus and surprise in your thesis. The examples that follow illustrate the kinds of tension we have been discussing and show why tension is a key requirement for a good thesis.

Question	What effect has the telephone had on our culture?
Thesis Without Tension	The invention of the telephone has brought many advantages to our culture.
Thesis with Tension	Although the telephone has brought many advantages to our culture, it may also have contributed to the increase of violence in our society.

Question	Do reservations serve a useful role in contemporary Native American culture?
Thesis Without Tension	Reservations have good points and bad points.
Thesis with Tension	Although my friend Wilson Real Bird believes that reservations are necessary for Native Americans to preserve their heritage, the continuation of reservations actually degrades Native American culture.

In the first example, the thesis without tension (telephones have brought advantages to our culture) is a truism with which everyone would agree and hence lacks surprise. The thesis with tension places this truism (the reader's "before" view) in an "although" clause and goes on to make a risky or contestable assertion. The surprising idea that the telephone contributes to violence shakes up our old, complacent view of the telephone as a beneficent instrument, and gives us a new way to regard telephones.

In the second example, the thesis without tension may not at first seem tensionless because the writer sets up an opposition between good and bad points. But *almost anything* has good and bad points, so the opposition is not meaningful, and the thesis offers no element of surprise. Substitute virtually any other social institution (marriage, the postal service, the military, prisons), and the statement that it has good and bad points would be equally true. The thesis with tension, in contrast, is risky. It commits the writer to argue that reservations have degraded Native American culture and to oppose the counterthesis that reservations are needed to *preserve* Native American culture. The reader is twisted by the tension between two opposing views.

We have used the terms *stretching* and *twisting* to help you see various ways in which a thesis can have tension, but it is not important to make sharp distinctions between the two. Frequently, a thesis stretches and twists simultaneously. What *is* important is that you see that the writer's goal is to surprise the reader in some way, thereby bringing about some kind of change in the reader's view. A thesis can surprise a reader by doing the following:

- giving the reader new information or clarifying a confusing concept
- posing a dilemma by juxtaposing two or more differing answers to the same question or by finding paradoxes or contradictions in an area that others regard as nonproblematic
- identifying an unexpected effect, implication, or significance of something
- showing underlying differences between two concepts normally thought to be similar or underlying similarities between two concepts normally thought to be different
- showing that a commonly accepted answer to a question isn't satisfactory or that a commonly rejected answer may be satisfactory
- opposing a commonly accepted viewpoint, supporting an unpopular viewpoint, or otherwise taking an argumentative stance on an issue
- providing a new solution for a problem

FOR WRITING AND DISCUSSION

It is difficult to create thesis statements on the spot because a writer's thesis grows out of an exploratory struggle with a problem. However, through brief exploratory writing and talking it is sometimes possible to arrive at a thesis that is both surprising and arguable. Working individually, spend ten minutes freewriting on one of the following topics chosen by your class or the instructor:

competitive sports	mathematics education
commuting by automobile	television talk shows
homelessness	sex-education classes
gangs	zoos

Then, working in small groups or as a whole class, share your freewrites, looking for elements in each person's freewrite that surprise other members of the class. From the ensuing discussion, develop questions or problems that lead to one or more surprising thesis statements. Each thesis should be supportable through personal experiences, previous reading and research, or critical thinking; for example:

Topic	Competitive Sports.
Question	Is it psychologically beneficial to participate in competitive sports?
Surprising Thesis	Although we normally think that playing competitive sports is good for us psychologically, the psychological traits that coaches try to develop in athletes are like anorectic dieting.

■ SUPPORTING A THESIS: POINTS AND PARTICULARS

Of course, a surprising thesis is only one aspect of an effective essay. An essay must also persuade the reader that the thesis is sound as well as surprising. Although tabloid newspapers have shocking headlines ("Thigh cream found to be a cheap alternative to fossil fuel!" "Elvis captains UFO that buzzes home of Dennis Rodman!"), skepticism quickly replaces surprise when we discover that within the articles the claims are unsupported. A strong thesis, then, must both surprise a reader and be supported with convincing particulars.

In fact, the particulars are the flesh and bone of writing and comprise most of the sentences. A principle of closed-form prose is that these particulars are always connected clearly to points and that the points precede the particulars. In this section, we want to help you understand this principle more fully because it will give you a powerful conceptual understanding of what effective closed-form writing does.

How Points Convert Information to Meaning

When particulars are clearly related to a point, that point converts information to meaning. To put it another way, a point's function is to state a meaning. A particular's function is to support a point: Particulars constitute the evidence, data, details, specifics, examples, explanations, and so forth that develop a point and make it convincing. By themselves, particulars are inert information—mere data without meaning.

You can see this difference for yourself in the following exercise. Here is a short list of information about a room in Dorkfinkster Hall.

- Dingy paint is peeling from the walls.
- Several light bulbs are burned out.
- The windows are dirty.

To convert this list of information into a meaningful unit, you need to make a point. What point might a writer have in mind if she wanted to mention peeling paint, burned-out light bulbs, and dirty windows? Although lots of variations are possible, she might solve the problem like this:

> The rooms in Dorkfinkster Hall are poorly maintained. Dingy paint is peeling from the walls, several light bulbs are burned out, and the windows are dirty.

Here her opening sentence makes a point and thus gives meaning to the list of information.

Now try a variation of the same exercise. Consider the same list of information about a room in Dorkfinkster Hall. Add several more pieces of information that could also be plausibly true about the room.

Since all the particulars on the list imply poor maintenance, most people continue with this meaning as they invent new particulars for the list:

- There are dead flies on the window sills.
- The floors have stained splotches.
- Some of the desks are sticky with spilled pop.

However, the exercise itself doesn't specify "poor maintenance" information; it asks for any kind of information. So the following data about the room would also fit the task:

- The room is rectangular and contains fifty movable desks.
- The wall clock has black hands on a white face.
- The window frames are two inches wide.

Obviously, once people start listing raw information, they can keep going forever. But reasonable people don't like lists of raw information; they like meanings. Hence our minds naturally intuited "poor maintenance" in the original list and continued with poor maintenance data. In closed-form prose, writers need to state those meanings explicitly in point sentences. What we should see is that the point sentence "The rooms in Dorkfinkster Hall are poorly maintained" is not an individual datum about the room, but rather a writer-created generalization that states a meaning found in some of the data about the room—the burned-out light bulbs, the peeling paint, the filthy windows—but not in the other equally true data concerning the number of desks or the width of the window frames.

These examples should make clear that a sentence like "The rooms in Dork-finkster Hall are poorly maintained" is fundamentally different from a sentence like "There are fifty moveable desks in the room." The first sentence is a *point*, whereas the second is a *particular*—that is, a specific piece of information, a fact. Obviously, reasonable people seek some kind of coordination between points and particulars, some sort of weaving back and forth between them. Writing teachers use a number of nearly synonymous terms for expressing this paired relationship: points/particulars, generalizations/specifics; claims/evidence; ideas/details; interpretations/data, meaning/support.

By definition, the highest-level point sentence in an essay is called its *thesis statement* and the highest-level point sentence in a paragraph is its *topic sentence*. But in reality essays have many more levels of points than just the thesis statement and the topic sentences of paragraphs. Several paragraphs can work together to support a single major point while an individual paragraph might have several subpoints. As an example of how small blocks of meaning (a point with its supporting particulars) get nested into a larger essay, consider how our little mini-paragraph on Dorkfinkster Hall could function as part of a larger essay with this thesis: "The Administration at this college doesn't care about its students." Our hypothetical essay could have the following outline:

Thesis: The Administration at this college doesn't care about its students.

I.   Registration day is absolute chaos.
        [Particulars about problems with registration day]

II. Student services are inadequate.
        [Particulars about bad student services]

III. The physical plant is in bad shape.
   A. The Student Union Building is falling apart.
       1. Broken tables in the cafeteria
       2. Moldy smell in the game room
       3. Restrooms have leaky plumbing
   B. Dorkfinkster Hall is poorly maintained.
       1. Peeling paint on the walls
       2. Burned out light bulbs
       3. Windows dirty

As this outline shows, the writer has three complaints: registration day is chaos, student services are inadequate, and the physical plant is in bad shape. Our mini-paragraph on Dorkfinkster Hall now functions as support for the writer's last main point.

How Removing Particulars Creates a Summary

What we have shown, then, is that skilled writers weave back and forth between generalizations and specifics. The generalizations form a network of higher-level and lower-level points that develop the thesis; the particulars (specifics) support each of the points and subpoints in turn. In closed-form prose, the network of points is easily discernible because points are clearly highlighted with transitions and main points are placed prominently at the heads of paragraphs. (In open-form prose, generalizations are often left unstated, creating gaps where the reader must actively fill in meaning.)

If you remove most of the particulars from a closed-form essay, leaving only the network of points, you will have written a summary or abstract of the essay. As an example, reread the civil engineer's letter to the editor arguing against the feasibility of wind-generated power (pp. 12–13). The writer's argument can be summarized in a single sentence:

> Wind-generated power is not a reasonable alternative to other forms of power in the Pacific Northwest because wind power is unreliable, because there are major unsolved problems involved in the design of wind generation facilities, and because the environmental impact of building thousands of wind towers would be enormous.

What we have done in this summary is remove the particulars, leaving only the high-level points that form the skeleton of the argument. The writer's thesis remains surprising and contains tension, but without the particulars the reader has no idea whether to believe the generalizations or not. The presence of the particulars is thus essential to the success of the argument.

FOR WRITING AND DISCUSSION

Compare Rockwood's original letter with the one-sentence summary just given and then note how Rockwood uses specific details to support each point. How do these particulars differ from paragraph to paragraph? How are they chosen to support each point?

How to Use Your Knowledge About Points and Particulars When You Revise

The lesson to learn here is that in closed-form prose writers regularly place a point sentence in front of detail sentences. When a writer begins with a point, readers interpret the ensuing particulars not as random data, but rather as *evidence* in support of that point. The writer depends on the particulars to make the point credible and persuasive.

This insight may help you clarify two of the most common kinds of marginal comments that readers (or teachers) place on writers' early drafts. If your draft has a string of sentences giving data or information unconnected to any stated point, your reader is apt to write in the margin, "What's your point here?" or "Why are you telling me this information?" "How does this information relate to your thesis?" Conversely, if your draft tries to make a point that isn't developed with particulars, your reader is apt to write marginal comments such as "Evidence?" "Development?" "Could you give an example?" and "More details needed."

Don't be put off by these requests; they are a gift. It is common in first drafts for main points to be unstated, buried, or otherwise disconnected from their details and for supporting information to be scattered confusingly through the draft or missing entirely. Having to write point sentences obliges you to wrestle with your intended meaning: Just what am I trying to say here? How can I nutshell that in a point? Likewise, having to support your points with particulars causes you to wrestle with the content and shape of your argument: What particulars will make this point convincing? What further research do I need to do to find these particulars? In Part Three of this text, which is devoted to advice about composing and revising, we show how the construction and location of point sentences are essential for reader clarity. Part Three also explains various composing and revising strategies that will help you create effective networks of points and particulars.

Moving Up and Down the Scale of Abstraction

We have said, then, that writers weave back and forth between points and particulars. But the distinction between points and particulars is a matter of context: A point in one context can be a particular in another. For example, the sentence "The rooms in Dorkfinkster Hall are poorly maintained" is a point in relationship to the specific details about dirty windows and burned out light bulbs, but it is a particular in relationship to the larger point "This college doesn't care about its students." What matters is the relative position of sentences along a scale of abstraction. As an illustration of such a scale, consider the following list of words, descending from the abstract to the specific:

living creature

animal

mammal

cow

Holstein

Twyla

old sleepy-eyed Twyla chewing her cud

This scale takes you from a general word that encompasses all living creatures down to a specific phrase, the details of which represent one specific cow—old sleepy-eyed Twyla.

In descriptive and narrative prose, writers often use sensory details very low on the scale of abstraction. Note how shifting down the scale improves the vividness of the following passage:

Mid-scale	The awkward, badly dressed professor stood at the front of the room.
Low on the scale	At the front of the room stood the professor, a tall, gawky man with inch-thick glasses, an enormous Adam's apple, wearing a manure brown jacket, burgundy and gray plaid pants, a silky vest with what appeared to be "scenes from an aquarium" printed on it, and a polka dot blue tie.

The details in the more specific passage help you experience the writer's world. They don't just tell you that the professor was dressed weirdly; they *show* you.

Academic or professional prose also often uses particulars that are low on the scale of abstraction—statistics, facts, quotations, or specific examples. Civil engineer David Rockwood uses low-on-the-scale numerical data about the size and number of wind towers to convince readers that wind generation of electricity entails environmental damage. But particulars don't always have to be concrete sensory details (such as the colors of the professor's tie and jacket) or highly specific factual or numerical data (such as those used in Rockwood's letter). Some kinds of writing remain at fairly high levels of abstraction, especially in academic prose on theoretical or philosophical topics. Yet even the most theoretical kind of prose will include several layers on the scale. Each of the assignment chapters in Part Two of this text gives advice on finding the right kinds and levels of particulars to support each essay.

FOR WRITING AND DISCUSSION

Working as individuals, what kinds of particulars could you use to support each of the provided points? Share your results as a whole class or in small groups. This exercise is a warm-up for the brief writing assignment at the end of this chapter.

1. The weather was beautiful yesterday.
2. I was shocked by the messiness of Bill's dorm room.
3. Advertising in women's fashion magazines creates a distorted and unhealthy view of beauty.
4. Although freewriting looks easy, it is actually quite difficult.
5. At the introductory level, chemistry is much more abstract than physics.

CHAPTER SUMMARY

In this chapter, we have highlighted the importance of drafting as a problem-solving process in which the writer seeks a surprising thesis and convincing details. To achieve surprise, the writer develops a thesis aimed at changing the reader's view of a topic. A surprising thesis is characterized by tension, created either from stretching the reader's understanding in a new direction or from twisting the reader's beliefs in a contrary direction. In addition to presenting a surprising thesis, a writer needs to support the thesis through a network of points, each point backed up by particulars. By omitting the particulars, a writer can create a summary of a closed-form piece. Writers weave back and forth between generalizations and specifics by moving up and down the ladder of abstraction.

BRIEF WRITING PROJECT

The brief writing assignment for this chapter gives you practice generating particulars to support a point. To make it easier, we've supplied the point sentence. This assignment teaches an essential concept: effective closed-form writing supports points with particulars.

> Write one full paragraph that uses specific details to support the provided point sentence. Begin your paragraph with the point sentence and then use the body of the paragraph to provide specific supporting details. Your paragraph should be between 150 and 250 words in length. For your point sentence, choose any one of the following (or another point sentence provided by your instructor):
>
> - Directly or indirectly, anyone who is not a vegetarian causes animals to suffer.
> - Although the college library looks as though it is a good place to study, it has many distractions that lure you from your work.
> - Although doing X looks easy, it actually requires remarkable skill. (For X, substitute any activity of your choice; for example, "Although playing center midfielder in soccer looks easy, it actually requires remarkable athletic skill.")
> - Although X works reasonably well, it has one major problem—_____. (For X substitute anything of your choice, e.g., "Although the interior of my new car is generally well designed, it has one major problem—awkward controls." or "Although the registration system at our school works reasonably well, it has one major problem: Most students find it almost impossible to locate their advisor." The idea is to use convincing details to persuade readers that a problem exists.
> - The most memorable trait of (person's name) is X. (e.g., "The most memorable trait of my grandfather was his sense of humor." or "The most memorable trait of my sister is her incredible athletic ability." Then use specific details to illustrate the trait.)

The purpose of this assignment is to help you appreciate the difference between generalizations and specifics. This assignment provides you with a generalization or the frame for a generalization that you can apply to your own topic. Your task is to provide the supporting particulars that convince the reader of the truth of the generalization. For this assignment, your particulars will probably take the form of specific observations, facts, or examples. Here is a student paragraph written for this assignment.

Student Example

Although my new stereo receiver produces a pleasant sound and has ample power and volume, it has one major problem: poor design of the controls. The on/off switch in the upper left-hand corner is small and easy to confuse with two switches that control the main and remote speakers. If you hit the main speaker switch instead of the on/off switch, the sound will go off and you will think you have turned off the amplifier. When you try to turn it on again (by hitting the on/off switch), you will not hear any sound and will think the system is broken. This problem wouldn't be so bad if the tuning dial were always lit—that way you would know if the amplifier was turned on or not. But no light appears on the face of the receiver unless it is set in the "tuner" mode. Another problem with the controls is that the preset tuning buttons for radio stations are so small and close together that you have to use your little finger to push them. In the dark, they aren't lit, so I have to keep a little flashlight next to the amplifier to change radio stations at night. Finally, the volume control isn't gradual enough. The slightest movement of the knob changes the volume dramatically so that it is very difficult to adjust the sound to just the right level. (236 words)

Main point sentence

First subpoint: on/off switch confused with other switches

Details supporting first subpoint

Second subpoint: tuning buttons are too hard to use

Details supporting second subpoint

Third subpoint: volume controls not gradual

Solving Rhetorical Problems

Purpose, Audience, and Genre

WHAT YOU WILL LEARN IN THIS CHAPTER

In this chapter you will learn how writing is motivated by both internal and external factors. When you analyze your rhetorical situation, you discover how decisions about your purpose, audience, and genre affect the content, structure, and style of what you write. In particular, you will learn the following:

■ How to write for different purposes
■ How to analyze your audience
■ How to recognize different genres
■ How to make decisions about structure and style based on analysis of your purpose, audience, and genre
■ How to vary your style and construct an appropriate voice

It is amazing how much so-called writing problems clear up when the student really cares, when he is realistically put into the drama of somebody with something to say to somebody else.

—James Moffett, *Writing Teacher and Theorist*

In Chapter 3, we characterized composing as a problem-solving process requiring multiple drafts. We focused on subject-matter problems, in particular, the writer's struggle to find a surprising thesis and convincing details. In this chapter we explore ways in which writers' structural and stylistic choices are influenced by their rhetorical situations. We begin by discussing occasions that impel people to write. We then analyze three key variables of rhetorical context—purpose, audience, and genre—and show how these variables affect choices about structure and style.

▨ MOTIVATING OCCASIONS, OR WHY AM I WRITING THIS PIECE?

We said in Chapter 1 that people naturally enjoy posing and pursuing subject-matter problems. It is less clear whether people naturally enjoy writing about those problems. It is interesting to ask yourself when putting words on paper, "Why am I sitting here writing an essay when I could be doing something else?"

If asked, Why *do* you write? many of you might well answer, "Because teachers like you tell me to." Perhaps from first grade on, writing—or at least writing for school—has not been pleasant for you. Left to your own desires, you might have avoided school writing as diligently as you avoided canned spinach or bad hair days.

For others, writing school essays may have been—at least on occasion—deeply satisfying. Perhaps there was something about the assignment, the subject matter, or the environment created by the teacher that engaged you. On those occasions you may have immersed yourself in the writing project, written with care, and rewritten until you had fulfilled standards higher than those you would have set on your own. Even when there is an element of compulsion in the writing situation, you can claim ownership of the project and grow in the act of writing.

What we are suggesting is that there are two different motivations for writing—an external compulsion and an internal creative desire. Many of you might think that the first of these motivations—compulsion or coercion—is peculiar to school situations in which teachers assign papers and set deadlines. But you should know that the element of external compulsion felt so keenly in school writing is present in nearly every writing situation. Even poets report that writing can be a laborious process, provoked as often by ego, dumb habit, publishers' deadlines, or even greed, as by a burning vision. Eighteenth-century English writer Samuel Johnson, regarded by many as the first professional writer in Western culture, claimed that "No man but a blockhead ever wrote but for money." Yet he managed to write compellingly and artfully on everything from politics to language.

Most writing, whether it's done by students, artists, or businesspeople, is the product of mixed motives, some more or less voluntary, others downright coercive. Consider a middle manager requested by a company vice-president to write a report explaining why his division's profits are down. The manager is motivated by several factors: he wants to provide sound causal explanations for the financial decline, which will help the company set a course to remedy the situation; he wants to avoid looking bad or at least appearing to be solely responsible for the dip in profits; he wants to impress the vice-president in the hope that she will promote him to upper management; he wants to understand and articulate for himself just how this lamentable state of affairs came about; he wants each sentence to say just what he wants it to say; and so on.

College students' motivations for writing are often as complex as those of our hypothetical middle manager. Perhaps your writing is occasioned by an assignment and a deadline set by an instructor. But that rarely tells the whole story. In part, you write because you are engaged by an intellectual problem and want to say something significant about that problem; in part, you want to produce a well-written essay; in part, you want to please the teacher and get a good grade; in part, you want to improve your writing, and so forth. However arbitrary or artificial a college writing assignment might seem, it is really no more so than the writing occasions you will encounter outside college, when you must often write on tight deadlines for purposes specified by others. Given this fact, we believe that your best chance of writing successfully in college is to become engaged with the intellectual problem specified in the assignment. When you care about your ideas, you begin to imagine readers who care about them also (as opposed to imagining a teacher looking for mistakes), and you write to have an impact on those readers. The external motivations for writing are real and inescapable, but developing an internal motivation for writing—the desire to say something significant about your topic to an audience for a purpose—will help you produce your best work.

FOR WRITING AND DISCUSSION

Think of a time when you actually wanted to write something. What did you write and why did you find it satisfying? If this experience was a school assignment, what was it about the assignment, the subject matter, the classroom environment, the teacher, or you that awakened in you an internal motivation for writing? Prior to class discussion, spend several minutes freewriting about the occasion, exploring what made you feel internally motivated to write. Then, working in small groups or as a whole class, share your experiences with classmates. As a class, can you make any generalizations about the kinds of occasions or experiences that make a person want to write something? (If you cannot recall such an occasion, then recall the most hideous writing experience you've had and recount the elements that made it particularly gruesome. Why did the occasion fail to motivate you internally?)

◪ THE ELEMENTS OF RHETORICAL CONTEXT: PURPOSE, AUDIENCE, AND GENRE

We have said that the best motivation for writing is the desire to say something significant about a substantive problem to an audience that cares about your ideas. But while writing you must also wrestle with rhetorical problems. What you say about your topic, how you organize and develop your ideas, what words you choose, and what voice and tone you adopt are all determined by your rhetorical context. In this section, we discuss in detail three important components of rhetorical context—purpose, audience, and genre.

Purpose

In analyzing your rhetorical context, you should start by asking: What is my purpose? Or, to put it another way: What effect do I want to have on my readers? What change do I want to bring about in their understanding of my subject? In most instances, you can write a one-sentence, nutshell answer to your question about purpose.

> My purpose is to share with my reader my successful struggle with dyslexia.
>
> My purpose is to raise serious doubts in my reader's mind about the value of the traditional grading system.
>
> My purpose is to inform my reader about the surprising growth of the marijuana industry in the midwestern farm states.
>
> My purpose is to explain how Northrop Frye's view of *Hamlet* fails to account for several key features of the text.
>
> My purpose is to convince readers that the potential bad consequences of mail-order marriages require governments to regulate the mail-order bride industry.
>
> My purpose is to persuade the general public that wind-generated electricity is not a practical energy alternative in the Pacific Northwest.

In closed-form academic articles, technical reports, and other business and professional pieces, writers typically place explicit purpose statements in the introduction. In most other forms of writing, they formulate purpose statements behind the scenes—the writer keeps a purpose statement in mind and uses it to achieve focus and direction, but seldom states it explicitly.

Writers' purposes generally fall into six broad categories. Situating your writing project within one or more of these categories can help you understand how to approach your task.

Writing to Express or Share (Expressive Purpose)

When you adopt this general purpose, you place your own life—your personal experiences and feelings—at the center of your reader's attention. You express in words what it is like to be you, to see or feel the world your way. Writing expressively in a diary, journal, or personal notebook has therapeutic value because it gives you the opportunity to vent your feelings and explore your thoughts. Often, however, you may choose to write expressively to move or touch a reader, to share your experiences and feelings with others—with friends or relatives through letters or with strangers through formal autobiographical essays or personal reflections.

Expressive writing usually follows the impulse to share rather than to argue or disagree. It says, in effect, "While you read my story or my reflections, you can momentarily cease being you and become me for a while, seeing the world through my eyes. My words might cause you to see the world differently, but my goal isn't to change you, just to help you appreciate the uniqueness of my experience." Instead of creating surprise through an argumentative thesis, expressive writing achieves surprise by offering the reader access to the private experiences of another human being.

Expressive writing usually falls near the open end of our closed-to-open continuum. When an expressive purpose is joined to a literary one (which we will describe shortly) the writer produces autobiographical pieces that function in a literary way, using image, plot, character, and symbol.

Writing to Inquire or Explore (Exploratory Purpose)

Although exploratory writing is closely linked to expressive writing, it usually focuses more on subject-matter problems than on the writer's life. You use exploratory writing to wade into complexity via freewriting, idea mapping, journal keeping, note taking, e-mail exchanges, letter writing, drafting, and any other writing that probes a subject and deepens your thinking. Its goal is to help you ask questions, explore possible answers, consider opposing views, pursue conflicting trains of thought, expand and clarify your thinking, and generally delay closure on a question in order to work your way through the complexity of your subject.

Exploratory writing is usually unfinished, behind-the-scenes work not intended to be read by others, but it sometimes results in a formal, finished product. In these cases, the writing aims to *pose* or *deepen a problem*, to muddy waters that the reader thought were clear. It doesn't *support* a thesis; it *seeks* a thesis. It perplexes the reader by revealing new questions about a topic, by showing how various approaches to that topic are unsatisfactory or how certain aspects of a topic are more problematic than previously supposed. Because exploratory writing often takes a narrative shape, dramatizing the process of the writer's thinking about a subject, it usually falls toward the open end of the closed-to-open continuum.

Writing to Inform or Explain (Informative Purpose)

When your purpose is informative, you see yourself as more knowledgeable than your reader about your topic. You create surprise by enlarging the reader's view of a topic, providing new ideas and information based on your own experiences or research. When you write to inform, you adopt the role of teacher in relation to your reader. You imagine that the reader will trust your authority and not dispute what you say. Although informative writing usually has a closed-form structure, it may fall anywhere along the continuum from closed to open.

Writing to Analyze or Interpret (Analytical Purpose)

When your purpose is analytical, you examine aspects of a subject that puzzle your reader and offer tentative ways to resolve these puzzles. Analytical writing requires you to think critically about a problematic text, set of data, or other phenomenon. Your goal is to clarify your reader's understanding of this problematic subject. You surprise your reader with a new or more illuminating way of seeing, thinking about, or understanding the subject.

Analytical writing, often laced with informative elements, constitutes the most common kind of academic prose. It typically takes a closed-form structure. The introduction poses a question, and the body presents the writer's solution. The reader generally regards the solution as *tentative,* so the writer must support it with reasons and evidence or other justifying arguments. Unlike informative writing, which positions the writer as an expert, analytical writing generally assumes that writer and reader are equally well informed and equally engaged with the puzzling phenomenon. Analytical writing presupposes a more skeptical audience than does informative prose. The writer might not expect readers to argue back, but will certainly expect them to test his or her ideas against their own experience and hypotheses.

Writing to Persuade (Persuasive Purpose)

When your purpose is persuasive, you enter a conversation in which people disagree with each other about answers to a given question. You think of your audience as judges, jurors, or other decision makers, who must be convinced that your answer to the question is sounder than other answers. Persuasive writing addresses a controversial problem, to which there are several alternative answers with supporting reasons and evidence. When you write to persuade, you aim to surprise the reader with your own reasons and evidence or other appeals that will change the reader's beliefs or actions.

Persuasive writing can fall anywhere along the closed-to-open continuum. It may have a closed-form structure of reasons and evidence set out in a logical point-by-point format, or it may have a very open structure—a powerful story or a collage of emotionally charged scenes might be extremely persuasive in influencing a reader's views on an issue.

When writing persuasively, writers usually imagine skeptical readers vigorously questioning their claims. The only way they can effectively anticipate and respond to these questions is to understand alternative positions on the issue—including understanding the values, assumptions, and beliefs of the people who hold alternative views—and either refute these views, concede to them, or compromise with them. This emphasis on countering or accommodating alternative views and on appealing to the values and beliefs of the reader distinguishes persuasive writing from most analytical writing.

Writing to Entertain or Give Aesthetic Pleasure (Literary Purpose)

Sometimes writers focus not on themselves (expressive prose), nor on the subject matter (exploratory, informative, and analytical prose), nor on the reader (persuasive prose), but on the artistic shaping of language. When you adopt a literary purpose, you treat language as a medium, such as paint or clay. You explore its properties and its sound and rhythms. We typically think of literary writing as fiction or poetry, but nonfiction prose can also use literary techniques. Such prose is often called *literary nonfiction* or *belletristic prose.* Literary nonfiction usually combines a literary purpose with one or more other purposes, for example, an expressive purpose (an autobiographical essay about a turning point in your life) or an exploratory purpose (your contemplation of the cosmic meanings of a spider web).

FOR WRITING AND DISCUSSION

As a class, choose one of the following topic areas or another provided by your instructor. Then imagine six different writing situations in which a hypothetical writer would compose an essay about the selected topic. Let each situation call for a different purpose. How might a person write about the selected topic with an expressive purpose? An exploratory purpose? An informative purpose? An analytical purpose? A persuasive purpose? A literary purpose? How would each essay surprise its readers?

baseball	cats	hospices or nursing homes*
homelessness	garbage	dating or marriage
advertising	newspapers	gays in the military

Working on your own or in small groups, create six realistic scenarios, each of which calls for prose in a different category of purpose. Then share your results as a whole class. Here are two examples based on the topic "hospices."

Expressive Purpose	Working one summer as a volunteer in a hospice for dying cancer patients, you befriend a woman whose attitude toward death changes your life. You write an autobiographical essay about your experiences with this remarkable woman.
Analytic Purpose	You are a hospice nurse working in a home-care setting. You and your colleagues note that sometimes family members cannot adjust psychologically to the burden of living with a dying person. You decide to investigate this phenomenon. You interview "reluctant" family members in an attempt to understand the causes of their psychological discomfort so that you can provide better counseling services as a possible solution. You write a paper for a professional audience analyzing the results of your interviews.

Audience

In our discussion of purpose, we have already had a lot to say about audience. What you know about your readers—their familiarity with your subject matter, their reasons for reading, their closeness to you, their values and beliefs—affects most of the choices you make as a writer.

In assessing your audience, you must first consider what to them is old information and what is new information. You'll ask questions like these: What in my

---

*If this topic interests you, see how student writer Sheridan Botts wrote about hospices, first with an exploratory purpose (Chapter 8, pp. 174–77), and later with a persuasive purpose (Chapter 16, pp. 401–3).

essay will be old and familiar and what will be new, challenging, and surprising? How much background will my readers need? What can I assume they know and don't know? What is their current view of my topic that I am trying to change?

On a related note, you will also need to consider your audience's methods and reasons for reading. Imagine that you are a marketing manager and you want to persuade your harried boss to increase your research budget. You picture your boss sitting at her desk, people waiting to see her, phone ringing, a pile of memos, reports, and proposals in the in box. Consequently, you fashion a budget request with a tightly closed structure. Your document must be clear, concise, and well designed for her immediate comprehension and assent. The same reader in a different mood and setting may turn to a different kind of prose. In the evening, your harried boss might relax in an easy chair, sip a cup of tea, and reach for her favorite magazine. Is she most concerned now with speedy comprehension and quick access to needed information? Probably not. She's more likely to be interested in leisurely reading, perhaps an open-form piece on, say, bicycling in Italy. And she may well savor the way a passage is written, pausing to reflect on the scene it evokes.

Now consider how a change in audience can affect the content of a piece. Suppose you want voters in your city to approve a bond issue to build a new baseball stadium. If most members of your audience are baseball fans, you can appeal to their love of the game, the pleasure of a new facility, and so forth. But non–baseball fans won't be moved by these arguments. To reach them, you must tie the new baseball stadium to their values. You can argue that a new stadium will bring new tax revenues to the city, clean up a run-down area, revitalize local businesses, or stimulate the tourist industry. Your purpose remains the same, to persuade taxpayers to fund the stadium, but the content of your argument changes if your audience changes.

A change in audience can change a writer's purpose as well. A graduate student we know who studies wildlife management developed a technique for using a net gun to capture mountain goats so that researchers could place radio collars around their necks. He wrote several articles based on his expertise. For fellow specialists who studied mountain goats, he wrote a scientific article showing that capturing mountain goats with a net gun was more effective than drugging them with a dart gun (informative and analytical purposes). For the audience of a popular outdoors magazine, he wrote a personal-action narrative about shooting a net gun from a hovering helicopter (expressive and literary purpose). And because he was also concerned with preserving natural habitats for mountain goats, he wrote letters to legislators using data gathered from the radio collars to argue for restrictions on wilderness development (persuasive purpose).

In college, you are often writing for an audience of one—your instructor. However, most instructors try to read as a representative of a broader audience. To help college writers imagine these readers, many instructors try to design writing assignments that provide a fuller sense of audience. They may ask you to write for the readers of a particular magazine or journal, or they may create case assignments with a built-in audience (for example, "You are an accountant in the firm of Numbers and Fudge; one day you receive a letter from . . . "). If your instructor does not specify an audience, you can generally assume what we like to call the generic academic audience—student peers who have approximately the same level of knowledge and expertise in the field as you do, who are engaged by the question you address, and who want to read your writing to be surprised in some way.

Assessing Your Audience

In any writing situation, you can use the following questions to help you make decisions about content, form, and style:

1. Who is going to read what I write? A specific individual? A specific group with special interests? Or a general readership with wide-ranging interests and backgrounds?
2. What relationship do I have with these readers? Do I and my readers have an informal, friendly relationship or a polite, formal one? Is my readers' expertise in my general subject area greater, less, or equal to mine?
3. How much do my readers already know about the specific problem I address? How much background will I have to provide?
4. How much interest do my readers bring to my topic? Do I need to hook readers with a vivid opening and use special techniques to maintain their interest throughout? Or are they interested enough in the problem I am examining that the subject matter itself will drive their reading? (In persuasive writing, particularly in writing that proposes a solution to a problem, you may need to shock your readers into awareness that the problem exists.)
5. What are my audience's values, beliefs, and assumptions in relation to my topic? If I am writing on a controversial issue, will my readers oppose my position, be neutral to it, or support it? To which of their values, beliefs, or assumptions can I appeal? Will my position unsettle or threaten my audience or stimulate a strong emotional response? (Because a concern for audience is particularly relevant to persuasive writing, we will treat these questions in more depth in Chapters 14 through 16.)

Posing these questions will not lead to any formulaic solutions to your writing problems, but can help you develop strategies that will appeal to your audience and enable you to achieve your purpose.

FOR WRITING AND DISCUSSION

Working on your own, imagine that you enjoyed a fun party last weekend. (a) Describe that party in a letter to a close friend, inventing the details needed to show your friend how great the party was. (b) Describe the same party in a letter to a parent (or some other person whose differences from your friend would lead to a different description.) Note: You may substitute any other event or phenomenon that you would describe in different ways to different audiences.

Then, in small groups or as a class, share excerpts from your two letters. What changes did you make in your description as a result of changes in your audience?

Genre

The term *genre* refers to broad categories of writing that follow certain conventions of style, structure, and approach to subject matter. Literary genres include the short story, the novel, the epic poem, the limerick, the sonnet, and so forth. Nonfiction prose has its own genres: the business memo, the technical manual, the scholarly article, the scientific report, the popular magazine article (each magazine, actually, has its own peculiar conventions), the five-paragraph theme (a school genre), the newspaper editorial, the cover letter for a job application, the legal contract, the advertising brochure, and so forth.

The concept of genre creates strong reader expectations and places specific demands on writers. How you write any given letter, report, or article is influenced by the structure and style of hundreds of previous letters, reports, or articles written in the same genre. If you wanted to write for *Reader's Digest,* for example, you would have to use the conventions that appeal to its older, conservative readers: simple language, subjects with strong human interest, heavy reliance on anecdotal evidence in arguments, an upbeat and optimistic perspective, and an approach that reinforces the conservative ethos of individualism, self-discipline, and family. If you wanted to write for *Seventeen* or *Rolling Stone,* however, you would need to use quite different conventions.

To illustrate the relationship of a writer to a genre, we sometimes draw an analogy with clothing. Although most people have a variety of different types of clothing in their wardrobe, the genre of activity for which they are dressing (Saturday night movie date, job interview, wedding) severely constrains their choice and expression of individuality. A man dressing for a job interview might express his personality through choice of tie or quality and style of business suit; he probably wouldn't express it by wearing a bicycle helmet and mismatched shoes. Even when people deviate from a convention, they tend to do so in a conventional way. For example, teenagers who do not want to follow the genre of "teenager admired by adults" form their own genre of purple hair and pierced body parts. The concept of genre raises intriguing and sometimes unsettling questions about the relationship of the unique self to a social convention or tradition.

These same kinds of questions and constraints perplex writers. For example, academic writers usually follow the genre of the closed-form scholarly article. This highly functional form achieves maximum clarity for readers by orienting them quickly to the article's purpose, content, and structure. Readers expect this format, and writers have the greatest chance of being published if they meet these expectations. In some disciplines, however, scholars are beginning to publish more experimental, open-form articles. They may slowly alter the conventions of the scholarly article, just as fashion designers alter styles of dress.

The genre of the scholarly article varies enormously from discipline to discipline, both in the kinds of questions that specialists pose about their subject matter and in the style and structure of articles. As a specific example of a genre that many college students regularly encounter, we introduce you here to the *experimental report*. This genre is commonly used in fields that conduct empirical research, such as the physical or social sciences, nursing, medicine, business, engineering, education, and other fields.

The Experimental Report

An experimental report, sometimes called a scientific or technical report, is a formal paper addressed primarily to professionals who are interested in the results of an investigation. Its readers want to know why the investigation was undertaken, how it was conducted, what was learned, and whether the findings are significant and useful. Experimental reports usually follow a standard five-part format:

1. *Introduction.* This section explains the purpose of the investigation, what problem was addressed and what makes the problem both problematic and significant. The introduction often includes a review of the literature, which summarizes previous research addressing the same or a related problem. In many scientific disciplines, it is conventional to conclude the introduction with a hypothesis, a tentative answer to the question, which the investigation confirms or disconfirms.

2. *Methods.* Sometimes called *methodology* or *procedures,* the methods section details in cookbook fashion how the investigators conducted the research. It provides enough details so that other researchers can replicate the investigation. This section usually includes the following subsections: (a) research design, (b) apparatus and materials, and (c) procedures followed.

3. *Findings (results).* This section presents the empirical results of the investigation, the data discovered in the experiment. The findings may be displayed in figures, tables, graphs, or charts. Usually, the findings are not interpreted in this section.

4. *Discussion of findings.* This section is the main part of the experimental report. It explains the significance of the findings by relating what was discovered back to the problem set out in the introduction and detailing how the investigation did or did not accomplish its original purpose, that is, whether it answered the questions outlined in the introduction. (Did it confirm/disconfirm the writer's hypothesis?) This section also discusses the usefulness and significance of the findings and explores new questions raised by the experiment.

5. *Conclusions and recommendations.* This last section focuses on the main points learned from the investigation and, in some cases, on the practical applications of the investigation. If the investigation was a pure research project, this section often summarizes the most important findings and recommends areas for further research. If the investigation was aimed at mak-

ing a practical decision (for example, an engineering design decision), this section recommends appropriate actions.

You can tell from this description that the experimental report has a very closed form. Note, however, that the thesis is delayed until the discussion section, which reveals through the writer's analysis of the findings whether the original hypothesis was confirmed or disconfirmed.

FOR WRITING AND DISCUSSION

1. On page 63, we offered you a brief description of the conventions governing *Reader's Digest* articles, which appeal mainly to older, conservative readers. For this exercise, prepare similar descriptions of the conventions that govern articles in several other magazines, such as *Rolling Stone, Sports Illustrated, Cosmopolitan, Details, The New Yorker,* or *Psychology Today.* Each person should bring to class a copy of a magazine that he or she enjoys reading. The class should then divide into small groups according to similar interests. Your instructor may supply a few scholarly journals from different disciplines. In preparing a brief profile of your magazine, consider the following:

   - Scan the table of contents. What kinds of subjects or topics does the magazine cover?
   - Look at the average length of articles. How much depth and analysis are provided?
   - Consider the magazine's readership. Does the magazine appeal to particular political or social groups (liberal/conservative, male/female, young/old, white collar/blue collar, in-group/general readership)?
   - Look at the advertisements. What kinds of products are most heavily advertised in the magazine? Who is being targeted by these advertisements? What percentage of the magazine consists of advertisements?
   - Read representative pages, including introductions, of some articles. Would you characterize the prose as difficult or easy? Intellectual or popular? Does the prose use the jargon, slang, or other language particular to a group? Are the paragraphs long or short? How are headings, inserts, visuals, and other page-formatting features used? Is the writing formal or informal?
   - Think about what advice you would give a person who wanted to write a freelance article for this magazine.

2. Imagine that someone interested in hospices (see the example in the For Writing and Discussion exercise on p. 60) wanted to write an article about hospices for your chosen magazine. What approach would the

> writer have to take to have a hospice-related article published in your magazine? There may be no chance of this happening, but be creative. Here is an example:
>
> > Ordinarily *Sports Illustrated* would be an unlikely place for an article on hospices. However, *SI* might publish a piece about a dying athlete in a hospice setting. It might also publish a piece about sports memories of dying patients or about watching sports as therapy.

▨ RHETORICAL CONTEXT AND DECISIONS ABOUT STRUCTURE

So far in this chapter we have examined purpose, audience, and genre as components of a writer's rhetorical context. In this section and the next, our goal is to help you appreciate how these variables influence a writer's choices regarding structure and style. Although there is no formula that allows you to determine an appropriate structure and style based on particular purposes, audiences, and genres, there are some rules of thumb that can help you make decisions. Let's look first at structure.

Because most academic, business, and professional writing uses a closed-form structure, we spend a significant portion of this text advising you how to write such prose. However, you also need to be able to open up your prose on occasion, and to that end you need to practice writing at different positions on the continuum. The following advice will help you decide when closed or open forms are more appropriate.

When is closed-form prose most appropriate?

- When your focus is on the subject matter itself and your goal is to communicate efficiently to maximize clarity. In these cases, your purpose is usually to inform, to analyze, or to persuade.
- When you imagine your audience as a busy or harried reader who needs to be able to read quickly and process ideas rapidly. Closed-form prose is easy to summarize; moreover, a reader can speed read closed-form prose by scanning the introduction and then glancing at headings and the openings of paragraphs, where writers place key points.
- When the conventional genre for your context is closed-form writing, and you choose to meet, rather than break, readers' expectations.
- When you encounter any rhetorical situation that asks you to assert and support a thesis in response to a problem or question.

When is a more open form desirable?

- When you want to delay your thesis rather than announce it in the introduction, for example, to create suspense. A delayed thesis structure is less combative and more friendly; it conveys an unfolding "let's think through this together" feeling.

■ When your purpose is expressive, exploratory, or literary. These purposes tend to be served better through narrative rather than through thesis-with-support writing.

■ When you imagine your audience reading primarily for enjoyment and pleasure. In this context you can often wed a literary purpose to another purpose.

■ When the conventional genre calls for open-form writing, for example, autobiographical narratives, character sketches, or personal reflective pieces. Popular magazine articles often have a looser, more open structure than do scholarly articles or business reports.

■ When you are writing about something that is too complex or messy to be captured in a fixed thesis statement, or when you feel constrained by the genre of thesis with support.

▨ RHETORICAL CONTEXT AND DECISIONS ABOUT STYLE

Writers need to make choices not only about structure but also about style. By *style*, we mean the choices you make about how to say something. Writers can say essentially the same thing in a multitude of ways, each placing the material in a slightly different light, subtly altering meaning, and slightly changing the effect on readers. In this section we illustrate more concretely the many stylistic options open to you and explain how you might go about making stylistic choices.

Factors that Affect Style

As we shall see, style is a complex composite of many factors. We can classify the hundreds of variables that affect style into four broad categories.

1. *Ways of shaping sentences:* long/short, simple/complex, many modifiers/few modifiers, normal word order/frequent inversions or interruptions, mostly main clauses/many embedded phrases and subordinate clauses.
2. *Types of words:* abstract/concrete, formal/colloquial, unusual/ordinary, specialized/general, metaphoric/literal, scientific/literary.
3. *The implied personality projected by the writer (often called* **persona**): expert/layperson, scholar/student, outsider/insider, political liberal/conservative, neutral observer/active participant.
4. *The writer's implied relationship with the reader and the subject matter (often called* **tone**): intimate/distant, personal/impersonal, angry/calm, browbeating/sharing, informative/entertaining, humorous/serious, ironic/literal, passionately involved/aloof.

Recognizing and Creating Style or "Voice"

When discussing style, writing teachers often use the terms *style* and *voice* interchangeably. We can distinguish the two terms by thinking of style as analyzable textual features on the page (number of words in a sentence, number of main and subordinate clauses, use of active or passive voice, use of first, second, or third person, and so forth) and of voice as the reader's impression of the writer projected from the page—a combination of the image that you try to portray and the attitude you take toward your subject matter. Through your stylistic choices, you create an image of yourself in your reader's mind. This image, sometimes called a *persona*, can be cold or warm, humorous or serious, stuffy or lively, and so forth. It is your persona that readers like or dislike, trust or distrust. It is your tone (that is, your implied attitude toward your audience and subject) that engages and interests your readers or turns them off, that inspires or antagonizes them.

An Example of Varying Voices and Styles

To help you get a sense of different voices and styles, we try our hand at illustrating a few. In this section, rather than drawing examples from published sources, we imitate different styles and voices ourselves—both to show you that doing so can be fun and to let you see how stylistic variations on the same subject matter can produce different effects. Imagine the following scenario: One Farrago Pomp, a rising light in the educational community, has developed a new teaching method that he calls the critical visionary method of instruction. He has conducted several studies to demonstrate its effectiveness, and now other scholars are beginning to join the conversation that Pomp has initiated. First we present the introduction to a hypothetical scholarly article written in a formal academic style by a critic of Pomp, one Dr. Elwit Morganthorpe.

Formal Academic Style

Variations in pedagogical methodology are widely reported in the literature, and it is to be assumed that such variations will continue so long as empirical research yields less than unanimous consensus concerning the psychological and environmental factors that influence learning and cognition. Nevertheless, the work of F. Pomp (see especially 1989; 1992b; 1995) has firmly established the trance-inducing methodology embodied in his "Critical Visionary Method of Instruction" as among the most influential of the last two decades. Indeed, a recent review of the literature reveals that eighty-four articles—virtually all of which make elaborate claims for the efficacy of Pomp's approach—were published in the last three years alone.

Yet Pomp's work is being called increasingly into question. Shovit (1994) and Stuffit (1995) recently questioned a number of Pomp's underlying premises, while Ehrbag's (1994) pioneering empirical study raised serious doubts about Pomp's methodology. For that reason a rigorous research agenda was undertaken to put Pomp's claims to a definitive test in 26 college classrooms around the country. The results of this study are reported herein. The findings, while confirming a few of Pomp's less ambitious claims, show significantly sparser learning gains overall than those claimed in the literature.

—Elwit Morganthorpe, "Dimming the Vision: A Critical
Evaluation of Pomp's 'Visionary Method of Instruction'"

Next is the introduction to a conference presentation by another Pomp skeptic, Elmira Eggwhite, addressed to an academic audience. It is still an academic paper, but in a conversational rather than a formal style.

Informal Academic Style

A lot of teachers these days have been experimenting with Farrago Pomp's Visionary Method, and many have reported good results. (I am told that more than eighty articles supporting Pomp's work have been published in the last three years.) So I decided to try out some of Pomp's methods myself—with disastrous results. I admit that I have no weighty evidence to support my own less than enthusiastic assessment of VM—just one semester's experience with thirty first-year students in a writing class at Weasel College. I sincerely tried to make the method work. I read Pomp meticulously and tried to follow his suggestions exactly when I induced the trances, including use of drums, mantras, and synthetic sea music. In short, I employed Pomp's method with as much conviction as a normally credulous human being could muster.

As I'll show in the rest of this paper, Pomp's method had dismal effects on my students' writing and evoked extremely negative reactions to the more evangelical aspects of the approach. As one of my students put it: "Trances are for summer camp, not the classroom."

—Elmira Eggwhite, "Waking Up from Pomp's Trance"

In our final example, we switch all three variables of rhetorical context: purpose, audience, and genre. In this example the writer's purpose is not to analyze or evaluate Pomp's methods, but to write an informative piece on the visionary method movement. The audience consists of general readers rather than scholars. The genre is an upbeat popular magazine aimed at a youthful audience.

Popular Magazine Style

What's new in the college classroom these days? Retro hairdos and plastic pumps, you say. Tattoos and nose rings? True true, but what are people actually doing in those classrooms? Anything new about the way today's students are being taught?

Most definitely, say our campus correspondents. The latest rage is Vision. Or, more properly, Visionary Method.

According to Farrago Pomp, the man who invented the Visionary Method, his approach will be the mainstay of the 21st century classroom.

The tall, bearded Pomp explained the genesis of his approach at an early morning interview between numerous cups of double espresso.

"The idea for the Visionary Method hit me," says Pomp, "during a drum ceremony in my men's group."

"I realized that the old methods—tedious studying, often in weary isolation—didn't work. Knowledge should be imbibed, or quaffed in heady drafts, amidst chanting circles of fellow Visionaries," said Pomp, gesturing frantically for another espresso.

It appears, however, that not all of Pomp's colleagues are beating the same drum. Professor Elwit Morganthorpe has been leading a pack of educators throwing sand and water on Pomp's sacred campfires. "Pomp's methods are bogus," says Morganthorpe, citing his own comprehensive investigation of the Visionary Method. "Drum ceremonies can never replace old-fashioned studying."

In the meantime, thousands of college students are chanting their way through their college courses. Heady stuff indeed for those of us who got through college by memorizing textbooks and solving equations. What we wouldn't have given to be able to walk into our philosophy class and chug-a-lug some Spinoza. . . .

—"Drum Rolls, Please: Learning in the New Age"

FOR WRITING AND DISCUSSION

Working in small groups or as a whole class, analyze the differences in the styles of these three samples. How do the differences in styles create different voices—that is, what features of the writing make each voice sound different? How are differences in style a result of differences in the writer's purpose, audience, or genre?

Creating Your Writer's Voice

What is an appropriate writer's voice? For most college assignments, finding a voice close to your speaking voice is a good idea. In most rhetorical situations, it is to your advantage to project a trustworthy, credible, well-informed, thoughtful, and fair persona. We often ask our students to approximate their "natural" speaking voices in their writing to develop a conversational academic style—perhaps something similar to the second Pomp example—to avoid the stiffness of the formal style or the breezy glibness of the popular magazine style. By *natural*, we mean a voice that strives to be plain and clear while retaining the engaging quality of a person who is enthusiastic about the subject.

Of course, as you become an expert in a discipline, you often need to move toward a more scholarly voice. For example, the prose in an academic journal article can be extremely dense in its use of technical terms and complex sentence structure, but expert readers in that field understand and expect this voice. When writers wish to reach a wider range of readers outside a specialized field, they take on a plainer voice, using simpler diction and less complex sentences. Students sometimes try to imitate a dense academic style before they have achieved the disciplinary expertise to make the style sound natural: The result can seem pretentiously stilted and phony. Writing with clarity and directness within your natural range will usually create a more pleasing and powerful voice.

Often the persona you project—especially your credibility and trustworthiness—is conveyed in subtle ways. In an academic article, the overt function of footnotes, citations, and a bibliography is to enable other scholars to track down the cited sources. A covert function, however, is to create an air of authority for you, the writer, to assure readers that you have done your homework and are fully knowledgeable and informed. Judicious use of the discipline's specialized language can have a similar effect.

Your persona is also reflected in your manuscript's form, appearance, and editorial correctness. Sloppy or inappropriately formatted manuscripts, grammatical errors, misspelled words, and other problems send a signal to the reader that you are unprofessional and perhaps untrustworthy and undependable. Printing a manuscript in unconventional fonts or with faint type is inappropriate for academic and professional situations. In all contexts, grammatical errors and misspellings signal a lack of care.

Another factor in creating a trustworthy persona, especially in analytical and persuasive writing, is how you treat alternative views. Do you acknowledge the existence of views different from your own? If you do not, readers of analytical prose may sense that you are uninformed or less than rigorous; readers of persuasive prose may perceive you as unfair or not credible. And when you do acknowledge differing views, do you summarize them fairly and treat them with dignity, or do you ridicule them? In some contexts, ridiculing an opponent works well (for example, if you are fanning the enthusiasm of readers who already share your views), but in other contexts it is disastrous (for example, if you want to change the views of those who disagree with you). How you acknowledge differing views is a particularly important concern in persuasive writing, as we explain in detail in Chapter 14.

You need to recognize that almost every choice you make as a writer influences the way readers perceive who you are, what your beliefs and assumptions are, and how you view reality. Once you recognize this perhaps unsettling truth— that your writing always conveys an image of you as the writer—you will be better able to control the choices you make and to construct a persona that fits your purpose, your audience, and your genre.

Practicing Different Styles Through Creative Imitation

One effective way to understand and appreciate different writers' styles is to try to imitate them. This rhetorical practice—called creative imitation—has a long history beginning with the rhetoricians of classical Greece and Rome. When you do creative imitation, you examine a passage from an expert stylist and try to emulate it. You substitute your own subject matter, but you try to imitate the exact grammatical structures, lengths and rhythms of the sentences, and the tones of the original passage. The long-range effect of creative imitation is to expand your stylistic choices; the more immediate effect is to increase your skill at analyzing a writer's style. Most practitioners find that creative imitation encourages surprising insights into their own subject matter (when seen through the lens of the original writer's style) as well as a new understanding of how a particular piece of writing creates its specific effects.

You begin a creative imitation by asking questions such as these: What is distinctive about the sentences in this passage of writing? How do choices about sentence length and complexity, kinds of words, figures of speech, and so forth create a writer's voice? After close examination of the passage, you then think of your own subject matter that could be appropriately adapted to this writer's style.

To help you understand creative imitation, we provide two examples. In the first, the writer, Victoria Register-Freeman, is exploring how relations between young men and women today threaten to undo some of this century's progress toward gender equality. In the section of her article that precedes this passage,

Register-Freeman explains how she, as a single mother, taught her boys to cook, sew, do laundry, and "carry their weight domestically." But then, as she explains in this passage, teenage girls undid her attempts at creating gender equality:*

Register-Freeman Passage

Then came puberty and hunkhood. Over the last few years, the boys' domestic skills have atrophied because handmaidens have appeared en masse. The damsels have driven by, beeped, phoned and faxed. Some appeared so frequently outside the front door they began to remind me of the suction-footed Garfields spread-eagled on car windows. While the girls varied according to height, hair color and basic body type, they shared one characteristic. They were ever eager to help the guys out.

—Victoria Register-Freeman, "My Turn: Hunks and Handmaidens"

Register-Freeman's voice projects the image of a concerned mother and feminist social critic. Her tone includes a range of attitudes: serious, personal, factual, ironic, frustrated. Note how this passage begins and ends with short, clipped sentences. The second sentence states a problem that the next three sentences develop with various kinds of details. The third sentence includes a series of colorful verbs; the fourth uses a metaphor (the ever-present girls compared to Garfields on car windows). The fifth sentence builds to the point in the sixth sentence, which is delivered bluntly and simply.

Here is one writer's attempt at a creative imitation:

Creative Imitation of Register-Freeman

Then came prosperity and popularity. Over the last ten years, Seattle's special charms have faded because expansion has occurred too rapidly. Traffic has multiplied, thickened, amplified and slowed. Traffic jams appeared so often on the freeways and arterials they began to remind me of ants swarming over spilled syrup. While the congestion varies according to time, seasons, and weather conditions, it has one dominant effect. It is increasingly threatening to spoil the city's beauty.

In our second passage, an excerpt from Louise Erdrich's essay "A Woman's Work: Too Many Demands, and Not Enough Selves," the writer, of Native American descent, mourns the death of her grandfather.

Erdrich Passage

My maternal grandfather—tribal chairman, powwow dancer, a man of subtle humor and intelligence—dies after years of wandering in a dark place. His illness was cruel and took nearly two decades to destroy him. He disappears cell by cell, losing his sense of time and place slowly, and then weakening still further, so there is no clear moment of obvious loss—only the tiny and incremental lacks, the odd habits becoming the completely irrational then frightening.

—Louise Erdrich, "A Woman's Work: Too Many Demands, and Not Enough Selves"

*You can read Register-Freeman's complete article in Chapter 6, pages 128–29.

Here Erdrich's tone is sad and serious. The passage begins with her personal loss and then probes the gradual evolution of this personal loss over the years. A close look at this passage reveals that the first sentence includes a series of renaming phrases, placed between dashes, that interrupt the statement of its main idea. The second sentence, with two parts, is fairly simple, but the third sentence is long. It begins with a simple statement, adds two *-ing* descriptive phrases (participial phrases), and then continues with "so there is no clear moment of obvious loss" followed by more piled-up descriptive details set off with a dash. The switch from present to past to present tense in this passage contributes to the experience of slow death and increasing grief that Erdrich wants the reader to share.

Now here is how one writer applied Erdrich's style to the loss of forests around her parent's home:

Creative Imitation of Erdrich

The forests around my parents' home—old growth, dense firs, a mantle of tall spires and greenness—fall after months of invasions with powerful machinery. The logging was devastating and took almost five years to annihilate them. They vanish patch by patch, forfeiting their place and majesty steadily, and then crumbling even more, so there is no specific day of complete denuding—only the spotty and increasing bareness, the stark hills appearing more brown and finally raw.

FOR WRITING AND DISCUSSION

1. Do your own creative imitations of the passages from Register-Freeman and Erdrich.
2. Choose one or more of the following three passages for creative imitation. Begin by jotting down all the specific observations you can make about the stylistic features of the passage. Use the list of factors that contribute to style on page 67 to help you. Then choose a topic that matches the topic of the original in its degree of lightness or seriousness and its depth. Explore your topic by presenting it using the sentence structures and kinds of words used in the original. Try to imitate the original phrase by phrase and sentence by sentence. You may find it helpful to use a dictionary and thesaurus.

   a. Africa is mystic; it is wild; it is a sweltering inferno; it is a photographer's paradise, a hunter's Valhalla, an escapist's Utopia. It is what you will, and it withstands all interpretations. It is the last vestige of a dead world or the cradle of a shiny new one. To a lot of people, as to myself, it is just "home." It is all of these things but one thing—it is never dull.
      —Beryl Markham, "Flying Elsewhere," *West with the Night*

   b. I went up in the ferris wheel for the last ride before being thrown into seventh grade. It went up into the stars and fell back to earth and rose again, and I had a magnificent vision, or think I did, though it's hard to remember if it was that year with the chocolate cake or the next one with the pigs getting loose. The ferris wheel is the same year after year. It's like all one ride to me: we go up and I think of people I knew who are dead and I smell fall in the air, manure, corn dogs, and we drop down into blazing light and blaring music. Every summer I'm a little bigger, but riding the ferris wheel, I feel the same as ever, I feel eternal.

—Garrison Keillor, "State Fair," *A Prairie Home Companion*

c. The disease was bubonic plague, present in two forms: one that infected the bloodstream, causing the buboes and internal bleeding, and was spread by contact; and a second, more virulent pneumonic type that infected the lungs and was spread by respiratory infection. The presence of both at once caused the high mortality and speed of contagion. So lethal was the disease that cases were known of persons going to bed well and dying before they woke, of doctors catching the illness at a bedside and dying before the patient.

—Barbara Tuchman, "This Is the End of the World," *A Distant Mirror*

◪ SUMMARY OF CHAPTER 4 AND PART ONE

In this chapter we have examined how the elements of rhetorical context influence structure and style. We began by looking at the three key variables of rhetorical context—purpose, audience, and genre—and then considered how these variables influenced the writer's choices about structure and style.

This chapter concludes Part One, "A Rhetoric for College Writers." Together the chapters of Part One give you a background about how writers pose problems, how they pursue them through exploratory writing and talking, and how they try to solve them during the process of composing and revising. Particularly writers try to solve subject-matter problems by seeking a surprising thesis supported with convincing particulars. Simultaneously they try to solve rhetorical problems regarding structure and style by considering issues of purpose, audience, and genre. This background knowledge should prepare you to tackle the writing assignments of Part Two. Further help for your Part Two assignments is provided in Part Three, which gives nuts and bolts instruction on composing and revising.

BRIEF WRITING PROJECT

This assignment asks you to try your hand at translating a piece of writing from one rhetorical context to another. As background, you need to know that each month's *Reader's Digest* includes a section called "News from the World of Medicine," which contains one or more mini-articles reporting on recent medical research. The writers of these pieces scan articles in medical journals, select items of potential interest to the general public, and translate them from a formal scientific style into a popular style. Here is a typical example of a *Reader's Digest* mini-article.

> Cheese could be one secret of a healthy, cavity-free smile, according to a recent study by a professor of dentistry at the University of Alberta in Edmonton, Canada.
>
> In the study, John Hargreaves found that eating a piece of hard cheese the size of a sugar cube at the end of a meal can retard tooth decay. The calcium and phosphate present in the cheese mix with saliva and linger on the surface of the teeth for up to two hours, providing protection against acid attacks from sweet food or drink.
>
> —Penny Parker, "For Teeth, Say Cheese"

Now compare this style with the formal scientific style in the following excerpts, the introduction and conclusion of an article published in the *New England Journal of Medicine.*

> *Introduction:* The past 10 years have witnessed major changes in our understanding of the pathophysiologic mechanisms underlying vascular occlusion and considerable progress in the clinical assessment of aspirin and other antiplatelet agents. The purpose of this review is to describe a rational basis for antithrombotic prophylaxis and treatment with aspirin. Basic information on the molecular mechanism of action of aspirin in inhibiting platelet function will be integrated with the appropriate clinical pharmacologic data and the results of randomized clinical trials. . . .
>
> *Conclusions:* Aspirin reduces the incidence of occlusive cardiovascular events in patients at variable risk for these events. Progress in our understanding of the molecular mechanism of the action of aspirin, clarification of the clinical pharmacology of its effects on platelets, and clinical testing of its efficacy at low doses have contributed to a downward trend in its recommended daily dose. The present recommendation of a single loading dose of 200–300 mg followed by a daily dose of 75–100 mg is based on findings that this dose is as clinically efficacious as higher doses and is safer than higher doses. The satisfactory safety profile of low-dose aspirin has led to ongoing trials of the efficacy of a combination of aspirin and low-intensity oral anti-coagulants in high-risk patients. Finally, the efficacy of a cheap drug such as aspirin in preventing one fifth to one third of all important cardiovascular events should not discourage the pharmaceutical industry from attempting to develop more effective antithrombotic drugs, since a sizeable proportion of these events continue to occur despite currently available therapy.
>
> —Carlo Patrono, "Aspirin as an Antiplatelet Drug"

Assume that you are a writer of mini-articles for the medical news section of *Reader's Digest.* Translate the findings reported in the article on aspirin into a *Reader's Digest* mini-article.

Although the style of the medical article may seem daunting at first, a little work with a good dictionary will help you decipher the whole passage. The original article by Dr. Patrono followed the experimental report format described on pages 64–65 and included sections entitled "Introduction," "Methods," "Findings," "Discussion," and "Conclusions." We have reprinted here most of the introduction and the complete conclusions section. Because Patrono's conclusion summarizes the important findings reported and analyzed in the body of the report, these two sections provide all the information you need for your mini-article.

Writing Projects

part T W O

c h a p t e r   5

Seeing Rhetorically
The Writer as Observer

◪ ABOUT SEEING RHETORICALLY

One time-honored way to begin a writing course is to have students observe a scene and describe it in dense, sensory language. On the surface, this seems a simple and pleasurable enough exercise. But consider what happens to this traditional task when it is given a rhetorical twist. Suppose we asked you to write *two* descriptions of the same scene from different angles of vision (for example, different perspectives, moods, or rhetorical purposes) and then to analyze how the two descriptions differed. We could then ask you to reflect on the extent to which any description of a scene is influenced by the prior experiences, beliefs, moods, and purposes of the observer. Recast in this way, the task requires you to reflect on your degree of responsibility for what you see and to acknowledge the impossibility of arriving at a single, objective account of the scene.

We take this self-reflective twist as our point of departure for this chapter. As soon as you realize that your perceptions of the world shape as well as record that world, you are ready to play a more active role in the learning process and to use writing as a way of seeing and a mode of learning. Your writing assignment for this chapter falls into a category that we call *writing to learn.* Such assignments seldom result in self-contained essays. More often they result in thought exercises that help you learn a concept and then reflect on your learning.

One goal of this writing assignment is to raise the issue of angle of vision versus objectivity in writing. Angle of vision is a factor in all kinds of writing, not just in description. Consider an example from the world of statistics. At one point in a recent baseball season, the Seattle Mariners had the following twelve-game sequence of wins and losses: seven consecutive losses; two wins; one loss; two wins. On the same day in the local papers, two different sports writers summed up the Mariners' record as follows:

> **Reporter 1**   The surging Mariners have now won four out of their last five games.
>
> **Reporter 2**   The struggling Mariners have won only four of their last twelve games.

These two accounts raise some interesting questions. Are they equally factual? Are they equally true? Is there a term that would sum up the Mariners' recent record more accurately than "surging" or "struggling"? (By "recent" do we mean the last five games or the last twelve? Why not the last eight or the last eighteen?)

This example illustrates what we mean by *seeing rhetorically*. To see something rhetorically is to interpret it, that is, to see it as meaningful. To see data as meaningful entails asserting a point about it ("The Mariners are struggling" or "The Mariners are surging") and identifying data that account for that conclusion (to go back twelve games, which explains "struggling," or to go back five games, which explains "surging"). Before we develop this explanation in more detail, we would like you to experience for yourself the dilemma of having to see rhetorically.

■ EXPLORING RHETORICAL OBSERVATION

You are an assistant professor of management in the School of Business at Ivy Lite College. One day you receive a letter from a local bank requesting a confidential evaluation of a former student, one Neal Weasel, who has applied for a job as a management trainee. The bank wants your assessment of Weasel's intelligence, aptitude, dependability, and ability to work with people. You haven't seen Neal for several years, but you remember him well. Here are some of the facts and impressions you recall about Mr. Weasel.

- Very temperamental student, seemed moody, something of a loner.
- Long hair and very sloppy dress—seemed like a misplaced street person; often twitchy and hyperactive.
- Absolutely brilliant mind; took lots of liberal arts courses and applied them to business.
- Wrote a term paper relating different management styles to modern theories of psychology—the best undergraduate paper you ever received. You gave it an A+ and remember learning a lot from it yourself.
- Had a strong command of language—the paper was very well written.
- Good at mathematics; could easily handle all the statistical aspects of the course.
- Frequently missed class and once told you that your class was boring.
- Didn't show up for the midterm. When he returned to class later, he said only that he had been out of town. You let him make up the midterm, and he got an A.
- Didn't participate in a group project required for your course. He said the other students in his group were idiots.
- You thought at the time that Weasel didn't have a chance of making it in the business world because he had no talent for getting along with people.
- Other professors held similar views of Weasel—brilliant, but rather strange and hard to like; an odd duck.

You are in a dilemma because you want to give Weasel a chance (he's still young and may have had a personality transformation of some sort), but you also don't want to damage your own professional reputation by falsifying your true impression.

Working individually at your desk for ten minutes or so, compose a brief letter assessing Weasel; use details from the list to support your assessment. Try to convey a positive impression, but remain honest. Then, working in small groups or as a whole class, share your letters. Pick out representative examples ranging from most positive to least positive and discuss how the letters achieve their different rhetorical effects. To what extent does honesty compel you to mention some or all of your negative memories? Is it possible to mention negative items without emphasizing them? How?

WRITING PROJECT

Your writing project for this chapter is to write two descriptions and an analysis. The assignment has two parts.*

Part A: Find a place on or near campus where you can sit and observe for fifteen or twenty minutes in preparation for writing a focused description of the scene that will enable your readers to see what you see. Here is the catch. You are to write *two* descriptions of the scene. Your first description must convey a favorable impression of the scene, making it appear pleasing or attractive. The second description must convey a negative, or unfavorable, impression, making the scene appear unpleasant or unattractive. Both descriptions must contain only factual details and must describe exactly the same scene from the same location at the same time. It's not fair, in other words, to describe the scene in sunny weather and then in the rain or otherwise to alter factual details. Each description should be one paragraph long (approximately 125–175 words).

Part B: Attach to your two descriptions an analysis (approximately 400–500 words) that explains how your two equally factual descriptions create two contrasting impressions of the same subject. What did you do differently to create the contrasting effects in the two descriptions? In the conclusion of your analysis, address the question "So what?" by exploring what you have learned about reading and writing from composing your two descriptions. Help your readers see what is significant about your thought exercise.

Part A of the assignment asks you to describe the same scene in two different ways, giving your first description a positive tone and the second description a

---

*For this assignment, we are indebted to two sources: (1) Richard Braddock, *A Little Casebook in the Rhetoric of Writing* (Englewood Cliffs, NJ: Prentice-Hall, 1971), and (2) Kenneth Dowst, "Kenneth Dowst's Assignment," in William E. Coles, Jr., and James Vopat (eds.), *What Makes Writing Good?* (Lexington, MA: D. C. Heath, 1985), pp. 52–57.

negative one. You can choose from any number of scenes: the lobby of a dormitory or apartment building, a view from a park bench or from your dormitory or apartment window, the entrance to campus, a crowd at a basketball game, a busy street, a local eating or drinking spot, a scene in a lecture hall, a person studying at a library table, whatever. Part B of the assignment asks you to reflect on what you did to convey a positive or negative impression. Did you include details in one scene that you omitted from the other? Did you choose words with different connotations or use different figures of speech? Did you arrange details in different order or alter sentence structure for different emphasis? The assignment concludes by prompting you to reflect further on what you learned from this exercise about seeing rhetorically.

More discussion of this assignment, as well as a student example of two contrasting descriptions, occurs later in this chapter. As we noted earlier, this assignment results in a thought exercise rather than in a self-contained essay that requires an introduction, transitions between parts, and so forth. You can label your sections simply "Descriptions" and "Analysis."

◢ UNDERSTANDING OBSERVATIONAL WRITING

In this section we explore the extent to which the writer's angle of vision shapes the language he or she chooses, or, to put it inversely, how the chosen language creates an angle of vision. We also explore the complex relationship between perception and belief by showing how previous knowledge, cultural background, interests, values, and beliefs may influence perceptions.

How Observational Writing Reflects an Angle of Vision

To see how observational or descriptive writing reflects an angle of vision, let's look at several examples. Our first is the opening of a newspaper feature article in which a freelance writer describes his bicycle tour through the Prudhoe Bay area of Alaska.

> The temperature is 39 degrees. The going is slow but finally I am in motion. The bike churns through big rocks and thick gravel that occasionally suck the wheels to a dead halt.
>
> Sixty miles to the east lies the Arctic National Wildlife Refuge, a place ARCO describes as "a bleak and forbidding land where temperatures plunge to more than 40 degrees below zero and the sun is not seen for nearly two months each year." To me, the refuge is 19.5 million acres of unspoiled wilderness believed to contain crude oil and natural gas fields.
>
> Prudhoe Bay production is on the decline, and oil corporations are salivating over the prospect of drilling on the 125-mile-long stretch of coastal plain within the refuge.
>
> This area is the principal calving ground for the 180,000-member porcupine caribou herd that annually migrates to this windswept plain, seeking relief from insects.

The refuge also provides habitat for grizzlies, wolves, musk oxen, wolverines and arctic foxes. Polar bears hunt over the ice and come ashore. Millions of waterfowl, seabirds and shorebirds nest here.

—Randal Rubini, "A Vicious Cycle"

The opening of this article juxtaposes the author's view of the Arctic National Wildlife Refuge (ANWR) and ARCO's view. ARCO, a major oil-refining company, describes the ANWR as a "bleak and forbidding land where temperatures plunge to more than 40 degrees below zero and the sun is not seen for nearly two months each year." In contrast, Rubini describes it as "unspoiled wilderness," the habitat of caribou, grizzly bears, shorebirds, and other wildlife.

FOR WRITING AND DISCUSSION

Working as a whole class or in small groups, address the following questions:

1. How does each description reflect an angle of vision that serves the political interests of each party? (Hint: How does ARCO's description make the ANWR seem like a good place to drill for oil? How does Rubini's description make it seem like a bad place to drill for oil?)
2. What is the rhetorical effect of the word "salivating" in the third paragraph? How does Rubini's choice of that word serve his interests?

Appreciating how a writer's choice of words and selection of details reflects an angle of vision can help you read any text from a position of strength. One key is to pay attention to what is *omitted* from a text as well as to what is included. For example, ARCO's descriptive passage about the ANWR omits reference to the animals, keeping the reader focused on the bleak and frigid landscape. In contrast, Rubini's description of the ANWR omits references to the Alaskan economy or the U.S. need for domestic oil, keeping the reader focused instead on the ANWR's beauty and wildlife. Neither perspective is necessarily dishonest; each is true in a limited way. In any writing, writers necessarily—whether consciously or unconsciously—include some details and exclude others. Their choices are driven by their sense of audience and purpose and most important, by their "situatedness" in the world, which creates a predisposition toward a particular perspective or angle of vision. By noting what is *not there*, a reader can begin to detect that angle of vision and analyze it. The reader sees the piece of writing not as the whole truth, but as a constructed piece with a rhetorical effect (that is, with a persuasive power) created by its angle of vision.

The rhetorical effect of observational writing is even more clear in our next example, consisting of excerpts from the works of two female anthropologists studying the role of women in the !Kung* tribe of the African Kalahari (sometimes called

---

*The word *!Kung* is preceded by an exclamation point in scholarly work to indicate the unique clicking sound of the language.

the Bushmen). Anthropologists have long been interested in the !Kung because they still hunt and forage for food in the manner of their prehistoric ancestors.

Here is how anthropologist Lorna Marshal describes !Kung women's work:

Marshal's Description

Women bring most of the daily food that sustains the life of the people, but the roots and berries that are the principal plant foods of the Nyae Nyae !Kung are apt to be tasteless, harsh and not very satisfying. People crave meat. Furthermore, there is only drudgery in digging roots, picking berries, and trudging back to the encampment with heavy loads and babies sagging in the pouches of the karosses: there is no splendid excitement and triumph in returning with vegetables.

—Lorna Marshal, *The !Kung of Nyae Nyae*

And here is how a second anthropologist describes women's work:

Draper's Description

A common sight in the late afternoon is clusters of children standing on the edge of camp, scanning the bush with shaded eyes to see if the returning women are visible. When the slow-moving file of women is finally discerned in the distance, the children leap and exclaim. As the women draw closer, the children speculate as to which figure is whose mother and what the women are carrying in the karosses. [. . .]

!Kung women impress one as a self-contained people with a high sense of self-esteem. There are exceptions—women who seem forlorn and weary—but for the most part, !Kung women are vivacious and self-confident. Small groups of women forage in the Kalahari at distances of eight to ten miles from home with no thought that they need the protection of the men or of the men's weapons should they encounter any of the several large predators that also inhabit the Kalahari.

—P. Draper, "!Kung Women: Contrasts in Sexual Egalitarianism in Foraging and Sedentary Contexts"

As you can see, these two anthropologists "read" the !Kung society in remarkably different ways. Marshal's thesis is that !Kung women are a subservient class relegated to the heavy, dull, and largely thankless task of gathering vegetables. In contrast, Draper believes that women's work is more interesting and requires more skill than other anthropologists have realized. Her thesis is that there is an egalitarian relationship between men and women in the !Kung society.

The source of data for both anthropologists is careful observation of !Kung women's daily lives. But the anthropologists are clearly not seeing the same thing. When the !Kung women return from the bush at the end of the day, Marshal sees their heavy loads and babies sagging in their pouches, whereas Draper sees the excited children awaiting the women's return.

So, which view is correct? That's a little like asking whether the Mariners are surging or struggling or whether the ANWR is bleak or teeming with animals. All writers necessarily present their own perspectives on their subjects; the alternative would be to list only facts—but even then you would have to decide which facts to list and in what order. As soon as you begin interpreting the facts—making inferences, reaching judgments, asserting meanings—you create a view of your subject from your own angle of vision. As a reader you should realize that all texts filter reality by privileging some aspects of the subject and suppressing others. When you realize that no text gives you the whole truth, but only the author's version of the truth, you can learn to read more critically, to be aware of the writer's point of view, and to be alert to how the writer's choice of words, use of metaphor, style, and arrangement of text urge you to narrow your view of the subject until it coincides with the writer's own angle of vision.

This doesn't mean that there is no such thing as truth. It means that no one writer can give you the complete picture and that you must actively seek alternative points of view, do further research, ask more questions, and confront the subject's complexity. If you wanted to do further study of women's roles in !Kung society, for example, some additional questions you might want to ask are the following: Were the two anthropologists studying the same !Kung groups at the same time? Are there aspects of male and female behaviors in !Kung society on which most anthropologists agree? What other information about male and female roles would be helpful and how could it be obtained? Should some terms, such as *male dominance* and *subservient role*, be defined more clearly?

Conducting a Simple Rhetorical Analysis

Our discussion of two different views of the ANWR and two different views of the role of women in !Kung society shows how a seemingly objective description of a scene reflects a specific angle of vision that can be revealed through analysis. Rhetorically, a description subtly persuades the reader toward the author's angle of vision. This angle of vision isn't necessarily the author's "true self" speaking, for authors *create* an angle of vision through rhetorical choices they make while composing.

We hope you will discover this insight for yourself while doing the assignment for this chapter. This assignment asks you first to compose two contrasting descriptions of the same scene (Part A) and then to explain how your two equally true descriptions create contrasting rhetorical effects (Part B). This latter task constitutes a rhetorical analysis of your two descriptions. In this section we describe five textual strategies writers often use (consciously or unconsciously) to create the persuasive effect of their texts. Each strategy creates textual differences that you can discuss in your rhetorical analysis.

Strategy 1: Writers Can State Their Meaning or Intended Effect Directly

Often writers state their point or angle of vision openly so that readers do not need to infer the writer's meaning or intentions. For example, the first anthropologist says that "there is only drudgery in digging roots" while the second anthropologist says "!Kung women impress one as a self-contained people with a high sense of self-esteem." The first writer announces her meaning directly—women's work is drudgery; in contrast, the second writer announces a more positive meaning.

Strategy 2: Writers Can Select Details that Convey Their Intended Effect and Omit Those that Don't

Another strategy for creating an angle of vision (and therefore influencing a reader's view) is to select details that further the writer's purpose and omit those that do not. For example, the details selected by Marshal, the first anthropologist, focus on the tastelessness of the vegetables and the heaviness of the women's loads, creating an overall impression of women's work as thankless and exhausting. The details chosen by Draper, the second anthropologist, focus on the excitement of the children awaiting their mothers' return and the fearlessness of the women as they forage "eight to ten miles from home," creating an impression of self-reliant women performing an essential task. As a specific example, Marshal includes the detail "babies sagging in the pouches of the karosses" while Draper includes "clusters of children standing on the edge of camp." The different details create different rhetorical effects.

Strategy 3: Writers Can Choose Words with Connotations that Convey Their Intended Effect

Writers can also influence readers through their choice of words. Because words carry emotional connotations as well as denotative meanings, any given word is a kind of lens that filters its subject in a certain way. Marshal chooses words connoting listlessness and fatigue, such as *drudgery, trudging, heavy,* and *sagging.* In contrast, Draper chooses words connoting energy: the children *scan* the bush, *leap and exclaim,* and *speculate,* while the women *forage.*

Strategy 4: Writers Can Use Figurative Language that Conveys Their Intended Effect

Figurative language—metaphors, similes, and analogies that compare or equate their subject to something else—can profoundly affect perception of a subject. When Rubini writes that oil companies are "salivating" for new oil-drilling opportunities, the reader's negative image of drooling dogs is transferred subconsciously to the oil companies. If those same companies were said to be "exploring new paths toward American independence from foreign oil," the reader might see them in a quite different light.

Strategy 5: Writers Can Create Sentence Structures that Convey Their Intended Effect

Another subtle way to control the rhetorical effect of a passage is through sentence structure. By placing key words and phrases in emphatic positions (for example, at the end of a long sentence, in a short sentence surrounded by long sentences, or in a main clause rather than a subordinate clause), writers can emphasize some parts of the passage while de-emphasizing others. Consider the difference in emphasis of these two possible sentences for a letter of recommendation for Neal Weasel (from the exercise on pp. 80–81).

> Although Neal Weasel was often moody and brusque in my classes, he is surely a genius.

> Although Neal Weasel is surely a genius, he was often moody and brusque in
> my classes.

Most readers will agree that the first version emphasizes Neal's brilliance and the
second version emphasizes his less than peachy personality. The passages are
equally factual—they both contain the same information—but they subtly convey
different impressions.

Next consider how the first anthropologist, Marshal, uses sentence structure
to create a negative feeling about !Kung women's plant-gathering role:

> Women bring most of the daily food that sustains the life of the people, but
> the roots and berries that are the principal plant foods of the Nyae Nyae !Kung
> are apt to be tasteless, harsh and not very satisfying. People crave meat.

Here the writer's emphasis is on meat as highly desirable (the short sentence,
"People crave meat," in an environment of long sentences is especially emphatic)
and on vegetables as "tasteless, harsh and not very satisfying" (these words occur
in the stress position at the end of a long sentence). We could rewrite this passage,
keeping the same facts, but creating a quite different rhetorical effect.

> Although the !Kung people crave meat and consider the plant food of the
> Kalahari tasteless, harsh, and not very satisfying, the women nevertheless pro-
> vide most of the daily food that sustains the life of the people.

In this version, the emphasis is on how the women sustain the life of the people—
a point presented in a nonstressed position in the original passage.

FOR WRITING AND DISCUSSION

What follows is a student example of two contrasting descriptions written for the assignment in this chapter. Read the descriptions carefully. Working individually, analyze the descriptions rhetorically to explain how the
writer has created contrasting impressions through overt statements of
meaning, selection and omission of details, word choice, figurative language,
and sentence structure. You will do the same thing for your own two descriptions in Part B of your assignment. Spend approximately ten minutes
freewriting your analysis. Then, working in small groups or as a whole class,
share your analyses, trying to reach agreement on examples of how the
writer has created different rhetorical effects by using the five strategies just
described.

Description 1—Positive Effect

Light rain gently drops into the puddles that have formed along the
curb as I look out my apartment window at the corner of 14th and East
John. Pedestrians layered in sweaters, raincoats, and scarves and guarded
with shiny rubber boots and colorful umbrellas sip their steaming hot
triple-tall lattes. Some share smiles and pleasant exchanges as they hurry
down the street, hastening to work where it is warm and dry. Others,

smelling the aroma of French roast espresso coming from the coffee bar next to the bus stop, listen for the familiar rumbling sound that will mean the 56 bus has arrived. Radiant orange, yellow, and red leaves blanket the sidewalk in the areas next to the maple trees that line the road. Along the curb a mother holds the hand of her toddler, dressed like a miniature tugboat captain in yellow raincoat and pants, who splashes happily in a puddle.

Description 2—Negative Effect

A solemn grayness hangs in the air, as I peer out the window of my apartment at the corner of 14th and East John. A steady drizzle of rain leaves boot-drenching puddles for pedestrians to avoid. Bundled in rubber boots, sweaters, coats, and rain-soaked scarves, commuters clutch Styrofoam cups of coffee as a defense against the biting cold. They lift their heads every so often to take a small sip of caffeine, but look sleep-swollen nevertheless. Pedestrians hurry past each other, moving quickly to get away from the dismal weather, the dull grayness. Some nod a brief hello to a familiar face, but most clutch their overcoats and tread grimly on, looking to avoid puddles or spray from passing cars. Others stand at the bus stop, hunched over, waiting in the drab early morning for the smell of diesel that means the 56 bus has arrived. Along the curb an impatient mother jerks the hand of a toddler to keep him from stomping in an oil-streaked puddle.

Using Rhetorical Knowledge to Become a Strong Reader

Knowing how to analyze a text rhetorically can help you become a stronger reader. The more you understand how a text works, the more you can appreciate its particular point of view. Learning to ask what is *not* in the text, why the text is constructed *this* way and not *that* way, or why the writer took this particular point of view and not another enables you to identify the forces that shape what a writer sees and opens up the possibility for you to challenge and speak back to the text.

Reading written texts in this way prepares you to "read" many other human artifacts—body language, advertising images, architecture, classroom seating arrangements, party behaviors—in a similar way. You can learn to ask questions like the following:

What news items are *not* included on page 1 of today's paper? What belief or value system (and whose) causes this story to be front-page news while relegating that story to page 4?

When I read *Mademoiselle* or *Seventeen,* what products are *not* being advertised in its pages? Why?

Why does a party in the Philippines typically include all the host's neighbors and relatives whereas a party in the United States typically includes just one social group (for example, teens, but not uncles, aunts, and neighbors)? How do differences in who is invited or not invited to parties reflect differences in cultures?

We return to such questions in subsequent chapters. For now, keep in mind that the exercise of creating two different descriptions of the same scene can open up new ways of asking questions about countless things in the world around you.

Which Comes First, Perception or Interpretation?

So far we have been examining how writers, in observing a certain scene from their unique angle of vision, create a rhetorical effect through language choices. What we have saved for last is a crucial chicken-and-egg question: Which comes first, the writer's perception or the writer's interpretation? For example, did the two anthropologists begin their observations of the !Kung people with no pre-conceived theories or notions, letting their interpretations arise from their observations, or did they start with a theory or hypothesis, which in turn determined what they saw? This is a truly knotty problem, for, as we try to show in this section, it is difficult to draw a clear line between observation and interpretation; what you see and what you are predisposed to see are complexly intertwined.

On the face of it, terms such as *observation, perception,* and *seeing* seem non-problematic. Objects are objects, and the process of perceiving an object—assuming that you aren't imbibing mind-altering drugs—is immediate and automatic. However, perception is never a simple matter. Consider what we call the expert–novice phenomenon. Experts on any given subject notice details about that subject that a novice overlooks. An experienced birdwatcher can distinguish dozens of kinds of swallows by subtle differences in size, markings, and behaviors, whereas a non-birdwatcher sees only a group of birds of similar size and shape. Similarly, people observing an unfamiliar game (for example, an American watching cricket or a Nigerian watching baseball) don't know what actions or events have meaning and hence don't know what to look for. Psychologists have found that after observing an inning of baseball, avid baseball fans remember numerous details about plays on the field, but people unfamiliar with the game remember none of these details, although they may have vivid recollections of people in the stands or of a player's peculiar mannerisms. In short, prior knowledge or absence of it causes people to see different things.

Cultural differences also affect perception. An American watching two Japanese business executives greet each other might not know that they are participating in an elaborate cultural code of bowing, eye contact, speech patterns, and timing of movements that convey meanings about social status. An Ethiopian newly arrived in the United States and an American sitting in a doctor's office will see different things when the nurse points to one of them to come into the examination room. The American notices nothing remarkable about the scene; he or she may remember what the nurse was wearing or something about the wallpaper. The Ethiopian, however, is likely to remember the nurse's act of pointing, a gesture of rudeness used in Ethiopia only to beckon children or discipline dogs. Again, observers of the same scene see different things.

Sometimes your beliefs and values are so powerful that they create blind spots. You won't notice data that contradict them. You may perceive contradictory data at some level, but if they don't register on your mind as significant, you disregard them. In this vein, a syndicated columnist explains why people who favor gun control and people who oppose it have trouble communicating with each other; they each filter out information that contradicts their own beliefs.

> The gun control advocates keep large files on every case of careless gun use they can find.
> But they don't have any records of people successfully defending themselves against criminals.
> At the same time, the National Rifle Association has thick files on honest citizens using guns to kill, wound or capture criminals.
> But under F in its file cabinets, there is nothing about family gun tragedies.
>
> —Mike Royko, *Chicago Tribune*

The lesson here is that people note and remember whatever is consistent with their worldview much more readily than they note and remember whatever is inconsistent with that view. What you believe is what you see.

To really see something that is familiar to you, to get beyond your beliefs about a subject in order to recognize aspects of it that are inconsistent with those beliefs, you may need to "defamiliarize" it, to make it strange. Many artists try to defamiliarize familiar objects by seeing them from unfamiliar perspectives, sometimes even distorting the object to disrupt ordinary ways of seeing. An artist might draw something upside down, or a writer might write about an event from the point of view of someone he or she considers loathsome—whatever it takes to wipe away "the film of habit" from the object. The writing project for this chapter will get you to see your scene in unfamiliar ways.

READINGS

The readings in this section raise issues about observation as a rhetorical act. The first, by American humorist Mark Twain, shows how his perception of the Mississippi River changed when he became a steamboat pilot.

MARK TWAIN
TWO WAYS OF SEEING A RIVER

Now when I had mastered the language of this water and had come to know every 1
trifling feature that bordered the great river as familiarly as I knew the letters of the alphabet, I had made a valuable acquisition. But I had lost something, too. I had lost something which could never be restored to me while I lived. All the grace, the beauty,

the poetry, had gone out of the majestic river! I still kept in mind a certain wonderful sunset which I witnessed when steamboating was new to me. A broad expanse of the river was turned to blood, in the middle distance the red hue brightened into gold, through which a solid log came floating, black and conspicuous; in one place a long, slanting mark lay sparkling upon the water; in another the surface was broken by boiling, tumbling rings, that were as many-tinted as an opal; where the ruddy flush was faintest, was a smooth spot that was covered with graceful circles and radiating lines, ever so delicately traced; the shore on our left was densely wooded and the somber shadow that fell from this forest was broken in one place by a long, ruffled trail that shone like silver, and high above the forest wall a clean-stemmed dead tree waved a single leafy bough that glowed like a flame in the unobstructed splendor that was flowing from the sun. There were graceful curves, reflected images, woody heights, soft distances, and over the whole scene, far and near, the dissolving lights drifted steadily, enriching it every passing moment with new marvels of coloring.

2 I stood like one bewitched. I drank it in, in a speechless rapture. The world was new to me and I had never seen anything like this at home. But as I have said, a day came when I began to cease from noting the glories and the charms which the moon and the sun and the twilight wrought upon the river's face; another day came when I ceased altogether to note them. Then, if that sunset scene had been repeated, I should have looked upon it without rapture, and should have commented upon it inwardly after this fashion: "This sun means that we are going to have wind to-morrow; that floating log means that the river is rising, small thanks to it; that slanting mark on the water refers to a bluff reef which is going to kill somebody's steamboat one of these nights, if it keeps on stretching out like that; those tumbling 'boils' show a dissolving bar and a changing channel there; the lines and circles in the slick water over yonder are a warning that that troublesome place is shoaling up dangerously; that silver streak in the shadow of the forest is the 'break' from a new snag and he has located himself in the very best place he could have found to fish for steamboats; that tall dead tree, with a single living branch, is not going to last long, and then how is a body ever going to get through this blind place at night without the friendly old landmark?"

3 No, the romance and beauty were all gone from the river. All the value any feature of it had for me now was the amount of usefulness it could furnish toward compassing the safe piloting of a steamboat. Since those days, I have pitied doctors from my heart. What does the lovely flush in a beauty's cheek mean to a doctor but a "break" that ripples above some deadly disease? Are not all her visible charms sown thick with what are to him the signs and symbols of hidden decay? Does he ever see her beauty at all, or doesn't he simply view her professionally and comment upon her unwholesome condition all to himself? And doesn't he sometimes wonder whether he has gained most or lost most by learning his trade?

Thinking Critically About "Two Ways of Seeing a River"

1. Earlier in this chapter we asked which comes first, knowledge or perception? What seems to be Twain's view of the relationship between knowledge and perception?
2. Do you agree with Twain that professionals such as doctors or riverboat pilots lose the ability to see the beauty in the subjects they study?

The second reading consists of two eyewitness accounts of an event that occurred on the Congo River in Africa in 1877.* The first account is by the famous British explorer Henry Morton Stanley, who leads an exploration party of Europeans into the African interior. The second account is by the African tribal chief Mojimba, as told orally to a Belgian missionary, Fr. Frassle, who recorded his story. The conflicting accounts suggest the complexity of what happens when different cultures meet for the first time.

HENRY MORTON STANLEY'S ACCOUNT

We see a sight that sends the blood tingling through every nerve and fibre of the body . . . a flotilla of gigantic canoes bearing down upon us. A monster canoe leads the way . . . forty men on a side, their bodies bending and swaying in unison as with a swelling barbarous chorus they drive her down towards us . . . the warriors above the manned prow let fly their spears. . . . But every sound is soon lost in the ripping crackling musketry. . . . Our blood is up now. It is a murderous world, and we feel for the first time that we hate the filthy vulturous ghouls who inhabit it. . . . We pursue them . . . and continue the fight in the village streets with those who have landed, hunt them out into the woods, and there only sound the retreat, having returned the daring cannibals the compliment of a visit.

MOJIMBA'S ACCOUNT

When we heard that the man with the white flesh was journeying down the [Congo] we were open-mouthed with astonishment. . . . He will be one of our brothers who were drowned in the river. . . . We will prepare a feast, I ordered, we will go to meet our brother and escort him into the village with rejoicing! We donned our ceremonial garb. We assembled the great canoes. . . . We swept forward, my canoe leading, the others following, with songs of joy and with dancing, to meet the first white man our eyes had beheld, and to do him honor. But as we drew near his canoes there were loud reports, bang! bang! And fire-staves spat bits of iron at us. We were paralyzed with fright . . . they were the work of evil spirits! "War! That is war!" I yelled. . . . We fled into our village—they came after us. We fled into the forest and flung ourselves on the ground. When we returned that evening our eyes beheld fearful things: our brothers, dead, dying, bleeding, our village plundered and burned, and the water full of dead bodies. The robbers and murderers had disappeared.

Thinking Critically About the Two Accounts

Our purpose in presenting these two accounts is to raise the central problem examined in this chapter: To what extent is objectivity possible in language? Can a "truth" be discovered that transcends the perspective of an individual writer?

*These readings are taken from Donald C. Holsinger, "A Classroom Laboratory for Writing History," *Social Studies Review* 31,1 (1991): 59–64. The role-playing exercise following the readings is also adapted from this article.

1. How do the two accounts differ? How does each observer create a persuasive effect by using one or more of the five strategies described on pages 85–87 (overt statement of meaning, selection/omission of details, connotations of words, figurative language, ordering and shaping of sentences)?
2. What is common to both accounts? Focusing on common elements, try to establish as many facts as you can about the encounter.
3. As a class, try the following role-playing exercise.

   Background: You are a newspaper reporter who enjoys a global reputation for objectivity, accuracy, and lack of bias. You write for a newspaper that has gained a similar reputation and prides itself on printing only the truth. Your editor has just handed you two eyewitness accounts of an incident which has recently occurred in central Africa. You are to transform the two accounts into a brief front-page article (between 60 and 90 words) informing your readers what happened. You face an immediate deadline and no time to seek additional information.

   Task: Each class member should write a 60–90 word newspaper account of the event, striving for objectivity and lack of bias. Then share your accounts.

4. As a class, play the believing and doubting game with this assertion: "It is possible to create an objective and unbiased account of the Congo phenomenon."
5. If you are interested in how historians wrestle with conflicting accounts and the problem of objectivity, see Jane Tompkins's " 'Indians' ": Textualism, Morality, and the Problem of History" (in Chapter 8, pp. 177–85). To what extent does Tompkins believe it is possible to get a verifiable account of what Native Americans were like when the Puritans arrived in North America in the seventeenth century?

◨ COMPOSING YOUR ESSAY

Since the assignment for this chapter has two parts—Part A, calling for two contrasting descriptions, and Part B, calling for a rhetorical analysis—we will address each part separately.

Generating and Exploring Ideas for Your Two Descriptions

When you think about description, it sometimes helps to imagine yourself as the companion of a recently blinded person. Suppose that you were to become that person's eyes, describing your scene so fully that your blind companion could share your experience of seeing it. Then your blind companion, having a newly heightened sense of hearing, touch, and smell, could enrich your own perceptions so that the two of you, pooling your perceptions, could work together to create a richly detailed description of the scene. In your writing, good description should also be packed with sensory detail—sights, sounds, smells, textures, even on occasion tastes—all contributing to a dominant impression that gives the description focus.

After you have chosen a subject for your two descriptions, observe it intensely for fifteen or twenty minutes. One way to train yourself to notice sensory details is to create a sensory chart, with one column for your pleasant description and one column for your unpleasant description.

Pleasant Impression	Unpleasant Impression
Sight/eyes	Sight/eyes
Sound/ears	Sound/ears
Odor/nose	Odor/nose
Touch/fingers	Touch/fingers
Taste/tongue	Taste/tongue

As you observe your scene, note details that appeal to each of the senses and then try describing them first positively (left column) and then negatively (right column). One student, observing a scene in a local tavern, made these notes in her sensory chart:

Taste/tongue	Taste/tongue
salted and buttered popcorn	salty, greasy popcorn
frosty pitchers of beer	half-drunk pitchers of stale, warm beer
big bowls of salted-in-the-shell peanuts on the tables	mess of peanut shells and discarded pretzel wrappers on tables and floor

Sound/ears	Sound/ears
hum of students laughing and chatting	din of high-pitched giggles and various obnoxious frat guys shouting at each other from across the room
the juke box playing oldies but goodies from the early Beatles	juke box blaring out-of-date music

Shaping and Drafting Your Two Descriptions

Once you have observed your scene and made your sensory chart, compose your two descriptions. You will need to decide on an ordering principle for your descriptions. It generally makes sense to begin with an overview of the scene to orient your reader.

> From the park bench near 23rd and Maple, one can watch the people strolling by the duck pond.

> By 8:00 on any Friday night, Pagliacci's Pizzeria on Broadway becomes one of the city's most unusual gathering places.

Then you need a plan for arranging details. There are no hard and fast rules here, but there are some typical practices. You can arrange details in the following ways:

- by spatially scanning from left to right or from far to near
- by using the written equivalent of a movie zoom shot; begin with a broad overview of the scene, then move to close-up descriptions of specific details

Compose your pleasant description, selecting and focusing on details that convey a positive impression. Then compose your unpleasant description. Each description should comprise one fully developed paragraph (125–175 words).

Using *Show* Words Rather than *Tell* Words

In describing your scenes, use *show* words rather than *tell* words. *Tell* words interpret a scene without describing it. They name an interior, mental state, thus telling the reader what emotional reaction to draw from the scene.

Tell Words

There was a *pleasant* tree in the back yard.

There was an *unpleasant* tree in the back yard.

In contrast, *show* words describe a scene through sensory details appealing to sight, sound, smell, touch, and even taste. The description itself evokes the desired effect without requiring the writer to state it overtly.

Show Words

A *spreading elm* tree *bathed* the back yard with *shade.*   *[evokes positive feelings]*

An *out-of-place elm, planted too close to the house, blocked our view* of the *mountains.)*   *[evokes negative feelings]*

Whereas show words are particulars that evoke the writer's meaning through sensory detail, tell words are abstractions that announce the writer's intention directly (strategy 1 on p. 85). An occasional tell word can be useful, but show words operating at the bottom of the "scale of abstraction" (see Chapter 3, pp. 50–51) are the flesh and muscle of descriptive prose.

Inexperienced writers often try to create contrasting impressions of a scene simply by switching tell words.

Weak: Overuse of *Tell* Words

The smiling merchants happily talked with customers trying to get them to buy their products.   *[positive purpose]*

The annoying merchants kept hassling customers trying to convince them to buy their products.   *[negative purpose]*

In this example, the negative words *annoying* and *hassling* and the positive words *smiling* and *happily* are tell words; they state the writer's contrasting intentions, but they don't describe the scene. Here is how the student writer revised these passages using show words.

Strong: Conversion to *Show* Words

One of the merchants, selling thick-wooled Peruvian sweaters, nodded approvingly as a woman tried on a richly textured, blue cardigan in front of the mirror. *[positive purpose]*

One of the merchants, hawking those Peruvian sweaters that you find in every open-air market, tried to convince a middle-aged woman that the lumpy, oversized cardigan she was trying on looked stylish. *[negative purpose]*

Here are some more examples taken from students' drafts before and after revision:

Draft with *Tell* Words	Revision with *Show* Words
Children laugh and point animatedly at all the surroundings.	Across the way, a small boy taps his friend's shoulder and points at a circus clown.
The wonderful smell of food cooking on the barbecue fills my nose.	The tantalizing smell of grilled hamburgers and buttered corn on the cob wafts from the barbecue area of the park, where men in their cookout aprons wield forks and spatulas and drink Budweisers.
The paintings on the wall are confusing, dark, abstract, demented, and convey feelings of unhappiness and suffering.	The paintings on the wall, viewed through the smoke-filled room, seem confusing and abstract—the work of a demented artist on a bad trip. Splotches of black paint are splattered over a greenish-yellow background like bugs on vomit.

Revising Your Two Descriptions

The following revision hints will help you improve your first draft.

1. ***Do the two descriptions focus on the same scene at the same time?*** The rules for the assignment ask you to use only factual details observable in the same scene at the same time. It violates the spirit of the assignment to have one scene in the rain and another in the sunshine, or to have one scene at a winning basketball game and another at a losing game.
2. ***Do you use plenty of "show" words and few "tell" words?*** Inexperienced writers tend to rely on tell words rather than show words. Go through your draft identifying words that describe internal mental states (*pleasant, happy, depressing, annoying, pretty, ugly,* and so forth). These are tell words, most of which should be eliminated. Rewrite the passages by actually describing what you see, hear, smell, touch, and taste.
3. ***Can the focus on a dominant impression be improved through more effective word choice?*** Can you improve the focus on each description's dominant impression by choosing naming and action words with stronger connotations? For example, consider synonyms for the generic word *shoe*. Most people wear shoes, but only certain people on certain occasions wear wing tips or pumps or sandals. Among words for kinds of sandals, *Birkenstocks* carries

a different connotation from *Tevas* or *thongs* or *strappy espadrilles with a faux-metallic finish.* Search your draft for places where you could substitute more colorful or precise words for a generic word to convey your dominant impression more effectively.

Generating and Exploring Ideas for Your Rhetorical Analysis

Part B of the assignment asks you to write a rhetorical analysis of your two descriptions in which you explain the strategies you used to create different rhetorical effects. Your analysis should answer questions like these:

1. Did you state your intended meaning overtly in each description through the use of "tell" words? Give examples.
2. Did you include different details in each description? Why? Illustrate.
3. Did you select words with positive connotations in one description and negative connotations in the other? Illustrate.
4. Did you use figurative language differently in the two descriptions? Why? Illustrate?
5. Did you vary sentence structure in the two descriptions to emphasize positive details in one and negative details in the other? Illustrate.
6. What other strategies did you use?

Your rhetorical analysis should be organized as a brief essay with a thesis statement and good paragraph structure. One effective approach is to begin with a thesis statement that forecasts the rhetorical strategies you used. Then illustrate your analysis with examples and brief quotations from your two descriptions.

The last part of the rhetorical analysis should be your reflection on what you learned from doing this assignment. In effect, you are answering your reader's "So what?" question. "So you wrote two different descriptions," your reader might say. "Why are you telling me this? What's your point?" Your reader needs an answer to this question to understand the larger implications—the value—of what he or she has read. In sharing your two descriptions of a scene, what larger point do you want to make about writing and reading? What is the surprise (new knowledge? new understanding about description?) that you want to bring your reader?

What did you learn? To help you generate ideas for this section, try freewriting your responses to the following questions:

1. What are the most important things you learned from reading this chapter and writing your two descriptions?
2. How has reading this chapter and doing this writing project affected the way you now read other texts, for example, the newspaper or readings from your other courses?
3. Did the need to slant your descriptions affect the way you observed? How so? Do you think you could write a single objective description of your scene that would be better than the two paragraphs you wrote? Why?

4. What are the most important questions that this chapter raises in your mind? What does it make you think about?

Freewriting for several minutes in response to each of these questions should give you enough material for your final reflection on what you learned.

Shaping and Drafting Your Rhetorical Analysis

The structure of your analysis is prescribed by the assignment: (a) a rhetorical analysis of the difference between your two descriptions, and (b) a final reflection on what you learned.

Revising Your Rhetorical Analysis

When you have written a draft of your rhetorical analysis, share it with your classmates to get insights about how best to revise it. Your goal at the revision stage is to discover the ideas that you want to communicate and then to make those ideas as clear as possible for readers. The following guidelines for peer reviewers should be helpful.

g   u   i   d   e   l   i   n   e   s

for Peer Reviewers

Instructions for peer reviews, including use of these guidelines, are provided in Chapter 17, pages 429–35. To write a peer review for a classmate, use your own paper, numbering your responses to correspond to the questions on the guidelines. At the head of your paper place the author's name and your own name, as shown.

Author's Name: _____

Peer Reviewer's Name: _____

I. Read the draft at a normal reading speed from beginning to end. As you read, do the following:
   A. Place a wavy line in the margin next to any passages that you find confusing, that contain something that doesn't seem to fit, or that otherwise slow down your reading.
   B. Place a "Good!" in the margin next to any passages where you think the writing is particularly strong or interesting.
II. Read the draft again slowly and answer the following questions by writing brief explanations of your answers.

A. The two descriptions:
   1. Are there differences in the time or place of the two descriptions or other differences in "fact" (change in the weather, in what people are doing, or so forth)? If so, alert the writer to redo at least one of the descriptions.
   2. Are the two descriptions clearly of the same scene but from different angles of vision? Could the two descriptions be made more parallel, sketched more boldly, or made more detailed and vivid?
   3. Where does the writer use show words effectively? How many of the five senses are appealed to? Where could the writer replace tell words with show words or improve the specificity of show words?
   4. If the writer has relied primarily on one or two methods of creating contrast (overt interpretation, selection or omission of details), how might he or she use other methods (contrasting word choice, contrasting figurative language, changes in sentence structure)?
B. Analysis section:
   1. How might the writer improve the ideas or structure of the analysis?
   2. Does the analysis show how the writer has used several or all of the five strategies explained on pages 85–87? Are there strategies used that the writer doesn't discuss?
   3. Where could the writer use more or better examples to illustrate differences in overt commentary, selection or omission of details, word choice, figurative language, and sentence structure?
   4. What could be added or changed in the analysis?
C. "So what?" section:
   1. Has the writer explained what he or she has learned from seeing rhetorically? Do the insights seem interesting? Are they clear?
   2. Which, if any, of the writer's points could be better developed or illustrated?
D. Sum up what you see as the chief strengths and problem areas of this draft.
   1. Strengths
   2. Problem areas
III. Read the draft one more time. Place a check in the margin wherever you notice problems in grammar, spelling, or mechanics (one check per problem).

Reading Rhetorically
The Writer as
Strong Reader

◤ ABOUT READING RHETORICALLY

Many new college students are surprised by the amount, range, and difficulty of reading they have to do in college. Every day they are challenged by reading assignments ranging from scholarly articles and textbooks on complex subject matter to primary sources, such as Plato's dialogues or Darwin's *Voyage of the Beagle.*

The goal of this chapter is to help you become a more powerful reader of academic texts, prepared to take part in the conversations of the disciplines you study. To this end, we explain two kinds of thinking and writing essential to your college reading: first, your ability to listen carefully to a text, to recognize its parts and their functions, and to summarize its ideas; and second, your ability to formulate strong responses to texts by interacting with them, either by agreeing with, interrogating, or actively opposing them.

To interact strongly with texts, you must learn how to read them both with and against the grain. When you read *with the grain* of a text, you see the world through its author's perspective, open yourself to the author's argument, apply the text's insights to new contexts, and connect its ideas to your own experiences and personal knowledge. When you read *against the grain* of a text, you resist it by questioning its points, raising doubts, analyzing the limits of its perspective, or even refuting its argument. We say that readers who respond strongly to texts in this manner read *rhetorically;* that is, they are aware of the effect a text is intended to have on them, and they critically consider that effect, entering into or challenging the text's intentions.

◤ EXPLORING RHETORICAL READING

As an introduction to rhetorical reading, we would like you to read Dr. Andrés Martin's "On Teenagers and Tattoos," which appeared in the *Journal of the American Academy of Child and Adolescent Psychiatry,* a scholarly publication. Before reading the article, complete the following opinion survey. Answer each question using a 1–5 scale, with 1 meaning "strongly agree" and 5 meaning "strongly disagree."

1. For teenagers, getting a tattoo is like following any other fad, such as wearing the currently popular kind of shoe or hairstyle.
2. Teenagers get tattoos primarily as a form of asserting independence from parents and other adults.
3. Teenagers get tattoos on the spur of the moment and usually don't consider the irreversibility of marking their skin.
4. Teenagers who get tattoos are expressing deep psychological needs.
5. A psychiatry journal can provide useful insights into teen choices to tattoo their bodies.

When you have finished rating your degree of agreement with these statements, read Martin's article, using whatever notetaking, underlining, or highlighting strategies you normally use when reading for a class. When you have finished reading, complete the exercises that follow.

READING

▼

ANDRÉS MARTIN, M.D.
ON TEENAGERS AND TATTOOS

> The skeleton dimensions I shall now proceed to set down are copied verbatim from my right arm, where I had them tattooed: as in my wild wanderings at that period, there was no other secure way of preserving such valuable statistics.
>
> —*Melville/Moby Dick CII*

1   Tattoos and piercings have become a part of our everyday landscape. They are ubiquitous, having entered the circles of glamour and the mainstream of fashion, and they have even become an increasingly common feature of our urban youth. Legislation in most states restricts professional tattooing to adults older than 18 years of age, so "high end" tattooing is rare in children and adolescents, but such tattoos are occasionally seen in older teenagers. Piercings, by comparison, as well as self-made or "jailhouse" type tattoos, are not at all rare among adolescents or even among schoolage children. Like hairdo, makeup, or baggy jeans, tattoos and piercings can be subject to fad influence or peer pressure in an effort toward group affiliation. As with any other fashion statement, they can be construed as bodily aids in the inner struggle toward identity consolidation, serving as adjuncts to the defining and sculpting of the self by means of external manipulations. But unlike most other body decorations, tattoos and piercings are set apart by their irreversible and permanent nature, a quality at the core of their magnetic appeal to adolescents.

Adolescents and their parents are often at odds over the acquisition of bodily dec- 2
orations. For the adolescent, piercings or tattoos may be seen as personal and beautifying statements, while parents may construe them as oppositional and enraging
affronts to their authority. Distinguishing bodily adornment from self-mutilation may indeed prove challenging, particularly when a family is in disagreement over a teenager's
motivations and a clinician is summoned as the final arbiter. At such times it may be
most important to realize jointly that the skin can all too readily become but another
battleground for the tensions of the age, arguments having less to do with tattoos and
piercings than with core issues such as separation from the family matrix. Exploring
the motivations and significance underlying tattoos (Grumet, 1983) and piercings can
go a long way toward resolving such differences and can become a novel and additional way of getting to know teenagers. An interested and nonjudgmental appreciation
of teenagers' surface presentations may become a way of making contact not only in
their terms but on their turfs: quite literally on the territory of their skins.

The following three sections exemplify some of the complex psychological under- 3
pinnings of youth tattooing.

Identity and the Adolescent's Body

Tattoos and piercing can offer a concrete and readily available solution for many 4
of the identity crises and conflicts normative to adolescent development. In using such
decorations, and by marking out their bodily territories, adolescents can support their
efforts at autonomy, privacy, and insulation. Seeking individuation, tattooed adolescents can become unambiguously demarcated from others and singled out as unique.
The intense and often disturbing reactions that are mobilized in viewers can help to effectively keep them at bay, becoming tantamount to the proverbial "Keep Out" sign
hanging from a teenager's door.

Alternatively, [when teenagers feel] prey to a rapidly evolving body over which they 5
have no say, self-made and openly visible decorations may restore adolescents' sense
of normalcy and control, a way of turning a passive experience into an active identity.
By indelibly marking their bodies, adolescents can strive to reclaim their bearings within
an environment experienced as alien, estranged, or suffocating or to lay claim over their
evolving and increasingly unrecognizable bodies. In either case, the net outcome can
be a resolution to unwelcome impositions: external, familial, or societal in one case; internal and hormonal in the other. In the words of a 16-year-old girl with several facial
piercings, and who could have been referring to her body just as well as to the position
within her family. "If I don't fit in, it is because *I* say so."

Incorporation and Ownership

Imagery of a religious, deathly, or skeletal nature, the likenesses of fierce animals 6
or imagined creatures, and the simple inscription of names are some of the time-tested
favorite contents for tattoos. In all instances, marks become not only memorials or recipients for clearly held persons or concepts: they strive for incorporation, with images
and abstract symbols gaining substance on becoming a permanent part of the individual's skin. Thickly embedded in personally meaningful representations and object relations, tattoos can become not only the ongoing memento of a relationship, but at
times even the only evidence that there ever was such a bond. They can quite literally
become the relationship itself. The turbulence and impulsivity of early attachments and
infatuations may become grounded, effectively bridging oblivion through the visible
reality of tattoos.

7   *Case Vignette.* A, a 13-year-old boy, proudly showed me his tattooed deltoid. The coarsely depicted roll of the dice marked the day and month of his birth. Rather disappointed, he then uncovered an immaculate back, going on to draw for me the great "piece" he envisioned for it. A menacing figure held a hand of cards: two aces, two eights, and a card with two sets of dates. A's father had belonged to "Dead Man's Hand," a motorcycle gang named after the set of cards (aces and eights) that the legendary Wild Bill Hickock had held in the 1890s when shot dead over a poker table in Deadwood, South Dakota. A had only the vaguest memory of and sketchiest information about his father, but he knew he had died in a motorcycle accident: the fifth card marked the dates of his birth and death.

8   The case vignette also serves to illustrate how tattoos are often the culmination of a long process of imagination, fantasy, and planning that can start at an early age. Limited markings, or relatively reversible ones such as piercings, can at a later time scaffold toward the more radical commitment of a permanent tattoo.

The Quest for Permanence

9   The popularity of the anchor as a tattoo motif may historically have had to do less with guild identification among sailors than with an intense longing for rootedness and stability. In a similar vein, the recent increase in the popularity and acceptance of tattoos may be understood as an antidote or counterpoint to our urban and nomadic lifestyles. Within an increasingly mobile society, in which relationships are so often transient—as attested by the frequencies of divorce, abandonment, foster placement, and repeated moves, for example—tattoos can be a readily available source of grounding. Tattoos, unlike many relationships, can promise permanence and stability. A sense of constancy can be derived from unchanging marks that can be carried along no matter what the physical, temporal, or geographical vicissitudes at hand. Tattoos stay, while all else may change.

10   *Case Vignette.* A proud father at 17, B had had the smiling face of his 3-month-old baby girl tattooed on his chest. As we talked at a tattoo convention, he proudly introduced her to me, explaining how he would "always know how beautiful she is today" when years from then he saw her semblance etched on himself.

11   The quest for permanence may at other times prove misleading and offer premature closure to unresolved conflicts. At a time of normative uncertainties, adolescents may maladaptively and all too readily commit to a tattoo and its indefinite presence. A wish to hold on to a current certainty may lead the adolescent to lay down in ink what is valued and cherished one day but may not necessarily be in the future. The frequency of self-made tattoos among hospitalized, incarcerated, or gang-affiliated youths suggests such motivations: a sense of stability may be a particularly dire need under temporary, turbulent, or volatile conditions. In addition, through their designs teenagers may assert a sense of bonding and allegiance to a group larger than themselves. Tattoos may attest to powerful experiences, such as adolescence itself, lived and even survived together. As with Moby Dick's protagonist Ishmael, they may bear witness to the "valuable statistics" of one's "wild wandering(s)": those of adolescent exhilaration and excitement on the one hand; of growing pains, shared misfortune, or even incarceration on the other.

12   Adolescents' bodily decorations, at times radical and dramatic in their presentation, can be seen in terms of figuration rather than disfigurement, of the natural body being through them transformed into a personalized body (Brain, 1979). They can often be understood as self-constructive and adorning efforts, rather than prematurely

subsumed as mutilatory and destructive acts. If we bear all of this in mind, we may not only arrive at a position to pass more reasoned clinical judgment, but become sensitized through our patients' skins to another level of their internal reality.

References

Brain, R. (1979). *The Decorated Body.* New York: Harper & Row.

Grumet, G. W. (1983). Psychodynamic implications of tattoos. *Am J Orthopsychiatry* 53:482–492.

Postreading Exercises

1. Summarize in one or two sentences Martin's main points.
2. Freewrite your response to this question: In what way, if any, has Martin's article caused me to reconsider my answers to the opinion survey?
3. Working in small groups or as a whole class, compare the notetaking strategies you used while reading this piece. (a) How many people wrote marginal notes? How many underlined or highlighted? (b) Compare the contents of these notes. Did people highlight the same passage or different passages? (c) Individually, look at your annotations and highlights and try to decide why you wrote or marked what you did. Share your reasons for making these annotations. The goal of this exercise is to make you more aware of your thinking processes as you read.
4. Working as a whole class or in small groups, share your responses to the questionnaire and to the postreading questions. To what extent did this article change people's thinking about the reasons teenagers choose to tattoo their bodies? What were the most insightful points in this article?
5. Assume that you are looking for substantial, detailed information about teenagers and tattooing. What parts of this article leave you with unanswered questions? Where would you like to have more explanation or examples?

WRITING PROJECT

Write a "summary/strong response" essay that includes: (a) a summary (approximately 150–250 words) of a reading specified by your instructor and (b) a strong response to that reading in which you speak back to that reading from your own critical thinking, personal experience, and values. As you formulate your own response, consider both the author's ideas and the author's rhetorical choices concerning audience, purpose, genre, and style. Think of your response as your analysis of how the text tries to influence its readers rhetorically and how your wrestling with the text has expanded and deepened your thinking about its ideas.

The skills this assignment develops are crucial for academic writers. You will learn how to summarize an article, including how to quote brief passages, how to use attributive tags to cue your reader that you are reporting someone else's ideas rather than your own, and how to cite the article using (in this case) the Modern Language Association (MLA) documentation system. You will use these skills any time you write a research paper, term paper, or any other scholarly work that uses sources. But you will also learn how to contribute your own ideas to a conversation. Weak readers passively report what other people have said. Strong readers see themselves as contributors to the conversation, capable of analyzing and evaluating texts, speaking back to other authors, and thinking actively for themselves.

◢ UNDERSTANDING RHETORICAL READING

In this section we contrast the kinds of difficulties college students encounter when they read academic texts with the fluent reading practices of experts. We then show you how to read a text both with the grain and against the grain—skills you will need to summarize a text and respond to it strongly.

What Makes College-Level Reading Difficult

The difficulty of college-level reading stems in part from the complexity of the subject matter. Whatever the subject—from international monetary policies to cold fusion—you have to wrestle with new and complex materials that might perplex anyone. But in addition to the daunting subject matter, several other factors contribute to the difficulty of college-level reading.

Vocabulary

Many college-level readings—especially primary sources—contain unfamiliar technical language. The Martin text, for example, assumes that you understand such technical terms as *identity consolidation, normative, individuation,* and *object relations.* In some contexts you can look up a difficult word in the dictionary. But in academia, words often carry specialized meanings that evoke a whole history of conversation and debate that may be inaccessible even through a specialized dictionary. *Existentialism, Neoplatonic, postmodernism, Newtonian,* and *Keynesian,* for example, are code words for attitudes or positions in a complex conversation. No dictionary could capture all the nuances of meaning that these words carry in those conversations. You will not fully understand them until you are initiated into the disciplinary conversations that gave rise to them.

Unfamiliar Rhetorical Context

Another cause of difficulty, especially in primary materials, is lack of familiarity with the text's original rhetorical context. As we explained in Part One, writers write to an audience for a purpose; the purpose results from some motivating occasion or event. Unless you know something about a text's purpose, occasion, and intended audience (that is, unless you know the conversation to which the text belongs), you may well be left floundering. Sometimes the rhetorical context is easy to figure out, as in the case of the Martin article (he is offering advice to psychiatrists about how to counsel tattooed teens and their families effectively). But why did Plato write his dialogues? What conversation was Freud joining when he began interpreting dreams? Whom was Einstein opposing when he proposed his theory of relativity? The more you can learn about a text's rhetorical context, through internal clues or through outside research, the easier it is to read and respond to the text.

Unfamiliar Genre

In Chapter 4 we discussed genre in our analysis of a writer's rhetorical context. In your college reading you will encounter a wide range of genres, such as textbooks, scholarly articles, scientific reports, historical documents, newspaper articles, op-ed pieces, and so forth. Each of these genres makes different demands on readers and requires a different reading strategy. An unfamiliar genre adds to the difficulty of reading.

Lack of Background Knowledge

Writers necessarily make assumptions about what their readers know. If you lack background knowledge, you may have trouble interpreting the writer's ideas and fully understanding the text. Your understanding of Martin, for example, would be more complete if you had a background in adolescent psychology and psychiatric therapy.

FOR WRITING AND DISCUSSION

The importance of background knowledge can be easily demonstrated any time you dip into past issues of a news magazine or try to read articles about an unfamiliar culture. Consider the following passage from a 1986 *Newsweek* article. How much background knowledge do you need before you can fully comprehend this passage? What cultural knowledge about the United States would a student from Ethiopia or Indonesia need?

Throughout the NATO countries last week, there were second thoughts about the prospect of a nuclear-free world. For 40 years nuclear weapons have been the backbone of the West's defense. For almost as long American presidents have ritually affirmed their desire to see the world rid of them. Then, suddenly, Ronald Reagan and Mikhail Gorbachev came close to actually doing it. Let's abolish all nuclear ballistic missiles in the next 10 years, Reagan said. Why not all nuclear weapons, countered Gorbachev. OK, the president responded, like a man agreeing to throw in the washer-dryer along with the house.

What if the deal had gone through? On the one hand, Gorbachev would have returned to Moscow a hero. There is a belief in the United States that the Soviets need nuclear arms because nuclear weapons are what make them a superpower. But according to Marxist-Leninist doctrine, capitalism's nuclear capability (unforeseen by Marx and Lenin) is the only thing that can prevent the inevitable triumph of communism. Therefore, an end to nuclear arms would put the engine of history back on its track.

On the other hand, Europeans fear, a nonnuclear United States would be tempted to retreat into neo-isolationism.

—Robert B. Cullen, "Dangers of Disarming," *Newsweek*

Working in small groups or as a class, identify words and passages in this text that depend on background information or knowledge of culture for complete comprehension.

Reading Processes Used by Experienced Readers

In Chapter 17, we describe the difference between the writing processes of experts and those of beginning college writers. There are parallel differences between the reading processes of experienced and inexperienced readers, especially when they encounter complex materials. In this section we discuss some of the skills used by experienced readers.

Varying Strategies to Match Reading Goals

Unlike novices, experienced readers vary their reading speed and strategies according to their goals. Experienced readers sometimes scan texts for a piece of information and other times scrutinize every word. Robert Sternberg, a cognitive psychologist, asked subjects to read four different passages for four different purposes: (1) scanning for a piece of information, (2) skimming for main ideas, (3) reading for complete comprehension, and (4) reading for detailed analysis. The researcher discovered that experienced readers varied their reading speed appropriately, spending the most time with passages they had to analyze in detail and the least time with those requiring only scanning or skimming. Inexperienced readers, in contrast, read all four passages at the same speed, spending too much or too little time on three of the four readings.

FOR WRITING AND DISCUSSION

Suppose you are doing a research project on a question of interest to you. So far you have located several books and a dozen or so articles on your topic. Working in small groups or as a whole class, create hypothetical scenarios in which you would, on different occasions, read material at all four reading speeds. When would you scan material? When would you skim for main ideas only? When would you read a text carefully from beginning to end? When would you pore over a text line by line?

Varying Strategies to Match Genre

Experienced readers also match their reading strategies to the genre of the piece being read. They use conventions of the genre to select the portions of the text that are most important to their purposes. To illustrate, let's look at how experienced readers read scientific or technical reports, a genre described in Chapter 4. Such reports typically contain five sections: introduction, methods (procedures), findings, discussion of findings, and conclusions and recommendations.

Experts seldom read a scientific report from beginning to end. A common approach is to read the introduction section (which explains the research question being examined, often reviews the literature surrounding the question, and presents the hypothesis), move to the discussion section, and then read the conclusions and recommendations section. These sections carry the study's argument by showing to what extent the findings help answer the research question. Most experts would turn to the methods and findings sections only after determining that the research was relevant to their work and generally helpful. They would read these sections primarily to determine how carefully and thoughtfully the research was done. (Debates about scientific research often focus on the research design and methodology.)

Other genres, too, demand special ways of reading, which you will develop through experience. For now, it is important simply to recognize that different genres use different conventions, which, in turn, invite different ways of reading.

Adopting a Multidraft Reading Process

Just as people may mistakenly believe that experienced authors compose effortlessly in one sitting, they also may mistakenly believe that expert readers comprehend a text perfectly with one rapid reading. Deceived by speed-reading advertisements, many students push themselves to read more quickly rather than more carefully. Experts, however, adjust their reading speed to the text's level of difficulty. As they read, they struggle to make the text comprehensible. They hold confusing passages in mental suspension, having faith that later parts of the essay may clarify earlier parts. They "nutshell" passages, often writing gist statements in the margins. A gist statement is a brief indication of the paragraph's function or purpose in the argument or a brief summary of the paragraph's content. Experts reread difficult texts two and three times, treating their first pass as an approximation or rough draft. They interact with the text by asking questions, expressing disagreement, and linking the text with other readings or with personal experience.

Students often don't allot enough study time for this kind of careful reading and rereading, thus depriving themselves of the challenges that will help them grow as readers. The rest of this chapter will show you how to struggle effectively with a challenging text.

Improving Your Own Reading Process

Here are some general strategies you can use to improve your ability to read any kind of college-level material.

1. *Slow down or speed up, depending on your goals.* First, decide why you are reading the material and what you will need to do with it. If you are

looking through several articles to find those that relate to a specific research topic, then you probably want to skim quickly through them. But many of your assignments will demand close, detailed reading. In these instances, follow the strategies of experts, reading with pen in hand and allotting time to reread a text if it is particularly difficult, treating first readings as first drafts.

2. *Reconstruct the rhetorical context.*   Train yourself to ask questions such as these: Who is this author? What audience is the author targeting? What occasion prompted this writing? What is the author's purpose? Any piece of writing makes more sense if you think of its author as a real person writing for some real purpose within a real historical context. Often you can reconstruct the rhetorical context from clues within the text. Encyclopedias and biographical dictionaries can also help you establish a rhetorical context.

3. *Join the text's conversation by exploring your views on the issues before reading.*   To determine the text's issues before reading it through, note the title, read the first few paragraphs carefully, and skim the opening sentences of all paragraphs. Try to appreciate from the outset what conversation the text is joining and consider your own views on the issue. This sort of personal exploration at the prereading stage both increases your readiness to understand the text and enhances your ability to enjoy it. We tried to create this experience for you by designing the brief prereading questionnaire for the Martin piece.

4. *Lose your highlighter; find your pen.*   Relying on those yellow highlighters or underlining with a pen or pencil can be a good strategy when your sole concern is to note main ideas, but in other cases it can make you too passive. When you read for full comprehension and detailed analysis, highlighting can lull you into thinking that you are reading actively when you aren't. Next time you get the urge to highlight a passage, write in the margin why you think it's important. Is it a major new point in the argument? A significant piece of support? A summary of the opposition? A particularly strong or particularly weak point? Use the margins to summarize, protest, question, or assent—but don't just color the pages. If you are reading a text that you can't write in (for example, a library book), make your "marginal notes" in a reading log keyed to the text's pages.

5. *Get the dictionary habit.*   Get in the habit of looking up words when you can't tell their meaning from context. One strategy is to make small tick marks next to words you're unsure of and look them up after you've finished reading so that you don't break your concentration.

6. *Recognize when lack of background information is the source of your difficulty.*   Sometimes you simply have to live a while with fuzzy passages that refer to concepts or phenomena that you don't understand. Write a question in the margin to make note of the concept, term, or reference you can't understand and then continue to do the best you can with the rest of the text. After you finish your reading, you can consult encyclopedias, other library resources, or knowledgeable peers to fill gaps in your knowledge.

7. ***Try "translating" difficult passages.***   When you stumble over a difficult passage, try translating it into your own words. Converting the passage into your own language will force you to focus on the precise meanings of words. Although your translation may not be exactly what the author intended, you will see more clearly where the sources of confusion lie and what the likely range of meanings might be.

8. ***Read both with the grain and against the grain.***   When you read with the grain, you are a compliant reader who tries to read the text the way the author intended. When you read against the grain, you are a resistant reader who asks unanticipated questions, pushes back, and reads the text in ways unforeseen by the author. Using the believing/doubting game introduced in Chapter 2 as a metaphor, reading with the grain means to believe the text; reading against the grain means to doubt it. When you share the author's belief system, it is sometimes difficult to resist the text; when you oppose the author's belief system, it is sometimes hard to be compliant. Nevertheless, strong readers try to develop their ability to read in both ways. A good strategy is to write in the margins what the text prompts you to think as you read—your surprises, insights, questions, and objections.

9. ***Continue the conversation after you read.***   After you've read a text, try completing the following statements in a journal:
   - Before reading this text, I believed this about the topic:

     _____

   - But after reading the text, my view has changed in these ways:

     _____

   - Although the text has persuaded me that _____,
     I still have these doubts: _____
   - The most significant questions this text raises for me are these:

     _____

   - The most important insights I have gotten from reading this text are these:

     _____

How to Write a Summary

In the rest of this chapter, we are going to show you how to apply these active reading skills to writing about complex texts. One of the skills you will need and use most in your college courses—and later in your career and life as a citizen—is the ability to produce accurate, thoughtful, and informed responses to what you have read. Writing a summary fosters a close encounter between you and the text and demonstrates your understanding of it.

We turn now to the nuts and bolts of reading a text when your goal is a full and detailed comprehension of its arguments. When you write a summary, you practice reading with the grain of a text. In summarizing, you "listen" actively to the text's author, showing that you understand the author's point of view by restating his or her argument as completely and fairly as possible. Sometimes you will need to compose a stand-alone summary of your own piece of writing, as when professionals are asked to write *abstracts* or *executive summaries* of an experimental report, proposal, or paper to be presented at a scholarly conference. Most commonly, however, you will need to summarize the views of other writers, particularly when you imagine readers who have not read a text that you want to refer to in your own writing. The summary gives your readers a condensed view of the other writer's argument, which you can then use as support for your own views or as a starting point for analysis or disagreement.

The process for summarizing outlined in the following steps will help you read more actively and accurately. As you become a more experienced reader and writer, you'll follow these steps without thinking about them.

Reading for Both Structure and Content

Step 1: The first time through, read the text fairly quickly for general meaning. If you get confused, keep going; later parts of the text might clarify earlier parts.

Step 2: Reread the text carefully. As you read, write gist statements in the margins for each paragraph. A *gist statement* is a brief indication of the paragraph's function or purpose in the text or a brief summary of the paragraph's content. Sometimes it is helpful to think of these two kinds of gist statements as "what it does" statements and "what it says" statements.* A "what it does" statement specifies the paragraph's function—for example, "summarizes an opposing view," "introduces another reason," "presents a supporting example," "provides statistical data in support of a point," and so on. A "what it says" statement captures the main idea of a paragraph by summarizing the paragraph's content.

When you first practice detailed readings of a text, you might find it helpful to write complete *does* and *says* statements on a separate sheet of paper rather than in the margins until you develop the internal habit of appreciating both the function and content of parts of an essay. Here are *does* and *says* statements for selected paragraphs in Andres Martin's essay on teenage tattooing (pp. 101–4).

> *Paragraph 1: Does:* Introduces the subject and sets up the argument. *Says:* The current popularity of tattoos and piercings is partly explained as an aid toward finding an identity, but the core or their appeal is their irreversible permanence.
>
> *Paragraph 2: Does:* Narrows the focus and presents the thesis. *Says:* To counsel families in disagreement over tattoos, psychiatrists should exhibit a nonjudgmental appreciation of teen tattoos and use them to understand teenagers better.
>
> *Paragraph 4: Does:* Discusses the first complex motivation behind youth tattooing. *Says:* Teens use tattoos to handle identity crises and to establish their uniqueness from others.

---

*For our treatment of "what it does" and "what it says" statements, we are indebted to Kenneth A. Bruffee, *A Short Course in Writing,* 2nd ed. (Cambridge, MA: Winthrop, 1980).

Paragraph 5: Does: Elaborates on the first motivation, the identity issue. *Says:* Tattoos provide teens with a sense of control over their changing bodies and over an environment perceived as adverse and domineering.

Paragraph 11: Does: Complicates the view of teens' use of tattoos to find permanence and belonging. *Says:* Although tattoos may unrealistically promise the resolution to larger conflicts, they may at least record the triumphs and miseries of adolescent turbulence, including gang and prison experience.

Paragraph 12: Does: Sums up the perspective and advice of the article. *Says:* Psychiatrists should regard adolescent tattoos positively as adornment and self-expression and employ tattoos to help understand teens' identities and sense of reality.

You may occasionally have difficulty writing a *says* statement for a paragraph because you may have trouble deciding what the main idea is, especially if the paragraph doesn't begin with a closed-form topic sentence. One way to respond to this problem is to formulate the question that you think the paragraph answers. If you think of chunks of the text as answers to a logical progression of questions, you can often follow the main ideas more easily. Rather than writing *says* statements in the margins, therefore, some readers prefer writing *says* questions. *Says* questions for the Martin text may include the following: What is the most constructive approach clinicians can take to teen tattooing when these tattoos have become the focus of family conflict? What psychological needs and problems are teenagers acting out through their tattoos? Why does the permanence of tattoos appeal to young people?

No matter which method you use—*says* statements or *says* questions—writing gist statements in the margins is far more effective than underlining or highlighting for helping you recall the text's structure and argument.

Step 3: After you have analyzed the article paragraph by paragraph, try locating the article's main divisions or parts. In longer closed-form articles, writers often forecast the shape of their essays in their introductions or use their conclusions to sum up main points. Although Martin's article is short, it uses both a forecasting statement and subheads to direct readers through its main points. The article is divided into several main chunks as follows:

- Introductory paragraphs, which establish the problem to be addressed and narrow the focus to a clinical perspective (paragraphs 1–2)
- A one-sentence organizing and predicting statement (paragraph 3)
- A section explaining how tattoos may help adolescents establish a unique identity (paragraphs 4–5)
- A section explaining how tattoos help teens incorporate onto their bodies a symbolic ownership of something important to them (paragraphs 6–8)
- A section explaining how tattoos represent and satisfy teens' search for permanence (paragraphs 9–11)
- A conclusion that states the thesis explicitly and sums up Martin's advice to fellow psychiatrists (paragraph 12)

Instead of listing the sections, you might prefer to make an outline or tree diagram of the article showing its main parts.

Writing Your Summary

Once you have written gist statements or questions in the margins and clarified the text's structure by creating an outline or diagram, you are ready to write a summary. Typically, summaries range from 100 to 250 words, but sometimes writers compose summaries as short as one sentence. The order and proportions of your summary can usually follow the order and proportions of the text. However, if the original article has a delayed thesis or other characteristics of open-form writing, you can rearrange the order and begin with the thesis. With prose that has many open-form features, you may also have to infer points that are more implied than expressed.

A summary of another author's writing—when it is incorporated into your own essay—makes particular demands on you, the writer. A successful summary should do the following:

- Represent the original article accurately and fairly.
- Be direct and concise, using words economically.
- Remain objective and neutral, not revealing your own ideas on the subject but rather only the original author's points.
- Give the original article balanced and proportional coverage.
- Use your own words to express the original author's ideas.
- Keep your reader informed through attributive tags (such as *according to Martin* or *Martin argues that*) that you are expressing someone else's ideas, not your own.
- Possibly include quotations for a few key terms or ideas from the original, but quote sparingly.
- Be a unified, coherent piece of writing in its own right.
- Be properly cited and documented so that the reader can find the original text.

Some of these criteria for a successful summary are challenging to meet. For instance, to avoid interjecting your own opinions, you will need to choose your words carefully, including the verbs you use in attributive tags. Note the subtle differences between these pairs of verbs: *Smith argues* versus *Smith rants; Jones criticizes* versus *Jones attacks; Brown asserts* versus *Brown leaps to the conclusion.* In each pair, the second verb, by moving beyond neutrality, reveals your own judgment of the author's ideas.

When you incorporate a summary into your own writing, it is particularly important to distinguish between the author's ideas and your own—hence the importance of frequent attributive tags, which tell the reader that these ideas belong to Smith or Jones or Brown rather than you. If you choose to copy any of the author's words directly from the text, you need to use quotation marks and cite the quotation using an appropriate documentation system. Chapter 22 provides a full discussion of how to summarize, paraphrase, or quote sources; how to work them smoothly into your own writing; and how to avoid plagiarism.

The following example, which summarizes Martin's article on teenagers and tattoos, uses the MLA documentation system.

Summary of Martin Article

Identification of the article, journal and author

In "On Teenagers and Tattoos," published in The American Academy of Child and Adolescent Psychiatry, Dr. Andrés Martin advises fellow

Thesis of article

psychiatrists to think of teenage tattooing not as a fad or as a form of self-mutilation but as an opportunity for clinicians to understand

Attributive tag

teenagers better. Martin examines three different reasons that teenagers

Transition

get tattoos. First, he argues that tattoos help teenagers establish unique

Attributive tag

identities by giving them a sense of control over their evolving bodies

Transition and attributive tag

and over an environment perceived as adverse and domineering. Second, he believes that a tattooed image often symbolizes the teen's relationship to a significant concept or person, making the relationship more visible

Transition and attributive tag

and real. Finally, says Martin, because teens are disturbed by modern

Inclusion of short quotation from article. MLA documentation style; number in parentheses indicates page number of original article where quotation is found

society's mobility and fragmentation and because they have an "intense longing for rootedness and stability" (861), the irreversible nature of tattoos may give them a sense of permanence. Martin concludes that tattoos can be a meaningful record of survived teen experiences. He

Attributive tag

Attributive tag

Another short quotation

encourages therapists to regard teen tattoos as "self-constructive and adorning efforts," rather than as "mutilatory and destructive acts" (861)

Brackets indicate that the writer changed the material inside the brackets to fit the grammar and context of the writer's own sentence

and suggests that tattoos can help therapists understand "another level of [teenagers'] internal reality" (861). [195 words]

Works Cited

Martin article cited completely using MLA documentation form; in a formal paper, the "works cited" list begins on a new page

Martin, Andrés. "On Teenagers and Tattoos." Journal of the American Academy of Child and Adolescent Psychiatry 36 (1997): 860-61.

FOR WRITING AND DISCUSSION

Imagine that the context of a research paper you are writing calls for a shorter summary of the Martin article than the one presented here (which is approximately 195 words, including attributive tags). To practice distilling the main ideas of an article to produce summaries of different lengths, first write a 100-word summary of "On Teenagers and Tattoos." Then reduce your summary further to 50 words. Discuss the principles you followed in deciding what to eliminate or how to restructure sentences to convey the most information in the fewest number of words.

How to Write a Strong Response

In college and professional life, you will often need more than a clear understanding of the main ideas you have read. You will also need to engage with this reading at a deeper level by writing strong responses. To respond strongly to a text means to carry on an interactive dialogue with it in a conscious and purposeful manner. You can interact strongly with a text by reading it with the grain, against the grain, or anywhere along a continuum ranging from enthusiastic agreement and assimilation to outright anger and disbelief.

When you read with the grain of a text, you practice what psychologist Carl Rogers calls *empathic listening,* in which you try to see the world through the author's eyes, role-playing as much as possible the author's intended audience, adopting its beliefs and values, and acquiring its background knowledge. Reading with the grain requires your willingness to extend the author's project, to support the author's thesis or point of view or method with new evidence from your own personal experiences, other readings, or research; you focus on how this text endows you with a new understanding of this subject.

When you read against the grain of a text, you challenge, question, resist, and perhaps even rebut the author's ideas. Your strong response often consists of pointed queries to the author that challenge the author's reasoning, sources, examples, or choice of language. Your talking back to the text might take the form of counterexamples, a mentioning of the points that the author has overlooked or omitted, and alternative lines of reasoning.

Most often, a strong response to a text will consist of both with-the-grain and against-the-grain interactions. Perhaps you find that you agree with parts of the text and disagree with others. Perhaps the text poses questions you have never considered. Such texts can stretch your thinking and, if you allow them to, can cause you to grow and change. When we say that a strong response involves speaking back to a text, we don't necessarily mean opposing it. We mean adding your voice to the conversation the text is part of.

What Should a Strong Response Do?

In a strong response you speak back to an author as if you were joining him or her in a conversation. The key is to think of several main points you want to add to the conversation, sketch out those points in an initial thesis statement, and prepare to develop those points one at a time. A strong response is truly strong when it includes both rhetorical points (points about why, to whom, and how the text is written) and subject matter points.

When you join an author in conversation, you need to have a good sense of the context, purpose, and style of the original reading. At least one of your main points should consider how the author tries to influence his or her audience. You should look first at what the author of the text is trying to accomplish. You can then comment on the author's purpose, audience, genre, and stylistic choices. You can read with the grain by affirming the effectiveness of the author's rhetorical strategies, or you can read against the grain by questioning and challenging these strategies from your own perspective. Consider questions such as these:

- What is the author's purpose in writing the text?
- Who is the intended audience?
- What is the genre and how does that genre restrict/limit readership, style and purpose?
- What change does the author hope to make in the audience's view of the topic?
- What persuasive strategies does the author use (amount of and kinds of evidence, strategies of reasoning, selection/omission of details, word choices, figurative language, and stylistic choices)?

In some cases, your strong response might consist entirely of a rhetorical analysis, especially if the text you are analyzing is particularly interesting or complex rhetorically. But often you will want to respond to the text in other ways as well. The strong response gives you an opportunity to add your own voice to the conversation of ideas stimulated by the text. (Think of the text as having thrown you a ball and now you have to throw it back.) Here are some examples of the kinds of ways you can speak back to the author's ideas:

- Agree with one of the author's points and support it using new evidence from personal experience or knowledge.
- Identify a new insight you have gotten from the text and illustrate it, perhaps by applying it to a different context.
- Disagree with or raise doubts about one of the author's points by using counter-evidence from your own personal experience or knowledge.
- Fill in a gap in the text by adding your own theory, hypothesis, explanation, or analysis; show the value of adding something that the author overlooked or left out.
- Develop one or more questions, issues, or problems raised for you by the text. How does the text cause you to question your own understanding of the text's subject matter or to question your own values, assumptions, or beliefs?

- Evaluate the usefulness of the text, its applicability to other contexts, its limitations based on the writer's bias or narrowness, or the potential consequences of its ideas.

Student Example of a "Summary/Strong Response" Essay

Before giving you some tips on how to discover ideas for your strong response, we show you an example of a student essay for this chapter: a "summary/ strong response" essay. Note that the essay begins by identifying the question under discussion: Why do teenagers get tattoos? It then summarizes the article by Andrés Martin.* Immediately following the summary, the student writer states his thesis, followed by the strong response, which contains both rhetorical and subject matter points.

Why Do Teenagers Get Tattoos? A Response to Andrés Martin
Sean Barry (student)

My sister has one. My brother has one. I have one. Just take a stroll downtown and you will see how commonplace it is for someone to be decorated with tattoos and hung with piercings. In fact, hundreds of teenagers, every day, allow themselves to be etched upon or poked into. What's the cause of this phenomenon? Why do so many teenagers get tattoos? *[Introduces topic and sets context]*

Dr. Andrés Martin has answered this question from a psychiatrist's perspective in his article "On Teenagers and Tattoos," published in *The American Academy of Child and Adolescent Psychiatry.* Martin advises fellow psychiatrists to think of teenage tattooing as a constructive opportunity for clinicians to understand teenagers better. Martin examines three different reasons that teenagers get tattoos. First, he argues that tattoos help teenagers establish unique identities by giving them a sense of control over their evolving bodies and over an environment perceived as adverse and domineering. Second, he believes that a tattooed image often symbolizes the teen's relationship to a significant concept or person, making the relationship more visible and real. Finally, says Martin, because teens are disturbed by modern society's mobility and fragmentation and because they have an "intense longing for rootedness and stability" (103), the irreversible nature of tattoos may give them a sense of permanence. Martin concludes that tattoos can be a meaningful record of survived teen experiences. *[Summary of Martin's article]*

Although Martin's analysis has relevance and some strengths, I think he overgeneralizes and over-romanticizes teenage tattooing, leading him to overlook other causes of teenage tattooing such as commercialization and teenagers' desire to identify with a peer group as well as achieve an individual identity. *[Thesis statement]*

Some of Martin's points seem relevant and realistic and match my own experiences. I agree that teenagers sometimes use tattoos to establish their own identities. When my brother, sister, and I all got our tattoos, we were partly asserting our own independence from our parents. Martin's point about the symbolic significance of a tattoo image also connects with my experiences. A Hawaiian guy in my dorm has a fish tattooed on his back, which he says represents his love of the ocean and the spiritual experience he has when he scuba dives. *[With-the-grain point in support of Martin's ideas]*

*In this essay the student writer uses a shortened version of his 195-word summary used as an illustration on page 114.

Rhetorical point about Martin's audience, purpose, and genre that has both with-the-grain and against-the-grain elements

Martin, speaking as a psychiatrist to other psychiatrists, also provides psychological insights into the topic of teen tattooing even though this psychological perspective brings some limitations, too. In this scholarly article, Martin's purpose is to persuade fellow psychiatrists to think of adolescent tattooing in positive rather than judgmental terms. Rather than condemn teens for getting tattoos, he argues that discussion of the tattoos can provide useful insights into the needs and behavior of troubled teens (especially males). But this perspective is also a limitation because the teenagers he sees are mostly youths in psychiatric counseling, particularly teens struggling with the absence of or violent loss of a parent and those who have experience with gangs and prison-terms. This perspective leads him to over-generalize. As a psychological study of a specific group of troubled teens, the article is informative. However, it does not apply as well to most teenagers who are getting tattoos today.

Against-the-grain rhetorical point: Barry analyzes Martin's use of quotations from Moby Dick

Besides over-generalizing, Martin also seems to romanticize teenage tattooing. Why else would a supposedly scientific article begin and end with quotations from *Moby Dick*? Martin seems to imply a similarity between today's teenagers and the sailor hero Ishmael who wandered the seas looking for personal identity. In quoting *Moby Dick*, Martin seems to value tattooing as a suitable way for teenagers to record their experiences. Every tattoo, for Martin, has deep significance. Thus, Martin casts tattooed teens as romantic outcasts, loners, and adventurers like Ishmael.

Transition to writer's own analysis

In contrast to Martin, I believe that teens are influenced by the commercial nature of tattooing, which has become big business aimed at their age group. Every movie or television star or beauty queen who sports a tattoo sends the commercial message that tattoos are cool: "A tattoo will help you be successful, sexy, handsome, or attractive like us." Tattoo parlors are no longer dark dives in seedy, dangerous parts of cities, but appear in lively commercial districts; in fact, there are several down the street from the university. Teenagers now buy tattoos the way they buy other consumer items.

Against-the-grain point: writer's alternative theory

Against-the-grain point: writer's second theory

Furthermore, Martin doesn't explore teenagers' desire not only for individuality but also for peer group acceptance. Tattooing is the "in" thing to do. Tattooing used to be defiant and daring, but now it is popular and more acceptable among teens. I even know a group of sorority women who went together to get tattoos on their ankles. As tattooing has become more mainstreamed, rebels/trendsetters have turned to newer and more outrageous practices, such as branding and extreme piercings. Meanwhile, tattoos bring middle-of-the-road teens the best of both worlds: a way to show their individuality and simultaneously to be accepted by peers.

Conclusion and summary

In sum, Martin's research is important because it examines psychological responses to teen's inner conflicts. It offers partial explanations for teens' attraction to tattoos and promotes a positive, noncritical attitude toward tattooing. But I think the article is limited by its overgeneralizations based on the psychiatric focus, by its tendency to romanticize tattooing, by its lack of recognition of the commercialization of tattooing, and by its under-emphasis on group belonging and peer pressure. Teen tattooing is more complex than even Martin makes it.

Works Cited

Complete citation of article in MLA format

Martin, Andrés. "On Teenagers and Tattoos." *Journal of the American Academy of Child and Adolescent Psychiatry* 36 (1997): 860–61. Rpt. in *The Allyn and Bacon Guide to Writing*. John D. Ramage and John C. Bean. 2nd ed. Boston, MA: Allyn and Bacon, 2000. 101–04.

How to Think of Ideas for Your Strong Response

In the student example just shown, Sean Barry makes a number of points. He analyzes the rhetorical context of Martin's original article by pointing out some of the limitations of a psychiatric point of view and exploring the implications of the *Moby Dick* references; he supports two of Martin's points using his own personal examples; and he argues that Martin—perhaps influenced by his romantic view of tattoos—fails to appreciate the impact on teenagers of the commercialization of tattooing and the importance of peer group acceptance. Clearly, Sean Barry illustrates what we mean by being a strong reader.

How can you develop the aptitude and habits of strong reading? Here are some strategies you can practice when preparing to write your own summary/strong response essay.

Make Strong Marginal Notations as You Read

A strong reader thinks actively while reading. She not only tries to understand the author's ideas but also interacts with the text (as if in dialogue with the author) and records ideas and reactions while reading. A portion of Sean Barry's annotations of the Martin article, showing both with- and against-the-grain reading comments is shown in Figure 6.1.

Identify "Hot Spots" in the Text

Most texts will create "hot spots" for you (each reader's hot spots are apt to be different). By "hot spot" we mean a quotation or passage that you especially notice, either because you agree or disagree with it or because it triggers memories or other associations. Or perhaps the hot spot strikes you as particularly thought provoking. Perhaps it raises a problem or is confusing yet suggestive. Go back through the text and copy out short quotations that intrigue you (or place an asterisk next to longer passages); then freewrite your responses to these hot spots.

Write Out Questions Triggered by the Text

Almost any text triggers questions as you read. A good way to begin formulating a strong response is simply to write out several questions that the text caused you to think about. Then explore your responses to those questions through freewriting. Sometimes the freewrite will trigger more questions.

Consent to the Text's Perspective

As you read, try to suspend your own belief system and enter fully into the author's position. Put into play the believing part of the believing and doubting game discussed in Chapter 2. Consider what thinking about the subject in this way enables you to perceive that you haven't thought of before. Write comments back to the text that acknowledge the points where this text surprises you, enriches your thinking, or enlarges your perspective. Brainstorm for examples from your own personal experience or knowledge that support the author's argument. Read intensely with the grain.

ANDRÉS MARTIN, M.D.
ON TEENAGERS AND TATTOOS

Quotation from a novel?

The skeleton dimensions I shall now proceed to set down are copied verbatim from my right arm, where I had them tattooed: as in my wild wanderings at that period, there was no other secure way of preserving such valuable statistics.

—*Melville/Moby Dick CII*

A strange beginning for a scientific article

What do 19th-century sailors have to do with late 20th-century teens?

Idea here: the body as a concrete record of experience?

Larger tattooing scene?

Tattoos and piercings have become a part of our everyday landscape. 1 They are ubiquitous, having <u>entered the circles of glamour</u> and the <u>mainstream of fashion,</u> and they have even become an increasingly common feature of our urban youth. Legislation in most states restricts professional tattooing to adults older than 18 years of age, so "high end" tattooing is rare in children and adolescents, but such tattoos are occasionally seen in older teenagers. Piercings, by comparison, as well as self-made or "jailhouse" type tattoos, are not at all rare among adolescents or even among schoolage children. Like hairdo, makeup, or baggy jeans, tattoos and piercings can be subject to fad influence or peer pressure in an effort toward group affiliation. As with any other fashion statement, they can be construed as bodily aids in the inner struggle toward identity consolidation, serving as adjuncts to <u>the defining and sculpting of the self</u> by means of external manipulations. But unlike most other body decorations, tattoos and piercings are set apart by their irreversible and permanent nature, a quality at the core of their magnetic appeal to adolescents.

I like the phrase "the defining and sculpting of the self"—sounds creative, like art

This idea is surprising and interesting. It merits lots of discussion.

Which teenagers? All teenagers?

Adolescents and their parents are often at odds over the acquisition of 2 bodily decorations. For the adolescent, piercings or tattoos may be seen as personal and beautifying statements, while parents may construe them as oppositional and enraging affronts to their authority. Distinguishing <u>bodily adornment</u> from <u>self-mutilation</u> may indeed prove challenging, particularly when a family is in disagreement over a <u>teenager's motivations</u> and a clinician is summoned as the final arbiter. At such times it may be most important to realize jointly that the skin can all too readily become but another battleground for the tensions of the age, arguments having less to do with tattoos and piercings than with core issues such as separation from the family matrix. Exploring the motivations and significance belying tattoos (Grumet, 1983) and piercings can go a long way toward resolving such differences and can become a novel and additional way of getting to know teenagers. An interested and nonjudgmental appreciation of teenagers' surface presentations may become a way of making contact not only in their terms but on their turfs: quite literally on the territory of their skins.

The following three sections exemplify some of the complex psychological underpinnings of youth tattooing. 3

These terms show the main opposing views on tattoos.

Is he speaking only to psychiatrists? Does this clinical perspective have other applications?

Good open-minded, practical approach to teen tattoos

I like Martin's focus on complexity

FIGURE 6.1   Student Marginal Notes on Martin's Text

Deny the Text's Perspective

Now, reading again, remain skeptical of the text and resist its argument. Put into play the doubting side of the believing and doubting game. Show what might be harmful or dangerous in adopting the author's perspective. Brainstorm for examples from your own personal experience or knowledge that raise doubts about the author's argument. Question the author's values, beliefs, or assumptions. Read intensely against the grain.

Articulate Your Difference from the Intended Audience

In some cases you can read strongly by articulating how you differ from the text's intended audience. As we show in Chapter 4, experienced writers try to imagine their audience. They ask: What are my audience's values? How interested in and knowledgeable about my topic is my audience? Eventually, the author makes decisions about audience, in effect "creates" the audience, so that the text reveals both an image of the author and of its intended reader.

Your own experiences, arising from your gender, class, ethnicity, sexual orientation, political and religious beliefs, interests, values, and so forth, may cause you to feel estranged from the author's imagined audience. If the text seems written for straight people and you are gay, or for Christians and you are a Muslim or an atheist, or for environmentalists and you grew up in a small logging community, you may well resist the text. Sometimes your sense of exclusion from the intended audience makes it difficult to read a text at all. For example, a woman student of our acquaintance once brought a class to a standstill by slamming the course anthology on her desk and exclaiming, "How can you people stand reading this patriarchal garbage!" She had become so irritated by the authors' assumption that all readers shared their male-oriented values that she could no longer bear to read the selections.

When you differ significantly from the text's assumed audience, you can often use this difference to question the author's underlying assumptions, values, and beliefs.

FOR WRITING AND DISCUSSION

What follows is a short passage by writer Annie Dillard in response to a question about how she chooses to spend her time. This passage often evokes heated responses from our students.

> I don't do housework. Life is too short. . . . I let almost all my indoor plants die from neglect while I was writing the book. There are all kinds of ways to live. You can take your choice. You can keep a tidy house, and when St. Peter asks you what you did with your life, you can say, "I kept a tidy house, I made my own cheese balls."

Individual task: Read the passage and then briefly freewrite your reaction to it. *Group task:* Working in groups or as a whole class, develop answers to the following questions:

1. What values does Dillard assume her audience holds?
2. What kinds of readers are apt to feel excluded from that audience?
3. If you are not part of the intended audience for this passage, what in the text evokes resistance?

Articulate Your Own Purpose for Reading

You may sometimes read a text against the grain if your purposes for reading differ from what the author imagined. Normally you read a text because you share the author's interest in a question and want to know the author's answer. In other words, you usually read to join the author's conversation. But suppose that you wish to review the writings of nineteenth-century scientists to figure out what they assumed about nature (or women, or God, or race, or capitalism). Or suppose that you examine a politician's metaphors to see what they reveal about his or her values, or analyze *National Geographic* for evidence of political bias. In these cases, you will be reading against the grain of the text. In a sense, you would be "blindsiding" the authors—while they are talking about topic X, you are observing them for topic Y.

You can see this strategy at work in literary critic Jane Tompkins' " 'Indians': Textualism, Morality, and the Problem of History" (see pp. 177–85). Tompkins, assigned to teach a course in early American literature, wanted to find out as much as she could about the relationship between Puritans and Native Americans in colonial New England. So she turned to a famous 1950s scholarly work by Perry Miller on the Puritan mind. Here is her brief account of her reading experience:

> My research began with Perry Miller. Early in the preface to *Errand into the Wilderness*, while explaining how he came to write his history of the New England mind, Miller writes a sentence that stopped me dead. He says that what fascinated him as a young man about his country's history was "the massive narrative of the movement of European culture into the vacant wilderness of America." "Vacant?" Miller, writing in 1956, doesn't pause over the word "vacant," but to people who read his preface thirty years later, the word is shocking. In what circumstances could someone proposing to write a history of colonial New England *not* take into account the Indian presence there?

This experience—reading a sentence that "stopped [her] dead"—sets Tompkins off on her own research project: "How do historians examining colonial New England portray Indians?" As she reads historian after historian, her interest isn't in the research problems posed by the authors but in her own research problem: How does this author portray Indians? This method of resistant reading is very common in academia.

Ask Generic Strategic Questions

The essence of reading strongly, then, is to read critically and to pose questions. Here are generic strategic questions you can ask to generate ideas for your strong response:

- How is the author trying to change his or her intended readers' view of the topic? What rhetorical strategies does the author use to influence the intended audience?
- How has this author changed my view of this topic? What do I have to give up or lose in order to change my view? What do I gain? How do the author's rhetorical strategies affect me?
- What is excluded from this author's text? All writers must select certain details to include in their texts and others to exclude. By looking at what is omitted from a text, you can often ascertain something about the author's value system.
- How can I question this author's data, evidence, and supporting arguments? If I am not persuaded by the author's data and evidence, why not? What is missing? What can be called into question?
- How can I question the author's values, beliefs, and assumptions, both stated and unstated? Conversely, how does this text cause me to question my own values, beliefs, and assumptions?
- How can I use this author's ideas for my own purposes? What new insights have I gained? What new ways of thinking can I apply to another context?

Consider Your Purpose(s) for Writing

In imagining possibilities for different kinds of strong responses, consider again the various purposes for writing that we developed in Chapter 4. Most of these purposes suggest approaches you might take in composing your strong response: to express, to explore, to inform, to analyze, and to persuade. (In fact, potentially a strong response could even take the form of a poem or short story: that is, have a literary purpose.)

For a strong response essay, you most likely will be doing some or all of the following: expressing your personal reaction to the text from the perspective of your own life, exploring your ideas and questions prompted by the text, informing readers of new or different data related to the text's subject matter, analyzing the author's ideas and rhetorical choices, and persuading a reader to think as you do about the text. You may focus primarily on one of these purposes, or you may choose to encompass and combine several purposes.

READINGS

This section contains four essays that invite strong responses. The first is easy to classify as closed form; the remaining three resist simple classification in that they include some features of open-form prose (occasional implicit points and narrative elements). Each piece will prompt personal and intellectual grappling with the author's ideas and beliefs. Each piece also calls attention to the author's rhetorical strategies, making you reflect on his or her audience, purpose, and stylistic choices. Your instructor may choose one of these pieces as the subject of your assignment for this chapter. Because your task is to summarize your assigned piece and respond strongly to it, we omit the questions for analysis that typically accompany readings elsewhere in the text.

The first reading originally appeared in the conservative political journal *The National Review* in October 1988. Written by Richard Lynn, a professor of psychology, this article stirred considerable public discussion and has particularly influenced the Republican party's views on education—for example, their advocacy of a standardized curriculum, of school vouchers to stimulate competition among schools, and higher standards for student achievement.

RICHARD LYNN
WHY JOHNNY CAN'T READ, BUT YOSHIO CAN

There can be no doubt that American schools compare poorly with Japanese schools. In the latter, there are no serious problems with poor discipline, violence, or truancy; Japanese children take school seriously and work hard. Japanese educational standards are high, and illiteracy is virtually unknown. 1

The evidence of Japan's high educational standards began to appear as long ago as the 1960s. In 1967 there was published the first of a series of studies of educational standards in a dozen or so economically developed nations, based on tests of carefully drawn representative samples of children. The first study was concerned with achievement in math on the part of 13- and 18-year-olds. In both age groups the Japanese children came out well ahead of their coevals in other countries. The American 13-year-olds came out second to last for their age group; the American 18-year-olds, last. In both age groups, European children scored about halfway between the Japanese and the Americans. 2

Since then, further studies have appeared, covering science as well as math. The pattern of results has always been the same: the Japanese have generally scored first, the Americans last or nearly last, and the Europeans have fallen somewhere in between. In early adolescence, when the first tests are taken, Japanese children are two or three years ahead of American children; by age 18, approximately 98 per cent of Japanese children surpass their American counterparts. 3

Meanwhile, under the Reagan Administration, the United States at least started to take notice of the problem. In 1983 the President's report, *A Nation at Risk,* described the state of American schools as a national disaster. A follow-up report issued by the then-secretary of education, Mr. William Bennett, earlier this year claims that although some improvements have been made, these have been "disappointingly slow." 4

An examination of Japan's school system suggests that there are three factors responsible for its success, which might be emulated by other countries: a strong national curriculum, stipulated by the government; strong incentives for students; and the stimulating effects of competition between schools. 5

The national curriculum in Japan is drawn up by the Department of Education. It covers Japanese language and literature, math, science, social science, music, moral education, and physical education. From time to time, the Department of Education requests advice on the content of the curriculum from representatives of the teaching pro- 6 fession, industry, and the trade unions. Syllabi are then drawn up, setting out in detail the subject matter that has to be taught at each grade. These syllabi are issued to school principals, who are responsible for ensuring that the stipulated curriculum is taught in their schools. Inspectors periodically check that this is being done.

7   The Japanese national curriculum ensures such uniformly high standards of teaching that almost all parents are happy to send their children to the local public school. There is no flight into private schools of the kind that has been taking place in America in recent years. Private schools do exist in Japan, but they are attended by less than 1 per cent of children in the age range of compulsory schooling (six to 15 years).

8   This tightly stipulated national curriculum provides a striking contrast with the decentralized curriculum of schools in America. Officially, the curriculum in America is the responsibility of school principals with guidelines from state education officials. In practice, even school principals often have little idea of what is actually being taught in the classroom.

9   America and Britain have been unusual in leaving the curriculum so largely in the hands of teachers. Some form of national curriculum is used throughout Continental Europe, although the syllabus is typically not specified in as much detail as in Japan. And now Britain is changing course: legislation currently going through Parliament will introduce a national curriculum for England and Wales, with the principal subjects being English, math, science, technology, a foreign language, history and geography, and art, music, and design. It is envisioned that the new curriculum will take up approximately 70 per cent of teaching time, leaving the remainder free for optional subjects such as a second foreign language, or extra science.

10   Under the terms of the new legislation, schoolchildren are going to be given national tests at the ages of seven, 11, 14, and 16 to ensure that the curriculum has been taught and that children have learned it to a satisfactory standard. When the British national curriculum comes into effect, America will be left as the only major economically developed country without one.

11   To achieve high educational standards in schools it is necessary to have motivated students as well as good teachers. A national curriculum acts as a discipline on teachers, causing them to teach efficiently, but it does nothing to provide incentives for students, an area in which American education is particularly weak.

12   One of the key factors in the Japanese education system is that secondary schooling is split into two stages. At the age of 11 or 12, Japanese children enter junior high school. After three years there, they take competitive entrance examinations for senior high schools. In each locality there is a hierarchy of public esteem for these senior high schools, from the two or three that are regarded as the best in the area, through those considered to be good or average, down to those that (at least by Japanese standards) are considered to be poor.

13   The top schools enjoy national reputations, somewhat akin to the famous English schools such as Eton and Harrow. But in England the high fees exacted by these schools mean that very few parents can afford them. Consequently there are few candidates for entry, and the entrance examinations offer little incentive to work for the great mass of children. By contrast, in Japan the elite senior high schools are open to everyone. While a good number of these schools are private (approximately 30 per cent nationwide, though in some major cities the figure is as high as 50 per cent), even these schools are enabled, by government subsidies, to keep their fees within the means of a large proportion of parents. The public schools also charge fees, but these are nominal, amounting to only a few hundred dollars a year, and loans are available to cover both fees and living expenses.

Thus children have every expectation of being able to attend the best school they can qualify for; and, hence, the hierarchical rankings of senior high schools act as a powerful incentive for children preparing for the entrance examinations. There is no doubt that Japanese children work hard in response to these incentives. Starting as early as age ten, approximately half of them take extra tuition on weekends, in the evenings, and in the school holidays at supplementary coaching establishments known as *juku,* and even at that early age they do far more homework than American children. At about the age of 12, Japanese children enter the period of their lives known as *examination hell:* during this time, which lasts fully two years, it is said that those who sleep more than five hours a night have no hope of success, either in school or in life. For, in addition to conferring great social and intellectual status on their students, the elite senior high schools provide a first-rate academic education, which, in turn, normally enables the students to get into one of the elite universities and, eventually, to move into a good job in industry or government. 14

Although Japanese children are permitted to leave school at the age of 15, 94 per cent of them proceed voluntarily to the senior high schools. Thus virtually all Japanese are exposed in early adolescence to the powerful incentive for academic work represented by the senior-high-school entrance examinations. There is nothing in the school systems of any of the Western countries resembling this powerful incentive. 15

The prestige of the elite senior high schools is sustained by the extensive publicity they receive from the media. Each year the top hundred or so schools in Japan are ranked on the basis of the percentage of their pupils who obtain entry to the University of Tokyo, Japan's most prestigious university. These rankings are widely reported in the print media, and the positions of the top twenty schools are announced on TV news programs, rather like the scores made by leading sports teams in the United States and Europe. At a local level, more detailed media coverage is devoted to the academic achievements of all the schools in the various localities, this time analyzed in terms of their pupils' success in obtaining entry to the lesser, but still highly regarded, local universities. 16

Thus, once Japanese 15-year-olds have been admitted to their senior high schools, they are confronted with a fresh set of incentives in the form of entrance examinations to universities and colleges, which are likewise hierarchically ordered in public esteem. After the University of Tokyo, which stands at the apex of the status hierarchy, come the University of Kyoto and ten or so other highly prestigious universities, including the former Imperial Universities in the major provincial cities and the technological university of Hitosubashi, whose standing and reputation in Japan resembles that of the Massachusetts Institute of Technology in the United States. 17

Below these top dozen institutions stand some forty or so less prestigious but still well-regarded universities. And after these come numerous smaller universities and colleges of varying degrees of standing and reputation. 18

To some extent the situation in Japan has parallels in the United States and Europe, but there are two factors that make the importance of securing admission to an elite university substantially greater in Japan than in the West. In the first place, the entire Japanese system is geared toward providing lifelong employment, both in the private sector and in the civil service. It is practically unheard of for executives to switch from one corporation to another, or into public service and then back into the private sector, as in the United States and Europe. Employees are recruited directly out of college, and, needless to say, the major corporations and the civil service recruit virtually entirely from the top dozen universities. The smaller Japanese corporations operate along the same lines, although they widen their recruitment net to cover the next forty 19 or so universities in the prestige hierarchy. Thus, obtaining entry to a prestigious university is a far more vital step for a successful career in Japan than it is in the United States or Europe.

20   Secondly, like the elite senior high schools, the elite universities are meritocratic. The great majority of universities are public institutions, receiving substantial government subsidies. Again, as with the senior high schools, fees are quite low, and loans are available to defray expenses. In principle and to a considerable extent in practice, any young Japanese can get into the University of Tokyo, or one of the other elite universities, provided only that he or she is talented enough and is prepared to do the work necessary to pass the entrance examinations. Knowing this, the public believes that *all* the most talented young Japanese go to one of these universities—and, conversely, that anyone who fails to get into one of these schools is necessarily less bright. Avoiding this stigma is, of course, a further incentive for the student to work hard to get in.

21   The third significant factor responsible for the high educational standards in Japan is competition among schools. This operates principally among the senior high schools, and what they are competing for is academic reputation. The most prestigious senior high school in Japan is Kansei in Tokyo, and being a teacher at Kansei is something like being a professor at Harvard. The teachers' self-esteem is bound up with the academic reputation of their schools—a powerful motivator for teachers to teach well.

22   In addition to this important factor of self-esteem, there is practical necessity. Since students are free to attend any school they can get into, if a school failed to provide good-quality teaching, it would no longer attract students. In business terms, its customers would fade away, and it would be forced to close. Thus the essential feature of the competition among the Japanese senior high schools is that it exposes the teachers to the discipline of the free-enterprise system. In the case of the public senior high schools, the system can be regarded as a form of market socialism in which the competing institutions are state-owned but nevertheless compete against each other for their customers. Here the Japanese have been successfully operating the kind of system that Mikhail Gorbachev may be feeling his way toward introducing in the Soviet Union. The Japanese private senior high schools add a further capitalist element to the system insofar as they offer their educational services more or less like firms operating in a conventional market.

23   The problem of how market disciplines can be brought to bear on schools has been widely discussed in America and also in Britain ever since Milton Friedman raised it a quarter of a century or so ago, but solutions such as Friedman's voucher proposal seem as distant today as they did then. Although the proposal has been looked at sympathetically by Republicans in the United States and by Conservatives in Britain, politicians in both countries have fought shy of introducing it. Probably they have concluded that the problems of getting vouchers into the hands of all parents, and dealing with losses, fraud, counterfeits, and so forth, are likely to be too great for the scheme to be feasible.

24   The Japanese have evolved a different method of exposing schools to market forces. Subsidies are paid directly to the schools on a per-capita basis in accordance with the number of students they have. If a school's rolls decline, so do its incomes, both from subsidies and from fees. This applies to both the public and private senior high schools, although the public schools obviously receive a much greater proportion of their income as subsidies and a smaller proportion from fees.

25   A similar scheme is being introduced in Britain. The Thatcher government is currently bringing in legislation that will permit public schools to opt out of local-authority control. Those that opt out will receive subsidies from the central government on the

basis of the number of students they have. They will then be on their own, to sink or swim.

There is little doubt that this is the route that should be followed in America. The exposure of American schools to the invigorating stimulus of competition, combined with the introduction of a national curriculum and the provision of stronger incentives for students, would work wonders. Rather than complaining about Japanese aggressiveness and instituting counterproductive protectionist measures, Americans ought to be looking to the source of Japan's power.   26

Our second reading appeared as an opinion piece in a recent issue of *Newsweek*. Its author, Victoria Register-Freeman, is an English teacher. In this piece, she employs her language skills to speak out from her position as a mother, career woman, and supporter of gender equality.

VICTORIA REGISTER-FREEMAN
HUNKS AND HANDMAIDENS

Rhett, my 19-year-old son, went from Tom Sawyer to Tom Cruise around 15, about the time his voice changed. Suddenly, the family phone recorder began to fill up with breathless messages from what his older brother referred to as "Rhett's Gidgets," flaxen-haired surfer girls from a nearby beach. Like fruit flies they appeared in dense buzzing masses with exotic names like Shaunna, Tiffany, Kendra and Kimberly.   1

I was prepared for this metamorphosis because it had happened to Rhett's older brother Robert at about the same age. My first inkling of the change came in a pizza parlor during a post-basket-ball-game dinner. Since I could not decide between black olives and anchovies, Robert gave his order first. The waitress, an attractive Madonna clone, went into great detail with him concerning salad dressings, crust types, cheese consistencies, toppings, whether he wanted ice with his Coke, did he live in the neighborhood, was there *anything* else he might want. When he smiled and shook his head, she floated off toward the kitchen, totally forgetting to take my order. Next to my son, I had become invisible.   2

I was stunned. Like most American moms, I had been so blinded by the sight of my offspring in ripped jeans and SAVE THE MANATEE T shirts, and so deafened by numerous arguments over the acceptable decibel level of Beastie Boys CDs, that I was slow to recognize my firstborn had become heartthrob material.   3

Nevertheless, it was true, and it became equally true for his younger brother. Through some quirks of DNA, my ex-husband and I—two average-appearing adults— spawned genetic celebrities: square-jawed, pearl-toothed, mahogany-haired, 6-foot-5-inch slabs of guy flesh whose casual glance seems to turn many otherwise articulate young women into babbling Barbies.   4

I'm not proud of this. Wasn't the motherhood manifesto for women of my generation to abolish stereotypes? Weren't '90s men supposed to be fully functioning members of a newly designed home team, a mutually supportive, multiskilled unit? I thought so. Many of my friends thought so too. We've done our part to raise our sons as full-   5 fledged "new" team members—competent, caring individuals who can do more around the house than crush cans for the recycling bin and put a new plastic liner in the garbage pail.

6   Both of my sons learned early to make an edible lasagna, toss a salad, sew on buttons, grocery-shop and separate the whites from the darks at laundry time. They could iron a shirt as well as rebound a basketball or kick a soccer goal. Growing up in a single-mom household for much of their lives, they really had to carry their weight domestically. And they did—for a while.

7   Then came puberty and hunkhood. Over the last few years, the boys' domestic skills have atrophied because handmaidens have appeared en masse. The damsels have driven by, beeped, phoned and faxed. Some appeared so frequently outside the front door they began to remind me of the suction-footed Garfields spread-eagled on car windows. While the girls varied according to height, hair color and basic body type, they shared one characteristic. They were ever eager to help the guys out.

8   For example, Robert's freshman year at college, I arrived home from work one day to hear the sound of a vacuum. The sound intrigued me because Robert, home on spring break, was sprawled on the sofa reading the swimsuit edition of *Sports Illustrated* and Rhett was at crew practice. I daydreamed briefly that my fantasy had been realized and the dust wads under the bed had generated a cleaning lady. I strode back to the bedroom, briefcase in hand, but there was no one there but Bonnie, Robert's current girlfriend. Yes, it was *cum laude* Bonnie of the Titian curls and the Always on Time Term Paper. Bonnie was vacuuming Robert's room—known in our family as The Room From Hell. This meant she had been on this project for most of the afternoon, because there hadn't been any visible floor in Robert's room for more than a year.

9   I pulled the plug on the Kenmore. "What are you doing, Bonnie?" I inquired gently. She replied that she was cleaning Robert's room for him. She did not see the broader implications. I sat down slowly on the unwrinkled bed, my entire life as a postmodern woman passing before my eyes. It was a psychic near-death experience; I felt I was on the Disorient Express for good this time. I explained to her that Robert held the high-school record for rebounds in a single basketball game. His motor skills were intact. He could clean his own room. It was his choice. He chose not to do so. He chose instead to lounge in the living room and undress Kathy Ireland with his eyes.

10   Bonnie, despite her 140 IQ, seemed perplexed. Her green eyes widened. Her brow furrowed. After all Robert had mentioned his room was a mess and it seemed so natural to . . . This is the frightening thing I've noticed about my home-grown hunks. Females don't require enough "real" help from them. My sons do not have to employ many of the skills I've so painstakingly taught them during our time together. Young women take one look at the guys and stand in line to become the chosen one to clean rooms, pick up laundry, fry chicken, lend money, drop dates with girlfriends, rent videos, treat for drinks.

11   This is not the way it was supposed to be—the reason I read 50 books on raising males in the new world order. This is not the payoff I would like for spending years in a support group for single moms with sons. But I'm realistic. I've done my part. It's up to the others—the girlfriends, cohabitants, main squeezes or wives—to insist that the hunks carry their fair share of the domestic load. Despite catchy commercials to the contrary, bringing home the bacon *and* frying it can get irksome. Besides, the hunks—like many of their cohorts—have seen their moms work hard to survive economically. They know what women can do; they respect that ability and—at some subterranean level—they're hard-wired to help. We, the Elvis-era moms, have done the best we can. It's now up to Tiffany, Kendra and Kimberly.

The following essay, by prolific environmental writer Edward Abbey, first appeared in 1971 in *Beyond the Walls: Essays from the Outside*. His view of Lake Powell, formed on the border of Utah and Arizona by the damming of Glen Canyon, has helped stimulate a growing anti-dam movement among environmentalists.

EDWARD ABBEY

THE DAMNATION OF A CANYON

There was a time when, in my search for essences, I concluded that the canyon-land country has no heart. I was wrong. The canyonlands did have a heart, a living heart, and that heart was Glen Canyon and the golden, flowing Colorado River.   1

In the summer of 1959 a friend and I made a float trip in little rubber rafts down through the length of Glen Canyon, starting at Hite and getting off the river near Gunsight Butte—The Crossing of the Fathers. In this voyage of some 150 miles and ten days our only motive power, and all that we needed, was the current of the Colorado River.   2

In the summer and fall of 1967 I worked as a seasonal park ranger at the new Glen Canyon National Recreation Area. During my five-month tour of duty I worked at the main marina and headquarters area called Wahweap, at Bullfrog Basin toward the upper end of the reservoir, and finally at Lee's Ferry downriver from Glen Canyon Dam. In a number of powerboat tours I was privileged to see almost all of our nation's newest, biggest and most impressive "recreational facility."   3

Having thus seen Glen Canyon both before and after what we may fairly call its damnation, I feel that I am in a position to evaluate the transformation of the region caused by construction of the dam. I have had the unique opportunity to observe first-hand some of the differences between the environment of a free river and a powerplant reservoir.   4

One should admit at the outset to a certain bias. Indeed I am a "butterfly chaser, googly eyed bleeding heart and wild conservative." I take a dim view of dams; I find it hard to learn to love cement; I am poorly impressed by concrete aggregates and statistics in the cubic tons. But in this weakness I am not alone, for I belong to that ever-growing number of Americans, probably a good majority now, who have become aware that a fully industrialized, thoroughly urbanized, elegantly computerized social system is not suitable for human habitation. Great for machines, yes: But unfit for people.   5

Lake Powell, formed by Glen Canyon Dam, is not a lake. It is a reservoir, with a constantly fluctuating water level—more like a bathtub that is never drained than a true lake. As at Hoover (or Boulder) Dam, the sole practical function of this impounded water is to drive the turbines that generate electricity in the powerhouse at the base of the dam. Recreational benefits were of secondary importance in the minds of those who conceived and built this dam. As a result the volume of water in the reservoir is continually being increased or decreased according to the requirements of the Basin States Compact and the power-grid system of which Glen Canyon Dam is a component.   6

The rising and falling water level entails various consequences. One of the most obvious, well known to all who have seen Lake Mead, is the "bathtub ring" left on the   7 canyon walls after each drawdown of water, or what rangers at Glen Canyon call the Bathtub Foundation. This phenomenon is perhaps of no more than aesthetic importance; yet it is sufficient to dispel any illusion one might have, in contemplating the scene, that you are looking upon a natural lake.

8   The utter barrenness of the reservoir shoreline recalls by contrast the aspect of things before the dam, when Glen Canyon formed the course of the untamed Colorado. Then we had a wild and flowing river lined by boulder-strewn shores, sandy beaches, thickets of tamarisk and willow, and glades of cottonwoods.

9   The thickets teemed with songbirds: vireos, warblers, mockingbirds and thrushes. On the open beaches were killdeer, sandpipers, herons, ibises, egrets. Living in grottoes in the canyon walls were swallows, swifts, hawks, wrens and owls. Beaver were common if not abundant: not an evening would pass, in drifting down the river, that we did not see them or at least hear the whack of their flat tails on the water. Above the river shores were the great recessed alcoves where water seeped from the sandstone, nourishing the semi-tropical hanging gardens of orchid, ivy and columbine, with their associated swarms of insects and birdlife.

10   Up most of the side canyon, before damnation, there were springs, sometimes flowing streams, waterfalls and plunge pools—the kind of marvels you can now find only in such small scale remnants of Glen Canyon as the Escalante area. In the rich flora of these laterals the larger mammals—mule deer, coyote, bobcat, ring-tailed cat, gray fox, kit fox, skunk, badger and others—found a home. When the river was dammed almost all of these things were lost. Crowded out—or drowned and buried under mud.

11   The difference between the present reservoir, with its silent sterile shores and debris choked side canyons, and the original Glen Canyon, is the difference between death and life. Glen Canyon was alive. Lake Powell is a graveyard.

12   For those who may think I exaggerate the contrast between the former river canyon and the present man-made impoundment, I suggest a trip on Lake Powell followed immediately by another boat trip on the river below the dam. Take a boat from Lee's Ferry up the river to within sight of the dam, then shut off the motor and allow yourself the rare delight of a quiet, effortless drifting down the stream. In that twelve-mile stretch of living green, singing birds, flowing water and untarnished canyon walls—sights and sounds a million years older and infinitely lovelier than the roar of motorboats—you will rediscover a small and imperfect sampling of the kind of experience that was taken away from everybody when the oligarchs and politicians condemned our river for purposes of their own.

13   Lake Powell, though not a lake, may well be as its defenders assert the most beautiful reservoir in the world. Certainly it has a photogenic backdrop of buttes and mesas projecting above the expansive surface of stagnant waters where the speedboats, houseboats and cabin cruisers play. But it is no longer a wilderness. It is no longer a place of natural life. It is no longer Glen Canyon.

14   The defenders of the dam argue that the recreational benefits available on the surface of the reservoir outweigh the loss of Indian ruins, historical sites, wildlife and wilderness adventure. Relying on the familiar quantitative logic of business and bureaucracy, they assert that whereas only a few thousand citizens even ventured down the river through Glen Canyon, now millions can—or will—enjoy the motorized boating and hatchery fishing available on the reservoir. They will also argue that the rising waters behind the dam have made such places as Rainbow Bridge accessible by powerboat. Formerly you could get there only by walking (six miles).

This argument appeals to the wheelchair ethos of the wealthy, upper-middle-class 15
American slob. If Rainbow Bridge is worth seeing at all, then by God it should be easily, readily, immediately available to everybody with the money to buy a big powerboat.
Why should a trip to such a place be the privilege only of those who are willing to walk
six miles? Or if Pikes Peak is worth getting to, then why not build a highway to the top
of it so that anyone can get there? Anytime? Without effort? Or as my old man would
say, "By Christ, one man's just as good as another—if not a damn sight better."

It is quite true that the flooding of Glen Canyon has opened up to the motorboat 16
explorer parts of side canyons that formerly could be reached only by people able to
walk. But the sum total of terrain visible to the eye and touchable by hand and foot has
been greatly diminished, not increased. Because of the dam the river is gone, the inner
canyon is gone, the best parts of the numerous side canyons are gone—all hidden beneath hundreds of feet of polluted water, accumulating silt, and mounting tons of trash.
This portion of Glen Canyon—and who can estimate how many cubic miles were
lost?—*is no longer accessible to anybody.* (Except scuba divers.) And this, do not forget, was the most valuable part of Glen Canyon, richest in scenery, archaeology, history, flora and fauna.

Not only has the heart of Glen Canyon been buried, but many of the side canyons 17
above the fluctuating waterline are now rendered more difficult, not easier, to get into.
This because the debris brought down into them by desert storms, no longer carried
away by the river, must unavoidably build up in the area where flood meets reservoir.
Narrow Canyon, for example, at the head of the impounded waters, is already beginning to silt up and to amass huge quantities of driftwood, some of it floating on the surface, some of it half afloat beneath the surface. Anyone who has tried to pilot a
motorboat through a raft of half-sunken logs and bloated dead cows will have his own
thoughts on the accessibility of these waters.

Second, the question of costs. It is often stated that the dam and its reservoir have 18
opened up to the many what was formerly restricted to the few, implying in this case
that what was once expensive has now been made cheap. Exactly the opposite is true.

Before the dam, a float trip down the river through Glen Canyon would cost you a 19
minimum of seven days' time, well within anyone's vacation allotment and a capital
outlay of about forty dollars—the prevailing price of a two-man rubber boat with oars,
available at any army-navy surplus store. A life jacket might be useful but not required,
for there were no dangerous rapids in the 150 miles of Glen Canyon. As the name implies, this stretch of the river was in fact so easy and gentle that the trip could be and
was made by all sorts of amateurs: by Boy Scouts, Camp Fire Girls, stenographers,
schoolteachers, students, little old ladies in inner tubes. Guides, professional boatmen,
giant pontoons, outboard motors, radios, rescue equipment were not needed. The Glen
Canyon float trip was an adventure anyone could enjoy, on his own, for a cost less than
that of spending two days and nights in a Page motel. Even food was there, in the water:
the channel catfish were easier to catch and a lot better eating than the striped bass
and rainbow trout dumped by the ton into the reservoir these days. And one other thing:
at the end of the float trip you still owned your boat, usable for many more such casual
and carefree expeditions.

What is the situation now? Float trips are no longer possible. The only way left for 20
the exploration of the reservoir and what remains of Glen Canyon demands the use of
a powerboat. Here you have three options: (1) buy your own boat and engine, the necessary auxiliary equipment, the fuel to keep it moving, the parts and repairs to keep it
running, the permits and licenses required for legal operation, the trailer to transport it;

(2) rent a boat; or (3) go on a commercial excursion boat, packed in with other sightseers, following a preplanned itinerary. This kind of play is only for the affluent.

21   The inescapable conclusion is that no matter how one attempts to calculate the cost in dollars and cents, a float trip down Glen Canyon was much cheaper than a powerboat tour of the reservoir. Being less expensive, as well as safer and easier, the float trip was an adventure open to far more people than will ever be able to afford motorboat excursions in the area now.

22   All of the foregoing would be nothing but a futile exercise in nostalgia (so much water over the dam) if I had nothing constructive and concrete to offer. But I do. As alternate methods of power generation are developed, such as solar, and as the nation establishes a way of life adapted to actual resources and basic needs, so that the demand for electrical power begins to diminish, we can shut down the Glen Canyon power plant, open the diversion tunnels, and drain the reservoir.

23   This will no doubt expose a dreary and hideous scene: immense mud flats and whole plateaus of sodden garbage strewn with dead trees, sunken boats, the skeletons of long-forgotten, decomposing water-skiers. But to those who find the prospect too appalling, I say give nature a little time. In five years, at most in ten, the sun and wind and storms will cleanse and sterilize the repellent mess. The inevitable floods will soon remove all that does not belong within the canyons. Fresh green willow, box elder and redbud will reappear; and the ancient drowned cottonwoods (noble monuments to themselves) will be replaced by young of their own kind. With the renewal of plant life will come the insects, the birds, the lizards and snakes, the mammals. Within a generation—thirty years—I predict the river and canyons will bear a decent resemblance to their former selves. Within the lifetime of our children Glen Canyon and the living river, heart of the canyonlands, will be restored to us. The wilderness will again belong to God, the people and the wild things that call it home.

Our last reading is by Patricia J. Williams, a well-known African-American professor of law at Columbia University, legal scholar, and social critic. In this essay, which comes from her book *The Alchemy of Race and Rights* (1991), she explores racial identity and the problems of representing racial identity in a publication process that submerges, erases, and distorts that identity.

PATRICIA J. WILLIAMS

THE DEATH OF THE PROFANE: A COMMENTARY ON THE GENRE OF LEGAL WRITING

1   Buzzers are big in New York City. Favored particularly by smaller stores and boutiques, merchants throughout the city have installed them as screening devices to reduce the incidence of robbery: if the face at the door looks desirable, the buzzer is pressed and the door is unlocked. If the face is that of an undesirable, the door stays locked. Predictably, the issue of undesirability has revealed itself to be a racial determination. While controversial enough at first, even civil-rights organizations backed

down eventually in the face of arguments that the buzzer system is a "necessary evil," that it is a "mere inconvenience" in comparison to the risks of being murdered, that suffering discrimination is not as bad as being assaulted, and that in any event it is not all blacks who are barred, just "17-year-old black males wearing running shoes and hooded sweatshirts."[1]

The installation of these buzzers happened swiftly in New York; stores that had always had their doors wide open suddenly became exclusive or received people by appointment only. I discovered them and their meaning one Saturday in 1986. I was shopping in Soho and saw in a store window a sweater that I wanted to buy for my mother. I pressed my round brown face to the window and my finger to the buzzer, seeking admittance. A narrow-eyed, white teenager wearing running shoes and feasting on bubble gum glared out, evaluating me for signs that would pit me against the limits of his social understanding. After about five seconds, he mouthed "We're closed," and blew pink rubber at me. It was two Saturdays before Christmas, at one o'clock in the afternoon; there were several white people in the store who appeared to be shopping for things for *their* mothers.

I was enraged. At that moment I literally wanted to break all the windows of the store and *take* lots of sweaters for my mother. In the flicker of his judgmental gray eyes, that saleschild had transformed my brightly sentimental, joy-to-the-world, pre-Christmas spree to a shambles. He snuffed my sense of humanitarian catholicity, and there was nothing I could do to snuff his, without making a spectacle of myself.

I am still struck by the structure of power that drove me into such a blizzard of rage. There was almost nothing I could do, short of physically intruding upon him, that would humiliate him the way he humiliated me. No words, no gestures, no prejudices of my own would make a bit of difference to him; his refusal to let me into the store—it was Benetton's, whose colorfully punnish ad campaign is premised on wrapping every one of the world's peoples in its cottons and woolens—was an outward manifestation of his never having let someone like me into the realm of his reality. He had no compassion, no remorse, no reference to me; and no desire to acknowledge me even at the estranged level of arm's-length transactor. He saw me only as one who would take his money and therefore could not conceive that I was there to give him money.

In this weird ontological imbalance, I realized that buying something in that store was like bestowing a gift, the gift of my commerce, the lucre of my patronage. In the wake of my outrage, I wanted to take back the gift of appreciation that my peering in the window must have appeared to be. I wanted to take it back in the form of unappreciation, disrespect, defilement. I wanted to work so hard at wishing he could feel what I felt that he would never again mistake my hatred for some sort of plaintive wish to be included. I was quite willing to disenfranchise myself, in the heat of my need to revoke the flattery of my purchasing power. I was willing to boycott Benetton's, random white-owned businesses, and anyone who ever blew bubble gum in my face again.

My rage was admittedly diffuse, even self-destructive, but it was symmetrical. The perhaps loose-ended but utter propriety of that rage is no doubt lost not just to the young man who actually barred me, but to those who would appreciate my being barred only as an abstract precaution, who approve of those who would bar even as they deny that they would bar *me*.

---

[1]"When 'By Appointment' Means Keep Out," *New York Times*, December 17, 1986, p. B1. Letter to the Editor from Michael Levin and Marguerita Levin, *New York Times*, January 11, 1987, p. E32.

7   The violence of my desire to burst into Benetton's is probably quite apparent. I often wonder if the violence, the exclusionary hatred, is equally apparent in the repeated public urgings that blacks understand the buzzer system by putting themselves in the shoes of white storeowners—that, in effect, blacks look into the mirror of frightened white faces for the reality of their undesirability; and that then blacks would "just as surely conclude that [they] would not let [themselves] in under similar circumstances."[2] (That some blacks might agree merely shows that some of us have learned too well the lessons of privatized intimacies of self-hatred and rationalized away the fullness of our public, participatory selves.)

8   On the same day I was barred from Benetton's, I went home and wrote the above impassioned account in my journal. On the day after that, I found I was still brooding, so I turned to a form of catharsis I have always found healing. I typed up as much of the story as I have just told, made a big poster of it, put a nice colorful border around it, and, after Benetton's was truly closed, stuck it to their big sweater-filled window. I exercised my first-amendment right to place my business with them right out in the street.

9   So that was the first telling of this story. The second telling came a few months later, for a symposium on Excluded Voices sponsored by a law review. I wrote an essay summing up my feelings about being excluded from Benetton's and analyzing "how the rhetoric of increased privatization, in response to racial issues, functions as the rationalizing agent of public unaccountability and, ultimately, irresponsibility." Weeks later, I received the first edit. From the first page to the last, my fury had been carefully cut out. My rushing, run-on-rage had been reduced to simple declarative sentences. The active personal had been inverted in favor of the passive impersonal. My words were different; they spoke to me upsidedown. I was afraid to read too much of it at a time— meanings rose up at me oddly, stolen and strange.

10   A week and a half later, I received the second edit. All reference to Benetton's had been deleted because, according to the editors and the faculty advisor, it was defamatory; they feared harassment and liability; they said printing it would be irresponsible. I called them and offered to supply a footnote attesting to this as my personal experience at one particular location and of a buzzer system not limited to Benetton's; the editors told me that they were not in the habit of publishing things that were unverifiable. I could not but wonder, in this refusal even to let me file an affadavit, what it would take to make my experience verifiable. The testimony of an independent white bystander? (a requirement in fact imposed in U.S. Supreme Court holdings through the first part of the century[3]).

11   Two days *after* the piece was sent to press, I received copies of the final page proofs. All reference to my race had been eliminated because it was against "editorial policy" to permit descriptions of physiognomy. "I realize," wrote one editor, "that this was a very personal experience, but any reader will know what you must have looked like when standing at that window." In a telephone conversation to them, I ranted wildly about the significance of such an omission. "It's irrelevant," another editor explained in a voice gummy with soothing and patience; "It's nice and poetic," but it doesn't "advance the discussion of any principle. . . . This is a law review, after all." Frustrated, I accused him of censorship; calmly he assured me it was not. "This is just a matter of style," he said with firmness and finality.

---

[2]*New York Times,* January 11, 1987, p. E32.

[3]See generally *Blyew v. U.S.,* 80 U.S. 581 (1871), upholding a state's right to forbid blacks to testify against whites.

Ultimately I did convince the editors that mention of my race was central to the whole sense of the subsequent text; that my story became one of extreme paranoia without the information that I am black; or that it became one in which the reader had to fill in the gap by assumption, presumption, prejudgment, or prejudice. What was most interesting to me in this experience was how the blind application of principles of neutrality, through the device of omission, acted either to make me look crazy or to make the reader participate in old habits of cultural bias. **12**

That was the second telling of my story. The third telling came last April, when I was invited to participate in a law-school conference on Equality and Difference. I retold my sad tale of exclusion from Soho's most glitzy boutique, focusing in this version on the law-review editing process as a consequence of an ideology of style rooted in a social text of neutrality. I opined: **13**

Law and legal writing aspire to formalized, color-blind, liberal ideals. Neutrality is the standard for assuring these ideals; yet the adherence to it is often determined by reference to an aesthetic of uniformity, in which difference is simply omitted. For example, when segregation was eradicated from the American lexicon, its omission led many to actually believe that racism therefore no longer existed. Race-neutrality in law has become the presumed antidote for race bias in real life. With the entrenchment of the notion of race-neutrality came attacks on the concept of affirmative action and the rise of reverse discrimination suits. Blacks, for so many generations deprived of jobs based on the color of our skin, are now told that we ought to find it demeaning to be hired, based on the color of our skin. Such is the silliness of simplistic either-or inversions as remedies to complex problems.

What is truly demeaning in this era of double-speak-no-evil is going on interviews and not getting hired because someone doesn't think we'll be comfortable. It is demeaning not to get promoted because we're judged "too weak," then putting in a lot of energy the next time and getting fired because we're "too strong." It is demeaning to be told what we find demeaning. It is very demeaning to stand on street corners unemployed and begging. It is downright demeaning to have to explain why we haven't been employed for months and then watch the job go to someone who is "more experienced." It is outrageously demeaning that none of this can be called racism, even if it happens only to, or to large numbers of, black people; as long as it's done with a smile, a handshake and a shrug; as long as the phantom-word "race" is never used.

The image of race as a phantom-word came to me after I moved into my late godmother's home. In an attempt to make it my own, I cleared the bedroom for painting. The following morning the room asserted itself, came rushing and raging at me through the emptiness, exactly as it had been for twenty-five years. One day filled with profuse and overwhelming complexity, the next day filled with persistently recurring memories. The shape of the past came to haunt me, the shape of the emptiness confronted me each time I was about to enter the room. The force of its spirit still drifts like an odor throughout the house.

The power of that room, I have thought since, is very like the power of racism as status quo: it is deep, angry, eradicated from view, but strong enough to make everyone who enters the room walk around the bed that isn't there, avoiding the phantom as they did the substance, for fear of bodily harm. They do not even know they are avoiding; they defer to the un-seen shapes of things with subtle responsiveness, guided by an impulsive awareness of nothingness, and the deep knowledge and denial of witchcraft at work.

The phantom room is to me symbolic of the emptiness of formal equal opportunity, particularly as propounded by President Reagan, the Reagan Civil Rights Commission and the Reagan Supreme Court. Blindly formalized constructions of equal opportunity are the creation of a space that is filled in by a meandering stream of unguided hopes, dreams, fantasies, fears, recol-lections. They are the presence of the past in imaginary, imagistic form—the phantom-roomed exile of our longing.

It is thus that I strongly believe in the efficacy of programs and paradigms like affirmative action. Blacks are the objects of a constitutional omission which has been incorporated into a theory of neutrality. It is thus that omis-sion is really a form of expression, as oxymoronic as that sounds: racial omission is a literal part of original intent; it is the fixed, reiterated prophecy of the Founding Fathers. It is thus that affirmative action is an affirmation; the affirmative act of hiring—or hearing—blacks is a recognition of individu-ality that re-places blacks as a social statistic, that is profoundly intercon-nective to the fate of blacks and whites either as sub-groups or as one group. In this sense, affirmative action is as mystical and beyond-the-self as an initiation ceremony. It is an act of verification and of vision. It is an act of social as well as professional responsibility.

14   The following morning I opened the local newspaper, to find that the event of my speech had commanded two columns on the front page of the Metro section. I quote only the opening lines: "Affirmative action promotes prejudice by denying the status of women and blacks, instead of affirming them as its name suggests. So said New York City attorney Patricia Williams to an audience Wednesday."[4]

15   I clipped out the article and put it in my journal. In the margin there is a note to myself: eventually, it says, I should try to pull all these threads together into yet another law-review article. The problem, of course, will be that in the hierarchy of law-review citation, the article in the newspaper will have more authoritative weight about me, as a so-called "primary resource," than I will have; it will take precedence over my own citation of the unverifiable testimony of my speech.

16   I have used the Benetton's story a lot, in speaking engagements at various schools. I tell it whenever I am too tired to whip up an original speech from scratch. Here are some of the questions I have been asked in the wake of its telling:

17   Am I not privileging a racial perspective, by considering only the black point of view? Don't I have an obligation to include the "salesman's side" of the story?

18   Am I not putting the salesman on trial and finding him guilty of racism without giv-ing him a chance to respond to or cross-examine me?

19   Am I not using the store window as a "metaphorical fence" against the potential of his explanation in order to represent my side as "authentic"?

20   How can I be sure I'm right?

21   What makes my experience the real black one anyway?

[4]"Attorney Says Affirmative Action Denies Racism, Sexism," *Dominion Post* (Morgantown, West Vir-ginia), April 8, 1988, p. B1.

Isn't it possible that another black person would disagree with my experience? If so, doesn't that render my story too unempirical and subjective to pay any attention to?   22

Always a major objection is to my having put the poster on Benetton's window. As one law professor put it: "It's one thing to publish this in a law review, where no one can take it personally, but it's another thing altogether to put your own interpretation right out there, just like that, uncontested, I mean, with nothing to counter it."   23

◼ COMPOSING YOUR SUMMARY/STRONG RESPONSE ESSAY

Generating and Exploring Ideas for Your Summary

Once you have selected the piece you will use for this assignment, your first task is to read it carefully to get as accurate an understanding of the article as you can. Remember that summarizing is the most basic and preliminary form of reading with the grain of a text.

1. The first time through, read the piece for general meaning. Follow the argument's flow without judgment or criticism, trying to see the world as the author sees it.
2. Reread the piece slowly, paragraph by paragraph, writing "what it does" or "what it says" gist statements in the margins for each paragraph or writing out the question that you think each paragraph answers. We recommend that you supplement these marginal notations by writing out a complete paragraph-by-paragraph *does/says* analysis modeled after our example on pages 111–12.
3. After you've analyzed the piece paragraph by paragraph, locate the argument's main divisions or parts and create an outline or tree diagram of the main points.

Shaping, Drafting, and Revising Your Summary

Once you have analyzed the article carefully paragraph by paragraph and understand its structure, you are ready to write a draft. If the piece you are summarizing is closed form, you can generally follow the order of the original article, keeping the proportions of the summary roughly equivalent to the proportions of the article. Begin the essay by identifying the question or problem that the reading addresses. Then state the article's purpose or thesis and summarize its argument point by point. If the article has a delayed thesis or some features of open-form prose, then you may have to rearrange the original order to create a clear structure for readers.

Count the number of words in your first draft to see if you are in the 150–250 word range specified by the assignment. When you revise your summary, follow the criteria presented on page 113. Also use the Guidelines for Peer Reviewers (pp. 140–41) as a checksheet for revision.

Generating and Exploring Ideas for Your Strong Response

After you have written your summary, your next step is to engage with the text on a deeper level. Read more deeply with the grain—beyond merely understanding the article—by believing its values and applying its principles to other contexts. Then read against the grain. Your strong response will most likely include both with-the-grain and against-the-grain observations and will discuss both the author's ideas and his or her other rhetorical strategies.

1. Begin by making strong marginal notations in the text. Identify and praise interesting points; relate the text to your own ideas and experiences; note your reactions, especially where you are surprised or disturbed by "hot spots"; doubt evidence, raise problems, jot down counterexamples.
2. List questions that the text raises in your mind or identify several hot spots that particularly attracted your notice (see p. 119). Pick the most promising of these questions or hot spots and freewrite your responses to them.
3. Do a rhetorical analysis of the text by exploring your answers to the questions on page 116 describing the "rhetorical analysis" component of a strong response.
4. For some texts, it is useful to articulate the differences between you and the text's intended audience. How does your "position"—in terms of gender, class, ethnicity, sexual orientation, or value system—make you different from the reader the text assumes? Also identify your purpose for reading the text if your purpose differs from that of the original author's intended audience. (For example, Andrés Martin imagined an audience of psychiatrists whose purpose for reading was to improve their ability to counsel teenagers with tattoos. In contrast, student writer Sean Barry's purpose was to get insights on the broad social question of why teenagers get tattoos.)
5. Freewrite your responses to the generic strategic questions listed on pages 122–23.

Shaping and Drafting Your Strong Response

Based on these explorations, draft a strong response to the reading. Typically, a strong response will be organized as follows:

- *Thesis statement* (one- or two-sentence assertion of the main points you want to make in response to the article). Your thesis may appear at the end of the summary paragraph or may be placed in its own mini-paragraph following the summary.
- A series of developed strong response points, including your response to the author's ideas and rhetorical choices. This section typically contains both with-the-grain and against-the-grain elements. At least one of your points should address the author's rhetorical choices and strategies. Your strong response constitutes your own voice in the conversation raised by the text.

Revising Your Strong Response

In revising your strong response, you will find that peer reviews are especially helpful, both in generating ideas and in locating places that need expansion and development. As you revise, think about how well you have incorporated ideas from your initial explorations and how you can make your essay clearer and more meaningful to readers.

g   u   i   d   e   l   i   n   e   s

for Peer Reviewers

Instructions for peer reviews are provided in Chapter 17 (pp. 429–35). To write a peer review of a classmate's essay, use your own paper, numbering your responses to correspond to the questions on the guidelines. At the head of your responses place the author's name and your own name, as shown:

Author's name: _____

Peer reviewer's name: _____

I. Read the draft at normal reading speed from beginning to end. As you read, do the following:
   A. Place a wavy line in the margin next to any passages where you get confused or find something that doesn't seem to fit or otherwise slowed down your reading.
   B. Place a *Good!* in the margin next to any passages where you think the writing is particularly strong or interesting.
II. Read the draft again slowly and answer the following questions by writing brief explanations of your answers.
   A. The summary:
      1. Is the summary as comprehensive, balanced, and accurate as possible?
      2. Is it fair and neutral, and does it avoid injecting the writer's own views?
      3. Does it use attributive tags effectively?
      4. If it includes quotations, are they properly identified and cited?
      5. Does the summary read smoothly, with appropriate transitions between ideas?
      6. What suggestions do you have for improving the summary?
   B. The strong response:
      1. Does the writer's thesis statement set up several focused points about the text's rhetorical strategies and ideas?
      2. Does the body of the strong response follow the points predicted in the thesis?

3. Has the writer applied his or her own critical thinking to the text's rhetorical strategies and ideas by questioning the text, analyzing it, evaluating it, arguing for and against it, or extending its argument?
4. Where do you as reader need more clarification or support for the writer's rhetorical points and subject matter points?
5. How could the strong response be improved by adding points, developing points, or making points in a different way?

C. Sum up what you see as the chief strengths and problem areas of this draft:
   1. Strengths
   2. Problem areas

III. Finally, read the draft one more time. This time place a check in the margin next to any places where you noticed problems in grammar, spelling, or mechanics. (One check per problem.)

c h a p t e r 7

Writing an Autobiographical Narrative

◤ ABOUT AUTOBIOGRAPHICAL NARRATIVE

The assignment in this chapter asks you to write an autobiographical narrative about something significant from your own life. But rather than state the significance up front in a thesis, you let it unfold in storylike fashion. This narrative structure places autobiographical writing on the open end of the closed-to-open form continuum, making it more like literary nonfiction than like an academic essay. Consequently, we advise you to consult Chapter 19, which discusses the features of open-form prose, prior to writing your assignment for this chapter. The student pieces "Making My Mark" and "Masks" in this chapter and "Berkeley Blues" in Chapter 19 were written for an assignment like the one in this chapter.

Don't let the term *literary* scare you. It simply refers to basic techniques, such as dialogue, specific language, and scene-by-scene construction, that you use when sharing stories, telling jokes, or recounting experiences to friends. These are the most natural and universal of techniques, the ones that peoples of all cultures have traditionally used to pass on their collective wisdom in myths, legends, and religious narratives.

In addition to telling stories to entertain and to preserve wisdom, we use them to reveal ourselves. In this regard, autobiographical writing, like certain forms of conversation, fills a very basic need in our daily lives—the need for intimacy or nontrivial human contact. One of the best measures we have of our closeness to other human beings is our willingness or reluctance to share with them our significant life stories, the ones that reveal our aspirations or humiliations.

We also use others' stories, particularly during adolescence, to monitor our own growth. Many of us once read (and still read) the stories of such people as Anne Frank, Helen Keller, Malcolm X, and Laura Ingalls Wilder in search of attitudes and behaviors to emulate. Reading their stories becomes a way of critiquing and understanding our own stories.

At this point, you might be thinking that your own life lacks the high drama of these authors' lives. In the context of holocausts and race wars, your own story may seem unworthy of recounting. Perhaps you're thinking that unless you've gone parasailing in the Pacific, bilked a savings and loan, saved a politician from an assassin's bullet, or survived a fall off the Sears Tower, you haven't done anything significant enough to write about. In this chapter we try to give you another view of significance—one that gets at the heart of what it means to write a story.

To our way of thinking, significance is not a quality out there in the events of your life; it's in the sensibility that you bring to those events and the way you write about them. When you mistakenly equate significance with singularity (it never happened to anyone else) or its public importance (what happened here made history), you misunderstand the power of a good writer to render any sort of event significant.

Many of the events your audience will find most interesting are those ordinary occurrences that happen to everyone. All of us have experienced a first day at school, a rival or sibling who seemed to best us at every turn, a conflict with a parent. But everyone enjoys hearing good writers describe their unique methods of coping with and understanding these universal situations. It is precisely because readers have experienced these things that they can project themselves easily into the writer's world. This chapter shows you how to write an autobiographical story by finding a significant moment in your life and by writing about it compellingly using literary techniques.

◩ EXPLORING AUTOBIOGRAPHICAL NARRATIVE

One of the premises of this book is that good writing is rooted in the writer's perception of a problem. Problems are at the center not only of thesis-based writing, but also of narrative writing. In effective narration, the problem usually takes the form of a *contrary,* two or more things in opposition—ideas, characters, expectations, forces, worldviews, or whatever. Three kinds of contraries that frequently form the plots of autobiographical narratives are the following:

1. *Old self versus new self.*   The writer perceives changes in himself or herself as a result of some transforming moment or event.
2. *Old view of person X versus new view of person X.*   The writer's perception of a person (favorite uncle, friend, childhood hero) changes as a result of some revealing moment; the change in the narrator's perception of person X also indicates growth in self-perception.
3. *Old values versus new values that threaten, challenge, or otherwise disrupt the old values.*   The writer confronts an outsider who challenges his or her worldview, or the writer undergoes a crisis that creates a conflict in values.

Prior to class discussion, freewrite for ten minutes about episodes in your own life that fit one or more of these typical plots. Then, working in small groups or as a whole class, share your discoveries. Your goal is to begin seeing that each of your lives is a rich source of stories.

For the moment think of *significant* not as "unusual" or "exciting," but as "revealing" or "conveying an unexpected meaning or insight." Thought of in this way, a significant moment in a story might be a gesture, a remark, a smile, a way of walking or tying a shoe, a piece of clothing, or an object in a purse or pocket. Invent a short scene in which a gesture, smile, or brief action reverses one character's feelings about, or understanding of, another character.

1. You think that Maria has led a sheltered life until _____.
2. You think Pete is a gruff, intimidating thug until _____.
3. Ken (Julia) seemed the perfect date until _____.

In each case, think of specific details about one revealing moment that reverses your understanding. Here is an example of a scene.

> My dad seemed unforgivingly angry at me until he suddenly smiled, turned my baseball cap backward on my head, and held up his open palm for a high five. "Girl, if you don't change your ways, you're going to be as big a high school screw-up as your old man."

WRITING PROJECT

Write a narrative essay about something significant in your life, using the literary strategies of plot, character, and setting. Develop your story through the use of contraries, creating tension that moves the story forward and gives it significance. You can discuss the significance of your story explicitly, perhaps as a revelation, or you can imply it (we discuss and illustrate each of these strategies later in this chapter). Use specific details and develop contraries that create tension.

This assignment calls for a *story*. In Chapter 19, we argue that a narrative qualifies as a story only when it depicts a series of connected events that create for the reader a sense of tension or conflict that is resolved through a new understanding or change in status. (See the discussion of minimal story in Chapter 19, pp. 488–93.) Your goal for this assignment is to write a story about your life that fulfills these criteria. The rest of this chapter will help you every step of the way.

◢ UNDERSTANDING AUTOBIOGRAPHICAL WRITING

Autobiographical writing may include descriptions of places and people and depictions of events that are more entertaining than enlightening. However, the spine of most autobiographical writing is a key moment or event, or a series of key moments or events, that shape or reveal the author's emerging character or growth in understanding.

Autobiographical Tension: The Opposition of Contraries

Key events in autobiography are characterized by a contrariety of opposing values or points of view. These oppositions are typically embodied in conflicts between characters or in divided feelings within the narrator. The contrariety in a story can often be summed up in statements such as these:

> My best friend from the eighth grade was suddenly an embarrassment in high school.

> My parents thought I was too young to drive to the movies when in fact I was ready to ride off with Iggy's Motorcycle Maniacs.

> My boyfriend thought I was mad about his being late for dinner when in fact I was mad about things he could never understand.

An autobiographical piece without tension is like an academic piece without a problem or a surprising thesis. No writing is more tedious than a pointless "So what?" narrative that rambles on without tension. (You can read such a narrative in the discussion of "and then" writing in Chapter 19, pp. 491–93. It's a good example of what *not* to do for this assignment.)

Like the risky thesis statement in closed-form writing, contrariety creates purpose and focus for open-form writing. It functions as an organizing principle, helping the writer determine what to include or omit. It also sets a direction for the writer. When a story is tightly wound and all the details contribute to the story line, the tension moves the plot forward as a mainspring moves the hands of a watch. The tension is typically resolved when the narrator experiences a moment of recognition or insight, vanquishes or is vanquished by a foe, or changes status.

Using the Elements of Literary Narrative to Generate Ideas

The basic elements of a literary narrative that work together to create a story are plot, character, setting, and theme. In this section we show how you can use each of these elements to help think of ideas for your autobiographical story.

Plot

By *plot* we mean the basic action of the story, including the selection and sequencing of scenes and events. Most autobiographical plots revolve around how the writer came to be who he or she is. Often stories don't open with the earliest chronological moment; they may start *in medias res* ("in the middle of things") at a moment of crisis and then flash backward to fill in earlier details that explain the origins of the crisis. What you choose to include in your story and where you place it are concerns of plot. The amount of detail you choose to devote to each scene is also a function of plot. How a writer varies the amount of detail in each scene is referred to as a plot's *pacing*.

Plots typically unfold in the following stages: (a) an arresting opening scene; (b) the introduction of characters and the filling in of background; (c) the building of tension or conflict through oppositions embedded in a series of events or scenes;

(d) the climax or pivotal moment when the tension or conflict comes to a head; and (e) reflection on the events of the plot and their meaning.

To help you recognize story-worthy events in your own life, consider the following list of pivotal moments that have figured in numerous autobiographical narratives:

■ Moments of enlightenment or coming to knowledge: understanding a complex idea for the first time, recognizing what is meant by love or jealousy or justice, mastering a complex skill, seeing some truth about yourself or your family that you previously haven't seen

■ Passages from one realm to the next: from innocence to experience, from outsider to insider or vice versa, from child to adult, from novice to expert, from what you once were to what you now are

■ Confrontation with the unknown or with people or situations that challenged or threatened your old identity and values

■ Moments of crisis or critical choice that tested your mettle or your system of values

■ Choices about the company you keep (friends, love interests, cliques, larger social groups) and the effects of those choices on your integrity and the persona you project to the world

■ Problems maintaining relationships without compromising your own growth or denying your own needs

■ Problems accepting limitations and necessities, such as the loss of dreams, the death of intimates, the failure to live up to ideals, or living with a chronic illness or disability

■ Contrasts between common wisdom and your own unique knowledge or experience: doing what people said couldn't be done, failing at something others said was easy, finding value in something rejected by society, finding bad consequences in something widely valued

FOR WRITING AND DISCUSSION

Prior to class, use one or more of these pivotal-moment categories as an aid to brainstorm ideas for your own autobiographical essay. Then choose one of your ideas to use for your plot, and freewrite possible answers to the following questions:

1. How might you begin your story?
2. What events and scenes might you include in your story?
3. How might you arrange them?
4. What would be the climax of your story (the pivotal moment or scene)?
5. What insights or meaning might you want your story to suggest?

Then share your ideas and explorations with classmates. Help each other explore possibilities for good autobiographical stories. Of course, you are not yet committed to any pivotal moment or plot.

Character

Which characters from your life will you choose to include in your autobiography? The answer to that question depends on the nature of the tension that moves your story forward. Characters who contribute significantly to that tension or who represent some aspect of that tension with special clarity belong in your story. Whatever the source of tension in a story, a writer typically chooses characters who exemplify the narrator's fears and desires or who forward or frustrate the narrator's growth in a significant way.

Sometimes writers develop characters not through description and sensory detail but through dialogue. Particularly if a story involves conflict between people, dialogue is a powerful means of letting the reader experience that conflict directly. The following piece of dialogue, taken from African-American writer Richard Wright's classic autobiography, *Black Boy,* demonstrates how a skilled writer can let dialogue tell the story, without resorting to analysis and abstraction. In the following scene, young Wright approaches a librarian in an attempt to get a book by Baltimore author and journalist H. L. Mencken from a whites-only public library. He has forged a note and borrowed a library card from a sympathetic white coworker and is pretending to borrow the book in his coworker's name.

> "What do you want, boy?"
> As though I did not possess the power of speech, I stepped forward and simply handed her the forged note, not parting my lips.
> "What books by Mencken does he want?" she asked.
> "I don't know ma'am," I said avoiding her eyes.
> "Who gave you this card?"
> "Mr. Falk," I said.
> "Where is he?"
> "He's at work, at the M—— Optical Company," I said. "I've been in here for him before."
> "I remember," the woman said. "But he never wrote notes like this."
> Oh, God, she's suspicious. Perhaps she would not let me have the books? If she had turned her back at that moment, I would have ducked out the door and never gone back. Then I thought of a bold idea.
> "You can call him up, ma'am," I said, my heart pounding.
> "You're not using these books are you?" she asked pointedly.
> "Oh no ma'am. I can't read."
> "I don't know what he wants by Mencken," she said under her breath.
> I knew I had won; she was thinking of other things and the race question had gone out of her mind.
>
> —Richard Wright, *Black Boy*

It's one thing to hear *about* racial prejudice and discrimination; it's another thing to *hear* it directly through dialogue such as this. In just one hundred or so words of conversation, Wright communicates the anguish and humiliation of being a "black boy" in the United States in the 1920s.

Another way to develop a character is to present a sequence of moments or scenes that reveal a variety of behaviors and moods. Imagine taking ten photographs of your character to represent his or her complexity and variety and then arranging them in a collage. Your narrative can create a similar collage using verbal descriptions. Sheila Madden uses this strategy in "Letting Go of Bart," a story in the Readings section of this chapter.

FOR WRITING AND DISCUSSION

If you currently have ideas for the story you plan to write, consider now the characters who will be in it. If you haven't yet settled on a story idea, think of memorable people in your life. Explore questions such as these: Why are these characters significant to you? What role did they play in forwarding or frustrating your progress? Given that role, which of their traits, mannerisms, modes of dress, and actions might you include in your account? Could you develop your character through dialogue? Through a collage of representative scenes? After you have considered these questions privately, share your responses to them either as a whole class or in groups. Help each other think of details to make your characters vivid and memorable.

Setting

Elements of setting are selected as characters are selected, according to how much they help readers understand the conflict or tension that drives the story. When you write about yourself, what you notice in the external world often reflects your inner world. In some moods you are apt to notice the expansive lawn, beautiful flowers, and swimming ducks in the city park; in other moods you might note the litter of paper cups, the blight on the roses, and the scum on the duck pond. The setting typically relates thematically to the other elements of a story. In "Berkeley Blues" (Chapter 19, pp. 486–87), for example, the author contrasts the swimming pools and sunsets of his hometown to the grit and darkness of inner-city Berkeley. The contrast in settings mirrors the contrast in the worldviews of the high school debaters and the homeless person who confronts them.

FOR WRITING AND DISCUSSION

On your own, freewrite about possible settings to include in your autobiographical narrative. Describe one of these settings fully. What do you see? Hear? Smell? Why is this setting appropriate for your story? Can you imagine two contrasting settings that reflect the contraries or oppositions in your story? Alternatively, picture in your mind one of the characters you thought of in the exercise above. Now, imagine this character in a setting that reveals his or her significance—in a kitchen baking a pie, on the front steps of a porch laughing with neighbors, in an open field running barefoot, in the backyard working on an old engine, in a cluttered office standing by the watercooler. Picture a photograph of your character in this setting. Freewrite your description of that photograph.

Then, share your descriptive freewrites with classmates, discussing how your settings might be used in your autobiographical narrative.

Theme

The word *theme* is difficult to define. Themes, like thesis statements, organize the other elements of the essay. But a theme is seldom stated explicitly and never proved with reasons and factual evidence. Readers ponder—even argue about—themes, and often different readers are affected very differently by the same theme. Some literary critics view theme as simply a different way of thinking about plot. To use a phrase from critic Northrop Frye, a plot is "what happened" in a story, whereas the theme is "what happens" over and over again in the story and others like it. To illustrate this distinction, we summarize a selection from William Least Heat Moon's autobiographical narrative, which you will read in the next section, from two perspectives.

Plot perspective   It's the story of a man's experience exploring the old U.S. highways. Getting lost one day, he eats a sandwich at a beautiful mountain overlook and then wanders into an Oregon town, where he meets a couple driving a huge motor home and trailer. The story ends with his unpleasant encounter with these people, who mistake him for a dangerous vagrant.

Theme perspective   It's the story of the contrast between a view of life that dreads change, error, and difference and a view of life that welcomes error and the unexpected as a possibility for growth and new understanding. Although the narrator is discouraged by people's small-mindedness, the essay affirms difference and openness.

As you can see, the thematic summary goes beyond the events of the story to point toward the larger significance of those events. Although you may choose not to state your theme directly for your readers, you need to understand that theme to organize your story. This understanding usually precedes and guides your decisions about what events and characters to include, what details and dialogue to use, and what elements of setting to describe. But sometimes you need to reverse the process and start out with events and characters that, for whatever reason, force themselves on you, and then figure out your theme after you've written for a while. In other words, theme may be something you discover as you write.

FOR WRITING AND DISCUSSION

Using the ideas you have brainstormed from previous exercises in this chapter, choose two possible ideas for an autobiographical narrative you might write. For each, freewrite your response to this question: What is the significance of this story for me? (Why did I choose this story? Why is it important to me? Why do I want to tell it? What am I trying to show my reader?)

In class, share your freewrites. All the exercises in this section are designed to generate discussion about the elements of autobiographical narrative and to encourage topic exploration.

READINGS

Now that we have examined some of the key elements of autobiographical writing, let's look at some particular examples.

The first reading is taken from basketball player Bill Russell's autobiography, *Second Wind*. In this passage, Russell tells about a life-changing event that happened during his junior year in high school.

BILL RUSSELL
FROM *SECOND WIND*

During my junior year in high school, in 1950, I had a mystical revelation. One day while I was walking down the hall from one class to another, by myself, as usual, it suddenly dawned on me that it was all right to be who I was.   1

The thought just came to me: "Hey, you're all right. Everything is all right." The idea was hardly earthshaking, but I was a different person by the time I reached the end of the hall. Had I been methodical I would have immediately written down my thoughts. Over and over again I received the idea that everything was all right about me—so vividly that the thought seemed to have colors on it. I remember looking around in class to make sure the other kids didn't think I was acting strange.   2

Those moments in the hall are the closest I've come to a religious experience. For all I know, it may have actually been one. A warm feeling fell on me out of nowhere. I wondered why the idea hadn't occurred to me before; everything seemed to fall into place, the way it does for a kid when he first understands simple multiplication.   3

Everybody remembers the "Aha!" sensation when a good idea hits you. I remember sitting in a logic class at the University of San Francisco, puzzling over something the priest had been explaining to us for the previous few days. Then it came to me. Bells went off; the mental pleasure was so great that I jumped as if someone had pinched me and yelled "Hey!"   4

The priest said, "Congratulations, Mr. Russell. You have just had your first real and complete thought. How does it feel?" He was patronizing me, but I didn't care because he had just given me a new way of seeing things.   5

What I saw in the hallway at high school that day was more than just an idea; it was a way out of self-rejection. In the four years since my mother had died, everybody I encountered felt that there was something wrong with me. Worse, I *agreed* with them.   6

I was clumsy at everything. When I opened a soup can, it felt as if I was trying to take apart a watch with a sledgehammer. I was insulted all the time. At my first and only football practice the coach lined up players to run over me all afternoon, and then complained to the team that he'd gotten the "bum of the family" instead of my brother, who was a star football player at a rival high school. I dropped football, swallowed my pride and went out for the cheerleading team. I didn't even make that. I was the classic ninety-pound weakling—except that nobody would have dreamed of using my picture in an advertisement.

7   The white cops in Oakland stopped me on the streets all the time, grilled me and routinely called me "nigger." Whenever they said it, it put me in such a state that I would shrivel up inside and think, "Oh, God. They're right." I gave everybody the benefit of the doubt—friends who ignored me, strangers who were mean—because I thought they were probably justified.

8   All this changed after that trip down the hall.

Thinking Critically About *Second Wind*

Perhaps the first thing the reader realizes about Russell's narrative is that the significant event is hardly an event at all—just a revelation that came to him while he was walking down the hall. So tiny and noneventful is the event itself that Russell spends very little time describing it. Instead, most of this passage (and the several pages that follow it) recounts Russell's mental journey through the significance of the event; it is short on action and long on reflection. The tension arises from a clash between the poles of a major contrariety: the contrast between Russell's old self and his new self.

Notice that this essay shares many of the features of open-ended, narrative-based prose discussed in Chapters 4 and 19:

- Lack of initial mapping with occasional gaps created by unexpected transitions (Russell's first sentence prepares the reader only for a "mystical revelation," not for the account of self-acceptance that follows)
- Use of flashbacks and flash-forwards (Russell opens the story with a moment of revelation in his junior year of high school, flashes forward to an analogous moment of revelation in a college logic class, then flashes back to events that occurred between the death of his mother when he was twelve and his moment of revelation at sixteen)
- Use of analogy and figurative language ("everything seemed to fall into place, the way it does for a kid when he first understands simple multiplication")
- Use of details more than generalizations to make points (Russell conveys the point that he was a victim of prejudice through specifics: "The white cops in Oakland stopped me on the streets all the time, grilled me and routinely called me 'nigger.' ")

For a different approach to narrative, consider this excerpt from the book *Blue Highways: A Journey in America* by William Least Heat-Moon (pseudonym for

William Trogdon), a writer of Native American heritage. Least Heat-Moon's book is an autobiographical account of his travels along the back roads of America. It interweaves disparate strands of thought—facts about the land and geography, word derivations, science, history, literary quotations, social observations, and his own pleasant and unpleasant experiences. In this excerpt, the writer describes one of his days on the road. Unlike Bill Russell's overt thematic commentary in the preceding piece, here Least Heat-Moon's thematic commentary is subtler and requires more reader interpretation. Notice how the setting is an essential part of the story.

WILLIAM LEAST HEAT-MOON
FROM *BLUE HIGHWAYS: A JOURNEY IN AMERICA*

Lassen Peak is a kind of bookend to the bottom of the Cascade Range that runs single-file toward the Canadian border, where Mount Baker props up the other end. In between—preeminently—are Rainer, St. Helens, Adams, Hood, and Shasta. Their symmetric conical peaks average nearly twelve thousand feet and retain snowy summits all year; what's more, they are part of the most volcanically active range in the coterminous states. 1

Highway 89 wound among the volcanic dumpings from Lassen that blasted Hat Creek valley about three hundred times between 1914 and 1917. Scrub covered the ash, cinders, and lava as the wasteland renewed itself; yet even still it looked terribly crippled. Off the valley floor, California 299 climbed to ride the rim of the Pit River gorge. I ate a sandwich at the edge of a deep rift that opened like jaws to expose rocks so far below they were several hundred million years older than the ones I sat on. From the high edge I looked down on the glossy backs of swallows as they glided a thousand feet, closed their wings like folded fans, and plummeted into the abyss. It was a wild, mad, silent, spectacular descent of green iridescence that left me woozy. 2

Again on the road, I drove up a lumpy, dry plateau, all the while thinking of the errors that had led me to Hat Creek. The word *error* comes from a Middle English word, *erren*, which means "to wander about," as in the knight errant. The word evolved to mean "going astray" and that evolved to mean "mistake." As for *mistake*, it derives from Old Norse and once meant "to take wrongly." Yesterday, I had been mistaken and in error, taking one wrong road after another. . . . 3

I never found Lookout. In dry and dusty Tulelake, I bought groceries, then crossed into Oregon, where the Cascades to the west blocked a froth of storm clouds; but for the mountains, I would have been in rain again. A town of only fifteen thousand somehow spread across the entire bottom of a long valley; when I saw the reach of Klamath Falls, I kept going. U.S. 97 was an ordeal of cars and heavy trucks. I don't know whether Oregonians generally honk horns or whether they had it in for me, but surely they honked. Later, someone said it was part of the "Keep Moving, Stranger" campaign. I turned off into the valley at the first opportunity, an opportunity numbered route 62 that ran to Fort Klamath, a town that began in 1863 as an Army post with the mission of controlling hostile Klamath Indians, who has succeeded for years in keeping settlers out of their rich valley. Keep moving, stranger. 4

5   Drawn as always to the glow of neon in the dusk, I stopped at a wooden cafe. No calendars, otherwise perfect. In front sat an Argosy landcruiser (the kind you see in motel parking lots) with an Airstream trailer attached; on top of the Argosy was a motorboat and on the front and back matched mopeds. Often I'd seen the American propensity to take to the highway with as many possessions as a vehicle could carry—that inclination to get away from it all while hauling it all along—but I stood amazed at this achievement of transport called a vacation. Although the Argosy side windows were one-way glass (to look and not get looked at back), in the trailer I saw pine paneling, Swiss cupboards, and a self-cleaning oven. What the owner really wanted was to drive his 3-BR-splitfoyer so he wouldn't have to leave the garage and basement behind.

6   A man with a napkin tucked to his belt came out of the cafe. A plump woman, lately beyond the Midol years, face fearful like the lady who has just discovered the heartbreak of psoriasis, watched from the cafe.

7   "What's up, chum?" the man said.

8   "I couldn't believe this outfit. You are one well-prepared family. This little highway's not really big enough for you, is it?"

9   He relaxed at what he took as sympathy. "Tried a damned back road."

10   We went inside, and I heard the woman whisper, "His type make me nervous." She'd read about people like me and stared in a bold, contemptuous way she never would have used had she been alone. I tried to check my own irritation. She probably wasn't a bad sort; she had her good side. Surely she had studied the Gospel According to Heloise and knew by rote the six helpful hints for removing catsup stains.

11   The food was ordinary, prices high, the waitress unpleasant, and, on top of that, I got reviled by people who could afford life at six-miles-per-gallon. I paid and left. The couple came out, hoisted themselves into the Argosy, and clicked locks against my type. Just above the legal maximum, off they went, those people who took no chances on anything—including their ideas—getting away from them. After all, they read the papers, they watched TV, and they knew America was a dangerous place.

Thinking Critically About *Blue Highways*

Unlike Russell, who comments extensively on the significance of his experience, William Least Heat-Moon expects the reader to connect the narrator's thoughts and sights early in the day with the brief unpleasant scene at the wooden café later that evening. For the narrator, much of his experience is embedded in the geographical and historical details that frame the story.

1. What do you see as the main contraries (tensions, conflicts, oppositions) in this piece?
2. What is the significance of paragraph 3, in which the narrator describes the derivation and history of the word *error*?
3. In Chapter 19 we say that an element of a minimal story is *connectedness*. How are the details in the first half of the excerpt (paragraphs 1–4) connected to the encounter with the Argosy landcruiser couple? Particularly, how is the narrator's encounter with the couple related to his description of the landscape and nature in paragraphs 1 and 2 and his discussion of the "Keep Moving, Stranger" campaign in paragraph 4 (which also includes the sentence about the Klamath Indians)?

4. What memory-soaked images (see Chapter 19, pp. 498–99) are called to mind by "Argosy landcruiser," "matched mopeds," "one-way glass," "pine paneling," "Swiss cupboards, and a self-cleaning oven," "3-BR-splitfoyer," "beyond the Midol years," and "the heartbreak of psoriasis"? Because William Least Heat-Moon is referring to architectural and advertising details and products of the 1970s and 1980s, you may need to do some historical reconstruction to recover their significance.

5. From the moment the narrator parks his van at the café and inspects the trailer rig, his observations and his exchanges with the couple are loaded with irony. How many layers of opposite meanings can you detect in his descriptions and dialogue? (See Chapter 19 on ironic points of view, pp. 495–96.)

6. What other examples can you find in Least Heat-Moon's piece of specific words, revelatory words, and figurative words? (See Chapter 19, pp. 496–500.)

FOR WRITING AND DISCUSSION

Imagine yourself twenty years in the future describing the room where you live now (your dorm room or apartment, or, if you live at home, the room that is most your own). What specific words, revelatory words, and memory-soaked words will be most likely to make this room come to life in your imagination? What details about styles of architecture and furniture, room decorations, posters and pictures on the wall, stereo or computer equipment, clothes, and so on will most trigger old associations and memories? List these details and then share them with classmates.

The next example was written for a first-year composition course by a student writer who wishes to remain anonymous.

MASKS

Her soft, blond hair was in piggytails, as usual, with ringlets that bounced whenever she turned her head. As if they were springs, they could stretch, then shrink, then bounce, excited by the merest movement of her head. Never was there a hair that wasn't enclosed in those glossy balls which always matched her dress. I knew the only reason she turned her head was so they'd bounce. Because it was cute. Today, she wore a pink dress with frills and lace and impeccably white tights. Her feet, which swayed back and forth underneath her chair, were pampered with shiny, black shoes without a single scuff. She was very wise, sophisticated beyond her kindergarten years.   1

I gazed at her and then looked down at my clothes. My green and red plaid pants and my yellow shirt with tiny, blue stars showed the day's wear between breakfast, lunch, and recess. Showing through the toe of my tenny runners was my red sock.   2

3   At paint time, I closely followed behind her, making sure I painted at the easel next to hers. She painted a big, white house with a white picket fence and a family: Mom, Dad, and Daughter. I painted my mom, my brother, and myself. I, then, painted the sky, but blue streaks ran down our faces, then our bodies, ruining the picture.

4   The next day, I wore my hair in piggytails. I had done it all by myself, which was obvious due to my craftsmanship. She pointed and giggled at me when I walked by. I also wore a dress that day but I didn't have any pretty white tights. The boys all gathered underneath me when I went on the monkeybars to peak at my underwear to chant, "I see London, I see France, I see Tiffy's underpants."

5   When the day was done, she ran to the arms of her mother that enveloped her in a loving and nurturing hug. She showed her mother her painting, which had a big, red star on it.

6   "We'll have to put this up on the refrigerator with all of your others," her mother said. I had thrown my painting away. I looked once more at the two of them as they walked hand in hand towards their big, white house with a white picket fence. I trudged to my babysitter's house. I wouldn't see my mother until six o'clock. She had no time for me, for my paintings, for my piggytails. She was too busy working to have enough money to feed my brother and me.

7   Digging absently through books and folders, I secretly stole a glance at her, three lockers down. Today she wore her Calvins and sported a brand new pair of Nikes. As always, at the cutting edge of fashion. If I wanted Nikes, I could pay for them myself, or so said my mother. In the meantime, I had to suffer with my cheap, treadless Scats. As I searched for a pen, her giggle caught my attention. Three of her friends had flocked around her locker. I continued searching for a pen but to no avail. I thought of approaching and borrowing one but I was fearful that they would make fun of me.

8   "Jim and Brad called me last night and both of them asked me to go to the show. Which one should I pick?" she asked. My mom wouldn't let me go out on dates until I was a sophomore in high school. We were only in seventh grade and she was always going out with guys. Not that it mattered that I couldn't date, yet. Nobody had ever asked me out.

9   "My hair turned out so yucky today. Ick," she commented. She bent down to grab a book and light danced among the gentle waves of her flowing, blond mane. Her radiant brown eyes and adorable smile captivated all who saw her. Once captured, however, none was allowed past the mask she'd so artfully constructed to lure them to her. We were all so close to her, so far away. She was so elusive, like a beautiful perfume you smell but can't name, like the whisper that wakes you from a dream and turns out to belong to the dream.

10   As she walked into the library, I heard a voice whisper, "There she is. God, She's beautiful." She was wearing her brown and gold cheerleader outfit. Her pleated skirt bounced off her thighs as she strutted by. Her name, "Kathy," was written on her sweater next to her heart and by it hung a corsage. As she rounded the corner, she flicked her long, blond curls and pivoted, sending a ripple through the pleats of the skirt. She held her head up high, befitting one of her social standing: top of the high school food chain. She casually searched the length of the library for friends. When she reached the end of the room, she carefully reexamined every table, this time less casually. Her smile shaded into a pout. She furrowed her face, knitting her eyebrows together, and saddening her eyes. People stared at her until she panicked.

She was bolting toward the door when she spotted me. She paused and approached my table. Putting on her biggest smile, she said, "Oh hi! Can I sit by you?" Thrilled at the possibility of at last befriending her, I was only too happy to have her sit with me. As she sat down, she again scanned the expanse of the library.   11

"So, who does the varsity basketball team play tonight?" I asked.   12

"Great Falls Central," she replied. "Make sure you're there! . . . How's the Algebra assignment today?!"   13

"Oh, it's okay. Not too tough," I said.   14

"John always does my assignments for me. I just hate Algebra. It's so hard."   15

We stood up in silence, suddenly painfully aware of our differences. She glanced in the reflection of the window behind us, checked her hair, then again scanned the room.   16

"There's Shelly! Well, I'll see you later," she said.   17

She rose from the table and fled to her more acceptable friend.   18

The next day, she walked down the hall surrounded by a platoon of friends. As we passed, I called out "Hi!" but she turned away as if she didn't know me, as if I didn't exist.   19

I, then, realized her cheerleader outfit, her golden locks, her smile were all a mask. Take them away and nothing but air would remain. Her friends and their adoration were her identity. Without them she was alone and vulnerable. I was the powerful one. I was independent.   20

Thinking Critically About "Masks"

1. What are the main contrarieties in this piece?
2. This piece focuses on the narrator's movement toward a significant recognition. What is it she recognizes? If you were a peer reviewer for this writer, would you recommend eliminating the last paragraph, expanding it, or leaving it as it is? Why?
3. Where does this writer use details with particular effectiveness?

The next example uses mainly dialogue, dramatic scenes, and a humorous tone (the writer's attitude toward the subject) to convey its theme. It was written by a student writer who was responding to the assignment in this chapter.

CHRIS KORDASH (STUDENT)

MAKING MY MARK

Junior high has to be one of the worst times when it comes to identity. For all I cared, I would have been an elf just as long as everyone else thought elves were cool. I remember my first day of junior high as if it were yesterday: the guys suddenly seemed six feet tall, and the girls, wow. These were not girls; they were mature women. I decided that I was going to make my mark in this place.   1

The first couple of weeks were rough. The mature women, or so I thought at the time, were going for guys with facial hair. I thought facial hair belonged only to dads in their late thirties. These girls were way out of my league—for the time being.   2

3   One day as I was staring at this girl, Mandy, in my English class an all too familiar nasally voice interrupted.

4   "She is pretty cute, huh?"

5   "Yeah," I replied.

6   "Give it up, man. She is way out of your league," he chuckled.

7   "Oh, yeah, how far out of my league will she be when she hears that I can drive?"

8   Josh was a wiry Italian who had been congested, or so it seemed, his entire life. This really added to the nasally effect. Josh and I had known each other through elementary school and because we had the same ambition—popularity with chicks—we latched on in junior high. Josh and I figured we had to devise a plan that would set us apart from the rest of the guys—put us on a higher level. We figured that having a car would easily solve our problem. We started spreading some talk about our driving, and sure enough it grabbed people's attention. The only problem was that no one had actually seen us in this supposed car. As time passed our story grew harder and harder to keep up.

9   It was time to act, to turn talk into fact. My parents were going a couple of hundred miles out of town for the weekend, and I knew where Dad kept the spare keys to his Porsche. If we failed with our plan, our reputations would be lost forever. The Friday that my folks were to leave we told the kids in the "cool crowd" that we might stop by their party in my dad's Porsche.

10   "No way."

11   "Bullshit." And then the clincher.

12   "That would be so cool," said Mandy. Now there was not a doubt in my mind about what I was going to do.

13   At around midnight, we called the party to warn them that we were coming down. For ultimate coolness all we had to do was drive up to their house in that car and pull into their driveway. As the garage door opened we watched it unfold a 1990 Porsche 9285. The car seemed to glow from the dim light on the garage door. As we made ourselves comfortable in the seats, we sat in a moment of silence. Thoughts were racing in my head. I kept telling my mind to shut up, that driving this car wasn't that hard. I figured that the extensive video game driving and the one time driving with my dad on a back road would be plenty. Plus it was an automatic. How hard was that? As I slid the key into the ignition and gave it a turn, a horrendous roar emerged from the engine.

14   "Let's roll," I exclaimed.

15   Driving in town was as easy as I had thought. It was so late there was no traffic. I knew the basics: red means stop and green means go. We passed the house where the party was and made a couple of turns around the block. The lights were all out. I decided to pull into the driveway, hoping to see the car lights, hear the car, and come out. Nothing. Everyone was asleep.

16   "You're kidding me, right?" I said to Josh. We left a note under the front door and bailed home.

17   Our first attempt at ultimate coolness had fizzled. I still had something to prove and luckily we had a day and a half with a car before my parents returned. Saturday I woke up and called Josh around noon. Because I lived in a rural area it took Josh a little while to get there and he had to be home at five, which meant we had only a little time in the car. Looking out at the wetness, we decided that the rain would get the Porsche totally muddy if we took it out. Our other option was the old Suburban. The Burb, as it is known today, is black and looks like a machine straight out of hell with large tires and a three-inch lift.

"We can get some serious off-roading in this," I said to Josh. I thought we ought to practice before we went cruising for chicks. 18

We excitedly hopped in and set to the logging roads in back of our house. I felt I was handling this automatic fine. Mud was flying, and we were cruising along without a worry in the world. Not wanting to get stuck, we decided to hit the gravel roads. As I turned onto a road, I discovered one of the coolest things, fishtailing. Talk about fun. We began doing roadies, laughing wildly and really getting into this driving. Because it was getting late, we decided to cruise on back to my house. After we turned around, I popped in my Metallica tape for the ride back. I floored it and started to cruise home. I had revved it up to 70 mph when I hit a turn. The back slid out and the car slipped sideways down the road. I slammed on the brakes and tried to correct, but it was useless. The Burb slid to a fifteen-foot embankment and rolled. We rolled three and a half times, or at least that is what I remember. I was on the roof and Josh was suspended from his seat when the car stopped rolling. I helped him unlatch himself and we crawled out. As I stared at the banged-up, overturned car, my weak laugh turned into an hysterical bawl. Josh ended up running home, leaving me by myself. At least the cool people would like me, right? 19

I am sure that you can imagine the reaction of my parents. It is a side of them that is really nice to avoid. In a matter of days, the entire school knew about what had happened. This experience stuck with me socially for about four years. I would meet new people and the first thing they would snicker would be, "Hey, didn't you roll your parents' Suburban?" 20

Well, the goal that I set at the beginning of junior high was met. I definitely made my mark. 21

Thinking Critically About "Making My Mark"

1. What are the main contrarieties in this piece?
2. How does this piece build to a pivotal moment?
3. In this narrative, how does Kordash use irony (saying one thing and intending something else, often the opposite), exaggeration, and understatement (deliberately saying less in order to express much more) both to create humor and to convey his significant recognition? If you were a peer reviewer for this writer, would you recommend expanding the last paragraph or leaving it as it is? Why?
4. How does Kordash use dialogue and details to engage readers? How do the dialogue and details contribute to the theme?

The final example uses a collage technique (see pp. 147–48). Here the emphasis is so much on the character Bart that the narrator seems relatively unimportant, and you may wonder whether this piece is biography (the story of Bart) or autobiography (the story of the narrator). We include "Letting Go of Bart" in the category of autobiographical narrative because the way in which the writer, Sheila Madden, tells the story reveals her own growth in understanding, her own deepening of character.

SHEILA MADDEN
LETTING GO OF BART

1   Bart lies stiffly in bed, toes pointed downward like a dancer's, but Bart is far from dancing. When he tries to shift position, his limbs obey spasmodically because his nervous system has been whipsawed by the medications he has been taking for years to control the various manifestations of AIDS.

2   He is wearing diapers now, for incontinence—the ultimate indignity. An oxygen tube is hooked into his nose, morphine drips into his arm; his speech is slurred.

3   But Bart is not confused. He is intensely irritable and has been the terror of his nurses. Though he has a great self-deprecating grin, I haven't seen it for weeks.

4   I can't say a proper goodbye because he is never alone. I would like to pray silently by his bedside, meditating; but even if I could, he would barely tolerate it. Bart has no god.

5   I remember the day a tall, good-looking young man popped into the open door of the downstairs apartment I was fixing up in my San Francisco home. That late afternoon, I was tiredly putting the last coat of paint on the walls with the help of a couple of friends. Bart had seen the for-rent sign in the window and just walked in. Within moments he had all three of us laughing uproariously as he put a deposit in my hand. I had asked the angels for help in finding a decent renter; the angels had responded. Bart and I would get on famously.

6   For one thing, Bart managed to fix or overlook the unfinished bits in the apartment. He and his father built a fine, much-needed deck on the back garden, charging me only for the lumber. He made the small apartment look spacious, arranging the furniture skillfully, backlighting the sofas. And he was prompt with the rent.

7   However, Bart was far more than a satisfactory renter. He was a fine singer and a member of the symphony chorus. When he practiced, his rich baritone would sail up the stairs, smoothing the airways, never ruffling them.

8   He asked permission to put a piano in his apartment, and I agreed nervously. Because he was a beginner on the instrument, I feared endless, fumbling scales disturbing my peace. It never happened. He played softly, sensitively, and always at reasonable hours.

9   I attended some of his concerts and met his friends. At times we joined forces at parties upstairs or downstairs, but somehow we never got in each other's hair.

10   He was a skillful ballroom dancer. Once he agreed to stand in as partner for my visiting sister when we attended a Friday dance at the Embarcadero Plaza—although the prospect could not have thrilled him.

11   Another time I disabled my tape deck by spraying it with WD-40 and ran downstairs for help. Bart came up immediately, scolding me roundly for putting oil on such a machine. Then he spent the better part of an hour wrapping matchsticks in cotton batting (for lack of a better tool), degreasing the heads with rubbing alcohol, and putting all to rights.

12   Bart had family problems; I had them. We commiserated. Bart was an ally, a compatriot, a brother.

13   I suspected Bart was gay; but we never talked about it, although he knew I was working in the AIDS fields as a counselor and that it was a nonissue with me.

14   Then one day he got a bad flu, which turned into a deep, wracking cough that did not go away. I worried about it, having heard such coughs in the AIDS patients

I dealt with daily. I encouraged him to see a doctor, and he did, making light of his visit.

Finally the cough receded, but psychically so did Bart. I saw him hardly at all for the next three months. When I did, he seemed somber and abstracted. 15

However, my life was hectic at the time. I didn't pay attention, assuming his problem was job dissatisfaction; I knew his boss was a constant thorn in his side. One day he told me that he was changing jobs and moving to Napa, an hour's drive away. I rejoiced for him and cried for myself. I would miss Bart. 16

Our lives separated. Napa might as well have been the moon. Over a two-year period we talked once or twice on the phone, and I met him once for dinner in the city. 17

Then one night my doorbell rang unexpectedly, and Bart came in to tell me of his recovery from a recent bout of pneumocystis pneumonia. "I'm out of the closet, willy-nilly," he said. 18

I was stunned. I had put him in the "safe" category, stuffing my fears about the telltale cough. It must have been then that he learned his diagnosis. For the next 24 hours I cried off and on, inconsolably, for Bart and probably for all the others I had seen die. 19

Now he is at the end, an end so fierce there is nothing to do but pray it will come quickly. Bart is courageous, his anger masking fear. He has thus far refused to let the morphine dull his consciousness. His eyes, hawklike, monitor all that is going on around him. Angels, who once brought him, take him home. 20

Thinking Critically About "Letting Go of Bart"

Madden's technique is to create her portrait of Bart through a collection of scenes: Bart lying stiffly in bed; Bart popping into the apartment to put down a rent deposit; Bart fixing up the apartment and building a deck with his father; Bart singing and playing piano; Bart taking Madden's sister to a ballroom dance; Bart cleaning Madden's tape deck; Bart coughing. The scenes are selected to show, rather than tell about, Bart's personality. The way in which Madden remembers the scenes and movingly describes them indicates the depth of her own feelings.

FOR WRITING AND DISCUSSION

To generate more ideas for an autobiographical narrative, each class member should do the following exercise independently and then share the results with the rest of the class.

1. Have you ever had a moment of revelation when the world suddenly seemed different to you—as did Bill Russell? If you have, freewrite about this experience.

2. Have you ever had an encounter with people whose values differed remarkably from your own, as did William Least Heat-Moon in *Blue Highways*? If so, freewrite about this encounter, imagining specific details and dialogue that show the difference between your perspective and someone else's. How did this encounter help you reach a new understanding about yourself or your values?

3. Have you ever changed your view of a person in a way analogous to the narrator's reassessment of the cheerleader in "Masks"? If so, freewrite about this character. What details reveal this person before and after your moment of reassessment?

4. Have you ever had an experience, like Chris Kordash's in "Making My Mark," that turned out so opposite from what you intended that it has become a significant part of your maturation? If so, freewrite about this experience, including a dramatic description of your goal and the event that upset that goal.

5. Have you ever known a person whose presence in your life made an important difference to you, as did Bart to Sheila Madden? If you have, freewrite about this character, imagine a series of scenes that might create a collage effect.

◪ COMPOSING YOUR ESSAY

In deciding what to write about, keep in mind the basic requirement for a good story: it must portray a sequence of connected events driven forward by some tension or conflict that results in a recognition or new understanding. Not every memorable event in your life will lend itself to this sort of structure. The most common failing in faulty narratives is that the meaning of the event is clearer to the narrator than to the audience. "You had to be there," the writer comments, when a story just doesn't have the expected impact on an audience.

But it's the storyteller's job to *put the reader there* by providing enough detail and context for the reader to *see* why the event is significant. If an event didn't lead to any significant insight, understanding, knowledge, change, or other kind of difference in your life, and if you really had to be there to appreciate its significance, then it's a poor candidate for an autobiographical narrative.

Generating and Exploring Ideas

Choosing a Plot

For some of you, identifying a plot—a significant moment or insight arising out of contrariety—will present little problem; perhaps you have already settled on an idea you generated in one of the class discussion exercises earlier in this chapter. However, if you are still searching for a plot idea, you may find the following list helpful:

■ A time when you took some sort of test that conferred new status on you (Red Cross lifesaving exam, drivers' test, SAT, important school test, entrance exam, team tryout). If you failed, what did you learn from it or how did it shape you? If you succeeded, did the new status turn out to be as important as you expected it would be?

■ A situation in which your normal assumptions about life were challenged (an encounter with a foreign culture, a time when you ran away from home or got lost, a time when a person you'd stereotyped surprised you).

■ A time when you left your family for an extended period or forever (going to college, getting married, entering the military, leaving one parent for another after their divorce).

■ A time that plunged you into a crisis (being the first person to discover a car crash, seeing a robbery in progress, being thrown in with people who are repugnant to you, facing an emergency).

■ A situation in which you didn't fit or didn't fulfill others' expectations of you, or a situation in which you were acknowledged as a leader or exceeded others' expectations of you (a summer job, membership on a team, a tough class, a new role).

■ A time when you overcame your fears to do something for the first time (first date, first public presentation).

■ A situation in which you learned how to get along amicably with another human being, or a failed relationship that taught you something about life (your first extended romantic relationship, your relationship with a difficult sibling, relative, teacher, or boss).

■ A time when a person who mattered to you (parent, romantic interest, authority figure) rejected you or let you down, or a time when you rejected or let down someone who cared for you.

■ A time when you made a sacrifice on behalf of someone else or someone else made a sacrifice in your name (parent or spouse who took on a second job to help you through school).

■ A time when you were irresponsible or violated a principle or law and thereby caused others pain (you shoplifted or drank when underage and were caught; you failed to look after someone entrusted to your care).

■ A time when you were criticized unjustly or given a punishment you didn't deserve (you were accused of plagiarizing a paper that you'd written).

■ A time when you were forced to accept defeat or death or the loss of a dream or otherwise learned to live with reduced expectations.

■ A time when you lived out a fantasy.

Thickening the Plot

Once you've identified an event about which you'd like to write, you need to develop ways to show readers what makes that event particularly story worthy. In thinking about the event, consider the following questions:

■ What makes the event so memorable? What particulars, what physical details come most readily to mind when you think back on the event?

- What are the major contrarieties that gave the event tension? Did it raise a conflict between two or more people? Between their worldviews? Between before and after versions of yourself?
- How can you make the contrarieties memorable and vivid to the reader? What scenes can you create? What words could your characters exchange?
- Is there a moment of insight, recognition, or resolution that would give your plot a climax?
- What is the significance of the story? How does it touch on larger human issues and concerns? What makes it something your reader will relate to? What is its theme?

Shaping and Drafting

When stuck, writers often work their way into a narrative by describing in detail a vividly recalled scene, person, or object. This inductive approach is common with many creative processes. You may or may not include all the descriptive material in your final draft, but in the act of writing exhaustively about this one element, the rest of the story may begin to unfold for you and forgotten items and incidents may resurface. In the course of describing scenes and characters, you will probably also begin reflecting on the significance of what you are saying. Try freewriting answers to such questions as "Why is this important?" and "What am I trying to do here?" Then continue with your rough draft.

Revising

Once you've written a draft, you need to get down to the real work of writing—rewriting. Revisit your prose critically, with an eye toward helping your reader share your experience and recognize its significance. Chapter 19, as well as the following guidelines for peer reviewers, will be of particular help during revision.

g u i d e l i n e s

for Peer Reviewers

Instructions for peer reviews, including use of these guidelines, are provided in Chapter 17, pages 429–35. To write a peer review for a classmate, use your own paper, numbering your responses to correspond to the questions on the guidelines. At the head of your paper place the author's name and your own name, as shown.

Author's Name: _____

Peer Reviewer's Name: _____

I. Read the draft at normal reading speed from beginning to end. As you read, do the following:
   A. Place a wavy line in the margin next to any passages that you find confusing, that contain something that doesn't seem to fit, or that otherwise slow down your reading.
   B. Place a "Good!" in the margin next to any passages where you think the writing is particularly strong or interesting.

II. Read the draft again slowly and answer the following questions by writing down brief explanations of your answers.
   A. Plot: What are the contrarieties, tensions, or conflicts (internal and/or external) in this story?
      1. How might the writer heighten or clarify the tension between contrarieties? Do you have to wait too long before the main tension of the story becomes clear?
      2. How might the writer improve the structure or pacing of scenes and the connection between these events? If you were to expand or reduce the treatment given to any events, which would you change and why?
      3. How could the writer use chronological order, flashbacks, or flashforwards more effectively?
   B. Characters: Are the characters and their functions in the story vivid and compelling?
      1. How might the writer portray characters more effectively? What details or information do you the reader need to know or see to understand and be engaged with these characters?
      2. Do you have a clear sense of which characters you sympathize with?
      3. Where might the writer use dialogue more effectively to reveal character and advance the plot?
   C. Setting: Is the setting adequately described with details to make the narrative's conflicts and characters interesting? What more do you need to know or see about the setting?
   D. Theme: What do you see as the *So what?* or significance of this story, and does it come through in a memorable and surprising way?
      1. Could refining the treatment of the conflicts, characters, or setting help the reader appreciate the thematic significance of the story more?
      2. Should the revelation or interpretation of the narrative be made more explicit or be left more for readers to grasp on their own?
   E. Could the writer use the title and opening paragraphs of the story more effectively to hook the reader's interest and prepare for the story to follow?
   F. Briefly summarize in a list what you see as the chief strengths and problem areas in the draft.

III. Read the draft one more time. Place a check in the margin wherever you notice problems in grammar, spelling, or mechanics (one check per problem).

Writing an Exploratory Essay

◢ ABOUT EXPLORATORY WRITING

In Chapter 1, we said that to grow as a writer you need to love problems—to pose them and to live with them. Most academic writers testify that writing projects begin when they become engaged with a question or problem and commit themselves to an extensive period of exploration. During exploration, writers may radically redefine the problem and then later alter or even reverse their initial thesis.

As we noted in Chapters 2 and 3, however, inexperienced writers tend to truncate this exploratory process, committing themselves hastily to a thesis to avoid complexity. College professors say this tendency hinders their students' intellectual growth. Asserting a thesis commits you to a position. Asking a question, on the other hand, invites you to contemplate multiple perspectives, entertain new ideas, and let your thinking evolve. As management professor A. Kimbrough Sherman puts it, to grow as thinkers students need "to 'wallow in complexity' and work their way back out" (see p. 23).

To illustrate his point, Sherman cites his experience in a management class where students were asked to write proposals for locating a new sports complex in a major U.S. city. To Sherman's disappointment, many students argued for a location without first considering all the variables—impact on neighborhoods, building costs and zoning, availability of parking, ease of access, attractiveness to tourists, aesthetics, and so forth—and without analyzing how various proposed locations stacked up against the criteria they were supposed to establish. The students reached closure without wallowing in complexity.

The assignment for this chapter asks you to dwell with a problem, even if you can't solve it. You will write an essay with an exploratory purpose; its focus will be a question rather than a thesis. The body of your paper will be a narrative account of your thinking about the problem—your attempt to examine its complexity, to explore alternative solutions, and to arrive at a solution or answer. Your exploration will generally require outside research, so many instructors will assign sections of Part Four, "A Guide to Research," along with this chapter. The paper will be relatively easy to write because it will be organized chronologically, but you will have nothing to say—no process to report—unless you discover and examine the problem's complexity.

▨ EXPLORING EXPLORATORY WRITING

Through our work in writing centers, we often encounter students disappointed with their grades on essay exams or papers. "I worked hard on this paper," they tell us, "but I still got a lousy grade. What am I doing wrong? What do college professors want?"

To help you answer this question, consider the following two essays written for a freshman placement examination in composition at the University of Pittsburgh, in response to the following assignment:

> Describe a time when you did something you felt to be creative. Then, on the basis of the incident you have described, go on to draw some general conclusions about "creativity."

How would you describe the differences in thinking exhibited by the two writers? Which essay do you think professors rated higher?

Essay A

I am very interested in music, and I try to be creative in my interpretation of music. While in high school, I was a member of a jazz ensemble. The members of the ensemble were given chances to improvise and be creative in various songs. I feel that this was a great experience for me, as well as the other members. I was proud to know that I could use my imagination and feelings to create music other than what was written.

Creativity to me means being free to express yourself in a way that is unique to you, not having to conform to certain rules and guidelines. Music is only one of the many areas in which people are given opportunities to show their creativity. Sculpting, carving, building, art, and acting are just a few more areas where people can show their creativity.

Through my music I conveyed feelings and thoughts which were important to me. Music was my means of showing creativity. In whatever form creativity takes, whether it be music, art, or science, it is an important aspect of our lives because it enables us to be individuals.

Essay B

Throughout my life, I have been interested and intrigued by music. My mother has often told me of the times, before I went to school, when I would "conduct" the orchestra on her records. I continued to listen to music and eventually started to play the guitar and the clarinet. Finally, at about the age of twelve, I started to sit down and to try to write songs. Even though my instrumental skills were far from my own high standards, I would spend much of my spare time during the day with a guitar around my neck, trying to produce a piece of music.

Each of these sessions, as I remember them, had a rather set format. I would sit in my bedroom, strumming different combinations of the five or six chords I could play, until I heard a series which sounded particularly good to me. After this, I set the music to a suitable rhythm (usually dependent on my mood at the time), and ran through the tune until I could play it fairly easily. Only after this section was complete did I go on to writing lyrics, which generally followed along the lines of the current popular songs on the radio.

At the time of the writing, I felt that my songs were, in themselves, an original creation of my own; that is, I, alone, made them. However, I now see that, in this sense of the word, I was not creative. The songs themselves seem to be an oversimplified form of the music I listened to at the time.

In a more fitting sense, however, I *was* being creative. Since I did not purposely copy my favorite songs, I was, effectively, originating my songs from my own "process of creativity." To achieve my goal, I needed what a composer would call "inspiration" for my piece. In this case the inspiration was the current hit on the radio. Perhaps, with my present point of view, I feel that I used too much "inspiration" in my songs, but, at that time, I did not.

Creativity, therefore, is a process which, in my case, involved a certain series of "small creations" if you like. As well, it is something the appreciation of which varies with one's point of view, that point of view being set by the person's experience, tastes, and his own personal view of creativity. The less experienced tend to allow for less originality, while the more experienced demand real originality to classify something a "creation." Either way, a term as abstract as this is perfectly correct, and open to interpretation.

Working as a whole class or in small groups, analyze the differences between Essay A and Essay B. What might cause college professors to rate one essay higher than the other? What would the writer of the weaker essay have to do to produce an essay more like the stronger?

WRITING PROJECT

Choose a question, problem, or issue that genuinely perplexes you. At the beginning of your exploratory essay, explain why you are interested in this chosen problem and why you have been unable to reach a satisfactory answer. Then write a first-person, chronologically organized, narrative account of your thinking process as you investigate your question through library research, talking with others, and doing your own reflective thinking. You might also wish to interview people, if appropriate, and to draw on your own personal experiences, memories, and observations. Your goal is to examine your question, problem, or issue from a variety of perspectives, assessing the strengths and weaknesses of different positions and points of view. By the end of your essay, you may or may not have reached a satisfactory solution to your problem. You will be rewarded for the quality of your exploration and thinking processes. In other words, your goal is not to answer your question, but to report on the process of wrestling with it.

This assignment asks you to dwell with a problem—and not necessarily to solve that problem. Your problem may shift and evolve as your thinking progresses. What matters is that you actively engage with your problem and demonstrate why it is problematic.

Your instructor may choose to combine this writing project with a subsequent one (for example, a research paper based on one of the assignments in the remaining chapters in Part Two) to create a sustained project in which you write two pieces on the same topic. If so, then the essay for this chapter will prepare you to write a later analytical or persuasive piece. Check with your instructor to make sure that your chosen question for this project will work for the later assignment.

◪ UNDERSTANDING EXPLORATORY WRITING

As we have explained, this assignment calls for an essay with an *exploratory purpose* (see our discussion of purposes in Chapter 4, pp. 57–60). Exploratory writing generally has an open-form structure; the writer cannot assert a thesis and forecast a structure in the introduction (typical features of closed-form prose) because the thesis is unknown as the essay opens. Instead of following a closed-form, points-first structure, the essay narrates chronologically the process of the author's thinking about the problem.

The Essence of Exploratory Prose: Considering Multiple Solutions

The essential move of an exploratory essay is to consider multiple solutions to a problem or multiple points of view on an issue. The writer defines a problem, poses a possible solution, explores its strengths and weaknesses, and then *moves* on to consider another possible solution.

To show a mind at work examining multiple solutions, let's return to the two student essays you examined in the previous exploratory activity (pp. 166–67). The fundamental difference between Essay A and Essay B is that the writer of Essay B treats the concept of "creativity" as a true problem. Note that the writer of Essay A is satisfied with his or her initial definition.

> Creativity to me means being free to express yourself in a way that is unique to you, not having to conform to certain rules and guidelines.

The writer of Essay B, however, is *not* satisfied with his or her first answer and uses the essay to think through the problem. This writer remembers an early creative experience—composing songs as a twelve-year-old.

> At the time of the writing, I felt that my songs were, in themselves, an original creation of my own; that is, I, alone, made them. However, I now see that, in this sense of the word, I was not creative. The songs themselves seem to be an oversimplified form of the music I listened to at the time.

This writer distinguishes between two points of view: "On the one hand, I used to think this, but now, in retrospect, I think that." This move forces the writer to go beyond the initial answer to think of alternatives.

The key to effective exploratory writing is to create a tension between alternative views. When you start out, you might not know where your thinking process will end up; at the outset you might not have formulated an opposing, countering, or alternative view. Using a move such as "I used to think . . . , but now I think" or "Part of me thinks this . . . , but another part thinks that . . ." forces you to find something additional to say; writing then becomes a process of inquiry and discovery.

The second writer's dissatisfaction with the initial answer initiates a dialectic process that plays one idea against another, creating a generative tension. In contrast, the writer of Essay A offers no alternative to his or her definition of creativity. This writer presents no specific illustrations of creative activity (such as the specific details in Essay B about strumming the guitar), but presents merely space-filling abstractions ("Sculpting, carving, building, art, and acting are just a few more areas where people can show their creativity."). The writer of Essay B scores a higher grade, not because the essay creates a brilliant (or even particularly clear) explanation of creativity; rather, the writer is rewarded for thinking about the problem dialectically.

We use the term *dialectic* to mean a thinking process often associated with the German philosopher Hegel, who said that each thesis ("My act was creative") gives rise to an antithesis ("My act was not creative") and that the clash of these opposing perspectives leads thinkers to develop a synthesis that incorporates some features of both theses ("My act was a series of 'small creations' "). You initiate dialectic thinking any time you play Elbow's believing and doubting game (see Chapter 2, pp. 37–39) or use other strategies to place alternative possibilities side by side.

Essay B's writer uses a dialectic thinking strategy that we might characterize as follows:

1. Regards the assignment as a genuine problem worth puzzling over.
2. Considers alternative views and plays them off against each other.
3. Looks at specifics.
4. Continues the thinking process in search of some sort of resolution or synthesis of the alternative views.
5. Incorporates the stages of this dialectic process into the essay.

FOR WRITING AND DISCUSSION

1. According to writing theorist David Bartholomae, who analyzed several hundred student essays in response to the placement-examination question on p. 166, almost all the highest scoring essays exhibited a similar kind of dialectic thinking. How might the writer of the first

essay expand the essay by using the dialectic thinking processes just described?

2. Working individually, read each of the following questions and write out your initial opinion or one or two answers that come immediately to mind.

- Given the easy availability of birth-control information and the ready availability of condoms, why do you think there are so many teenage pregnancies?
- Why do U.S. students, on the average, lag so far behind their European and Asian counterparts in scholastic achievement?
- Should women be assigned to combat roles in the military?
- The most popular magazines sold on college campuses around the country are women's fashion and lifestyle magazines such as *Glamour, Seventeen, Mademoiselle*, and *Cosmopolitan*. Why are these magazines so popular? Is there a problem with these magazines being so popular? (Two separate questions, both of which are worth exploring dialectically.)

3. Choose one of these questions or one assigned by your instructor and freewrite for five or ten minutes using one or more of the following moves to stimulate dialectic thinking.

I used to think _____, but now I think _____.

Part of me thinks _____, but another part of me thinks _____.

On some days I think _____, but on other days I think _____.

The first answers that come to mind are _____, but as I think further I see _____.

My classmate thinks _____, but I think _____.

Your goal here is to explore potential weaknesses or inadequacies in your first answers, and then to push beyond them to think of new or different answers. Feel free to be wild and risky in posing possible alternative solutions.

4. As a whole class, take a poll to find out what the most common first-response answers were for each of the questions. Then share alternative solutions generated by class members during the freewriting. The goal is to pose and explore answers that go beyond or against the grain of the common answers. Remember, there is little point in arguing for an answer that everyone else already accepts.

READINGS

To help you appreciate exploratory essays, we include in this section two student essays and a professional article.

In the first essay, student writer Mary Turla explores the problem of mail-order brides. (You read some of Mary's early research journal entries in Chapter 1, p. 9.) She later developed this exploration into a research paper that appears as our student example in Chapter 22 (pp. 573–87).

▼

MARY TURLA (STUDENT)
MAIL-ORDER BRIDE ROMANCES: FAIRY TALE, NIGHTMARE, OR SOMEWHERE IN BETWEEN?

1   I first became interested in the issue of mail-order brides when I picked up the *Seattle Times* one afternoon and read that an angry Timothy Blackwell walked into the King County Courthouse and gunned down his wife, Susanna Remarata Blackwell, a mail-order bride (Haines and Sevens A1). I was outraged mainly because she was Filipina and so am I. I remember asking myself questions like, "Why did she become a mail-order bride? Why did Timothy Blackwell pick a wife out of a mail-order catalog? Is this prostitution?"

2   When I discussed the topic with my friends and fellow Pinays, the general feeling was that the mail-order bride business exploited vulnerable, poor women from the Third World. We felt that men who searched specifically for a foreign Asian bride wanted either a sex slave or a domestic slave, or maybe both. Basically, I felt the mail-order bride business should absolutely be abolished.

3   But then I spoke with my mother. And, I admit I wavered on my absolute intolerance of the process. She grew up in the Philippines and, although she wasn't a mail-order bride, I am sure she has met a few or has heard of such matches. I was surprised to find out that she had once played matchmaker for her friend in the Philippines and a male co-worker here in the States! "Life is so hard there," she explained. "We moved here to give our children a better life . . . opportunities and choices many back home don't have." Although I still did not feel entirely comfortable with the idea, I realized that maybe there were legitimate motivations for people using a mail-order bride service.

4   In my desire to form a justifiable position on the issue, I wanted to find out as much as I could about how the business worked, the profiles of the typical brides and grooms, and the social, cultural, or economic consequences. I also wanted to find out the role of Filipinas as mail-order brides. If this industry does create a negative image of the women involved (as sexual, submissive commodities), I better pay attention because I am Filipina American.

5   I went to the college library to start my investigation with a study of the Susanna Blackwell murder case. The question that kept nagging at me while I was reading the Blackwell articles was: Was the marital violence that led to her murder because she was a Filipina mail-order bride? Based on his testimony, Blackwell's anger toward his wife grew out of his belief that she had used him for his money and for getting American

citizenship. "From the beginning she wanted money . . . she wanted a green card," he said (Haines and Sevens A1). Throughout his testimony, Blackwell continually expressed his anger over the money he had spent on her. Susanna testified that Blackwell emotionally and physically abused her, as early as their courtship in 1993. In her statement to the police, Susanna said that she wanted to go back to the Philippines but that Timothy told her "to stay in the U.S. for two years and pay him $500 a month to repay the $10,000 he'd spent on her" (Haines and Sevens A6).

Many other questions ran through my mind. Are there many cases where domestic violence and mail-order marriages go hand-in-hand? Why did she marry him? Would Susanna Blackwell be dead if they had met through different means or if she wasn't Filipina? What are the implications for his emphasis on how much she had cost him? What were they both hoping for in this marriage? What is the new bride's status in her husband's country? After the murder, one *Seattle Times* headline read, "Gunman felt duped." In response, I say: Who was really in control? 6

The next logical piece of the puzzle was to find out what kind of men and women participate in the mail-order business: What are their hopes and expectations? What happens if those dreams aren't met? Unfortunately, I couldn't find any answers to these questions in our college library. Using INFOTRAC and other indexes in the library didn't yield any sources. However, being Filipina, I knew that the Filipino National Historical Society had its own specialized library in Seattle. I headed off to this library in hopes of finding psychological, cultural, or social perspectives on the mail-order industry within its archives. I was lucky because they had a file of information on the mail-order bride industry. 7

I found out that most of the men who subscribe to mail-order bride catalogs are Caucasian. According to a University of Texas study cited by Villipando, the median income of 265 subscribers to these catalogs was higher than average—65 percent with incomes higher than $20,000. The average age was 37 (50 percent being over 37), average height five feet seven inches, and most were college educated. Only five percent never finished high school (Villipando 6). 8

Article after article supported the idea that men choose Asian brides because they long for the traditional woman: she cooks and cleans and is subservient and loyal to her husband. Also the men are burnt out by both the women's movement and the American dating scene. The Japanese American Citizens League, a national civil rights group, confirms these findings in its recent position paper on mail-order brides. The group found the men to be "white, much older than the bride they choose, politically conservative, frustrated by the women's movement. They . . . find the traditional Asian value of deference to men reassuring" (Villipando 6). 9

Most of the women who take part in the mail-order service range from teenagers to women in their 40's. They come from disadvantaged families and may reside within underdeveloped countries. They see America as the land of opportunity and feel that American men may provide better for them and their families than they would be able to for themselves in their own countries. "It is the social and economic conditions in underdeveloped countries that drive women to participate. For many, marrying a North American means marrying upward in society" (Valdez 21). 10

After reading this information, I seriously questioned whether mail-order marriages could be successful based on the vulnerable position in which the woman is placed. She is a foreigner living a new life in a new country with new customs. Most often, she is left without nearby family or community support (vital in most Asian communities). Her immigrant status leaves her vulnerable to the threat of deportation and return to a 11 life of poverty. There is also the question of domestic abuse and who the bride will turn to if it occurs, if she speaks out at all. I also learned from the Blackwell murder case how much the threat of deportation becomes a part of domestic violence.

12   What bothered me most of all were the descriptions of women found in the mail-order catalogs. According to Villipando, the brochures put out by the mail-order bride industry create and perpetuate unrealistic images of real people. One brochure describing Filipino women reads: "They are raised to respect and defer to the male. . . . The young Oriental woman . . . derives her basic satisfactions from serving and pleasing her husband" (13). Another brochure reads: "Most, if not all are very feminine, loyal, loving . . . and virgins!" (13).

13   I decided that I wanted to see some of these brochures myself and realized that the mail-order bride companies might advertise on the Internet. Using the Hotbot search engine, I found ten companies with brochures on the web. One of these, with a homepage labeled "Forever Yours: the Write Connection," showed two pictures of beautiful young Asian women. It had the following text beneath the pictures:

> Have you ever dreamed of finding your ideal lady—loving, beautiful, and devoted? Are you looking for old-fashioned love in a liberated age? Then please take a few minutes, browse our site, and I sincerely promise that you can realize your dreams.

Timothy Blackwell bought into these images: "I had heard so much that these women were very sincere, very loving, very faithful. . . . I always admired Polynesian-type women with very long, straight black hair, and light brown skin" (Haines and Sevens A6).

14   Although there is a sense (thus far) that the women are more vulnerable than the men, I began feeling sympathy for both parties. Both are victims of romantic ideals. He searches for a docile, loyal, family-oriented, exotic, dark-haired fantasy. She longs for a big, strong American to save her from her desperate circumstances.

15   I then had the opportunity to speak with Ellen Ayaberra, commissioner for the Seattle Women's Commission and president of the Filipino American Political Action Group of Washington on her assessment of the issue. She believes that the mail-order bride industry should be abolished for three reasons. First, she sees it as legalized woman trafficking. Second, she adds that the media misrepresent the true image of the Filipino women as uneducated and naive instead of degree-holding professionals, as many of them are. And, third, she fears the consequences of the unrealistic expectations that both husband and bride bring to the relationship. Abeyerra said:

> [A mail-order marriage] is a union based on false expectations. . . . America is not always paradise, American men are not always heros. . . . Filipinas are educated, hardworking professionals who live, with few choices, in poverty . . . we are not dumb country girls.

16   I left the session and leave this paper wondering: Should we try to outlaw the mail-order bride industry completely or should we try to regulate it in some way? In all honesty, I hope to see it abolished because it seems to treat people like commodities or unrealistic romantic figures. It keeps people from being seen as they are: individual human beings. But I can see the other side too.

Works Cited

Ayaberra, Ellen. Personal interview. 26 Apr. 1995.

"Forever Yours: The Write Connection." *Forever Yours World Wide International* 13 July 1998 <http://www.4everyours.com/index2html>.

Haines, Thomas W., and Richard Sevens. "Gunman Felt Duped by Bride from the Start." *Seattle Times* 4 Mar. 1995: A1+.

Valdez, Marybeth. "Return to Sender: The Mail-Order Bride Business in the Philippines." *Philippine Review* May 1995: 5+.

Villipando, Venny. "The Business of Selling Mail-Order Brides." *San Diego Asian Journal* 1 Feb. 1990: 6–16.

Thinking Critically About "Mail-Order Bride Romances"

1. How does Mary Turla's exploratory paper reveal dialectic thinking?
2. What do you see as the chief strengths and weaknesses of Mary's exploration of the mail-order bride industry?
3. Mary uses only five research sources for this paper. In her final researched argument (pp. 573–87), however, she has fourteen sources—indicating that she felt the need to do more research. What additional questions or issues do you think Mary needs to investigate before she can make a strong argument to abolish or regulate the mail-order bride industry?

In this next essay, student writer Sheridan Botts explores problems related to the funding of hospices for the terminally ill. Because her professor assigned the exploratory essay as a first stage in writing a proposal argument (Chapter 16), this writer poses both content-oriented questions about hospices and rhetorical questions about the focus, purpose, and audience for her proposal paper. (Her final version, a proposal argument, appears on pp. 401–3.)

▼

SHERIDAN BOTTS (STUDENT)
EXPLORING PROBLEMS ABOUT HOSPICES

Last fall my brother-in-law, Charles, lay dying, and his mother, Betty, was overwhelmed with grief and responsibility. Charles wanted to die at home, not connected to tubes in the hospital, so Betty cared for him in his home with the help of a home care agency. At the same time as she was caring for him—helping him get sips of water, trying to meet his every need—she was terribly depressed. She had already lost one son, and now she was losing another. But she was unable to talk about her depression with her friends. When I called the home care agency to seek counseling help for Betty, they said, "Is she the patient? We can only care for the patient." And then, after Charles died, and Betty was bereft, she was on her own. No services were available to her from the home care agency. 1

If Charles had been with a hospice agency instead of a home care agency, Betty would have had help. A hospice would have helped Charles stay comfortable at home, and, in addition to the visits by nurses, social workers, and home health aides provided 2 by the home care agency, a hospice would have provided chaplain and volunteer helpers both for Charles and for Betty. Social workers or a chaplain would have helped Betty prepare for Charles's death—and after his death, helped her deal with her tremendous grief. Then, for the following year, a hospice would have offered Betty continuing help with grief—articles, a grief counseling group, and calls from volunteers.

3   So, this spring, when I started thinking about what to do my paper on, I thought of hospice. I wanted to learn more about the hospice movement and be able to clearly articulate the benefit of hospice programs. I had two interconnected writing assignments—this exploratory paper and then a follow-up persuasive argument. There were a lot of things I wanted to find out about hospice, but what was there to argue about in a persuasive paper? Perhaps I could persuade people about the benefits of hospice. But I already knew the benefits, and almost everyone agrees that hospices are valuable. So what issue about hospices is there to argue about? What persuasive essay is crying to be written?

4   I decided to find out more about the problems facing hospices, so I looked in the phone book under "Hospice," called Hospice of Seattle, and was referred to the Marketing Coordinator. I asked her if there was a hospice question that needed arguing and she said:

> Yes! Convince the private insurance companies to bill on a per diem basis instead of fee-for-service. Fee-for-service doesn't pay for social work, chaplain visits, volunteers, and grief counseling. You could really help hospices if you wrote a persuasive paper on that subject!

Ah ha! This was it! A meaningful project. Here was an opportunity to make a real difference, have an impact, learn more about hospices, and improve my writing. Here was a subject that was important, and to which I didn't have a ready answer. How could I convince insurance companies to pay for hospice on a per diem basis?

5   I got excited about convincing a real entity to do something real about a real issue. I called the National Hospice Organization and ordered information on hospice care. I then went to the library to see what else I could find. I looked up on Lycos and found Hospice Net. This web page included a description of the hospice concept: a comprehensive program of care to patients and families facing a life-threatening illness. From Hospice Net I found Hospice Hands, from Hospice of North Central Florida. The Hospice Hands web page included links to other pages and articles on hospice services, pain management, and ethical issues. These two pages were very helpful in finding a variety of hospice information on the Web. In addition to information on the Web, the library had many books on hospice. I especially enjoyed reading moving stories in *Final Passages: Positive Choices for the Dying and Their Loved Ones* (1992) about men and women who had received hospice care and how much it meant to them.

6   Although the websites and library books confirmed the value of hospice, they did not help me understand the problem of funding, and I started feeling frustrated. I then conducted an article search on Infotrac using the keyword "hospice."

7   The problem was that I didn't quite know what to look for because I didn't fully understand the implications of fee-for-service versus per diem payment. Just what is the difference? Why is there such a distinct preference for fee-for-service by insurance companies, and such a preference for per diem by hospices? Instead of seeking the answers in the library, I decided to try interviews. I made an appointment with a Medical Social Worker at Hospice of Seattle who helped patients sign up for insurance. She was great to talk to because she understood the issue clearly. She explained that with

fee-for-service, each visit to the patient's home by a nurse, social worker, home health aide, or therapist is paid for separately, but fee-for-service doesn't pay for everything the patient needs. Fee-for-service doesn't pay for the volunteer program (which has a paid Volunteer Coordinator), chaplains, grief care (the Grief Counselor coordinates volunteers to call on grief-stricken family members and mails packages throughout the year to family members). Also some insurance programs don't pay for social work. Hospice of Seattle pays for all these services, and tries to incorporate the cost into services that insurance *does* pay for. It seemed clear that fee-for-service did not benefit Hospice of Seattle.

According to the social worker, per diem payment works better for hospices. With per diem, the patient's insurance pays the hospice for each day of care the patient receives. This covers the costs better because the hospice can budget and plan better, can order the most appropriate services and supplies, can negotiate better rates with medical equipment companies, and can provide services not covered under fee-for-service. Per diem is also better for the family. They can be assured that their medical needs will be covered. There won't be unexpected surprises, or mounting co-payments. This justification of per diem sounded good to me. 8

Per diem did not seem to benefit the insurance company, however. Insurance companies want to minimize the cost for each patient, and get the most for their money. As long as patients are getting the care they need, if the insurance company can get away without paying, well, that sounds pretty good for the insurance company. 9

Uh oh. What if I couldn't come up with good reasons for insurance companies to pay per diem? What if it is to the advantage of the hospice, but *not* to the insurance company, to pay per diem? I asked the Hospice of Seattle Director for help and he gave me a paper, "Accessing Reimbursement: How to Bill Private Insurance," by Brenda Horne. Ms. Horne says, "Billing on a per visit (fee-for-service) basis does not provide adequate reimbursement levels to cover costs for the entire range of hospice services. Only per diem rates take into consideration the fact that hospice offers a unique range of services not available through any other health provider" (2). Unfortunately, the rationale focuses on the value to hospices rather than for insurance companies. The article didn't help me as much as I had hoped it would. 10

This is where I am now, somewhat discouraged. I have learned quite a bit about hospice care and I am even more convinced of the importance of providing this care for dying people. I have been frustrated, however, that I was not able to find more literature analyzing per diem billing. I have more papers to read, but I don't think they will shed light on this subject. The literature seems either to be about hospice care in general, or on the cost saving of hospice care over traditional medicine. The web pages, articles, and books don't get much into the specific question of the benefit of per diem over fee-for-service billing. Maybe that's why the Marketing Coordinator said that this would be a good paper to write. 11

I think my best hope in supporting per diem billing is to talk with more staff people at Hospice of Seattle. My guess is that per diem billing should have an advantage in keeping costs down; I need to investigate this justification for per diem billing and try to find other reasons that will persuade insurance companies to try the per diem approach. Now I have the question, but I still need to find a convincing answer. 12

Works Cited

Ahronheim, Judith, M.D., and Doron Weber. *Final Passages, Positive Choices for the Dying and Their Loved Ones.* New York: Simon, 1992.

Friedrichsen, Ann. Medical Social Worker, Hospice of Seattle. Personal interview. 18 Aug. 1998.

Horne, Brenda. "Accessing Reimbursement: How to Bill Private Insurance." Rec. 14th Annual Meeting and Symposium of the National Hospice Organization. Nashville. 31 Oct. 1992.

Hospice Net. 31 July 1998 <http://www.hospicenet.org>.

Hospice of North Central Florida. "Hospice Hands." 31 July 1998 <http://www. hospice-cares.com/welcome.html>.

Smith, Rodney. Hospice Director, Hospice of Seattle. Personal interview. 11 Sept. 1998.

Surla, Johanna. Marketing Coordinator, Hospice of Seattle. Personal interview. 14 July 1998.

Thinking Critically About "Exploring Problems About Hospices"

1. In Part One, we distinguished between two kinds of problems that writers face: content problems and rhetorical problems. Sheridan Botts wrestles with both problems throughout this exploratory paper. In your own words, what are the content problems that Sheridan examines and what are the rhetorical problems?

2. What are the chief strengths and chief weaknesses of her exploration so far?

3. What further research does Sheridan need to do before she can persuade insurance companies to pay hospices on a per diem basis?

The third example of exploratory writing is an excerpt from a scholarly article by literary critic Jane Tompkins. First published in the scholarly journal *Critical Inquiry,* Tompkins's article focuses on the problem of how different historians portray Native Americans. This problem was a surprise for Tompkins, who began her research in pursuit of another topic. Note how deftly Tompkins uses an open-form structure to recount both personal and scholarly revelations. Although it is too long to print in full here, the entire article follows the narrative shape of Tompkins's thinking process, beginning with the discovery and evolution of a "problem of my own."

▼

JANE TOMPKINS
"INDIANS": TEXTUALISM, MORALITY, AND THE PROBLEM OF HISTORY

1   When I was growing up in New York City, my parents used to take me to an event in Inwood Park at which Indians—real American Indians dressed in feathers and blankets—could be seen and touched by children like me. This event was always a disappointment. It was more fun to imagine that you *were* an Indian in one of the caves in

This passage introduces the problem by relating a childhood memory about Indians.

Inwood Park than to shake the hand of an old man in a headdress who was not overwhelmed at the opportunity of meeting you. After staring at the Indians for a while, we would take a walk in the woods where the caves were, and once I asked my mother if the remains of a fire I had seen in one of them might have been left by the original inhabitants. After that, wandering up some stone steps cut into the side of the hill, I imagined I was a princess in a rude castle. My Indians, like my princesses, were creatures totally of the imagination, and I did not care to have any real exemplars interfering with what I already knew.

I already knew about Indians from having read about them in school. Over and over   2
we were told the story of how Peter Minuit had bought Manhattan Island from the Indians for twenty-four dollars' worth of glass beads. And it was a story we didn't mind hearing because it gave us the rare pleasure of having someone to feel superior to, since the poor Indians had not known (as we eight-year-olds did) how valuable a piece of property Manhattan Island would become. Generally, much was made of the Indian presence in Manhattan; a poem in one of our readers began: "Where we walk to school today / Indian children used to play," and we were encouraged to write poetry on this topic ourselves. So I had a fairly rich relationship with Indians before I ever met the unprepossessing people in Inwood Park. I felt that I had a lot in common with them. They, too, liked animals (they were often named after animals); they, too, made mistakes—they liked the brightly colored trinkets of little value that the white men were always offering them; they were handsome, warlike, and brave and had led an exciting, romantic life in the forest long ago, a life such as I dreamed of leading myself. I felt lucky to be living in one of the places where they had definitely been. Never mind where they were or what they were doing now.

My story stands for the relationship most non-Indians have to the people who first   3
populated this continent, a relationship characterized by narcissistic fantasies of freedom and adventure, of a life lived closer to nature and to spirit than the life we lead now. As Vine Deloria, Jr., has pointed out, the American Indian Movement in the early seventies couldn't get people to pay attention to what was happening to Indians who were alive in the present, so powerful was this country's infatuation with people who wore loincloths, lived in tepees, and roamed the plains and forests long ago. The present essay, like these fantasies, doesn't have much to do with actual Indians, though its subject matter is the histories of European-Indian relations in seventeenth-century New England. In a sense, my encounter with Indians as an adult doing "research" replicates the childhood one, for while I started out to learn about Indians, I ended up preoccupied with a problem of my own.

This essay enacts a particular instance of the challenge poststructuralism poses to   4
the study of history. In simpler language, it concerns the difference that point of view makes when people are giving accounts of events, whether at first or second hand. The problem is that if all accounts of events are determined through and through by the observer's frame of reference, then one will never know, in any given case, what really happened.

I encountered this problem in concrete terms while preparing to teach a course in   5
colonial American literature. I'd set out to learn what I could about the Puritans' relations with American Indians. All I wanted was a general idea of what had happened between the English settlers and the natives in seventeenth-century New England; poststructuralism and its dilemmas were the furthest thing from my mind. I began, more or less automatically, with Perry Miller, who hardly mentions the Indians at all, then proceeded to the work of historians who had dealt exclusively with the European-Indian

This section explains the focus of this paper and then makes a transition to the academic problem it will explore.

Poststructuralism is a critical theory that, among other things, denies that truth can be directly understood and stated clearly.

This section provides an overview

encounter. At first, it was a question of deciding which of these authors to believe, for it quickly became apparent that there was no unanimity on the subject. As I read on, however, I discovered that the problem was more complicated than deciding whose version of events was correct. Some of the conflicting accounts were not simply contradictory, they were completely incommensurable, in that their assumptions about what counted as a valid approach to the subject, and what the subject itself was, diverged in fundamental ways. Faced with an array of mutually irreconcilable points of view, points of view which determined what was being discussed as well as the terms of the discussion, I decided to turn to primary sources for clarification, only to discover that the primary sources reproduced the problem all over again. I found myself, in other words, in an epistemological quandary, not only unable to decide among conflicting versions of events but also unable to believe that any such decision could, in principle, be made. It was a moral quandary as well. Knowledge of what really happened when the Europeans and the Indians first met seemed particularly important, since the result of that encounter was virtual genocide. This was the kind of past "mistake" which, presumably, we studied history in order to avoid repeating. If studying history couldn't put us in touch with actual events and their causes, then what was to prevent such atrocities from happening again?

of Tompkins's exploration of the problem.

Here Tompkins shows why her problem is problematic.

Here she shows why her problem is significant.

6   For a while, I remained at this impasse. But through analyzing the process by which I had reached it, I eventually arrived at an understanding which seemed to offer a way out. This essay records the concrete experience of meeting and solving the difficulty I have just described (as an abstract problem, I thought I had solved it long ago). My purpose is not to throw new light on antifoundationalist epistemology—the solution I reached is not a new one—but to dramatize and expose the troubles antifoundationalism gets you into when you meet it, so to speak, in the road.

This paragraph states the purpose of the essay and forecasts its exploratory shape.

Antifoundationalism rejects the notion that truth can be verified using laws, events, or texts.

7   My research began with Perry Miller. Early in the preface to *Errand into the Wilderness,* while explaining how he came to write his history of the New England mind, Miller writes a sentence that stopped me dead. He says that what fascinated him as a young man about his country's history was "the massive narrative of the movement of European culture into the vacant wilderness of America." "Vacant?" Miller, writing in 1956, doesn't pause over the word "vacant," but to people who read his preface thirty years later, the word is shocking. In what circumstances could someone proposing to write a history of colonial New England *not* take account of the Indian presence there?

Here Tompkins describes the start of her intellectual journey.

8   The rest of Miller's preface supplies an answer to this question, if one takes the trouble to piece together its details. Miller explains that as a young man, jealous of older compatriots who had had the luck to fight in World War I, he had gone to Africa in search of adventure. "The adventures that Africa afforded," he writes, "were tawdry enough, but it became the setting for a sudden epiphany" (p. vii). "It was given to me," he writes, "disconsolate on the edge of a jungle of central Africa, to have thrust upon me the mission of expounding what I took to be the innermost propulsion of the United States, while supervising, in that barbaric tropic, the unloading of drums of case oil flowing out of the inexhaustible wilderness of America" (p. viii). Miller's picture of himself on the banks of the Congo furnishes a key to the kind of history he will write and to his mental image of a vacant wilderness; it explains why it was just there, under precisely these conditions, that he should have had his epiphany.

9   The fuel drums stand, in Miller's mind, for the popular misconception of what this country is about. They are "tangible symbols of [America's] appalling power," a power that everyone but Miller takes for the ultimate reality (p. ix). To Miller, "the mind of man

In this section, Tompkins presents a series of particulars to illustrate the point that Miller had a biased and limited perspective that prevented him from truly "seeing" the Indians.

is the basic factor in human history," and he will plead, all unaccommodated as he is among the fuel drums, for the intellect—the intellect for which his fellow historians, with their chapters on "stoves or bathtubs, or tax laws," "the Wilmot Proviso" and "the chain store," "have so little respect" (p. viii, ix). His preface seethes with a hatred of the merely physical and mechanical, and this hatred, which is really a form of moral outrage, explains not only the contempt with which he mentions the stoves and bathtubs but also the nature of his experience in Africa and its relationship to the "massive narrative" he will write.

Miller's experiences in Africa are "tawdry," his tropic is barbaric because the jungle he stands on the edge of means nothing to him, no more, indeed something less, than the case oil. It is the nothingness of Africa that precipitates his vision. It is the barbarity of the "dark continent," the obvious (but superficial) parallelism between the jungle at Matadi and America's "vacant wilderness" that releases in Miller the desire to define and vindicate his country's cultural identity. To the young Miller, colonial Africa and colonial America are—but for the history he will bring to light—mirror images of one another. And what he fails to see in the one landscape is the same thing he overlooks in the other: the human beings who people it. As Miller stood with his back to the jungle, thinking about the role of mind in human history, his failure to see that the land into which European culture had moved was not vacant but already occupied by a varied and numerous population, is of a piece with his failure, in his portrait of himself at Matadi, to notice *who* was carrying the fuel drums he was supervising the unloading of. **10**

The point is crucial because it suggests that what is invisible to the historian in his own historical moment remains invisible when he turns his gaze to the past. It isn't that Miller didn't "see" the black men, in a literal sense, any more than it's the case that when he looked back he didn't "see" the Indians, in the sense of not realizing they were there. Rather, it's that neither the Indians nor the blacks *counted* for him, in a fundamental way. The way in which Indians can be seen but not counted is illustrated by an entry in Governor John Winthrop's journal, three hundred years before, when he recorded that there had been a great storm with high winds "yet through God's great mercy it did no hurt, but only killed one Indian with the fall of a tree." The juxtaposition suggests that Miller shared with Winthrop a certain colonial point of view, a point of view from which Indians, though present, do not finally matter. **11**

Here Tompkins describes the next step in her journey. Vaughan's book is explicitly about Puritans and Indians, so she expects it to answer questions that Miller didn't address.

A book entitled *New England Frontier: Puritans and Indians, 1620–1675,* written by Alden Vaughan and published in 1965, promised to rectify Miller's omission. In the outpouring of work on the European-Indian encounter that began in the early sixties, this book is the first major landmark, and to a neophyte it seems definitive. Vaughan acknowledges the absence of Indian sources and emphasizes his use of materials which catch the Puritans "off guard." His announced conclusion that "the New England Puritans followed a remarkably humane, considerate, and just policy in their dealings with the Indians" seems supported by the scope, documentation, and methodicalness of his project (*NEF,* p. vii). The author's fair-mindedness and equanimity seem everywhere apparent, so that when he asserts "the history of interracial relations from the arrival of the Pilgrims to the outbreak of King Philip's War is a credit to the integrity of both peoples," one is positively reassured (*NEF,* p. viii). **12**

Tompkins begins showing the reader why Vaughan is also

But these impressions do not survive an admission that comes late in the book, when, in the course of explaining why works like Helen Hunt Jackson's *Century of Dishonor* had spread misconceptions about Puritan treatment of the Indians, Vaughan finally lays his own cards on the table. **13**

The root of the misunderstanding [about Puritans and Indians] . . . lie[s] in a failure to recognize the nature of the two societies that met in seventeenth century New England. One was unified, visionary, disciplined, and dynamic. The other was divided, self-satisfied, undisciplined, and static. It would be unreasonable to expect that such societies could live side by side indefinitely with no penetration of the more fragmented and passive by the more consolidated and active. What resulted, then, was not—as many have held—a clash of dissimilar ways of life, but rather the expansion of one into the areas in which the other was lacking. [*NEF,* p. 323]

not a reliable source of truth about Indians.

14   From our present vantage point, these remarks seem culturally biased to an incredible degree, not to mention inaccurate: was Puritan society unified? If so, how does one account for its internal dissensions and obsessive need to cast out deviants? Is "unity" necessarily a positive culture trait? From what standpoint can one say that American Indians were neither disciplined nor visionary, when both these characteristics loom so large in the ethnographies? Is it an accident that ways of describing cultural strength and weakness coincide with gender stereotypes—active/passive, and so on? Why is one culture said to "penetrate" the other? Why is the "other" described in terms of "lack"?

In these transitional paragraphs, Tompkins shows how the reader plays an active role in shaping the meaning of a written text. The perspective of scholars who were deeply affected by the tumultuous cultural changes of the 1960s exposed Vaughan's racial biases. Finally, Tompkins leaves the scholars of the past behind, preparing us for "an entirely different picture of the European-Indian encounter."

15   Vaughan's fundamental categories of apprehension and judgment will not withstand even the most cursory inspection. For what looked like even-handedness when he was writing *New England Frontier* does not look that way anymore. In his introduction to *New Directions in American Intellectual History,* John Higham writes that by the end of the sixties

the entire conceptual foundation on which [this sort of work] rested [had] crumbled away. . . . Simultaneously, in sociology, anthropology, and history, two working assumptions . . . came under withering attack: first, the assumption that societies tend to be integrated, and second, that a shared culture maintains that integration. . . . By the late 1960s all claims issued in the name of an "American mind" were subject to drastic skepticism.

"Clearly," Higham continues, "the sociocultural upheaval of the sixties created the occasion" for this reaction. Vaughan's book, it seemed, could only have been written before the events of the sixties had sensitized scholars to questions of race and ethnicity. It came as no surprise, therefore, that ten years later there appeared a study of European-Indian relations which reflected the new awareness of social issues the sixties had engendered. And it offered an entirely different picture of the European-Indian encounter.

16   Francis Jennings's *The Invasion of America* (1975) rips wide open the idea that the Puritans were humane and considerate in their dealings with the Indians. In Jennings's account, even more massively documented than Vaughan's, the early settlers lied to the Indians, stole from them, murdered them, scalped them, captured them, tortured them, raped them, sold them into slavery, confiscated their land, destroyed their crops, burned their homes, scattered their possessions, gave them alcohol, undermined their systems of belief, and infected them with diseases that wiped out ninety percent of their numbers within the first hundred years after contact.

Here begins the third stage of Tompkins's journey. Now she is exploring the work of a post-1960s scholar with a radically different perspective on Puritans and Indians.

17   Jennings mounts an all-out attack on the essential decency of the Puritan leadership and their apologists in the twentieth century. The Pequot War, which previous historians had described as an attempt on the part of Massachusetts Bay to protect itself from the fiercest of the New England tribes, becomes, in Jennings's painstakingly

researched account, a deliberate war of extermination, waged by whites against Indians. It starts with trumped-up charges, is carried on through a series of increasingly bloody reprisals, and ends in the massacre of scores of Indian men, women, and children, all so that Massachusetts Bay could gain political and economic control of the southern Connecticut Valley. When one reads this and then turns over the page and sees a reproduction of the Bay Colony seal, which depicts an Indian from whose mouth issue the words "Come over and help us," the effect is shattering.

Tompkins begins showing how Jennings's view is also limited by his own perspective.

But even so powerful an argument as Jennings's did not remain unshaken by subsequent work. Reading on, I discovered that if the events of the sixties had revolutionized the study of European-Indian relations, the events of the seventies produced yet another transformation. The American Indian Movement, and in particular the founding of the Native American Rights Fund in 1971 to finance Indian litigation, and a court decision in 1975 which gave the tribes the right to seek redress for past injustices in federal court, created a climate within which historians began to focus on the Indians themselves. "Almost simultaneously," writes James Axtell, "frontier and colonial historians began to discover the necessity of considering the American natives as real determinants of history and the utility of ethnohistory as a way of ensuring parity of focus and impartiality of judgment." In Miller, Indians had been simply beneath notice; in Vaughan, they belonged to an inferior culture; and in Jennings, they were the more or less innocent prey of power-hungry whites. But in the most original and provocative of the ethnohistories, Calvin Martin's *Keepers of the Game,* Indians became complicated, purposeful human beings, whose lives were spiritually motivated to a high degree. Their relationship to the animals they hunted, to the natural environment, and to the whites with whom they traded became intelligible within a system of beliefs that formed the basis for an entirely new perspective on the European-Indian encounter. **18**

Before she moves to the fourth stage of her journey, Tompkins helps readers get their bearings by briefly reviewing the path she has taken.

Tompkins begins the fourth stage of her journey by summarizing the work of Calvin Martin, a modern scholar motivated by the desire to explore a problem: Why did the Indians willingly participate in the fur trade, a self-destructive pursuit?

Within the broader question of why European contact had such a devastating effect on the Indians, Martin's specific aim is to determine why Indians participated in the fur trade which ultimately led them to the brink of annihilation. The standard answer to this question had always been that once the Indian was introduced to European guns, copper kettles, woolen blankets, and the like, he literally couldn't keep his hands off them. In order to acquire these coveted items, he decimated the animal populations on which his survival depended. In short, the Indian's motivation in participating in the fur trade was assumed to be the same as the white European's—a desire to accumulate material goods. In direct opposition to this thesis, Martin argues that the reason why Indians ruthlessly exploited their own resources had nothing to do with supply and demand, but stemmed rather from a breakdown of the cosmic worldview that tied them to the game they killed in a spiritual relationship of parity and mutual obligation. **19**

The hunt, according to Martin, was conceived not primarily as a physical activity but as a spiritual quest, in which the spirit of the hunter must overmaster the spirit of the game animal before the kill can take place. The animal, in effect, *allows* itself to be found and killed, once the hunter has mastered its spirit. The hunter prepared himself through rituals of fasting, sweating, or dreaming which revealed the identity of his prey and where he can find it. The physical act of killing is the least important element in the process. Once the animal is killed, eaten, and its parts used for clothing or implements, its remains must be disposed of in ritually prescribed fashion, or the game boss, the "keeper" of that species, will not permit more animals to be killed. The relationship between Indians and animals, then, is contractual; each side must hold up its end of the bargain, or no further transactions can occur. **20**

What happened, according to Martin, was that as a result of diseases introduced into the animal population by Europeans, the game suddenly disappeared, began to **21** act in inexplicable ways, or sickened and died in plain view, and communicated their diseases to the Indians. The Indians, consequently, believed that their compact with the animals had been broken and that the keepers of the game, the tutelary spirits of each animal species whom they had been so careful to propitiate, had betrayed them. And when missionization, wars with the Europeans, and displacement from their tribal lands had further weakened Indian society and its belief structure, the Indians, no longer restrained by religious sanctions, in effect, turned on the animals in a holy war of revenge.

22   Whether or not Martin's specific claim about the "holy war" was correct, his analysis made it clear to me that, given the Indians' understanding of economic, religious, and physical processes, an Indian account of what transpired when the European settlers arrived here would look nothing like our own. Their (potential, unwritten) history of the conflict could bear only a marginal resemblance to Eurocentric views. I began to think that the key to understanding European-Indian relations was to see them as an encounter between wholly disparate cultures, and that therefore either defending or attacking the colonists was beside the point since, given the cultural disparity between the two groups, conflict was inevitable and in large part a product of mutual misunderstanding.

Tompkins speculates that Indians' perceptions of events differed so radically from those of European settlers' that "conflict was inevitable."

23   But three years after Martin's book appeared, Shepard Krech III edited a collection of seven essays called *Indians, Animals, and the Fur Trade,* attacking Martin's entire project. Here the authors argued that we don't need an ideological or religious explanation for the fur trade. As Charles Hudson writes,

Now Tompkins begins stage five of her journey, summarizing a collection of essays that run counter to Martin's way of thinking.

> The Southeastern Indians slaughtered deer (and were prompted to enslave and kill each other) because of their position on the outer fringes of an expanding modern world-system. . . . In the modern world-system there is a core region which establishes *economic* relations with its colonial periphery. . . . If the Indians could not produce commodities, they were on the road to cultural extinction. . . . To maximize his chances for survival, an eighteenth-century Southeastern Indian had to . . . live in the interior, out of range of European cattle, forestry, and agriculture. . . . He had to produce a commodity which was valuable enough to earn him some protection from English slavers.

24   Though we are talking here about Southeastern Indians, rather than the subarctic and Northeastern tribes Martin studied, what really accounts for these divergent explanations of why Indians slaughtered the game are the assumptions that underlie them. Martin believes that the Indians acted on the basis of perceptions made available to them by their own cosmology; that is, he explains their behavior as the Indians themselves would have explained it (insofar as he can), using a logic and a set of values that are not Eurocentric but derived from within Amerindian culture. Hudson, on the other hand, insists that the Indians' own beliefs are irrelevant to an explanation of how they acted, which can only be understood, as far as he is concerned, in the terms of a Western materialist economic and political analysis. Martin and Hudson, in short, don't agree on what counts as an explanation, and this disagreement sheds light on the preceding accounts as well. From this standpoint, we can see that Vaughan, who thought that the Puritans were superior to the Indians, and Jennings, who thought the reverse, are both, like Hudson, using Eurocentric criteria of description and evaluation. While all three critics (Vaughan, Jennings, and Hudson) acknowledge that Indians and Europeans behave differently from one another, the behavior differs, as it were, within the order of the same: all three assume, though only Hudson makes the assumption explicit, that an understanding of relations between the Europeans and the Indians must

Tompkins again helps readers get their bearings by summarizing her understanding of what she has learned up to this point in her journey.

Then she reiterates the basic poststructuralist dilemma posed

earlier: How can you get at the truth about an event when every account is biased?

Tompkins describes a new strategy for determining which perspectives are valid.

In the essay's final section, Tompkins works out her solution to the problem she has examined. Here the ellipses indicate a long section we have omitted in which she analyzes a variety of historical documents.

be elaborated in European terms. In Martin's analysis, however, what we have are not only two different sets of behavior but two incommensurable ways of describing and assigning meaning to events. This difference at the level of explanation calls into question the possibility of obtaining any theory-independent account of interaction between Indians and Europeans.

At this point, dismayed and confused by the wildly divergent views of colonial history the twentieth-century historians had provided, I decided to look at some primary materials. I thought, perhaps, if I looked at some firsthand accounts and at some scholars looking at those accounts, it would be possible to decide which experts were right and which were wrong by comparing their views with the evidence. Captivity narratives seemed a good place to begin, since it was logical to suppose that the records left by whites who had been captured by Indians would furnish the sort of first-hand information I wanted. . . . 25

After a while it began to seem to me that there was something wrong with the way I had formulated the problem. . . . 26

My problem presupposed that I couldn't judge because I didn't know what the facts were. All I had, or could have, was a series of different perspectives, and so nothing that would count as an authoritative source on which moral judgments could be based. But, as I have just shown, I did judge, and that is because, as I now think, I did have some facts. I seemed to accept as facts that ninety percent of the native American population of New England died after the first hundred years of contact, that tribes in eastern Canada and the northeastern United States had a compact with the game they killed, that Comanches had subjected a captive girl to casual cruelty, that King Philip smoked a pipe, and so on. It was only where different versions of the same event came into conflict that I doubted the text was a record of something real. And even then, there was no question about certain major catastrophes. I believed that four hundred Pequots were killed near Saybrook, that Winthrop was the Governor of the Massachusetts Bay Colony when it happened, and so on. My sense that certain events, such as the Pequot War, did occur in no way reflected the indecisiveness that overtook me when I tried to choose among the various historical versions. In fact, the need I felt to make up my mind was impelled by the conviction that certain things *had* happened that shouldn't have happened. Hence it was never the case that "what happened" was completely unknowable or unavailable. It's rather that in the process of reading so many different approaches to the same phenomenon I became aware of the difference in the attitudes that informed these approaches. This awareness of the interests motivating each version cast suspicion over everything, in retrospect, and I ended by claiming that there was nothing I could know. This, I now see, was never really the case. But how did it happen? 27

Tompkins acknowledges and demonstrates how her own method of reading all these documents reflects her own historical perspective.

Someone else, confronted with the same materials, could have decided that one of these historical accounts was correct. Still another person might have decided that more evidence was needed in order to decide among them. Why did I conclude that none of the accounts was accurate because they were all produced from some particular angle of vision? Presumably there was something in my background that enabled me to see the problem in this way. . . . 28

What this means for the problem I've been addressing is that I must piece together the story of European-Indian relations as best I can, believing this version up to a point, that version not at all, another almost entirely, according to what seems reasonable and 29 plausible, given everything else that I know. And this, as I've shown, is what I was already doing in the back of my mind without realizing it, because there was nothing else I *could* do. If the accounts don't fit together neatly, that is not a reason for rejecting them all in favor of a metadiscourse about epistemology; on the contrary, one encounters contradictory facts and divergent points of view in practically every phase of life, from deciding whom to marry to choosing the right brand of cat food, and one decides as best one can given the evidence available. It is only the nature of the academic situation which makes it appear that one can linger on the threshold of decision in the name of an epistemological principle. What has really happened in such a case is that the subject of debate has changed from the question of what happened in a particular instance to the question of how knowledge is arrived at. The absence of pressure to decide what happened creates the possibility for this change of venue.

30   The change of venue, however, is itself an action taken. In diverting attention from the original problem and placing it where Miller did, on "the mind of man," it once again ignores what happened and still is happening to American Indians. The moral problem that confronts me now is not that I can never have any facts to go on, but that the work I do is not directed toward solving the kinds of problems that studying the history of European-Indian relations has awakened me to.

Thinking Critically About " 'Indians' "

1. Tompkins's essay is about her struggle to find out "what had happened between the English settlers and the natives in seventeenth-century New England." Explain in your own words why Tompkins's study of various historians didn't lead to a direct answer to her question.

2. Tompkins's journey begins with her shocked revelation that historian Perry Miller (one of the great U.S. historians writing in the 1950s) didn't "see" the Indians. He talks instead about the movement of European culture into the "vacant wilderness" of America. To try to understand Miller, Tompkins reads his discussion of his experience in Africa. Tompkins concludes: "[W]hat is invisible to the historian in his own historical moment remains invisible when he turns his gaze to the past." What does Tompkins mean? How does Miller's preface support her claim?

3. Trace the competing theses of each of the historians that Tompkins reads. How does Tompkins show that each thesis is "determined through and through by the observer's frame of reference"?

4. One fact on which historians agree is that Native Americans participated in the fur trade by exchanging furs for guns, copper kettles, and woolen blankets. Historians disagree, however, on why Native Americans sold furs to the white traders. What is the traditional explanation? How does Calvin Martin's explanation (in *Keepers of the Game*) differ from the traditional view? How does Charles Hudson attack Martin?

5. In the final section of her essay, Tompkins explains her own solution to the dilemma she has explored. In your own words, how does she resolve her dilemma? Do you find her resolution satisfactory? How does her resolution give rise to the "moral dilemma" she poses in her last sentence?

■ COMPOSING YOUR EXPLORATORY ESSAY

Generating and Exploring Ideas

Your process of generating and exploring ideas is, in essence, the *subject matter* of your exploratory paper. This section should help you get started and keep going.

Keeping a Research Log

Since this assignment asks you to create a chronologically organized account of your thinking process, you will need to keep a careful, detailed record of your investigation. The best tool for doing so is a research log or journal in which you take notes on your sources and record your thinking throughout the process.

As you investigate your issue, keep a chronologically organized account that includes notes on your readings, interviews, and significant conversations, plus explorations of how each of these sources, new perspectives, or data influence your current thinking. Many writers keep a double-entry notebook that has a "notes" section, in which you summarize key points, record data, copy potentially usable quotations verbatim, and so forth, and a "reflections" section, in which you write a strong response to the reading exploring how it advanced your thinking, raised questions, or pulled you in one direction or another. (For an example, see "Sam's Notes on *Newsweek* Article" on pages 188–89.)

As you write your exploratory essay, your research log will be your main source for details—evidence of what you were thinking at regular intervals throughout the process.*

Exploring Possible Problems for Your Essay

Your instructor may assign you a specific problem to explore. If not, then your first step is to choose a question, problem, or issue that currently perplexes you. Perhaps a question is problematic to you because you haven't studied it (How serious is the problem of global warming? How can we keep pornography away from children on the Internet?) or because the available factual data seem conflicting and inconclusive (Should postmenopausal women take supplemental estrogen?), or because the problem or issue draws you into an uncomfortable conflict of values (Should we legalize drugs? Where do I stand on abortion?).

The key to this assignment is to choose a question, problem, or issue *that truly perplexes you.* The more clearly readers sense your personal engagement with the problem, the more likely they are to be engaged by your writing. Note: If your instructor pairs this assignment with a later one, be sure that your question is appropriate for the later assignment. Check with your instructor.

---

*For those of you majoring in science or engineering, this research log is similar to the laboratory notebooks that are required parts of any original research in science or industry. Besides recording in detail the progress of your research, these notebooks often serve as crucial data in patent applications or liability lawsuits. Doctors and nurses keep similar logs in their medical records file for each patient. This is a time-honored practice. In Mary Shelley's early nineteenth-century novel *Frankenstein,* the monster learns about the process of his creation by reading Dr. Frankenstein's laboratory journal.

Here are several exercises to help you think of ideas for this essay.

Exploration Exercise 1.   In your research log, make a list of issues or problems that both interest and perplex you. Then choose two or three of your issues and freewrite about them for five minutes or so, exploring questions such as these: Why am I interested in this problem? What makes the problem problematic? What makes this problem significant? Share your list of questions and your freewrites with friends and classmates. Discussing questions with friends often stimulates you to think of more questions yourself or to sharpen the focus of questions you have already asked.

Exploration Exercise 2.   If your exploratory essay is paired with a subsequent assignment, look at the invention exercises for that assignment to help you ask a question that fits the context of the final paper you will write.

Exploration Exercise 3.   A particularly valuable kind of problem to explore for this assignment is a public controversy. Often such issues involve complex disagreements about facts and values that merit careful, open-ended exploration. This assignment invites you to explore and clarify where you stand on such complex public issues as gay marriages, overcrowded prisons, the Endangered Species Act, funding of Medicare or Social Security, public funding of the arts, and so forth. These issues make particularly good topics for persuasive papers or formal research papers, if either is required in your course. For this exercise, look through a current newspaper or weekly newsmagazine and in your research log make a list of public issues that you would like to know more about. Use the following trigger question:

> I don't know where I stand on the issue of _____.

Share your list with classmates and friends.

Formulating a Starting Point

After you've chosen a problem or issue, write a research-log entry identifying the problem or issue you have chosen and explaining why you are perplexed by and interested in it. You might start out with a sharp, clearly focused question (for example, "Should the United States eliminate welfare payments for single mothers?"). Often, however, formulating the question turns out to be part of the *process* of writing the exploratory paper. Many writers don't start with a single, focused question but rather with a whole cluster of related questions swimming in their heads. This practice is all right—in fact, it is healthy—as long as you have a direction in which to move after the initial starting point. Even if you do start with a focused question, it is apt to evolve as your thinking progresses.

For this exercise, choose the question, problem, or issue you plan to investigate and write a research-log entry explaining how you got interested in that question and why you find it both problematic and significant. This will be the *starting point* for your essay; it might even serve as the rough draft for your introduction. Many instructors will collect this exploration as a quick check on whether you have formulated a good question that promises fruitful results.

Here is how one student, Sam, wrote the starting-point entry for his research log.

Sam's Starting Point Research-Log Entry

I want to focus on the question of whether women should be allowed to serve in combat units in the military. I became interested in the issue of women in combat through my interest in gays in the military. While I saw that gays in the military was an important political issue for gay rights, I, like many gays, had no real desire to be in such a macho organization. But perhaps that was just the point—we had the opportunity to break stereotypes and attack areas most hostile to us.

Similarly, I wonder whether feminists see women in combat as a crucial symbolic issue for women's rights. (I wonder too whether it is a *good* symbol, since many women value a less masculine approach to the world.) I think my instinct right now is that women should be allowed to serve in combat units. I think it is wrong to discriminate against women. Yet I also think America needs to have a strong military. Therefore, I am in a quandary. If putting women in combat wouldn't harm our military power, then I am fully in favor of women in combat. But if it would hurt our military power, then I have to make a value judgment. So I guess I have a lot to think about as I research this issue. I decided to focus on the women issue rather than the gay issue because it poses more of a dilemma for me. I am absolutely in favor of gays in the military, so I am not very open-minded about *exploring* that issue. But the women's issue is more of a problem for me.

Continuing with Research and Dialectic Thinking

After you have formulated your starting point, you need to proceed with research, keeping a research log that records both your reading notes and your strong-response reflections to each reading.

After Sam wrote his starting-point entry, he created an initial bibliography by searching his college library's INFOTRAC. He decided to try keeping his research log in a double-entry format. What follows is his research-log entry for the first article he read, a piece from *Newsweek*.

Sam's Notes on *Newsweek* Article

Notes

Hackworth, David H. "War and the Second Sex." *Newsweek* 5 Aug. 1991: 24–28.

- Ideals in conflict are equality and combat readiness.
- Acknowledges women's bravery, competence, and education (uses the Gulf War as an example). Admits that there are some women as strong and fit as the strongest men (gives some examples), but then argues that allowing even these women in combat is the type of experimentation that the army doesn't need right now. (He says women already have plenty of jobs open for them in noncombat units).
- Biggest problem is "gender norming"—having different physical standards for men and women. A 22-year-old female is allowed three more minutes

than a 22-year-old male to run two miles; men have to climb a 20-foot rope in 30 seconds; women can take 50 seconds.

- One of Hackworth's big values is male bonding. He points to "male bonding" as a key to unit cohesion. Men have been socialized to think that women must be protected. He uses Israel as an example:

  "The Israeli Army put women on the front lines in 1948. The experiment ended disastrously after only three weeks. It wasn't that the women couldn't fight. It was that they got blown apart. Female casualties demoralized the men and gutted unit cohesion." (pp. 26–27)

- Another major problem is pregnancy causing women to leave a unit. He says that 10 to 15 percent of servicewomen wear maternity uniforms in a given year. During the Gulf War, pregnancy rates soared. 1200 pregnant women were evacuated from the gulf (p. 28) during the war. On one destroyer tender, 36 female crew members got pregnant (p. 28). These pregnancies leave vacancies in a unit that can destroy its effectiveness.

- He claims that women soldiers themselves had so many complaints about their experiences in the Gulf War (fraternization, sexual harassment, lack of privacy, primitive living conditions) that they said "don't rush to judgment on women in combat" (p. 28).

Reflections

Some challenging points, but not completely convincing. His biggest reason for opposing women in combat is harm to unit morale, but this isn't convincing to me. The Israeli example seems like unconvincing evidence seeing how those soldiers' attitudes in 1948 reflected a much different society.

Issue of pregnancy is more convincing. A pregnant woman, unlike a father-to-be, cannot continue to fill her role as a combat soldier. I was shocked by the number of pregnancies during the Gulf War and by the extent (although Hackworth doesn't give statistics) of the fraternization (he says the army passed out over a million condoms—p. 28).

I am also bothered by the gender-norming issue. It seems to me that there ought to be some absolute standards of strength and endurance needed for combat duty and the military ought to exclude both men and women who don't meet them. This would mean that a lower percentage of women than men would be eligible, but is that discrimination?

Where do I now stand? Well, I am still leaning toward believing that women should be allowed to serve in combat, but I see that there are a number of sub-questions involved. Should physical standards for combat positions be the same for men and women? Will the presence of women really hurt morale in a mostly male unit? Should women be given special consideration for their roles as mothers? How serious a problem is pregnancy? I also see another problem: Should physically eligible women be *required* (e.g., drafted) to serve in combat the same way men are drafted into combat positions? And I still want to know whether this is a crucial issue for the women's rights movement.

In the next section we see how Sam converts material from his research log into a draft of his exploratory essay.

Shaping and Drafting

Your exploratory essay should offer accounts of your search procedures (useful conversations with friends, strategies for tracking down sources, use of indexes or computer searches, strokes of good fortune at stumbling on good leads, and so forth) and your thought processes (what you were discovering, how your ideas were evolving). Drawing on your research log, you can share your frustration when a promising source turned out to be off the mark or your perplexity when a conversation with a friend over late-night espresso forced you to rethink your views. Hook your readers by making your exploratory essay read like a detective story. Consider giving your account immediacy by quoting your thoughts at the very moment you wrote a log entry. The general shape of an exploratory essay can take the following pattern:

1. Starting point: you describe your initial problem, why you are interested in it, why it is problematic, why it is worth pursuing.
2. New input: you read an article, interview someone, pose an alternative solution.
   a. Summarize, describe, or explain the new input.
   b. Discuss the input, analyzing or evaluating it, playing the believing and doubting game with it, exploring how this input affects your thinking.
   c. Decide where to go next—find an alternative view, pursue a subquestion, seek more data, and so forth.
3. More new input: you repeat step 2 for your next piece of research.
4. Still more new input.
5. Ending point: you sum up where you stand at the point when the paper is due, how much your thinking about the issue has changed, whether or not you've reached a satisfactory solution.

Here is how Sam converted his starting-point entry (see p. 188) and his first research entry (pp. 188–89) into the opening pages of his exploratory essay.

Should Women Be Allowed to Serve in Combat Units?

Sam Scofield

At first, I wanted to explore the issue of gays in the military. But since I am a gay man I already knew where I stood on that issue and didn't find it truly problematic *for myself*. So I decided to shift my question to whether women should be allowed to serve in combat units. I wasn't sure whether feminists see the issue of women in combat the same way that gays see the military issue. Is it important to the feminist cause for women to be in combat? Or should feminists seek a kind of political order that avoids combat and doesn't settle issues through macho male behavior? In my initial thinking, I was also concerned about maintaining our country's military strength. In my "starting point" entry of my research log, I recorded the following thoughts:

> If putting women in combat wouldn't harm our military power, then I am fully in favor of women in combat. But if it would hurt our military power, then I have to make a value judgment.

So I decided that what I should do first is find some general background reading on the women in combat question. I went to the library, plugged the key words "woman and combat" into our online INFOTRAC database, and found a dozen entries just for the last two years. I went to the stacks and found the most familiar magazine in my initial list: *Newsweek*.

I began with an article by a retired Air Force colonel, David H. Hackworth. Hackworth was opposed to women in combat and focused mainly on the standard argument I was expecting—namely that women in combat would destroy male bonding. He didn't provide any evidence, however, other than citing the case of Israel in 1948.

> The Israeli Army put women on the front lines in 1948. The experiment ended disastrously after only three weeks. It wasn't that the women couldn't fight. It was that they got blown apart. Female casualties demoralized the men and gutted unit cohesion. (26–27)

However, this argument wasn't very persuasive to me. I thought that men's attitudes had changed a lot since 1948 and that cultural changes would allow us to get used to seeing both men and women as *people* so that it would be equally bad—or equally bearable—to see either men or women wounded and killed in combat.

But Hackworth did raise three points that I hadn't anticipated, and that really set me thinking. First he said that the military had different physical fitness requirements for men and women (for example, women had three minutes longer to run two miles than did men [25]). As I said in my research log, "It seems to me that there ought to be some absolute standards of strength and endurance needed for combat duty and the military ought to exclude both men and women who don't meet them." A second point was that an alarming number of female soldiers got pregnant in the Gulf War (1200 pregnant soldiers had to be evacuated [28]) and that prior to the war about 10–15 percent of female soldiers were pregnant at any given time (28). His point was that a pregnant woman, unlike a father-to-be, cannot continue to fill her role as a combat soldier. When she leaves her unit, she creates a dangerous gap that makes it hard for the unit to accomplish its mission. Finally, Hackworth cited lots of actual women soldiers in the Gulf War who were opposed to women in combat. They raised issues such as fraternization, sexual harassment, lack of privacy, and primitive living conditions.

Although Hackworth didn't turn me against wanting women to be able to serve in combat, he made the issue much more problematic for me. I now realized that this issue contained a lot of sub-issues, so I decided to focus first on the two major ones for me: (1) How important is this issue to feminists? This concern is crucial for me because I want to support equal rights for women just as I want to do so for gays or ethnic minorities. And (2) How serious are the pregnancy and strength-test issues in terms of maintaining military strength?

As I read the rest of the articles on my list, I began paying particular attention to these issues. The next article that advanced my thinking was. . . .

Revising

Because an exploratory essay describes the writer's research and thinking in chronological order, most writers have little trouble with organization. When they revise, their major concern is often to improve their essay's interest level by keeping it focused and lively. Exploratory essays grow tedious if the pace crawls too slowly or if extraneous details appear. They also tend to become too long, so that condensing and pruning become key revision tasks. The draft here is actually Sam's second draft; the first draft was a page longer and incorporated many more details and quotations from the Hackworth article. Sam eliminated these because he realized that his purpose was not to report on Hackworth, but to describe the evolution of his own thinking. By condensing the Hackworth material, Sam saved room for the ideas he discovered later.

Peer reviewers can give you valuable feedback about the pace and interest level of an exploratory piece. They can also help you achieve the right balance between external details (how you did the research, to whom you talked, where you were) and mental details (what you were thinking about). As you revise, make sure you follow proper stylistic conventions for quotations and citations (see Chapter 22).

g u i d e l i n e s
for Peer Reviewers

Instructions for peer reviews, including use of these guidelines, are provided in Chapter 17, pages 429–35. To write a peer review for a classmate, use your own paper, numbering your responses to correspond to the questions on the guidelines. At the head of your paper place the author's name and your own name, as shown.

Author's Name: _____

Peer Reviewer's Name: _____

 I. Read the draft at a normal reading speed from beginning to end. As you read, do the following:
    A. Place a wavy line in the margin next to any passages that you find confusing, that contain something that doesn't seem to fit, or that otherwise slow down your reading.
    B. Place a "Good!" in the margin next to any passages where you think the writing is particularly strong or interesting.
 II. Read the draft again slowly and answer the following questions by writing brief explanations of your answers.
    A. Posing the problem:
       1. Does the essay have an effective title that identifies the problem to be examined and engages your interest? How might the title be improved?

2. Has the writer posed the initial problem effectively, showing why it is interesting, problematic, and significant?
3. Does the opening provide cues showing that the writer's purpose is to explore a question rather than argue a thesis? How could the writer improve the opening section of the paper?

B. Narrating the exploration:
1. Is the body of the paper organized chronologically so that the reader sees the gradual development of the writer's thinking?
2. How has the writer revealed the stages or changes in his or her thinking about the problem?
3. Has the writer done enough research to explore the problem? Are there additional ideas or perspectives that you think the writer should consider? Are there ideas that you would like to challenge? Can you make suggestions for further research?
4. How might the writer improve the clarity or structure of the draft?
5. Does the ending of the essay sum up the evolution of the writer's thinking and clarify why the writer has or has not resolved the problem?

C. Sum up what you see as the chief strengths and problem areas of this draft.
1. Strengths
2. Problem areas

III. Read the draft one more time. Place a check in the margin wherever you notice problems in grammar, spelling, or mechanics (one check per problem).

Writing an Informative (and Surprising) Essay

▰ ABOUT INFORMATIVE (AND SURPRISING) WRITING

Throughout this text we have encouraged the habit of considering alternative solutions to a problem. This chapter shows you how to amplify that habit through the use of a powerful rhetorical strategy for thesis-based essays: the *problem/ expected answer/surprising reversal* pattern. This pattern creates tension between your own thesis and one or more opposing views.

The concept of *surprising reversal* spurs you to go beyond the commonplace to change your reader's view of a topic. As we discussed in Chapters 3 and 4, writers of thesis-based prose usually try to change a reader's view in one of three ways, corresponding to three of the broadly defined purposes of writing.

1. *Informative purpose:* *enlarging* readers' views of a topic by providing new information or otherwise teaching them something about the topic they didn't know ("People my parents' age commonly think that men with tattoos are sleezy, macho bikers or waterfront sailors, but I will show them that many younger people get tattoos for deeply personal and spiritual reasons.")
2. *Analytical or interpretive purpose:* *clarifying* readers' views of a topic by bringing critical thinking to bear on problematic data or on a problematic text ("Most people think that this jeans ad reveals a liberated woman, but on closer inspection we see that the woman fulfills traditional gender stereotypes.")
3. *Persuasive purpose:* *restructuring* readers' views of a topic by causing them to choose the writer's position rather than a competing position on a controversial issue ("Many readers believe that the federal government should legalize cocaine and heroin, but I will show that legalizing such drugs would be disastrous.")

The surprising reversal pattern occurs whenever you contrast your reader's original view of a topic with your own new or surprising view. The pattern's power isn't that it tells you what to say about the topic or how to organize the main body of your essay. Its power is that it automatically gives your thesis tension. It pushes your view up against the commonplace or expected views that are likely to be shared by your audience. Although the assignment for this chapter is limited to the first purpose listed (writing to inform), the surprising reversal pattern works well also for the purposes of analysis or persuasion. You may find yourself using variations of this pattern for the remaining essay assignments in Part Two.

◪ EXPLORING INFORMATIVE (AND SURPRISING) WRITING

Your goal for this activity is to discover unique knowledge or experience that gives each member of your class an uncommon perspective on some topic.

For the first part of this task, work privately at your desk for five or ten minutes. Consider one of the following trigger questions:

> Based on my personal experience, reading, research, or observation, what information or knowledge do I have about X that is different from the popular view of X?

or

> Although people commonly regard X this way, my personal experience, observation, or research shows X to be this other way.

In response to these trigger questions, brainstorm as many possible Xs as you can, using freewriting, idea mapping, or simple list making. Here are some examples from recent students.

> Most people think that having an alcoholic mother would be the worst thing that could happen to you, but my mother's disease forced our family closer together.

> Most people think that Native Americans lived in simple harmony with the earth, but my research reveals that they often "controlled" nature by setting fire to forests to make farming easier or to improve hunting.

> Most people think of pawnshops as sleazy, disreputable places, but my experience shows pawn shops can be honest, wholesome businesses that perform a valuable social service.

> Most people think of the film *Frankenstein* as a monster movie about science gone amuck, but to the gay community it holds a special and quite different meaning.

> Most people believe that operating your own AM radio station would be both illegal and expensive, but my research has revealed a cheap and legal way to become a disk jockey on your own AM station.

After everyone has brainstormed at least a few such statements, work in small groups or as a whole class to refine and share ideas. Most people think of many more possibilities once they begin hearing what their classmates are saying. Keep helping classmates until everyone in the class has at least one satisfactory topic.

WRITING PROJECT

Write a short informative essay following the surprising reversal pattern. Imagine an audience of general readers who hold a common view of your topic. Your purpose is to give them a new, surprising view. Pose a question, provide the commonly accepted answer to the question, and then give your own surprising answer, based on information derived from personal experience, observation, or research.

This assignment asks you to use your own personal experiences, observation, or research to enlarge your reader's view of a subject in a surprising way. The introduction of your essay should engage your reader's interest in a question and provide needed background or context. Do not put your thesis early in the introduction; instead, delay it until after you have explained the common, expected answer to your opening question. This delay in presenting the thesis creates a slightly open-form feel that readers often find engaging.

You might wonder why we call this assignment informative writing rather than persuasive writing, since we emphasize reversing a reader's view. The difference is in the kind of question posed and the reader's stance toward the writer. In persuasive writing the question being posed is controversial (Should drugs be legalized? Is the greenhouse effect currently warming the earth?), with strong, rational arguments on all sides. Often, disputes about values are as prevalent as disputes about facts. When writing persuasive prose, you imagine a resistant reader who may argue back.

With informative prose, the stakes are lower, and you can imagine a more trusting reader willing to learn from your experiences or research. You are enlarging your reader's view of the topic by presenting unexpected or surprising information, but you aren't necessarily saying that the common view is wrong, nor are you initiating a debate. In the examples in the preceding exploratory activity, the student writers aren't arguing whether alcoholic mothers are good or bad, whether all pawnshops are honest, or whether it is right to get a tattoo or build a personal radio station. They are simply offering readers new, unexpected, and expanded views of their topics.

For this assignment, avoid controversial issues that engender debate (save these issues for the chapters on persuasion, Chapters 14–16), and focus on how you, through your personal experience or research, can enlarge your reader's view of a topic by providing unexpected or surprising information.

◢ UNDERSTANDING INFORMATIVE (AND SURPRISING) WRITING

When we speak of informative writing aimed at surprise, we mean thesis-based prose that is consciously intended to surprise the reader with an unexpected view. Such an essay represents only one kind of informative writing. Other kinds include encyclopedia articles, technical manuals, budget reports, experimental observations, instruction sheets, and many kinds of college textbooks—all of which convey detailed information without being thesis based and without intending to surprise the reader with an unexpected view. Readers turn to these other forms of informative writing when they need straightforward factual information. Often in your college and professional career you will be called upon to write straightforward informative prose without the surprising reversal pattern.

The essay you will write for this assignment is thus more provocative, more like the kinds of self-contained essays published in magazines or journals, for which the audience isn't ready-made, as it is for a budget report or a case observation in nursing. Your essay will need to hook your readers and sustain their interest by showing them a surprising new way of seeing your subject.

Because of its power to hook and sustain readers, examples of surprising reversal essays can be found in almost any publication—from scholarly journals to easy-reading magazines. Here, for example, are abstracts of several articles from the table of contents pages of recent issues of *Atlantic Monthly*.

"Reefer Madness" by Eric Schlosser

Marijuana has been pushed so far out of the public imagination by other drugs, and its use is so casually taken for granted in some quarters of society, that one might assume it had been effectively decriminalized. In truth, the government has never been tougher on marijuana offenders than it is today. In an era when violent criminals frequently walk free or receive modest jail terms, tens of thousands of people are serving long sentences for breaking marijuana laws.

"The Sex-Bias Myth in Medicine" by Andrew G. Kadar

A view has gained wide currency that men's health complaints are taken more seriously than those of women, and that medical research has benefited men more than it has women. "In fact," the author writes, "one sex does appear to be favored in the amount of attention devoted to its medical needs. . . . That sex is not men, however."

" 'It's Not the Economy, Stupid' " by Charles R. Morris

The conventional assumption, on which national elections often turn, is that one of the President's jobs is to "manage" the American economy: to make detailed economic actions that have precise results. But the truth is, the author writes, that managing the economy in this sense is far beyond any President's power—and, indeed, beyond the power of economics.

"Midlife Myths" by Winifred Gallagher

The idea that middle age is a dismal stage of life—scarred by traumas of personal crisis and physical change—is both firmly entrenched and almost completely untrue. The image in many Americans' minds, the author writes, is derived "not from the ordinary experiences of most people but from the unusual experiences of a few."

Each of these articles asserts a surprising new position that counters a commonly held view.

Common View	Surprising View
Because marijuana laws are no longer enforced, marijuana use has effectively become decriminalized.	The government has never been tougher on marijuana offenders than it is today.
More research dollars are spent on men's diseases than on women's diseases.	The reverse is true: more money is spent on women's diseases.
One of the president's jobs is to manage the economy by taking detailed economic action.	The economy is too complicated to be controlled by presidential action.
Middle age is a dismal stage of life.	The widespread notion of midlife crises is a myth based on the unusual experiences of the few.

A similar pattern is often found in scholarly academic writing, which has the following typical underlying shape:

> Whereas scholar A says X, scholar B says Y, and scholar C says Z, my research reveals Q.

Because the purpose of academic research is to advance knowledge, an academic article almost always shows the writer's new view against a background of prevailing views (what previous scholars have said).

READINGS

To help you understand the surprising reversal pattern in more detail, let's look at some complete essays. We begin with an easy-reading piece from *America West Airlines Magazine*. The topic, tarantulas, is particularly relevant to travelers on America West Airlines, which has a hub in Arizona, where tarantulas are plentiful. Note that the writer's strategy is to sum up the common view of these creatures and then to counter it with his own thesis.

LEO W. BANKS

NOT GUILTY: DESPITE ITS FEARSOME IMAGE, THE TARANTULA IS A BENIGN BEAST

If an insect ever had an image problem, it is the tarantula. Big, dark and hairy, tarantulas cause even the bold among us to back up a little and shiver reflexively. 1

No doubt that's part of the reason why Hollywood has made the creepy crawlies a movie-industry tradition. In the not-so-subtle 1955 sci-fi film *Tarantula*, for example, a scientist grows a 100-foot-tall version that chews up cars. The horror doesn't end until air force pilots hose the giant bug with napalm. 2

3   Science fiction isn't the only culprit. In *Dr. No,* the usually composed James Bond goes into a frenzy after being awakened by a tarantula crawling on his shoulder. Bond won the duel by frantically smashing the bug with a shoe.

4   These days Hollywood pays about $75 a day to rent a tarantula, a cheap price for such a grand and terrifying illusion. Illusion is the key word, for virtually everything the movies want the public to believe about tarantulas is false. The unexciting truth is that they are relatively benign insects. "The occurrence of humans being bitten by tarantulas is almost nonexistent," says Howard Lawler, curator of small animals at the Arizona-Sonora Desert Museum in Tucson, Arizona. "You have to practically hold one against your body or press it in your hand to make it bite you."

5   And when tarantulas do bite, the sensation is about as severe as an ant bite or bee sting. What's more, scientists say tarantula venom isn't especially potent and rarely is employed in defensive bites against humans. Instead, tarantulas save their venom, which is also a digestive enzyme, for use against natural prey. "Some people have a reaction to [the venom], but for others it's no problem," says Mike Carrington, a Tucson pet store owner. "I've been bitten several times and it doesn't bother me at all."

6   Found in much of the Southern and Western United States, tarantulas live in burrows—cylindrical foot-deep holes in the ground that usually are lined with silk. Life expectancy is 10 years for males and 25 years for females, who never venture farther than 6 feet from their burrows.

7   The spiders typically feed on crickets, grasshoppers and even small mice. Because of their bad eyesight, they rely on vibration-sensing organs in their feet to pick up the movements of passing prey. "In the darkness, if you drop a beetle from 6 feet above the head of a tarantula resting near its burrow, the tarantula will, in a millisecond, race out and grab it and return to the burrow," says Steve Prchal, president of Sonoran Arthropod Studies Inc., a non-profit organization in Tucson dedicated to public education about insects.

8   Predators, even large ones, often find tarantulas more than a match. If confronted by a curious fox, for example, a tarantula will scoop the hairs off its abdomen and toss them into the fox's eyes. The hairs, which are sharp and contain a venom, irritate and usually distract the animal long enough to allow the tarantula to escape.

9   Ironically, the male tarantula's worst enemy is probably the female. "If she is hungry enough, the female will sometimes try to eat the male during mating," Prchal says. As a defense, males have small hooks on their forelegs that can be used to grab the female's fangs to keep from being bitten.

10   Besides the bad rap they've received in Hollywood, these easygoing beasts also have been the villains of nursery rhymes—"Little Miss Muffet," for example—and folklore. One prominent superstition dates back to the Dark Ages in Europe, when people bitten by wolf spiders thought they had to dance hysterically and sweat out the creature's venom in order to survive. The ritual was called the Tarantula Dance.

11   But probably the biggest reason tarantulas are so feared is their appearance. Besides being ugly, they sport fangs that are sometimes a half-inch long and curled at the bottom. And, by spider standards, tarantulas are huge. "I have one male who, if you laid him flat, would reach 11 inches across," says Carrington, who keeps seven pet tarantulas. "Most people who come to the house don't mind my tarantulas, but my mother-in-law won't go anywhere near them."

12   Pet stores sell tarantulas, a practice discouraged by scientists, for between $7 and $35. But sales are irregular because the insects are commonly found in the wild, especially during the spring-summer mating season.

In fact, they're so plentiful that former Tucson bar owner Jack Sheaffer remembers   13
some nights when he couldn't keep tarantulas from coming into his establishment. It
made for some interesting encounters that speak not to the insect's Hollywood image,
but to its true nature. "Tarantulas never hurt anything," Sheaffer, says. "They just
wanted to come in and say hello. Once I found one snoozing in a cash box. He was a
friendly little critter."

Thinking Critically About "Not Guilty"

What ideas does Banks present as the common view of tarantulas? Where and
how does he present his thesis statement?

Banks's essay follows a formula frequently used in travel magazines: it gives
travelers a new view of a local phenomenon. What popular misconceptions might
there be about places, people, ways of life, or other phenomena in your own hometown or region? You might consider a similar topic for your own surprising
reversal essay. Working as a whole class or in small groups, brainstorm misconceptions that travelers or newcomers have about phenomena in your area or about
another area with which you are familiar.

Whereas the preceding piece is intended as light reading for airplane travelers, our next example—taken from the left-leaning political magazine *Utne
Reader*—is aimed at readers interested in the environment, the labor movement,
poverty, and other social issues. It illustrates a short informative piece using research data for support.

▬▬▬▬▬▼▬▬▬▬▬

ELAINE ROBBINS
THE NEW ECO *MOOOOVEMENT*

*Common view
that cows are
environmentally
harmful*

Environmentalists have long regarded cows as Public Enemy No. 1 in the Ameri-   1
can West. They are blamed for everything from degrading public lands and destroying
wildlife habitat to wasting energy (it takes five pounds of grain to produce one pound
of beef). Even their belching is environmentally incorrect: The methane gas they expel
contributes to the greenhouse effect.

*Thesis: Asserts
the surprising
counterview
that cows are
beneficial to the
environment*

But some ranchers and university researchers who are pioneering holistic land   2
management techniques assert that cattle grazing can actually improve the health of
grasslands. Cattle hooves till the earth, creating stable soil cover, and grazing can remove old plant material and stimulate the growth of beneficial perennial grasses. As
Dan Daggett, author of *Beyond the Rangeland Conflict: Toward a West That Works*,
points out in *Yes! A Journal of Positive Futures* (Fall 1997), this new research—and its
practical application—may hold the keys to saving our vanishing grasslands.

*Informal citation
of source—
common in
magazines that
are not scholarly
journals*

On a ranch in central Nevada, for example, a desolate 10-acre slope was suc-   3
cessfully reseeded by simply scattering hay and allowing the herd to graze and tram-
ple and fertilize it. A few months later, a tract that once barely supported tumbleweeds
had sprouted thigh-high grass. "Tests revealed that their cow-cultivated mine site had
produced more grass than some of their neighbors' irrigated hay fields—and had done
it on less than six inches of moisture," Daggett writes.

4   Former Zimbabwean wildlife manager Allan Savory has taught this cultivation method to thousands of ranchers throughout the West after making similar observations on the savannas of Africa. While the grazing of domestic cattle often leaves the land ruined, migrating herds who feed and leave actually improve the soil.

5   Some environmentalists regard these arguments as a thinly veiled attempt to create positive PR for the embattled cow at a time when various interests are duking it out in Washington over a hike in public land grazing fees. "I don't deny that Savory grazers have revolutionized [ranching]," says Dan Heinz, a grazing consultant for several environmental groups. "But they also need to realize that extended rest can have benefits, too." *Anticipates an objection*

6   On another front, environmental groups such as the Nature Conservancy have begun working with ranchers to fight a common enemy: suburban sprawl. They want to preserve large open tracts of land, which they consider critical corridors for migrating wildlife. *Cites another way that ranchers can contribute to improving the environment*

7   Such a partnership could be good news for the American rancher, who, if overgrazing continues, could find himself relegated to Marlboro ads and coffee-table books. Those ranchers who work to keep the entire ecosystem healthy may be the ones who survive in the long run.

Thinking Critically About "The New Eco *Moooovement*"

1. Explain in your own words what is surprising about this essay.
2. Paragraph 5 raises a problem: When is information simply factual truth and when is it a partial or limited truth serving the writer's cause? (Chapters 5 and 6 on rhetorical observing and reading explore this problem extensively.) Explain in your own words why some environmentalists see the research of Daggett and Savory as "positive PR for the embattled cow." How could a researcher or scholar try to resolve this controversy?

Our next reading is by student writer Cheryl Carp, whose experience doing volunteer outreach in a maximum security prison enabled her to reverse stereotyped ideas about prisoners. She wrote the following essay for her freshman English class.

▼

CHERYL CARP (STUDENT)
BEHIND STONE WALLS

1   For about eight hours out of every month I am behind the stone walls of the Monroe State Penitentiary. No, that's not the sentencing procedure of some lenient judge; I am part of a group of inmates and outsiders who identify themselves as Concerned Lifers. Concerned Lifers is an organization operating both inside and outside of prison walls. Inside Monroe there are close to thirty men who take part in the organization and its activities, all of whom have been given life sentences. Concerned Lifers outside the prison visit the prisoners, take part in the organization's meetings, and then split into

various small groups for personal conversation. I became involved in this exciting group as a personal sponsor (able to visit the prison alone for special activities) after attending my first meeting inside Monroe State Penitentiary. That first drive to Monroe seemed to take forever. Looking out the window of that twelve-seater van filled with apprehensive first-time volunteers, I kept my eyes on the evening sky and tried to imagine what it would be like to be shut up in prison for life, never to see this beautiful scenery again. I was not scared, but I was nervous and could feel my pulse rate steadily rise as I began to see the green and white road signs to the prison. As the van slowly climbed the hill to the guard tower at the top, I wondered what it would be like to visit this maximum security prison.

Many people believe that visiting a prison would be frightening. Most people typically picture dangerous men lurking in every corner. The guards are yelling and the men are fighting; the men are covered with tattoos, probably carrying concealed razor blades and scowling menacingly. People think that prisons are a haven for rampant homosexuality and illegal drugs. Common belief is that the inmates are like locked animals, reaching out between the iron bars of their cages. These men are seen as sex-starved, eagerly waiting for a female body to enter their domain. The atmosphere is one of suspense, with sub-human men ready at any moment to break free and run. People I've spoken to express a fear of danger to themselves and almost a threat to their lives. They wonder how I have the nerve to do it.   2

But visiting a prison to me is an uplifting experience, far from frightening. Since that initial visit, I have returned many times to organize and participate in a clown group. The clown group is made up of about twenty of the inmates in the Concerned Lifers group and myself. The prisoners meet and rehearse once a week, and I join them every other week to critique their progress, give them pointers, and do various exercises to improve their ability.   3

The only frightening part of a visit is getting through all the guards and their red tape. Last week I drove up the hill to the guard tower, identified myself and my affiliation, and was told to "park to the left" by a disembodied voice coming from a loudspeaker. After going through many metal security doors, being checked by a metal detector that even picks up the nails in your shoes, and being escorted by numerous guards, I finally got to be with the people I had come to see.   4

The most enjoyable, exciting, and friendly time I spend at the prison is the time I spend with the boys. These people are no longer "the prisoners" or "the inmates," but are now individuals. Visiting the prison is not a frightening experience because the men inside become people, people full of emotions, creativity, and kindness. These qualities are evident in the activities and projects these men become involved in or initiate themselves. For example, one young lifer named Ken became interested in Japanese paper folding—origami. In order to pursue his interest in origami, he requested a book on the subject from the prison librarian and proceeded to teach himself. A few weeks later, I saw origami creations everywhere—flowers, dragons, and birds—all made by the guys and all done carefully and beautifully. Ken had taught his fellow inmates. Another great thing that this group has undertaken is the sponsorship of four children through an orphan relief program. The men make almost nothing at their various jobs within the prison, but what they do make they are more than willing to share, something many of us never seem to "get around to."   5

It is true that the men value the presence of a female, but not for sexual reasons. The men inside Monroe are hungry for outside companionship and understanding. They're hungry for a woman's viewpoint and conversation. They have treated me as a friend, valued my conversation, and never made sexual advances. The men behind the   6 walls are reaching through their bars not menacingly, but pleadingly—begging the outside world to take a good look at them. The men need to be looked at as people and as fellow humans in this world. Most of them are aching for a second chance at life and relationships. This is not a place for outsiders to fear, but a place to which outsiders can bring light, hope, and understanding.

7   My point is not to condone the crimes that these men may have committed in the past, but to look to the present and the future by seeing these men not as "inmates," but as individual people trying to succeed in the kind of life they now have to live.

Thinking Critically About "Behind Stone Walls"

1. What is the common view of prisoners that Cheryl Carp attempts to reverse?
2. What is her own surprising view?
3. What are the strengths and weaknesses of Cheryl's essay?

FOR WRITING AND DISCUSSION

Perhaps reading the essays by Banks, Robbins, and Carp has stimulated you to think of more possible essay topics that employ the surprising reversal pattern. The goal of this exercise is to continue brainstorming possible topics.

Form small groups. Assign a group recorder to make a two-column list, with the left column headed "Common view of X" and the right column headed "Groupmate's surprising view." Brainstorm ideas for surprising reversal essay topics until every group member has generated at least one entry for the right-hand column. Avoid repeating the topics you developed in the opening exploratory activity (p. 195). Here is a sample list entry.

Common View of X	Groupmate's Surprising View
Football offensive lineman is a no-brain, repetitive job requiring size, strength, and only enough brains and athletic ability to push people out of the way	Jeff can show that being an offensive lineman is an interesting job that requires mental smarts as well as size, strength, and athletic ability.

To help stimulate ideas, you might consider topic areas such as the following:

- *People:* computer programmers, homeless people, cheerleaders, skateboarders, gang members, priests or rabbis, feminists, housespouses, mentally ill or developmentally disabled persons.
- *Activities:* washing dishes, climbing mountains, wrestling, modeling, gardening, living with a chronic disease or disability, owning a certain breed of dog, riding a subway at night, entering a dangerous part of a city.
- *Places:* particular neighborhoods, particular buildings or parts of buildings, local attractions, junkyards, places of entertainment, summer camps.

> ■ *Other similar categories:* groups, animals and plants, and so forth; the list is endless.
>
> Next, go around the room sharing the topics you have generated with the entire class. Remember that you are not yet committed to writing about any of these topics.

Before we begin offering suggestions for composing your essay, let's look at one more example of a surprising reversal essay. This one moves up the reading dial a bit from the easy-reading airline-travel piece by Leo Banks to a more serious reading station. The article is by David Quammen, who regularly writes about nature for *Outside* magazine. As you will see shortly, this information is important because it gives you some clues about Quammen's intended audience. This article is also about Arizona spiders—written in Tucson, the same locale used by Banks—yet it couldn't be more different from Banks's article. Whereas Banks writes with a simple informative purpose, Quammen combines his informative purpose with a more complex exploratory one.

▼

DAVID QUAMMEN
THE FACE OF A SPIDER:
EYEBALL TO EYEBALL WITH THE GOOD,
THE BAD, AND THE UGLY

1   One evening a few years ago I walked back into my office after dinner and found roughly a hundred black widow spiders frolicking on my desk. I am not speaking metaphorically and I am not making this up: a hundred black widows. It was a vision of ghastly, breathtaking beauty, and it brought on me a wave of nausea. It also brought on a small moral crisis—one that I dealt with briskly, maybe rashly, in the dizziness of the moment, and that I've been turning back over in my mind ever since. I won't say I'm *haunted* by those hundred black widows, but I do remember them vividly. To me, they stand for something. They stand, in their small synecdochical way, for a large and important question.

2   The question is, How should a human behave toward the members of other living species?

3   A hundred black widows probably sounds like a lot. It is—even for Tucson, Arizona, where I was living then, a habitat in which black widows breed like rabbits and prosper like cockroaches, the females of the species growing plump as huckleberries and stringing their ragged webs in every free corner of every old shed and basement window. In Tucson, during the height of the season, a person can always on short notice round up eight or ten big, robust black widows, if that's what a person wants to do. But a hundred in one room? So all right, yes, there was a catch: These in my office were newborn babies.

4   A hundred scuttering bambinos, each one no bigger than a poppyseed. Too small still for red hourglasses, too small even for red egg timers. They had the aesthetic virtue of being so tiny that even a person of good eyesight and patient disposition could not make out their hideous little faces.

5   Their mother had sneaked in when the rains began and set up a web in the corner beside my desk. I knew she was there—I got a reminder every time I dropped a pencil and went groping for it, jerking my hand back at the first touch of that distinctive, dry, high-strength web. But I hadn't made the necessary decision about dealing with her. I knew she would have to be either murdered or else captured adroitly in a pickle jar for relocation to the wild, and I didn't especially want to do either. (I had already squashed scores of black widows during those Tucson years but by this time, I guess, I was going soft.) In the meantime, she had gotten pregnant. She had laid her eggs into a silken egg sac the size of a Milk Dud and then protected that sac vigilantly, keeping it warm, fending off any threats, as black widow mothers do. While she was waiting for the eggs to come to term, she would have been particularly edgy, particularly unforgiving, and my hand would have been in particular danger each time I reached for a fallen pencil. Then the great day arrived. The spiderlings hatched from their individual eggs, chewed their way out of the sac, and started crawling, brothers and sisters together, up toward the orange tensor lamp that was giving off heat and light on the desk of the nitwit who was their landlord.

6   By the time I stumbled in, fifty or sixty of them had reached the lampshade and rappelled back down on dainty silk lines, leaving a net of gossamer rigging between the lamp and the Darwin book (it happened to be an old edition of *Insectivorous Plants,* with marbled endpapers) that sat on the desk. Some dozen others had already managed dispersal flights, letting out strands of buoyant silk and ballooning away on rising air, as spiderlings do—in this case dispersing as far as the bookshelves. It was too late for one man to face one spider with just a pickle jar and an index card and his two shaky hands. By now I was proprietor of a highly successful black widow hatchery.

7   And the question was, How should a human behave toward the members of other living species?

8   The Jain religion of India has a strong teaching on that question. The Sanskrit word is *ahimsa,* generally rendered in English as "noninjury" or the imperative "do no harm." *Ahimsa* is the ethical centerpiece of Jainism, an absolute stricture against the killing of living beings—*any* living beings—and it led the traditional Jains to some extreme forms of observance. A rigorously devout Jain would burn no candles or lights, for instance, if there was danger a moth might fly into them. The Jain would light no fire for heating or cooking, again because it might cause the death of insects. He would cover his mouth and nose with a cloth mask, so as not to inhale any gnats. He would refrain from cutting his hair, on grounds that the lice hiding in there might be gruesomely injured by the scissors. He could not plow a field, for fear of mutilating worms. He could not work as a carpenter or a mason, with all that dangerous sawing and crunching, nor could he engage in most types of industrial production. Consequently the traditional Jains formed a distinct socioeconomic class, composed almost entirely of monks and merchants. Their ethical canon was not without what you and I might take to be glaring contradictions (vegetarianism was sanctioned, plants as usual getting dismissive treatment in the matter of rights of life), but at least they took it seriously. They lived by it. They tried their best to do no harm.

9   And this in a country, remember, where 10,000 humans died every year from snakebite, almost a million more from malaria carried in the bites of mosquitoes. The

black widow spider, compared to those fellow creatures, seems a harmless and innocent beast.

But personally I hold no brief for *ahimsa,* because I don't delude myself that it's   10
even theoretically (let alone practically) possible. The basic processes of animal life, human or otherwise, do necessarily entail a fair bit of ruthless squashing and gobbling. Plants can sustain themselves on no more than sunlight and beauty and a hydroponic diet—but not we animals. I've only mentioned this Jainist ideal to suggest the range of possible viewpoints.

Modern philosophers of the "animal liberation" movement, most notably Peter   11
Singer and Tom Regan, have proposed some other interesting answers to the same question. So have writers like Barry Lopez and Eugene Linden, and (by their example, as well as by their work) scientists like Jane Goodall and John Lilly and Dian Fossey. Most of the attention of each of these thinkers, though, has been devoted to what is popularly (but not necessarily by the thinkers themselves) considered the "upper" end of the "ladder" of life. To my mind, the question of appropriate relations is more tricky and intriguing—also more crucial in the long run, since this group accounts for most of the planet's species—as applied to the "lower" end, down there among the mosquitoes and worms and black widow spiders.

These are the extreme test cases. These are the alien species who experience   12
human malice, or indifference, or tolerance, at its most automatic and elemental. To squash or not to squash? Mohandas Gandhi, whose own ethic of nonviolence owed much to *ahimsa,* was once asked about the propriety of an antimalaria campaign that involved killing mosquitoes with DDT, and he was careful to give no simple, presumptuous answer. These are the creatures whose treatment, by each of us, illuminates not just the strength of emotional affinity but the strength, if any, of principle.

But what is the principle? Pure *ahimsa,* as even Gandhi admitted, is unworkable.   13
Vegetarianism is invidious. Anthropocentrism, conscious or otherwise, is smug and ruinously myopic. What else? Well, I have my own little notion of one measure that might usefully be applied in our relations with other species, and I offer it here seriously despite the fact that it will probably sound godawful stupid.

Eye contact.   14

Make eye contact with the beast, the Other, before you decide upon action. No kid-   15
ding, now, I mean get down on your hands and knees right there in the vegetable garden, and look that snail in the face. Lock eyes with that bull snake. Trade stares with the carp. Gaze for a moment into the many-faceted eyes—the windows to its soul—of the house fly, as it licks its way innocently across your kitchen counter. Look for signs of embarrassment or rancor or guilt. Repeat the following formula silently, like a mantra: "This is some mother's darling, this is some mother's child." *Then* kill if you will, or if it seems you must.

I've been experimenting with the eye-contact approach for some time myself. I   16
don't claim that it has made me gentle or holy or put me in tune with the cosmic hum, but definitely it has been interesting. The hardest cases—and therefore I think the most telling—are the spiders.

The face of a spider is unlike anything else a human will ever see. The word "ugly"   17
doesn't even begin to serve. "Grotesque" and "menacing" are too mild. The only adequate way of communicating the effect of a spiderly countenance is to warn that it is "very different," and then offer a photograph. This trick should not be pulled on loved ones just before bedtime or when trying to persuade them to accompany you to the Amazon.

18   The special repugnant power of the spider physiognomy derives, I think, from fangs and eyes. The former are too big and the latter are too many. But the fangs (actually the fangs are only terminal barbs on the *chelicerae,* as the real jaw limbs are called) need to be large, because all spiders are predators yet they have no pincers like a lobster or a scorpion, no talons like an eagle, no social behavior like a pack of wolves. Large clasping fangs armed with poison glands are just their required equipment for earning a living. And what about those eight eyes—big ones and little ones, arranged in two rows, all bugged-out and pointing every-whichway? (My wife the biologist offers a theory here: "They have an eye for each leg, like us—so they don't *step* in anything.") Well, a predator does need good eyesight, binocular focus, peripheral vision. Sensory perception is crucial to any animal that lives by the hunt and, unlike insects, arachnids possess no antennae. Beyond that, I don't know. I don't *know* why a spider has eight eyes.

19   I only know that, when I make eye contact with one, I feel a deep physical shudder of revulsion, and of fear, and of fascination; and I am reminded that the human style of face is only one accidental pattern among many, some of the others being quite drastically different. I remember that we aren't alone. I remember that we are the norm of goodness and comeliness only to ourselves. I wonder about how ugly I look to the spider.

20   The hundred baby black widows on my desk were too tiny for eye contact. They were too numerous, it seemed, to be gathered one by one into a pickle jar and carried to freedom in the backyard. I killed them all with a can of Raid. I confess to that slaughter with more resignation than shame, the jostling struggle for life and space being what it is. I can't swear I would do differently today. But there is this lingering suspicion that I squandered an opportunity for some sort of moral growth.

21   I still keep their dead and dried mother, and their vacated egg sac, in a plastic vial on an office shelf. It is supposed to remind me of something or other.

22   And the question continues to puzzle me: How should a human behave toward the members of other living species?

23   Last week I tried to make eye contact with a tarantula. This was a huge specimen, all hairy and handsomely colored, with a body as big as a hamster and legs the size of Bic pens. I ogled it through a sheet of plate glass. I smiled and winked. But the animal hid its face in distrust.

Thinking Critically About "The Face of a Spider"

This article is meaty enough to justify a closer look. Before we comment on it, take a few moments to explore your own reactions to the following questions:

1. This article is closer to the open end of our closed-to-open continuum than are the other readings in this chapter. Quammen clearly highlights his question up front: "How should a human behave toward the members of other living species?" But he delays his answer—"I sprayed them with a can of Raid"—until the end of the article. Why? How did the absence of a thesis up front affect your experience in reading the article?
2. We sometimes use Quammen's dilemma in our classes without having students read the article. We ask students what they would do if they found

hundreds of baby black widow spiders crawling across their desks. The most common answer we get, by margins of 10 to 1, is "Spray those suckers with a can of Raid." In other words, the surprising answer in Quammen's article is really the expected, common answer in our classes. So, to whom is Quammen writing?

3. Quammen's audience is apparently familiar with words such as *synecdochical* (we hope you looked it up), and they apparently know the people mentioned in paragraph 11 (animal liberationists Peter Singer and Tom Regan; nature writers Barry Lopez and Eugene Linden; and scientists Jane Goodall, John Lilly, and Dian Fossey). Quammen assumes that his readers are so familiar with these people's viewpoints that he needs only a single sentence to refresh their memories:

> Most of the attention of each of these thinkers . . . has been devoted to what is popularly (but not necessarily by the thinkers themselves) considered the 'upper' end of the 'ladder' of life.

Are you familiar with any of these thinkers? If not, then what do you surmise their views are, based on the context of Quammen's piece?

4. What do you think Quammen is getting at when he uses the term "eye contact"? How is this a surprising reversal of what the audience expects? How does it lead to his decision to poison the spiders? How does it lead to his uncertainty as to whether Raid was the right answer?

Quammen's essay can teach us a lot about how writers work. By delaying his thesis, Quammen keeps us in suspense about how he is going to solve his problem and invites us to participate with him in thinking through it. The mood he creates—one of inquiring openness rather than confident certainty—is an effect of shifting from closed-form writing to more open-form writing.

In shaping his essay, Quammen sets up two interrelated problems: the immediate problem of what to do about the spiders, and the broad philosophical problem of how humans should behave toward other living species.

To appreciate this essay's surprising reversal, you have to appreciate Quammen's audience—well-educated, typically liberal environmentalists interested in such issues as the rift between humans and the earth's other living creatures. This audience is likely to be sympathetic toward Peter Singer's arguments against eating animals and to be familiar with Barry Lopez's essays on wolves, Jane Goodall's work with chimpanzees, and Dian Fossey's (*Gorillas in the Mist*) passionate defense of mountain gorillas against bounty hunters. Quammen's intention is to push such readers toward a dilemma. "I know," his prose implies, "that you ecologically minded readers won't bring harm to wolves, or salmon, or spotted owls, or mountain gorillas, but what about a deskful of black widow spiders?" To such an audience, a can of Raid has the same symbolic resonance as a chainsaw. Both symbolize Western man's (we use the patriarchal term intentionally) passion for control over nature. The essay thus raises profound questions about the boundaries of our concern for nonhumans. It surprises us—even haunts us—in any number of ways.

◼ COMPOSING YOUR ESSAY

This assignment asks for an informative essay that surprises the reader with new information. Your new information can come either from your own personal experience (as Cheryl Carp uses her personal experience to reverse the common view of lifers) or from research (as Leo Banks uses both library and interview research to reverse the common view of tarantulas and as Elaine Robbins uses her reading of Daggett to reverse common views about the ecological destructiveness of cows).

As you write your essay, keep in mind that *surprise* is a relative term based on the relationship between you and your intended audience. You don't have to surprise everyone in the world, just those who hold a common view of your topic. Cheryl Carp writes to those classmates who have never been inside a prison; Leo Banks writes to airline travelers who have only a Hollywood understanding of tarantulas; Elaine Robbins writes to ecologically minded environmentalists with a dim view of cows; and David Quammen writes to similar folks with a philosophical bent toward animal liberation.

Additionally, your surprising view doesn't necessarily have to be diametrically opposed to the common view. Perhaps you think the common view is *incomplete* or *insufficient* rather than dead *wrong*. Instead of saying, "View X is wrong, whereas my view, Y, is correct," you can say, "View X is correct and good as far as it goes, but my view, Y, adds a new perspective." In other words, you can also create surprise by going a step beyond the common view to show the reader something new.

Generating and Exploring Ideas

When you write something outside a school setting, you are usually prompted to do so in one of two ways. Sometimes you are prompted by a particular rhetorical occasion that dictates your subject matter and purpose—a notice from a collection agency prompts you to protest a bill; your boss needs a proposal for the next sales meeting; your grandmother complains to your parents that you never write to her. On other occasions, you are motivated to write for your own internal reasons, creating your own context and selecting your own subject matter and purpose—you write in a daily journal to express your ideas and feelings; you write a poem or short story to satisfy a creative urge; you write to your representative in Congress to support or oppose impending legislation; or you write a freelance article on safety tips for hitchhikers to see if you can be published in a magazine.

This present assignment, although it gives you an in-school mandate to write something, is designed to simulate the second kind of prompting. We'd like you to experience what it's like to write when you have an almost unlimited choice of subject matter and potential audiences. Part of the point of this assignment is to help you see how experienced writers finally settle on a particular topic under those circumstances. This assignment encourages you to determine how your unique experiences, observations, or research gives you an angle on a topic that differs from the common view.

The For Writing and Discussion exercises in this chapter have been designed to help you brainstorm and select a topic for this assignment. Look back over these exercises, and see if they help you choose a topic. If not, here is one more exercise that might help you get started.

Exploration Task

With its emphasis on enlarging your audience's view with something unexpected or surprising, this assignment invites you to focus on your audience when selecting your topic. To write a surprising reversal essay, you need to know the common views about a topic, reflected in your audience's conversations. This exercise asks you to eavesdrop on conversations inside and outside class. Instead of entering into a conversation, listen to it intently. What in the conversation leaves you dissatisfied? What are the participants leaving out? Where are they too shallow? Where do they over- or underemphasize a point or focus too narrowly? If you could join this conversation anonymously by saying what you really think at a deep level, what might you say?

Freewrite for several minutes about a conversation that bothered you in some way. When you finish the freewrite, ask yourself if you have a surprising view that you could *add* to that conversation.

Shaping and Drafting

The surprising reversal pattern requires two main movements: an exposition of the common or expected answers to a question, and the development of your own surprising answer to that question. In addition, your essay needs an introduction that presents the question to be addressed and a separate conclusion that finishes it off.

Both Cheryl Carp and David Quammen use distinct introductory sections to provide a context and ask the essay's focusing question. Carp's lead provokes curiosity ("For about eight hours out of every month I am behind the stone walls of the Monroe State Penitentiary"), provides explanatory background on Concerned Lifers, and then poses the question that gave rise to her essay—one that she imagines her readers are asking:

> As the van slowly climbed the hill to the guard tower at the top, I wondered
> what it would be like to visit this maximum security prison.

Quammen opens his essay with a stunning lead ("One evening a few years ago I walked back into my office after dinner and found roughly a hundred black widow spiders frolicking on my desk"). He then explains how this event created "a small moral crisis" and presents, in its own separate paragraph, the essay's focusing question:

> The question is, How should a human behave toward the members of other living species?

In contrast, Leo Banks uses the common view of tarantulas as his lead, fusing his introduction with his exposition of the common view. Rather than stating the essay's question explicitly ("What is the true nature of the tarantula?"), he simply implies it when he presents his thesis:

> Illusion is the key word, for virtually everything the movies want the public to believe about tarantulas is false.

Both methods are effective.

As you go through these moves in your essay, your principal challenge is to maintain your reader's interest. You can do this by developing general statements with colorful, specific details. Cheryl Carp uses details from personal experience (green-and-white road signs, a disembodied voice emanating from a loudspeaker, origami dragons); Leo Banks uses research data about tarantulas (details about tarantula venom and so forth) as well as quotations from spider experts and local Arizonans; Robbins uses precise details about cows hooves, their belching, and their trampling of the ground; Quammen's essay is distinguished by its precise narrative and its descriptive sensory details (the explanation of how the baby spiders happened to be crawling on his desk and the description of the face of a spider, for example).

All four essays make extensive use of supporting examples. Banks uses a James Bond movie and a 1955 sci-fi film to support his point about the common Hollywood view of tarantulas; Robbins uses the central Nevada ranch and ranching in Zimbabwe; Carp uses the story of Ken's teaching his fellow inmates how to make origami flowers and dragons to illustrate her point about the inmates' humanity and creativity; Quammen provides a series of examples to make the point that devout Jains will not harm any animal (for example, they will not cut hair for fear of harming lice). Your essay will need these kinds of supporting examples and details.

As a way of helping you generate ideas and overcome writer's block, we offer the following five questions. Questions 1, 2, and 4 are planning questions that will help you create broad point sentences to form your essay's skeletal framework. These questions call for one-sentence generalizations. Questions 3 and 5 are freewriting prompts to help you generate supporting details. For these questions, freewrite rapidly, either on paper or at your computer. Following each question, we speculate about what Carp, Banks, Robbins, and Quammen might have written if they had used the same questions to help them get started on their respective essays.

1. ***What question does your essay address?*** (Carp might have said, "What is it like to visit lifers in a maximum security prison?" Banks might have said, "Do tarantulas deserve their scary reputation?" Robbins might have said, "But do cows really harm the environment?" Quammen might have said, "How

should I treat a deskful of baby black widow spiders? And how should humans behave toward other creatures?")

2. *What is the common, expected, or popular answer to this question?*
(Carp might have said, "Visiting these lifers will be scary because lifers are sex-starved, dangerous people." Banks might have said, "Tarantulas are poisonous, nightmarish creatures." Robbins might have said, "Cows destroy wildlife habitat, degrade public land, and waste energy." Quammen might have said, "My audience expects me to offer an ecologically sound solution to the spider problem that reflects my respect and concern for all of earth's creatures.")

3. *Why do you believe this is the expected answer? Who holds the views that it reflects?*   Expand on these views by developing them with supporting examples and details. (Carp might have brainstormed details about concealed razor blades, drugs, prison violence, the fear of her friends, and so on. Banks's freewrites might have focused on the sci-fi and James Bond films and other misconceptions about tarantulas. Robbins would have remembered complaints against cows in environmental conversations. Quammen's freewriting might have centered on the Jain religion and other respect-all-earth's-creatures movements.)

4. *What is your own surprising view?*   (Carp might have answered, "Visiting the prison is uplifting because prisoners can be kind, creative, and generous." Banks might have answered, "Tarantulas are peaceful creatures with a largely painless bite and harmless venom." Robbins might have said, "Cows can improve the health of grasslands and help preserve large open tracts of land to fight suburban sprawl." Quammen might have answered, "My look-them-in-the-eye theory allows me to spray these spiders with Raid.")

5. *What examples and details support this view? Why do you hold this view? Why should a reader believe you?*   Writing rapidly, spell out the evidence that supports your point. (Carp would have done a freewrite on all the experiences she had that changed her views about prisoners. Later she would have selected the most powerful ones and refined them for her readers. Banks would have spilled out all his evidence that tarantulas don't deserve their bad reputation. Robbins would have cited new research data. Quammen would have explored his theory about looking creatures in the eye, experimentally applying it to black widows.)

Once you finish exploring your response to these five trigger questions, you will be well on the way to composing a first draft of your essay. Now finish writing your draft fairly rapidly without worrying about perfection.

Revising

Once you have your first draft on paper, the goal is to make it work better first for yourself and then for your readers. If you discovered ideas as you wrote, you may need to do some major restructuring. Check to see that the question you are addressing is clear. Do you state it directly, as do Carp and Quammen, or simply imply it, as do Banks and Robbins? Make sure that you distinguish between the common view and your own surprising view. Do you put your meanings up front, using point sentences at the head of each section and near the beginning of every paragraph? Carp's, Banks's, and Robbins's essays are closed-form pieces with no narrative suspense about the writer's thesis or the essay's structure; Quammen purposely violates some of the rules for closed-form writing to create suspense. Which strategy are you using? Check to see that you have colorful details and plenty of examples and illustrations.

As you revise, follow the suggestions in Chapter 17 for improving your own revising processes. At some point in the middle of your writing process, you will want to road-test your draft by trying it out on readers who can give you valuable insights for further revision. Chapter 17 also has suggestions for conducting peer reviews and gives advice on how to incorporate feedback from readers into your subsequent drafts. Remember to save editing matters for late in the process, attending first to the global concerns of ideas, structure, and overall development.

We conclude this chapter with peer review guidelines that sum up the features to look for in your essay and remind you of the criteria your instructor will use in evaluating your work.

g u i d e l i n e s

For Peer Reviewers

Instructions for peer reviews, including use of these guidelines, are provided in Chapter 17, pages 429–35. To write a peer review for a classmate, use your own paper, numbering your responses to correspond to the questions on the guidelines. At the head of your paper place the author's name and your own name, as shown.

Author's Name: _____

Peer Reviewer's Name: _____

I. Read the draft at a normal reading speed from beginning to end. As you read, do the following:
   A. Place a wavy line in the margin next to any passages that you find confusing, that contain something that doesn't seem to fit, or that otherwise slow down your reading.
   B. Place a "Good!" in the margin next to any passages where you think the writing is particularly strong or interesting.
II. Read the draft again slowly and answer the following questions by writing down brief explanations for your answers.

A. Introduction:
 1. What does the introduction do to capture your interest and set up the question to be addressed? How might the writer enliven or clarify the opening?
 2. Does the writer effectively describe the common or expected view of the topic? Can you think of any additional supporting examples, illustrations, or details that would help the writer develop the common view more vividly? Is this *your* view of the topic?
 3. Does the essay have an effective title? How could the title and the introduction be improved?
B. Thesis:
 1. Does the writer have a thesis statement asserting his or her surprising view? Where does the writer locate the thesis? Is the location effective?
 2. Do you find the writer's thesis surprising? Why or why not?
C. Surprising view:
 1. Does the writer effectively explain his or her surprising view? Can you think of additional supporting examples, illustrations, or details that would help the writer more vividly develop this surprising view?
 2. How might the writer improve the clarity or structure of the draft?
D. Sum up what you see as the chief strengths and problem areas of this draft.
 1. Strengths
 2. Problem areas
III. Read the draft one more time. Place a check in the margin wherever you notice problems in grammar, spelling, or mechanics (one check per problem).

c h a p t e r **10**

Analyzing Images

■ ABOUT ANALYZING IMAGES

This chapter asks you to analyze the persuasive power of images. We are surrounded by images that have designs on us, that urge us to buy things, go places, believe ideas, and so forth. Often the messages of these images are fairly subtle. Information brochures rely on carefully shot photographs of people and places to enhance a subject's image (consider the photographs of the campus included in your college catalog); news photographs editorialize their content (during the Vietnam War a newspaper photograph of a naked Vietnamese child running screaming toward the photographer turned many Americans against the war); and paintings and visual arts cause us literally to see new things ("There was no yellow fog in London until Turner painted it," according to Oscar Wilde). But the most powerful and pervasive images in our culture come to us through the medium of magazine and television advertisements. This chapter focuses on helping you learn to analyze the persuasive nature of these images.

By *images* we mean both the advertisements' pictures themselves and also the images of self and society that they project. When we discuss the persuasive nature of ads we can ask both: How does this ad persuade me to buy this product? and How does this ad persuade me to be a certain kind of person, to adopt a certain self-image, or to strive for certain values?

This chapter is the first of four chapters on writing to analyze. As you may recall from Chapter 4, when you write to analyze you apply your own critical thinking to a puzzling object or to puzzling data. Your goal is to raise interesting questions about the object or data being analyzed—questions that perhaps your reader hasn't thought to ask—and then to provide tentative answers to those questions through close examination of the object or data. The word *analysis* derives from a Greek word meaning "to dissolve, loosen, or undo." Metaphorically, analysis means to divide or dissolve the whole into its constituent parts, to examine these parts carefully, to look at the relationships among them, and then to use this understanding of the parts to better understand the whole—how it functions or what it means. Synonyms for writing to analyze might be writing to interpret, to clarify, or to explain.

What you will develop through this chapter is the ability to understand and explain the persuasive power of advertisements. We will look at the constituent parts of these advertisements—setting, furnishings, and props; characteristics of the models, including their clothes, gestures, hair, facial expressions, and poses; camera angle and lighting; the interplay between the visual images and the verbal copy—and ask how all these parts working together contribute to the rhetorical effect of the advertisement. Along the way, we raise questions about how advertisements shape our sense of who we are and what we value.

Because advertising is such a broad and complex subject, any discussion of it raises numerous interconnected questions concerning the ethics of advertising, the nature of a consumer economy, the complexity and challenge of running a successful business, and what modern critics sometimes call the "social construction of the self," that is, the way messages in the culture create our sense of self and others. Critics of advertising point to its harmful effects (hooking young women on dieting, inciting young men to steal in order to buy $150 basketball shoes), while supporters of advertising point to its benefits (making capitalism work, funding radio and television, undermining communist economies by creating a longing for Western consumer products). All these are areas for exploration and debate.

◰ EXPLORING IMAGE ANALYSIS

Working on your own, freewrite your responses to the following questions:

1. Can you recall a time when a magazine or TV advertisement directly influenced you to buy a product? Describe the occasion and try to recall the specifics of how the ad influenced you.
2. According to a communications professor, Sut Jhally, many critics of advertising claim that "it is a tool whereby consumers are controlled and manipulated by the producers of goods (on whose behalf advertising is waged) to desire things for which they have no real need." To what extent has advertising made you desire things that you don't need? Give some examples. How did the advertisements work on you? What techniques did they use?
3. Has advertising ever influenced your values or your image of what you want to be? For example, an ad may not have caused you to buy a product (a particular perfume or brand of coffee), but has an ad made you long for certain values or experiences (to ride a horse through the pounding surf, to have a romantic encounter in a European café)? As a specific example, one of the authors of this text remembers one summer morning when he and his seven-year-old daughter ate their breakfast cereal on their front porch, cereal bowls cupped in their hands, as a direct result of a Grapenuts advertisement. Can you think of similar experiences?

In small groups or as a whole class, share your freewrites. From the ensuing discussion, create a list of specific ways in which magazine or TV advertisements have been successful in persuading members of your class (a) to buy a product, (b) to value something they didn't need, and (c) to embrace particular values or long for certain experiences.

For further exploration, read the following introduction to a brief article with the headline "Attention Advertisers: Real Men Do Laundry." This article appeared in a recent issue of *American Demographics,* a magazine that helps advertisers target particular audiences based on demographic analysis of the population.

> Commercials almost never show men doing the laundry, but nearly one-fifth of men do at least seven loads a week. Men don't do as much laundry as women, but the washday gap may be closing. In the dual-career 1990's laundry is going unisex.
>
> Forty-three percent of women wash at least seven loads of laundry a week, compared with 19 percent of men, according to a survey conducted for Lever Brothers Company, manufacturers of Wisk detergent. Men do 29 percent of the 419 million loads of laundry Americans wash each week. Yet virtually all laundry-detergent advertising is aimed at women.

Working in small groups, create an idea for a laundry detergent ad to be placed in a men's magazine such as *Playboy, Sports Illustrated, Field and Stream,* or *Esquire.* Draw a rough sketch of your ad that includes the picture, the placement of words, and a rough idea of the content of the words. Pay particular attention to the visual features of your ad—the models, their age, ethnicity, social status or class, and dress; the setting, such as a self-service laundry or a home laundry room; and other features. When you have designed a possible approach, explain why you think your ad will work.

WRITING PROJECT

> Choose two magazine or TV advertisements that sell the same kind of product but appeal to different audiences (for example, a car advertisement aimed at men and one aimed at women; a cigarette ad aimed at upper-middle-class consumers and one aimed at working-class consumers; a clothing ad from *The New Yorker* and one from *Rolling Stone*). Describe the ads in detail so that an audience can easily visualize them without actually seeing them. Analyze the advertisements and explain how each appeals to its target audience. To what values does each ad appeal? How is each ad constructed to appeal to those values? In addition to analyzing the rhetorical appeals made by each ad, you may also wish to evaluate or criticize the ads, commenting on the images they convey of our culture.

This assignment asks you to analyze two different advertisements that are for the same kind of product but appeal to different audiences. Seeing the contrasts in the ads will heighten your awareness of how advertisers vary their appeals to reach different target audiences. For example, Budweiser beer and Pyramid ale are aimed at two different segments of the beer market and the kinds of appeals they use are very different. Companies often vary their appeals for the same product by gender. The Coors beer advertisements in *Glamour* or *Redbook* often differ from the Coors advertisements in *Playboy* or *Sports Illustrated*. Similarly, advertisers often vary their appeals to reach African-American, Hispanic, or Asian markets. This assignment asks you to explain how these appeals are targeted and created.

◪ UNDERSTANDING IMAGE ANALYSIS

Advertisements use images in subtle ways. Although some advertisements are primarily informational—explaining why the company believes its product is superior—most advertisements involve parity products, such as soft drinks, deodorants, breakfast cereals, toothpaste, and jeans. *Parity* products are products that are roughly equal in quality to their competitors and can't be sold through any rational or scientific proof of superiority.

Advertisements for parity products usually use psychological and motivational strategies to associate a product with a target audience's (often subconscious) dreams, hopes, desires, and wishes. The ads play on the idea that the product will magically dispel subconscious fears and anxieties or magically deliver on values, desires, and dreams. Using sophisticated research techniques, advertisers study how people's fears, dreams, and values differ according to their ethnicity, gender, educational level, socioeconomic class, age, and so forth; this research allows advertisers to tailor their appeals precisely to a target audience.

Every feature of an expensive ad, down to the tiniest detail, is the result of conscious choice. Therefore, you must pay close attention to every detail: Why is the hair this way rather than that way? Why these clothes rather than other clothes? Why these body positions rather than other body positions? Why this facial expression rather than another facial expression? Why these words rather than other words? Why this camera angle rather than another camera angle? And so forth.

Targeting Specific Audiences

Much of the market research on which advertisers rely is based on an influential demographic tool developed by SRI Research called the VALS™ (*values and lifestyle system*).* This system divides consumers into three basic categories, with further subdivisions.

1. *Needs-driven consumers.* Poor, with little disposable income, these consumers generally spend their money only on basic necessities.
   - *Survivors:* Live on fixed incomes or have no disposable income. Advertising seldom targets this group.

*Our discussion of the VALS™ is adapted from Harold W. Berkman and Christopher Gibson, *Advertising*, 2nd ed. (New York: Random House, 1987), pp. 134–37.

- *Sustainers:* Have very little disposable income, but often spend what they have impulsively on low-end, mass-market items.
2. ***Outer-directed consumers.***   These consumers want to identify with certain in-groups, to "keep up with the Joneses" or to surpass them.
   - *Belongers:* Believe in traditional family values and are conforming, non-experimental, nostalgic, and sentimental. They are typically blue collar or lower middle class, and they buy products associated with mom, apple pie, and the American flag.
   - *Emulators:* Are ambitious and status conscious. They have tremendous desire to associate with currently popular in-groups. They are typically young, have at least moderate disposable income, are urban and upwardly mobile, and buy conspicuous items that are considered "in."
   - *Achievers:* Have reached the top in a competitive environment. They buy to show off their status and wealth and to reward themselves for their hard climb up the ladder. They have high incomes and buy top-of-the-line luxury items that say "success." They regard themselves as leaders and persons of stature.
3. ***Inner-directed consumers.***   Marching to their own drummers, these consumers are individualistic and buy items to suit their own tastes rather than to symbolize their status.
   - *I-am-me types:* Are young, independent, and often from affluent backgrounds. They typically buy expensive items associated with their individual interests (such as mountain bikes, stereo equipment, or high-end camping gear), but may spend very little on clothes, cars, or furniture.
   - *Experiential types:* Are process-oriented and often reject the values of corporate America in favor of alternative lifestyles. They buy organic foods, make their own bread, do crafts and music, value holistic medicine, and send their children to alternative kindergartens.
   - *Socially conscious types:* Believe in simple living and are concerned about the environment and the poor. They emphasize the social responsibility of corporations, take on community service, and actively promote their favorite causes. They have middle to high incomes and are usually very well educated.

No one fits exactly into any category, and most people exhibit traits of several categories, but advertisers are interested in statistical averages, not individuals. When a company markets an item, it enlists advertising specialists to help target the item to a particular market segment. Budweiser is aimed at belongers, expensive imported beers at achievers, and microbrewery beers at either experiential types or emulators (if microbeers are currently "in"). To understand more precisely the fears and values of a target group, researchers can analyze subgroups within each of these VALS segments by focusing specifically on women, men, children, teenagers, young adults, or retirees or on specified ethnic or regional minorities. Researchers also determine what kinds of families and relationships are valued in each of the VALS segments, who in a family initiates demand for a product, and who in a family makes the actual purchasing decisions. Thus ads aimed at belongers depict traditional families; ads aimed at I-am-me types may depict more ambiguous relationships. Advertisements aimed at women can be particularly complex because of women's conflicting social roles in our society. When advertisers target the broader category of gender, they sometimes sweep away VALS distinctions and try to evoke more deeply embedded emotional and psychological responses.

FOR WRITING AND DISCUSSION

You own a successful futon factory that has marketed its product primarily to experiential types. Your advertisements have associated futons with holistic health, spiritualism (transcendental meditation, yoga), and organic wholesomeness (all-natural materials, gentle people working in the factory, incense and sitar music in your retail stores, and so forth). You have recently expanded your factory and now produce twice as many futons as you did six months ago. Unfortunately, demand hasn't increased correspondingly. Your market research suggests that if you are going to increase demand for futons you have to reach other VALS segments.

Working in small groups, develop ideas for a magazine or TV advertisement that might sell futons to one or more of the other target segments in the VALS system. Your instructor can assign a different target segment to each group, or each group can decide for itself which target segment constitutes the likeliest new market for futons.

Groups should then share their ideas with the whole class.

Analyzing an Advertisement

When you analyze an advertisement, you need to examine it in minute detail. Here are some suggestions for analyzing magazine advertisements. The same strategies can be applied to television advertisements, but TV ads are more complex because they add dialogue, multiple scenes, music, and so forth.

1. *Examine the setting, furnishings, and props.*
   a. List all furnishings and props. If the ad pictures a room, look carefully at such details as the kind and color of the rug; the subject matter of paintings on the walls; the styles of picture frames, curtains, and furniture; the objects on tables; the general arrangement of objects (Is the room neat and tidy or does it have a lived-in look?); the room's feeling (Is it formal? Warm? Casual?); and so forth. Almost all details are purposely chosen; almost nothing is accidental.
   b. What social meanings and values are attached to the objects you listed in (a)? In a den, for example, duck decoys and fishing rods have a connotation different from that of computers and fax machines. It makes a difference whether a dog is a Labrador retriever, an English sheepdog, a toy poodle, or a mutt. What symbolic meanings or associations do vari-

ous props have? A single rose connotes romance or elegance, a bouquet of daisies suggests freshness, and a hanging fuchsia suggests earthy naturalness. Always ask why the ad maker includes one particular prop rather than another.

2. *Consider the characters, roles, and actions.*

    a. Create the story of the ad. Who are the people? What are their relationships? Why are they here? What are they doing? Note details about the clothing and accessories of all the models; pay special attention to hairstyles, because popular culture invests hair with great significance (hence the anxiety created by a bad hair day). Note the poses and gestures of models as well as their positioning and relative sizes. For further advice on what to look for when analyzing the people in advertisements, consult Gillian Dyer's discussion of the manner and actions of characters in ads (pp. 229–31).

    b. Ask what social roles are being played and what values appealed to. Are the gender roles traditional or nontraditional? Are the relationships between people romantic, erotic, friendly, formal, uncertain? What are the power relationships between characters? In most ads, men are larger than women and occupy a stronger position (the woman looking up at the man, the man looking directly at someone or into the camera while the woman averts her eyes), but sometimes these roles are reversed. Either choice is deliberate.

3. *Examine the photographic effects.*   Some advertisements use highly artistic photographic techniques. Parts of the ad may be in crisp focus and others slightly blurred; camera angle or filters may have been used to create special effects. Why? Frequently, photographs are cropped so that only parts of a body are shown. Research suggests that women's bodies are more often cropped than are men's. It is not unusual to see photographs of women's arms, feet, ears, lips, or eyes, but it is rare to see similar photographs of men. What does this difference suggest about the culture's view of men and women? Many ads consist of a large picture with a small insert picture at the top or bottom; the insert often includes one of the characters from the large picture in a different role or pose. Ask how the insert comments on the large picture or how the insert and the large picture otherwise interrelate.

4. *Analyze words and copy.*   The words in advertisements are chosen with extreme care, and special attention is given to connotations, double entendres, and puns. In well-made ads the words and pictures combine for a unified effect. Pay attention to both the message of the words and their visual effect on the page (placement, relative size, and so forth).

Sample Analysis of an Advertisement

As an example of how a specific ad persuades, consider the contrast between the beer ads typically aimed at men (showing women in bikinis fulfilling adolescent male sexual fantasies or men on fishing trips or in sports bars) with the "Sam

Sam and Me.

Me and Sam? We're just friends. Best friends, actually, since Mrs. Ainsley's first grade class when I let the hamster loose and Sam took the rap for me. I mean Sam's seen me in braces and I've seen him eat pizza. There's just way too much history here. Sam's my friend. The one I go to when I really need someone to talk to. I bring the Coors Light and Sam brings his shoulder. And sometimes it's Sam bringing the Coors Light and I'm doing the listening. Me and Sam? Together? I've never even thought about it. Okay, so I've thought about it.

Coors Light.
Just between friends.

and Me" Coors Light ad (above), which ran in a variety of women's magazines. Rather than associating beer drinking with a wild party, this ad associates beer drinking with the warm friendship of a man and woman and with just a hint of potential romance. The ad shows a man and a woman, probably in their early to mid-twenties, in relaxed conversation; they are sitting casually on a tabletop, with their legs resting on chair seats. The woman is wearing casual pants, a summery cotton top, and informal shoes. Her braided, shoulder-length hair has a healthy, messed appearance, and one braid comes across the front of her shoulder. She is turned away from the man, leans on her knees, and holds a bottle of Coors Light. Her sparkling eyes are looking up, and she smiles happily, as if reliving a pleasant memory. The man is wearing slacks, a cotton shirt with the sleeves rolled up, and scuffed tennis shoes with white socks. He also has a reminiscing smile on his face, and he leans on the woman's shoulder. The words "Coors Light. Just between friends" appear immediately below the picture next to a Coors Light can.

This ad appeals to women's desire for close friendships and relationships. Everything about the picture signifies long-established closeness and intimacy—old friends rather than lovers. The way the man leans on the woman shows her strength and independence. Additionally, the way they pose, with the woman slightly forward and sitting up more than the man, results in their taking up equal space in the picture. In many ads featuring male-female couples the man appears larger and taller than the woman; this picture signifies mutuality and equality.

The words of the ad help you interpret the relationship. Sam and the woman have been friends since the first grade, and they are reminiscing about old times. The relationship is thoroughly mutual. Sometimes he brings the Coors Light and sometimes she brings it; sometimes she does the listening and sometimes he does; sometimes she leans on his shoulder and sometimes he leans on hers. Sometimes the ad says, "Sam and me"; sometimes it says "me and Sam." Even the "bad grammar" of "Sam and me" (rather than "Sam and I") suggests the lazy, relaxed absence of pretense or formality.

These two are reliable old buddies. But the last three lines of the copy leave just a hint of potential romance. "Me and Sam? Together? I've never even thought about it. Okay, so I've thought about it." Whereas beer ads targeting men portray women as sex objects, this ad appeals to women's desire for relationships and for romance that is rooted in friendship rather than sex.

And why the name Sam? Students in our classes have hypothesized that Sam is a "buddy" kind of name rather than a romantic hero name. Yet it is more modern and more interesting than other buddy names such as Bob or Bill or Dave. "A Sam" said one of our students, "is more mysterious than a Bill." Whatever associations the name strikes in you, be assured that the ad makers spent hours debating possible names until they hit on this one. For an additional example of an ad analysis, see the sample student essay (pp. 232–34).

FOR WRITING AND DISCUSSION

Examine any of the other magazine ads reprinted in this chapter, or ads brought to class by students or your instructor, and analyze them in detail, paying particular attention to setting, furnishings, and props; characters, roles, and actions; photographic effects; and words and copy. Prior to discussion, freewrite your own analysis of the chosen ad.

Cultural Issues Raised by Advertisements

There isn't space here to examine in depth the numerous cultural issues raised by advertisements, but we can introduce you to a few of them and provide several tasks for exploratory writing and talking.

In 1979, the influential sociologist and semiotician* Erving Goffman published a book called *Gender Advertisements,* arguing that the way in which women are pictured in advertisements removes them from serious power. In many cases, Goffman's point seems self-evident. Women in advertisements are often depicted in frivolous, childlike, exhibitionistic, sexual, or silly poses that would be considered undignified for a man, such as the "Of Sound Body" Zenith ad (p. 225). Women in advertisements are often fun to look at or enthralling to "gaze" at, but seldom call for serious attention. What distinguishes Goffman's work is his analysis of apparently positive portrayals of women in advertisements. He points out tiny details that differentiate the treatment of men from that of women. For example, when men hold umbrellas in an ad, it is usually raining, but when women hold umbrellas, it is for decoration; men grip objects tightly, but women often caress objects or cup them in a gathering in or nurturing way. Female models dance and jump and wiggle in front of the camera (like children playing), whereas male models generally stand or sit in a dignified manner. Even when trying to portray a powerful and independent woman, ads reveal cultural signs that the woman is subordinate.

FOR WRITING AND DISCUSSION

To see what Goffman is getting at, we invite you to explore this issue in the following sequence of activities, which combine class discussion with invitations for exploratory writing.

1. Bring to class advertisements for clothing, perfumes, or accessories from recent fashion and beauty magazines, such as *Glamour, Elle, Mademoiselle,* and *Vogue.* Ask male students to assume the postures of the women in the ads. How many of the postures, which look natural for women, seem ludicrous when adopted by men? To what extent are these postures really natural for women? Freewrite your responses to this exercise.

2. Examine the Zenith advertisement on page 225. How might Erving Goffman argue that this ad subordinates women? Do you agree that this ad reflects the inferior status of women in U.S. culture? Why or why not? Freewrite your response in preparation for class discussion.

3. A highly popular advertisement for cognac that ran several years ago shows three male business executives, ranging in age from the early thirties to early fifties, sitting in an upscale bar overlooking a subway

*A *semiotician* is a person who studies the meanings of signs in a culture. A *sign* is any human-produced artifact or gesture that conveys meaning. It can be anything from a word to a facial expression to the arrangement of chairs at a dinner table.

station (see the "The World's Most Civilized Spirit" Hennessy ad, p. 226). The men are wearing power suits; one man has removed his jacket and rolled up the sleeves on his striped oxford shirt, revealing

his power tie and expensive suspenders. He is reaching for cashew nuts in a cut-glass bowl. The three men are sipping cognac from expensive brandy snifters. The copy at the top of the ad reads, "When the 8:05 isn't leaving until 8:55." What the ad reveals, then, are powerful business leaders at the end of a business day, which is—conspicuously—

close to 8:00 p.m., not 5:00. Since the 8:05 train has been delayed, the men relax, enjoy each other's company, and sip fine cognac.

Freewrite or discuss your responses to this question: Would this ad work if you replaced the male business executives with female executives? Why or why not?

4. Imagine a comparable ad featuring female models that appeals to women's desire to be seen as competent, empowered corporate leaders in today's business environment. Freewrite your ideas for such an ad, addressing the following questions: (a) What product would the ad be selling? (b) What kind of model or models would you choose for your ad? Of what age? From what ethnic group? With what look? (c) What setting and props would you use? (d) How would the models be dressed? What would their hairstyles be? How would they pose? What would they be doing? (e) What might the ad copy say? (f) In what magazines would you publish your ad?

5. Bring to class examples of advertisements that portray women in a particularly positive and empowered way—ads that you think couldn't be deconstructed even by Erving Goffman, to show the subordination of women in our culture. Share your examples with the class and see if they agree that these ads place women on a par with men.

6. After everyone in the class has examined several recent advertisements in a variety of magazines, ask individuals or groups to look at some advertisements from magazines from the 1950s. (Most college libraries have old copies of *Time* or *Life*.) Then hold a class debate on the following question:

> RESOLVED: In recent years advertising has made enormous gains in portraying women as strong, independent, intelligent, and equal with men in their potential for professional status.

READINGS

Vance Packard's *The Hidden Persuaders* is one of the most significant books ever written on advertising. Published in 1957, it brought to public awareness the extent to which advertisers were applying findings from psychological studies in their attempts to influence consumer behavior. In a chapter entitled "Marketing Eight Hidden Needs," Packard provided convincing evidence that advertisers were trying to manipulate the middle class by appealing to eight psychological needs: emotional security, reassurance of worth, ego gratification, something for moms to love once their kids are grown, a sense of power, a sense of roots, a sense of immortality, and creative outlets. The excerpt that follows focuses on this last need—creative outlets. Although Packard was not a feminist, his observations reveal many of the subtle expectations and limitations that society placed on the roles of middle-class women during the *I Love Lucy,* and *Leave It to Beaver* era. *The Hidden Persuaders* laid the groundwork for subsequent studies of gender and advertising and remains a standard reference for those who pursue this fascinating subject.

VANCE PACKARD
FROM *THE HIDDEN PERSUADERS*

Selling creative outlets.   The director of psychological research at a Chicago ad   1
agency mentioned casually in a conversation that gardening is a "pregnancy activity." When questioned about this she responded, as if explaining the most obvious thing in the world, that gardening gives older women a chance to keep on growing things after they have passed the child-bearing stage. This explains, she said, why gardening has particular appeal to older women and to men, who of course can't have babies. She cited the case of a woman with eleven children who, when she passed through menopause, nearly had a nervous collapse until she discovered gardening, which she took to for the first time in her life and with obvious and intense delight.

Housewives consistently report that one of the most pleasurable tasks of the home   2
is making a cake. Psychologists were put to work exploring this phenomenon for merchandising clues. James Vicary made a study of cake symbolism and came up with the conclusion that "baking a cake traditionally is acting out the birth of a child" so that when a woman bakes a cake for her family she is symbolically presenting the family with a new baby, an idea she likes very much. Mr. Vicary cited the many jokes and old wives tales about cake making as evidence: the quip that brides whose cakes fall obviously can't produce a baby yet; the married jest about "leaving a cake in the oven"; the myth that a cake is likely to fall if the woman baking it is menstruating. A psychological consulting firm in Chicago also made a study of cake symbolism and found that "women experience making a cake as making a gift of themselves to their family," which suggests much the same thing.

The food mixes—particularly the cake mixes—soon found themselves deeply in-   3
volved in this problem of feminine creativity and encountered much more resistance than the makers, being logical people, ever dreamed possible. The makers found themselves trying to cope with negative and guilt feelings on the part of women who felt that use of ready mixes was a sign of poor housekeeping and threatened to deprive them of a traditional source of praise.

In the early days the cake-mix packages instructed, "Do not add milk, just add   4
water." Still many wives insisted on adding milk as their creative touch, overloaded the cakes or muffins with calcium, and often the cakes or muffins fell, and the wives would blame the cake mix. Or the package would say, "Do not add eggs." Typically the milk and eggs had already been added by the manufacturer in dried form. But wives who were interviewed in depth studies would exclaim: "What kind of cake is it if you just need to add tap water!" Several different psychological firms wrestled with this problem and came up with essentially the same answer. The mix makers should always leave the housewife something to do. Thus Dr. Dichter counseled General Mills that it should start telling the housewife that she and Bisquick *together* could do the job and not Bisquick alone. Swansdown White Cake Mix began telling wives in large type: "You Add Fresh Eggs . . ." Some mixes have the wife add both fresh eggs and fresh milk.

5   Marketers are finding many areas where they can improve sales by urging the prospective customer to add his creative touch. A West Coast firm selling to home builders found that although its architects and designers could map houses to the last detail it was wise to leave some places where builders could add their own personal touch. And Dr. Dichter in his counseling to pharmaceutical houses advised them that in merchandising ready-mixed medical compounds they would be wise to leave the doctors ways they could add personal touches so that each doctor could feel the compound was "his own."

Thinking Critically About *The Hidden Persuaders*

1. Packard's explanation of how Bisquick advertisers used psychological research to make their ads more effective suggests both the complexity and the sophistication of the "science" of advertising. Bring to class examples of contemporary advertisements that use psychological motivations in subtle ways. Share your examples with classmates and discuss the strategies employed in the ads.

2. Very few advertisements for stereo equipment are found in women's magazines, although women now constitute a large segment of stereo buyers. Why don't the ads for stereo equipment found in men's magazines, such as *GQ* and *Esquire,* appeal to women? How might you design a stereo advertisement with a strong appeal to women?

Many of the points addressed in our earlier discussion about analyzing advertisements are explained in greater detail in an influential book published in 1982, *Advertising as Communication,* by Gillian Dyer, a British professor of communication. The following excerpt from that book focuses on what models' nonverbal behaviors are meant to communicate. Again, although Dyer is attempting merely to present observations rather than to promote a feminist point of view, the findings inevitably hone in on gender distinctions and their societal implications. The citations of Erving Goffman refer to the book we mentioned earlier, *Gender Advertisements* (p. 224).

GILLIAN DYER
ON MANNER AND ACTIVITY

Manner

1   Manner indicates behaviour or emotion at any one time, and is manifest in three main codes of non-verbal communication.

2   1. *Expression.* The face and facial expression are a particular focus of attention in ads. Most expressions are based on socially learned, conventionalized cultural codes, which vary from culture to culture. The expression is meant to underwrite

the appeal of a product and arouse our emotions. Normally the expression of the "actor" will be positive, contented, purposeful, delighted, happy, gleeful, etc. There is considerable empirical evidence to suggest that in our society women smile more than men—both in reality and in commercial scenes. Women are often depicted in a childlike state of expectation and pleasure. They frequently seem to be too easily pleased in ads, as Goffman suggests:

> If television commercials are to be believed, most American women go into uncontrollable ecstasies at the sight and smell of tables and cabinets that have been lovingly caressed with long-lasting, satin-finish, lemon-scented, spray-on furniture polish. Or they glow with rapture at the blinding whiteness of their wash—and the green-eyed envy of their neighbours . . . (1979, p. 68).

In cosmetic ads in glossy fashion magazines the model's look might be cool and naughty as she looks the reader in the eye. Other typical expressions in ads may be seductive, alluring, coy, kittenish, inwardlooking, thoughtful, pensive, carefree, out-going, comic, maternal or mature.

2. *Eye contact.* The attention of the actor in an ad is significant whether it be directed towards audience/camera (person to viewer eye contact), at an object (product), towards other people in the ad or to the middle-distance (detached, distant). Goffman discusses the ritual of withdrawing one's gaze, mental drifting and social dissociation under the general description *licensed withdrawal.* He remarks that

> Women more than men . . . are pictured engaged in involvements which remove them psychologically from the social situation at large leaving them unoriented in it and to it, and presumably, therefore, dependent on the protectiveness and good will of others who are (or might come to be) present. (1979, p. 57)

Covering the face or mouth with the hands is one way of hiding an emotion like remorse, fear, shyness or laughter. The aversion of the eyes and lowering of the head can indicate withdrawal from a scene and symbolize dependency and submissiveness. In many advertisements women are shown mentally drifting while in close physical contact with a male as if his mental and physical alertness were enough for both of them. Women may focus their attention on the middle distance, on some object (like the product) or on a piece of the man's clothing. Women are sometimes seen with a dreamy luxuriating look in their eyes. Eyes may be covered up or shaded by hair, hats, hands, dark glasses. Similarly, blinking or winking have great cultural significance. However, an equally important feature in ads is the shielding of everything but the eyes so that the person can observe an event without actually participating in it; some ads show women coyly peeping from behind fans, curtains, objects or products.

3. *Pose.* This can be static or active and sometimes corresponds to expression. Poses can be composed, relaxed, leisurely, passive, leaning, seductive, snuggling. Bodies can be vertical or horizontal. An individual can use another to act as a shield or as an object to lean against, or rest hands or legs on. Pose is also related to social position and status, hence women are often seen in a lower position than the man, for instance sitting at their feet.

4. *Clothes.* These are obviously extremely important carriers of meaning in ads, even when they are not the object being sold. They can range from the formal

(regimental or work costume), to the informal (leisure, relaxation, sports wear), and can be smart, sophisticated, glamorous, elegant, trendy or comfortable and casual. They can of course sum up a "look," e.g. the "twenties" look.

Activity

6   Body gestures, movement and posture can be related to what the actor is doing.

7   1. *Touch.* The finger brought to the mouth or face can signify thoughtfulness but of a dissociated kind; women and children are often shown with the tips of their fingers in the mouth. Finger to finger touching similarly implies dissociation. Women more than men are pictured touching, or delicately fingering objects, tracing their outline, caressing their surfaces. This ritualistic touching is different from functional touching like grasping or holding. Hand-holding can be a significant gesture in ads and often is used to allow the man to protect or direct the woman. Self-touching is again something that women do more than men; it conveys the impression of narcissism, admiring one's own body and displaying it to others, so that everyone can share the admiration of this delicate and precious thing. Sometimes the act of touching is displaced onto things—sun, wind or water on the naked body when sunbathing or swimming. The feel of clothes against the skin—satins, silks, furs—is conveyed as a pleasurable thing.

8   2. *Body movement.* This might be quite functional, i.e. simply related to what the actor is doing—cleaning the kitchen floor, making beds, filling up the car with petrol, playing football, gardening. These movements may be exaggerated, ridiculous or child-like, calling into question the competence of the performer. Bodies, particularly women's, are often not treated seriously, either through what Goffman calls "ritual subordination" (that is lowering the body in front of others more superior, lying or sitting down, ritually bending the knee or lowering the head) *or* through puckishness and clowning. An example of body movement is where two people are engaged in "mock assault" and this is sometimes seen in advertisements, men usually playing these games on women.

9   3. *Positional communication.* The relationships between actors and actors, actors and objects are extremely significant, and are shown by their position within the frame of a picture. Superiority, inferiority, equality, intimacy and rank can be signified by people's position, size, activity and their relationship to the space around them, the furniture and to the viewer/consumer. Close-up shots, for instance, are meant to signify more intimacy and identification than long-shots.

Thinking Critically About "On Manner and Activity"

1. Your instructor will choose an advertisement for analysis. Observe the ad closely, paying attention to expression, eye contact, pose, clothes, touch, body movement, and positional communication. How would a change in any of these features affect the ad's impact and "meaning"?

2. Dyer explains that the manner and activity of males and females in advertisements differ significantly. What are some of these differences? Can you find these differences illustrated in the advertisements that you and your classmates have been examining?

3. Do you agree with Dyer and Goffman that these differences are culturally significant, that is, that they reveal (and subtly reinforce) a cultural belief that women are subordinate to men?

The final reading is a student essay written in response to the assignment in this chapter. It contrasts the strategies of two different cigarette ads to make smoking appear socially desirable despite public sentiment to the contrary.

STEPHEN BEAN (STUDENT)
HOW CIGARETTE ADVERTISERS ADDRESS THE STIGMA AGAINST SMOKING: A TALE OF TWO ADS

Any smoker can tell you there's a social stigma attached to smoking in this country. With smokers being pushed out of restaurants, airports, and many office buildings, how could anyone not feel like a pariah lighting up? While never associated with the churchgoing crowd, smoking is increasingly viewed as lower class or as a symbol of rebellion. Smoking has significantly decreased among adults while increasing among teenagers and young adults in recent years—a testament to its growing status as an affront to middle- and upper-class values. Cigarette advertisers are sharply tuned into this cultural attitude. They must decide whether to overcome the working-class/rebellious image of smoking in their advertisements or use it to their advantage. The answer to this question lies in what type of people they want an ad to target—the young? the rich? the poor?—and in what values, insecurities, and desires they think this group shares. Two contrasting answers to these questions are apparent in recent magazine ads for Benson and Hedges cigarettes and for Richland cigarettes. 1

The ad for Benson and Hedges consists of a main picture and a small insert picture below the main one. The main picture shows five women (perhaps thirty years old) sitting around, talking, and laughing in the living room of a comfortable and urbane home or upscale apartment. The room is filled with natural light and is tastefully decorated with antique lamps and Persian rugs. The women have opened a bottle of wine, and a couple of glasses have been poured. They are dressed casually but fashionably, ranging from slightly hip to slightly conservative. One woman wears a loose, black, sleeveless dress; another wears grungesque boots with a sweater and skirt. One of the women, apparently the hostess, sits on a sofa a bit apart from the others, smiles with pleasure at the conversation and laughter of her friends, and knits. Two of the women are smoking, and three aren't. No smoke is visible coming from the cigarettes. Underneath the main picture is a small insert photograph of the hostess—the one knitting in the main picture—in a different pose. She is now leaning back in pleasure, apparently after the party, and this time she is smoking a cigarette. Underneath the photos reads the slogan "For people who like to smoke." 2

The ad for Richland cigarettes shows a couple in their late twenties sitting in a diner or perhaps a tavern off the freeway. The remains of their lunch—empty burger and fries baskets, a couple of beer bottles—lie on the table. They seem to be talking leisurely, 3 sharing an after-meal smoke. The man is wearing black jeans and a black T-shirt. The woman is wearing a pinkish skirt and tank top. Leaning back with her legs apart she sits in a position that signals sexuality. The slogan reads, "It's all right here." And at the bottom of the ad, "Classic taste. Right price." Outside the window of the diner you can see a freeway sign slightly blurred as if from heated air currents.

4   Whom do these different advertisements target? What about them might people find appealing? Clearly the Benson and Hedges ad is aimed at women, especially upper-middle-class women who wish to appear successful. As the media have noted lately, the social stigma against smoking is strongest among middle- and upper-class adults. My sense of the B&H ad is that it is targeting younger, college-educated women who feel social pressure to quit smoking. To them the ad is saying, "Smoking makes you no less sophisticated; it only shows that you have a fun side too. Be comfortable doing whatever makes you happy."

5   What choices did the advertisers make in constructing this scene to create this message? The living room—with its antique lamps and vases, its Persian rugs and hardcover books, and its wall hanging thrown over what appears to be an old trunk—creates a sense of comfortable, tasteful, upscale living. But figuring out the people in the room is more difficult. Who are these women? What is their story? What brought them together this afternoon? Where did their money come from? Are these professional women with high-paying jobs, or are they the wives of young bankers, attorneys, and stockbrokers? One woman has a strong business look—short hair feathered back, black sleeveless dress—but why is she dressed this way on what is apparently a Saturday afternoon? In contrast, another woman has a more hip, almost grunge look—slightly spiky hair that's long in the back, a loose sweater, a black skirt, and heavy black boots. Only one woman wears a wedding ring. It seems everything about these women resists easy definition or categorization. The most striking image in the ad is the hostess knitting. She looks remarkably domestic, almost motherly, with her knees drawn close, leaning over her knitting and smiling to herself as others laugh out loud. Her presence gives the scene a feeling of safety and old-fashioned values amidst the images of independence. Interestingly, we get a much different image of the hostess in the second insert picture placed just above the B&H logo. This picture shows the hostess leaning back pleasurably on the couch and smoking. The image is undeniably sexual. Her arms are back; she's deeply relaxed; the two top buttons of her blouse are open; her hair is slightly mussed; she smokes languidly, taking full pleasure in the cigarette, basking in the party's afterglow.

6   The opposing images in the advertisement (knitting/smoking, conservative/hip, wife/career, safe/independent, domestic/sexual) mean that these women can't easily be defined—as smokers or as anything else. For an ad promoting smoking, the cigarettes themselves take a back seat. In the main picture the cigarettes are hardly noticeable; the two women holding cigarettes do so inconspicuously and there is no visible smoke. The ad doesn't say so much that it is good to smoke, but that it is okay to smoke. Smoking will not make you less sophisticated. If anything, it only shows that you have an element of youth and fun. The slogan, "For people who like to smoke," targets nonsmokers as much as it does smokers—not so much to take up smoking but to be more tolerant of those who choose to smoke. The emphasis is on choice, independence, and acceptance of others' choices. The ad attacks the social stigma against smoking; it eases the conscience of "people who like to smoke."

7   While the B&H ad hopes to remove the stigma attached to smoking, the Richland ad feasts on it. Richland cigarettes aren't for those cultivating the upper-class look. The ad goes for a rebellious, gritty image, for beer drinkers, not wine sippers. While the story

of the women in the B&H ad is difficult to figure out, the Richland ad gives us a classic image: a couple on the road who have stopped at a diner or tavern. Here the story is simpler: a man and woman being cool. They are going down the freeway to the big city. I picture a heavy American cruising car parked out front. Everything about the ad has a gritty, blue-collar feel. They sit at a booth with a Formica tabletop; the walls are bare, green-painted wood. The man is dressed in black with a combed-back, James Dean haircut. The woman wears a pink skirt with a tank top; her shoulder-length hair hasn't been fussed over, and she wears a touch of makeup. Empty baskets and bottles cluttering the table indicate they had a classic American meal—hamburgers, fries, and a beer—eaten for pleasure without politically correct worries about calories, polyunsaturated fats, cruelty to animals, or cancer. While the sexual imagery in the B&H ad is subtle, in the Richland ad it is blatant. The man is leaning forward with his elbows on the table; the woman is leaning back with her legs spread and her skirt pushed up slightly. Her eyes are closed. They smoke leisurely, and the woman holds the cigarette a couple of inches from her expecting lips. The slogan, "It's all right here," is centered beneath the woman's skirt. Smoking, like sex, is about pure pleasure—something to be done slowly. Far from avoiding working-class associations with smoking, this ad aims to reinforce them. The cigarettes are clearly visible, and, unlike the cigarettes in the B&H ad, show rings of rising smoke. This ad promotes living for the moment. The more rebellious, the better.

So we see, then, two different ways that cigarette companies address the stigma   8 against smoking. The B&H ad tries to eliminate it by targeting middle-class, college-educated women. It appeals to upscale values, associating cigarette smoking with choice, and showing that "people who like to smoke" can also knit (evoking warm, safe images of domestic life) or lean back in postparty pleasure (evoking a somewhat wilder, more sexual image). In contrast, the Richland ad exploits the stigma. It associates smoking with on-the-road freedom, rebellion, sexuality, and enjoyment of the moment. The smoke visibly rising from the cigarettes in the Richland ad and noticeably absent from the Benson and Hedges ad tells the difference.

Thinking Critically About "A Tale of Two Ads"

1. Stephen Bean argues that the Benson and Hedges and the Richland ads use very different appeals to encourage their target audiences to smoke. What are the appeals he cites? Do you agree with Stephen's analysis?

2. Collect a variety of cigarette ads from current magazines and analyze their various appeals. How do the ads vary according to their intended audience? Consider ads targeted at men versus women or at audiences from different VALS segments.

3. What do you see as the strengths and weaknesses of Stephen's essay?

◢ COMPOSING YOUR ESSAY

Generating and Exploring Ideas

Your first task is to find two ads that sell the same general product to different target audiences or that make appeals to noticeably different value systems.

Look for ads that are complex enough to invite detailed analysis. Then, analyze the ads carefully, using the strategies suggested in Analyzing an Advertisement (pp. 220–21) and Dyer's ideas from "On Manner and Activity" (pp. 229–31). The sample student essay (pp. 232–34) provides an example of the kind of approach you can take.

If you get stuck, try freewriting your responses to the following questions: (a) What attracted your attention to this ad? (b) Whom do you think this ad targets? Why? (c) What props and furnishings are in this ad, and what values or meanings are attached to them? (d) What are the characters like, what are they doing, and why are they wearing what they are wearing and posed the way they are posed? (e) Is there anything worth noting about camera angle or photographic effects? (f) How do the words of the ad interplay with the picture? (g) How would the ad be less effective if its key features were changed in some way? (h) Overall, to what fears, values, hopes, or dreams is this ad appealing?

Shaping and Drafting

Your essay should be fairly easy to organize at the big-picture level, but each part will require its own organic organization depending on the main points of your analysis. At the big-picture level, you can generally follow a structure like this:

I. Introduction (hooks readers' interest, gives background on how ads vary their appeals, asks the question your paper will address, and ends with initial mapping in the form of a purpose or thesis statement)
II. General description of the two ads
  A. Description of ad 1
  B. Description of ad 2
III. Analysis of the two ads
  A. Analysis of ad 1
  B. Analysis of ad 2
IV. Conclusion (returns to the big picture for a sense of closure; makes final comments about the significance of your analysis or touches in some way on larger issues raised by the analysis)

We recommend that you write your rough draft rapidly, without worrying about gracefulness or about correctness or even about getting all your ideas said at once. Many people like to begin with the description of the ads and then write the analysis before writing the introduction and conclusion. After you have written your draft, put it aside for a while before you begin revising. We recommend that you ask classmates for a peer review of your draft early in the revising process.

Revising

Most experienced writers have to make global changes in their final drafts when they revise, especially when they are doing analytical writing. The act of writing a rough draft generally leads to the discovery of more ideas. You may also realize that many of your original ideas aren't clearly developed or that the draft feels scattered and unorganized.

g u i d e l i n e s
for Peer Reviewers

Instructions for peer reviews, including use of these guidelines, are provided in Chapter 17, pages 429–35. To write a peer review for a classmate, use your own paper, numbering your responses to correspond to the questions on the guidelines. At the head of your paper place the author's name, and your own name, as shown.

Author's Name: _____

Peer Reviewer's Name: _____

   I. Read the draft at a normal reading speed from beginning to end. As you read, do the following:
     A. Place a wavy line in the margin next to any passages that you find confusing, that contain something that doesn't seem to fit, or that otherwise slow down your reading.
     B. Place a "Good!" in the margin next to any passages where you think the writing is particularly strong or interesting.
  II. Read the draft again slowly and answer the following questions by writing brief explanations of your answers.
     A. Introduction:
       1. Is the title appropriate for an academic analysis? Does it suggest the thesis and focus of the paper and pique your interest? How might the title be improved?
       2. What does the writer do to capture your interest, provide needed background, and set up the question to be addressed?
       3. Does the thesis statement, purpose statement, or forecasting statement provide the big picture for both the description and the analysis of the two ads? How might the writer improve the introduction?
     B. Description of the ads:
       1. Does the writer describe the ads in an interesting and vivid manner? How could this description help you "see" the ads more clearly?
       2. In what ways do the ads appeal to different audiences or have different value systems? What makes the ads complex enough to justify an analysis?
     C. Analysis of the ads:
       1. How does the analysis of the ads shed light on and build on the description of the ads?

2. How many of the following features does the writer discuss? Which could be added to deepen and complicate the analysis?
   a. Setting, props, and furnishings: how they indicate lifestyle and socioeconomic status; appeal to certain values; carry certain cultural associations or meanings; serve as symbols.
   b. Characters, roles, and actions: the story of the ad; power relationships and status of the characters; gender, age, or ethnic roles followed or violated; the significance of clothing and accessories, of hair and facial expressions, and of posing, positioning, and gestures.
   c. Photographic effects: lighting, camera angle, cropping, focus?
   d. Language and wording of the ad's copy: its overt message; feelings, mood and values communicated through connotations, double entendres, and so forth; visual layout of copy?
3. Does the analysis interpret the ads convincingly? Do any details of the ads contradict the analysis? Do you disagree with the writer's view of these ads?
4. Do you have any suggestions for making the body of the paper clearer, better organized, or easier to follow? Where might the writer better apply the principles of clarity from Chapter 18 (starting with the big picture; putting points before particulars; using transitions; following the old/new contract)?

D. Sum up what you see as the chief strengths and problem areas of this draft.
   1. Strengths
   2. Problem areas

III. Read the draft one more time. Place a check in the margin wherever you notice problems in grammar, spelling, or mechanics (one check per problem).

Analyzing Numerical Data

■ ABOUT NUMERICAL ANALYSIS

Most people have mixed feelings about numerical and graphic data. On the one hand, people venerate these data for their capacity to express large chunks of reality economically and impartially and respect their unique power to persuade. On the other hand, people also harbor a deep suspicion of numbers. Everyone has seen hucksters and self-promoters manipulate data for their own ends.

Our goal in this chapter grows out of this ambivalence and is basically twofold. We want (1) to make you more respectful of the unique power of numerical data to represent reality broadly and objectively, and (2) to nurture in you a healthy skepticism about conclusions drawn from numbers.

■ EXPLORING NUMERICAL ANALYSIS

Suppose that you are researching changes in the public image of teenagers over the last two decades. As part of your research, you wish to examine the way teenagers are portrayed in the media. You come across the following article appearing in *USA Today* on November 8, 1985. Read this brief article; then answer the questions that follow.

READING

HELP TROUBLED TEENS—
DON'T FORGET THEM

The USA's teen-agers are in trouble.   1

Too many of them are pregnant. Too many are drunk. Too many are strung out on   2
drugs. Too many are criminals. Too many die, because of homicide or suicide.

3   Some are poor kids, on the street corners of The Bronx or Watts, sneaking marijuana cigarettes and wobbling off to school. Some are rich kids, in San Rafael or Scarsdale, raiding the liquor closet, mixing booze and pills.

4   Some are young and pregnant. In the high schools of small towns or large cities. Some will never see 18, victims of homicide or suicide in Detroit or Dallas.

5   Last week a blue-ribbon committee, the Business Advisory Commission of the Education Commission of the States released some startling statistics about teen-agers.

6   Twenty-two percent of them—14 million—live in poverty. More than 1 million get pregnant each year, and most do not marry. About 700,000 dropped out of school last year.

7   On Wednesday, a new survey of high school seniors showed 30 percent had used illegal drugs in the past month; 37 percent had indulged in heavy drinking.

8   People under 21 account for more than half of all arrests in serious crimes. And the teen-age suicide rate is up 150 percent since 1950.

9   Why would a group of business and government leaders worry about the USA's young people?

10   They worry that if too many of our kids are lost to drugs or booze, there will be a shortage of skilled labor. But beyond that, they realize that if these mixed-up kids don't get help, huge numbers of them will never lead productive lives. And the rest of us will pay the bill for their failures.

11   Business already spends $40 billion a year to train workers. In some cases, it has been forced to teach young people things they should have learned in elementary school.

12   The business group calls these kids "disconnected"—cut off from school or work. As many as 15 percent of all teens may be in trouble, lost, unable to live productive lives?

13   What can be done about it?

14   Nothing, some say. They argue there will always be a small number of underachievers or misfits—so don't waste time, energy, or money helping them.

15   That view, besides being callous, is terribly short-sighted. If today's teens don't contribute to our society, then they will take from it—and the rest of us will pay for it.

16   Some solutions are just common sense. Restore discipline and accountability in the schools. Get parents involved in education. Crack down on drug and alcohol abuse. Give them a sense of values.

Working in small groups or as a whole class, explore your answers to the following questions:

1. What view of U.S. teenagers emerges from this article?
2. How does the writer's use of statistical data contribute to the rhetorical effect of the article?
3. Consider some of the writer's specific uses of statistics:
   - "More than 1 million get pregnant each year, and most do not marry." Why does the writer use a raw number here (1 million) rather than a percentage? What percent of all teenagers get pregnant? [*Note:* A clue early in the article will help you compute the total number of teenagers. The writer says that 14 million equals 22 percent of the whole.] What does the writer mean by "most"?

- ■ "And the teen-age suicide rate is up 150 percent since 1950." The writer had several choices here: citing the actual raw number of teenage suicides; citing the percentage of teenagers who committed suicide; or citing the increase in the rate of suicide measured from any base year. Why does the writer choose the last option? Why do you suppose he or she starts from the base year 1950 rather than, say, 1930 or 1960?
- ■ "People under 21 account for more than half of all arrests in serious crimes." Why does the writer choose to focus on *arrests* for serious crimes rather than *convictions*? (Can you think of occasions where the police automatically suspect teenagers, arrest them, and then later release them?) How serious is "serious"?
- ■ "As many as 15 percent of all teens may be in trouble, lost, unable to live productive lives?" This sentence is powerful rhetorically, but when you examine it, what does it really say? Where did the 15 percent come from? What about the weasel words *as many as* and *may*? How would you define *in trouble*?

4. How could you derive data from this article to argue that teenagers are not in trouble?

WRITING PROJECT

Find a short article that relies heavily on numerical data for its argument. (The two articles on the minimum wage on pp. 256–58 are suitable for this assignment.) In your paper, analyze the writer's rhetorical choices in selecting and shaping the data. How do the writer's decisions about the selection and representation of data help persuade readers toward the writer's point of view?

The assignment asks you to analyze how a writer's choices in selecting and representing data influence the reader's perception. In using numerical data, writers regularly make decisions about what data to select (and hence to omit) and how to display it (raw numbers versus percentages, real numbers versus adjusted numbers, pie charts versus tables, and so forth). Your task in this assignment is to unpack and analyze a writer's rhetorical decisions in selecting and displaying numerical data. Vicki Alexander's paper (pp. 253–55) is an example of a student essay written to this assignment. It analyzes the *USA Today* article on teenagers that you just read.

■ UNDERSTANDING NUMERICAL ANALYSIS

What Do We Mean by "Data"?

Before we discuss more specifically the basic tools of data analysis and how to get data to "talk," we need to explain what we mean by data and where they fit into the realm of understanding. *Data* are representations, in the form of numbers, words, or graphics, of facts or events in the real world. For the purposes of this chapter, we focus on data in their numeric and graphical forms. In its raw form, each piece of data represents one fact or event. For example, each piece of raw data used to calculate the Consumer Price Index (CPI) represents the current price of one of several hundred types of consumer goods based on a sampling from a variety of stores.

Data are rarely used in raw form. The power of data derives from your ability to compress and combine them, to express a profusion of raw data as a single datum. As Figure 11.1 shows, raw data undergo several transformations before they emerge as a single number, such as the CPI.

The Consumer Price Index is a single number that allows us to compare over time the cost of buying the basic goods that Americans routinely consume. The starting point for the index is 100, which currently signifies the CPI for the base period of 1982–1984. A CPI of 150 means that basic living expenses—food, transportation, housing, medical care, and so on—cost one-and-a-half times more than they did in the 1982–1984 base period.

The value of a figure such as the CPI is that it functions as a gauge by which to measure large-scale economic change. Workers in many industries use the CPI to determine whether their wages are keeping up with increases in the cost of living. For instance, if the CPI has increased by 20 percent since the last contract, but wages have increased by only 10 percent during the same period, workers will use these data to negotiate salary increases in their next contract to make up that gap.

The representative nature of data allows a writer to deal with facts and events economically. By comparing the CPI at two points in time, as we just did, we conveyed a great deal in a few words. Figure 11.2 (page 242) uses fictional data to plot CPI against wages for a single occupational category. This graph presents data even more economically. If we wanted to see the implications of our comparison for workers in a particular field, we could create a graph with two lines, one tracing

FIGURE 11.1   Types of Data

Raw Data	Bread X	Detergent Y
Store A	$1.04	$1.89
Store B	1.29	1.75
Store C	1.43	1.59
Intermediate Data	Bread X	Detergent Y
Average price,		
Stores A–Z	$1.25	$1.74

Cumulative Data

Combined average current price of all sampled products.

Comparative Data

Current average combined price of all sampled products measured against average combined price of similarly sampled products in months or years past.

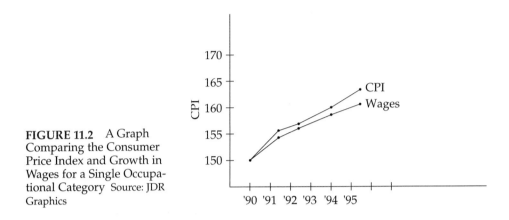

FIGURE 11.2 A Graph Comparing the Consumer Price Index and Growth in Wages for a Single Occupational Category Source: JDR Graphics

the growth of the CPI over the past several years, the other tracing the growth of wages in the particular field. At a glance the reader would know a great deal about how these workers had been doing for an extended period of time.

This economy of expression also poses some real dangers. Because it reveals so much with so few words or lines, data can be used to misrepresent—intentionally or unintentionally—a large number of facts or events at a single stroke. This power accounts for public mistrust of numerical data and those who use them, embodied in popular sayings such as, "Figures don't lie, but liars do figure" and "There are three kinds of lies: lies, damned lies, and statistics."

Those who gather, use, and analyze data regularly have their own language for expressing degrees of data manipulation. *Teasing* and *tweaking* data are usually legitimate attempts to portray data in a better light; *massaging* data may involve a bit of subterfuge, but is still within acceptable limits; when the line is crossed and manipulation turns into outright, conscious misrepresentation, however, people say the data have been *cooked*—an unsavory fate for data and people alike. The existence of a well-developed language for describing degrees of manipulation underscores the prevalence of such practices. If you are to use data responsibly and protect yourself from others' abuses of them, it's important to understand how to analyze them.

Basic Tools of Data Analysis

In this section, we discuss some of the most common tools for data analysis and offer advice on when to use them and how to read them. We'll look specifically at tables, line graphs, bar graphs, and pie charts and discuss the rhetorical effects created by each.

Tables

One of the simplest means for making data visible to your audience is a table. Halfway between a picture and a list, a table presents numerical data in columns (vertical groupings) and rows (horizontal groupings), thereby allowing us to see relationships relatively quickly. Figure 11.3 (page 244) depicts a table with summary information on U.S. family income (before taxes) based on the 1989, 1992, and 1995 Survey of Consumer Finances (SCF). It offers snapshots of family income broken out by selected characteristics.

You read tables in two directions: from the top down and from left to right. The title of the table is usually at the top. In this case, the title "Before-tax family income for previous year, by selected characteristics of families, 1989, 1992, and 1995 and percentage of families who saved, 1992 and 1995," tells us the subject of the table—U.S. family income and savings—and the principle means used to organize the table's contents—family characteristics and time.

The first row of the table tells us that the columns of the table will be grouped by survey year ("1989," "1992," "1995"). The second row of the table tells us the different statistics to be presented for each of the survey years ("Median," "Mean," "Percentage of Families"). We then move to the top of the far left column, where we find "Family Characteristic." Immediately below "Family Characteristic" we find the data broken down by age, education level, race or ethnicity, current work status, housing status of the head of household, and family net worth. Reading across each row, we see a series of numbers telling us the median and mean income for the people in each category and the percentage of families who fall in that category. Thus, in 1989 the median income for a family with a head of household less than thirty-five years old was $25,800. The mean income for that same group was $35,400. That same group accounted for 27.2 percent of the number of families participating in the 1989 survey.

When you read a table, avoid the temptation simply to plunge into all the numbers. After you've read the title and headings to make basic sense of what the table is telling you, try randomly selecting several numbers in the table and saying aloud what those numbers "mean" to be sure you understand what the table is really about.

FOR WRITING AND DISCUSSION

It is obvious from Figure 11.3 that income in the United States is unequally distributed. Looking at the table we see that median and mean income vary depending on education levels, race and ethnicity, job status, housing status, and net worth. Much political debate is focused on how to interpret this inequality. Is the unequal distribution of income a social problem or not? Using the information contained in Figure 11.3, which pieces of data would you point toward to argue that the unequal distribution of income is not a serious social problem? Which data from the table suggest that the unequal distribution of income is a serious social problem?

Line Graphs

At first glance, line graphs seem significantly simpler to read than tables. Sometimes we literally see the significance of a line graph at a glance. A line graph achieves this simplicity by converting numerical data into a series of points on an

FIGURE 11.3 An Example of a Table

Before-tax Family Income for Previous Year, by Selected Characteristics of Families, 1989, 1992, and 1995, and Percentage of Families Who Saved, 1992 and 1995 (thousands of 1995 dollars except as noted).

Family characteristic	1989			1992				1995			
	Median	Mean	Percentage of families	Median	Mean	Percentage of families who saved	Percentage of families	Median	Mean	Percentage of families who saved	Percentage of families
All families	**31.8** (n.a.)	**49.8** (n.a.)	**100.0**	**29.1** (.8)	**43.5** (1.3)	**57.1**	**100.0**	**30.8** (.6)	**44.3** (1.3)	**55.0**	**100.0**
Age of head (years)											
Less than 35	25.8	35.4	27.2	26.8	33.1	59.3	25.8	26.7	31.9	56.4	24.8
35–44	46.3	61.8	23.4	39.1	50.8	57.1	22.8	39.1	48.3	54.1	23.2
45–54	45.7	77.4	14.4	45.5	61.5	59.0	16.2	41.1	64.8	57.6	17.8
55–64	32.1	52.7	13.9	31.6	53.3	59.0	13.2	36.0	52.9	58.5	12.5
65–74	19.3	38.6	12.0	19.3	31.4	53.8	12.6	19.5	37.0	49.6	11.9
75 and more	16.7	28.5	9.0	14.9	25.3	49.2	9.4	17.3	27.3	51.5	9.8
Education of head											
No high school diploma	16.7	23.8	24.3	13.4	19.0	38.3	20.4	15.7	21.9	42.7	19.0
High school diploma	27.3	36.2	32.1	25.8	32.7	56.9	29.9	26.7	35.2	50.9	31.6
Some college	36.0	50.3	15.1	30.5	40.3	59.5	17.7	29.8	39.9	54.2	19.0
College degree	51.4	87.0	28.5	48.6	70.8	67.8	31.9	46.3	70.4	67.5	30.5
Race or ethnicity of head											
White non-Hispanic	37.3	56.9	75.1	33.4	47.8	60.9	75.1	33.3	48.6	58.9	77.5
Nonwhite or Hispanic	18.0	28.5	24.9	20.1	30.3	45.6	24.9	21.0	29.5	41.8	22.5
Current work status of head											
Professional, managerial	55.5	76.6	16.9	50.9	69.8	68.9	16.8	54.4	72.7	67.9	15.9
Technical, sales, clerical	35.2	43.6	13.4	35.8	41.6	64.5	14.8	34.4	46.2	56.3	14.9
Precision production	47.6	50.9	9.6	36.1	43.4	65.6	7.0	41.1	43.8	60.0	8.2
Machine operators and laborers	30.9	35.4	10.6	29.1	34.1	57.6	10.0	32.9	35.6	60.9	13.1
Service occupations	19.3	25.8	6.6	21.3	28.7	51.5	6.2	21.1	27.2	50.2	6.6
Self-employed	48.1	111.0	11.2	48.6	82.2	59.2	10.9	39.0	79.0	62.3	9.7
Retired	17.3	28.4	25.0	16.5	24.9	48.0	26.0	17.5	27.3	46.1	25.0
Other not working	9.0	17.6	6.7	12.3	22.9	41.6	8.2	12.3	19.9	31.4	6.5
Housing status											
Owner	41.1	62.8	63.8	37.8	53.0	63.0	63.9	38.1	54.6	60.9	64.7
Renter or other	17.6	26.9	36.2	19.0	26.5	46.6	36.1	18.8	25.5	44.3	35.3
Net worth (1995 dollars)											
Less than 10,000	13.9	19.2	27.8	14.8	19.8	39.3	27.0	15.4	18.9	36.0	25.8
10,000–24,999	27.1	29.5	9.3	26.2	29.5	52.5	10.4	25.7	28.4	54.1	10.0
25,000–49,999	29.6	33.6	10.1	25.8	30.4	50.0	11.4	32.0	33.9	48.2	11.6
50,000–99,999	36.0	39.5	14.6	32.8	35.9	61.3	15.3	35.2	38.2	57.8	16.9
100,000–249,999	42.9	52.2	21.6	40.9	48.0	67.6	20.7	39.4	47.6	64.4	21.3
250,000 and more	72.0	128.4	16.5	70.0	106.5	78.6	15.2	68.4	111.6	78.2	14.4

NOTE. Dollars converted to 1995 values with the consumer price index (CPI) for all urban consumers. Standard errors in parentheses. The 1989 survey did not ask families whether they had saved in the preceding year.

imaginary grid created by horizontal and vertical axes, and then by connecting those points. The resulting line gives us a picture of the relationship between whatever is represented on the horizontal (x) axis and whatever is represented on the vertical (y) axis. Although they are extremely economical, graphs can't convey the same richness of information that tables can. They are most useful when your focus is on a single relationship.

To illustrate how graphs work, consider Figure 11.4, which contains a graphic representation of one relationship from the table in Figure 11.3; in this case, median family income and its relationship to the age of head of household. To determine what this graphic is telling you, you must first clarify what's represented on the two axes. In this case the x axis represents "Age of Head" while the y axis represents "Median Income." The first point on the y axis indicates that the median income for a family with a head of household less than 35 years old is $26,700. By the time the head of household is between ages forty-five and fifty-four, however, the median income of his or her family is $41,100. By the time the head of household is seventy-five or more years old, however, median income has fallen to $17,300.

So what does this graph tell us? How would we generally characterize the nature of the relationship between the x axis and the y axis? In simple English, we might translate this relationship to something like the following: "People have low income early in life, high income in the middle, and low income in retirement."

You can apply the "truth" of this graph to your own situation or that of friends and family members. Young families, with individuals just beginning their careers, often have trouble making ends meet. Later in life, after they have become established in their careers, income levels rise. Finally, people who have retired earn no salary but still receive some income in the form of Social Security, pension payments, stock dividends, or interest payments on savings. Political conservatives often use this relationship to argue that the inequality of income in the United

FIGURE 11.4   Example of a Line Graph

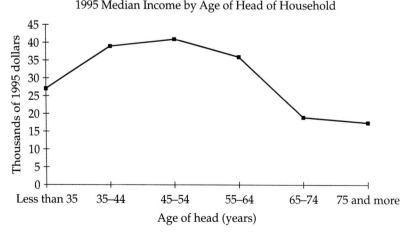

States is not a significant problem. They argue that the inequality of income simply reflects a natural pattern of lifetime income earnings.

Bar Graphs

Bar graphs use bars of varying length and width, extending either horizontally or vertically, to contrast two or more quantities. As with any graphic presentation, you should read from the top down, being especially careful to note the graph's title. Most bar graphs also have *legends,* or explanations of how to read the graph. Bars are typically shaded in various hues, crosshatched, left clear, or filled in with slanting lines, to differentiate among the quantities or items being compared. The legend identifies what quantity or item each bar represents.

The bar graph in Figure 11.5 is based on data contained in Figure 11.3. The title tells us that the purpose of the graph is to contrast "Median Income by Race or Ethnicity." The legend, in turn, shows us which quantity each of the bars in the graph represents: the lightly shaded bar represents median income for nonwhites or Hispanics, the dark bar represents median income for non-Hispanic whites.

The power of this visual is that it shows the median income for multiple groups across time. Had the survey split the sample to a finer level, it would have been easy to reflect the income levels of several different groups for each of the survey years. By placing values for each group beside the other, bar graphs are particularly useful for making comparisons. Figure 11.5 shows that non-Hispanic white median income was at least one and a half times the median income of nonwhites and Hispanics. Liberals often use comparisons such as this to argue that

FIGURE 11.5   Example of a Bar Graph

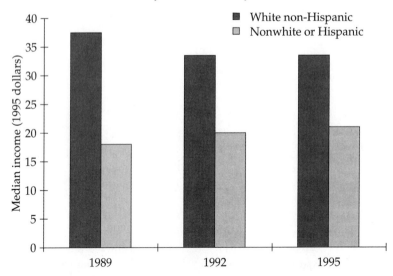

the income inequality in the United States is a problem. Many argue that the income inequality in the United States stems from racial discrimination.

Pie Charts

Pie charts, as their name suggests, depict different percentages of a total (the pie) in the form of slices. At tax time, pie charts are a favorite way of depicting all the different places that your tax dollars go. If your main point is to demonstrate that a particular portion of a whole is disproportionately large—perhaps you're arguing that too many of our tax dollars are spent on Medicaid or defense—the pie chart can demonstrate that at a glance. (Conversely, of course, it can also demonstrate that some other part of the whole is undersized relative to other shares.) The effectiveness of pie charts diminishes as we add more slices. In most cases, you'll begin to confuse readers if you include more than five or six slices.

Figures 11.6 and 11.7 show pie charts based on data taken from Figure 11.3. Figure 11.6 features two pie charts. The left pie shows the percentages of family heads from the 1995 sample according to their level of education. The right pie shows the percentage of income received by family heads within those same education levels. Thus, from the left pie, we see that 30 percent of the family heads from the 1995 sample had college degrees. From the right pie, we see that that same group received 49 percent of the total income from the 1995 sample. Similarly, 19 percent of the sample had no high school education. That group earned only 9 percent of the income. This presentation of the data contained in Figure 11.3 certainly highlights the importance of a college education. It could further be used to support an argument for increased financial support for higher education.

Figure 11.7 is similar to Figure 11.6. Like Figure 11.6, it uses two pie charts to show percentages of families in different groups, this time " Net Worth," and the

FIGURE 11.6 Example of a Pie Chart

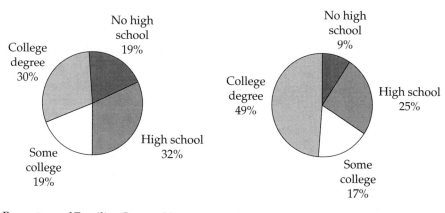

Percentage of Families Grouped by
Head of Household Education Level

Percentage of Income Grouped by
Head of Household Education Level

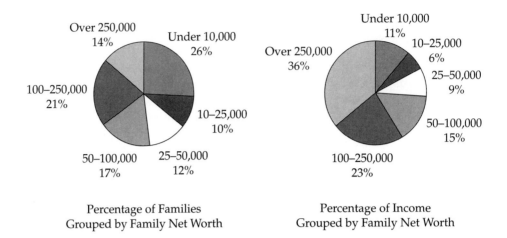

Percentage of Families
Grouped by Family Net Worth

Percentage of Income
Grouped by Family Net Worth

FIGURE 11.7   Another Example of a Pie Chart

share of income each group receives. For example, 14 percent of the families surveyed in 1995 had a family net worth in excess of $250,000. That same group re-
ceived 36 percent of the total survey income. Likewise, 26 percent of the sample
had a net worth under $10,000. That group earned only 6 percent of the survey in-
come. The data presented in Figure 11.7 might be used to show not only the *inequality* of the U.S. income distribution, but also the *inequity* of the U.S. income
distribution. Figure 11.7 suggests that the rich get richer and the poor get poorer.

Shaping Data for Specific Effects

As a reader and daily consumer of numerical data (and as a user of numerical data on many occasions as a writer), you need to be acutely aware of the ways
in which data can sometimes entice you into drawing hasty and erroneous conclusions about the world. You must also take care not to be fooled by people who
intentionally manipulate data to lead you to a wrong conclusion. In what follows
we review several choices writers make in shaping data for a desired rhetorical effect. The difference between shaping such data legitimately and shaping it intentionally to mislead an audience is a matter of degree, not kind. Everyone
inevitably *shapes* data according to his or her goals and perspectives; the question
is, How much shaping is legitimate?

Using Data Selectively

Throughout this book, we've remarked on the human tendency to see the
world selectively, depending on the viewer's situatedness and purposes in observing or seeking out information. Whether you are conducting secondary research by examining numerical data gathered by others or conducting primary
research by gathering the data themselves, people tend to select data that support

their points. In selecting data to support your argument (and in analyzing data used by others), you should apply the time-honored criteria for evaluating data: *recency, scope,* and *relevance.*

Recency is an important criterion, first, because the subjects that people research (crime rates, economic trends, public opinions, etc.) tend to change over time, and, second, because data-based studies build on earlier studies. If a recent study contradicts an earlier study, then the writers of the later study typically base their rejection of the earlier study on such factors as flawed methodology or technical improvements in data gathering unavailable to earlier researchers.

However, newer isn't *always* better. A later study may ignore earlier studies or may not have been as rigorously conducted. Conscientious writers cite the latest *reliable* studies, whereas manipulative writers cite the latest studies that support their position.

Scope is also a significant measure of a study's value. In most cases, the greater the scope of the research, the more cases, respondents, or experiments it's based on, the more likely that its conclusions are valid. Some small, well-crafted studies are perfectly legitimate also. Bigger isn't *always* better. The care with which a study's subjects are chosen and with which various variables are taken into account is more critical than size.

Relevance is the third vital criterion for data selection. Charging data with irrelevance is probably the most common critique offered. In arguments about handgun controls, for example, proponents cite studies of low homicide rates in countries with strong gun-control laws, whereas opponents reject the relevance of such studies on the grounds that many cultural differences, and not differences in laws, account for the disparate homicide rates.

Using Graphics for Effect

Anytime you present numerical data pictorially, the potential for enhancing the rhetorical presence of your argument, or for manipulating your audience outright, increases markedly. By *presence,* we mean the immediacy and impact of your material. As you have seen, raw numbers by their nature are abstract. But numbers turned into pictures are very immediate. Graphs, charts, and tables help an audience see at a glance what long strings of statistics can only hint at.

You can have markedly different effects on your audience according to how you design and construct a graphic. For example, by coloring one variable prominently and enlarging it slightly, a graphic artist can greatly distort the importance of that variable. Although such depictions may carry warnings that they are not to scale, the visual impact is often more memorable than the warning.

One of the subtlest ways of controlling an audience's perception of a numerical relationship is through the presentation of the grids on the x and y axes of a line graph. Consider the graph in Figure 11.8, which depicts the monthly net profits of an ice cream sandwich retailer. Looking at this graph, you'd think that the net profits of Bite O' Heaven were themselves shooting heavenward. But if you were considering investing in an ice cream sandwich franchise yourself, you would want to consider how the graph was constructed. Note the quantity assigned

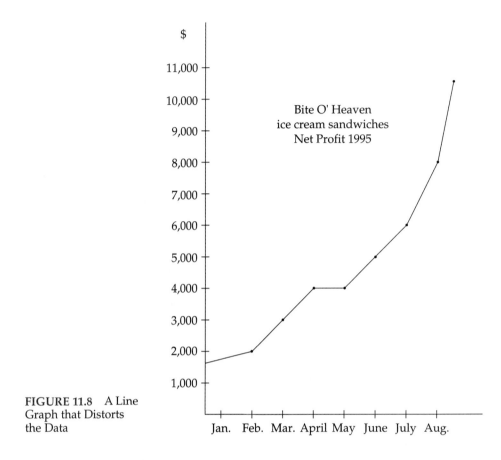

FIGURE 11.8 A Line Graph that Distorts the Data

to each square on the grid. Although the graph does represent the correct quantities, the designer's choice of increments leads to a wildly inflated depiction of success. If the Bite O' Heaven folks had chosen a larger increment for each square on the vertical axis, say, $5,000 instead of $1,000, the company's rise in profitability would appear as in Figure 11.9. You can easily distort or overstate a rate of change on a graph by consciously selecting the quantities assigned to each scale unit on the horizontal or vertical axis.

Another way to create a rhetorical effect with a line graph is to vary the scope of time it covers. Note that the graphs in Figures 11.8 and 11.9 cover net sales from January through August. What do you think might be typical sales figures for this company from September through December?

Using Numbers Strategically

The choice and design of a graphic can markedly affect your audience's perception of your subject. You can also influence your audience through the kinds of numbers you use: raw numbers versus percentages; raw numbers versus adjusted numbers (for example, wages "adjusted for inflation"); use of a mean ver-

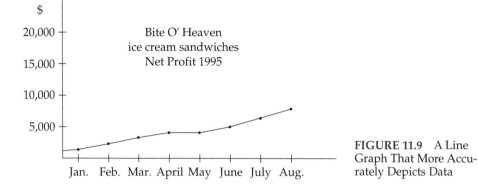

FIGURE 11.9   A Line Graph That More Accurately Depicts Data

sus a median; or a statistical presentation versus a narrative one. The choice always depends on the audience you are addressing and the purpose you want to achieve.

One of the most frequent choices you have to make as a writer is whether to cite raw numbers or percentages, rates, or some sort of adjusted numbers. In some cases a raw number will be more persuasive than a percentage. If you were to say that the cost of attending a state college would increase at a rate 15 percent greater than the CPI over the next decade, most audiences would be lost—few would know how to translate that number into terms they could understand. But if you said that in the year 2007, the cost of attending a state college for one year would be about $21,000, you would surely grab your audience's attention. So, if you were a financial planner trying to talk a young couple into saving money for their children's college education, you would be more prone to use the raw number than the percentage increase; but if you were a college administrator trying to play down the increasing costs of college to a hostile legislator, you might well use the percentage increase.

FOR WRITING AND DISCUSSION

A recent proposal to build a new ballpark in Seattle, Washington, yielded a wide range of statistical arguments. The following statements are all reasonably faithful to the same facts:

- The ballpark will be funded by raising the sales tax from 8.2 percent to 8.3 percent over a twenty-year period.
- The sales tax increase is one-tenth of one percent.
- This increase represents an average of $7.50 per person per year—about the price of a movie ticket.
- This increase represents $750 per five-person family over the twenty-year period of the tax.
- This is a $250-million tax increase for the residents of the Seattle area.

How would you describe the costs of the proposed ballpark if you opposed the proposal? How would you describe the costs if you supported the proposal?

READINGS

The first reading is taken from a question–answer column in which science writer Bryant Stamford explains how the labels on low-fat milk can mislead consumers.

▼

BRYANT STAMFORD

UNDERSTAND CALORIES, FAT CONTENT IN FOOD

Q: There was a story in the national news on 2 percent low-fat milk. I think I   1
understand the concept about the difference between fat content as weight
and as calories. Something about this conversion still escapes me, however.
In plain English, can you explain the conflict surrounding low-fat milk?

—*J. H., St. Johns, Mich.*

A: Millions of Americans think that 2 percent milk is low in fat. The label even says   2
"low-fat." Sorry, but 2 percent milk actually is very high in fat, with 37.5 percent of its
calories (kcals) coming from fat.

How can they get away with trying to pass off this fatty product as low-fat? The an-   3
swer has to do with how the fat content is reported. Food manufacturers who don't want
you to know their products are loaded with fat will report the fat content by weight.

Here is a simple example: Let's assume a bottle contains 99 grams of water. Water   4
has no calories and passes through the body quickly and easily. We add 1 gram of fat
to the water, making 100 total grams. The 1 gram of fat contains calories and stays in
the body after being digested. The water, in effect, serves merely as a carrier for the fat.

In reporting the fat content of this watery mix, we can report it by weight or by calo-   5
ries. The choice makes a profound difference in our perception of the mix.

If we report fat content by weight, we see that, because only 1 gram out of 100 is   6
fat, the mix is only 1 percent fat, or 99 percent fat-free. This is the way a manufacturer
would want you to see it, and that's why they would tell you the fat content by weight.

But when fat is reported by calories, it is a much different story. This product con-   7
tains 9 calories, because 1 gram of fat contains 9 calories.

Since all 9 calories are in the form of fat, this product is 100 percent fat. The dif-   8
ference between reporting a product as 1 percent fat (by weight) vs. 100 percent fat
(by calories) speaks for itself.

Now let's apply this concept to milk. Since milk is mostly water, reporting fat by   9
weight will always grossly underestimate the actual fat content. In 2 percent milk, out

of 100 grams of total weight, 2 grams will be fat. Thus, it can be reported as 98 percent fat-free.

10   It's an entirely different story when reporting fat content by calories.

11   One cup of 2 percent milk contains 5 grams of fat and 120 calories. Here is the calculation for determining fat content by calories.

12   Five grams of fat times 9 calories equal 45 calories of fat. Of the 120 total calories, 45 are from fat. Forty-five divided by 120 equals .375. Then, .375 times 100 equals 37.5 percent fat.

13   The story is just as bad for whole milk, which is 3.3 percent fat by weight, but 48 percent fat by calories.

14   You can apply this formula to other food as well.

15   Meat, for example, may contain a high proportion of water, and, therefore, reporting fat content by weight grossly underestimates the actual fat content. Your confusion may arise from the fact that there is no "typical" conversion factor, or constant, that can be applied to all food to convert the fat content by weight to fat content by calories.

16   The reason is that foods vary in water content. The greater the water content, the more diluted will be the fat content when reported by weight.

17   Thus, you must use the formula for each food to determine the actual fat content by calories.

18   The bottom line is buyer beware. Unless you are armed with a little information, chances are you will be misled every time.

Thinking Critically About "Understand Calories, Fat Content in Food"

1. In calling 2 percent milk "low fat," do you think the manufacturer is telling the truth, tweaking the data, massaging the data, or cooking the data? Why?
2. Reporting fat content as a percentage of weight or calories is analogous to numerous other statistical dilemmas. What other situations can you think of in which different ways of calculating the numbers will lead to significant differences in results?

Our second reading, by Vicki Alexander, was written for the assignment in this chapter. It analyzes the article on teenagers in *USA Today* on pages 238–39.

VICKI ALEXANDER (STUDENT)
TROUBLE WITH TEENS OR WITH NUMBERS?

1   The author of the *USA Today* editorial "Help Troubled Teens—Don't Forget Them" argues that the nation's teens are besieged with problems. The editorial primarily uses statistics to support its claims. Initially, the editorial may seem persuasive, but if readers examine it closely, they may discern ways the editorial distorts perceptions of the teen population.

The first specific statistic offered about teens is that "twenty-two percent of them— 14 million—live in poverty." This is a grim statistic, but it is hard to tell what it means. How many of these are teenagers living in families below the poverty level and how many are teenagers who are independent of their parents but not yet earning very much money? It's logical to expect that teenagers working part time or full time at low-paying jobs wouldn't earn enough money to be above the poverty level. As teens age and gain experience, their incomes will certainly increase. Thus, while this statistic may seem disturbing, it is likely that for lots of teens, their poverty is only temporary. Certainly it doesn't mean that they are "underachievers" or "misfits" as the article seems to imply.

2

The next statistic the editorial presents is "more than 1 million get pregnant each year." A million pregnancies sounds alarming; however, the percentage this number represents is actually surprisingly low. The percentage can be calculated by using the information in an earlier statistic that 14 million teenagers comprise 22 percent of the teen population. Rounded off, the total size of the teen population is 63 million. Therefore, the one million referred to here constitutes only about 1.6 percent of the teen population. The writer chooses to say 1 million rather than 1.6 percent because the raw number has a greater persuasive impact. The writer again uses only a raw number— 700,000—when reporting how many teens dropped out of school last year. When this number is converted to a percentage, the statistic is surprising only because it is so small: just about 1 percent dropped out of school.

3

The editorial's next piece of evidence to support its thesis that teens are troubled is the statement: "On Wednesday a new survey of high school seniors showed 30 percent had used illegal drugs in the past month; 37 percent had indulged in heavy drinking." Who conducted this survey? These figures seem not to be part of the study done by the "blue-ribbon committee" identified earlier. Research can only be as credible as its source, but no source of this study is identified. Furthermore, although the editorial is supposedly about teenagers in general, this statistic focuses just on high school seniors, a quite different population. High school seniors are more likely than younger teens to use illegal drugs and excessive alcohol, so limiting the statistics to only high school seniors may falsely inflate these statistics. Other information is excluded that could also help readers better interpret the statistics on high school seniors' drug and alcohol use. What constitutes "heavy drinking"? And when was the study done? Perhaps it was conducted soon after prom or graduation, when seniors would be especially tempted to use illegal drugs or excessive alcohol at parties marking these events.

4

The statistic that "people under 21 account for more than half of all arrests in serious crimes" changes the population group once more: from all teens to just high school seniors to those up through age 20. The source of these findings is also unclear: Is it the blue-ribbon committee first cited, or another study? "More than half" is imprecise, perhaps representing a number just minimally greater than half. Also, the statistic refers to arrests, not convictions. If police officers have the same negative assumptions about teens that the writer of this editorial has, innocent teens may often be subjected to arrests which do not result in convictions.

5

The final statistic given presents information using a unit of measurement not used before in the editorial: "The teenage suicide rate is up 150 percent since 1950." Why didn't the writer use raw numbers or percentages as elsewhere in the editorial? According to the U.S. Department of Health and Human Services, the teen suicide

6

rate when this editorial was published was .01 percent, that is, one-hundredth of 1 percent. Clearly it is more alarming to say the suicide rate has gone up 150 percent than to say it has risen from .0067 percent to .01 percent. One must wonder too why the writer selected 1950 as the year for comparison. Perhaps the teen suicide rate has stayed the same or decreased in recent years, and the writer could only make the problem seem significantly worse by stretching back many decades. Finally, the suicide figures for 1950 may not be accurate. Because of the conservatism of the time, it's likely that suicide was underreported as a cause of death more often than it would be now.

7   Ideally, teens would not have any of the problems referred to in this *USA Today* editorial. Teens deserve social support even if only a few of them are poor, pregnant, drug or alcohol addicted, or convicted of crimes. Clearly, even one teen suicide is too many. Yet this is not the writer's point. Instead, the writer distorts readers' perceptions of the teen population. By changing the units of statistical measurement, the identity of the population being studied, and the source of the statistics, as well as by omitting important information that can put the statistics about teens into perspective, the editorial reinforces falsely negative stereotypes of most teenagers.

Thinking Critically About "Trouble with Teens or with Numbers?

1. Read again the article that student writer Vicki Alexander analyzes—the *USA Today* editorial "Help Troubled Teens—Don't Forget Them" (pp. 238–39). Most readers find that article persuasive in its depiction of teenagers in trouble. How does the editorialist use statistics persuasively?
2. How does Vicki Alexander's analysis undermine the persuasiveness of the editorial's statistics?
3. Which parts of Alexander's analysis seem strongest to you? Which parts are weakest?

Our last readings take alternative points of view on the wisdom of raising the minimum wage. The first article, an op-ed piece by John Burbank, the executive director of the Seattle-based Economic Opportunity Institute, supports Initiative 688, which was on the 1998 ballot. Passed overwhelmingly by Washington voters, this initiative gave the state of Washington the nation's most liberal minimum wage statute. The second article, from *Fortune* magazine, opposes minimum wage statutes. It was written by David R. Henderson, a research fellow with the conservative Hoover Institute and an economics professor at the Naval Postgraduate School.

Because your instructor may ask you to analyze these two pieces for your assignment for this chapter, we forego our customary critical thinking questions. As you read them, pay close attention to how each uses statistics rhetorically to persuade you toward the writer's point of view.

JOHN BURBANK

THE MINIMUM WAGE: MAKING WORK PAY

The Economic Opportunity Institute strongly supports Initiative 688 to increase the 1 minimum wage. A full-time worker at the current minimum wage earns $10,500 a year, 15 percent below the poverty level for a family of three. At the national level, over 30 percent of workers earn wages below the poverty level. What is worse, Washington has the lowest minimum wage in the region—lower even than poorer states like Idaho.

Raising the minimum wage to $6.50 per hour would simply tie the minimum wage 2 to the poverty level. A hard week's work should pay enough to keep your family at least at or above the poverty line.

A common refrain of those who oppose raising the minimum wage is that minimum- 3 wage workers are usually just teenagers working part-time to pay for movies, gas and fast food. But let's look at who really earns the minimum wage in America. According to the conservative Employment Policies Institute, 71 percent of minimum-wage workers are over 20 years old and fewer than 30 percent live with their parents. Furthermore, almost 40 percent of minimum-wage earners are the sole source of income for their households and fully 50 percent of minimum-wage workers live in households whose total income is less than $27,000.

According to a University of Washington study on the minimum wage, 83 percent of 4 minimum-wage workers in Washington work more than 20 hours a week, with 43 percent holding full-time jobs. In addition, an overwhelming majority (72 percent) of minimum-wage earners are women, many of whom are working to support their families.

But what about the economic effects of raising the minimum wage? Opponents 5 argue that raising the minimum wage will force businesses to cut costs by laying off employees. But the Economic Policy Institute looked at the effects that raising the federal minimum wage in 1996 and 1997 had on employment. What they found was that these minimum-wage increases had a statistically insignificant effect on jobs.

A 1998 study conducted by the Center on Budget and Policy Priorities on the effects of Oregon's minimum-wage increases in 1997 and 1998 shows similar results. 6 This study discovered that positive job growth occurred in the retail trade industry (the industry with the largest proportion of minimum-wage workers). In fact, the job growth in this industry kept pace with the overall employment growth in Oregon.

Furthermore, minimum-wage workers do not cause inflation. Their extremely small 7 share of dollars within the overall Washington economy eliminates a minimum-wage increase as a factor for inflation. The evidence is piling up: Raising the minimum wage does not cause inflation nor reduce jobs.

In fact, raising the minimum wage can actually benefit businesses. Specifically, 8 raising the minimum wage can lead to lower turnover rates, job vacancies are filled more quickly, and workers receive better training since they are receiving a higher wage. All of these factors increase worker productivity, which in turn stimulates economic growth. And everyone—businesses, workers and consumers—benefits from economic growth. Especially in low-income areas, the added disposable income from minimum-wage workers creates an important economic stimulus for local businesses.

Raising the minimum wage has a strong and positive impact for parents leaving 9 welfare and re-entering the work force. In the three years before Oregon raised its minimum wage in 1997 and 1998, the average starting wage of welfare recipients fell 5 percent. But after Oregon raised its minimum, the average wage for welfare recipients rose

76 cents per hour. Furthermore, Oregon's welfare caseload declined faster than any other state. The higher minimum wage certainly makes returning to the labor market more feasible for parents with a family to support.

10   Most importantly, minimum-wage workers are underpaid for the value of their work. In 1968, the value of the minimum wage was one and one-half times greater than it is now. Given that in the past 30 years productivity has increased over 40 percent, minimum-wage workers are grossly underpaid compared to the value of their labor benchmarked by the 1968 minimum wage. Today, many employers are simply hiding behind the minimum wage to underpay their workers. That is not right.

DAVID R. HENDERSON
MINIMUM WAGE + $1 = MORE POVERTY

1   Amazing fact: Even as you read this—even as each new stanza of that bizarre epic, the Clintoniad, is written—there are politicians in Washington actually trying to change, you know, laws. It's true, and in the case of minimum wage policy, it's unfortunate. When they're not distancing themselves from the President, Democrats in Congress are quietly agitating to raise the minimum wage from $5.15 to $6.15 over the next two years and will probably try to attach a higher minimum to a spending bill this fall.

2   The minimum wage is a bad idea that keeps coming back, despite the efforts of economists everywhere to kill it. The vast majority of economists oppose the minimum wage on the grounds that it destroys jobs for unskilled workers. For every 20% increase in the minimum wage, most economists believe, employment of teenagers and young adults falls by about 2% to 4%. A new study published by the National Bureau of Economic Research in Cambridge, Mass., enormously strengthens the economists' case against the minimum wage. The study, done by David Neumark of Michigan State University, Mark Schweitzer of the Federal Reserve Bank of Cleveland, and William Wascher of the Federal Reserve Board of Governors, finds that increases in the minimum wage also increase the number of families below the poverty line.

3   One common justification for raising the minimum wage is that since the ensuing job loss is so small, it's a good way of increasing the income of the unskilled, many of whom are in poor families. In other words, if a 20% minimum wage increase throws only 2% of youths out of work, doesn't that mean that the other 98% get a 20% pay increase? Actually, no. Neumark et al. point out that in the real world, when the government raises the minimum wage, the majority of youths are usually earning well above the new minimum, so most youths will see little or no pay increase after the wage hike. If the minimum goes up, only those who had been earning less than the new limit could possibly enjoy a raise.

4   In fact it is these very low-paid youths—who are supposed to benefit from a wage hike—who suffer the job losses, as the study illustrates with wage data from 1995, before the minimum wage went from $4.25 to $5.15. In that year there were 19 million workers ages 16 to 24, of whom about four million earned somewhere between $4.25 and $5.14, and therefore stood to receive raises. Now apply the minimum wage/job loss ratio described above and use the low end of the consensus estimate—that a 20% increase in the minimum wage reduces youth employment overall by at least 2%. Since the 1995 case involved a 21% minimum wage hike, about 2%, or 380,000, of all young

workers lost their jobs. But when you focus only on the 4 million workers directly affected by the wage hike, the tradeoff looks a lot worse: 380,000 jobs now translates to 9%.

The study also looks at state governments, which sometimes impose their own 5 minimum wages. Neumark et al. use census data to estimate the effects on family income when a state's minimum wage is set above the federal minimum. They find that within a year of an increase in a state's minimum wage, there was a 4.5% increase in the number of families with incomes below the poverty level. So the net effect of increasing the minimum wage has been to increase poverty rather than to decrease it.

Why would this effect occur a year after the minimum wage increase rather than 6 right away? For two reasons. First, when the minimum wage increases, employers take time to adjust their methods of production. That is to say, it takes time for fast-food joints to buy new burger-flipping machinery that requires one teenager to operate rather than two. Second, low-wage jobs turn over quickly, so employers who don't like firing (i.e., most of them) tend to wait for turnover and attrition to do the job for them.

In answer to the usual leftish defense of the minimum wage as a boon to the urban 7 poor, liberal MIT economist Paul Samuelson once asked, "What good does it do a black youth to know that an employer must pay him $2 an hour if the fact that he must be paid that amount is what keeps him from getting a job?" The problem isn't raising the minimum wage; the problem is, and always has been, the minimum wage itself.

◪ COMPOSING YOUR ESSAY

Generating and Exploring Ideas

The first step in composing this essay is to analyze your chosen article carefully, isolating all the statistics. Pick out representative examples of data that contribute to the persuasiveness of the article. Then consider alternative ways that the data could have been presented—as raw numbers, say, rather than as percentages, or as a line graph rather than a pie chart.

Pay particular attention to what is not included and to various contexts that may suggest a different interpretation or explanation of the data from that presented in the article. Also question the source of the data, looking especially at its recency, scope, and relevance.

Shaping and Drafting

This essay calls for a closed-form structure with a clear thesis in the introduction. A good way to organize this essay is to follow the strategy used by Vicki Alexander, who devotes a paragraph or block of paragraphs to each statistic she chooses to analyze.

Revising

Once you've developed a thesis and written a draft, you are ready to road-test it on readers to determine what works and what is confusing or undeveloped. The following Guidelines for Peer Reviewers can serve as a checklist for your revision.

g u i d e l i n e s

For Peer Reviewers

Instructions for peer reviews, including use of these guidelines, are provided in Chapter 17, pages 429–35. To write a peer review for a classmate, use your own paper, numbering your responses to correspond to the questions on the guidelines. At the head of your paper place the author's name and your own name, as shown.

Author's Name: _____

Peer Reviewer's Name: _____

I. Read the draft at a normal reading speed from beginning to end. As you read, do the following:
   A. Place a wavy line in the margin next to any passages that you find confusing, that contain something that doesn't seem to fit, or that otherwise slow down your reading.
   B. Place a "Good!" in the margin next to any passages where you think the writing is particularly strong or interesting.
II. Read the draft again slowly and answer the following questions by writing down brief explanations for your answers.
   A. Introduction:
      1. Does the title focus the paper and pique your interest?
      2. Does the writer briefly summarize the article being analyzed and present a clear thesis about how the use of statistics creates a rhetorical effect?
      3. Could the thesis be more clear, precise, forceful, or risky?
   B. Analysis:
      1. Does the author choose specific statistics from the article and show how the writer's selection or presentation of the data produces a desired rhetorical effect?
      2. Do you agree with the author's analysis? Are there additional details from the article that you think the author should discuss? Where are the ideas weak, undeveloped, or confusing?
      3. How could the author improve the clarity and structure of the draft?
   C. Sum up what you see as the chief strengths and problem areas of this draft.
      1. Strengths
      2. Problem areas
III. Read the draft one more time. Place a check in the margin wherever you notice problems in grammar, spelling, or mechanics (one check per problem).

Analyzing a Short Story

▨ ABOUT LITERARY ANALYSIS

You've no doubt had more than one experience analyzing literature. Unhappily, some of these experiences were probably unenlightening, even exasperating. Perhaps the whole process struck you as arbitrary; the teacher assigned one meaning to a work or passage when many others seemed equally possible. Or perhaps your teacher chose to discuss a work whose contents seemed far removed from your own experience and whose language sounded like some sort of Klingon code. Our goal in this chapter is to demonstrate that analyzing literature is neither arbitrary nor useless, and—done right—can even be pleasurable. Analyzing literature isn't all that different from analyzing other texts or events, so you already have most of the skills you need to do it well.

To begin understanding literary analysis, try to think of literature not so much as a collection of great books to be read, but rather as a way of reading. Or, put another way, you can choose to read anything literally or literarily. When you read something *literally,* you attempt to reduce its meaning to one clear set of statements and disregard other possible ways of reading the text. When you read something *literarily,* you read it playfully and openly, trying to see in it a wide range of possible meanings. When you read literarily, you can convert almost anything into literature—at least in a playful sense—even the back of a cereal box.

To help you understand the distinction we're drawing, consider the following analogy. A literal reading of an imaginative text is like a bad package tour of an exotic land. Picture a bus filled with bored American tourists slowly making its way through winding, narrow streets in search of the local Hilton. Centuries-old architectural wonders slip past unnoticed; the raucous sounds and pungent smells of the marketplace go unremarked.

As the few who aren't dozing stare out the windows, they catch glimpses of men in flowing robes greeting each other with embraces and kisses to the cheek—the tourists are perplexed. This is not how members of the class "male" are supposed to dress and act. Later, when they pass women haggling with street vendors, they are appalled. "They wouldn't last long with that sort of attitude at our local supermarket," one tourist assures another. They agree that this is a very strange place and they'll be glad to get back to the normal world where men touch hands, not cheeks, to greet each other and women use coupons, not persuasion, to get a deal on food.

The first step in moving beyond a literal to a literary reading of a text, or a country, is to get off the bus and open yourself up to the otherness of the text. You have to experience it on its own terms, which means reading it carefully, then noticing and examining your reactions to what you have read. You have to stop being a tourist and become instead a traveler, who goes alone, by foot, into foreign lands and lives for an extended time among the natives, trying to learn their language and ways. Travelers aren't driven by a desire to have been somewhere so they can tell others that they were there. Instead, they are driven by curiosity, a sense of wonder, a knack for recognizing resemblances in a world of apparent differences, and a capacity for being enthralled by the differences they do find.

To be a traveler rather than a tourist, you need to be an active participant in the process of constructing meaning from a text. Whereas tourists tend to write brief "We're here!" notes on postcards to friends, travelers are more likely to keep extensive journals to help them remember and understand their experiences. They reflect on what they see and on relationships between what they see, do, and feel one day to what they've seen, done, or felt in the past or to what others have reported seeing, doing, and feeling in the same place.

In this way, travelers interpret what they experience. Interpretive writing differs from other forms of writing most notably in its degree of tentativeness. An interpretation focuses on an ambiguous aspect of a text or experience and says, "Here's what I think is most probable." Unlike a traditional argument, which obligates the writer to refute other points of view, an interpretation may simply point out alternative explanations of the ambiguity and then focus on the writer's own interpretation.

◪ EXPLORING LITERARY ANALYSIS

As we have noted, any sort of text can be read either literally or literarily. However, texts do tend to invite one kind of reading over another. The following Navajo legend contains several signals that invite us to read literarily rather than literally. As you read through this piece, note where those signals occur.

READING

RETOLD BY EVELYN DAHL REED
THE MEDICINE MAN

1   There is a telling that, in the beginning, when the animals first came up from the darkness to live above the ground, Coyote was sent ahead by Thought Woman to carry a buckskin pouch far to the south.

"You must be very careful not to open the pouch," she told him, "or you will be punished."   2

For many days, Coyote ran southward with the pouch on his back. But the world was new, and there was nothing to eat along the way, so he grew very hungry. He wondered if there might be food in the pouch. At last, he took it from his back and untied the thongs. He looked inside and saw nothing but stars. Of course, as soon as he opened the pouch the stars all flew up into the sky, and there they are to this day.   3

"Now look what you've done," said Thought Woman. "For now you shall always get into trouble everywhere you go."   4

And because Coyote disobeyed, he was also made to suffer with the toothache. When the other animals were asleep, he could only sit and howl at the stars. Thus, he has been crying ever since the beginning of the world.   5

Sometimes he would ask the other animals to cure him, but they would only catch the toothache from him, and they, too, would cry.   6

One day he met Mouse, who lived in a little mound under the chaparral bush. "Friend Mouse," begged Coyote, "can you cure me of this toothache?"   7

Now it happened that while digging underground, as is his habit, Mouse had come upon a sweet-smelling root and had put it with the other herbs in the pouch he always carried. He was said to be very wise in the use of herbs.   8

"I don't know," said Mouse, "but I have just found a new root, and it may be that it will help you." He rubbed the root on Coyote's swollen cheek, and in a little while the toothache was gone.   9

This is how it happened that coyotes never hunt or kill field mice.   10

1. List the signals in the text that led you to read this story literarily as opposed to literally. Summarize the most important differences between how you read this story and how you read the introduction to this chapter.
2. Devise questions about the legend that you think might produce different responses among your classmates. For example: Why is the woman named Thought Woman? Why is Thought Woman a female and not a male?
3. Explain why you think these questions will evoke different responses.

WRITING PROJECT

Your writing project for this chapter has two parts—a formal essay and a series of reading-log entries that will prepare you to write your formal essay. Your entries in your reading log will give you an opportunity to explore your own ways of reading and responding to the story and then to compare your interpretations with those of your classmates. Your essay should use traditional closed-form writing to present your analysis and interpretation. Use it to present your answer to *your* problematic question about the story.

Essay Assignment

Pose an interpretive question about a short story and respond to it analytically, showing your readers how the text of the story supports your interpretation. All class members will analyze the same story—either one of the stories in the readings section of this chapter or another story provided by your instructor. In the introduction to your essay, pose an interesting, problematic, and significant question about the story, one that can be answered several different ways according to the evidence in the text. Look for a question that might lead to differences of opinion among your classmates and that offers readers new insights into the story.

Your task in this assignment is not to discover the right way to interpret the text, but to explain *your* way of reading some aspect of it. In the introduction, make clear just what question you are putting to the text and why. Then, in the body of your paper, explain your own response to this question, contrasting your answer with other possible interpretations that have been proposed by your classmates or that you yourself have considered. Without disputing the alternative interpretations, concentrate on showing your reader how you arrived at *your* interpretation and why you think that interpretation is valuable. Use details from the story for support.

Reading Log Assignment

To help you settle on a good question for your paper and to develop and share ideas, we have interspersed throughout the chapter a series of reading-log questions for you to use in exploring the text. Your reading log will help you the most if you write in response to each freewriting task when you come to it in the text. (There are fifteen in all.) The sequence and timing of the early entries are important, so do not read ahead. Keep your notebook and pen with you as you read, and when you come to a reading-log question, stop and respond to it at that time.

The reading-log entries will help you pose a good question about your assigned short story. Good literary questions call attention to problematic details of the text, stimulate conversation, and provoke readers to return to the text to reread and rethink. You know you will have a good question if your classmates disagree about the answer and contribute their own differing views to the conversation. Sharing your reading-log entries with classmates will help you generate and sustain a productive discussion about the short story.

◼ UNDERSTANDING LITERARY ANALYSIS

The Truth of Literary Events

As an introduction to literary analysis, let's return to "Medicine Man" and consider several questions that it, and other texts of its sort, pose to the reader. First, in what sense is the story true? What advantages are there to expressing a view of truth in a literary, rather than in a literal way? Why might someone choose to tell such a story rather than to approach the world scientifically? What other stories does "Medicine Man" remind you of? How is it different from those stories? How are the characters in the story like and unlike characters you've known in real life?

"Medicine Man" is immediately recognizable as literary; it's difficult, if not impossible, to read it literally. Animals can't talk, and galaxies can't be carted about in a buckskin pouch. We either make a leap of faith and license the author to play fast and loose with our conventional understanding of reality, or we put the story down, dismayed that anyone could think we'd be gullible enough to buy this twaddle.

The events of the story are presented to us as if they actually happened. We know better, but we go along with the ruse in order to enjoy the story. We know that when we read these sorts of texts, we can't demand a one-to-one correspondence between the words we read and the things, persons, and events to which they supposedly refer. We must read instead with what the poet Coleridge called "a Willing Suspension of Disbelief."

Suspending disbelief does not mean erasing it. While we're reading literarily, we are to some degree consciously suppressing skepticism and nagging doubts, leftovers of our literal-minded selves. While we're reading "Medicine Man," we never really forget that coyotes can't talk. But if coyotes could talk, we can imagine them talking as this coyote talks. The coyote in this story is true not because it literally existed, but because it resembles coyotes of our world and coyotes in other stories we've read. So we put aside our skepticism and focus on the resemblance.

Both ways of looking at the story—literal and literary—are open to us, and we consciously choose one over the other. Choosing between a literary and a literal reading is similar to choosing between two ways of looking at an optical illusion. For example, you can look at the drawing in Figure 12.1 as either two profiles or a vase—but you can't see both at once. Until you see both possibilities, you might get stuck seeing it literally as one thing and one thing only. After you've seen it both ways, you're always conscious of that other way of seeing it.

FIGURE 12.1   An Optical Illusion: Two Profiles or a Vase?

This both/and principle applies not only to the events of a fictional story, but also to the language of literature. When we encounter a simile announcing that "love is like a red, red rose," we never quite forget that roses aren't really love; we know that the word *like* keeps love and roses forever apart in the very act of bringing them together. To read literarily isn't to cease reading literally so much as it is to read both/and—*both* literally *and* literarily. The stories we read are both true and false; the metaphors we encounter are both one thing (*loveredredrose*) and two different things (*love* [an abstract noun] and *red, red rose* [two adjectives intensifying a concrete noun]); the optical illusion in Figure 12.1 is both two profiles and a vase—we just can't see it both ways simultaneously.

We read *as if* normally suspicious stories were true and *as if* metaphoric language allowed members of two completely different classes to hop their categorical fences and become some barely imaginable third thing. In this regard, the "as if" of literary language is like the magical "let's pretend" of childhood, which allowed us to become action heroes, television characters, or historical or legendary figures; to die, marry, become parents, and have careers; to talk freely in character and out—and then to pop back to reality for a peanut butter sandwich and a nap.

Reading the Story

We ask you now to read the short story your instructor has designated for this assignment. Let the following reading-log tasks help you become a traveler in the story rather than a tourist. Task 1 asks you to stop several times along the way as you read. Tasks 2 and 3 should be written immediately after you finish reading.

Reading-Log Task 1	As you read your assigned story, stop at several points and predict what you think will happen in the rest of the story. Make your first stop fairly early in the story, choose a second stopping place in the middle, and stop a third time near the end. In each case, predict what is going to happen in the rest of the story and note what in the text causes you to make your prediction. Freewrite for three or four minutes each time you stop.
Reading-Log Task 2	As soon as you finish your reading, write down your immediate responses to the text—how it made you feel or think, what emotions it triggered, what issues it raised. Freewrite for five minutes.
Reading-Log Task 3	Write down (a) what most interested you about the story and (b) the most important question you're left with after reading the text. Freewrite for a couple of minutes after several minutes of reflecting.

FOR WRITING AND DISCUSSION

As a whole class or in small groups, share your responses to the reading-log tasks. Because you will need to begin your formal essay for this assignment with a problematic question, pay particular attention to your classmates' responses to (b) in Task 3—the most important question raised by the text. Perhaps you have a tentative answer you would like to propose to someone else's question.

Writing (About) Literature

We put "about" in parentheses in this heading because in a sense, to write about literature is to write literature. When you read literarily you are an active co-creator of the text just as a musician is a co-creator of a concerto. Musicians and literary readers don't completely reinvent composers' notes and authors' words every time they play or read them. Composers and writers provide abundant cues to signal how they wish to be played or read and to limit possible interpretations of their work. But in the process of performing another's text, readers and musicians give those words and notes a meaning unique to that particular performance. And in some cases, their renditions may depart considerably from the originator's intentions.

This reading as performance is quite different from the more passive process of literal reading. Whereas the literal reader expects to find unambiguous, universally shared meaning in the text, the literary reader anticipates having to create meaning, which then must be justified to other readers and modified by them. For the literal reader, meaning is a commodity that is extracted intact from the text much as gold nuggets are sluiced from a stream. For the literary reader, meaning is more like a quilt constructed from bits and pieces of the text by many people, who consult and argue and admire each others' skill and change each others' minds about which pieces to include and where to put them.

To participate in the reading process actively, to "write" your version of a text, you need to know the kinds of questions you might ask of it. To help you, we briefly summarize four critical elements of a literary text and the kinds of questions each element suggests. (For additional discussion of these elements, and of open-form writing in general, refer to Chapter 7 and Chapter 19.)

Asking Questions About Plot

Plot refers to the sequence of critical events in the story. The key term here is *critical*. A plot summary does not include everything that happens in a story; it focuses on the elements that most directly move the action of the story forward. One method of analyzing the plot is to begin by identifying what you see as the most critical single event or moment in a story. What is the most pivotal point, the one that prior events lead up to and that subsequent events derive from? Different readers are apt to pick different moments, indicating differences in the way they read the story. Your task is to identify your own choice and to be prepared to defend it. Remember, you are *performing* the story, not trying to figure out some unambiguous right meaning. As long as you have a rationale for your decision, you are acting as a literary critic.

Reading-Log Task 4 What is the single most important moment or event in your assigned story? Why do you see this moment as important or crucial? Freewrite for about ten minutes.

FOR WRITING AND DISCUSSION

As a whole class or in small groups, share your responses to Task 4. Which events did you choose and what are your arguments for selecting them? Take notes about how your classmates' interpretations differ.

Asking Questions About Characters

Characters are the people who make the decisions that forward the plot and whose fortunes change as a result of the plot. You can understand characters in a text only in relationship to each other and to the direction of change in the text. The major character, sometimes called the *protagonist*, is typically the one most responsible for forwarding the plot. In action stories, these characters are pretty static; Dirty Harry or Batman may undergo occasional physical changes and disguises, but their characters tend not to grow or deepen. In other kinds of stories, the major character may change significantly in terms of fortune, insight, or understanding. Which characters change in the story you are examining? How do they change? Which characters do not change? Why do the characters change or not change?

To examine the characters' relationships with each other, you might start with the protagonist and consider the other characters according to how they help or hinder the protagonist. Characters may contribute to the plot by overt action or inaction, by recognizing or failing to recognize something of significance, by adapting to the situation of the story or by being inflexible. They can guide or misguide the protagonist, be a friend or foe, share or threaten the protagonist's values or beliefs, and so forth. What tensions, contrasts, and differing points of view do you see among the characters?

Reading-Log Task 5 Who do you think is the most important character in the story? How does this character change or grow as the story progresses? How do the other characters promote or inhibit change in the main character? How do they help you see and understand the changes? Freewrite for 10–15 minutes.

FOR WRITING AND DISCUSSION

Share your reading-log entries and note differences in the interpretations of various members of the class. Remember that you are not seeking the one right answer to these questions. You are trying to determine how *you* read this story.

Asking Questions About Setting

Although a setting is sometimes little more than a backdrop, like a black curtain behind a speaker on a stage, it can also serve to amplify or help explain the events and motivations of a story. Sometimes the setting acts as a symbol or serves the same function in a story that theme music serves in a movie, underscoring the text's primary themes and moods. A story could be set at the edge of a dark forest, on an ascent up a mountain, or in an inner city, with action moving back and forth between remote vacant lots and a warm kitchen. Sometimes setting plays an active role in the text, functioning almost as a character. A setting could thwart the protagonist's efforts to bring about change or to survive; for example, the collapse of a bridge could prevent a character from crossing a river. Does setting play a role in the story you are analyzing? If so, how would you characterize that role? Could you picture the events of the text taking place in a significantly different setting? Why or why not?

Asking Questions About Point of View

Perhaps the toughest element to perceive in a fictional work is point of view. It does not exist out there on the page, as do character and plot. Point of view is the filter through which the reader views the action of a story. In some cases the impact of point of view on your perception of a character or event is obvious; in other cases it is not. The point of view can trick you into seeing an event in a particular way that you will have to revise when you realize that the narrator's perspective was limited, biased, or ironic. Often the narrator's values and perceptions are different from those of the author; you should never assume that the narrator of the story and the author are the same.

The two primary elements of point of view are time and person. Most stories are told in the past tense, a significant number in the present tense, and a few in the future tense. An almost equal number of stories are told in the first person (in which case the narrator is usually an actor in the story, although not always the main character) as in the third person (in which case the narrator tells the story from a position outside the tale). All choices of tense and person affect the reader's perception of a story. For example, a story told in the first-person present tense ("We ride back from the hunt at dusk") has an immediacy that a story told in the third-person past ("They rode back from the hunt at dusk") does not have. You learn about a first-person narrator both from what the narrator does or says in the plot and from how the narrator tells the story—what he or she includes or omits, the sentence structure, tone, or figures of speech that he or she adopts, and so forth. A third person narrator may be objective (the narrator sees only the external actions of characters) or omniscient (the narrator can enter the minds and feelings of various characters). Sometimes a third-person narrator is omniscient with respect to one character but objective toward others.

Narrators can provide a full and complete sense of a given character (by entering that character's mind as an omniscient narrator) or a partial view only (by observing the character from the outside). Some stories feature multiple points of view through multiple narrators. For example, one character may discover a journal written by another character or may listen to a story told by another character.

The surest path to understanding point of view is to start with your feelings and attitudes toward characters and events and then to examine the extent to which point of view contributes to those attitudes. Do you trust the narrator? Do you like the narrator? Has the narrator loaded the dice, causing you to see characters or events in strongly slanted ways? Is the narrator scrupulously objective or ironic to the point that you're not quite sure what to make of his or her observations?

To ask questions about point of view, begin by asking whether the narrative is first or third person. Then ask whether the narrator's perspective is omniscient or limited. Does the narrator reveal bias or irony? Do you feel that there is more to the story than the narrator is telling you? What does the narrator leave out? How are the narrator's perceptions different from your own?

Reading-Log Task 6	Is there anything worth noting about your assigned story's setting? What are the settings, how do settings change, and what role do these settings play in your reading of the story? Freewrite for ten minutes on your ideas about the importance of setting in the story.
Reading-Log Task 7	What is the story's point of view? Does the narrator play a role in the story? Is the narrator's way of seeing part of what the story is about? Freewrite for ten minutes on any ideas you generate by contemplating the story's point of view.

FOR WRITING AND DISCUSSION

Share your reading-log entries with your class and note differences in interpretations.

Asking Questions About Theme

If a plot is what happens in a story, then theme is the significance of what happens. Your response to the question "So what?" after reading a story represents your notion of the story's theme. Sometimes, a theme is obvious—the main characters might discuss it, or the author might even state it outright. Often, however, a theme is veiled, and you have to infer it from the words and deeds of the characters.

One way to discover theme is simply to reflect on your immediate responses to characters or on passages that affected you particularly strongly. Consider questions such as these: How did this story change your view of something or the way you feel about something? Is this story trying to reveal something about racism? About endurance in time of trial? About growth from one phase of life to another? About appearance versus reality? About conflicts between the individual and family? About exterior loss and interior gain? About rebellion from society? About what's really valuable versus what appears to be valuable? About establishing values in a confusing world?

Reading-Log Task 8	Reread your response to Task 2, your first attempt to articulate ideas related to the story's theme. Then complete one of

the following statements: (a) After further reflection on my assigned story, I think the author is trying to say something to readers about _____. (b) Here is what this story makes me think about and see: _____. Freewrite for fifteen minutes.

You can often gain valuable insights into a story's theme by examining the connections among the various literary elements we have been discussing. These points of intersection may also help you generate significant interpretive questions.

Reading-Log Task 9   Look again at the place in the story that you identified in Task 4 as its most important moment or event. (a) What role do the elements of *character* that you identified in Task 5 play in this crucial passage? (b) Do elements of the story's *setting* contribute to your understanding of the importance of this passage? How do these details add to its impact? (c) How does *point of view* contribute to a reader's sense of the importance of the events and/or description in this passage? (d) Does your analysis of the interconnections of these literary elements give you new ideas or raise new questions for you about the story's *theme*? Freewrite for fifteen minutes.

FOR WRITING AND DISCUSSION

Share your responses to reading-log tasks 8 and 9 with your class and note differences in the ways in which members of the class read this story.

READINGS

We include in this section two short stories to test your analytical skills. Because analyzing short stories requires you to pose your own interesting questions about a text, we do not provide any analysis questions following the stories. In addition, we include a student essay written to the same assignment.

Our first reading is "Everyday Use (for your grandmama)" by contemporary African-American writer Alice Walker. It appeared in *In Love and Trouble: Stories of Black Women* in 1973.

ALICE WALKER
EVERYDAY USE (FOR YOUR GRANDMAMA)

I will wait for her in the yard that Maggie and I made so clean and wavy yesterday   1
afternoon. A yard like this is more comfortable than most people know. It is not just a yard. It is like an extended living room. When the hard clay is swept clean as a floor

and the fine sand around the edges lined with tiny, irregular grooves, anyone can come and sit and look up into the elm tree and wait for the breezes that never come inside the house.

2   Maggie will be nervous until after her sister goes: she will stand hopelessly in corners, homely and ashamed of the burn scars down her arms and legs, eying her sister with a mixture of envy and awe. She thinks her sister has held life always in the palm of one hand, that "no" is a word the world never learned to say to her.

3   You've no doubt seen those TV shows where the child who has "made it" is confronted, as a surprise, by her own mother and father, tottering in weakly from backstage. (A pleasant surprise, of course: What would they do if parent and child came on the show only to curse out and insult each other?) On TV mother and child embrace and smile into each other's faces. Sometimes the mother and father weep; the child wraps them in her arms and leans across the table to tell how she would not have made it without their help. I have seen these programs.

4   Sometimes I dream a dream in which Dee and I are suddenly brought together on a TV program of this sort. Out of a dark and soft-seated limousine I am ushered into a bright room filled with many people. There I meet a smiling, gray, sporty man like Johnny Carson who shakes my hand and tells me what a fine girl I have. Then we are on the stage and Dee is embracing me with tears in her eyes. She pins on my dress a large orchid, even though she has told me once that she thinks orchids are tacky flowers.

5   In real life I am a large, big-boned woman with rough, man-working hands. In the winter I wear flannel nightgowns to bed and overalls during the day. I can kill and clean a hog as mercilessly as a man. My fat keeps me hot in zero weather. I can work outside all day, breaking once to get water for washing; I can eat pork liver cooked over the open fire minutes after it comes steaming from the hog. One winter I knocked a bull calf straight in the brain between the eyes with a sledge hammer and had the meat hung up to chill before nightfall. But of course all this does not show on television. I am the way my daughter would want me to be: a hundred pounds lighter, my skin like an uncooked barley pancake. My hair glistens in the hot bright lights. Johnny Carson has much to do to keep up with my quick and witty tongue.

6   But that is a mistake. I know even before I wake up. Who ever knew a Johnson with a quick tongue? Who can even imagine me looking a strange white man in the eye? It seems to me I have talked to them always with one foot raised in flight, with my head turned in whichever way is farthest from them. Dee, though. She would always look anyone in the eye. Hesitation was no part of her nature.

7   "How do I look, Mama?" Maggie says, showing just enough of her thin body enveloped in pink skirt and red blouse for me to know she's there, almost hidden by the door.

8   "Come out into the yard," I say.

9   Have you ever seen a lame animal, perhaps a dog run over by some careless person rich enough to own a car, sidle up to someone who is ignorant enough to be kind to him? That is the way my Maggie walks. She has been like this, chin on chest, eyes on ground, feet in shuffle, ever since the fire that burned the other house to the ground.

10   Dee is lighter than Maggie, with nicer hair and a fuller figure. She's a woman now, though sometimes I forget. How long ago was it that the other house burned? Ten, twelve years? Sometimes I can still hear the flames and feel Maggie's arms sticking to me, her hair smoking and her dress falling off her in little black papery flakes. Her eyes

seemed stretched open, blazed open by the flames reflected in them. And Dee. I see her standing off under the sweet gum tree she used to dig gum out of; a look of concentration on her face as she watched the last dingy gray board of the house fall in toward the red-hot brick chimney. Why don't you do a dance around the ashes? I'd wanted to ask her. She had hated the house that much.

I used to think she hated Maggie, too. But that was before we raised the money, the church and me, to send her to Augusta to school. She used to read to us without pity; forcing words, lies, other folks' habits, whole lives upon us two, sitting trapped and ignorant underneath her voice. She washed us in a river of make-believe, burned us with a lot of knowledge we didn't necessarily need to know. Pressed us to her with the serious way she read, to shove us away at just the moment, like dimwits, we seemed about to understand.   11

Dee wanted nice things. A yellow organdy dress to wear to her graduation from high school; black pumps to match a green suit she'd made from an old suit somebody gave me. She was determined to stare down any disaster in her efforts. Her eyelids would not flicker for minutes at a time. Often I fought off the temptation to shake her. At sixteen she had a style of her own: and she knew what style was.   12

I never had an education myself. After second grade the school was closed down. Don't ask my why: in 1927 colored asked fewer questions than they do now. Sometimes Maggie reads to me. She stumbles along good-naturedly but can't see well. She knows she is not bright. Like good looks and money, quickness passed her by. She will marry John Thomas (who has mossy teeth in an earnest face) and then I'll be free to sit here and I guess just sing church songs to myself. Although I never was a good singer. Never could carry a tune. I was always better at a man's job. I used to love to milk till I was hooked in the side in '49. Cows are soothing and slow and don't bother you, unless you try to milk them the wrong way.   13

I have deliberately turned my back on the house. It is three rooms, just like the one that burned, except the roof is tin; they don't make shingle roofs any more. There are no real windows, just some holes cut in the sides, like the portholes in a ship, but not round and not square, with rawhide holding the shutters up on the outside. This house is in a pasture, too, like the other one. No doubt when Dee sees it she will want to tear it down. She wrote me once that no matter where we "choose" to live, she will manage to come see us. But she will never bring her friends. Maggie and I thought about this and Maggie asked me, "Mama, when did Dee ever *have* any friends?"   14

She had a few. Furtive boys in pink shirts hanging about on washday after school. Nervous girls who never laughed. Impressed with her they worshiped the well-turned phrase, the cute shape, the scalding humor that erupted like bubbles in lye. She read to them.   15

When she was courting Jimmy T she didn't have much time to pay to us, but turned all her faultfinding power on him. He *flew* to marry a cheap city girl from a family of ignorant flashy people. She hardly had time to recompose herself.   16

When she comes I will meet—but there they are!   17

Maggie attempts to make a dash for the house, in her shuffling way, but I stay her with my hand. "Come back here," I say. And she stops and tries to dig a well in the sand with her toe.   18

It is hard to see them clearly through the strong sun. But even the first glimpse of leg out of the car tells me it is Dee. Her feet were always neat-looking, as if God himself had shaped them with a certain style. From the other side of the car comes a short,   19 stocky man. Hair is all over his head a foot long and hanging from his chin like a kinky mule tail. I hear Maggie suck in her breath. "Uhnnnh," is what it sounds like. Like when you see the wriggling end of a snake just in front of your foot on the road. "Uhnnnh."

20   Dee next. A dress down to the ground, in this hot weather. A dress so loud it hurts my eyes. There are yellows and oranges enough to throw back the light of the sun. I feel my whole face warming from the heat waves it throws out. Earrings gold, too, and hanging down to her shoulders. Bracelets dangling and making noises when she moves her arm up to shake the folds of the dress out of her armpits. The dress is loose and flows, and as she walks closer, I like it. I hear Maggie go "Uhnnnh" again. It is her sister's hair. It stands straight up like the wool on a sheep. It is black as night and around the edges are two long ponytails that rope about like small lizards disappearing behind her ears.

21   "Wa-su-zo-Tean-o!" she says, coming in on that gliding way the dress makes her move. The short stocky fellow with the hair to his navel is all grinning and he follows up with "Asalamalakim, my mother and sister!" He moves to hug Maggie but she falls back, right up against the back of my chair. I feel her trembling there and when I look up I see the perspiration falling off her chin.

22   "Don't get up," says Dee. Since I am stout it takes something of a push. You can see me trying to move a second or two before I make it. She turns, showing white heels through her sandals, and goes back to the car. Out she peeks next with a Polaroid. She stoops down quickly and lines up picture after picture of me sitting there in front of the house with Maggie cowering behind me. She never takes a shot without making sure the house is included. When a cow comes nibbling around the edge of the yard she snaps it and me and Maggie *and* the house. Then she puts the Polaroid in the back seat of the car, and comes up and kisses me on the forehead.

23   Meanwhile Asalamalakim is going through the motions with Maggie's hand. Maggie's hand is as limp as a fish, and probably cold, despite the sweat, and she keeps trying to pull it back. It looks like Asalamalakim wants to shake hands but wants to do it fancy. Or maybe he don't know how people shake hands. Anyhow, he soon gives up on Maggie.

24   "Well," I say. "Dee."

25   "No, Mama," she says. "Not 'Dee,' Wangero Leewanika Kemanjo!"

26   "What happened to 'Dee'?" I wanted to know.

27   "She's dead," Wangero said. "I couldn't bear it any longer, being named after the people who oppress me."

28   "You know as well as me you was named after your aunt Dicie," I said. Dicie is my sister. She named Dee. We called her "Big Dee" after Dee was born.

29   "But who was *she* named after?" asked Wangero.

30   "I guess after Grandma Dee," I said.

31   "And who was she named after?" asked Wangero.

32   "Her mother," I said, and saw Wangero was getting tired. "That's about as far back as I can trace it," I said. Though, in fact, I probably could have carried it back beyond the Civil War through the branches.

33   "Well," said Asalamalakim, "there you are."

34   "Uhnnnh," I heard Maggie say.

35   "There I was not," I said, "before 'Dicie' cropped up in our family, so why should I try to trace it that far back?"

36   He just stood there grinning, looking down on me like somebody inspecting a Model A car. Every once in a while he and Wangero sent eye signals over my head.

37   "How do you pronounce this name?" I asked.

"You don't have to call me by it if you don't want to," said Wangero.   38

"Why shouldn't I?" I asked. "If that's what you want us to call you, we'll call you."   39

"I know it might sound awkward at first," said Wangero.   40

"I'll get used to it," I said. "Ream it out again."   41

Well, soon we got the name out of the way. Asalamalakim had a name twice as   42
long and three times as hard. After I tripped over it two or three times he told me to just
call him Hakim-a-barber. I wanted to ask him was he a barber, but I didn't really think
he was, so I didn't ask.

"You must belong to those beef-cattle peoples down the road," I said. They said   43
"Asalamalakim" when they met you, too, but they didn't shake hands. Always too busy:
feeding the cattle, fixing the fences, putting up salt-lick shelters, throwing down hay.
When the white folks poisoned some of the herd the men stayed up all night with rifles
in their hands. I walked a mile and a half just to see the sight.

Hakim-a-barber said, "I accept some of their doctrines, but farming and raising cat-   44
tle is not my style." (They didn't tell me, and I didn't ask, whether Wangero (Dee) had
really gone and married him.)

We sat down to eat and right away he said he didn't eat collards and pork was un-   45
clean. Wangero, though, went on through the chitlins and corn bread, the greens and
everything else. She talked a blue streak over the sweet potatoes. Everything delighted
her. Even the fact that we still used the benches her daddy made for the table when we
couldn't afford to buy chairs.

"Oh, Mama!" she cried. Then turned to Hakim-a-barber. "I never knew how lovely   46
these benches are. You can feel the rump prints," she said, running her hands underneath her and along the bench. Then she gave a sigh and her hand closed over
Grandma Dee's butter dish. "That's it!" she said. "I knew there was something I wanted
to ask you if I could have." She jumped up from the table and went over in the corner
where the churn stood, the milk in it clabber by now. She looked at the churn and
looked at it.

"This churn top is what I need," she said. "Didn't Uncle Buddy whittle it out of a   47
tree you all used to have?"

"Yes," I said.   48

"Uh huh," she said happily. "And I want the dasher, too."   49

"Uncle Buddy whittle that, too?" asked the barber.   50

Dee (Wangero) looked up at me.   51

"Aunt Dee's first husband whittled the dash," said Maggie so low you almost   52
couldn't hear her. "His name was Henry, but they called him Stash."

"Maggie's brain is like an elephant's," Wangero said, laughing. "I can use the churn   53
top as a centerpiece for the alcove table," she said, sliding a plate over the churn, "and
I'll think of something artistic to do with the dasher."

When she finished wrapping the dasher the handle stuck out. I took it for a moment   54
in my hands. You didn't even have to look close to see where hands pushing the dasher
up and down to make butter had left a kind of sink in the wood. In fact, there were a
lot of small sinks; you could see where thumbs and fingers had sunk into the wood. It
was beautiful light yellow wood, from a tree that grew in the yard where Big Dee and
Stash had lived.

After dinner Dee (Wangero) went to the trunk at the foot of my bed and started ri-   55
fling through it. Maggie hung back in the kitchen over the dishpan. Out came Wangero
with two quilts. They had been pieced by Grandma Dee and then Big Dee and me had
hung them on the quilt frames on the front porch and quilted them. One was in the Lone
Star pattern. The other was Walk Around the Mountain. In both of them were scraps of

dresses Grandma Dee had worn fifty and more years ago. Bits and pieces of Grandma Jarrell's Paisley shirts. And one teeny faded blue piece, about the size of a penny matchbox, that was from Great Grandpa Ezra's uniform that he wore in the Civil War.

56   "Mama," Wangero said sweet as a bird. "Can I have these old quilts?"

57   I heard something fall in the kitchen, and a minute later the kitchen door slammed.

58   "Why don't you take one or two of the others?" I asked. "These old things was just done by me and Big Dee from some tops your grandma pieced before she died."

59   "No," said Wangero. "I don't want those. They are stitched around the borders by machine."

60   "That'll make them last better," I said.

61   "That's not the point," said Wangero. "These are all pieces of dresses Grandma used to wear. She did all this stitching by hand. Imagine!" She held the quilts securely in her arms, stroking them.

62   "Some of the pieces, like those lavender ones, come from old clothes her mother handed down to her," I said, moving up to touch the quilts. Dee (Wangero) moved back just enough so that I couldn't reach the quilts. They already belonged to her.

63   "Imagine!" she breathed again, clutching them closely to her bosom.

64   "The truth is," I said, "I promised to give them quilts to Maggie, for when she marries John Thomas."

65   She gasped like a bee had stung her.

66   "Maggie can't appreciate these quilts!" she said. "She'd probably be backward enough to put them to everyday use."

67   "I reckon she would," I said. "God knows I been saving 'em for long enough with nobody using 'em. I hope she will!" I didn't want to bring up how I had offered Dee (Wangero) a quilt when she went away to college. Then she had told me they were old-fashioned, out of style.

68   "But they're *priceless!*" she was saying now, furiously; for she has a temper. "Maggie would put them on the bed and in five years they'd be in rags. Less than that!"

69   "She can always make some more," I said. "Maggie knows how to quilt."

70   Dee (Wangero) looked at me with hatred. "You just will not understand. The point is these quilts, *these* quilts!"

71   "Well," I said, stumped. "What would *you* do with them?"

72   "Hang them," she said. As if that was the only thing you *could* do with quilts.

73   Maggie by now was standing in the door. I could almost hear the sound her feet made as they scraped over each other.

74   "She can have them, Mama," she said, like somebody used to never winning anything, or having anything reserved for her. "I can 'member Grandma Dee without the quilts."

75   I looked at her hard. She had filled her bottom lip with checkerberry snuff and it gave her face a kind of dopey, hangdog look. It was Grandma Dee and Big Dee who taught her how to quilt herself. She stood there with her hands hidden in the folds of her skirt. She looked at her sister with something like fear but she wasn't mad at her. This was Maggie's portion. This was the way she knew God to work.

76   When I looked at her like that something hit me in the top of my head and ran down to the soles of my feet. Just like when I'm in church and the spirit of God touches me and I get happy and shout. I did something I never had done before: hugged Maggie to me, then dragged her on into the room, snatched the quilts out of Miss Wangero's hands and dumped them into Maggie's lap. Maggie just sat there on my bed with her mouth open.

77   "Take one or two of the others," I said to Dee.

But she turned without a word and went out to Hakim-a-barber. 78

"You just don't understand," she said, as Maggie and I came out to the car. 79

"What don't I understand?" I wanted to know. 80

"Your heritage," she said. And then she turned to Maggie, kissed her, and said, "You 81
ought to try to make something of yourself, too, Maggie. It's really a new day for us.
But from the way you and Mama still live you'd never know it."

She put on some sunglasses that hid everything above the tip of her nose and her 82
chin.

Maggie smiled; maybe at the sunglasses. But a real smile, not scared. After we 83
watched the car dust settle I asked Maggie to me bring me a dip of snuff. And then the
two of us sat there just enjoying, until it was time to go in the house and go to bed.

Our next reading, "A Very Old Man with Enormous Wings" by Columbian
writer Gabriel García Márquez, is an example of magical realism. Magical realism
is a way of both seeing and knowing—a philosophy and a literary practice reflected by the writer's choice of fictional worlds. As a philosophy, magical realism
challenges the scientific and materialist assumptions of Western rationality, believing instead that reality should include what is marvelous, supernatural, un-
controllable, and mysterious. As a literary practice, magical realism blends the
fantastic and bizarre with the ordinary and everyday so that the magical occurrences seem real and believable. Magical realism is often associated with Latin
America because of its first appearance there, the numerous Latin American writers who practice it (among them Isabel Allende, Alejo Carpentier, Jorge Luis
Borges), and the peculiar way that Latin America itself represents a blend of native cultures with African and European traditions, of modern cities with untamed
nature, of mythic cyclical visions of history with social and political instability.
However, Kafka as well as many contemporary writers including Toni Morrison,
Louise Erdrich, and Salman Rushdie merge the marvelous with the everyday in
similarly disruptive ways. In "A Very Old Man with Enormous Wings," note the
numerous strange tensions or contradictions, often the result of yoking what is
"magical" with what is "real," that appear throughout this story.

GABRIEL GARCÍA MÁRQUEZ
A VERY OLD MAN WITH ENORMOUS WINGS

On the third day of rain they had killed so many crabs inside the house that Pelayo 1
had to cross his drenched courtyard and throw them into the sea, because the newborn
child had a temperature all night and they thought it was due to the stench. The world
had been sad since Tuesday. Sea and sky were a single ash-gray thing and the sands
of the beach, which on March nights glimmered like powdered light, had become a stew
of mud and rotten shellfish. The light was so weak at noon that when Pelayo was coming back to the house after throwing away the crabs, it was hard for him to see what it
was that was moving and groaning in the rear of the courtyard. He had to go very close

to see that it was an old man, a very old man, lying face down in the mud, who, in spite of his tremendous efforts, couldn't get up, impeded by his enormous wings.

2   Frightened by that nightmare, Pelayo ran to get Elisenda, his wife, who was putting compresses on the sick child, and he took her to the rear of the courtyard. They both looked at the fallen body with mute stupor. He was dressed like a ragpicker. There were only a few faded hairs left on his bald skull and very few teeth in his mouth, and his pitiful condition of a drenched great-grandfather had taken away any sense of grandeur he might have had. His huge buzzard wings, dirty and half-plucked, were forever entangled in the mud. They looked at him so long and so closely that Pelayo and Elisenda very soon overcame their surprise and in the end found him familiar. Then they dared speak to him, and he answered in an incomprehensible dialect with a strong sailor's voice. That was how they skipped over the inconvenience of the wings and quite intelligently concluded that he was a lonely castaway from some foreign ship wrecked by the storm. And yet, they called in a neighbor woman who knew everything about life and death to see him, and all she needed was one look to show them their mistake.

3   "He's an angel," she told them. "He must have been coming for the child, but the poor fellow is so old that the rain knocked him down."

4   On the following day everyone knew that a flesh-and-blood angel was held captive in Pelayo's house. Against the judgment of the wise neighbor woman, for whom angels in those times were the fugitive survivors of a celestial conspiracy, they did not have the heart to club him to death. Pelayo watched over him all afternoon from the kitchen, armed with his bailiff's club, and before going to bed he dragged him out of the mud and locked him up with the hens in the wire chicken coop. In the middle of the night, when the rain stopped, Pelayo and Elisenda were still killing crabs. A short time afterward the child woke up without a fever and with a desire to eat. Then they felt magnanimous and decided to put the angel on a raft with fresh water and provisions for three days and leave him to his fate on the high seas. But when they went out into the courtyard with the first light of dawn, they found the whole neighborhood in front of the chicken coop having fun with the angel, without the slightest reverence, tossing him things to eat through the openings in the wire as if he weren't a supernatural creature but a circus animal.

5   Father Gonzaga arrived before seven o'clock, alarmed at the strange news. By that time onlookers less frivolous than those at dawn had already arrived and they were making all kinds of conjectures concerning the captive's future. The simplest among them thought that he should be named mayor of the world. Others of sterner mind felt that he should be promoted to the rank of five-star general in order to win all wars. Some visionaries hoped that he could be put to stud in order to implant on earth a race of winged wise men who could take charge of the universe. But Father Gonzaga, before becoming a priest, had been a robust woodcutter. Standing by the wire, he reviewed his catechism in an instant and asked them to open the door so that he could take a close look at that pitiful man who looked more like a huge decrepit hen among the fascinated chickens. He was lying in a corner drying his open wings in the sunlight among the fruit peels and breakfast leftovers that the early risers had thrown him. Alien to the impertinences of the world, he only lifted his antiquarian eyes and murmured something in his dialect when Father Gonzaga went into the chicken coop and said good morning to him in Latin. The parish priest had his first suspicion of an impostor when he saw that he did not understand the language of God or know how to greet His ministers. Then he noticed that seen close up he was much too human; he had an unbearable smell of the outdoors, the back side of his wings were strewn with parasites and his main feathers had been mistreated by terrestrial winds, and nothing about him measured up

to the proud dignity of angels. Then he came out of the chicken coop and in a brief sermon warned the curious against the risks of being ingenuous. He reminded them that the devil had the bad habit of making use of carnival tricks in order to confuse the unwary. He argued that if wings were not the essential element in determining the difference between a hawk and an airplane, they were even less so in the recognition of angels. Nevertheless, he promised to write a letter to his bishop so that the latter would write to his primate so that the latter would write to the Supreme Pontiff in order to get the final verdict from the highest courts.

His prudence fell on sterile hearts. The news of the captive angel spread with such 6 rapidity that after a few hours the courtyard had the bustle of a marketplace and they had to call in troops with fixed bayonets to disperse the mob that was about to knock the house down. Elisenda, her spine all twisted from sweeping up so much marketplace trash, then got the idea of fencing in the yard and charging five cents admission to see the angel.

The curious came from far away. A traveling carnival arrived with a flying acrobat 7 who buzzed over the crowd several times, but no one paid any attention to him because his wings were not those of an angel but, rather, those of a sidereal° bat. The most unfortunate invalids on earth came in search of health: a poor woman who since childhood had been counting her heartbeats and had run out of numbers; a Portuguese man who couldn't sleep because the noise of the stars disturbed him; a sleepwalker who got up at night to undo the things he had done while awake; and many others with less serious ailments. In the midst of that shipwreck disorder that made the earth tremble, Pelayo and Elisenda were happy with fatigue, for in less than a week they had crammed their rooms with money and the line of pilgrims waiting their turn to enter still reached beyond the horizon.

The angel was the only one who took no part in his own act. He spent his time try- 8 ing to get comfortable in his borrowed nest, befuddled by the hellish heat of the oil lamps and sacramental candles that had been placed along the wire. At first they tried to make him eat some mothballs, which, according to the wisdom of the wise neighbor woman, were the food prescribed for angels. But he turned them down, just as he turned down the papal lunches that the penitents brought him, and they never found out whether it was because he was an angel or because he was an old man that in the end ate nothing but eggplant mush. His only supernatural virtue seemed to be patience. Especially during the first days, when hens pecked at him, searching for the stellar parasites that proliferated in his wings, and the cripples pulled out feathers to touch their defective parts with, and even the most merciful threw stones at him, trying to get him to rise so they could see him standing. The only time they succeeded in arousing him was when they burned his side with an iron for branding steers, for he had been motionless for so many hours that they thought he was dead. He awoke with a start, ranting in his hermetic language and with tears in his eyes, and he flapped his wings a couple of times, which brought on a whirlwind of chicken dung and lunar dust and a gale of panic that did not seem to be of this world. Although many thought that his reaction had been one not of rage but of pain, from then on they were careful not to annoy him, because the majority understood that his passivity was not that of a hero taking his ease but that of a cataclysm in repose.

Father Gonzaga held back the crowd's frivolity with formulas of maidservant in- 9 spiration while awaiting the arrival of a final judgment on the nature of the captive. But

sidereal: Coming from the stars.

the mail from Rome showed no sense of urgency. They spent their time finding out if the prisoner had a navel, if his dialect had any connection with Aramaic, how many times he could fit on the head of a pin,° or whether he wasn't just a Norwegian with wings. Those meager letters might have come and gone until the end of time if a providential event had not put an end to the priest's tribulations.

10   It so happened that during those days, among so many other carnival attractions, there arrived in town the traveling show of the woman who had been changed into a spider for having disobeyed her parents. The admission to see her was not only less than the admission to see the angel, but people were permitted to ask her all manner of questions about her absurd state and to examine her up and down so that no one would ever doubt the truth of her horror. She was a frightful tarantula the size of a ram and with the head of a sad maiden. What was most heart-rending, however, was not her outlandish shape but the sincere affliction with which she recounted the details of her misfortune. While still practically a child she had sneaked out of her parents' house to go to a dance, and while she was coming back through the woods after having danced all night without permission, a fearful thunderclap rent the sky in two and through the crack came the lightning bolt of brimstone that changed her into a spider. Her only nourishment came from the meatballs that charitable souls chose to toss into her mouth. A spectacle like that, full of so much human truth and with such a fearful lesson, was bound to defeat without even trying that of a haughty angel who scarcely deigned to look at mortals. Besides, the few miracles attributed to the angel showed a certain mental disorder, like the blind man who didn't recover his sight but grew three new teeth, or the paralytic who didn't get to walk but almost won the lottery, and the leper whose sores sprouted sunflowers. Those consolation miracles, which were more like mocking fun, had already ruined the angel's reputation when the woman who had been changed into a spider finally crushed him completely. That was how Father Gonzaga was cured forever of his insomnia and Pelayo's courtyard went back to being as empty as during the time it had rained for three days and crabs walked through the bedrooms.

11   The owners of the house had no reason to lament. With the money they saved they built a two-story mansion with balconies and gardens and high netting so that crabs wouldn't get in during the winter, and with iron bars on the windows so that angels wouldn't get in. Pelayo also set up a rabbit warren close to town and gave up his job as bailiff for good, and Elisenda bought some satin pumps with high heels and many dresses of iridescent silk, the kind worn on Sunday by the most desirable women in those times. The chicken coop was the only thing that didn't receive any attention. If they washed it down with Creolin° and burned tears of myrrh inside it every so often, it was not in homage to the angel but to drive away the dungheap stench that still hung everywhere like a ghost and was turning the new house into an old one. At first, when the child learned to walk, they were careful that he not get too close to the chicken coop. But then they began to lose their fears and got used to the smell, and before the child got his second teeth he'd gone inside the chicken coop to play, where the wires were failing apart. The angel was no less standoffish with him than with other mortals, but he tolerated the most ingenious infamies with the patience of a dog who had no illusions. They both came down with chicken pox at the same time. The doctor who took

---

fit on the head of a pin: An allusion to the medieval theological debate over how many angels could fit on the head of a pin.

Creolin: A cleanser and disinfectant.

care of the child couldn't resist the temptation to listen to the angel's heart, and he found so much whistling in the heart and so many sounds in his kidneys that it seemed impossible for him to be alive. What surprised him most, however, was the logic of his wings. They seemed so natural on that completely human organism that he couldn't understand why other men didn't have them too.

When the child began school it had been some time since the sun and rain had 12 caused the collapse of the chicken coop. The angel went dragging himself about here and there like a stray dying man. They would drive him out of the bedroom with a broom and a moment later find him in the kitchen. He seemed to be in so many places at the same time that they grew to think that he'd been duplicated, that he was repro- ducing himself all through the house, and the exasperated and unhinged Elisenda shouted that it was awful living in that hell full of angels. He could scarcely eat and his antiquarian eyes had also become so foggy that he went about bumping into posts. All he had left were the bare cannulae° of his last feathers. Pelayo threw a blanket over him and extended him the charity of letting him sleep in the shed, and only then did they notice that he had a temperature at night, and was delirious with the tongue twisters of an old Norwegian. That was one of the few times they became alarmed, for they thought he was going to die and not even the wise neighbor woman had been able to tell them what to do with dead angels.

And yet he not only survived his worst winter, but seemed improved with the first 13 sunny days. He remained motionless for several days in the farthest corner of the court- yard, where no one would see him, and at the beginning of December some large, stiff feathers began to grow on his wings, the feathers of a scarecrow, which looked more like another misfortune of decrepitude. But he must have known the reason for those changes, for he was quite careful that no one should notice them, that no one should hear the sea chanteys that he sometimes sang under the stars. One morning Elisenda was cutting some bunches of onions for lunch when a wind that seemed to come from the high seas blew into the kitchen. Then she went to the window and caught the angel in his first attempts at flight. They were so clumsy that his fingernails opened a furrow in the vegetable patch and he was on the point of knocking the shed down with the un- gainly flapping that slipped on the light and couldn't get a grip on the air. But he did manage to gain altitude. Elisenda let out a sigh of relief, for herself and for him, when she saw him pass over the last houses, holding himself up in some way with the risky flapping of a senile vulture. She kept watching him even when she was through cutting the onions and she kept on watching until it was no longer possible for her to see him, because then he was no longer an annoyance in her life but an imaginary dot on the horizon of the sea.

—Translated by Gregory Rabassa

The following student essay on Walker's "Everyday Use (for Your Grand- mama)" was written in response to this chapter's assignment. As you read it, con- sider what questions and comments you would have for its writer if you were in a peer review session together.

cannulae: The tubular pieces by which feathers are attached to a body.

BETSY WEILER (STUDENT)
WHO DO YOU WANT TO BE?
FINDING HERITAGE IN WALKER'S "EVERYDAY USE"

"You just don't understand."
"What don't I understand?"
"Your heritage" (276)

1   Whose heritage is Dee talking about? Is it her family's heritage or her ethnic heritage?

2   This exchange takes place near the end of Alice Walker's short story, "Everyday Use," when Dee is saying goodbye to her mother and her sister Maggie after a brief visit and an argument about some quilts. That visit was almost like a treasure hunt for Dee. It seems that Dee, who now has the name Wangero Leewanika Kemanjo, came to visit because she wants to try to identify herself with the past. She wants to take parts of a butter churn and some family quilts back home with her, but Mama says "no" about the quilts because she promised them to Maggie. Dee thinks that Maggie can't "appreciate" the quilts and is "backward enough to put them to everyday use" (275). This confrontation over the quilts suggests that Dee may have learned a lot in college about her ethnic background as an African American, but she does not understand or appreciate her own family's heritage.

3   At first, a reader might think that Dee/Wangero has come home to express her appreciation for her family's heritage. While Mama is waiting for her, she expects that Dee will want to tear down the family house because it is just like the one that burned down when she was a child there. Dee hated that house. But when Dee arrives, before she even tells her mother her new name, she begins taking "picture after picture" of her mother and Maggie, "making sure the house is included" in every one (273). It seems that Dee is proud to include the house in her heritage—but is it her ethnic heritage or her family heritage? What will she do with the pictures? Are they something to remember her family with or are they something "artistic" that she will use to display her ethnic heritage?

4   When Dee explains her new name to her mother, she seems to have forgotten part of her family heritage. Wangero says that "Dee" is "dead" because "I couldn't bear it any longer, being named after the people who oppress me" (273). After her mother explains that she is actually named after Aunt Dee and Grandma Dee, Wangero Leewanika Kemanjo may gain some appreciation of the family tradition because she says that Mama doesn't have to call her the new name "if you don't want to." But Mama shows her own respect for her own daughter by saying "I'll get used to it."

5   When the treasure hunt part of the visit begins after the dinner, Dee's concern for ethnic heritage becomes clear. Dee wants items from the past that she identifies with her ethnic heritage. She jumps up from the table and declares that she needs the churn top. She asks, "Didn't Uncle Buddy whittle it [the churn] out of a tree you all used to have?" (274). She is talking about the churn top in terms of family heritage, but when she says that she intends to use it as a centerpiece on an alcove table, the reader understands that for Dee the churn is more significant for the ethnic heritage it represents. Many blacks could not afford to buy butter, so they had to make it themselves. (In fact,

her mother is still using that churn to make butter.) She also wants the dasher from the churn. For Maggie and Mama, it is a tool in the present that represents family history. Maggie explains that Aunt Dee's first husband, Stash, whittled it; when Mama (the narrator) looks it over she notices the "small sinks" in the wood from the hands of people who had used it (including her own, no doubt). There is a strong contrast between their attitude toward the heirloom and Dee/Wangero's. She laughs at Maggie's story (family heritage), saying Maggie has a "brain like an elephant's" and announces that she herself will "think of something artistic to do with the dasher" (274). For all of them, the dasher represents the hard work blacks have had to struggle through, but for Mama and Maggie, it is a tool made by a family member to help with that work today. For Wangero it is an ethnic heritage object to display.

The final two items that Dee wants are the hand-stitched quilts that she digs out of   6
Mama's trunk. They represent family heritage because they contain pieces of her ancestor's clothing, including a tiny piece from the blue uniform of a great grandfather who fought in the Civil War. That family heritage is very strong for Mama, who was planning to give the quilts to Maggie as a wedding present. She remembers, but doesn't say anything, that Dee/Wangero had refused to take a quilt with her to college because they were old fashioned. Dee loses her temper over the idea of Maggie using the quilts on a bed because "in five years they'd be rags" (275). Mama says that then Maggie would make new ones. But Dee wants "*these* quilts," the ones with pieces of her own family's clothing. This may appear to be an appreciation of family heritage, but since Dee/Wangero wants to hang the quilts on the wall, not use them for a practical purpose, it seems that she wants to display a heritage that she doesn't want to live anymore.

Maggie is willing to give up the quilts, saying she can remember Grandma Dee   7
without them, but Mama grabs the quilts back from Dee. The conflict here is not only about remembering but also about how to remember. Although Dee wants to preserve the original quilts with their antique pieces, she keeps separating herself from the family heritage that created them.

As Dee gets into the car to leave, she puts on a pair of sunglasses that hide "every-   8
thing above the tip of her nose and her chin" (276). If, as the saying goes, the eyes are the windows to the soul, then Dee is hiding her soul. By wearing the sunglasses, Dee is hiding who she truly is and just wants to be identified with the color of her skin, her ethnic heritage. She tells Maggie that "it's really a new day for us" although "from the way you [. . .] live, you'd never know it" (276).

Mama and Maggie may live in a very old-fashioned setting, using old-fashioned   9
tools every day, but Dee/Wangero's attitude about her family and its heirlooms shows that actually she is the person who does not understand her heritage.

Thinking Critically About "Who Do You Want to Be? Finding Heritage in Walker's 'Everyday Use' "

1. The assignment for this chapter asks for an essay built around a problematic and significant interpretive question. Do you think that Betsy Weiler adequately addresses the assignment? Has she been successful in articulating a problematic question and indicating its importance for our understanding of the story?

2. Does Weiler's thesis statement respond adequately to the question? Does she supply enough details from the Walker story as evidence to support her

analysis? Would the paper be better with more analysis of literary elements? What would you suggest that she add? Should she cut some material?

3. What alternative answers to Weiler's interpretive question occur to you besides the ones she brings up? What evidence do you find in the text to support your analysis and interpretation?

4. What are the strengths and weaknesses of Weiler's essay? What recommendations would you have for improving this draft of the essay?

◢ COMPOSING YOUR ESSAY

The reading-log entries you've completed in conjunction with your assigned story should help you considerably when you start planning your essay. Begin that planning by writing out the question you will pose and explore in your paper. As we have seen, a good question, one that is problematic and significant, will be one that promotes engaged conversation and differing points of view. To help you decide on a question, the reading-log tasks in this section ask you to freewrite in response to several different "starter questions." After you decide on a question, you will need to explore ways to answer it, using textual details for support.

Generating and Exploring Ideas

To help you settle on a good problematic question for the introduction of your formal essay, we list several starter questions that focus on *turning points*—major changes in a story's character, plot, language, and point of view. You may want to begin with one of these questions and then refine it to make it more specific to the story.

After reviewing these questions, complete the two reading-log tasks that follow.

Turning-Point Starter Questions About a Short Story

1. Changes in character
   a. How do circumstances change for each character? What sets each change of circumstance in motion?
   b. How does each character's understanding or knowledge change?
   c. How does your attitude toward each character change?
   d. How does each character's relationship to other characters change?
2. Changes in language
   a. How does the dialogue change? Do characters talk to each other differently at any point?
   b. How does the tone of the language change? Does it become lighter or darker at given points?
   c. How do the metaphors and similes change? Is there a pattern to that change?

3. Changes in point of view
   a. How does the narrator's attitude toward the characters and events change? Does the narrator move closer or farther away from characters and events at any point?
   b. How credible is the narrator? If the narrator is not credible, at what point do you first suspect him or her of unreliability?
4. Changes in setting
   a. How does the time or place depicted in the text change? How are other changes in the text related to these changes?

Reading-Log Task 10	Using the turning-point starter questions to stimulate your thinking, pose five or six specific turning-point questions about your assigned story.
Reading-Log Task 11	Choose one of our turning-point questions and explore your own answer to it.

Looking at turning points is not the only way to pose questions about a text. A second list of starter questions focuses on other considerations, such as theme, values, and character. Review the questions and then complete the two reading log tasks that follow.

Additional Starter Questions
1. Why is the story's title appropriate (or inappropriate) in your view?
2. What does each of the major characters seek and want? What are each character's values?
3. Which character's beliefs and values are closest to your own? How so?
4. What or who blocks the characters from reaching their goals (remember, sometimes what blocks them may be inside them), and how much control do they have over achieving their ends?
5. How successful are the characters in achieving their goals and how do they respond to the outcome?
6. Among all the characters, who seems best to understand what happens and why?

Reading-Log Task 12	Pose two or three specific questions about your assigned story using these additional starter questions.
Reading-Log Task 13	Choose one of these questions and explore your responses to it through freewriting or idea mapping.

Choosing Your Problematic Question and Exploring Your Answer

You're now ready to choose the question that will initiate your essay and to explore your answer. For the final reading-log tasks, freewrite rapidly to spill your ideas onto the paper and avoid writer's block. Before you begin, read over what you have written so far in your reading log to help you get the juices flowing.

Reading-Log Task 14   Write out the question that you want to ask about your assigned short story. What makes this an interesting and problematic question? Why don't you and your classmates immediately agree on the answer?

Reading-Log Task 15   Freewriting as rapidly as you can, explore your answer to the question you asked in Task 12. Use textual details and your own critical thinking to create an argument supporting your answer.

Shaping and Drafting

Reading-log Tasks 14 and 15 give you a head start on a rough draft. The best way to organize your literary analysis is to follow the problem-thesis pattern of closed-form prose:

First, begin with an introduction that poses your question about the text and shows the reader why it is an interesting, problematic, and significant question. To show why your question is problematic, you may want to refer briefly to differing interpretations that your classmates have suggested or that you have considered. At the end of your introduction, be sure to include a thesis statement—a one-sentence summary answer to your question. Early in the introduction you may need to supply background about the story so that your reader can understand your question.

Second, write the main body of your essay, in which you develop and support your thesis using textual details and argument. There is no formula for organizing the body. The major sections will depend on your argument and the steps needed to make your case. If you haven't already summarized alternative interpretations in the introduction, you may choose to do so in the body. The key here is to create tension for your thesis and to demonstrate the significance of your interpretation.

Conclude by returning to your essay's big picture and suggesting why your answer to your opening question is significant. Does your analysis have larger implications for the story? What are they? What kind of changed view of the story do you want to effect in your readers' minds? Why is this view important to you? You may choose to write about the different value systems or different ways of reading that distinguish *your* analysis of the story from that of some of your classmates.

Revising

After you have produced a good rough draft, let it sit for a while. Then try it out on readers, who can follow the Guidelines for Peer Reviewers. Based on your readers' advice, begin revising your draft, making it as clear as possible for your readers. Remember to start with the big issues and major changes and then to work your way down to the smaller issues and minor changes.

g u i d e l i n e s
for Peer Reviewers

Instructions for peer reviews, including use of these guidelines, are provided in Chapter 17, pages 429–35. To write a peer review for a classmate, use your own paper, numbering your responses to correspond to the questions on the guidelines. At the head of your paper place the author's name and your own name, as shown.

Author's Name: _____

Peer Reviewer's Name: _____

I. Read the draft at a normal reading speed from beginning to end. As you read, do the following:
   A. Place a wavy line in the margin next to any passages that you find confusing, that contain something that doesn't seem to fit, or that otherwise slow down your reading.
   B. Place a "Good!" in the margin next to any passages where you think the writing is particularly strong or interesting.

II. Read the draft again slowly and answer the following questions by writing down brief explanations of your answers.
   A. Introduction:
     1. Does the title arouse interest and forecast the problem to be addressed? How might the author improve the title?
     2. Does the introduction capture your interest, explain the question to be addressed, and suggest why it is both problematic and significant?
     3. Does the introduction conclude with the writer's thesis? Is the thesis surprising? How might the author improve the introduction?
   B. Analysis and interpretation:
     1. Has the writer effectively shown how his or her thesis is in tension with alternative interpretations or views?
     2. Is the organization clear? Does the writer helpfully forecast the whole, place points before particulars, use transitions, and follow the old/new contract as explained in Chapter 18? How might the author improve or clarify the organization?
     3. Has the author quoted from the story (or used paraphrase or other specific references to the text) sufficiently for you to understand how each of the author's points is grounded in the text? Are there other passages not cited that you think might better support the argument? What recommendations do you have for improving the author's use of supporting details?
     4. Where do you disagree with the author's analysis? What aspects of the story are left unexplained? What doesn't fit?

C. Sum up what you see as the chief strengths and problem areas of this
draft.
1. Strengths
2. Problem areas

III. Finally, read the draft one more time. Place a check in the margin next to any
places where you noticed problems in grammar, spelling, or mechanics (one
check per problem).

Investigating Questions About Cause and Consequence

◢ ABOUT CAUSAL ANALYSIS

When you conduct a *causal analysis*, you try to show how one event or phenomenon leads to another: What are the causes or consequences of X? When physical and social scientists conduct their research, they focus primarily on causal questions. What physical processes cause the HIV virus to destroy the immune system? Why are white teenage females seven times more likely to smoke than black teenage females? What are the consequences of a change in the money supply on an emergent capitalist economy? What causes one child to grow up gay and another straight? What is causing the decline of frog populations worldwide?

Questions about cause and consequence also dominate business and public life, where answers to these questions shape decisions about what a company or a government ought to do. What effects will privatization of prisons have on our justice system? Will curtailment of government welfare payments discourage teenage pregnancy? What will be the consequences of a flat income tax?

Throughout college, many of your assignments will ask you to investigate questions about causes and consequences. Perhaps you will conduct experiments to establish whether a specific variable causes a phenomenon, or you may study statistical methods for testing causal links between two phenomena. You will also engage in a variety of other activities—observing, reading, testing, surveying, comparing—to help you understand why and how things happen in nature and in culture. In this chapter, we will prepare you for these future activities by exploring how causal arguments are constructed and, by the same token, how they sometimes go awry.

◢ EXPLORING CAUSAL ANALYSIS

To help you appreciate why cause or consequence questions can require complex analysis, we invite you to consider one or more of the following causal questions. Working in small groups or as a whole class, brainstorm as many possible causes or consequences as you can for each of the phenomena. As you conduct your discussion, note moments of controversy, where people disagree about a cause or consequence, or moments of surprising insight, where someone argues for an unsuspected or overlooked cause or consequence.

1. Until fairly recently in Western culture, women considered beautiful were ample, rounded, and fleshy. Titian's famous *Lying Venus* suggests a standard of beauty entirely different from the Kate Moss look. Why did thinness in women come to be considered attractive?
2. In the 1990s in the United States, almost 30 percent of all babies were born to single mothers outside wedlock—a precipitous rise from the middle of the century, when illegitimacy constituted a severe social stigma. How do you explain the precipitous increase in the percentage of babies born outside marriage?
3. What would be the consequences of finding a cure for cancer?

WRITING PROJECT

Write an essay in which you analyze the causes or consequences of a puzzling event, trend, or phenomenon, or in which you argue for an unusual, over-looked, or unexpected cause or consequence.

Your writing assignment for this chapter is to pose a question about the causes or consequences of a puzzling or controversial event, trend, or phenomenon. The introduction to your essay should capture your readers' interest by describing the event, trend, or phenomenon you are about to investigate and by explaining why it is intriguing or controversial. The body of your essay presents your own causal analysis.

In writing your analysis, you should try to change your reader's view in some way—either by identifying and supporting an unexpected cause or consequence or by arguing against your reader's initial understanding or beliefs. If your opening question is particularly controversial, you may wish to begin by summarizing and rejecting views that you disagree with. In this case, your essay uses a "sur-prising reversal" strategy, in which you pose your thesis against a counterthesis: "My audience believes that the causes of this phenomenon are X and Y; however, I argue for an unusual or unexpected cause: Z." The rest of this chapter will help you write your essay by giving you more background about causal analysis and by providing suggestions for each stage of the writing process.

▊ UNDERSTANDING CAUSAL ANALYSIS

Most questions about cause and consequence can be classified into three categories:

1. ***One-time events:*** What is the *cause* of a one-time event (the crash of TWA Flight 800; the extinction of dinosaurs)? Or what will be *consequences* of a one-time event (adoption of a flat tax; rescinding affirmative action)?

2. ***Repeatable event or recurring phenomenon:*** What is the *cause* of a repeatable event or recurring phenomenon (math anxiety among females; high levels of diabetes among certain minority groups)? Or what will be the *consequences* of a repeatable event or recurring phenomenon (low self-esteem in children; violence in the schools)?

3. ***Trend:*** What is the *cause* of a trend (a decline in liquor sales nationwide; the increased popularity of body piercing and tattooing)? Or what will be the *consequences* of a trend (the increasing contempt for women in rap lyrics; increased societal acceptance of illegitimacy)?

In thinking about causal phenomena, we need first to distinguish between one-time events and recurrent events. Because one-time events have usually come and gone by the time we study them, it can be especially difficult to determine their causes. Some of the evidence may have disappeared, or witnesses may have faulty or conflicting memories of what happened. Moreover, we usually can't study the event scientifically by repeating it with different variables. Nor can we study multiple cases over long periods of time and establish sophisticated mathematical correlations between the outcome and various suspected causes.

As a further complication, many one-time events involve human beings, which raises a second set of nettlesome causal questions. First, humans have (or appear to have) free will, which means they don't always respond to external forces predictably. Whereas any two rocks, if dropped from a roof, will always fall at precisely the same speed, any two humans, placed in any two identical circumstances, may react in a bewildering variety of ways. Sometimes humans will respond oddly out of pure perversity, precisely to disappoint expectations.

Second, even when humans are acted on by forces outside their control, it may be difficult to determine if nurture (how they were raised or influenced by their environment) or nature (their genetic dispositions and body chemistry), or some combination of both, is at work. For example, why does Person A become an alcoholic while Person B does not?

Trends represent a kind of middle ground between one-time events and repeatable events. Many trends happen only once (the hula hoop craze of the 1950s; recent increased interest in alternative medicine), but because so many people are involved in a trend it is possible to interview them or study them as we do repeatable events.

With these distinctions and cautions in mind, let's turn to various ways of arguing that one event causes another.

Three Methods of Showing a Causal Relationship

To analyze causes and consequences, you need to convince your readers that phenomenon A did cause or will cause phenomenon B. In this section we examine three ways to argue that one event is linked causally to another: directly, inductively, or analogically.

Method 1: Explain the Causal Mechanism Directly

The most compelling form of causal argument explains directly, step by step, how a given event came (or comes) to be. For example, in a recent newspaper article on the health problems of female athletes, the writer, Monica Yant, noted the alarming tendency of top female athletes to develop severe health problems. This claim is surprising because people typically associate athletes with vigorous health. Yant used a carefully constructed argument to show how a successful young female athlete could become a victim of osteoporosis, a disease of the bones associated with elderly females. She forged the following chain of causes and consequences.

Starting Point	Successful young female athletes are driven by a fierce competitiveness to achieve at the highest levels.
Link A	A female athlete may diet rigorously to keep her weight down to give her an edge over the competition and to please her coach.
Link B	Rigorous dieting gradually becomes obsessive, leading to an abnormal loss of body fat.
Link C	Loss of body fat leads to decreased production of estrogen, which leads in turn to amenorrhea, an absence or marked decrease in menstrual periods.
Link D	Amenorrhea leads to a further drop in the woman's estrogen levels.
End Point	A low estrogen level leads to diminished bone mass and in extreme cases to osteoporosis.

Certainly you could raise additional questions about this causal chain. You could start further back, asking how these young athletes became so competitive and so concerned with their achievements, why they care so much about what their coaches think of them and why they need that external validation. Or you might want to know more precisely *how* low body fat leads to low estrogen and *how* low estrogen brings about low bone mass.

But the argument as it stands seems pretty persuasive, particularly because it is punctuated by quotations from authorities and examples of individual athletes. The writer's decisions about which causal links to include and where to start along the chain were based primarily on her perceptions of her audience. She knew she was writing for a general audience of newspaper readers, not a cadre of medical experts or psychologists, so she limited the technical information and began by discussing the medical problems of mature athletes rather than the psychological intricacies of their formative years.

FOR WRITING AND DISCUSSION

Working as a whole class or in small groups, try developing a chain of causal links to connect the following starting points with their specified end points.

Starting Point	End Point
Invention of the automobile	Redesign of cities
Invention of the automobile	Changes in sexual mores
Popularity of beef in the U.S.	Global warming
Invention of the cotton gin	American Civil War
Popularity of aerosol sprays	Increase in skin cancer

Method 2: Explain the Causal Link Through Inductive Methods

Induction is a form of reasoning by generalizing from a limited number of specific cases. If you regularly get a headache after eating white rice but not after eating brown rice, you might conclude *inductively* that white rice causes you to get headaches, even though you can't explain the causal mechanism directly. However, it is also possible that unusual coincidences are at work. Because inductive reasoning yields only probable truths, not certain ones, it can mislead you into false assumptions. We discuss this caution in more detail later in this chapter.

When you conduct an investigation of causes using inductive methods, you can take one of several approaches.

Naturalistic Inquiry.   In most cases, naturalistic inquiry involves first-person observation, supplemented by interviews and other sources of data. Although naturalistic inquiry is not as rigorous or objective as a controlled scientific experiment, it can offer powerful validation of hypotheses. If you wanted to figure out why people subject themselves to mosh pits at rock concerts, you could hurl yourself into a mosh pit and interview various concertgoers as a source of data and insights for your causal analysis.

For example, two German neurologists, puzzled by the fact that so many teenage girls faint at rock concerts, attended a concert and interviewed nearly four hundred fainters. Their conclusion? The biggest culprit was lack of sleep—the fainters had been too excited to sleep the night before the concert.

Scientific Experimentation.   You can reach more precise inductive conclusions by designing scientific experiments to control variables and test them one at a time. For example, scientists conducted a study to determine whether a tendency toward obesity is caused by some inherited metabolic defect, by lifestyle and diet choices, or by some combination of both. The medical team randomly selected people to participate in an experiment designed to identify which of many variables affect weight gain. Researchers placed all subjects in the same environment and gave each the same amount of food, proportioned by body weight, for a prolonged period of time. Some subjects gained weight; others lost weight.

The team noticed that two important variables seemed to have the greatest effect on weight gain or loss: gender and activity level. Women tended to gain more weight than men because they burned fewer calories (a finding that was already well established), and those who lost weight moved around more than those who gained weight (a finding that was less well established and, thanks to the study, assumed greater importance).

Correlation.   *Correlation* is a statistical term indicating the probability that two events or phenomenon will occur together. The higher the correlation, the greater the chance that the two events or phenomenon are linked causally rather than co-incidentally. But correlation can't tell us the direction of causality. X may cause Y, Y may cause X, or some unknown factor Z may cause both of them.

For example, various studies have shown a correlation between creativity and left-handedness. That is, when we compare the percentage of left-handed people in the general population to the percentage of left-handed people in the popula-tion of creative people, the latter percentage is two or three times higher than we'd expect. That's too high to be coincidental. (Folk wisdom appears to have arrived at a similar conclusion: in folk tales left-handedness is often associated with ec-centricity and imaginative behavior.) But does creativity cause left-handedness, or vice versa? Or is there some third factor that accounts for both? Some researchers have suggested that right brain dominance accounts for both left-handedness and creativity, although many scientists are unsatisfied with that explanation.

FOR WRITING AND DISCUSSION

Working individually or in small groups, develop plausible causal ex-planations for correlations between the following pairs of phenomena:

1. Blond or red hair | Tendency to develop skin cancer
2. Second born in large family | Tendency to be a peacemaker
3. High family income | Tendency for children to do well in school
4. Member of National Rifle Association | Tendency to favor mandatory sentencing of criminals
5. Blond or red hair | Tendency toward alcoholism

Method 3: Cite Precedents or Analogies

One of the most common ways to construct a causal argument is to compare the case you are analyzing to something else that is better known and less controversial to your audience. For example, when baseball fans in Seattle and Cincinnati wanted to build a new ballpark, they argued that new ballparks can revitalize downtown areas. As proof, they cited the Baltimore Orioles' Camden Yards ballpark, which had spurred a dramatic revitalization in Baltimore. Or to take an example from analogy, rather than precedent, people who argue that high-density apartments can cause stress disorders in humans cite studies that prove that mice develop stress disorders when placed in overcrowded cages. Causal arguments by analogy and precedent usually are logically weaker than direct or inductive arguments because the *dissim-ilarities* between the things being compared often outweigh the similarities. Seattle and Cincinnati might be very different from Baltimore; humans are not mice.

But for all their logical and empirical limitations, analogies and precedents often have a great emotional impact in that they explain unfamiliar or puzzling phenomena by connecting them to phenomena that people understand well. So long as they are plausible, analogies and precedents can be extremely persuasive. To make an important point, however, a writer rarely relies on analogy or precedent alone. Most writers provide additional evidence from direct or inductive arguments to strengthen a case.

The Mysterious Decline in Male Births: An Extended Example of a Causal Puzzle

As an example of a puzzling phenomenon about causality—one that has given rise to vigorous conversation among scientists—consider a trend recently reported in *Scientific American**: a slow and mysterious decline in the percentage of male births in the United States, Canada, and several European countries since 1970. Historically, male babies have outnumbered female babies by a ratio of 105 to 100. Scientists have speculated that this ratio has been needed to preserve the species because males tend to die earlier than females as a result of war, hunting, and other dangerous male activities. Since 1970, this ratio has slowly declined. Why?

One theory is that parents are having children at a later age and that older fathers tend to beget daughters rather than sons. A related theory is that the decline stems from a reduction in the frequency of sex. Studies show that conception occurring early in the menstrual cycle apparently results in a higher percentage of male births and that frequent intercourse results in pregnancies occurring early in the cycle. (The frequency of intercourse theory also helps explain the widely observed phenomenon that birth of male babies increases after major wars.)

But a different and more troubling theory for the decline of male births has also been proposed. Perhaps the cause is pollution. One research study shows that when men are exposed to high levels of certain pesticides, they are less able to produce sperm cells with Y chromosomes. (When sperm and egg unite, the woman contributes an X chromosome while the man can contribute either an X or Y chromosome. A combination of XX produces a female; an XY produces a male.) Other studies suggest that certain toxins produce greater miscarriages of male fetuses than female fetuses.

The effect of pollution on the ratio of male to female births was documented dramatically in Seveso, Italy, when a 1976 explosion of a chemical plant led to a temporary but severe abundance of dioxin in the atmosphere. Between 1977 and 1984, 74 babies were born to parents who had been exposed to high levels of toxins. Only 35 percent of these babies were male, and the nine couples with the highest dioxin counts in their systems produced no male babies at all. One researcher believes that the decline in the ratio of male births is a "sentinel health event" that provides an early warning of severe environmental hazards. Other researchers,

---

*The information in this section is taken from "Where Have All the Boys Gone?" *Scientific American*, July (1998), 22–23.

however, have not found a correlation between levels of pollution and a declining ratio of male to female births. Thus the phenomenon has not yet been fully explained. What the controversy reveals, however, is the intricacy and complexity of many causal questions.

Glossary of Causal Terms

Now that you've considered one causal argument, let's take a closer look at some of the language that has grown up around causal debates.

The fallacy of the oversimplified cause: In conducting a causal analysis, one is tempted to look for *the* cause of a phenomenon. But rarely is an event or phenomenon caused by a single factor; almost always multiple factors work together. A carefully constructed causal analysis explains why one causal factor made a more or less important contribution than another; rarely does the writer try to convince us that a single factor is solely responsible for an effect.

Immediate versus remote causes: Every causal chain links backward into the indefinite past. Immediate causes are those closest in time to the effect you are studying; remote causes are those further away in time. An immediate cause of Ken's failing an exam might be his wild partying over the weekend. A more remote cause might be his relationship with his parents that led to partying behavior in college. The more remote in time the cause is from its purported effect, the greater the arguer's burden of proof. On the flip side, it's all too easy to overemphasize an immediate cause and to treat it as *the* cause rather than one among many.

Precipitating versus contributing causes: Whereas remote and immediate causes have different temporal relationships to their effects, precipitating and contributing causes may coexist simultaneously. Contributing causes give rise to a precipitating cause, which triggers the effect. In Ken's case, his wild partying is the precipitating cause of his failing the exam; contributing causes are all the conditions that made partying a part of the college scene—a social structure that values partying, the availability of liquor, films such as *Animal House* that make partying cool, friends who kept bringing Ken another drink, and so on.

Necessary versus sufficient causes: A necessary cause is one that must be present for a given effect to occur. In Ken's case, someone's throwing a kegger was a necessary cause of Ken's wild partying (we assume that Ken wouldn't have gotten wasted by himself). A sufficient cause is one that, if present, always triggers the given effect. In Ken's case, the existence of a party isn't a sufficient cause for Ken to get drunk. (On many occasions, he has gone to parties and not drunk at all.) Another cause had to be present—perhaps Ken had just broken up with Barbie and was drowning his sorrow. In this case, the existence of a party and the breakup of a romantic relationship are together sufficient causes of his wild behavior. Sometimes a cause can be sufficient without being necessary. Ken's wild partying was a sufficient cause of his failing the examination, but it wasn't a necessary cause. (Ken could have failed the examination for many other reasons besides wild partying.)

Constraints: Sometimes an effect occurs not because X happened, but because another factor—a constraint—was removed. A constraint is a kind of negative cause, a factor whose presence limits possibilities and choices. Ken's wild partying may have been caused by the removal of a constraint—his parents. Likewise, if Ken's college had instituted severe penalties for partying, these rules may have constrained Ken from partying, and he would have aced his exam.

The **post hoc, ergo propter hoc** *fallacy ("After this, therefore because of this"):* The *post hoc* fallacy is the most common reasoning fallacy associated with causal arguments. You fall victim to this fallacy if you assume that event A causes event B because event A precedes event B. Perhaps Ken would accuse us of *post hoc* reasoning when we assumed that his failing the exam was caused by his wild partying the weekend before (the partying occurred and then the exam occurred). But, Ken might claim, he had studied thoroughly for the exam the week before, was well rested, and had no hangover. He flunked the test because he didn't see a whole set of questions on the back of the test sheet. (For further discussion of the *post hoc* fallacy, see p. 338.)

READINGS

The following readings show examples of student and professional writers analyzing causal questions and proposing causal claims. Our first article, by science writer David H. Levy, is not in itself a causal analysis. Rather, it explains why popular reports of scientific findings are often inaccurate and misleading. Because finding the truth about causal links is the goal of scientific research, it is important to understand how science works and why it is often misrepresented in the media.

DAVID H. LEVY

HOW TO MAKE SENSE OUT OF SCIENCE

New Drugs Kill Cancer
Devastation by El Niño a Warning
6:30 P.M. October 26, 2028: Could This Be the Deadline for the Apocalypse?

When these headlines appeared this year, their stories became the subjects of conversations around the world—talks spiced with optimism and confusion. Imagine the hopes raised in the millions battling cancer. Did the news mean these people never had   1 to worry about cancer again? Or that we *all* had to worry about a catastrophe from outer space or, more immediately, from *El Niño*?

2   Unfortunately, science doesn't work that way. It rarely arrives at final answers. People battling cancer or victims of *El Niño* may find this frustrating, but the truth is that Nature does not yield her secrets easily. Science is done in increments, where an idea is fashioned into an experiment, the outcome, one hopes, being an increase in knowledge.

3   Science is not a set of definitive results but a way of understanding the world around us. Its real work is slow. The scientific method, as many of us learned in school, is a gradual process that begins with a purpose or a problem or question to be answered. It includes a list of materials, a procedure to follow, a set of observations to make and, finally, conclusions to reach. In medicine, when a new drug is proposed that might cure or control a disease, it is first tested on a large random group of people, and their reactions are then compared with those of another random group not given the drug. All reactions in both groups are carefully recorded and compared, and the drug is evaluated. All of this takes time—and patience.

4   It's the *result* of course, that makes the best news—not the years of quiet backwater work that characterize the bulk of scientific inquiry. After an experiment is concluded or an observation is made, the result continues to be scrutinized. When it is submitted for publication, it goes to a group of scientist's colleagues, who review the work. If the work is important enough, just before the report is published in a professional journal or read at a conference, a press release is issued and an announcement is made to the world.

5   The world may think that the announcement signifies the end of the process, but it doesn't. A publication is really a challenge: "Here's my result. Prove me wrong!" Other researchers will then try to repeat the experiment, and the more often it works, the better the chances that the result is sound. Einstein was right when he said: "No amount of experimentation can ever prove me right; a single experiment can at any time prove me wrong."

6   In August 1996, NASA announced the discovery in Antarctica of a meteorite from Mars that might contain evidence of ancient life on another world. As President Clinton said that day, the possibility that life existed on Mars billions of years ago was potentially one of the great discoveries of our time.

7   After the excitement wore down and initial papers were published, other researchers began looking at samples from the same meteorite. Some concluded that the "evidence of life" was mostly contamination from Antarctic ice or that there was nothing organic at all in the rock.

8   Was this a failure of science, as some news reports trumpeted?

9   No! It was a good example of the scientific method working the way it is supposed to. Scientists spend years on research, announce their findings, and these findings are examined by other scientists. That's how we learn. Like climbing a mountain, we struggle up three feet and fall back two. It's a process filled with disappointments and reverses, but somehow we keep on moving ahead.

Thinking Critically About "How to Make Sense Out of Science"

1. In Chapter 4 we said that the content and style of a piece of writing are functions of the author's audience, purpose, and genre. How do a writer's audience, purpose, and genre for a scientific article in a research journal

differ from a writer's audience, purpose, and genre for a popular article or newspaper story?

2. In their pursuit of causal explanations, scientists move slowly, often trying to prove other scientists wrong. This faith in the scientific method is what characterizes mainstream medicine throughout the world. To mainstream scientists, a medical treatment becomes accepted practice when controlled studies show significantly better results than a placebo. Many people, how-ever, believe that other forms of medicine "work": acupuncture, homeopa-thy, faith healing, folk medicines, and so forth. What "proofs" provided by these alternative medical practices convince their adherents that these methods work?

Our next reading, published in *Mother Jones* magazine, offers a possible scien-tific explanation for the healing effect of homeopathy. A bar at the top of the arti-cle says: "While critics call homeopathy 'utter nonsense,' two studies may give the alternative medical practice some scientific validity."

MICHAEL CASTLEMAN
THE .02 PERCENT SOLUTION

In war, it often takes a disinterested third party to bring combatants to the peace table, and that may just be happening right now with mainstream physicians and prac-titioners of homeopathy, an alternative therapy based on diluted natural substances that has long been dismissed by the U.S. medical establishment as quackery. Though largely ignored by the media, the results of experiments by Shui-Yin Lo, a former vis-iting associate in chemistry at California Institute of Technology, may, after almost two centuries, finally begin to explain scientifically how homeopathy works.   1

First practiced by German doctor Samuel Hahnemann in the early 1800s as a non-toxic alternative to the standard medical practices of his day (bleeding, leeches, and mercury), the logic of homeopathy rests on two main principles. Hahnemann treated ailing people with microscopic doses of the same substances (herbs, minerals, animal parts) that would cause their symptoms in healthy people. He dubbed this the Law of Similars (which led to the term "homeopathy"). It appears to work not unlike modern vaccinations, which use a tiny amount of a deactivated germ to stimulate an immune response, and thus protect people from the disease caused by larger amounts of the same germ.   2

Hahnemann also believed that homeopathic medicines get stronger as they be-come more dilute. But this second homeopathic principle, which he called the Law of Potentization, directly contradicts a central tenet of pharmacology: the "dose-response relationship," the idea that to increase a drug's effect, you must use a larger dosage. Not so, according to homeopaths, who often claim good results with medicines so di-lute that in all probability they contain not a single molecule of the original substance—somehow "remembering" the diluted substance and retaining its "essence."   3

4   For anyone with even a passing acquaintance with pharmacology, the Law of Potentization is hard to swallow. Oncologist Wallace Sampson, a professor at Stanford, has dismissed it as "not biologically plausible." Any benefits, he says, are the result of "suggestion," and "a placebo effect." Stephen Barrett of Allentown, Pennsylvania, a board member of the National Council for Reliable Health Information, is even less kind, calling the theory "utter nonsense." If extremely diluted substances can impart their "essence" to water, Barrett argues, then "every substance encountered by a molecule of water might imprint an 'essence' that could exert powerful (and unpredictable) medicinal effects when ingested." (Homeopaths counter that homeopathic medicines require distilled water and vigorous shaking between dilutions.) Barrett, who considers homeopathy a fraud, says it should be banned.

5   But Lo's findings may bolster the homeopathic cause. Although he has nothing to do with the alternative therapy—and wants no part of it—his experiments appear to give its advocates some independent scientific support. Two years ago, Lo created extremely dilute solutions using a technique similar to Hahnemann's. Training an electron microscope on them, he discovered that in some cases the water contained bizarre ice crystals that didn't behave anything like the stuff that comes from the freezer. This strange new type of ice, which forms in solutions at temperatures well above freezing, gives off a unique electrical field. Lo calls these crystals "IE"—ice with an electrical field.

6   Building on Lo's work, Benjamin Bonavida, an immunology professor at the University of California-Los Angeles, discovered in 1997 that water with the biologically active IE crystals significantly increases the production of several components of the immune system—stimulating up to 100 times more biological activity than plain water.

7   The implication, maintains Dana Ullman, director of Homeopathic Educational Services in Berkeley, California, is that homeopathic medicines work by creating IE crystals that stimulate the immune system. Yet promoting this link may prove difficult. Ullman says the prejudice against homeopathy in the U.S. makes it impossible for any scientist here to undertake its study, asserting that the fear of being professionally ostracized is "equivalent to the Red scare."

8   Homeopathy did not always receive such a blanket condemnation from the American medical community. Brought here from Europe in 1825, it quickly won supporters among doctors fed up with bleeding, leeches, and mercury. By 1844, homeopaths had launched the American Institute of Homeopathy. Three years later, mainstream doctors formed the American Medical Association, which waged a fierce campaign against the alternative medicine. State legislatures began licensing only those physicians who had graduated from medical institutions like Johns Hopkins, and by 1948, the last homeopathic school in the nation closed. By the early 1970s, there were fewer than 100 homeopaths in the U.S.

9   Homeopathy has always fared far better in Europe, where many mainstream doctors include elements of homeopathy in their practice.

10   But during the past 25 years, the U.S. has witnessed a modest homeopathic renaissance. An estimated 5,000 health professionals now include homeopathy in their practices, and a growing body of research shows that homeopathic treatment produces real benefits.

11   A 1991 review of homeopathic studies, conducted by Dutch epidemiologists at the University of Limburg, concluded that homeopathy could be considered a "regular treatment for certain indications," including hay fever, pain, and respiratory conditions

(colds, flu, bronchitis, and sinus infections). In 1994, Scottish researchers studied 28 people whose asthma attacks were triggered primarily by exposure to household dust mites. Those taking homeopathic preparations suffered significantly fewer attacks than those taking placebos. Last year, German and American researchers analyzed 89 scientific studies of homeopathy worldwide, finding that homeopathy worked significantly better than placebos.

Homeopaths prescribe treatment based on a patient's individual symptoms. Two people with what mainstream doctors would consider the same illness might get different homeopathic medicines if their overall symptoms differ even slightly.   12

Homeopaths prescribe medicines that are altogether different from mainstream drugs. They usually come in the form of tiny pellets and have strange-sounding Latin names, ranging from the familiar—*Allium cepa* (onion), *Natrum mur* (sodium chloride, i.e., salt), or *Chamomilla* (chamomile)—to the bizarre or seemingly dangerous—*Rhus tox* (poison ivy), *Arsenicum* (arsenic), *Tabacum* (tobacco), or *Lachesis* (venom of the bushmaster snake). But proponents assert that they're not dangerous in homeopathic doses, and the Food and Drug Administration agrees. They're exempt from regulation and available over the counter at most health food stores.   13

For a national directory of licensed health professionals who use homeopathy, contact: Homeopathic Educational Services, 2124 Kittredge St., Berkeley, CA 94704, (510) 649-0294; or the National Center for Homeopathy, 801 N. Fairfax St., Suite 306, Alexandria, VA 22314, (703) 548-7790.   14

Thinking Critically About "The .02 Percent Solution"

1. Castleman's article uses all three of the methods for showing causal links discussed in previous pages: (1) explaining a causal chain directly, (2) using inductive methods, and (3) arguing by analogy. Find examples of these methods in the article.
2. You may have been surprised to read about the antipathy between the scientific community and homeopathy in the United States. Why does homeopathy receive "blanket condemnation" from mainstream medicine in America? Why do you think homeopathy might be better received in Europe?
3. This article appeared in *Mother Jones,* a magazine often associated with countercultural values, including alternative medicine. In the issue in which this article appeared, we counted fourteen pages of ads for health foods, herbal remedies, and organic extracts, as well as numerous ads for environmentally friendly products and natural fibers. The readers of *Mother Jones* are probably friendlier toward homeopathy than, say, readers of *The National Review,* a politically conservative magazine. Given the countercultural bias of *Mother Jones,* do you think Castleman's article is scientifically responsible, or is it an example of magazine copy aimed at promoting the values of advertisers?

The following article appeared in the *Christian Science Monitor.* Although written in the late 1980s, we have included it because its causal analysis seems as relevant today as ever. At the time of writing, the author, Walter S. Minot, was a professor of English at Gannon University in Erie, Pennsylvania.

WALTER S. MINOT
STUDENTS WHO PUSH BURGERS

1   A college freshman squirms anxiously on a chair in my office, his eyes avoiding mine, those of his English professor, as he explains that he hasn't finished his paper, which was due two days ago. "I just haven't had the time," he says.

2   "Are you carrying a heavy course load?"

3   "Fifteen hours," he says—a normal load.

4   "Are you working a lot?"

5   "No, sir, not much. About 30 hours a week."

6   "That's a lot. Do you have to work that much?"

7   "Yeah, I have to pay for my car."

8   "Do you really need a car?"

9   "Yeah, I need it to get to work."

10   This student isn't unusual. Indeed, he probably typifies today's college and high school students. Yet in all the lengthy analyses of what's wrong with American education, I have not heard employment by students being blamed.

11   I have heard drugs blamed and television—that universal scapegoat. I have heard elaborate theories about the decline of the family, of religion, and of authority, as well as other sociological theories. But nobody blames student employment. The world seems to have accepted the part-time job as a normal feature of adolescence. A parochial school in my town even had a day to honor students who held regular jobs, and parents often endorse this employment by claiming that it teaches the value of the dollar.

12   But such employment is a major cause of educational decline. To argue my case, I will rely on memories of my own high school days and contrast them with what I see today. Though I do have some statistical evidence, my argument depends on what anyone can test through memory and direct observation.

13   When I was in high school in the 1950s, students seldom held jobs. Some of us baby-sat, shoveled snow, mowed lawns, and delivered papers, and some of us got jobs in department stores around Christmas. But most of us had no regular source of income other than the generosity of our parents.

14   The only kids who worked regularly were poor. They worked to help their families. If I remember correctly, only about five people in my class of 170 held jobs. That was in a working-class town in New England. As for the rest of us, our parents believed that going to school and helping around the house were our work.

15   In contrast, in 1986 my daughter was one of the few students among juniors and seniors who didn't work. According to Bureau of Labor statistics, more than 40 percent of high school students were working in 1980, but sociologists Ellen Greenberger and Laurence Steinberg in "When Teenagers Work" came up with estimates of more than 70 percent working in 1986, though I suspect that the figure may be even higher now.

My daughter, however, did not work; her parents wouldn't let her. Interestingly,   16
some of the students in her class implied that she had an unfair advantage over them
in the classroom. They were probably right, for while she was home studying, they were
pushing burgers, waiting on tables, or selling dresses 20 hours a week. Working students have little time for homework.

I attended a public high school, while she attended a Roman Catholic preparatory   17
school whose students are mainly middle class. By the standards of my day, her classmates did not "have to" work. Yet many of them were working 20 to 30 hours a week.
Why?

They worked so that they could spend $60 to $100 a week on designer jeans, rock   18
concerts, stereo and video systems, and, of course, cars. They were living lives of luxury, buying items on which their parents refused to throw hard-earned money away.
Though the parents would not buy such tripe for their kids, the parents somehow convinced themselves that the kids were learning the value of money. Yet, according to Ms.
Greenberger and Mr. Steinberg, only about a quarter of these students saved money for
college or other long-term goals.

How students spend their money is their business, not mine. But as a teacher, I   19
have witnessed the effects of their employment. I know that students who work all
evening aren't ready for studying when they get home from work. Moreover, because
they work so hard and have ready cash, they feel that they deserve to have fun—instead
of spending all their free time studying.

Thus, by the time they get to college, most students look upon studies as a spare-   20
time activity. A survey at Pennsylvania State University showed that most freshmen believed they could maintain a B average by studying about 20 hours a week. (I can
remember when college guidebooks advised two to three hours of studying for every
hour in class—30 to 45 hours a week.)

Clearly individual students will pay the price for lack of adequate time studying,   21
but the problem goes beyond the individual. It extends to schools and colleges that are
finding it difficult to demand quantity or quality of work from students.

Perhaps the reason American education has declined so markedly is because   22
America has raised a generation of part-time students. And perhaps our economy will
continue to decline as full-time students from Japan and Europe continue to outper-
form our part-time students.

Thinking Critically About "Students Who Push Burgers"

1. Minot begins with the assumption that American education is in precipitous
   decline. (Numerous test results confirm this assumption; Americans lag
   behind their Asian and European counterparts to an alarming degree in
   their knowledge of mathematics, science, history, geography, and languages.) What theories concerning the causes of this decline does Minot
   acknowledge? Do you agree with his "surprising" cause: teenage
   employment?
2. If you don't think teenage employment is an immediate or precipitating
   cause of the decline in American test scores, what theory do you propose?
3. Do you agree with Minot that designer jeans, rock concerts, stereo and video
   systems, and cars are just "tripe" for kids?
4. How effective is Minot's use of evidence to support his theory?

Our final essay, by student writer Susan Meyers, was written for the assignment in this chapter. We have reproduced it exactly to demonstrate the manuscript form and documentation style of the APA system (American Psychological Association) for research papers. For a description of the APA system, see pages 557–72.

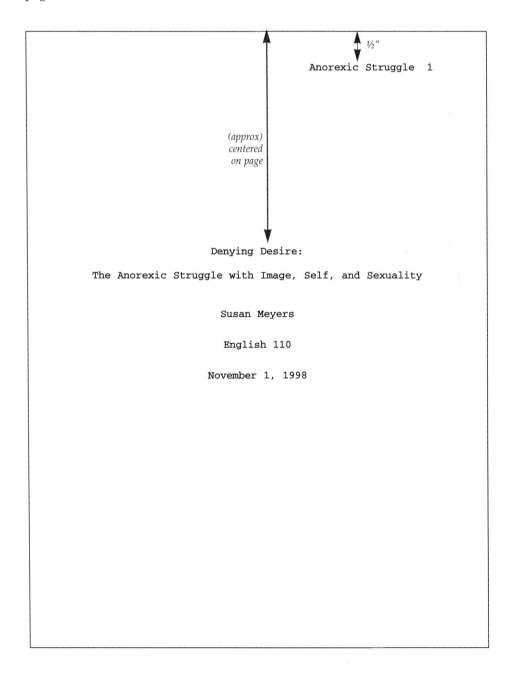

½"

Anorexic Struggle   1

(approx)
centered
on page

Denying Desire:

The Anorexic Struggle with Image, Self, and Sexuality

Susan Meyers

English 110

November 1, 1998

Anorexic Struggle 2

Denying Desire:

The Anorexic Struggle with Image, Self, and Sexuality

Imagine a disease without a clear diagnosis or cure. Not a virus, not a cancer. No enemy to trace and root out of the body. Imagine a self-inflicted disease that haunts you minute by minute. A disease that you control--just as it controls you.

Anorexia nervosa, a psychological disorder with physical consequences, is such a disease. As of 1998, according to the National Academy of Anorexia Nervosa and Associated Disorders, this eating disorder currently plagues more than seven million American teenage girls. In its online article "Anorexia Nervosa," the American Academy of Neurology describes anorexia as "a pathological fear of weight gain leading to faulty eating patterns, malnutrition, and usually excessive weight loss." Typical anorexics are healthy, attractive girls from successful families. Although public awareness of anorexia has risen since the 1980's, its cause and cure have continued to baffle physicians and psychologists, as well as parents, friends, and victims themselves (Landau, 1983).

Many theories about the cause of anorexia have been proposed. Some experts blame the advertising and entertainment industries for their startlingly thin models and actresses. Others argue that girls monitor their

Anorexic Struggle   3

food intake because they lack control in other areas of their lives. Still others blame perfectionist families or cite depression and low self-esteem as causes for anorexia. All these theories, however, lack a key element--the complex relationship that teenage girls have with sexual desire and desirability.

4   Blaming the media's thin role models is an especially popular explanation for anorexia in teenage girls (Zerbe, 1993). Sleek, slim, 5'10", 115-pound women are not good role models for girls just coming into an understanding about their bodies, say feminists and parents. As they reach their early teens, girls begin to flirt, date, and worry about their physical appearance. When the only images they have to compare themselves with are grossly disproportioned, it is not surprising that many girls develop unrealistic goals for their appearance.

5   Further, teens encourage each other to uphold and follow the standards set up by the media. Exercise and dieting are common topics of discussion among teenage girls, as are grooming and dating. While boys are encouraged to compete in football or hockey, girls tend to compete for the best bodies and boyfriends. The popular "blame the media and peer pressure" explanation, however, does not by itself fully address the reasons that girls value beauty and sexual desirability so highly.

6   A different theory about teenage anorexia cites the drastic changes during adolescence as a source of

anxiety and illness. According to this theory, teenagers
feel out of control as they make the shift from childhood to adulthood, so they seek to control the only
thing they think they can: their bodies (Landau, 1983).
Undoubtedly, girls (and boys) face many changes during
adolescence: shifts in relationships with parents, new
social standing and worries about the future, introduction to dating and sexuality, as well as physical and
hormonal changes. So much upheaval could certainly lead
one to feel panicked, helpless, or out of control. Such
feelings, coupled with sexual peer pressure and the
idealized female image described above, likewise could
certainly lead some girls to starve themselves. They
want both to reach the new standard that has been set
for them (a 5'10", 115-pound toned body), and they want
to hold onto and shape some part of their lives.

A more specific pressure that many anorexic girls
may be responding to is family. Statistically, anorexics
tend to be high-achieving "good girls [and] dutiful
daughters" (Pipher, 1994). Their families are strict,
close-knit, and success-driven, and often it is difficult for these daughters to separate psychologically
from their parents (Stierlin and Weber, 1989). Anorexia,
then, becomes both a way to strive for high goals
(female beauty expressed through extreme thinness) and
a means to act autonomously. As Melissa Dean, a former
anorexic and the daughter of a successful business

7

Anorexic Struggle   5

owner, explains, "My parents were really strict. I did
everything [for them]. I accomplished everything. I felt
like I had to do all this stuff. But [dieting] was the one
thing I could do by myself . . . I could make myself not
eat" (personal communication, August 25, 1998). The theory
of familial pressure has become very popular during the
80's and 90's, and deservedly so, since so many anorexic
girls come from traditional middle and upper class homes.
Like the theory of media pressure, however, it does not
explain why girls choose starvation and/or beauty to seek
their autonomy.

8   Still another theory is that anorexia stems from depression or low self-esteem. Proponents of this theory suggest
that uncertainty about physical, emotional, or relational
changes may cause many teenagers to lose self-confidence
and, possibly, to collapse into depression. Once these girls
feel depressed or inadequate, they look for a way to redeem
themselves: physical perfection (Kinoy et al., 1984). However, although depression and low self-esteem might be
present in an anorexic, they do not necessarily cause
anorexia. Depression, for example, sometimes causes people
to overeat rather than to starve themselves. Furthermore,
this theory, like the control theory, does not consider why
physical perfection becomes the chosen means of dealing with
depression or feelings of inadequacy. The question still
remains: Why is being physically desirable so intensely
important to some adolescent girls?

Anorexic Struggle   6

Perhaps a fuller understanding lies in a different direction. Perhaps anorexics don't pursue desirability but are rather avoiding it. Part of the traumatic shift from girlhood to womanhood is a movement from a presexual "neutral" self to a sexualized self that is an object of desire. During adolescence, American girls learn that in order to be good, successful women, they must inspire male desire while repressing their own; they are introduced to a double standard that favors male sexuality and represses women's desires. On the one hand, girls learn to seek male attention because having dates and boyfriends can increase their popularity or social status. But on the other hand, giving in to sexual pressures can turn them into outcasts; they may be labeled "sluts" (Orenstein, 1994). Further, they learn that, since men cannot be expected to control their sexual appetites, women must use mental willpower to overcome male pressures, as well as their own physical desires. As one mother explained to her daughter, " 'Your body wants one thing and your mind says another and you'll always feel that way' " (Orenstein, 1994). In this way, girls learn to hide their own desire while tantalizing it in males.

The shift from a largely desexualized girlhood to a highly sexualized adolescence and womanhood can easily lead to confusion, upset, and anger. Such stress can also compound anxieties about changes at home, school,

9

10

Anorexic Struggle   7

and in the body. Indeed, it can create a need to control something, to hold onto something; and sometimes that thing, whether victims know it or not, is girlhood. It has been argued that anorexics starve themselves in an unconscious effort to stunt their growth in order to remain girls (Landau, 1983), and, certainly, teenage anorexia does interfere with maturation and hormonal development. The thing that such girls resist, however, may not simply be physical change but rather the shift from a neutral self to an object of desire. As Sarah Lasseter, a former anorexic, related, "I hated the thought of sex. I didn't want a gender. I didn't want a body. I just wanted to be me" (personal communication, July 22, 1998). Such comments are heart-breaking, and it is a great misfortune that girls--and their teachers, parents, and doctors--do not consider the traumatic social conditioning that accompanies adolescence when they search out causes for anorexia. Instead of seeking desirability, some girls may actually be trying to escape it.

Anorexic Struggle   9

References

Anorexia nervosa. American Academy of Neurology [On-
line]. Retrieved October 10, 1998 from the World Wide
Web: http://www.aan.com/res/pig6.html

Kinoy, B., Miller, E. B., Atchley, J. A., & American
Anorexia/Bulimia Association. (1984). When will
we laugh again? Living and dealing with anorexia
nervosa and bulimia. New York: Columbia University
Press.

Landau, E. (1983). Why are they starving themselves?:
Understanding anorexia and bulimia. New York: Julian
Messner.

National Academy of Anorexia and Associated Disorders. (1998).
Who suffers from anorexia? Healthtouch Online [Online].
Retrieved October 11, 1998 from the World Wide Web:
http://www.healthtouch.com/level1/special/4Health.htm

Orenstein, P. & American Association of University
Women. (1994). Schoolgirls: Young women, self-esteem,
and the confidence gap. New York: Doubleday.

Pipher, M. B. (1994). Reviving Ophelia: Saving the
selves of adolescent girls. New York: Putnam.

Stierlin, H. & Weber, G. (1989). Unlocking the family
door: A systematic approach to the understanding and
treatment of anorexia nervosa. New York: Brunner/Mazel.

Zerbe, K. J. (1993). The body betrayed: Women, eating
disorders, and treatment. Washington, D.C.: American
Psychiatric Press.

Thinking Critically About "Denying Desire"

1. Meyers argues for a surprising cause of anorexia which she hints at but doesn't reveal until near the end. Does this organizational strategy work for you? Is her argument convincing?
2. If you were a peer reviewer for this essay, would you advise Meyers to eliminate the sentence fragments in her opening paragraph? Why or why not?
3. What do you see as the strengths and weaknesses of this paper?

◼ COMPOSING YOUR ESSAY

This assignment asks you to write a causal analysis in which you pose a question about a puzzling event, trend, or phenomenon and then explain and support your own understanding of its causes or consequences.

Generating and Exploring Ideas

Your first step is to select the event, trend, or phenomenon you intend to analyze. Your goal is to find a topic that is both puzzling enough and significant enough to engage your readers' interest and yet gives you plenty to say. Often it is helpful to explore several possibilities through freewriting or idea mapping before you settle on a final topic. The following suggestions will help you with the process.

Make a List of People's Unusual Likes and Dislikes

One fruitful subject for a causal argument is the causes of people's unusual likes or dislikes. For example: Why are people afraid of snakes (spiders, bats)? Why do many people fear public speaking (writing, computers)? Why do people like stamp collecting (rock climbing, raising tropical fish)? Make a list of unusual things that people you know like or dislike and freewrite about them for five minutes or so, speculating on the causes of this peculiar behavior. Naturalistic observation can help; or, you can interview people who have these puzzling tastes.

Make Lists of Puzzling Trends, One-Time Events, or Repeatable Phenomena

Another helpful brainstorming activity is to expand the lists of trends, one-time events, and repeatable phenomena on page 289. Think of as many ideas as you can and then select several to explore in more depth through freewriting. Consider working together with classmates since two heads (or three or four) are often better than one at the brainstorming stage.

Create Idea Maps to Explore Causes or Consequences

For this exercise we provide you with two columns; one lists events or trends for which you are to think of causes; the other lists hypothetical events for which you are to think of consequences. Create idea maps of causes or consequences for the problems or events. Begin by placing on your idea map the causes or consequences that people would commonly think of; then search for possible causes or consequences that the average person might not think of.

<table>
<tr><td>

Think of the Causes of

- the increase in smoking among children and teenagers
- the opposition of many Americans to gun-control legislation
- the urge to write graffiti on walls and in subway stations
- the small number of women in the skilled trades of carpentry, bricklaying, or plumbing
- the appeal of certain print or TV advertisements (choose some specific ads)
- the failure of soccer to capture a wide sports audience in the United States
- the popularity of TV talk shows
- the existence of homophobia or racism
- the failure or success of a TV series (choose one)

</td><td>

Think of the Consequences of

- destruction of rain forests
- universal health care in the United States
- increased social acceptance of suicide by the elderly or by persons with serious diseases
- a heavy tax on families with more than two children
- elimination of welfare benefits for unwed mothers
- a four-day workweek
- widespread use of the information highway
- legalizing marijuana, cocaine, and heroin
- allowing gay and lesbian marriages
- exhaustion of the world's supply of petroleum
- a change in a rule or regulation for a sport (choose a specific example)

</td></tr>
</table>

Explore Your Chosen Phenomenon Through Rapid Freewriting

Once you have chosen a puzzling phenomenon for your causal analysis paper, you can explore ideas and avoid writer's block by freewriting rapidly, spilling your initial ideas onto paper. These freewrites will make it easier to write a first draft and can reveal areas that may require more research or additional ideas. Try freewriting your responses to the following invention questions:

1. What is your chosen phenomenon? Describe it. If it is a trend, what is your evidence that the trend exists?
2. What personal experiences have you had with this phenomenon, either as a participant or as an observer? Describe those experiences.
3. Why are the causes of your phenomenon puzzling? Why is this an interesting or significant phenomenon to analyze?
4. What are the most common explanations for this phenomenon? What explanations do you think will first pop into your readers' minds?
5. Do you think these causes fully explain your phenomenon? What may be wrong, missing, or inadequate?
6. What do you see as the most important causes of this phenomenon? What is your evidence or support?
7. Are there alternative explanations that you think need to be examined and rejected? Why?

8. My ideas about the causes of this phenomenon will surprise my reader because _____. (Explore.)

Develop Ideas and Supporting Arguments Through Observation, Interviewing, or Other Forms of Research

Often your own personal experiences and critical thinking are all you need for a causal analysis. In other cases, research is necessary. It may be helpful to read about how other people have analyzed the causes of your phenomenon. (See Part Four for advice on research.)

You can also gather inductive evidence through naturalistic observation—by living among the people you are investigating, taking notes on their behavior, and asking them questions. Although a tape recorder might come in handy, all you really need to conduct a naturalistic inquiry is a pen and a notebook. Be sure to write down your impressions and quotations on the spot and carefully to note the time, place, and people involved. Soon after you're through observing, review your notes while they're still fresh in your mind and annotate them in the margins or on the facing page, categorizing them according to how they support or refute your initial hypotheses about causes.

Shaping and Drafting

Because your goal at this early discovery stage of drafting is to put your developing argument on paper, it will be useful for you to know some of the standard ways of organizing a causal argument. Later on, you may decide to adopt a different organizational pattern, but these standard ways will help you get started.

1. When your intention is to link your phenomenon to a cause (or consequence) by describing and explaining the links in a causal chain
   - Introduce the phenomenon, establishing (a) that it exists and (b) that it is worthy of analysis by being problematic and significant. Concentrate on engaging your reader's interest. Often readers need to be convinced that a problematic phenomenon exists before they become interested in its causes or consequences.
   - Present your thesis that this phenomenon has a surprising cause (or consequence).
   - Describe and explain each link in the causal chain.
2. When your intention is to explore the relative contribution of all causes to a phenomenon or all consequences of an event
   - Introduce the phenomenon, again demonstrating that it exists and showing why it is problematic or controversial. Engage your reader's interest.
   - Devote one section to each possible cause or consequence and support it with evidence. Arrange sections to present those causes most familiar to the audience first and those most surprising last.
   - If appropriate, describe alternative hypotheses and show why you are rejecting them.
3. When your purpose is to change your reader's view by arguing for a surprising or unexpected cause or consequence

- Introduce your phenomenon, establishing that it exists and may be even more prevalent than your reader thought, engage your reader's interest in the question, and summarize the commonplace explanation of causes that you assume your reader holds.
- One by one examine and reject, or show as inadequate or insufficient, the causes or consequences that your audience would normally assume or expect.
- Introduce your unexpected or surprising cause or consequence and argue for it.

Patterns 2 and 3 are similar in that they examine numerous possible causes or consequences. Pattern 2, however, tries to establish the relative importance of each cause or consequence, whereas Pattern 3 tries to discredit the audience's preconceived notions about these causes or consequences and then argues for a new, surprising cause or consequence.

Revising

Once you've selected your topic, written your draft, and discussed it with a member of your group, you're ready to do the major work of revising—converting your draft from something that works for you to something that works for readers. Because you will probably choose to write this paper near the closed end of the closed-to-open continuum, the revision suggestions in Chapter 18 are especially relevant: give the big picture first and refer to it often; place points before particulars (ensuring that paragraphs have topic sentences); use frequent transitions; and follow the old/new contract.

You should also seek out peer reviews, using the following guidelines.

---

g u i d e l i n e s

for Peer Reviewers

Instructions for peer reviews, including use of these guidelines, are provided in Chapter 17, pages 429–35. To write a peer review for a classmate, use your own paper, numbering your responses to correspond to the questions on the guidelines. At the head of your paper place the author's name and your own name, as shown.

Author's Name: _____

Peer Reviewer's Name: _____

  I. Read the draft at a normal reading speed from beginning to end. As you read, do the following:

    A. Place a wavy line in the margin next to any passages that you find confusing, that contain something that doesn't seem to fit, or that otherwise slow down your reading.

    B. Place a "Good!" in the margin next to any passages where you think the writing is particularly strong or interesting.

II. Read the draft again slowly and answer the following questions by writing brief explanations of your answers.

    A. Introduction:

       1. Is the title appropriate for an academic analysis? Does it predict the focus of the paper?

       2. Does the introduction capture your interest and set up the causal question to be addressed? How does it convince you that the phenomenon to be examined really exists and that answering the question will prove useful or will further your understanding?

       3. What is the writer's thesis in response to the question? Do you find the thesis surprising? Could the thesis be stated more clearly or include more tension and surprise?

    B. Analyzing the causes or consequences:

       1. Does the writer mention alternative explanations of the phenomenon? Does the writer persuade you to prefer his or her explanations to the alternatives?

       2. How does the writer make the argument that a given X causes Y? Could this argument be improved?

          a. If the writer describes the links in the causal chain, could these links be developed more convincingly?

          b. If the writer uses correlations, are they sound? Could the direction of cause be reversed or could an unnamed cause account for both X and Y?

          c. If the writer uses an analogy, is the analogy persuasive?

       3. How might the writer improve the structure and clarity of this draft? Where might the writer specifically apply the principles of clarity from Chapter 18?

       4. Where do you disagree with the writer's argument or have doubts or queries? If you could ask for one or more additional pieces of support for the writer's thesis, what would you ask for?

    C. Sum up what you see as the chief strengths and problem areas of this draft.

       1. Strengths

       2. Problem areas

III. Read the draft one more time. Place a check in the margin wherever you notice problems in grammar, spelling, or mechanics (one check per problem).

c h a p t e r 14

Writing a
Classical Argument

▚ ABOUT CLASSICAL ARGUMENT

The assignment for this chapter introduces you to a classical way of arguing in which you take a stand on an issue, offer reasons and evidence in support of your position, and summarize and respond to alternative views. Your goal is to persuade your audience, who can be initially perceived as either opposed to your position or undecided about it, to adopt your position or at least to regard it more openly or favorably.

The need for argument arises whenever members of a community disagree on an issue. Classical rhetoricians believed that the art of arguing was essential for good citizenship. If disputes can be resolved through exchange of perspectives, negotiation of differences, and flexible seeking of the best solutions to a problem, then nations won't have to resort to war or individuals to fisticuffs.

The study of argumentation involves two components: truth seeking and persuasion. By *truth seeking*, we mean a diligent, open-minded, and responsible search for the best course of action or solution to a problem taking into account all the available information and alternative points of view. By *persuasion*, we mean the art of making a claim on an issue and justifying it convincingly so that the audience's initial resistance to your position is overcome and they are moved toward your position.

These two components of argument seem paradoxically at odds: Truth seeking asks us to relax our certainties and be willing to change our views; persuasion asks us to be certain, to be committed to our claims, and to get others to change their views. We can overcome this paradox if we dispel two common but misleading views of argument. The most common view is that argument is a fight, as in "I just got into a horrible argument with my roommate." This view of argument as a fist-waving shouting match in which you ridicule anyone who disagrees with you (popularized by radio and television talk shows) entirely disregards argument as truth seeking, but it also misrepresents argument as persuasion because it polarizes people rather than promoting understanding, new ways of seeing, and change.

316

Another common but misleading view is that argument is pro/con debate modeled after high school or college debate matches or presidential debates. Although debating can be an excellent way to develop critical thinking skills, it misrepresents argument as a two-sided contest with winners and losers. Because controversial issues involve many different points of view, not just two, reducing an issue to pro/con positions distorts the complexity of the disagreement. Instead of thinking of *both* sides of an issue, we need to think of *all* sides. Equally troublesome, the debate image invites us to ask, "Who won the debate?" rather than "What is the best solution to the question that divides us?" The best solution might be a compromise between the two debaters or an undiscovered third position. The debate image tends to privilege the confident extremes in a controversy rather than the complex and muddled middle.

From our perspective, the best image for understanding argument is neither "fight" nor "debate" but instead the deliberations of a committee representing a wide spectrum of community voices charged with finding the best solution to a problem. From this perspective argument is both a *process* and *product*. As a process, argument is an act of inquiry characterized by fact finding, information gathering, and consideration of alternative points of view. As a product, it is someone's contribution to the conversation at any one moment—a turn taking in a conversation, a formal speech, or a written position paper such as the one you will write for this chapter. The goal of argument as process is truth seeking; the goal of argument as product is persuasion. When members of a diverse committee are willing to argue persuasively for their respective points of view but are simultaneously willing to listen to other points of view and to change or modify their positions in light of new information or better arguments, then both components of argument are fully in play.

We cannot overemphasize the importance of both truth seeking and persuasion to your professional and civic life. Truth seeking makes you an informed and judicious employee and citizen who delays decisions until a full range of evidence and alternative views are aired and examined. Persuasion gives you the power to influence the world around you, whether through letters to the editor on political issues or convincing position papers for business and professional life. Whenever an organization needs to make a major decision, those who can think flexibly and write persuasively can wield great influence.

▨ EXPLORING CLASSICAL ARGUMENT

An effective way to appreciate argument as both truth seeking and persuasion is to address an issue that is new to you and then watch how your own views evolve. Your initial position will probably reflect what social scientists sometimes call your personal *ideology*—that is, a network of basic values, beliefs, and assumptions that tend to guide your view of the world. However, if you adopt a truth-seeking attitude, your initial position may evolve as the conversation progresses. In fact, the conversation may even cause changes in some of your basic beliefs, since ideologies aren't set in stone and many of us have unresolved allegiance to competing ideologies that may be logically inconsistent (for example, a belief in freedom of speech combined with a belief that hate speech should be banned). In this exercise we ask you to keep track of how your views change and to note what causes the change.

The case we present for discussion involves ethical treatment of animals.

> *Situation:* A bunch of starlings builds nests in the attic of a family's house, gaining access to the attic through a torn vent screen. Soon the eggs hatch, and every morning at sunrise the family is awakened by the sound of birds squawking and wings beating against rafters as the starlings fly in and out of the house to feed the hatchlings. After losing considerable early morning sleep, the family repairs the screen. Unable to get in and out, the parent birds are unable to feed their young. The birds die within a day. Is this cruelty to animals?

1. Freewrite your initial response to this question. Was the family's act an instance of cruelty to animals (that is, was their act ethically justifiable or not)?
2. Working in small groups or as a whole class, share your freewrites and then try to reach a group consensus on the issue. During this conversation (argument as process), listen carefully to your classmates' views and note places where your own initial views begin to evolve.
3. So far we have framed this issue as an after-the-act yes/no question: Is the family guilty of cruelty to animals? But we can also frame it as an open-ended, before-the-fact question: "What should the family have done about the starlings in the attic?" Suppose you are a family member discussing the starlings at dinner prior to the decision to fix the vent screen. Make a list of your family's other options and try to reach class consensus on the two or three best alternative solutions.
4. At the end of the discussion, do another freewrite exploring how your ideas evolved during the discussion. What insights did you get into the twin components of argument: truth seeking and persuasion?

WRITING PROJECT

Write a position paper that takes a stand on a controversial issue. Your introduction will present your issue, provide background, and state the claim you intend to support. The body of your argument will summarize and respond to opposing views as well as present reasons and evidence in support of your own position. You will choose whether to summarize and refute opposing views before or after you have made your own case. Try to end your essay with your strongest arguments.

We sometimes call this assignment an argument in the *classical style* because it is patterned after the persuasive speeches of ancient Greek and Roman orators. In the terms of ancient rhetoricians, the main parts of a persuasive speech are the *exordium,* in which the speaker gets the audience's attention; the *narratio,* which provides needed background; the *propositio,* the speaker's proposition or thesis; the *partitio,* a forecast of the main parts of the speech, equivalent to a blueprint statement; the *confirmatio,* the speaker's arguments in favor of the proposition; the *confutatio,* the refutation of opposing views; and the *peroratio,* the conclusion that sums up the argument, calls for action, and leaves a strong last impression.

We cite these tongue-twisting Latin terms only to assure you that in writing a classical argument you are joining a time-honored tradition that links you to Roman senators on the capitol steps. From their discourse arose the ideal of a democratic society based on superior arguments rather than on superior weaponry. Although there are many other ways to persuade audiences, the classical approach is a particularly effective introduction to persuasive writing.

◪ UNDERSTANDING CLASSICAL ARGUMENT

Having introduced you to argument as both process and product, we now turn to the details of effective argumentation. To help orient you, we begin by describing the typical stages that mark students' growth as arguers.

Stages of Development: Your Growth as an Arguer

We have found that students in our argument classes typically proceed through identifiable stages as their argumentative skills increase. While these stages may or may not describe your own development, they suggest the skills you should strive to acquire.

- **Stage 1: Argument as personal opinion.** At the beginning of instruction in argument, students typically express strong personal opinions but have trouble justifying their opinions with reasons and evidence and often create short, undeveloped arguments that are circular, lack evidence, and insult those who disagree. The following freewrite, written by a student first confronting the starling case (p. 318), illustrates this stage.

    The family shouldn't have killed the starlings because that is really wrong! I mean that act was disgusting. It makes me sick to think how so many people are just willing to kill something for no reason at all. How are these parents going to teach their children values if they just go out and kill little birds for no good reason?!! This whole family is what's wrong with America!

This writer's opinion is passionate and heartfelt, but it provides no reasons and evidence why someone else should hold the same opinion.

- **Stage 2: Argument structured as claim supported by one or more reasons.** This stage represents a quantum leap in argumentative skill because the writer can now produce a rational plan containing point sentences (the reasons) and evidence (the particulars). The writer who produced the previous freewrite later developed a structure like this:

The family's act constituted cruelty to animals

- because the starlings were doing minimal harm
- because other options were available
- because the way they killed the birds caused needless suffering

- ***Stage 3: Increased attention to truth seeking.*** In Stage 3 students become increasingly engaged with the complexity of the issue as they listen to their classmates' views, conduct research, and evaluate alternative perspectives and stances. They are often willing to change their positions when they see the power of other arguments.
- ***Stage 4: Ability to articulate the unstated assumptions underlying their arguments.*** As we show later in this chapter, each reason in a writer's argument is based on an assumption, value, or belief (often unstated) that the audience must accept if the argument is to be persuasive. Often the writer needs to state these assumptions explicitly and support them. At this stage students identify and analyze their own assumptions and those of their intended audiences. Students gain increased skill at accommodating alternative views through refutation or concession.
- ***Stage 5: Ability to link an argument to the values and beliefs of the intended audience.*** In this stage writers are increasingly able to link their arguments to their audience's values and beliefs and to adapt structure and tone to the resistance level of their audience. Writers also appreciate how delayed-thesis arguments or other psychological strategies can be more effective than closed-form arguments when addressing hostile audiences.

The rest of this chapter will help you progress through these stages. Although you can read the rest of this chapter in one sitting, we recommend that you break your reading into sections, going over the material slowly and applying it to your own ideas in progress. Let the chapter's concepts and explanations sink in slowly, and return to them periodically for review. This section on "Understanding Classical Argument" contains the chapter's key instructional material and comprises a compact but comprehensive course in argumentation.

Creating an Argument Frame: A Claim with Reasons

Somewhere in the writing process, whether early or late, you need to create a frame for your argument. This frame includes a clear question that focuses the argument, your claim, and one or more supporting reasons. Often your reasons, stated as *because* clauses, can be attached to your claim to provide a working thesis statement.

Finding an Arguable Issue

At the heart of any argument is an issue, which we can define as a question that invites more than one reasonable answer and thus leads to perplexity or disagreement. This requirement excludes disagreements based on personal tastes where no shared criteria could be developed ("Baseball is more fun than soccer"). It also excludes purely private questions because issues arise out of disagreements in communities. When you are thinking of issues, ask what questions are currently being contested in one of the communities to which you belong (your family, neighborhood, religious or social group, workplace, classroom, dormitory, campus, hometown, state, region, nation, and so forth).

Issue questions are often framed as yes/no choices, especially when they appear on ballots or in courtrooms: Should gay marriage be legalized? Should the city pass the new school bond proposal? Is this defendant guilty of armed robbery? Just as frequently, they can be framed openly, inviting many different possible answers: What should our city do about skateboarders in downtown pedestrian areas? How can children be kept from pornography on the internet?

It is important to remember that framing an issue as a yes/no question does not mean that all points of view fall neatly into pro/con categories. Although citizens may be forced to vote yes or no on a proposed ballot initiative, they can support or oppose the initiative for a variety of reasons. Some may vote happily for the initiative, others vote for it only by holding their noses, and still others oppose it vehemently but for entirely different reasons. To argue effectively, you need to appreciate the wide range of perspectives from which people approach the yes/no choice.

How you frame your question will necessarily affect the scope and shape of your argument itself. In our exploratory exercise we framed the starling question in two ways: (1) Was the family guilty of cruelty to animals? and (2) What should the family do about the starlings? Framed in the first way, your argument would have to develop criteria for "cruelty to animals" and then argue whether the family's actions met those criteria. Framed in the second way, you could argue for your own solution to the problem ranging from doing nothing (wait for the birds to grow up, then fix the screen) to climbing into the attic and drowning the birds so that their death is quick and painless. Or you could word the question in a broader, more philosophical way: When are humans justified in killing an animal? Or you could focus on a subissue: When can an animal be labeled a "pest"?

FOR WRITING AND DISCUSSION

1. Working individually, make a list of several communities that you belong to and then identify one or more questions currently being contested within those communities. (If you have trouble, get a copy of your local campus and city newspapers or an organizational newsletter; you'll quickly discover a wealth of contested issues.) Then share your list with classmates.
2. Pick two or three issues of particular interest to you, and try framing them in different ways: as broad or narrow questions, as open-ended or yes/no questions. Place several examples on the chalkboard for class discussion.

Stating a Claim

Your claim is the position you want to take on the issue. It is your brief, one-sentence answer to your issue question:

The family was not ethically justified in killing the starlings.

The city should build skateboarding areas with ramps in all city parks.

You will appreciate argument as truth seeking if you find that your claim evolves as you think more deeply about your issue and listen to alternative views. Be willing to rephrase your claim to soften it or refocus it or even to reverse it as you progress through the writing process.

Articulating Reasons

Your claim, which is the position you take on an issue, needs to be supported by reasons and evidence. A *reason* (sometimes called a *premise*) is a subclaim that supports your main claim. In speaking or writing, a reason is usually linked to the claim with such connecting words as *because, therefore, so, consequently,* and *thus.* In planning your argument, a powerful strategy for developing reasons is to harness the grammatical power of the conjunction *because;* think of your reasons as *because* clauses attached to your claim. Formulating your reasons in this way allows you to create a thesis statement that breaks your argument into smaller parts, each part devoted to one of the reasons.*

Suppose, for example, that you are examining the issue "Should the government legalize hard drugs such as heroin and cocaine?" Here are several different points of view on this issue, each expressed as a claim with because clauses:

One View

Cocaine and heroin should be legalized

- because legalizing drugs will keep the government out of people's private lives.
- because keeping these drugs illegal has the same negative effects on our society that alcohol prohibition did in the 1920s.

Another View

Cocaine and heroin should be legalized

- because the subsequent elimination of the black market would cut down on muggings and robberies.
- because decriminalization would cut down on prison overcrowding and free police to concentrate on dangerous crime rather than finding drug dealers.
- because elimination of underworld profits would change the economic structure of the underclass and promote shifts to socially productive jobs and careers.

---

*The thesis statement for your essay could be your claim by itself or you could include in your thesis statement your main supporting reasons. For advice on how much of your supporting argument you should summarize in your thesis statement, see Chapter 18, pp. 476–78.

Still Another View

The government should not legalize heroin and cocaine

- because doing so will lead to an increase in drug users.
- because doing so will send the message that it is okay to use hard drugs.

Although the yes/no framing of this question seems to reduce the issue to a two-position debate, many different value systems are at work here. The first pro-legalization argument, libertarian in perspective, values maximum individual freedom. The second argument—although it too supports legalization—takes a community perspective valuing the social benefits of eliminating the black market. In the same way, people could oppose legalization for a variety of reasons.

FOR WRITING AND DISCUSSION

Working in small groups or as a whole class, generate a list of reasons for and against one or more of the following yes/no claims. State your reasons as because clauses. Think of as many because clauses as possible by imagining a wide variety of perspectives on the issue.

1. The school year for grades 1–12 should be lengthened to eleven months.
2. Marilyn Manson (and other such iconoclastic entertainers) serves a valuable social function.
3. Women's fashion/style magazines (such as *Glamour* and *Mademoiselle*) are harmful influences on teenage women.
4. The United States should replace its income tax with a national sales tax.
5. Medical insurance should cover alternative medicine (massage therapy, acupuncture, herbal treatments, and so forth).

Articulating Unstated Assumptions

So far, we have focused on the frame of an argument as a claim supported with one or more reasons. Shortly, we will proceed to the flesh and muscle of an argument, which is the evidence you use to support your reasons. But before turning to evidence, we need to look at another crucial part of an argument's frame: its *unstated assumptions*.

What Do We Mean by an Unstated Assumption?

Every time you link together a claim with a reason, you make a silent assumption that may need to be articulated and examined. Consider this argument:

The family was justified in killing the starlings because starlings are pests.

To support this argument, the writer would first need to provide evidence that starlings are pests (examples of the damage they do, and so forth). But the persuasiveness of the argument rests on the unstated assumption that it is okay to kill pests. If an audience doesn't agree with that assumption, then the argument flounders unless the writer articulates the assumption and defends it. The complete frame of the argument must therefore include the unstated assumption.

Claim: The family was justified in killing the starlings.

Reason: Because starlings are pests.

Unstated assumption: It is ethically justifiable to kill pests.

It is important to examine the unstated assumption behind any claim with reason *because you must determine whether your audience will accept that assumption. If not, you need to make it explicit and support it.* Think of the unstated assumption as a general principle, rule, belief, or value that connects the reason to the claim. It answers your reader's question, "Why, if I accept your reason, should I accept your claim?"

Here are a few more examples.

Claim with reason: Women should be allowed to join combat units because the image of women as combat soldiers would help society overcome gender stereotyping.

Unstated assumption: It is good to overcome gender stereotyping.

Claim with reason: The government should not legalize heroin and cocaine because doing so will lead to an increase in drug users.

Unstated assumption: It is bad to increase the number of drug users.

Claim with reason: The family was guilty of cruelty to animals in the starling case because less drastic means of solving the problem were available.

Unstated assumption: A person should choose the least drastic means to solve a problem.

FOR WRITING AND DISCUSSION

Identify the unstated assumptions for each of the following claims with reason.

1. Cocaine and heroin should be legalized because legalizing drugs will keep the government out of people's private lives.
2. The government should eliminate welfare payments to unwed mothers because doing so will reduce the illegitimacy rate.
3. After-school jobs are bad for high school students because they use up valuable study time.
4. We should strengthen the Endangered Species Act because doing so will preserve genetic diversity on the planet.
5. The Endangered Species Act is too stringent because it severely damages the economy.

Using Toulmin Terminology to Describe an Argument's Structure

Our explanation of argument structure is influenced by the work of philosopher Stephen Toulmin, who viewed argumentation as a dynamic courtroom drama where opposing attorneys exchanged arguments and cross-examinations before a judge and jury. The terms used by Toulmin to describe the structure of argument are widely accepted in rhetoric and composition studies and provide a handy vocabulary for discussing arguments. Toulmin called the unstated assumption behind a claim with reason the argument's *warrant*, based on our common word "warranty" for guarantee. If the audience accepts your warrant—that is, if they agree with your unstated assumption—then your argument is sound, or guaranteed. To put it another way, if your audience accepts your warrant, and if you can convince them that your reason is true, then they will accept your claim.

Besides the term *warrant*, Toulmin also uses the terms *grounds, backing, conditions of rebuttal*, and *qualifier*. We will explain these terms to you at the appropriate moments as we proceed.

Using Evidence Effectively

In Chapter 3 we showed you that the majority of words in a closed-form essay are particulars used to support points. If you think of reasons and warrants as the main points of your argument, then think of evidence as the supporting particulars. Each of your reasons will need to be supported by evidence. Toulmin's term for evidence in support of a reason is *grounds,* which we can think of as all the facts, data, testimony, statistics, subarguments and other details a writer can find to support a reason. The evidence and arguments used to support a warrant Toulmin calls *backing.* In this section we survey different kinds of evidence and show you how to incorporate that evidence into an argument, either as grounds to support a reason or as backing to support a warrant. Some arguments can be fleshed out with evidence based on your personal experience and observations. But most arguments require more formal evidence—the kind you gather from library or field research. (See Chapter 22 for a more elaborate treatment of how to use research sources in your own writing.)

Kinds of Evidence

The kinds of evidence most often used for the grounds and backing are the following.

Examples.   An example from personal experience can often be used to support a reason. Here is how one student writer, arguing that her church building needs to be remodeled, used a personal example to support a reason.

> Finally, Sacred Heart Church must be renovated immediately because the terrazzo floor that covers the entire church is very dangerous. Four Sundays ago, during 11:00 Mass, nine Eucharistic Ministers went up to the altar to prepare for distributing communion. As they carefully walked to their assigned post on the recently buffed terrazzo floor, a loud crash of crystal echoed through the church.

> A woman moving to her post slipped on the recently buffed floor, fell to the ground, hit her head on the marble, and was knocked unconscious. People rushed to her aid, thinking she was dead. Fortunately she was alive, only badly hurt. This woman was my mother.

Besides specific examples like this, writers sometimes invent hypothetical examples, or *scenarios,* to illustrate an issue or hypothesize about the consequences of an event. (Of course, you must signal your reader that the example or scenario is hypothetical.)

Summaries of Research.   Another common way to support an argument is to summarize research studies. Here is how a student writer used a summary statement to support his opposition to mandatory helmet laws for motorcycle riders:

> However, a helmet won't protect against head injury when one is traveling at normal traffic speeds. According to a U.S. Department of Transportation study, "There is no evidence that any helmet thus far, regardless of cost or design, is capable of rejecting impact stress above 13 mph" (Transportation Study, p. 8).*

Statistics.   Another common form of evidence is statistics. (For a detailed discussion of statistical data in arguments, see Chapter 11.) Here is how one writer uses statistics to argue that alcohol poses a more serious social problem than heroin or cocaine.

> The uproar about drugs is itself odd. In 1987, according to the Kerry subcommittee, there were 1,400 deaths from cocaine; in 1988, that figure had increased to 3,308. Deaths from *all* forms of illegal drugs total under 6,000. By contrast, 320,000 to 390,000 people die prematurely each year from tobacco and 100,000 to 200,000 from misuse of alcohol. Alcohol is associated with 40 percent of all suicide attempts, 40 percent of all traffic deaths, 54 percent of all violent crimes and 10 percent of all work-related injuries.

Testimony.   Writers can also use expert testimony to bolster a case. The following student essay uses testimony to support "comparable worth"—an economic policy intended to redress salary inequities between traditionally "male" and "female" job fields.

> Barbara Bergmann, professor of economics at the University of Maryland, has studied the comparable worth issue at length. If comparable worth were enacted, she points out, "Nobody's pay need go down. Nor will budgets or profits be wiped out" (9).†

Subarguments.   Sometimes writers support reasons not directly through data but through sequences of subarguments. Sometimes these subarguments develop a

---

*This student is using the APA (American Psychological Association) style for documenting sources. This quotation is found on page 8 of a document listed as "Transportation Study" in the References list at the end of the essay. See Chapter 22.

†This student is using the MLA (Modern Language Association) style for documenting sources. This quotation will be found on page 9 of an article authored by Barbara Bergmann and listed under Bergman in the Works Cited list at the end of the essay.

persuasive analogy, hypothesize about consequences, or simply advance the argument through a chain of connected points. In the following passage, taken from a philosophic article justifying torture under certain conditions, the author uses a subargument to support one of his main points—that a terrorist holding victims hostage has no "rights":

> There is an important difference between terrorists and their victims that should mute talk of the terrorist's "rights." The terrorist's victims are at risk unintentionally, not having asked to be endangered. But the terrorist knowingly initiated his actions. Unlike his victims, he volunteered for the risks of his deed. By threatening to kill for profit or idealism, he renounces civilized standards, and he can have no complaint if civilization tries to thwart him by whatever means necessary.

Rather than using direct empirical evidence, the author supports his point with a subargument showing how terrorists differ from victims and thus relinquish their claim to rights.

Reliability of Evidence

When you use empirical evidence, you can increase its persuasiveness by monitoring its recency, relevance, impartiality, and scope.

Recency.   As much as possible, and especially if you are addressing current issues in science, technology, politics, or social trends, use the most recent evidence you can find.

Relevance.   Ensure that the evidence you cite is relevant to the point you are making. For example, for many decades the medical profession offered advice about heart disease to their female patients based on studies of male subjects. No matter how extensive or how recent those studies, some of their conclusions are bound to be irrelevant for female patients.

Impartiality.   While all data must be interpreted and hence are never completely impartial, careful readers are aware of how easily data can be skewed. Newspapers, magazines, and journals often have political biases and different levels of respectability. Evidence you take from *Reader's Digest* or *The National Review* is apt to have a conservative bias, whereas evidence from *The Nation* or *Mother Jones* is apt to have a liberal bias. These sources often provide excellent data, but be aware that your readers may be wary of their objectivity. Generally, evidence associated with scientifically conducted studies is more highly regarded than evidence taken from second or third hand sources. Particularly problematic is information gathered from Internet websites, which are often unreliable and highly biased. See pages 370–77 for ideas on how to evaluate websites.

Sufficiency.   One of the most common reasoning fallacies is to make a sweeping generalization based on only one or two instances. The criterion of sufficiency (which means having enough examples to justify your point) helps you guard against hasty generalizations.

Addressing Objections and Counterarguments

Having looked at the frame of an argument (claim, reasons, and warrants) and at the kinds of evidence used to flesh out the frame, let's turn now to the important concern of anticipating and responding to objections and counterarguments. In this section, we show you an extended example of a student anticipating and responding to a reader's objection. We then describe a planning schema that can help you anticipate objections and show you how to respond to counterarguments either through refutation or concession. Finally we show how your active imagining of alternative views can lead you to qualify your claim.

Anticipating Objections: An Extended Example

In our earlier discussions of the starling case, we saw how readers might object to the argument "The family is justified in killing the starlings because starlings are pests." What rankles these readers is the unstated assumption (warrant) that it is okay to kill pests. Imagine an objecting reader saying something like this:

> It is *not* okay to get annoyed with a living creature, label it a "pest," and then kill it. This whole use of the term "pest" suggests that humans have the right to dominate nature. We need to have more reverence for nature. The ease with which the family solved their problem by killing living things sets a bad example for children. The family could have waited until fall and then fixed the screen.

Imagining such an objection might lead a writer to modify his claim. But if the writer remains committed to his claim, then he must develop a response. In the following example, in which a student writer argues that it is okay to kill the starlings, note (1) how the writer uses evidence to show that starlings are pests, (2) how he summarizes a possible objection to his warrant, and (3) how he supports his warrant with backing.

Student Argument Defending Reason and Warrant

Claim with reason

The family was justified in killing the starlings because starlings are pests. Starlings are nonindigenous birds that drive out native species and multiply rapidly. When I searched "starlings and pests" on the Alta Vista search engine, I discovered 161 websites dealing with starlings as pests. Starlings are hated by farmers and gardeners because huge flocks of them devour newly planted seeds in spring as well as fruits and berries at harvest. A flock of starlings can devastate a cherry orchard in a few days. As invasive nesters, starlings can also damage attics by tearing up insulation and defecating on stored items. Many of the website articles focused on ways to kill off starling populations. In killing the starlings, the family was protecting its own property and reducing the population of these pests.

Evidence that starlings are pests

Summary of a possible direction

Many readers might object to my argument, saying that humans should have a reverence for nature and not quickly try to kill off any creature they label a pest. Further, these readers might say that even if starlings are pests, the family could have waited until fall to repair the attic or found some other means of protecting their property without having to kill the baby starlings. I too would have waited until fall if the birds in the attic had been swallows or some other native species without starlings' destructiveness and propensity for unchecked population growth. But starlings should be compared to rats or mice. We set traps for rodents because we know the damage they cause when they nest in walls and attics. We don't get sentimental trying to save the orphaned rat babies. In the same way, we are justified in eliminating starlings as soon as they begin infesting our houses. Think of them not as chirpy little songsters but as rats of the bird world.

Response to the objection

In the preceding example, we see how the writer uses grounds to support his reason and then, anticipating his readers' objection to his warrant, summarizes that objection and offers backing. One might not be convinced by the argument, but the writer has done a good job trying to support both the reason and the warrant.

Using a Planning Schema to Anticipate Objections

The arguing strategy used by the previous writer was triggered by his anticipation of objections—what Toulmin calls *conditions of rebuttal.* Under conditions of rebuttal, Toulmin asks arguers to imagine various ways skeptical readers might object to a writer's argument or specific conditions under which the argument might not hold. The Toulmin system lets us create a planning schema that can help writers develop a persuasive argument.

This schema encourages writers to articulate their argument frame (reason and warrant) and then to imagine what could be used for grounds (to support the reason) and backing (to support the warrant). Equally important, the schema encourages writers to anticipate counterarguments by imagining how skeptical readers might object to the writer's reason or warrant or both. To create the schema, you simply make a chart headed by your claim with reason and then make slots for grounds, warrant, backing, and conditions of rebuttal. Then brainstorm ideas to put into each slot. Here is how another student writer used this schema to plan an argument on the starling case:

Claim with reason

The family showed cruelty to animals because the way they killed the birds caused needless suffering.

Grounds

I've got to show how the birds suffered and also how the suffering was needless. The way of killing the birds caused the birds to suffer. The hatchlings starved to death, as did the parent birds if they were trapped inside the attic. Starvation is very slow and agonizing. The suffering was also needless since other means were available such as calling an exterminator who would remove birds and either relocate them or kill them painlessly. If no other alternative was available, someone should have crawled into the attic and found a painless way to kill the birds.

Warrant

If it is not necessary to kill an animal, then don't; if it is necessary, then the killing should be done in the least painful way possible.

Backing

I've got to convince readers it is wrong to make an animal suffer if you don't have to. Humans have a natural antipathy to needless suffering—our feeling of unease if we imagine cattle or chickens caused to suffer for our food rather than being cleanly and quickly killed. If a horse is incurably wounded, we shoot it rather then letting it suffer. We are morally obligated to cause the least pain possible.

Conditions of rebuttal

How could a reader object to my reason? A reader could say that killing the starlings did *not* cause suffering. Perhaps hatchling starlings don't feel pain of starvation or die very quickly. Perhaps a reader could object to my claim that other means were available: There is no other way to kill the starlings—impossibility of catching a bunch of adult starlings flying around an attic. Poison may cause just as much suffering. Cost of exterminator is prohibitive.

How could a reader object to my warrant? Perhaps the reader would say that my rule to cause the least pain possible does not apply to animal pests. In class, someone said that worrying about the baby starlings was sentimental. Laws of nature condemn millions of animals each year to death by starvation or by being eaten alive by other animals. Humans occasionally have to take their place within this tooth-and-claw natural system.

How many of the ideas from this schema would the writer use in her actual paper? That is a judgment call based on the writer's analysis of audience. In every case, the writer should support the reason with evidence because supporting a claim with reasons and evidence is the minimal requirement of argument. But it is not necessary to state the warrant explicitly or provide backing for it unless the writer anticipates readers who doubt it.

The same rule of thumb applies to the need for summarizing and responding to objections and counterarguments: Let your analysis of audience be your guide. If we imagined the preceding argument aimed at readers who thought it was sentimental to worry about the suffering of animal pests, the writer should make her warrant explicit and back it. Her task would be to convince readers that humans have ethical responsibilities that exclude them from tooth-and-claw morality.

FOR WRITING AND DISCUSSION

Working individually or in small groups, create a planning schema for the following arguments: For each claim with reason: (a) imagine the kinds of evidence needed as grounds to support the reason; (b) identify the warrant; (c) imagine a strategy for supporting the warrant (backing); anticipate possible objections to the reason and to the warrant (conditions of rebuttal).

1. *Claim with reason:* Now that we are buying our first car together, we should buy a Jupiter 500 sedan because it is the most economical car on the road. (Imagine this argument aimed at your significant other, who wants to buy a Phantomjet 1000 sports car.)

2. *Claim with reason:* Gay marriage should be legalized because doing so will promote faithful monogamous relationships among gay people. (Imagine this argument aimed at a homophobic audience.)
3. *Claim with reason:* The government should eliminate welfare payments for unwed mothers because doing so would reduce the illegitimacy rate. (Imagine this argument aimed at liberals who support welfare payments to single mothers.)
4. *Claim with reason:* After-school jobs are bad for high school students because they use up valuable study time. (Aim this argument at a middle-class teenager who wants to get a job to earn extra spending money.)

Responding to Objections, Counterarguments, and Alternative Views Through Refutation or Concession

We have seen how a writer needs to anticipate alternative views that give rise to objections and counterarguments. Surprisingly, one of the best ways to approach counterarguments is to summarize them fairly. Make your imagined reader's best case against your argument. By resisting the temptation to distort a counterargument, you demonstrate a willingness to consider the issue from all sides. Moreover, summarizing a counterargument reduces your reader's tendency to say, "Yes, but have you thought of . . . ?" After you have summarized an objection or counterargument fairly and charitably, you must then decide how to respond to it. Your two main choices are to rebut it or concede to it.

Rebutting Opposing Views

When rebutting or refuting an argument, you can question the argument's reasons/grounds or warrant or both. In the following student example, the writer summarizes her classmates' objections to abstract art and then analyzes shortcomings in their reasons and grounds.

Some of my classmates object to abstract art because it apparently takes no technical drawing talent. They feel that artists turn abstract because they are not capable of the technical drafting skills that appear in Remington, Russell, and Rockwell pieces. Therefore they created an art form that anyone was capable of and that was less time consuming, and then they paraded it as artistic progress. But I object to the notion that these artists turned to abstraction because they lacked the ability to do representative drawing. Many abstract artists, such as Picasso, are excellent draftsmen, and their early pieces show very realistic drawing skill. As his work matured, Picasso became more abstract in order to increase the expressive quality of his work. *Guernica* was meant as a protest against the bombing of that city by the Germans. To express the terror and suffering of the victims more vividly, he distorted the figures and presented them in a black and white journalistic manner. If he had used representational images and color—which he had the skill to do—much of the emotional content would have been

lost and the piece probably would not have caused the demand for justice that
it did.

Conceding to Counterarguments

In some cases, an alternative view can be very strong. If so, don't hide that
view from your reader; summarize it and concede to it.

Making concessions to opposing views is not necessarily a sign of weakness;
in many cases, a concession simply acknowledges that the issue is complex and
that your position is tentative. In turn, a concession can enhance a reader's respect
for you and invite the reader to follow your example and weigh the strengths of
your own argument charitably. Writers typically concede to opposing views with
transitional expressions such as the following:

admittedly	I must admit that	I agree that	granted
even though	I concede that	while it is true that	

After conceding to an opposing view, you should shift to a different field
of values where your position is strong and then argue for those new values. For
example, adversaries of drug legalization argue plausibly that legalizing drugs
would increase the number of users and addicts. If you support legalization,
here is how you might deal with this point without fatally damaging your own
argument:

> Opponents of legalization claim—and rightly so—that legalization will lead
> to an increase in drug users and addicts. I wish this weren't so, but it is. Never-
> theless, the other benefits of legalizing drugs—eliminating the black market, re-
> ducing street crime, and freeing up thousands of police from fighting the war on
> drugs—more than outweigh the social costs of increased drug use and addic-
> tion, especially if tax revenues from drug sales are plowed back into drug educa-
> tion and rehabilitation programs.

The writer concedes that legalization will increase addiction (one reason for opposing legalization) and that drug addiction is bad (the warrant for that reason).
But then the writer redeems the case for legalization by shifting the argument to
another field of values (the benefits of eliminating the black market, reducing
crime, and so forth).

Qualifying Your Claim

The need to summarize and respond to alternative views lets the writer see an
issue's complexity and appreciate that no one position has a total monopoly on the
truth. Consequently, in the argument schema that we have adapted from Toulmin,
there is one final term that it is important to know: the *qualifier*. This term refers to
words that limit the scope or force of a claim to make it less sweeping and therefore less vulnerable. Consider the difference between the sentences "After-school
jobs are bad for teenagers" and "After-school jobs are often bad for teenagers." The
first claim can be refuted by one counterexample of a teenager who benefited from
an after-school job. Because the second claim admits exceptions, it is much harder

to refute. Unless your argument is airtight, you will want to limit your claim with qualifiers such as the following:

perhaps	maybe
in many cases	generally
tentatively	sometimes
often	usually
probably	likely
may or might (rather than is)	

You can also qualify a claim with an opening "unless" clause ("*Unless* your apartment is well soundproofed, you should not buy such a powerful stereo system.").

Appealing to *Ethos* and *Pathos*

When the classical rhetoricians examined ways that orators could persuade listeners, they focused on three kinds of proofs: *logos*, or the appeal to reason; *ethos*, or the appeal to the speaker's character; and *pathos*, or the appeal to the emotions and the sympathetic imagination. So far in this chapter we have focused on the logical appeals of *logos*. In this section we examine *ethos* and *pathos*. You can see how these three appeals are connected by visualizing a triangle with interrelated points labeled *message, writer/speaker,* and *audience* (Figure 14.1). Effective arguments consider all three points on this *rhetorical triangle.*

Appeal to *Ethos*

A powerful way to increase the persuasiveness of an argument is to gain your reader's trust. You appeal to *ethos* whenever your reader has confidence in your credibility and trustworthiness. In Chapter 4 we discussed how readers develop an image of the writer, the writer's persona, based on features of the writer's prose. For readers to accept your argument, they must perceive a persona that's knowledgeable, trustworthy, and fair. We suggest three ways to enhance your argument's ethos.

1. Demonstrate to your reader that you know your subject well. If you have personal experience with the subject, cite that experience. Reflect thoughtfully on your subject, citing research as well as personal experience, and summarize accurately and carefully a range of viewpoints.
2. Be fair to alternative points of view. Scorning an opposing view may occasionally win you favor with an audience predisposed toward your position, but it will offend others and hinder critical analysis. As a general rule, treating opposing views respectfully is the best strategy.
3. Build bridges toward your audience by grounding your argument in shared values and assumptions. Doing so will demonstrate your concern for your audience and enhance your trustworthiness. Moreover, rooting your argument in the audience's values and assumptions has a strong emotional appeal, as we explain in the next section.

Message

*(LOGOS: How can I make the argument
internally consistent and logical? How
can I find the best reasons and support
them with the best evidence?)*

Audience

*(PATHOS: How can I make the reader
open to my message? How can I best
engage my readers' emotions and
imagination? How can I appeal to
my readers' values and interests?)*

Writer or Speaker

*(ETHOS: How can I present myself
effectively? How can I enhance my
credibility and trustworthiness?)*

FIGURE 14.1   Rhetorical Triangle

Appeals to *Pathos*

Besides basing your argument on appeals to logos and ethos, you might also base it on an appeal to what the Greeks called *pathos.* Sometimes pathos is interpreted narrowly as an appeal to the emotions. This interpretation effectively devalues pathos because popular culture generally values reason above emotion. Although appeals to pathos can sometimes be irrational and irrelevant ("You can't give me a C! I need a B to get into med school, and if I don't I'll break my ill grandmother's heart."), they can also arouse audience interest and deepen understanding of an argument's human dimensions. Here are some ways to use pathos in your arguments.

Use Vivid Language and Examples.   One way to create pathos is to use vivid language and powerful examples. If you are arguing in favor of homeless shelters, for example, you can humanize your appeal by describing one homeless person.

> He is huddled over the sewer grate, his feet wrapped in newspapers. He blows on his hands, then tucks them under his armpits and lies down on the sidewalk with his shoulders over the grate, his bed for the night.

But if you are arguing for tougher laws against panhandling, you might let your reader see the issue through the eyes of downtown shoppers intimidated by "ratty, urine-soaked derelicts drinking fortified wine from a shared sack."

Find Audience-Based Reasons.   The best way to see pathos is not as an appeal to emotions but rather an appeal to the audience's values and beliefs. With its emphasis on warrants, Toulmin's system of analysis naturally encourages this kind of appeal. For example, in engineer David Rockwood's argument against wind-generated power (Chapter 1, pp. 12–13), Rockwood's final reason is that constructing wind generation facilities will damage the environment. To environmentalists, this reason has emotional as well as rational power because its warrant ("Preserving the environment is good") appeals to their values. It is an example of an audience-based reason, which we can define simply as any reason whose warrant the audience already accepts and endorses. Such reasons, because they hook into the beliefs and values of the audience, appeal to *pathos*.

When you plan your argument, seek audience-based reasons wherever possible. Suppose, for example, that you are advocating the legalization of heroin and cocaine. If you know your audience is concerned about their own safety in the streets, then you can argue that legalization of drugs will cut down on crime:

> We should legalize drugs because doing so will make our streets safer: It will cut down radically on street criminals seeking drug money, and it will free up narcotics police to focus on other kinds of crime.

If your audience is concerned about improving the quality of life for youths in inner cities, you might argue that legalization of drugs will lead to better lives for the current underclass:

> We should legalize drugs because doing so will eliminate the lure of drug trafficking that tempts so many inner-city youth away from honest jobs and into crime.

Or if your audience is concerned about high taxes and government debt, you might say:

> We should legalize drugs because doing so will help us balance federal and state budgets: It will decrease police and prison costs by decriminalizing narcotics; and it will eliminate the black market in drugs, allowing us to collect taxes on drug sales.

In each case, you would move people toward your position by connecting your argument to their beliefs and values.

Some Advanced Considerations

You have now finished reading what we might call a basic course in argumentation. In this final section, we discuss briefly some more advanced ideas about argumentation. Your instructor may want to expand on these in class, simply ask you to read them, or not assign this section at all. The three concepts we explore briefly are argument types, delayed-thesis and Rogerian arguments, and informal fallacies.

Argument Types

The advice we have given you so far in this chapter applies to any type of argument. However, scholars of argumentation have categorized arguments into several different types, each of which uses its own characteristic structures and ways of development. One way to talk about argument types is to divide them into truth issues and values issues.

Truth issues stem from questions about the way reality is (or was or will be). Unlike questions of fact, which can be proved or disproved by agreed-on empirical measures, issues of truth require interpretation of the facts. Does Linda smoke an average of twenty or more cigarettes per day? is a question of fact, answerable with a yes or a no. But the question, Why did Linda start smoking when she was fifteen? is a question of truth with many possible answers. Was it because of cigarette advertising? Peer pressure? The dynamics of Linda's family? Dynamics in the culture (for example, white American youths are seven times more likely to smoke than are African American youths)? Truth issues generally take one of the three following forms:

1. *Definitional issues.* Does this particular case fit into a particular category? (Is bungee jumping a "carnival ride" for purposes of state safety regulations? Is tobacco a "drug" and therefore under the jurisdiction of the Federal Drug Administration?)
2. *Causal issues.* What are the causes or consequences of this phenomenon? (Does the current welfare system encourage teenage pregnancy? Will the "three strikes and you're out" rule reduce violent crime?*)
3. *Resemblance or precedence issues.* Is this phenomenon like or analogous to some other phenomenon? (Was U.S. involvement in Bosnia like U.S. involvement in Vietnam? Is killing a starling like killing a rat?)

Rational arguments can involve disputes about values as well as truth. Family disagreements about what car to buy typically revolve around competing values: What is most important? looks? performance? safety? economy? comfort? dependability? prestige? Similarly, many public issues ask people to choose among competing value systems: Whose values should be adopted in a given situation? Those of corporations or environmentalists? of the fetus or the pregnant woman? of owners or laborers? of the individual or the state? Value issues usually fall in one of the following two categories:

---

*Although we placed our chapter on causes and consequences (Chapter 13) in the "writing to analyze" category, we could have placed it just as logically under "writing to persuade." The difference concerns the writer's perceived relationship to the audience. If you imagine your readers as decidedly skeptical of your thesis and actively weighing alternative theses, then your purpose is persuasive. However, if you imagine your readers as puzzled and curious—reading your essay primarily to clarify their own thinking on a causal question—then your purpose is analytical. The distinction here is a matter of degree, not of kind.

1. *Evaluation issues.*   How good is this particular member of its class? Is this action morally good or bad? (How effective was President Clinton's first year in office? Which computer system best meets the company's needs? Is the death penalty morally wrong? [See Chapter 15 for a fuller discussion of evaluation arguments.])
2. *Policy issues.*   Should we take this action? (Should Congress pass stricter gun-control laws? Should health-insurance policies cover eating disorders? [See Chapter 16 for a fuller discussion of policy issues.])

Delayed-Thesis and Rogerian Argument

Classical arguments are usually closed form with the writer's thesis stated prominently at the end of the introduction. Classical argument works best for neutral audiences weighing all sides of an issue or for somewhat opposed audiences who are willing to listen to other views. However, when you address a highly resistant audience, one where your point of view seems especially threatening to your audience's values and beliefs, classical argument can seem too blunt and aggressive. In such cases, a *delayed-thesis argument* works best. In such an argument you don't state your actual thesis until the conclusion. The body of the paper extends your sympathy to the reader's views, shows how troubling the issue is to you, and leads the reader gradually toward your position.

A special kind of delayed-thesis argument is called *Rogerian argument,* named after the psychologist Carl Rogers, who specialized in helping people with widely divergent views learn to talk to each other. The principle of Rogerian communication is that listeners must show empathy toward each other's world views and make every attempt to build bridges toward each other. In planning a Rogerian argument, instead of asking, "What reasons and evidence will convince my reader to adopt my claim?" you ask, "What is it about my view that especially threatens my reader? How can I reduce this threat?" Using a Rogerian strategy, the writer summarizes the audience's point of view fairly and charitably, demonstrating the ability to listen and understand the audience's views. She then reduces the threat of her own position by showing how both writer and resistant audience share many basic values. The key to successful Rogerian argument, besides the art of listening, is the ability to point out areas of agreement between the writer's and the reader's position. Then the writer seeks a compromise between the two views.

As an example, if you support a woman's right to choose abortion and you are arguing with someone completely opposed to abortion, you're unlikely to convert your reader, but you may reduce the level of resistance. You begin this process by summarizing your reader's position sympathetically, stressing your shared values. You might say, for example, that you also value babies; that you also are appalled by people who treat abortion as a form of birth control; that you also worry that the easy acceptance of abortion diminishes the value society places on human life; and that you also agree that accepting abortion lightly can lead to lack of sexual responsibility. Building bridges like these between you and your readers makes it more likely that they will listen to you when you present your own position.

Avoiding Informal Fallacies

Informal fallacies are instances of murky reasoning that can cloud an argument and lead to unsound conclusions. Because they can crop up unintentionally in anyone's writing, and because advertisers and hucksters often use them intentionally to deceive, it is a good idea to learn to recognize the more common fallacies.

Post Hoc, Ergo Proper Hoc *(After This, Therefore Because of This).*   This fallacy involves mistaking sequence for cause. Just because one event happens before another event doesn't mean the first event caused the second. The connection may be coincidental, or some unknown third event may have caused both of these events.

> Example   For years I suffered from agonizing abdominal itching. Then I tried Smith's pills. Almost overnight my abdominal itching ceased. Smith's pills work wonders.

Hasty Generalization.   Closely related to the *post hoc* fallacy is the hasty generalization, which refers to claims based on insufficient or unrepresentative data.

> Example   The food-stamp program supports mostly freeloaders. Let me tell you about my worthless neighbor.

False Analogy.   Analogical arguments are tricky because there are almost always significant differences between the two things being compared. If the two things differ greatly, the analogy can mislead rather than clarify.

> Example   You can't force a kid to become a musician any more than you can force a tulip to become a rose.

Either/Or Reasoning.   This fallacy occurs when a complex, multisided issue is reduced to two positions without acknowledging the possibility of other alternatives.

> Example   Either you are pro-choice on abortion or you are against the advancement of women in our culture.

Ad Hominem *("Against the Person").*   When people can't find fault with an argument, they sometimes attack the arguer, substituting irrelevant assertions about that person's character for an analysis of the argument itself.

> Example   Don't pay any attention to Fulke's views on sexual harassment in the workplace. I just learned that he subscribes to *Playboy.*

Appeals to False Authority and Bandwagon Appeals.   These fallacies offer as support for an argument the fact that a famous person or "many people" already support it. Unless the supporters are themselves authorities in the field, their support is irrelevant.

> Example   Buy Freeble oil because Joe Quarterback always uses it in his fleet of cars.
>
> Example   How can abortion be wrong if millions of people support a woman's right to choose?

Non Sequitur *("It Does Not Follow")*. This fallacy occurs when there is no evident connection between a claim and its reason. Sometimes a *non sequitur* can be repaired by filling in gaps in the reasoning; at other times, the reasoning is simply fallacious.

> Example   I don't deserve a B for this course because I am a straight-A student.

Circular Reasoning. This fallacy occurs when you state your claim and then, usually after rewording it, you state it again as your reason.

> Example   Marijuana is injurious to your health because it harms your body.

Red Herring. This fallacy refers to the practice of raising an unrelated or irrelevant point deliberately to throw an audience off the track. Politicians often employ this fallacy when they field questions from the public or press.

> Example   You raise a good question about my support for continuing the continuing military build-up in Bosnia. Let me tell you about my admiration for the bravery of our soldiers.

Slippery Slope. The slippery slope fallacy is based on the fear that one step in a direction we don't like inevitably leads to the next with no stopping place.

> Example   We don't dare send weapons to these guerrillas. If we do, we will next send in military advisers, then a special forces battalion, and then large numbers of troops. Finally, we will be in all-out war.

READINGS

Our first reading is by Edward I. Koch, former mayor of New York City and long-time active member of the Democratic Party. Generally associated with liberal politics, Koch here takes a conservative position on the death penalty, arguing that capital punishment affirms life. This article originally appeared in *The New Republic* in 1985.

▼

EDWARD I. KOCH
DEATH AND JUSTICE:
HOW CAPITAL PUNISHMENT AFFIRMS LIFE

1   Last December a man named Robert Lee Willie, who had been convicted of raping and murdering an eighteen-year-old woman, was executed in the Louisiana state prison. In a statement issued several minutes before his death, Mr. Willie said: "Killing people is wrong. . . . It makes no difference whether it's citizens, countries, or governments. Killing is wrong." Two weeks later in South Carolina, an admitted killer named Joseph Carl Shaw was put to death for murdering two teenagers. In an appeal to the

governor for clemency, Mr Shaw wrote: "Killing is wrong when I did it. Killing is wrong when you do it. I hope you have the courage and moral strength to stop the killing."

It is a curiosity of modern life that we find ourselves being lectured on morality by cold-blooded killers. Mr. Willie previously had been convicted of aggravated rape, aggravated kidnapping, and the murders of a Louisiana deputy and a man from Missouri. Mr. Shaw committed another murder a week before the two for which he was executed, and admitted mutilating the body of the fourteen-year-old girl he killed. I can't help wondering what prompted these murderers to speak out against killing as they entered the deathhouse door. Did their newfound reverence for life stem from the realization that they were about to lose their own? 2

Life is indeed precious, and I believe the death penalty helps to affirm this fact. Had the death penalty been a real possibility in the minds of these murderers, they might well have stayed their hand. They might have shown moral awareness before their victims died, and not after. Consider the tragic death of Rosa Velez, who happened to be home when a man named Luis Vera burglarized her apartment in Brooklyn. "Yeah, I shot her," Vera admitted. "She knew me, and I knew I wouldn't go to the chair." 3

During the twenty-two years in public service, I have heard the pros and cons of capital punishment expressed with special intensity. As a district leader, councilman, congressman, and mayor, I have represented constituencies generally thought of as liberal. Because I support the death penalty for heinous crimes of murder, I have sometimes been the subject of emotional and outraged attacks by voters who find my position reprehensible or worse. I have listened to their ideas. I have weighed their objections carefully. I still support the death penalty. The reasons I maintain my position can be best understood by examining the arguments most frequently heard in opposition. 4

1. The death penalty is "barbaric."

Sometimes opponents of capital punishment horrify with tales of lingering death on the gallows, of faulty electric chairs, or of agony in the gas chamber. Partly in response to such protests, several states such as North Carolina and Texas switched to execution by lethal injection. The condemned person is put to death painlessly, without ropes, voltage, bullets, or gas. Did this answer the objections of death penalty opponents? Of course not. On June 22, 1984, the *New York Times* published an editorial that sarcastically attacked the new "hygienic" method of death by injection, and stated that "execution can never be made humane through science." So it's not the method that really troubles opponents. It's the death itself they consider barbaric. 5

Admittedly, capital punishment is not a pleasant topic. However, one does not have to like the death penalty in order to support it any more than one must like radical surgery, radiation, or chemotherapy in order to find necessary these attempts at curing cancer. Ultimately we may learn how to cure cancer with a simple pill. Unfortunately, that day has not yet arrived. Today we are faced with the choice of letting the cancer spread or trying to cure it with the methods available, methods that one day will almost certainly be considered barbaric. But to give up and do nothing would be far more barbaric and would certainly delay the discovery of an eventual cure. The analogy between cancer and murder is imperfect, because murder is not the "disease" we are trying to cure. The disease is injustice. We may not like the death penalty, but it must be available to punish crimes of cold-blooded murder, cases in which any other form of punishment would be inadequate and, therefore, unjust. If we create a society in which injustice is not tolerated, incidents of murder—the most flagrant form of injustice—will diminish. 6

2. No other major democracy uses the death penalty.

7   No other major democracy—in fact, few other countries of any description—are plagued by a murder rate such as that in the United States. Fewer and fewer Americans can remember the days when unlocked doors were the norm and murder was a rare and terrible offense. In America the murder rate climbed 122 percent between 1963 and 1980. During the same period, the murder rate in New York City increased by almost 400 percent, and the statistics are even worse in many other cities. A study at M.I.T. showed that based on 1970 homicide rates a person who lived in a large American city ran a greater risk of being murdered than an American soldier in World War II ran of being killed in combat. It is not surprising that the laws of each country differ according to differing conditions and traditions. If other countries had our murder problem, the cry for capital punishment would be just as loud as it is here. And I daresay that any other major democracy where 75 percent of the people supported the death penalty would soon enact it into law.

3. An innocent person might be executed by mistake.

8   Consider the work of Hugo Adam Bedau, one of the most implacable foes of capital punishment in this country. According to Mr. Bedau, it is "false sentimentality to argue that the death penalty should be abolished because of the abstract possibility that an innocent person might be executed." He cites a study of the 7,000 executions in this country from 1893 to 1971, and concludes that the record fails to show that such cases occur. The main point, however, is this. If government functioned only when the possibility of error didn't exist, government wouldn't function at all. Human life deserves special protection, and one of the best ways to guarantee that protection is to assure that convicted murders do not kill again. Only the death penalty can accomplish this end. In a recent case in New Jersey, a man named Richard Biegenwald was freed from prison after serving eighteen years for murder; since his release he has been convicted of committing four murders. A prisoner names Lemuel Smith, who, while serving four life sentences for murder (plus two life sentences for kidnapping and robbery) in New York's Green Haven Prison, lured a woman corrections officer into the chaplain's office and strangled her. He then mutilated and dismembered her body. An additional life sentence for Smith is meaningless. Because New York has no death penalty statute, Smith has effectively been given a license to kill.

9   But the problem of multiple murder is not confined to the nation's penitentiaries. In 1981, 91 police officers were killed in the line of duty in this country. Seven percent of those arrested in the cases that have been solved had a previous arrest for murder. In New York City in 1976 and 1977, 85 persons arrested for homicide had a previous arrest for murder. Six of these individuals had two previous arrests for murder, and one had four previous murder arrests. During those two years the New York police were arresting for murder persons with a previous arrest for murder on the average of one every 8.5 days. This is not surprising when we learn that in 1975, for example, the median time served in Massachusetts for homicide was less than two and a half years. In 1976 a study sponsored by the Twentieth Century Fund found that the average time served in the United States for first-degree murder is ten years. The median time served may be considerably lower.

4. Capital punishment cheapens the value of human life.

10   On the contrary, it can be easily demonstrated that the death penalty strengthens the value of human life. If the penalty for rape were lowered, clearly it would signal a

lessened regard for the victim's suffering, humiliation, and personal integrity. It would cheapen their horrible experience, and expose them to an increased danger of recurrence. When we lower the penalty for murder, it signals a lessened regard for the value of the victim's life. Some critics of capital punishment, such as columnist Jimmy Breslin, have suggested that a life sentence is actually a harsher penalty for murder than death. This is sophistic nonsense. A few killers may decide not to appeal a death sentence, but the overwhelming majority make every effort to stay alive. It is by exacting the highest penalty for the taking of human life that we affirm the highest value of human life.

5. The death penalty is applied in a discriminatory manner.

This factor no longer seems to be the problem it once was. The appeals process   11
for a condemned prisoner is lengthy and painstaking. Every effort is made to see that the verdict and sentence were fairly arrived at. However, assertions of discrimination are not an argument for ending the death penalty but for extending it. It is not justice to exclude everyone from the penalty of the law if a few are found to be so favored. Justice requires that the law be applied equally to all.

6. Thou Shalt Not Kill.

The Bible is our greatest source of moral inspiration. Opponents of the death   12
penalty frequently cite the sixth of the Ten Commandments in an attempt to prove that capital punishment is divinely proscribed. In the original Hebrew, however, the Sixth Commandment reads "Thou Shalt Not Commit Murder," and the Torah specifies capital punishment for a variety of offenses. The biblical viewpoint has been upheld by philosophers throughout history. The greatest thinkers of the nineteenth century—Kant, Locke, Hobbes, Rousseau, Montesquieu, and Mill—agreed that natural law properly authorizes the sovereign to take life in order to vindicate justice. Only Jeremy Bentham was ambivalent. Washington, Jefferson, and Franklin endorsed it. Abraham Lincoln authorized executions for deserters in wartime. Alexis de Tocqueville, who expressed profound respect for American institutions, believed that the death penalty was indispensable to the support of social order. The United States Constitution, widely admired as one of the seminal achievements in the history of humanity, condemns cruel and inhuman punishment, but does not condemn capital punishment.

7. The death penalty is state-sanctioned murder.

This is the defense with which Messrs. Willie and Shaw hoped to soften the resolve   13
of those who sentenced them to death. By saying in effect, "You're no better than I am," the murderer seeks to bring his accusers down to his own level. It is also a popular argument among opponents of capital punishment, but a transparently false one. Simply put, the state has rights that the private individual does not. In a democracy, those rights are given to the state by the electorate. The execution of a lawfully condemned killer is no more than an act of murder than is legal imprisonment an act of kidnapping. If an individual forces a neighbor to pay him money under threat of punishment, it's called extortion. If the state does it, it's called taxation. Rights and responsibilities surrendered by the individual are what give the state its power to govern. This contract is the foundation of civilization itself.

Everyone wants his or her rights, and will defend them jealously. Not everyone,   14
however, wants responsibilities, especially the painful responsibilities that come with

law enforcement. Twenty-one years ago a woman named Kitty Genovese was assaulted and murdered on a street in New York. Dozens of neighbors heard her cries for help but did nothing to assist her. They didn't even call the police. In such a climate the criminal understandably grows bolder. In the presence of moral cowardice, he lectures us on our supposed failings and tries to equate his crimes with our quest for justice.

15   The death of anyone—even a convicted killer—diminishes us all. But we are diminished even more by a justice system that fails to function. It is an illusion to let ourselves believe that doing away with capital punishment removes the murderer's deed from our conscience. The rights of society are paramount. When we protect guilty lives, we give up innocent lives in exchange. When opponents of capital punishment say to the state, "I will not let you kill in my name," they are also saying to murderers: "You can kill in your *own* name as long as I have an excuse for not getting involved."

16   It is hard to imagine anything worse than being murdered while neighbors do nothing. But something worse exists. When those same neighbors shrink back from justly punishing the murderer, the victim dies twice.

Thinking Critically About "Death and Justice"

1. Skilled arguers use opening attention grabbers to create a desired rhetorical effect. Why does Koch begin with the material on Robert Lee Willie and Joseph Carl Shaw? What effect does he hope for? Does the opening work?
2. In supporting capital punishment, why does Koch choose to rebut opposing arguments rather than arguing more directly for his own position?
3. Consider carefully Koch's use of evidence. Sometimes he uses empirical evidence based on scholarly studies (for example, the study cited by Adam Bedau under point 3); sometimes he focuses on a single example (the cases of Biegenwald and Smith in point 3); sometimes he uses analogies (the comparison of murder to cancer under point 1). Where is his evidence most persuasive? Where is it least persuasive?
4. In citing the case of Lemuel Smith, Koch's logical point is complete once he tells us that Smith killed a corrections officer while serving a life sentence. Why does Koch also inform us he strangled her and mutilated and dismembered her body?
5. In paragraph 3 Koch states: "Had the death penalty been a real possibility in the minds of these murderers, they might well have stayed their hand." Although Koch's statement seems intuitively logical, most statistical studies show that the death penalty does not deter murder. Having no hard data to support his claim, Koch instead quotes Luis Vera. What is the rhetorical purpose of that quotation?
6. Koch chooses to list and number the objections to capital punishment. What is the rhetorical effect of having a numbered list?

Our next argument is a direct response to Koch. It also appeared in *The New Republic* in 1985. Its author, David Bruck, is a practicing attorney specializing in the legal defense of persons facing a death sentence. He has written numerous articles opposing the death penalty and particularly studies the problem of racial bias in sentencing.

DAVID BRUCK
THE DEATH PENALTY

Mayor Ed Koch contends that the death penalty "affirms life." By failing to execute murderers, he says, we "signal a lessened regard for the value of the victim's life." Koch suggests that people who oppose the death penalty are like Kitty Genovese's neighbors, who heard her cries for help but did nothing while an attacker stabbed her to death. 1

This is the standard "moral" defense of death as punishment: even if executions don't deter violent crime any more effectively than imprisonment, they are still required as the only means we have of doing justice in response to the worst of crimes. 2

Until recently, this "moral" argument had to be considered in the abstract, since no one was being executed in the United States. But the death penalty is back now, at least in the southern states, where every one of the more than thirty executions carried out over the last two years has taken place. Those of us who live in those states are getting to see the difference between the death penalty in theory, and what happens when you actually try to use it. 3

South Carolina resumed executing prisoners in January with the electrocution of Joseph Carl Shaw. Shaw was condemned to death for helping to murder two teenagers while he was serving as a military policeman at Fort Jackson, South Carolina. His crime, propelled by mental illness and PCP, was one of terrible brutality. It is Shaw's last words ("Killing was wrong when I did it. It is wrong when you do it. . . .") that so outraged Mayor Koch: he finds it "a curiosity of modern life that we are being lectured on morality by cold-blooded killers." And so it is. 4

But it was not "modern life" that brought this curiosity into being. It was capital punishment. The electric chair was J. C. Shaw's platform. (The mayor mistakenly writes that Shaw's statement came in the form of a plea to the governor for clemency: Actually Shaw made it only seconds before his death, as he waited, shaved and strapped into the chair, for the switch to be thrown.) It was the chair that provided Shaw with celebrity and an opportunity to lecture us on right and wrong. What made this weird moral reversal even worse is that J. C. Shaw faced his own death with undeniable dignity and courage. And while Shaw died, the TV crews recorded another "curiosity" of the death penalty—the crowd gathered outside the death-house to cheer on the executioner. Whoops of elation greeted the announcement of Shaw's death. Waiting at the penitentiary gates for the appearance of the hearse bearing Shaw's remains, one demonstrator started yelling, "Where's the beef?" 5

For those who had to see the execution of J. C. Shaw, it wasn't easy to keep in mind that the purpose of the whole spectacle was to affirm life. It will be harder still when Florida executes a cop-killer named Alvin Ford. Ford has lost his mind during his years of death-row confinement, and now spends his days trembling, rocking back and forth, and muttering unintelligible prayers. This has led to litigation over whether Ford meets a centuries-old legal standard for mental competency. Since the Middle Ages, the Anglo-American legal system has generally prohibited the execution of anyone who 6 is too mentally ill to understand what is about to be done to him and why. If Florida wins its case, it will have earned the right to electrocute Ford in his present condition. If it loses, he will not be executed until the state has first nursed him back to some semblance of mental health.[1]

7   We can at least be thankful that this demoralizing spectacle involves a prisoner who is actually guilty of murder. But this may not always be so. The ordeal of Lenell Jeter—the young black engineer who recently served more than a year of a life sentence for a Texas armed robbery that he didn't commit—should remind us that the system is quite capable of making the very worst sort of mistake. That Jeter was eventually cleared is a fluke. If the robbery had occurred at 7 P.M. rather than 3 P.M., he'd have had no alibi, and would still be in prison today. And if someone had been killed in that robbery, Jeter probably would have been sentenced to death. We'd have seen the usual execution-day interviews with state officials and the victim's relatives, all complaining that Jeter's appeals took too long. And Jeter's last words from the gurney would have taken their place among the growing literature of death-house oration that so irritates the mayor.

8   Koch quotes Hugo Adam Bedau, a prominent abolitionist, to the effect that the record fails to establish that innocent defendants have been executed in the past. But this doesn't mean, as Koch implies, that it hasn't happened. All Bedau was saying was that doubts concerning executed prisoners' guilt are almost never resolved. Bedau is at work now on an effort to determine how many wrongful death sentences may have been imposed: his list of murder convictions since 1900 in which the state eventually *admitted* error is some four hundred cases long. Of course, very few of these cases involved actual executions: the mistakes that Bedau documents were uncovered precisely because the prisoner was alive and able to fight for his vindication. The cases where someone is executed are the very cases in which we're least likely to learn that we got the wrong man.

9   I don't claim that executions of entirely innocent people will occur very often. But they will occur. And other sorts of mistakes already have. Roosevelt Green was executed in Georgia two days before J. C. Shaw. Green and an accomplice kidnapped a young woman. Green swore that his companion shot her to death after Green had left, and that he knew nothing about the murder. Green's claim was supported by a statement that his accomplice made to a witness after the crime. The jury never resolved whether Green was telling the truth, and when he tried to take a polygraph examination a few days before his scheduled execution, the state of Georgia refused to allow the examiner into the prison. As the pressure for symbolic retribution mounts, the courts, like the public, are losing patience with such details. Green was electrocuted on January 9, while members of the Ku Klux Klan rallied outside the prison.

10   Then there is another sort of arbitrariness that happens all the time. Last October, Louisiana executed a man named Ernest Knighton. Knighton had killed a gas station owner during a robbery. Like any murder, this was a terrible crime. But it was not premeditated, and is the sort of crime that very rarely results in a death sentence. Why was Knighton electrocuted when almost everyone else who committed the same offense was not? Was it because he was black? Was it because his victim and all 12 members of the jury that sentenced him were white? Was it because Knighton's court-appointed lawyer presented no evidence on his behalf at his sentencing hearing? Or maybe there's no reason except bad luck. One thing is clear: Ernest Knighton was

---

[1]AUTHOR'S NOTE: On June 26, 1986, the Supreme Court ruled against the State of Florida.

picked out to die the way a fisherman takes a cricket out of a bait jar. No one cares which cricket gets impaled on the hook.

Not every prisoner executed recently was chosen that randomly. But many were. And having selected these men so casually, so blindly, the death penalty system asks us to accept that the purpose of killing each of them is to affirm the sanctity of human life.   11

The death penalty states are also learning that the death penalty is easier to advocate than it is to administer. In Florida, where executions have become almost routine, the governor reports that nearly a third of his time is spent reviewing the clemency requests of condemned prisoners. The Florida Supreme Court is hopelessly backlogged with death cases. Some have taken five years to decide, and the rest of the Court's work waits in line behind the death appeals. Florida's death row currently holds more than 230 prisoners. State officials are reportedly considering building a special "death prison" devoted entirely to the isolation and electrocution of the condemned. The state is also considering the creation of a special public defender unit that will do nothing else but handle death penalty appeals. The death penalty, in short, is spawning death agencies.   12

And what is Florida getting for all of this? The state went through almost all of 1983 without executing anyone: its rate of intentional homicide declined by 17 percent. Last year Florida executed eight people—the most of any state, and the sixth highest total for any year since Florida started electrocuting people back in 1924. Elsewhere in the U.S. last year, the homicide rate continued to decline. But in Florida, it actually rose by 5.1 percent.   13

But these are just the tiresome facts. The electric chair has been a centerpiece of each of Koch's recent political campaigns, and he knows better than anyone how little the facts have to do with the public's support for capital punishment. What really fuels the death penalty is the justifiable frustration and rage of people who see that the government is not coping with violent crime. So what if the death penalty doesn't work? At least it gives us the satisfaction of knowing that we got one or two of the sons of bitches.   14

Perhaps we want retribution on the flesh and bone of a handful of convicted murderers so badly that we're willing to close our eyes to all of the demoralization and danger that come with it. A lot of politicians think so, and they may be right. But if they are, then let's at least look honestly at what we're doing. This lottery of death both comes from and encourages an attitude toward human life that is not reverent, but reckless.   15

And that is why the mayor is dead wrong when he confuses such fury with justice. He suggests that we trivialize murder unless we kill murderers. By that logic, we also trivialize rape unless we sodomize rapists. The sin of Kitty Genovese's neighbors wasn't that they failed to stab her attacker to death. Justice does demand that murderers be punished. And common sense demands that society be protected from them. But neither justice nor self-preservation demands that we kill men whom we have already imprisoned.   16

The electric chair in which J. C. Shaw died earlier this year was built in 1912 at the suggestion of South Carolina's governor at the time, Cole Blease. Governor Blease's other criminal justice initiative was an impassioned crusade in favor of lynch law. Any lesser response, the governor insisted, trivialized the loathsome crimes of interracial rape and murder. In 1912 a lot of people agreed with Governor Blease that a proper regard for justice required both lynching and the electric chair. Eventually we are going to learn that justice requires neither.   17

Thinking Critically About "The Death Penalty"

1. In this essay Bruck partly refutes Koch and partly makes his own arguments opposing the death penalty. In your own words, why does Bruck oppose capital punishment? Make a list of the reasons he uses.
2. Koch claims that the death penalty "affirms life." What rhetorical strategies does Bruck employ to persuade readers that the death penalty degrades life?
3. Imagine that Bruck and Koch are in the same room engaged not in a pro/con debate but in a search for the best understanding of each other's perspective. What common ground can you find between Koch and Bruck? Which of Koch's arguments would Bruck be most apt to agree with? Which of Bruck's arguments would be most compelling to Koch?
4. Why is it important to Bruck *when* J. C. Shaw uttered his condemnation of capital punishment?
5. A frequent claim-with-reason cited by opponents of capital punishment is this: "Capital punishment should be outlawed because innocent persons may be put to death." How does Koch rebut this argument? Where does Koch attack the reason and grounds and where does he attack the warrant? How does Bruck rebut Koch?
6. Before you read these two arguments, you probably had your own views on capital punishment. Locate one or two places where either Koch or Bruck caused you to change slightly your initial view.

In the following essay, former electrical engineer and mathematics teacher Diane Hunsaker argues against a current trend in teaching mathematics. This essay first appeared as a "My Turn" piece in *Newsweek.*

DIANE HUNSAKER
DITCH THE CALCULATORS

1   I sigh inwardly as I watch yet another student, this one a ninth grader, struggle with an advanced math problem that requires simple multiplication. He mentally grapples with 5×6, looks longingly at the off-limits calculator on the corner of my desk and finally guesses the answer: "35."

2   The proliferation of calculators in the classroom amazes me. The students I tutor tell me regularly that their teachers allow unlimited access to this tool. The National Council of Teachers of Mathematics actively encourages its use. Recently I attended a math seminar where the instructor casually stated that teachers, once reluctant to permit calculators in the classroom, had crossed this hurdle. Now "everyone" agrees on their importance, she said. The more I hear from the education establishment about the benefits of these devices in schools, the less surprised I am when middle- and high-school students who have difficulty with arithmetic call for tutoring in algebra and geometry. Having worked six years as an electrical engineer before switching to teaching, I

often suggest to my students that they consider technical and scientific careers, but I'm discouraged when I see an increasing number of kids who lack simple math skills.

Educators have many oft-repeated arguments in defense of calculators, but each one ignores the reason that we teach math in the first place. Math trains the mind. By this I mean that students learn to think logically and rationally, to proceed from known information to desired information and to become proficient with both numbers and ideas. These skills are something that math and science teach and are essential for adolescents to become thinking, intelligent members of society.

Some teachers argue that calculators let students concentrate on how to solve problems instead of getting bogged down with tedious computations. Having a calculator doesn't make it any easier for a student to decide how to attack a math problem. Rather, it only encourages him to try every combination of addition, subtraction, multiplication or division without any thought about which would be most appropriate. Some of my elementary-school children look at a word problem and instantly guess that adding is the correct approach. When I suggest that they solve the problem this way without a calculator, they usually pause and think before continuing. A student is much more likely to minimize his work by reflecting on the problem first if he doesn't have a calculator in his hand. Learning constructive methods for approaching confusing problems is essential, not just for math but for life.

A middle-school teacher once said to me, "So what if a student can't do long division? Give him a calculator, and he'll be fine." I doubt it. I don't know when memorization and repetitious problem-solving fell to such a low priority in education circles. How could we possibly communicate with each other, much less create new ideas, without the immense store of information in our brains?

Math is as much about knowing why the rules work as knowing what the rules are. A student who cannot do long division obviously does not comprehend the underlying principles. A true understanding of why often makes learning by rote unnecessary, because the student can figure out the rules himself. My students who view the multiplication tables as a list of unrelated numbers have much more difficulty in math than those who know that multiplication is simply repeated addition. Calculators prevent students from seeing this kind of inherent structure and beauty in math.

A student who learns to manipulate numbers mentally can focus on how to attack a problem and then complete the actual computations easily. He will also have a much better idea of what the answer should be, since experience has taught him "number sense," or the relationship between numbers.

A student who has grown up with a calculator will struggle with both strategies and computations. When youngsters used a calculator to solve 9 × 4 in third grade, they're still using one to solve the same problem in high school. By then they are also contending with algebra. Because they never felt comfortable working with numbers as children, they are seriously disadvantaged when they attempt the generalized math of algebra. Permitting extensive use of calculators invites a child's mind to stagnate. If we don't require students to do the simple problems that calculators can do, how can we expect them to solve the more complex problems that calculators cannot do?

Students learn far more when they do the math themselves. I've tutored youngsters on practice SAT exams where they immediately reach for their calculators. If they'd take a few seconds to understand the problem at hand, they most likely would find a simpler solution without using a crutch. I have also watched students erroneously enter a problem like 12 + 32 into their calculators as 112 + 32 and not bat an eye at the obviously incorrect answer. After all, they used a calculator, so it must be right!

10   Educators also rationalize that calculators are so inexpensive and commonplace that students must become competent in using them. New math texts contain whole sections on solving problems with a calculator. Most people, including young children, can learn its basic functions in about five minutes. Calculators do have their place in the world outside school and, to a limited extent, in higher-level math classes, but they are hardly educational tools.

11   Many teachers as well as students insist, "Why shouldn't we use calculators? They'll always be around, and we'll never do long division in real life." This may be true. It's also true of most math. Not many of us need to figure the circumference of a circle or factor a quadratic equation for any practical reason. But that's not the sole purpose of teaching math. We teach it for thinking and discipline, both of which expand the mind and increase the student's ability to function as a contributing individual in society: the ultimate goals of education.

Thinking Critically About "Ditch the Calculators"

1. In this article Diane Hunsaker enters an ongoing heated educational debate. What is her claim? What are her reasons?
2. Think about your own experiences with math from first grade through high school. Does Hunsaker's claim affirm or contradict your own experiences?
3. Where does Hunsaker mention and refute opposing viewpoints?
4. What grounds does Hunsaker give for her reasons? What does she do to make her evidence convincing?
5. Some of the stakes in this argument depend on the warrants related to the main claim with reasons. Where does the argument focus on warrants and backing? What makes Hunsaker's argument successful or unsuccessful?

In the next essay, Walt Spady, the owner of a boat dealership, opposes a local county's ban on "personal watercraft" (small, one-person powerboats analogous to motorcycles or snowmobiles) on lakes and bays. Spady's argument appeared as a guest editorial in a statewide newspaper.

WALT SPADY
A MISGUIDED BAN
ON PERSONAL WATERCRAFT

1   Well, they've gone and done it. The _____ County commissioners have passed an ordinance that excludes personal watercraft from their county. Effective last week, they've told me that if I operate my personal watercraft inside the county's boundaries, I'll be fined $50 the first time, $100 the second, and $250 the next.

2   It is the equivalent of the city of _____ saying that I can't ride a motorcycle down Main Street. And we're not talking about speeding or reckless behavior or endangering anyone. We're talking just operating a personal watercraft in _____ County, period.

This is a decision based on emotion and arrogance. It is a decision that is unilateral and confrontational, rather than cooperative and aimed at problem-solving. The County commissioners—at least the two who passed this measure—have said simply: "Go away." 3

They have said this to a segment of the boating population that now makes up one-third of all boating units sold [in this region]. There are about 17,000 owners of these small craft in [this state] and the number is growing. The commissioners have also said to a rental business in _____ County and to a number of family businesses all over the state that sell and service personal watercraft: "Go away." 4

They have said to large boats that use these craft for tenders: "Go away." These convenient and efficient little boats are used as tenders, for pleasure or beach cleanups, for skiing and for search-and-rescue and law enforcement. Are we all just to "Go away"? 5

A total ban on a widely used mode of transportation and recreation can hardly be considered a solution that serves a whole community. It's just not wise. It draws a line in the sand and provokes an adversarial response, which this action surely will. 6

A lot of reaction, and overreaction, to personal watercraft is based on two factors: noise and harm to the environment. 7

The fact is that a personal watercraft is no louder than a household vacuum . . . 75 dB's. The fact is that the _____ commissioners could cite no study that says personal watercraft are harmful to whales, dolphins, seals, or any other form of life, no more harmful than any other type of boat. Because they have no exposed prop, they are a great deal safer and more environmentally friendly than most boats. 8

The issue with personal watercraft, as it is with motorcycles, cars, trucks, airplanes, and hang gliders, is safe, responsible operation. The issue lies within the operator and not inherently in the vehicle itself. 9

I'd like to ask the county commissioners what they have tried first, in the way of training, education, signing, and public information, instead of jumping to a total ban. I also wonder what hotels, restaurants, campgrounds, and other tourist-oriented businesses think of banning such a large group of people. 10

The path that _____ County has taken is one of prohibition and punishment as opposed to education and regulation. 11

Last fall, the dealers in the state formed a network called the Personal Watercraft Safety Project. It is dedicated to safe, responsible use of personal watercraft. In the larger picture, we feel that boaters in general could use education in the areas of state law, tradition, and "rules of the road." 12

Our goal is to put as much information as we can into the hands of personal watercraft operators. We do that through person-to-person contact at the time of sale, videos, and brochures provided by manufacturers, safety checklists, posters, and instructional flyers. We'd like every personal watercraft operator in this state to have a short course on operation and safety, a wallet card, and a laminated on-board checklist. 13

This approach, we strongly believe, is much more effective, and in the interest of all of the citizens in this statewide community. It addresses an issue through education at a person-to-person and community level rather than simply saying: "Go away." 14

Thinking Critically About "A Misguided Ban on Personal Watercraft"

1. What is Spady's claim? How many supporting lines of reasoning does he develop? Can you summarize his supporting reasons as *because* clauses?

2. Where does Spady summarize opposing views? How does he respond to them? What are the strengths and weaknesses of his response?
3. Spady is the owner of a boat dealership, so he has an economic investment in promoting sales of personal watercraft. To what extent does your knowledge of Spady's profession color your reading of his argument? How successful is Spady in establishing an effective ethos?

In this last essay, first-year student Tiffany Linder enters an argument fiercely debated by environmentalists and the timber industry: the logging of old-growth forests.

TIFFANY LINDER (STUDENT)
SALVAGING OUR OLD-GROWTH FORESTS

1   It's been so long since I've been there I can't clearly remember what it's like. I can only look at the pictures in my family photo album. I found the pictures of me when I was a little girl standing in front of a towering tree with what seems like endless miles and miles of forest in the background. My mom is standing on one side of me holding my hand, and my older brother is standing on the other side of me, making a strange face. The faded pictures don't do justice to the real life magnificence of the forest in which they were taken—the Olympic National Forest—but they capture the awe my parents felt when they took their children to the ancient forest.

2   Today these forests are threatened by timber companies that want state and federal governments to open protected old growth forests to commercial logging. The timber industry's lobbying attempts must be rejected because the logging of old-growth forests is unnecessary, because it will destroy a delicate and valuable ecosystem, and because these rare forests are a sacred trust.

3   Those who promote logging of old-growth forests offer several reasons, but when closely examined, none is substantial. First, forest industry spokespeople tell us the forest will regenerate after logging is finished. This argument is flawed. In reality, the logging industry clear-cuts forests on a 50–80 year cycle, so that the ecosystem being destroyed—one built up over more than 250 years—will never be replaced. At most, the replanted trees will reach only one-third the age of original trees. Because the same ecosystem cannot rebuild if the trees do not develop to full maturity, the plants and animals that depend on the complex ecosystem—with its incredibly tall canopies and trees of all sizes and ages—cannot survive. The forest industry brags about replaceable trees but doesn't mention a thing about the irreplaceable ecosystems.

4   Another argument used by the timber industry, as forestry engineer D. Alan Rockwood has said in personal correspondence, is that "an old-growth forest is basically a forest in decline. . . . The biomass is decomposing at a higher rate than tree growth." According to Rockwood, preserving old-growth forests is "wasting a resource" since the land should be used to grow trees rather than let old ones slowly rot away, especially when harvesting the trees before they rot would provide valuable lumber. But the timber industry looks only at the trees, not at the incredibly diverse biosystem which the

ancient trees create and nourish. The mixture of young and old growth trees creates a unique habitat that logging would destroy.

Perhaps the main argument used by the logging industry is economic. Using the plight of loggers to their own advantage, the industry claims that logging old growth forests will provide jobs. They make all of us feel sorry for the loggers by giving us an image of a hardworking man put out of work and unable to support his family. They make us imagine the sad eyes of the logger's children. We think, "How's he going to pay the electricity bill? How's he going to pay his mortgage? Will his family become homeless?" We all see these images in our minds and want to give the logger his job so his family won't suffer, but in reality giving him his job back is only a temporary solution to a long-term problem. Logging in the old-growth forest couldn't possibly give the logger his job for long. For example, according to Peter Morrison of the Wilderness Society, all the old-growth forest in the Gifford Pinchot National Forest would be gone in three years if it were opened to logging (vi). What will the loggers do then? Loggers need to worry about finding new jobs now and not wait until there are no old-growth trees left.

Having looked at the views of those who favor logging of old-growth forests, let's turn to the arguments for preserving all old growth. Three main reasons can be cited. First, it is simply unnecessary to log these forests to supply the world's lumber. According to environmentalist Carl Sagoff, we have plenty of new-growth forest from which timber can be taken (89–90). Recently, there have been major reforestation efforts all over the United States, and it is common practice now for loggers to replant every tree that is harvested. These new-growth forests, combined with extensive planting of tree farms, provide more than enough wood for the world's needs. According to forestry expert Robert Sedjo (cited in Sagoff 90), tree farms alone can supply the world's demand for industrial lumber. Although tree farms are ugly and possess little diversity in their ecology, expanding tree farms is far preferable to destroying old-growth forests.

Moreover, we can reduce the demand for lumber. Recycling, for example, can cut down on the use of trees for paper products. Another way to reduce the amount of trees used for paper is with a promising new innovation, kenaf, a fast-growing, 15-foot-tall, annual herb that is native to Africa. According to Jack Page in *Planet Earth, Forest,* kenaf has long been used to make rope, and it has been found to work just as well for paper pulp (158).

Another reason to protect old-growth forests is the value of its complex and very delicate ecosystem. The threat of logging to the northern spotted owl is well known. Although loggers say "people before owls," ecologists consider the owls to be warnings, like canaries in mine shafts, that signal the health of the whole ecosystem. Evidence provided by the World Resource Institute shows that continuing logging will endanger other species. Also, Dr. David Brubaker, an environmental biologist at Seattle University, has said in a personal interview that the long term effects of logging will be severe. Loss of the spotted owl, for example, may affect the small rodent population, which at the moment is kept in check by the predator owl. Dr. Brubaker also explained that the old-growth forests also connect to salmon runs. When dead timber falls into the streams, it creates a habitat conducive to spawning. If the dead logs are removed, the habitat is destroyed. These are only two examples in a long list of animals that would be harmed by logging of old-growth forests.

Finally, it is wrong to log in old-growth forests because of their sacred beauty. When you walk in an old-growth forest, you are touched by a feeling that ordinary forests can't evoke. As you look up to the sky, all you see is branch after branch in a canopy of towering trees. Each of these amazingly tall trees feels inhabited by a spirit; it has its own personality. "For spiritual bliss take a few moments and sit quietly in the Grove of the Patriarchs near Mount Rainier or the redwood forests of Northern California," said Richard Linder, environmental activist and member of the National Wildlife Federation. "Sit silently," he said, "and look at the giant living organisms you're surrounded by; you can feel the history of your own species." Although Linder is obviously biased in favor of preserving the forests, the spiritual awe he feels for ancient trees is shared by millions of other people, who recognize that we destroy something of the world's spirit when we destroy ancient trees, or great whales, or native runs of salmon. According to Al Gore, "We have become so successful at controlling nature that we have lost our connection to it" (qtd. in Sagoff 96). We need to find that connection again, and one place we can find it is in the old-growth forests.

10   The old-growth forests are part of the web of life. If we cut this delicate strand of the web, we may end up destroying the whole. Once the old trees are gone, they are gone forever. Even if foresters replanted every tree and waited 250 years for the trees to grow to ancient size, the genetic pool would be lost. We'd have a 250-year-old tree farm, not an old-growth forest. If we want to maintain a healthy earth, we must respect the beauty and sacredness of the old-growth forests.

Works Cited

Brubaker, David. Interview. 25 Sept. 1998.

Linder, Richard. Interview. 12 Sept. 1998.

Morrison, Peter. *Old Growth in the Pacific Northwest: A Status Report.* Alexandria: Global Printing, 1988.

Page, Jack. *Planet Earth, Forest.* Alexandria: Time-Life, 1983.

Rockwood, D. Alan. E-mail to the author. 21–24 Sept. 1998.

Sagoff, Mark. "Do We Consume Too Much?" *Atlantic Monthly.* June 1997: 80–96.

World Resource Institute. "Old-Growth Forests in the United States Pacific Northwest." *Forest Resources* 13 Sept. 1998 <http://www.wri.org/biodiv>.

Thinking Critically About "Salvaging Our Old-Growth Forests"

1. What is the issue addressed in this argument? What is the writer's claim? What are the writer's main reasons in support of the claim?
2. How does this writer structure her argument to respond to alternative viewpoints? Does her summary of these arguments seem fair?
3. How does the writer appeal to readers' emotions, beliefs, and values?
4. What do you see as the strengths and weaknesses of this argument?

▨ COMPOSING YOUR ESSAY

Writing arguments deepens our thinking by forcing us to consider alternative views and to question the assumptions underlying our reasons and claim. Consequently, it is not unusual for a writer's position on an issue to shift—and even to reverse itself—during the writing process. If this happens to you, take it as a healthy sign of your openness to change, complexity, and alternative points of view. If writing a draft causes you to modify your views, it will be an act of discovery, not a concession of defeat.

Generating and Exploring Ideas

The tasks that follow are intended to help you generate ideas for your argument. Our goal is to help you build up a storehouse of possible issues, to explore several of these possibilities, and then to choose one for deeper exploration before you write your initial draft.

Make an Inventory of Issues that Interest You

Following the lead of the discussion exercise on page 321, make a list of various communities that you belong to and then brainstorm contested issues in those communities. You might try a trigger question like this: "When members of [X community] get together, what contested questions cause disagreements?" What decisions need to be made? What values are in conflict? What problems need to be solved?

Explore Several Issues

For this task, choose two or three possible issues from your previous list and explore them through freewriting or idea mapping. Try responding quickly to the following questions:

a. What is my position on this issue and why?
b. What are alternative points of view on this issue?
c. Why do people disagree about this issue? (Do people disagree about the facts of the case? about key definitions? about underlying values, assumptions, and beliefs?)
d. If I were to argue my position on this issue, what evidence would I need to gather and what research might I need to do?

Brainstorm Claims and Reasons

Choose one issue that particularly interests you and work with classmates to brainstorm possible claims that you could make on the issue. Imagining different perspectives, brainstorm possible reasons to support each claim, stating them as because clauses. See pages 322–23.

Conduct and Respond to Initial Research

If your issue requires research, do a quick bibliographic survey of what is available (see Chapter 21 if you need help with the library) and do enough initial reading to get a good sense of the kinds of arguments that surround your issue and of the alternative views that people have taken. Then freewrite your responses to the following questions.

1. What are the different points of view on this issue? Why do people disagree with each other?
2. Explore the evolution of your thinking as you did this initial reading. What new questions have the readings raised for you? What changes have occurred in your own thinking?

Conduct an In-Depth Exploration Prior to Drafting

The following set of tasks is designed to help you explore your issue in depth. Most students take one or two hours to complete these tasks; the time will pay off, however, because most of the ideas you will need for your rough draft will then be on paper.

1. Write out the issue your argument will address. Try phrasing your issue in several different ways, perhaps as a yes/no question and as an open-ended question. Try making the question broader, then narrower. (See the discussion of issue questions on pages 320–21.) Finally, frame the question in the way that most appeals to you.
2. Now write out your tentative answer to the question. This will be your beginning thesis statement or claim. Put a box around this answer. Next, write out one or more different answers to your question. These will be alternative claims that a neutral audience might consider.
3. Why is this a controversial issue? Is there insufficient evidence to resolve the issue, or is the evidence ambiguous or contradictory? Are definitions in dispute? Do the parties disagree about basic values, assumptions, or beliefs?
4. What personal interest do you have in this issue? How does the issue affect you? Why do you care about it? (Knowing why you care about it might help you get your audience to care about it.)
5. What reasons and evidence support your position on this issue? Freewrite everything that comes to mind that might help you support your case. This freewrite will eventually provide the bulk of your argument. For now, freewrite rapidly without worrying whether your argument makes sense. Just get ideas on paper.
6. Imagine all the counterarguments your audience might make. Summarize the main arguments against your position and then freewrite your response to each of the counterarguments. What are the flaws in the alternative points of view?
7. What kinds of appeals to *ethos* and *pathos* might you use to support your argument? How can you increase your audience's perception of your credibility and trustworthiness? How can you tie your argument to your audience's beliefs and values?
8. Why is this an important issue? What are the broader implications and consequences? What other issues does it relate to? Thinking of possible answers to these questions may prove useful when you write your introduction or conclusion.

Shaping and Drafting

Once you have explored your ideas, create a plan. Here is a suggested procedure.

Begin your planning by analyzing your intended audience. You could imagine an audience deeply resistant to your views or a more neutral, undecided audience acting like a jury. In some cases, your audience might be a single person, as when you petition your department chair to take an upper-division course when you are a sophomore. At other times, your audience might be the general readership of a newspaper, church bulletin, or magazine. When the audience is a general readership, you need to imagine from the start the kinds of reader you particularly want to sway. Here are some questions you can ask:

- *How much does your audience know or care about your issue?* Will you need to provide background? Will you need to convince them that your issue is important? Do you need to hook their interest? Your answers to these questions will particularly influence your introduction and conclusion.

- *What is your audience's current attitude toward your issue?* Are they deeply opposed to your position? If so, why? Are they neutral and undecided? If so, what other views will they be listening to? Classical argument works best with neutral or moderately dissenting audiences. Deeply skeptical audiences are best addressed with delayed-thesis or Rogerian approaches (see p. 337).

- *How do your audience's values, assumptions, and beliefs differ from your own?* What aspects of your position will be threatening to your audience? Why? How does your position on the issue challenge their own world view or identity? What objections will your audience raise toward your argument? Your answers to these questions will help determine the content of your argument and alert you to the extra research you may have to do to respond to audience objections.

- *What values, beliefs or assumptions about the world do you and your audience share?* Despite your differences with your audience, where can you find common links? How might you use these links to build bridges to your audience?

Your next step is to plan out an audience-based argument by seeking audience-based reasons or reasons whose warrants you can defend. Here is a process you can use:

1. Create a skeleton, tree diagram, outline, or flowchart for your argument by stating your reasons as one or more because clauses attached to your claim. Each because clause will become the head of a main section or *line of reasoning* in your argument.
2. Use the planning schema explained on pages 329–30 to plan each line of reasoning. If your audience accepts your warrant, concentrate on supporting your reason with grounds. If your warrant is doubtful, support it with back-

ing. Try to anticipate audience objections by exploring conditions for rebuttal, and brainstorm ways of addressing those objections.

3. Using the skeleton you created, finish developing an outline or tree diagram for your argument. Although the organization for each part of your argument will grow organically from its content, the main parts of a classical argument are as follows:

   a. *An introduction*, in which you engage your reader's attention, introduce your issue, and state your own position.

   b. *Background and preliminary material*, in which you place your issue in a current context and provide whatever background knowledge and definitions of key terms or concepts that your reader will need. (If this background is short, it can often be incorporated into the introduction.)

   c. *Arguments supporting your own position*, in which you make the best case possible for your views by developing your claim with reasons and evidence. This is usually the longest part of your argument, with a separate section for each line of reasoning.

   d. *Anticipation of objections and counterarguments*, in which you summarize fairly key arguments against your position. This section not only helps the reader understand the issue more clearly, but also establishes your *ethos* as a fair-minded writer willing to acknowledge complexity.

   e. *Response to objections through refutation or concession*, in which you point out weaknesses in opposing arguments or concede to their strengths.

   f. *A conclusion*, in which you place your argument in a larger context, perhaps by summarizing your main points and showing why this issue is an important one or by issuing a call to action.

This classical model can be modified in numerous ways. A question that often arises is where to summarize and respond to objections and counterarguments. Writers generally have three choices. One option is to handle opposing positions before you present your own argument. The rationale for this approach is that skeptical audiences may be more inclined to listen attentively to your argument if they have been assured that you understand their point of view. A second option is to place this material after you have presented your argument. This approach is effective for neutral audiences who don't start off with strong opposing views. A final option is to intersperse opposing views throughout your argument at appropriate moments. Any of these possibilities, or a combination of all of them, can be effective.

Another question often asked is the best way to order one's reasons. A general rule of thumb when ordering your own argument is to put your strongest reason last and your second strongest reason first. The idea here is to start and end with your most powerful arguments. If you imagine a quite skeptical audience, build bridges to your audience by summarizing alternative views early in the paper and concede to those that are especially strong. If your audience is neutral or undecided, you can summarize and respond to possible objections after you have presented your own case.

Revising

As you revise your argument, you need to attend both to the clarity of your writing (all the principles of closed-form prose described in Chapter 18) and also to the persuasiveness of your argument. As always, peer reviews are valuable, and especially so in argumentation if you ask your peer reviewers to role-play an opposing audience. The following Guidelines for Peer Reviewers can both assist your peer reviewers and help you with revision.

---

g   u   i   d   e   l   i   n   e   s

For Peer Reviewers

Instructions for peer reviews, including use of these guidelines, are provided in Chapter 17, pages 429–35. To write a peer review for a classmate, use your own paper, numbering your responses to correspond to the questions on the guidelines. At the head of your paper place the author's name and your own name, as shown.

Author's Name: _____

Peer Reviewer's Name: _____

I. Read the draft at a normal reading speed from beginning to end. As you read, do the following:
   A. Place a wavy line in the margin next to any passages that you find confusing, that contain something that doesn't seem to fit, or that otherwise slow down your reading.
   B. Place a "Good!" in the margin next to any passages where you think the writing is particularly strong or interesting.
II. Read the draft again slowly and answer the following questions by writing brief explanations of your answers.
   A. Introduction:
      1. Does the title announce the issue, reveal the writer's claim, or otherwise focus the reader's expectations and pique interest? How could the title be improved?
      2. How effectively does the opening introduce the issue, engage your interest, and convince you that the issue is significant and problematic? What would add clarity or appeal?
      3. Does the end of the introduction adequately forecast the argument and present the writer's claim? Could the statement of the claim be more focused, clear, or risky?

B. Arguing for the claim:
  1. Consider the overall structure: Does the structure of the argument effectively develop the claim? Can you discern the argument's main parts—background (if needed), supporting reasons (a main section for each line of reasoning), summary and refutation of alternative viewpoints, and conclusion? How could the structure be improved?
  2. Consider the support: For each line of reasoning, does the writer provide adequate grounds in the form of facts, examples, statistics, testimony, or other supporting details? Does the writer need to state warrants and develop backing? Where would you like more support for the writer's reasons?
  3. Consider *ethos* and *pathos:* Does the writer establish a trustworthy and credible persona? Where could the writer better appeal to the readers' emotions, beliefs, values?
  4. Consider the writer's summary and response to alternative viewpoints: Does the writer summarize opposing arguments fairly? Are there any important differing views that the writer hasn't considered? Does the writer offer adequate refutation of each opposing argument or otherwise respond to it effectively? How might the writer improve his or her treatment of opposing views?
  5. Does the conclusion bring a sense of completeness and closure to the argument?
  6. How might the writer improve the clarity of the draft? Where might the writer better apply the principles of clarity from Chapter 18?
C. Sum up what you see as the main strengths and problem areas of the draft.
  1. Strengths
  2. Problem areas
III. Read the draft one more time. Place a check in the margin wherever you notice problems in grammar, spelling, or mechanics (one check per problem).

c h a p t e r 15

Making an Evaluation

▧ ABOUT EVALUATIVE WRITING

Evaluation is a process of discernment and measurement that we are engaged in all the time. Frequently, in your college courses and later in your career, you will be asked to make evaluative decisions, and often the stakes will be high. As a premed major, should you take as many science courses as you can or choose a more rounded undergraduate program? As an undecided major, should you apply for a nonpaying summer internship that will give you valuable career experience or take a sales job at the mall that pays well? Later in your professional life, why should a business choose your advertising firm to manage its big campaign? Why should the CEO of the hospital agree to purchase the computer system that you recommend for the transcription department? To influence the communities to which you belong, your evaluations will often need to be justified cogently and persuasively in a written document.

This chapter instructs you in a systematic procedure for evaluating an object, event, person, idea, theory, or other phenomenon. Research suggests that most college assignments require some form of evaluative thinking. According to one study, college assignments typically take the form of "good/better/best" questions*:

Good:	Is X good or bad?
Better:	Which is better—X or Y?
Best:	Which is the best among available options? What is the best solution to a given problem?*

Even if an assignment isn't framed in this way, any thesis-based task requires behind-the-scenes evaluative thinking whenever it entails judgments about the quality of evidence, the reliability of sources, the consequences of a choice, and so forth. To appreciate the role of evaluative thinking in academic and professional

---

*The good/better/best example comes from Barbara E. Walvoord and Lucille P. McCarthy, *Thinking and Writing in College: A Naturalistic Study of Students in Four Disciplines.* (Urbana, IL: National Council of Teachers of English, 1990), p. 7.

life, consider the list of six crucial critical thinking skills that we introduced in Chapter 2 (p. 24). The last three of these skills are as follows:

4. The ability to imagine alternative solutions to the problem, to see different ways in which the question might be answered, and different perspectives for viewing it
5. The ability to analyze competing approaches and answers, to construct arguments for and against alternatives, and to choose the best solution in light of values, objectives, and other criteria that you determine and articulate
6. The ability to write an effective argument justifying your choice while acknowledging counterarguments

The thinking demanded by skills 5 and 6—analyzing alternative solutions, choosing the best solution based on criteria that you determine, and writing a justification of your choice—is what we mean by evaluative thinking.

As we will show, evaluative thinking requires two stages: (1) determining the criteria for the evaluation, and (2) matching the criteria to the thing being evaluated. Evaluations can be written with an informative purpose, an analytic purpose, or a persuasive purpose (see Chapter 4, pp. 57–60, for a discussion of purposes). A typical example of an informative evaluation is an article in *Consumer Reports*, to which a car buyer might turn to get unbiased data about a car's reliability, fuel economy, safety, and other factors. Typical examples of analytical evaluations include movie, book, or restaurant reviews. In a typical restaurant review, for example, the writer might describe the good and bad features of Elvis's House of Chili using such criteria as quality of cuisine, seating and atmosphere, friendliness of service, cost, and so forth.

In this book we have chosen to treat evaluative writing as persuasion, in which you imagine a community divided on an evaluation issue and therefore anticipate readers particularly resistant to your thesis. Evaluation issues frequently divide communities. The starling case in Chapter 14 was an evaluation issue focusing on whether the family's action in killing the starlings was ethically justified. Because evaluation issues are so common, students writing classical arguments for Chapter 14 may have chosen an evaluation issue for their arguments. All the skills of argument covered in Chapter 14 apply as well to this chapter, which simply looks at this specific kind of argument in more detail.

As we will show, evaluative questions become contested whenever community members disagree about what the criteria for judgment should be or about whether a specific case matches the criteria. Because evaluative arguments help communities make choices about actions, beliefs, or values, they are among the most important kinds of arguments to understand.

EXPLORING EVALUATIVE WRITING

To introduce you to evaluative thinking, we ask you as a classroom community to resolve a narrowly focused evaluative question designed to elicit criteria-match thinking. (By *criteria-match thinking,* we mean a thinking process in which you establish criteria for your evaluation and then match your specific case to those criteria.) As you apply the principles of truth seeking and persuasion to this issue, be aware of your thinking processes.

> *Situation:* You are a 10th grade social studies teacher. In your school building, the history and social studies classrooms have a large map of the Americas prominently displayed on a side wall. At a teachers' meeting, one of your colleagues proposes that in the history and social studies classrooms this traditional Americas map be replaced with an equivalent sized *inverted map* like the one shown in Figure 15.1 (p. 363). The question becomes, "Which of these two kinds of maps—the traditional one or the inverted one—is better for the front of a social studies classroom?" (As a class you may wish to establish a fuller context for this discussion by stipulating the size and location of the high school, thereby giving you more information about the class, ethnicity, and politics of its community.)

1. Freewrite your initial thoughts on this question and then share your freewrites in small groups or as a whole class.
2. Working in small groups or as a whole class, create the best arguments you can in favor of each map, framing each argument as a claim with reasons. State each reason as a *because* clause (for example, "The traditional map is better because . . . , because . . . etc.; then do the same for the inverted map).
3. Role-playing the teachers in this high school, reach consensus on this issue by holding a truth-seeking discussion in which participants make their best persuasive cases for their points of view but listen empathically to other points of view.
4. When the class reaches consensus on the issue, write the frame of the deciding argument on the chalkboard as a claim with *because* clauses. If you wish, you can also place a dissenting argument on the board. Then write out the warrant that links each reason to the claim (that is, the unstated assumption that the audience has to accept for the reason to have any force). As we will show in the next section, these warrants are actually statements of evaluative criteria for the argument.

WRITING PROJECT

Write an argument in which you evaluate something controversial. The opening of your essay should introduce your reader to the person, place, thing, event, or phenomenon that you are going to evaluate and show why its value is controversial or problematic. The body of your argument should establish criteria for evaluating your subject, and then show how your subject meets or does not meet the criteria. As with most other arguments, you should summarize opposing views and respond to them through either concession or refutation.

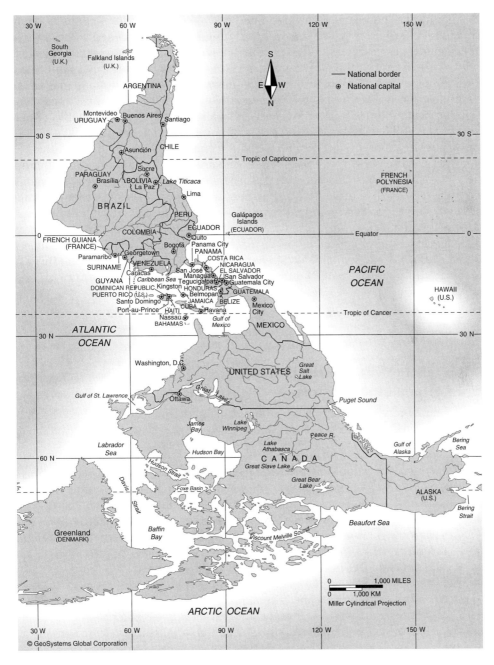

FIGURE 15.1   An Inverted Map

Map makers have traditionally placed north at the top of maps and south at the bottom. However, putting north on top is an arbitrary and conventional decision that has a subtle rhetorical effect. Because words like "top," "above," and "up" suggest superiority over words like "bottom," "below," and "down," a conventional map makes the northern hemisphere seem more important than the southern. An inverted map reverses this effect, placing the southern hemisphere in the privileged "upper" position. Geographically, the inverted map is completely accurate. All that changes is the viewer's perspective.

For this assignment, you need to find an evaluative question that invites controversy. For example: Is a flat income tax (graduated income tax, sales tax, sin tax on cigarettes) a good method of taxation? How effective is your school's general studies curriculum (football program, service learning program, writing center, registration system)? Are TV talk shows (news programs, sitcoms, soap operas) helpful or harmful to society? Is homeopathic medicine (chiropractic medicine, psychic healing) an effective approach to healing? Has the effect of the "three strikes and you're out" law (sexual predator laws, affirmative action, juvenile curfews, public-school dress codes) been good or bad?

The specific person, event, or phenomenon you choose to evaluate should be controversial or problematic, that is, there should be defensible evaluations of your subject that differ from your own evaluation. You must demonstrate that your evaluation makes more sense than these alternative evaluations. Thus this assignment asks you to produce something that is different from a typical movie, restaurant, or consumer product review that simply describes the subject being evaluated and explains its strengths and weaknesses. In contrast, this assignment asks you to change your reader's mind about the value of your chosen subject.

◼ UNDERSTANDING EVALUATION ARGUMENTS

The Criteria/Match Process of Evaluation Arguments

Evaluation arguments involve what we call a *criteria-match* process. The first step in this process is to establish criteria; the second step is to show how well your subject matches these criteria. Here are several examples:

- Which students should be awarded the prestigious Presidential Scholarships?
  Criteria task: What are the criteria for the Presidential Scholarship?
  Match task: Which of the candidates best meet the criteria?
- Is hospitalization an effective treatment program for eating disorders?
  Criteria task: What are the criteria for an effective treatment for eating disorders?
  Match task: Does hospitalization meet these criteria?
- Is *Nightmare on Elm Street* a great horror film?
  Criteria task: What are the criteria for a great horror film?
  Match task: Does *Nightmare on Elm Street* meet these criteria?
- Which is the better map for this high school's social studies classroom—a traditional map or an inverted one?
  Criteria task: What are the criteria for a better map in this context?
  Match task: Which map best meets the criteria?

In each of these cases, it is possible to articulate criteria, even though stakeholders in each issue might argue for different criteria or weight the criteria differently. For example, on the map issue one set of stakeholders might have argued this way:

Argument in Favor of Traditional Map

The traditional map is the better choice

- because it follows standard conventions for map making.
- because it is easier to comprehend quickly and will facilitate more thorough learning.
- because no costs are involved (we already own these maps and don't have to buy replacements).

The unstated assumptions (warrants) behind these reasons are that in choosing a map it is good to follow standard conventions, it is good to facilitate ease of comprehension, and it is good to keep costs low. In other words, this argument states that a good map should meet three criteria: (1) standard conventions, (2) ease of comprehension, and (3) minimal cost. Based on these criteria, the traditional map wins the argument hands down.

But another group of stakeholders might present a different argument:

Argument in Favor of Inverted Map

The inverted map is the better choice

- because it reveals how certain arbitrary conventions of mapmaking (e.g., putting north on top) can have a rhetorical effect on how we read the map.
- because it exposes Americans' ethnocentric assumptions about the "top" being superior to the "bottom."
- because it better promotes multicultural awareness and respect.

The warrants behind this argument establish a quite different set of criteria. To these stakeholders, a good map (1) reveals the rhetorical effect of arbitrary map conventions, (2) exposes ethnocentric assumptions, and (3) promotes multiculturalism. Based on these criteria, the inverted map wins hands down. Clearly, what is at issue in this dispute are the criteria themselves.

In other evaluation disputes, it is the application of criteria (the match argument) that causes disagreement. Consider a family deciding what used car to buy. They might agree on the criteria—let's say, (1) low cost, (2) safety, and (3) reliability. But they might disagree whether a specific car meets the criteria. In terms of cost, car A may be initially cheaper than car B but may get lower gas mileage and have a higher frequency of repair record. It would not be clear, then, whether car A or car B best meets the cost criterion.

FOR WRITING AND DISCUSSION

Whenever you evaluate something you first need to establish criteria—that is, for any given class of items, you have to determine the qualities, traits, behaviors, or features that constitute excellence for members of that class. Then you need to match those criteria to a single member of that class—the thing you are evaluating. The following simple exercise will give you practice in thinking in this systematic, two-stage way.

1. Working individually, make a list of criteria that are important to you in choosing a career. These criteria are apt to differ from person to person. Some people might place "high income" at the top of their list, while others might put "adventure," or "being outdoors," or "time for family and leisure" at the top. Then rank-order your criteria from highest to lowest priority.
2. Share your criteria lists in small groups or as a whole class. Then write on the chalkboard two or three representative lists of criteria.
3. Finally, write several different careers on the board and match them to the lists of criteria. Which possible careers come out tops for you? Which ones come out tops based on the criteria lists placed on the board? Possible careers to consider include these: grade school/high school teacher, lawyer, auto mechanic, airplane pilot, bus driver, military officer, engineer, computer technician, insurance salesperson, accountant, small business owner, plumber, commercial artist, homemaker, nurse/physician/dentist, chiropractor/optometrist, social worker, police officer.
4. When disagreements arise, try to identify whether they are disagreements about criteria or disagreements about the facts of a given career.

The Role of Purpose and Context in Determining Criteria

Ordinarily, criteria are based on the purpose of the class to which the thing being evaluated belongs. For example, if you asked a professor to write a recommendation for you, he or she would need to know what you were applying for—a scholarship? internship in a law office? Peace Corp volunteer? summer job in a national park? The qualities of a successful law office intern differ substantially from those of a successful Peace Corps worker in Uganda. The recommendation isn't about you in the abstract but about you fulfilling the purposes of the class "law office intern" or "Peace Corps volunteer." Similarly, if you were evaluating a car, you would need to ask, "a car for what purpose"?—reliable family transportation? social status (if so, what social group?)? environmental friendliness?

However, decisions about purpose are always affected by context. A union member, in buying a car, might specify an American-made car while a subscriber to *Mother Jones* magazine might specify high gas mileage and low pollution. To see how context influences criteria, consider a recent review of Seattle's soup kitchens appearing in a newspaper produced by homeless people. In most contexts, restaurant reviews focus on the quality of food. But in this review the highest criterion was the sense of dignity and love extended to homeless people by the staff.

Or consider the wider context of the map issue discussed earlier. The teachers might well pay attention to how administrators, parents, and school board members would react to a change of maps in the history classrooms. Would some people ridicule the teachers for their politically correct agenda? Would others applaud the teachers for championing multiculturalism and diversity? Would new, untenured teachers, drawn into the conflict, risk alienating key administrators or powerful senior teachers? Sometimes a tiny act that seems inconsequential at the time can become a symbolic battleground for clashing political forces.

FOR WRITING AND DISCUSSION

1. Working in small groups or as a whole class, how would you evaluate the Spice Girls or Madonna in the class "popular entertainer"? How about the class "role model for women"?
2. Working individually, identify several different classes that you belong to such as the class "son or daughter," "math student," "employee," "party animal," "friend." Choose one category in which you would rate yourself high or low. What are the criteria for excellence in that category? How do you meet or not meet these criteria? (You do not need to share your results unless you want to.)
3. As a whole class or in small groups, discuss how this individual exercise helped you realize how criteria for excellence vary when you place the same item into different classes with different purposes.

Other Considerations in Establishing Criteria

Establishing the criteria for evaluation arguments can entail other considerations besides purpose and context. We examine these considerations in this section.

The Problem of Apples and Oranges

To avoid the problem of apples and oranges, try to place the thing you are evaluating into the smallest applicable class. That way, apples compete only with other apples, not with the next larger class "fruit" (where they have to go head to head against bananas and peaches), nor to a neighboring class "orange." You would therefore evaluate Kobe Bryant against other basketball players rather than against golfers and race car drivers. And if you were to evaluate a less talented basketball player, you might do so within the subclass of "point guard" or "power forward" or "off-the-bench scorer" rather than the general class "basketball player."

In the readings for this chapter, the student writer evaluating the film *Picnic at Hanging Rock* had to place it in the narrow class "art film" to distinguish it from Hollywood blockbuster films or other subclasses of film. Clearly, the criteria for a successful art film are different from those for a horror film, an action film, or a dramatic comedy.

The Problem of Standards: What's Commonplace Versus What's Ideal?

When we determine criteria, we often encounter the problem of what's commonplace versus what's ideal. Do we praise something because it is better than average, or do we condemn it because it is less than ideal? Do we hold to absolute standards or to common practice? Do we censure someone for paying a house-keeper under the table to avoid taxes (failure to live up to an ideal), or do we over-look this behavior because it is so common? Is it better for high schools to pass out free contraceptives because teenagers are having sex anyway (what's *commonplace*), or is it better not to pass them out in order to support abstinence (what's *ideal*)?

There is no easy way to decide which standard to use. The problem with the "ideal" is that nothing may ever measure up. The problem with the "common-place" is that we may lower our standards and slip into a morally dangerous rel-ativism. In deciding which standard to follow, we need to recognize the limitations of each, to make the best choice we can, and to use the same standard for all items being evaluated.

The Problem of Necessary, Sufficient, and Accidental Criteria

In identifying criteria, we often recognize that some are more important than others. Suppose you said, "I will be happy with any job so long as it puts food on my table and gives me time for my family." In this case the criteria "adequate in-come" and "time for family," taken together, are *sufficient,* meaning that once these criteria are met, the thing being rated meets your standard for excellence. Suppose you said instead, "I am hard to please in my choice of a career, which must meet many criteria. But I definitely will reject any career that doesn't put enough food on my table or allow me time for my family." In this case the criteria of "adequate income" and "time for family" are *necessary* but not *sufficient,* meaning that these two criteria have to be met for a career to meet your standards, but that other cri-teria must be met also.

Besides necessary and sufficient criteria, there are also *accidental* criteria, which are added bonuses but not essential. For example, you might say something like, "Although it's not essential, having a career that would allow me to be out-side a lot would be nice." In this case "being outside" is an *accidental* criteria (nice but not required). (The terms *necessary* and *sufficient* are also used in causal argu-ments; see pp. 295–96.)

The Problem of Seductive Empirical Measures

Empirical data can help you evaluate all sorts of things. If you are buying an au-tomobile, you can be helped a great deal by knowing the numbers for its horsepower and acceleration, for its fuel economy and frequency-of-repair record, and for its po-tential resale value. But sometimes the need to make defensible evaluative decisions leads people to empirical measures that disastrously oversimplify complex matters. Every year, for example, new crops of potential professional athletes are scrutinized minutely for their records in the forty-yard dash, the bench press, the vertical leap, and so forth. Every year, some of the people who max out on these empirical mea-sures flop ingloriously in actual competition because they lack qualities that are dif-ficult if not impossible to measure empirically, whereas other athletes, with more modest scores, achieve great success thanks to these same invisible qualities.

Quantifiable measures can be helpful, of course. But they are so concrete and they make comparisons so easy that they can seduce you into believing that you can make complex judgments by comparing numbers. It's all too easy to fall into the trap of basing college admissions on SAT scores, scholarships on grade-point averages, or the success of a government policy on tax dollars saved.

The Problem of Cost

A final problem in establishing criteria is cost. A given X may be far superior to any other X's in its class, but it may also cost far more. Before you move from evaluating an X to acting on your evaluation (by buying, hiring, or doing X), you must consider cost, whether it is expressed as dollars, time, or lost opportunity. There's little question, for example, that a Lexus is superior to a Nissan Sentra according to most automotive criteria. But are the differences sufficient to justify the additional thirty thousand or so dollars that the Lexus costs?

Using Toulmin's System to Develop Evaluation Arguments

In Chapter 14, we presented a language for talking about argument based on the terminology of philosopher Stephen Toulmin. We explained how you can examine any claim with reason from the perspective of *grounds* (evidence to support the reason), *warrant* (the unstated assumption that links the reason to your claim), *backing* (an argument to support the warrant if needed), *conditions of rebuttal* (ways that a skeptical audience might refute your argument by attacking your reason and grounds or your warrant), and *qualifier* (a limiting phrase to reduce the sweep of your claim). Because the warrants for an evaluation argument are typically statements of your criteria, this system can easily be applied to evaluation arguments.

Let's say that you are the student member of a committee to select a professor for an outstanding teaching award. Several members of the committee want to give the award to Professor M. Mouse, a popular sociology professor at your institution. You are opposed. One of your lines of reasoning is that Professor Mouse's courses aren't rigorous. Here is how you could develop this line of reasoning using the planning schema explained in Chapter 14.

Claim with Reason
Professor Mouse does not deserve the teaching award because his courses aren't rigorous.

Grounds
I need to provide evidence that his courses aren't rigorous. From the dean's office records, I have discovered that 80 percent of his students get As or high Bs; a review of his syllabi shows that he requires little outside reading and only one short paper; he has a reputation in my dorm of being fun but easy.

Warrant
Having rigorous academic standards is a necessary criterion for the university teaching award.

Backing
I need to show why I think rigorous academic standards are necessary. Quality of teaching should be measured by amount that students learn. Good teaching is

more than a popularity contest. Good teachers draw high-level performance from their students and motivate them to put time and energy into learning. High standards lead to the development of skills that are demanded in society.

Conditions of Rebuttal

How could someone attack my reason and grounds? Might a person say that Mouse has high standards? Could someone show that students really earned the high grades? Are the students I talked to not representative? Could someone say that Mouse's workload and grading patterns meet or exceed the commonplace behavior of faculty in his department? *How could someone attack my warrant*? Could someone argue that rigorous academic standards aren't as important as other criteria—that this is an accidental not a necessary criterion? Could a person say that Mouse's goal—to inspire interest in sociology—is best achieved by not loading students down with too many papers and too much reading, which can appear like busywork? (I'll need to refute this argument.) Could someone say that the purpose of giving the university teaching award is public relations and it is therefore important to recognize widely popular teachers who will be excellent speakers at banquets and other public forums?

Qualifier

Rather than saying that Professor Mouse doesn't deserve the award, perhaps it would be better for me to say that he is a weak candidate or even a generally strong candidate except for one notable weakness.

Conducting an Evaluation Argument: An Extended Example of Evaluating Websites

Now that we have explored some potential difficulties in establishing and defending criteria for an evaluation, let's consider in more detail the process of evaluative thinking. One increasingly complex area requiring evaluation is researchers' use of the World Wide Web. Because anyone with a knowledge of hypertext markup language (HTML) can create a website and because there are very few controls or editorial checks on Web material, the quality of Web information can vary from gold to garbage. Moreover, the Web has an inconsistent fluidity. Some websites are regularly maintained, others are never updated, and still others appear one day and are gone the next without a trace.

To make matters more complex, there are many different kinds of websites, each with a different purpose: personal homepages, created by individuals for their own purposes; business/marketing websites, aimed at attracting and serving customers; informational/government websites, aimed at providing basic data from traffic information to bills being debated in Congress; news websites, aimed at supplementing coverage in other media; and advocacy websites, sponsored by organizations attempting to influence public opinion on disputed issues (often indicated by *.org* at the end of their URL address).

When you evaluate a site, you must consider both your own purpose in using the site and the purpose of the individuals or organization that created it. For example, if you were evaluating a business website, you might choose as your criteria its ease of use, the appeal of its design, its links to relevant external or internal sites, and the richness of its content. If you were evaluating personal homepages—perhaps with the intention of creating your own—you might consider aesthetic or design criteria, looking at how decorative or functional the art is, how clear the icons are, and how much the creativity adds to or detracts from the document: in short, what makes a "cool" or appealing site.

But your task becomes much more complicated when you want to use the Web for research—for example, when you wish to find sources for a research paper or conduct your own investigation of a complex issue. Part of the Web's value lies in its openness to voices and viewpoints that might not appear in traditional print media. However, this freedom and accessibility also create a problem: how do you sort out the good stuff from the junk? When you visit a website, how do you determine its source and purpose and its reliability to see if it fits your needs? Faced with these dilemmas, professional scholars and librarians have developed criteria for evaluating websites for research purposes. In general, these lists specify criteria like the following:

Criteria for Evaluating the Quality of Websites*

Criterion 1: Authority
- The site identifies the author.
- The site indicates the author's occupation, position, education, experience, and credentials.
- Introductory material reveals the author's motivation for publishing this information on the Internet.
- The site provides contact information for the author or producer such as an e-mail or organization address.

Criterion 2: Objectivity or Clear Disclosure of Advocacy
- The site's purpose to inform, explain, and/or persuade is clear.
- The site is explicit about declaring its point of view.
- The site indicates whether the author is affiliated with a specific organization, institution, or association.
- The site indicates whether it is directed toward a specific audience.

Criterion 3: Coverage
- The scope or topics covered by the site are clear.
- The site exhibits a suitable depth and comprehensiveness for its purpose.
- Sufficient evidence is provided to support the ideas and opinions presented.

Criterion 4: Accuracy
- The source of the information is stated; you can tell whether this information is original or taken from someplace else.

---

*For these criteria, which represent our composite of a number of such criteria worked out by librarians, we are indebted to Andrea Bartelstein, UWired Librarian at the University of Washington, Seattle, Washington. See her Resource page for additional references on evaluating Internet resources: "R545: Teaching Students to Think Critically about Internet Resources." http://weber.u.washington.edu/~libr560/NETEVAL

■ The facts appear to be accurate; most of all, you can verify this information by comparing this source with other sources in the field.

Criterion 5: Currency
■ Dates are included in the website and indicate whether they are the dates of the information itself, of its placement on the website, or of revising and updating the website.
■ The information is current, or at least still relevant, for the site's purpose.

Now let's assume that you want to conduct a research investigation and your topic is whether English should be made the official language of the United States. Your goal is to explore all sides of this issue and then write your own position paper. After examining books and print articles on this subject, you now wish to supplement your research by searching the Web. Now you must determine which websites will enhance your investigation by providing valuable background information and factual data as well as different arguments and perspectives. In other words, which sites offer you reliable and responsible information? When you type the keywords "English official language" into your search engine, you discover a variety of websites: news web pages, government documents (for example, the bill to declare English as the official U.S. language), online forums, and numerous advocacy sites ranging from organizations to personal opinion pages. You need to distinguish among this wide assortment of advocacy websites to determine which ones will lend the most credibility and substance to the position you will take.

Three of the websites that you have found are titled "U.S. English," "English as the Official Language," and "English for the Children." All three of these sites promote the adoption of English as the official language. Like other advocacy literature published in magazines, pamphlets, street corner handouts, and political advertisements, these sites promote a cause, fueling the enthusiasm of supporters while trying to win new adherents. Thus, you are not expecting to find objectivity here. Instead, the value of these sites lies in how well they clarify and present their positions, how well they present data and evidence in support of their positions, and how well they give you a full context for perspectives and points of view in support of their cause.

How do these websites match the criteria just presented? From our perspective, one of these sites constitutes a highly credible and responsible source, one of these measures up poorly, and one is problematic.

In our opinion, the best website among our three is "U.S. English" (http://www.us-english.org/index.html). Its homepage is shown in Figure 15.2. The visual appearance of the homepage, with its attractive logo and its inclusion of notices of awards for "outstanding website" and "one of the best Politics and Government sites on the Web," gives the reader an immediate sense of professionalism. Moreover, the site meets our criteria for authority, clear disclosure of advocacy, coverage, accuracy, and currency. This site's authority is conveyed on the homepage by identifying the organization's founder, the late Senator S. I. Hayakawa of California, and its chairman/CEO, Mauro E. Mujica, an immigrant committed to the cause of English fluency for all Americans.

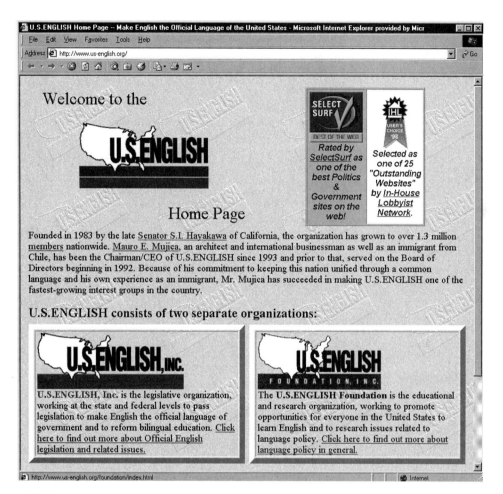

FIGURE 15.2 Homepage of U.S. English

In its introductory material, the site also forthrightly discloses its point of view—advocating political action and educational policies to keep "this nation unified through a common language." Through clear statements of scope and clear links, this site systematically presents its coverage of relevant issues and its own position on these issues. For instance, links direct the reader to two suborganizations: the legislative organization, U.S. English, Inc., which works both at the state and federal levels; and the U.S. English Foundation, Inc., which focuses on language policy, education, and research. If you then follow these links, you will see an equally clear statement of these organizations' goals and activities. All parts of this site seek to provide information while at the same time making a strong case for the political, educational, and social agenda of U.S. English. For instance, under the link to U.S. English, Inc., the site provides a list of questions frequently asked about this issue and succinctly states its answers. Although the site does not document its sources in scholarly fashion, it does convey a sense of accuracy in that its facts have a context and can be verified by going to other sources. The currency of the site is established by the statement that it was last updated on 09/01/98 (we accessed the cite on 09/23/98). If you end up arguing for English as an official language, this site could provide supporting evidence in the form of national surveys, testimonies before the U.S. Congress, editorials by well-known people, and historical background such as the text of the Treaty of Guadalupe Hidalgo and facts about the political status of Puerto Rico. If you end up opposing English as the official language, this site will help you understand alternative viewpoints.

In contrast, the website entitled "English as the Official Language" (http://www.homepages.dsu.edu/turnerm//mainpage.htm) seems minimally useful as a research source and meets none of our criteria (see Figure 15.3). It lacks authority because, although it names the writers who established the page, it doesn't give their credentials or reasons why Web users should regard them as knowledgeable. The site consists of three position papers and lists five other links to consult on this topic. The appearance of *.edu* (for *education*) in the URL suggests that the writers are students, and we suspect that the writers have simply put the papers they wrote for some college course onto the Web. Student papers can be useful documents if they are well researched, thoughtful, and carefully revised and edited for professionalism. But the grammatical mistakes and misspellings on this homepage suggest hasty, unprofessional work.

The site also fails to disclose its purpose or a defined point of view. In fact, it is unclear what motivated these students to put their papers on the Web. The unclear purpose and scope also contribute to the impression of uneven, haphazard coverage. The three student papers take a stand in favor of English as the official language, but the logic behind the links is difficult to reconstruct. Neither the link "Chronology of the Official English Movement" nor the link "Talking Points" is accessible; these sites appear to be dead. U.S. English and English First are two major advocacy organizations worth consulting. The link to Edward M. Chen, a representative of the American Civil Liberties Union, pulls up his eleven-page speech delivered to the United States House of Representatives and ends with detailed notes. This document could be very useful in grasping the main points of the opposition to English as the official language of the United States.

Although the student papers list some print and Web sources that might be worth pursuing, the papers are meagerly researched. Because the content of this site is insubstantial, there isn't much to check for accuracy. As for currency, the website was apparently constructed in 1997, based on the date of one of the student papers, but otherwise no dates are provided for this site. In sum, measured against the website criteria, this site might lead you to some useful material but is basically weak in its authority, disclosure of advocacy, coverage, accuracy, and currency.

Our last example website is harder to evaluate than the previous two. Its homepage, entitled "English for the Children" (http://www.onenation.org) is shown in Figure 15.4. In the following exercise, we invite you to evaluate this

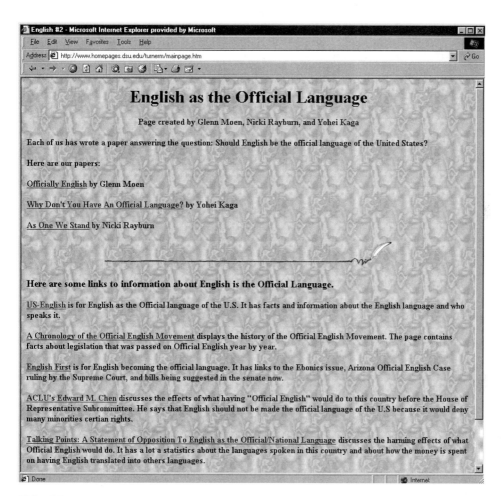

FIGURE 15.3   Homepage of English as the Official Language

homepage (you can't evaluate the site itself without accessing it online and examining its links). In the readings section of this chapter, student writer Casey James evaluates the complete site.

FOR WRITING AND DISCUSSION

1. Working as a whole class or in small groups, evaluate the homepage for "English for the Children." How logical and clear is its layout? What do you think you would find if you clicked on "People" or "Analysis" or "E-mail"? Based on the homepage itself, how well do you think the site will meet the criteria of

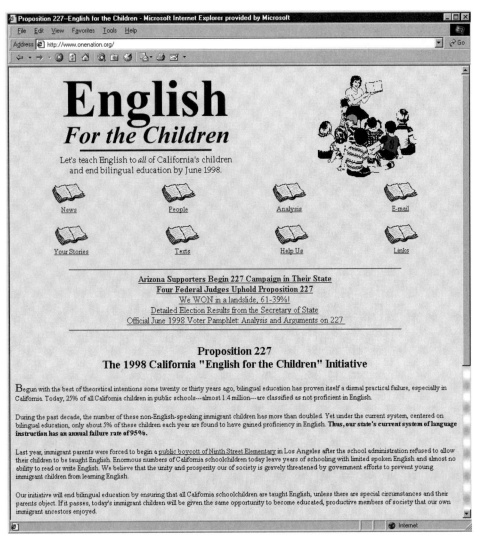

FIGURE 15.4 Homepage of English for the Children

authority, objectivity or clear disclosure of advocacy, accuracy, currency, and coverage?
2. Working in small groups, investigate two websites on one of the following topics (your instructor may assign a different topic to each group): tobacco, AIDS, immigration, the Holocaust, steroids and sports, animal testing (animal rights), alcoholism, alternative medicine, abortion, Internet censorship, or similar controversial issues. Evaluate each

website against the criteria: authority, objectivity or disclosure of advocacy, accuracy, currency, and coverage. Determine if you would consider the information provided in each website reliable and responsible enough to be used to enhance an argument on the website's topic.
3. Share your discoveries and evaluations with the whole class.

READINGS

Our first reading aims at changing its readers' assessment of the children's television program *Sesame Street*. It posits just one criterion—A good children's program should not be sexist—and then focuses exclusively on demonstrating that *Sesame Street* is sexist. Its authors are both attorneys and mothers of young children.

DIANE HELMAN AND PHYLLIS BOOKSPAN

Sesame Street: Brought to You by the Letters M-A-L-E

1   A recent report released by the American Association of University Women, "How Schools Shortchange Women," finds that teachers, textbooks and tests are, whether intentionally or unintentionally, giving preferential treatment to elementary-school boys. As a result, girls who enter school with equal or better academic potential than their male counterparts lose confidence and do not perform as well.

2   An earlier study about law students, published in the *Journal of Legal Education,* found a similar disparity. "Gender Bias in the Classroom" found that male law students are called upon in class more frequently than females, speak for longer periods of time and are given more positive feedback by law professors.

3   The article raised some disturbing questions about whether women and men receive truly equal education in American law schools.

4   Unfortunately, this insidious gender bias appears long before our children enter school and pervades even the television show *Sesame Street*. Yes, *Sesame Street* is sexist! But, just as in the story of the emperor and his new clothes, many of us do not notice the obvious.

5   The puppet stars of the show, Bert and Ernie, and all the other major *Sesame Street* animal characters—Big Bird, Cookie Monster, Grover, Oscar the Grouch, Kermit the Frog and Mr. Snuffleupagus—are male. Among the secondary characters, including Elmo, Herry Monster, Count VonCount , Telemonster, Prairie Dawn and Betty Lou, only a very few are girls.

6   The female Muppets always play children, while the males play adult parts in various scenes. In a recently aired skit "Squeal of Fortune," this disparity is evident when the host of the show introduces the two contestants. Of Count VonCount of Transylvania the host asks, "What do you do for a living?" to which the count responds

authoritatively, "I count!" Of Prairie Dawn, he inquires, "And how do you spend your day?" Sure, it would be silly to ask a schoolgirl what she does for a living. But none of the female Muppets on *Sesame Street* are even old enough to earn a living.

Further, almost all the baby puppet characters on *Sesame Street* are girls. For example, Snuffie's sibling is Baby Alice; in books, Grover's baby cousin is a girl, and when Herry Monster's mother brings home the new baby—it's a girl. Since babies are totally dependent and fairly passive, the older (male) relatives take care of them and provide leadership.

Also, the female Muppets almost never interact with each other. In sharp contrast, consequential and caring friendships have been fully developed between male Muppets: Ernie and Bert; Big Bird and Snuffie; even Oscar the Grouch and his (male) worm, Squirmy.

Any parent of toddlers or preschoolers can testify that the "girls" on *Sesame Street* are not very popular. Children ask their parents for Bert and Ernie dolls, not Baby Alice. Is this just because the girls are not marketed via books, tapes, placemats and toy dolls the same way the boys are? Or is it that the *Sesame Street* writers simply have not developed the girls into the same types of lovable, adorable personalities that belong to the main characters?

Interestingly and peculiarly, the minor "girls" look more human than most of the well-loved animal roles. They are not physically cuddly, colorful or bizarre, as are the more important male characters. Prairie Dawn has ordinary blonde hair and brown eyes—nothing even remotely similar to Big Bird's soft yellow feathers or Cookie Monster's wild, bright blue, mane.

Yes, we believe that *Sesame Street* is one of the best shows on television for small children. Our children—boys and girls—are regular viewers. In addition to its educational value, lack of violence and emphasis on cooperation, the adult characters on the show are admirably balanced in terms of avoiding sexual stereotypes.

But even the best of the bunch has room for improvement. Just as elementary through professional school educators must learn to be more sensitive to subtle and unintentional gender bias, so too should the folks at Children's Television Network. We can stop sexism from seeping into our children's first "formal" educational experience.

The message was brought to you by the letter F: fairness for females.

Thinking Critically About *Sesame Street*

1. This essay spends no time on the criteria part of the argument ("Sexism is bad") and all its time on the match argument ("*Sesame Street* exhibits sexism"). Why do the authors feel no need to defend the criterion?
2. Do the authors convince you that *Sesame Street* is sexist?
3. If you agree with the argument that *Sesame Street* is sexist, should that criterion be sufficient for undermining the popular assessment of *Sesame Street* as a model educational program for children?

Our next reading is by cultural critic Elayne Rapping. It first appeared in *Progressive* magazine, a leftist publication that strongly supports labor and working-class issues.

ELAYNE RAPPING
IN PRAISE OF ROSEANNE

1   The other night, while flipping among the three nightly network news broadcasts, I stopped—as I often do—to check out the *Roseanne* rerun Fox cleverly schedules during that time slot in New York. And, as often happens, I found myself sticking around longer than I intended, watching the Conners wiggle their way through whatever crisis had hit their Kmart window fan that day.

2   On the three more respectable networks, the Dow Jones averages rise and fall; Congress and the courts hand down weighty decisions in lofty prose; the official weapons of state are deployed, around the globe and in the inner cities, to preserve democracy and the American way. But in the Conner residence, where most things are either in disrepair or not yet paid for, it is possible to glimpse—as it rarely is on the newscasts themselves—how the fallout from such headlines might actually affect those who are relatively low in the pecking order.

3   On CBS, NBC, ABC, and CNN, the problems of the women who make headlines are not likely to sound familiar to most of us. Zoë Baird may be struggling with the servant issue. Hillary may have misplaced her capital-gains records. The Queen of England may be embroiled in royal-family dysfunction. But Roseanne, matriarch of the shabby Conner household, will be coping with less glamorous trauma—unemployment, foreclosure, job stress, marital power struggles, unruly and unmotivated kids—in a less dignified but more realistic style.

4   I am a big fan of Roseanne—Barr, Arnold, Conner, whatever. So are my female and working-class students, who invariably claim her as their own and hang on to her for dear life as they climb the ladder of class and professional achievement—an effort in which their parents have so hopefully invested everything they own. But it recently occurred to me that I have never—in the many years I've regularly analyzed and commented on American popular culture—written a single word about her. Nor have I read many, outside the trashy tabloids, where her personal life and public persona are regularly recorded and described.

5   In the last year, I've read dozens of academic and popular articles, and two whole books, about *The Cosby Show.* Archie Bunker and *All in the Family* have been appraised and analyzed endlessly. Even *Murphy Brown* and *The Mary Tyler Moore Show* are taken seriously in ever-broadening academic and journalistic circles. Not to mention the well-structured, post-structural Madonna, long the darling of feminist critics and academics.

6   What is it about these other media icons that makes them somehow more "respectable" subjects of intellectual analysis, more suitable to "serious" discourse? What is it about Roseanne that makes her so easy to ignore or write off, despite her (to me) obvious talent, originality, political *chutzpah,* and power? Gender and appearance are surely part of it; but I suspect that class—position as well as attitude—is the major factor. Bill Cosby's Cliff Huxtable, Mary Tyler Moore's Mary Richards, Candice Bergen's Murphy Brown are all well-turned-out, well-educated liberal professionals. And the grungy, working-class Archie Bunker, far from scoring points for his class, is always beaten down by the liberal, professional mentality of everyone else on the show. As for Madonna, while she is certainly not respectable, she makes up for it by being blond, chic, and gorgeous, which, in our culture, covers a multitude of social sins.

But Roseanne is a different story, far more unassimilable into mainstream-media   7
iconography than any of these others. Fat, sloppy, foul-mouthed, and bossy, she is just
a bit too unrepentantly, combatively proud of her gender and class position and style
to be easily molded into the "moving' on up" mode of American mass media. She isn't
"movin' up" to anywhere. She is standing pat, week after week on her show—and a lot
of the rest of the time in a lot of other places—speaking out for the dignity and the rights
of those the media have set out to shame into invisibility or seduce into endless, self-
hating efforts at personal transformation. With her bad hair and baggy pants and oversized shirts from the lower level of the mall, with her burned meat loaf and tuna
casseroles and Mallomars, with her rough language and politically incorrect childrearing methods, with her dead-end minimum-wage jobs, Roseanne has gone further than
Madonna or almost anyone else I can think of at turning the hegemonic norms of the
corporate media on their heads. But few of the intellectual writing classes have seen fit
to credit, much less celebrate, her for it. So I will.

To appreciate Roseanne's unlikely ascent into prime-time stardom, it's useful to   8
place her within the generic traditions of the family sitcom. Roseanne is not a descen-
dant of the pristine line of virginal wife/mothers who have set the norms for such characters from the days of June Cleaver to the present. No sweetly submissive smiles or
politely helpful suggestions to hubby and kids for her. She is one of a rarer breed, the
one invented and defined by Lucille Ball in *I Love Lucy,* in which the female protagonist is more Helpmeet from Hell than from Heaven.

The parallels between these two women are interesting, and reveal a lot about what   9
has and hasn't changed for the women—white, working-class, and poor—who make up
the female majority in this country (although you'd never know it from watching TV).
Both were, and are, popular and powerful beyond the dreams of almost any woman performer of their times. And yet both eschewed the traditional feminine, white, middle-
class persona dictated by the norms of their days, preferring to present themselves as
wild women, out of bounds, loud, funny, and noisy—all attributes which sexist culture
beats out of most of us very early on. In a world in which females are enjoined not to
take up too much space, not to make "spectacles" of ourselves, not to "disturb" but to
contain "the peace," women like Roseanne and Lucy have always been frightening, repulsive, even indecent. That's why they so appall us even as, consciously or subconsciously, we are drawn to them.

I used to cringe when I watched *I Love Lucy* as a child. She filled me with embar-   10
rassment because she was so stereotypically "hysterical," so much a failure in her endless efforts to move out of the confines of traditional femininity and its many indignities
(indignities otherwise kept hidden by the Stepford-like types of Donna Reed and June
Cleaver).

I was far more comfortable, as a middle-class girl, with the persona created by   11
Mary Tyler Moore—first as the frustrated dancer/wife in *The Dick Van Dyke Show* and
later as the first real career woman in her own show. Unlike Lucy, Mary Richards was
perfectly groomed and mannered. She was sweetly deferential in her apologetic efforts
at assertiveness; embarrassingly grateful for every nod of respect or responsibility from
her boss, "Mr. Grant." Ambitious, yes, but never forgetful of the "ladylike" way of moving up the corporate ladder, one dainty, unthreatening step at a time. Where Lucy em-
barrassed, Mary was soothing. No pratfalls or dumb disguises for her.

But through Roseanne, I've come to see the very improper Lucy differently. For her   12
time, after all, she was a real fighter against those feminine constraints. She tried to *do*
things and she tried to do them with other women, against the resistance of every man
on the show. She was not well groomed, did not live in tasteful elegance, did not sup-

port and help her husband at business and social affairs—far from it. She was full of energy and rebelliousness and, yes, independence—to a point.

13   But of course she always failed, and lost, and made a fool of herself. Her show was pure slapstick fantasy, because, back then, the things she was trying to achieve were so far from imaginable that someone like her could only exist in a farcical mode. But, as Roseanne's very different way of playing this kind of woman shows, that is no longer true.

14   Like Lucy, Roseanne is loud, aggressive, messy, and ambitiously bossy. Roseanne, too, has close relationships with other women. And Roseanne, too, is larger than life, excessive, to many frightening and repulsive. But her show is no fantasy. It is the most realistic picture of gender, class, and family relations on television today. And that's because Roseanne herself is so consciously political, so gender- and class-conscious, in every detail of her show.

15   No more the harried husband rolling his eyes at his wife's antics. Where other sitcoms either ignore feminism and reproduce traditional relations or, perhaps worse, present perfectly harmonious couples—like the Huxtables—for whom gender equity comes as naturally as their good looks, Roseanne and Dan duke it out over gender and power issues as equals who seem really to love, respect, and—not least—get angry at each other.

16   Nor does Roseanne need to think up crazy schemes for achieving the impossible— a project outside the home. Roseanne, like most of us, needs to work. The jobs she is forced to take—sweeping in a hair salon, waiting tables in malls and diners, working on an assembly line—are very like the ones Lucy nabbed and then messed up, to the wild laughter of the audience. But for Roseanne the humor is different. Roseanne fights with sexist, overbearing bosses, lashes out at her kids because she's stressed out at work, moonlights to get them through the rough days when Dan is out of work. And if these things are funny to watch, they are also deeply revealing of social and emotional truths in the lives of women and working-class families today.

17   The most touching and impressive thing about this series—and the main reason for its popularity—is its subtle presentation of progressive "messages" in a way that is neither preachy nor condescending to audiences. Much was made of the famous episode in which Roseanne was kissed by a lesbian character. (And it is surely a tribute to Roseanne's integrity and clout that this first lesbian kiss got past Standards and Practices[1] because of her.) But the kiss itself was really no big deal. Lots of shows will be doing this kind of one minute/one scene "Wow, did you see that?" thing soon enough.

18   Sitcoms are, indeed, informed by liberal values, and they do, indeed, tend to preach to us about tolerance and personal freedom. Lesbianism, as an idea, an abstraction, a new entry on the now very long list of liberal tolerances to which the professional middle classes must pay lip service, was bound to hit prime time soon anyway. What made the Roseanne "lesbian episode" remarkable and radically different from the usual liberal sitcom style of tackling such issues was not the kiss itself but the startlingly honest discussions about homosexuality that followed the kiss, between Dan and his young son D.J.; and then between Dan and Roseanne, in bed.

19   This segment was politically audacious because it *did not* lecture the vast majority of Americans who are, yes, queasy about homosexuality. It presented them with a

---

[1]*Standards and Practices:* network censors.

mirror image of their own confusion and anxiety, and led them to a position of relative comfort about it all, by sympathizing with their very real concern about radical social and sexual change.

This is how the show attacks all its difficult issues, sensational and mundane. Much   20
has been made of Roseanne's way of yelling at her kids, even hitting them on at least one occasion. Clearly, this is not how parents, since Dr. Spock, have been told to be-have, and for obvious and good reason. Nonetheless, we all do these things on occa-sion. (And those who don't, ever, probably have other serious parenting problems.) To pretend that parents don't do that—as most sitcoms do—is to condescend to viewers who know that this goes on everywhere, and who have, themselves, done it or at least fought the urge.

On *Roseanne,* such behavior is neither denied nor condemned; it is talked about   21
and analyzed. After hitting her son, for example, Roseanne apologizes and confesses, heartbreakingly, that she was herself beaten as a child and that it was wrong then and wrong now. It is this kind of honesty about negative feelings—especially when they are placed in the kind of social and economic context this show never slights—that makes the positive feelings of love and mutual respect within this battered, battling family so very believable.

Which brings me, unavoidably, to the issue of Roseanne Arnold herself, as a pub-   22
lic persona—surely the major factor in the public unease about her. There are two "Roseannes"—both media images constructed cleverly and carefully by Arnold herself. "Roseanne Conner" is, as Arnold herself says, "much nicer." She is the sitcom version of how someone overcomes personal and economic difficulty and not only survives but thrives. She comes from a long line of show-business satirists whose humor was based on social and political truth. Like the Marx Brothers and Charlie Chaplin, she is the lov-able outsider sneaking into the polite world to expose its hypocrisy and phoniness.

That is the fictional "Roseanne" of sitcom fame. The other persona, "Roseanne Barr   23
Arnold"—the woman who appears in tabloids, talk shows, news shows, and comedy clubs—is far more outrageous, more dangerous. She is the ultimate bad girl, the woman who shouts out to the entire world every angry, nasty, shameful truth and emotion she feels about the lives of women, especially poor women, in America today.

Much of what Roseanne confesses to—about incest, wife abuse, mental illness,   24
obesity, prostitution, lesbianism—makes people uncomfortable. It's tacky, embarrass-ing, improper, déclassé to discuss these issues in public. But so was much of what we Second Wave feminists and student activists and antiwar protesters and others insisted upon talking about and confessing to and doing in the 1960s. So is what Anita Hill insisted—in much classier style but to no less shock and outrage—on throwing at us from the Senate hearing rooms. So is almost every political statement and action that rocks the reactionary boats of institutionalized power and authority.

And like those other actions and statements, Roseanne's antics are inherently po-   25
litical, radical, salutary. For in speaking out about her hidden demons and ghosts and scars—as a woman, a working-class person, a victim of family and institutional abuse—she speaks *for* the myriad damaged and disempowered souls, mostly still silent and in-visible, who also bear the scars of such class, gender, and age abuse.

My timing, as I write this, couldn't be worse, of course. The tabloids are currently   26
ablaze with the latest, and most unfortunate, of Arnold brouhahas. Roseanne, having loudly accused her husband of infidelity and spousal abuse, filed for divorce, then al-most immediately rescinded the statements and reconciled with her husband, only to file for divorce again a few weeks later.

27   I am neither shocked nor disillusioned by this. Every abused woman I have ever known has attempted, unsuccessfully, to leave her destructive relationship many times, before finally finding the strength and support to make the break. This, after all, is the very essence of the abuse syndrome. Only Roseanne, as usual, has chosen to play it out, in all its gory details, in the spotlight.

28   I'm a Roseanne fan. I like her show and marvel at her compassion and intelligence, at what she manages to get away with. I like her style—even when she offends me and makes me nervous (which she often does)—because the world needs loud-mouthed unattractive women with brains, guts, a social conscience, and a sense of humor. There are few enough of them who make it through puberty with their spirits and energies intact.

Thinking Critically About "In Praise of Roseanne"

1. One of the rules of evaluation is to place the thing being evaluated in the smallest possible class. In much of this article, Rapping tries to determine the category that Roseanne belongs to. Why is that a problem? How does Roseanne differ from the heroines of most other TV sitcoms?

2. Rapping is surprised to discover some similarities between Roseanne and Lucy in the 1950s show *I Love Lucy.* How are these women similar?

3. This essay does not announce its criteria in a tightly closed-form fashion. You may need to read the essay carefully a second time to tease out the criteria Rapping uses. What are these criteria? To put it another way, why does Rapping like Roseanne the character and *Roseanne* the TV show?

4. Who is the audience for this essay? What is the alternative assessment of Roseanne that Rapping is arguing against?

5. Are you persuaded by Rapping's argument? If you don't think *Roseanne* is an excellent television sitcom, what alternative criteria would you use to make your own assessment?

Our next essay, by student writer Sarah Erickson, evaluates the film *Picnic at Hanging Rock* as an art film.

SARAH ERICKSON (STUDENT)
Picnic at Hanging Rock as an Art Film

1   Peter Weir's film *Picnic at Hanging Rock* (1975) opens ambiguously. A silent announcement informs viewers that three girls and their teacher disappeared without a trace while on a picnic in 1901. The camera focuses on the Australian bush and a monolithic rock on a hot summer day. Eerie panpipe music strikes up. Several teenage schoolgirls in their nightshifts and corsets are shown dressing for the day. Unlike Weir's recent American films—*The Dead Poets Society* (1989) and *The Truman Show* (1998)—and definitely unlike blockbuster thrillers, *Picnic at Hanging Rock* immediately

defies mainstream classification. Some people in our class thought the film was "strange," "slow," or "hard to understand," and they evaluated it as an unsuccessful movie. However, this Australian film should be evaluated as an art film because of its nonformulaic and unpredictable plot and its heavy use of symbolism to convey its themes and characters. Moreover, it is an excellent art film because it uses the elements effectively to provoke thought and create ambiguity.

While most mainstream popular films feature action-packed plots that follow a problem-climax-resolution pattern and clear, boldly developed characters, successful art films meet distinctly different criteria. An art film has no defined form. It is original, often unpredictable, and can be interpreted in many different ways depending on the viewers. Symbolism is used to connect ideas, but the interpretation is left up to the imagination of the viewer. In order to make sense of an art film, the viewer must analyze the characters, settings, and recurring themes. A good art film is original, mysterious, and ambiguous.

Picnic at Hanging Rock takes place in 1901 in Australia at two main locations: Appleyard College, a boarding school for wealthy girls, and Hanging Rock, an ancient geological formation. When the girls go on a Valentine's Day picnic to Hanging Rock, four girls—Marion, Irma, Edith, and their leader, beautiful, adventurous Miranda—disregard the prohibitions and explore Hanging Rock. Miss McCraw, the mathematics teacher, also heads up to the towering cliffs. While the girls are climbing, they seem to be in a trance. Later in the afternoon Miss McCraw and these girls, except for Edith who has fled back to the picnic, have vanished. One girl, Sarah, the school's only charity case, has been forced to miss the picnic by Mrs. Appleyard, the headmistress. Sarah, an orphan, depends on Miranda, but before leaving for the picnic, Miranda has cryptically advised Sarah to learn to live without her. In the second half of the film, two young men—Michael Fitzhubert and his coachman Albert Crundall—search exhaustively for the girls, whom they had seen earlier, and eventually Albert finds Irma unconscious in a cave. Irma is unable to explain what happened that dreadful day, and the school, the townspeople who have formed a search party, and the audience are left to wonder about the disappearance. When the school's reputation suffers from this incident and Sarah is unable to pay her tuition, Mrs. Appleyard becomes increasingly cruel to her. At the end of the movie, both Sarah and Mrs. Appleyard die strangely.

Picnic at Hanging Rock meets the first criterion of a good art film in that it follows no set formula and is unpredictable. The mysterious deaths or disappearances of the characters leave the ending of the movie up to the viewer's imagination. Nobody knows exactly what has happened. The possible conclusions are endless. Did the three girls and Miss McCraw commit suicide? Were they kidnapped and molested? Did they discover another world at the top of the mysterious rock? Did they find, or become, a part of a higher state of being? Who knows? The viewer must decide. Sarah is found dead in the greenhouse, and the headmistress dies at the base of Hanging Rock. Did they commit suicide? Did one kill the other? These questions do not have definite answers, either. These unresolved questions illustrate the open-endedness and thought-provoking unpredictability, which are appropriate for a successful art film.

A good art film also relies on symbolism more than direct statements and action to convey its themes. Symbolism permeates *Picnic at Hanging Rock*. Miranda is the most symbolic character. While climbing the rock, she is the first one to take off her stockings, something totally inappropriate for women in the early 1900s. She represents sensuality; perhaps that is why she mesmerizes Michael Fitzhubert, who cannot forget her. Miranda also has an adventurous spirit that refuses to be bound by class and gender restrictions. After shooting a scene of Miranda, the camera often focuses on a swan. Weir uses the swan to symbolize Miranda: both are beautiful, wild, and free, showing female sexuality at odds with restrictive Victorian standards. The swan is also elusive—appearing and flying away. Similarly, Miranda and reality are elusive and illusory in this film.

6   Another set of interrelated symbols are prominent in this film. Appleyard College is used to represent the sophisticated, wealthy British elite. Hanging Rock, on the other hand, represents Australia. In its raw form, the rock is magnificent, mysterious, untamed, and dangerous. As powerful nature, it dominates the action and overwhelms the civilized British intruders. Like the bush and the Aborigines, the rock is wild, free, and original. Unlike the beauty that Miranda portrays, the rock is beautiful in its own sense. The symbolism shows the clash between Appleyard College and the rock, which hardly seem able to exist in the same vicinity.

7   The film also displays the difference between the wealthy English elite and the poorer Australian-born characters. The lower-class Australians are subordinate in their own land and yet, as Albert's success in finding Irma on the rock indicates, are more able to survive than the upper-class British, who are imperiled in this harsh, mysterious land that is not their own.

8   Many mysteries and questions arise in this film. In the opening scenes, Miranda speaks Edgar Allan Poe's line: "What we see and what we seem, are but a dream. A dream within a dream." Later the Australian-born gardener at Appleyard College comments: "Some questions got answers and some haven't." With lines like these and all its scenes, the film challenges basic artistic formulas and sparks curiosity in the viewer's mind while it maintains its focus on illusion, contrasts, and mystery. In its lack of resolution and its symbolism, the film preserves its ambiguity. Weir's film meets and exceeds all the criteria for a good art film. So what did actually happen at Hanging Rock?

Thinking Critically About *"Picnic at Hanging Rock* as an Art Film"

1. What criteria does Sarah Erickson use for evaluating *Picnic at Hanging Rock*?
2. In writing about literature, students are generally advised not to include plot summaries of the story they are analyzing. Why do you suppose Erickson chooses to summarize the plot of this film?
3. What evidence does she supply to support the idea that this movie is "an excellent example of an art film"?
4. Where do you find this argument convincing? What weaknesses do you see and how could this evaluative argument be made stronger?

Our final reading is an evaluation of the website "English for the Children" discussed earlier in this chapter. For a view of this site's homepage, see Figure 15.4, page 376.

CASEY JAMES (STUDENT)
A DIFFICULT WEBSITE

1   What is the connection between the movement to make English the official language of the United States and bilingual education? What are the main political, social, and educational issues involved in bilingual education? Seeking answers to these

questions, I examined the website entitled "English for the Children" (http://www. onenation.org/). However, this site did not provide ready or clear answers to these questions. Although "English for the Children" has useful information, it is difficult and time-consuming to find because this site is inefficiently laid out. As measured against the criteria for websites presented in *The Allyn & Bacon Guide to Writing,* this site does a poor job of presenting its authority; it lacks clarity and support in its coverage, and it gives a poor impression of its accuracy and currency.

This site fails to measure up to the authority criteria by burying some important in-   2
formation and presenting other information in a confusing manner. The second page of this site indicates that English for the Children is a suborganization of One Nation/One California. The end of the site does provide a mailing address and an e-mail address along with the name of the author of the site, but it doesn't give the author's position or credentials. The reader also wonders who the heads of this organization are. Only the link "People" supplies information about the campaign's leadership, and only much searching of additional links eventually produces biographical sketches of the leaders of the nonprofit organization One Nation/One California as well as some published writings by them.

It also takes much time to figure out how this advocacy site frames and develops   3
its argument; in fact, the scope and depth of the site's coverage are problematic. The first problem with the coverage of the site is that the homepage, instead of explaining its scope, plunges readers into a confusing discussion of bilingual education. "English for the Children" is the homepage of an initiative, Proposition 227. Much searching of links enables the reader to figure out that this initiative seeks to replace bilingual education in California with what it calls "sheltered immersion in English."

A second problem is that this site initially bombards the reader with a series of un-   4
supported claims: bilingual education has failed, particularly in California; bilingual education is part of a government effort to prevent immigrant children from learning English; Proposition 227 promotes a program that will ensure that these children learn English; people across the political spectrum and immigrants as well as people born here support this initiative. A few numbers and percentages are given to back up a few of these claims; however, no sources are mentioned. The site doesn't explain how proficiency in English is measured or by whom.

The "Analysis" link, which finally leads readers to an explanation of the issues in-   5
volved, actually raises more questions without satisfactorily answering them. For example, the link "For Bilingual Education 'Local Control' Means 'Status Quo' " shows that many California school district officials still believe in bilingual education. The reader is left with an apparent contradiction: this site claims wide support for its position, yet most California educators continue to support bilingual education. Why? Do they only care about jobs and money, as is implied? These arguments need more explanation and evidence. The coverage in this site seems to be more aimed at reaffirming the opinions of supporters than at convincing others to embrace this cause.

The site also gives a poor impression of its accuracy and currency. The opening   6
lines of this site establish a specific political purpose: to rally California voters to vote against bilingual education in the June 1998 election. However, urging readers to vote for an election that is long past does not impress them with the thought or professionalism behind this site. (I visited the site five months after the election.) Neither the introductory page itself nor the link "Falsehoods and Facts about 'English for the Children' " has been updated since the June 1998 election. Thus, although the link "News" includes very recent articles from leading California newspapers, the overall

impression of this site is that it needs to be revised and more uniformly tended and organized.

7   Given a lot of time, much delving into the links, and much thought work on my part, I finally found some material that begins to help me answer my initial questions. However, because the site is poorly organized and unclear in its authority, coverage, accuracy, and currency, it seems to be designed for people within the cause who are already involved in the organization. The reader and researcher new to this issue will need patience and persistence in using this site because it exhibits vagueness and inefficiency in meeting the website criteria.

Thinking Critically About "A Difficult Website"

1. What evidence does Casey James provide to show that this website only minimally meets the criteria used in the text?
2. Do you find James's evaluation persuasive?

◢ COMPOSING YOUR ESSAY

Generating and Exploring Ideas

If you have not already chosen an evaluation issue, try creating idea maps with spokes chosen from among the following (or any other categories you can think of):

People: athletes, political leaders, musicians, entertainers, clergy

Science and technology: weapons systems, word-processing programs, spreadsheets, automotive advancements, treatments for diseases

Media: news programs, TV shows, radio stations, advertisements, websites

Government and world affairs: economic policies, Supreme Court decisions, laws or legal practices, government customs or practices, foreign policies

The arts: movies, books, buildings, paintings, music

Your college or university: courses, teachers, curricula, administrative policies, financial aid systems

The world of work: jobs, company operations, dress codes, systems of compensation, hiring policies, supervisors

Another good idea for finding a topic is to think of a recent review with which you disagree—a movie review, a restaurant review, a review of an art exhibit or play, or a sportswriter's assessment of a team or player.

Once you have chosen a possible topic, freewrite your responses to each of the following questions as a means of exploring ideas for your argument.

1. To what class does your X belong? Choose the smallest relevant class. (Instead of asking, "Is Joe Smith a good athlete?" ask "Is Joe Smith a good college basketball player?" or, even better, "Is Joe Smith a good college point guard?")

2. Determine the criteria you will use for your evaluation. Begin by listing the purposes of the class and then use freewriting or idea mapping to explore the qualities a member of that class has to have to achieve those purposes. What objections is your audience likely to raise about your criteria? How will you justify your criteria?
3. Which of your criteria is the most important? Why?
4. Evaluate your subject by matching it to each of the criteria. Explore why your subject does or does not match each of the criteria. Your freewriting for this exercise will yield most of the ideas you will need for your argument.

Shaping and Drafting

For your first draft, consider trying the following format. Many evaluation arguments follow this shape, and you can always alter the shape later if it seems too formulaic for you.

1. Introduce your issue and show why evaluating X is problematic or controversial.
2. Summarize and respond to opposing or alternative views.
3. Present your own argument.
   a. State criterion 1 and defend it if necessary.
   b. Show that X meets/does not meet the criterion.
   c. State criterion 2 and defend it if necessary.
   d. Show that X meets/does not meet the criterion.
   e. Continue with additional criteria and match arguments.
4. Sum up your evaluation.

Revising

A good way to revise an evaluation argument, as well as other kinds of arguments, is to analyze your lines of reasoning using Toulmin's system. For each element of your evaluation, examine your use of grounds, warrant (criteria), backing, and conditions for rebuttal. Let your revision reflect your deeper sense of your argument resulting from this analysis.

g u i d e l i n e s
for Peer Reviewers

Instructions for peer reviews, including use of these guidelines, are provided in Chapter 17, pages 429–35. To write a peer review for a classmate, use your own paper, numbering your responses to correspond to the questions on the guidelines. At the head of your paper place the author's name and your own name, as shown.

Author's Name: _____

Peer Reviewer's Name: _____

I. Read the draft at a normal reading speed from beginning to end. As you read, do the following:
   A. Place a wavy line in the margin next to any passages that you find confusing, that contain something that doesn't seem to fit, or that otherwise slow down your reading.
   B. Place a "Good!" in the margin next to any passages where you think the writing is particularly strong or interesting.
II. Read the draft again slowly and answer the following questions by writing brief explanations of your answers.
   A. Introduction:
      1. Does the title effectively focus the reader's expectations and pique interest?
      2. Does the introduction capture your interest, provide needed background, identify a controversial evaluative issue, and present the writer's claim?
      3. Is the claim appropriately focused and contestable? Is it an evaluative claim?
      4. How might the writer improve the introduction?
   B. The Criteria-Match Argument:
      1. What criteria does the writer use for evaluating X? Does the writer convincingly establish or defend these criteria?
      2. Do you accept the writer's criteria and agree with the way the writer weights their relative importance? How could the writer improve the criteria argument?
      3. What evidence does the writer present to show that the X being evaluated meets or fails to meet each criterion? Is the evidence persuasive? How could the writer improve the match argument?
      4. Where does the writer anticipate and summarize alternative views? Is the summary fair? How does the writer respond to these alternative views? How could the writer's refutation or response be improved?
      5. How do you react to the ideas in this draft? Where are they weak? What would you add or change to strengthen the argument?
      6. How might the writer improve the structure of the draft? Where might the writer better apply the principles of clarity from Chapter 18?
   C. Sum up what you see as the chief strengths and problem areas of this draft.
      1. Strengths
      2. Problem areas
III. Read the draft one more time. Place a check in the margin wherever you notice problems in grammar, spelling, or mechanics (one check per problem).

Proposing a Solution

◾ ABOUT PROPOSAL WRITING

Proposal arguments call an audience to action. They make a claim that some action *should* or *ought* to be done. Sometimes referred to informally as *should arguments*, proposals are among the most common kinds of arguments that you will write or read.

Some proposals aim to solve local, practical matters. For example, one of the student proposals in this chapter advocates that a soundproof door be installed in a dorm recreation room to create a quiet study area (see pp. 397–400). Practical proposals generally target a specific audience (usually the person with power to act on the proposal) and are typically introduced with a "letter of transmittal," in which the writer briefly summarizes the proposal, explains its purpose, and courteously invites the reader to consider it.

The rhetorical context of practical proposals makes effective document design essential. An effective design (layout, neatness, clear headings, flawless editing) helps establish the writer's *ethos* as a quality-oriented professional and makes the reading of the proposal as easy as possible. In many areas of business and industry, effective practical proposals are crucial for financial success. Many kinds of businesses—for example, construction and engineering firms, ad agencies, university research teams, nonprofit agencies, and others—generate most of their revenue from effective, competitive proposals.

Other kinds of proposals (often called *policy proposals*) are aimed at more general audiences instead of specific decision makers. These proposals typically address issues of public policy with the aim of swaying public support toward the writer's proposed solution. Policy proposals might address the problem of prison overcrowding, out-of-control health care costs, gang violence, declining SAT scores, fetal-alcohol-syndrome babies, Internet pornography and children, poverty, and so forth.

If the problem you are addressing is already well known to your audience, then *should* arguments can follow the shape of classical arguments described in Chapter 14, in which you introduce the issue, present the claim, provide supporting reasons for the claim, summarize and respond to alternative views, and provide a conclusion. If you wrote an argument for Chapter 14, you may well have chosen a proposal issue. Tiffany Linder's argument in that chapter (pp. 351–53), in which she argues that "all logging of old-growth forests should be banned," is a proposal argument.

In many cases, however, the problem you wish to address is *not* already known to your audience (or the audience doesn't take the problem seriously). The writer in effect must *create* the issue being addressed, calling the reader's attention to a problem and then proposing a course of action. The rest of this chapter focuses on strategies for this latter type of proposal, in which part of the writer's task is to convince readers that a problem exists, that it is serious, and that some action must be taken to resolve it.

◢ EXPLORING PROPOSAL WRITING

The following activity introduces you to the thinking processes involved in writing a proposal argument.

1. In small groups, identify and list several major problems facing students in your college or university.
2. Decide among yourselves which problems are most important and rank them in order of importance.
3. Choose your group's number one problem and explore answers to the following questions. Group recorders should be prepared to present answers to the class as a whole.
    a. Why is the problem a problem?
    b. For whom is the problem a problem?
    c. How will these people suffer if the problem is not solved? Give specific examples.
    d. Who has the power to solve the problem?
    e. Why hasn't the problem been solved up to this point?
    f. How can the problem be solved? Create a proposal for a solution.
    g. What are the probable benefits of acting on your proposal?
    h. What costs are associated with your proposal?
    i. Who will bear these costs?
    j. Why should this proposal be enacted?
    k. What makes this proposal better than alternative proposals?
4. As a group, draft an outline for a proposal argument in which you do the following:
    a. Describe the problem and its significance.
    b. Propose your solution to the problem.
    c. Justify your proposal by showing how the benefits of adopting it outweigh the costs.

5. Recorders for each group should write the group's outline on the board and be prepared to present the group's argument orally to the class.

WRITING PROJECT

Call your audience's attention to a problem, propose a solution to that problem, and present a justification for your solution. You have two choices (your instructor may limit you to just one): (a) create a *practical* proposal, with a letter of transmittal proposing a nuts-and-bolts solution to a local problem; or (b) write a more general *policy* proposal, addressing a public issue, in the form of a bylined feature editorial for a particular (state, local, or college) newspaper. For (b), your instructor might ask you to do substantial research and model your proposal after a magazine or journal article.

All proposals have one feature in common—they offer a solution to a problem. For every proposal, there is always an alternative course of action, including doing nothing. Your task as a proposal writer is threefold: You must demonstrate that a significant problem exists; propose a solution to the problem; and justify the solution, showing that benefits outweigh costs and that the proposed solution will fix the problem better than alternative solutions would. Accordingly, a proposal argument typically has three main parts.

1. ***Description of the problem.***   The description often begins with background. Where does the problem show up? Who is affected by the problem? How long has the problem been around? Is it getting worse? You may add an anecdote or some kind of startling information or statistics to give the problem *presence*. Typically, this section also analyzes the problem. What are its elements? What are its causes? Why hasn't it been solved before? Why are obvious solutions not adequate or workable? Finally, the description shows the problem's significance. What are the negative consequences of not solving the problem?

2. ***Proposal for a solution.***   This section describes your solution and shows how it would work. If you don't yet have a solution, you may choose to generate a *planning proposal*, calling for a committee or task force to study the problem and propose solutions at a later date. The purpose of a planning proposal is to call attention to a serious problem. In most cases, however, this section should propose a detailed solution, showing step by step how it would solve the problem and at what cost.

3. ***Justification.***   Here you persuade your audience that your proposal should be enacted. Typically you show that the benefits of your proposal outweigh the costs. You also need to show why your proposed solution is better than alternatives. Point out why other possible approaches would not solve the problem, would provide fewer benefits, or would cost significantly more than your proposal.

◩ UNDERSTANDING PROPOSAL WRITING

As we have noted, proposal arguments focus on identifying a problem and then proposing and justifying a solution. In this section we look first at some of the distinctive demands of proposal writing. We then show you a powerful strategy for developing the justification section of a proposal.

Special Demands of Proposal Arguments

To get the reader to take action—the ultimate purpose of a proposal—requires you to overcome some difficult challenges. Here we examine the special demands that proposal arguments make on writers and offer suggestions for meeting them.

Creating Presence

To convince readers that a problem really exists, you must give it *presence;* that is, you must help readers *see* and *feel* the problem. Writers often use anecdotes or examples of people suffering from the problem or cite startling facts or statistics to dramatize the problem. For example, a student proposing streamlined checkout procedures in the hotel where she worked gave presence to her problem by describing a family that missed its flight home because of a slow checkout line. Her description of this family's frustration—including angry complaints overheard by people waiting to check in—convinced her boss that the problem was worth solving. To persuade your readers to act on your proposal, you need to involve them both mentally *and* emotionally in your argument.

Appealing to the Interest and Values of Decision Makers

Proposal writers sometimes appeal directly to readers' idealism, urging them to do the right thing. But writers also need to show how doing the right thing converges with their readers' own best interests. Show decision makers how acting on your proposal will benefit *them* directly. The author of the hotel checkout proposal argued that her solution would enhance customer satisfaction, an idea that her boss would find more compelling than the notion of making life easier for desk clerks.

Overcoming Inherent Conservatism

People are inherently resistant to change. One of the most famous proposals of all time, the Declaration of Independence, is notable for the way in which it anticipates its audience's resistance to change: "Prudence, indeed, will dictate that governments long established should not be changed for light and transient causes; and accordingly, all experience hath shown, that mankind are more disposed to suffer, while evils are sufferable, than to right themselves by abolishing the forms to which they are accustomed."

To restate this passage as folk wisdom, "Better the devil you know than the one you don't know." Most people expect the status quo to have its problems, flaws, and frustrations. They live with and adapt to familiar imperfections. Unless they can be persuaded that change will make things markedly better, they will "suffer, while evils are sufferable" rather than risk creating new, possibly insufferable evils.

The challenge of proving that something needs changing is compounded by the fact that the status quo often appears to be working. If its shortcomings were readily apparent, people would probably already have fixed them. It is much harder to stir an audience to action when the problem you depict entails lost potential (things could be better), rather than palpable evil (look at all the suffering).

Predicting Consequences

People also resist change because they fear unforeseen bad consequences and doubt predictions of good consequences. Everyone has experienced the disappointment of failed proposals: your favorite sports team makes a major trade—and finishes with a record worse than the one it had before the trade; a company you invested in went through a major reorganization—and promptly went into the red; voters elect a new leader who promises major reforms—and nothing happens. Although most people do not become true cynics, they are understandably cautious about accepting the rosy scenarios contained in most proposals.

To persuade your audience that your predictions are realistic, follow the strategies outlined in Chapter 13 for causal arguments. The more uncertain your proposal's consequences, the more clearly you must show *how* the proposal will bring about the consequences. Show the links in the chain and how each one leads to the next. Whenever possible, cite similar proposals that yielded the sorts of results you are predicting.

Evaluating Consequences

Compounding the problem of predicting consequences is the difficulty of figuring out whether those consequences are good or bad and for whom. For example, any alternative to the current health care system will contain changes that simultaneously advantage one segment of your audience (say, patients) and disadvantage another (say, doctors, insurance companies, or taxpayers). Indeed, if any health care proposal benefited all segments of your audience, it would probably have been adopted long ago.

It can also be difficult to identify the appropriate standard of measure to use in calculating a proposal's costs and benefits. Often you must try to balance benefits measured in apples against costs measured in oranges. For instance, suppose that a health care proposal will reduce the cost of insurance by limiting coverage. How would you balance the dollars saved on your insurance bill against the suffering of persons denied a potentially life-saving medical procedure? Some cost-benefit analyses try to reduce all consequences to one scale of measure—usually money. This scale may work well in some circumstances, but it can lead to grotesquely inappropriate conclusions in others.

These, then, are some of the challenges that face the proposal writer. With these in mind, we now set forth some strategies for making proposals as effective as possible.

Developing an Effective Justification Section

The distinctions between proposals and other kinds of arguments dictate a special variety of support for proposals. Experienced proposal writers often use a *three-approaches* strategy to help them develop their justification sections. They brainstorm justifying reasons by focusing sequentially on principles, consequences, and precedents or analogies. Figure 16.1 (on p. 396) explains each element in the sequence.

Each of these argumentation strategies was clearly evident in a recent public debate in Seattle, Washington, over a proposal to raise county sales taxes to build a new baseball stadium. Those favoring the stadium put forth arguments such as these:

> We should build the new stadium because preserving our national pastime for our children is important (*argument from principle*), because building the stadium will create new jobs and revitalize the adjacent Pioneer Square district (*arguments from consequence*), and because building the stadium will have the same beneficial effects on the city that building Camden Yards had in Baltimore (*argument from precedent*).

Those opposing the stadium created arguments using the same strategies:

> We should not build the stadium because it is wrong to subsidize rich owners and players with tax dollars (*argument from principle*), because building a stadium diverts tax money from more important concerns such as low income housing (*argument from consequence*), and because Toronto's experience with Skydome shows that once the novelty of a new stadium wears off attendance declines dramatically (*argument from precedent*).

FOR WRITING AND DISCUSSION

Working individually or in small groups, use the strategies of principle, consequence, and precedent/analogy to create *because* clauses that support (or oppose) the following proposal claims. Try to have at least one *because* clause from each of the strategies, but generate as many reasons as possible.

Example:

Claim	Spanking children should be made illegal.
Principle	Because it is wrong to cause bodily pain to children.
Consequence	Because it teaches children that it is okay to hit someone out of anger; because it causes children to obey rules out of fear rather than respect; because it can lead children to be abusive parents.
Analogy/ precedent	Because spanking a child is like throwing dishes or banging your fists against a wall—it relieves your anger but turns the child into an object.

Approach 1: *Argument from Principle*

Using this strategy, you argue that a particular action should be taken because doing so is right according to some value, assumption, principle, or belief that you share with your audience. For example, you might argue, "We should create publicly financed jobs for poor people because doing so is both charitable and just." The formula for this strategy is as follows:

We should (should not) do (this action) because (this action) is _____.

Fill in the blank with an appropriate adjective or noun specifying a belief or value that the audience holds: good, just, right, ethical, honest, charitable, equitable, fair, and so forth.

Approach 2: *Argument from Consequence*

Using this strategy, you argue that a particular action should (should not) be taken because doing so will lead to consequences that you and your audience believe are good (bad). For example, you might say, "We should create publicly financed jobs for poor people because doing so will provide them money for food and housing, promote a work ethic, and produce needed goods and services." The formula for this strategy is as follows:

We should (should not) do (this action) because (this action) will lead to these good (bad) consequences: _____, _____, _____, etc.

Think of consequences that your audience will agree are good or bad, as your argument requires.

Approach 3: *Argument from Precedent or Analogy*

Using a precedent strategy, you argue that a particular action should (should not) be taken because doing so is similar to what was done in another case, which proved to be successful (unsuccessful). For example, you might say, "We should create publicly financed jobs for poor people because doing so will alleviate poverty in this country just as a similar program has helped poor people in Upper Magnesia." Using an analogy strategy, you compare the proposed action with a similar action that your audience already accepts as good or bad. For example, "We should create publicly financed jobs for poor people because doing so is like teaching the poor how to fish rather than giving them fish." The formula for either strategy is as follows:

We should (should not) do (this action) because doing (this action) is like _____, which turned out to be good (bad).

Think of precedents or analogies that are similar to your proposed action and that have definite good (bad) associations for your audience.

FIGURE 16.1   The Three-Approaches Strategy for a Justification Section

1. Service learning courses should/should not be required for graduation.
2. Medical insurance should/should not cover psychological counseling for eating disorders.
3. Marijuana should/should not be legalized.
4. The school year for K–12 should/should not be extended to eleven months.

READINGS

The first reading is a practical proposal by a student writer. Because practical proposals are aimed at a specific audience, they are often accompanied by a letter of transmittal that introduces the writer, sets the context, and summarizes the proposal.

Campwell Hall, Room 1209
February 5, 1999

Ms. Terri Halliwell
Director of Residences
_____ University
City, State Zip

Dear Ms. Halliwell:

1   I am a student in Campwell Hall. Please find enclosed a proposal to make the study lounge on the twelfth floor more quiet. Although I enjoy living in Campwell Hall very much, I and many other students are frustrated by the absence of adequate quiet study areas for its residents. It is particularly difficult to concentrate in the twelfth floor study lounge because of disruptive noise from hallways, from elevators, and from students who are talking and watching television in the adjoining recreational lounge. My proposed solution is to add a soundproof door between the twelfth floor recreational lounge and the study lounge. This low-cost addition will create a quiet study place for twelfth floor residents.

2   Thank you for your consideration of my ideas.

Sincerely,

Theresa LaPorte

Following the letter of transmittal is the proposal's cover or title page.

A PROPOSAL TO CREATE A QUIET STUDY LOUNGE
ON THE TWELFTH FLOOR OF CAMPWELL HALL

Submitted to Ms. Terri Halliwell
Director of Residences

Theresa LaPorte
Campwell Resident

If this were the actual proposal, the first page would begin on a new page following the cover page.

Problem

Campwell Hall does not have adequate study areas for its residents. Although there are many places for students to study at Campwell, I will examine each area, then show how it is an unacceptable option. 1

The most common studying place for students is their dorm rooms. Unfortunately, though, many students cannot study in their rooms because noise carries easily through the thin, uninsulated walls. Also, students have different study habits from each other. For example, while one student may need silence, her roommate may need music in order to concentrate. 2

The floor lounges are another alternative. Occasionally, students can study in the floor lounges if the television is turned off and if no other students are taking study breaks. However, most floors have ruled that television watchers have priority in the lounges because other study rooms are available, and lounges are meant for relaxation. Therefore, floor lounges are rarely an option. 3

Another alternative might be the study lounge on the first floor of Campwell, but it is also an unacceptable option for several reasons. It is located in a corner on the ground floor, well beyond the normal flow of traffic. The room is out of both sight and sound ranges to anyone who is not in the study lounge. The west hall is lined by unprotected windows that can be opened enough to allow a fully grown person easily to crawl in or out. Also, to leave this room, one must exit through another empty room. Because of its location and because it is usually empty, this lounge is potentially dangerous at night, and it can be frightening, especially for women who are alone. 4

The final option is the twelfth floor study lounge. This lounge has four small study rooms and one large community study room. Although this 5

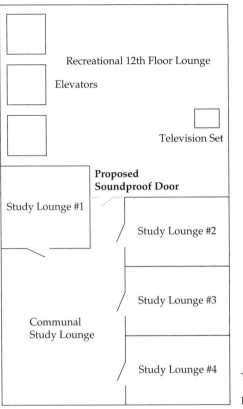

Recreational 12th Floor Lounge

Elevators

Television Set

**Proposed
Soundproof Door**

Study Lounge #1

Study Lounge #2

Study Lounge #3

Communal
Study Lounge

Study Lounge #4

Twelfth Floor Recreational Lounge and Study
Lounge Area

lounge is safe and has many nice features, it is impossible to concentrate in the study lounge because of external noises. The students themselves are usually quiet because they have come to this lounge to study. The problem is that there is no door between the twelfth floor recreational lounge and the study lounge (see diagram).

6   Consequently, frustrated students not only hear twelfth floor residents talking in the recreational lounge, but also elevators dinging, doors opening, and the television blaring. All of these external noises are magnified in a room that is otherwise silent.

7   In an informal survey of ten residents, I found that eight out of the ten thought that the communal study lounge on the twelfth floor was too noisy. Five out of ten students interviewed said that they often tried to study in the lounge, even though it was too noisy. An additional three out of ten students did not use the study lounge because it was so noisy.

Proposed Solution

8   The most practical solution to this problem is to soundproof the twelfth floor study lounge. According to Rick Smith, the Residence Hall Coordinator, building the door is a relatively simple process that could

be completed by a single person. The carpenter would first need to build an insulated wall around the door. Because the doorway is about twelve feet high, this wall would cost approximately $300. Next, the carpenter would put in a solid core door and frame. This would cost about $400 for the door, and $80 for the enclosure around it. The only additional charge would be for labor, which would cost approximately $800. The total proposed cost, therefore, is $1,580.

Justification

    The room cannot be completely soundproofed because the twelfth floor has a false ceiling that is merely plasterboard, but a hard core door and insulated wall would significantly reduce noises that come into the communal study lounge. This action would effectively solve the problem, as the small study rooms are already soundproofed, and no further repairs would be necessary.   9

    Although building a soundproof door would cost the Residence Hall Association of _____ University $1,580, other options which provide acceptable solutions to this problem are far less practical and much more expensive. For instance, the most effective solution would be to insulate and carpet each dorm room to eliminate noises coming from other rooms. This option is impractical because of the tremendous labor and expense. Another possible solution to the problem is to make the ground floor study lounge acceptable to all students by hiring a 24-hour monitor and possibly adding bars to cover the windows. This plan, too, is impractical because of its cost, since the expenses of a monitor for one year alone would exceed the one-time cost of a door. The last solution is to make the twelfth floor study lounge quieter without any remodeling. It would entail closing the twelfth floor lounge, removing the television, and banning conversation from the area. This option, too, is impractical. Twelfth floor residents would resent this decision, no one would be able to enforce the ruling, and the noise from the elevators and hallways would still remain. In comparison, building a soundproof door and wall is the most practical and least expensive choice.   10

    This new door would not only benefit the students who live in Campwell Hall, but it might also make life at _____ University more appealing to potential students. Campwell residents would then have the option of studying in a quiet, yet safe environment in their own hall. More importantly, though, this addition would demonstrate to Campwell residents, as well as potential students, that _____ University takes a serious approach to the academic goals of its students and wants them to get as much out of college and residential life as possible.   11

Thinking Critically About "A Proposal to Create a Quiet Study Lounge"

1. What strategies does Theresa LaPorte use to convince the residence director that a problem exists?
2. What strategies does Theresa use to convince administrators that the proposed solution is practical and cost effective?

3. How does Theresa try to tie her proposal to the values and beliefs of her audience—the director of residences in particular and university administrators in general?
4. If you were Ms. Terri Halliwell, the director of residences to whom this proposal is addressed (see Theresa's letter of transmittal), how effective would you find this proposal? What are its chief strengths and weaknesses?

The next proposal, also by a student writer, is a researched policy argument that addresses the issue of funding for hospices. To appreciate the origins of Sheridan Botts's argument, read her exploratory essay in Chapter 8 (pp. 174–77). The exploratory essay describes how Botts became interested in hospices, how she discovered the issue of funding (fee-for-service versus per diem funding), and how she wrestled to find an appropriate audience and focus for her ideas. The exploratory essay shows the writer struggling with a problem. The proposal argument that follows is the final product that emerged from that struggle. Because Botts imagined her arguments as an op-ed piece in a newspaper, she uses an informal documentation style. She supplied a separate references page to her instructor.

SHERIDAN BOTTS (STUDENT)
SAVING HOSPICES:
A PLEA TO THE INSURANCE INDUSTRY

1   Last fall my brother-in-law Charles lay dying, not in a sterile hospital room but in the warm and familiar surroundings of his own home, cared for by his mother Betty. Although the home care provision of Charles's private insurance paid for his medical expenses, it provided no services for Betty, who was overwhelmed with responsibility and grief. Tending her son hour by hour, Betty became terribly depressed. She had already lost one son and now had to watch another slowly die before her eyes.

2   If Charles's care had come from a hospice agency instead of a home care agency, Betty would have had help. Home care provides at-home clinician visits for nursing services, some social work, and personal attendant care. It is generally directed toward helping the patient get better and is strictly oriented toward the patient, not the family. In contrast, hospice care is holistic, comprehensive, and family centered, addressing the emotional needs of caregivers as well as the patient's medical needs. In Charles's case, hospice care would have provided, in addition to Charles's medical expenses, grief counseling for Betty, chaplain's visits, a variety of volunteer services, and assistance in helping the family make the dying person's last days a time of emotional bonding and support rather than loneliness and isolation.

3   Unfortunately, hospice care may not be available to the public in the future as long as the present system of insurance funding continues. Insurance companies often pay on a fee-for-service basis, meaning that each provided service must be preapproved and reimbursed separately. According to Rodney Smith, a local hospice director, the agency loses $900 per month for each hospice patient served on a fee-for-service basis. Hospices continue to provide services not reimbursed by private insurance

because they are committed to holistic care regardless of the family's ability to pay. However, as the cost of medical care increases, hospices risk insolvency if private insurance companies refuse to reimburse them fairly.

The solution to this problem is for private insurance companies to fund hospices   4
on a per diem rather than fee-for-service basis. With per diem, the patient's insurance pays the hospice for each day of care. Per diem rates are based on the total costs of providing hospice services divided by the total number of patients and days that services are provided. Medicare (the primary insurer of citizens 65 and older) has reimbursed hospices on a per diem basis for many years. This fair system now needs to be adopted by private insurance companies.

Although per diem funding would benefit the general public, insurance companies   5
fight it tooth and nail. Claims representatives from two different insurance companies told me that paying on a per diem basis would be giving hospices blank checks to provide all kinds of unnecessary services.

First, they explained that fee-for-service controls costs by allowing insurance companies to specify in advance which services will be funded and to limit indiscriminant   6
spending. But in actuality per diem payments would not give hospice agencies more money than they need. The per diem rate paid by Medicare averages the costs of care for patients who need few services with patients who need many services. It is true that a per diem rate would give hospices too much money for *some* patients, but also not nearly enough for other patients. Fair rates could be established that provided hospices with average costs.

The second objection to per diem payments raised by insurance companies is their   7
belief that medical insurance should pay only for the medical needs of the insured patient. They say that it is simply beyond the intended scope of medical insurance to pay for nonmedical care or for counseling for the patient's family.

I would say that this objection is based on an outdated view of medicine that treats   8
the patient as an isolated entity rather than as a human being in a network of family. Moreover, this view is shortsighted, since providing nonmedical services to the family can keep the patient at home, where costs are relatively cheap, rather than sending the patient to the hospital.

As an example of how helping the family can save an insurance company money,   9
consider the case of Randy and his daughter Sharon (not their real names) as told to me by a staff member of a local hospice. Randy, 85 years old, was dying of heart and lung disease and wanted to die at home, where Sharon cared for him. Having never been exposed to seriously ill persons, Sharon panicked in emergencies. Fortunately, their hospice provided Sharon with nursing consultation twenty-four hours a day, seven days a week. Several times in the middle of the night, Sharon phoned with terror in her voice. "I think Dad needs to go back to the hospital," she would say. "He's looking really bad." Over the phone the on-call nurse calmed Sharon, helped her figure out the right dose of pain medication, and convinced her that Randy would be better off at home. Moreover, counseling from a social worker helped Sharon accept the process of her father's dying. Without on-call nursing and counseling help—provided by hospice but not paid for by private insurance companies—Sharon would have called 911 during these emergencies and Randy would have been back in the hospital. The insurance company would have been stuck with huge hospital bills and Randy would have died in a strange place attached to tubes and machines.

Luckily for the future of hospices, studies are providing convincing data that per   10
diem reimbursement is cheaper for insurance companies in the long run. According to a 1994 study by Manard and Perrone, private insurance companies who adopted per

diem payments to hospices saved money while increasing benefits. In another study the same year, Mitchell compared hospice and nonhospice patient costs in the last three months of life. The average cost of medical care for hospice patients was $986, compared with $7,731 for nonhospice patients. These cost savings were attributed to the hospice team's teaching the family how to manage the patient at home (a nonmedical cost), providing constant, ongoing support for the family (another nonmedical cost), and providing optimal comfort care for the patient in the home setting. The enormous cost for nonhospice patients was caused by the frequency with which families sent the patient back to the hospital. Still another study, cited by Manard and Perrone, found that the grief counseling and support services offered to family members by hospices led to reduced use of hospital and clinic services.

11   But there is another reason why insurance companies should reimburse hospices equitably: It is the right and just thing to do. The psychological value of hospice care for the terminally ill and their families is undisputed. It is time that insurance companies recognized the value of psychological as well as physical care. There is something wrong with current medical practice when insurance companies will fund without question expensive technological treatments for a dying patient but will quibble at paying grief counseling for the patient's loved ones. Because the general public values hospice care, most private insurance companies in their advertising brochures boast of covering hospice care. But by excluding "nonmedical" services, they actually provide only home care, not hospice. If insurance companies claim they believe in the holistic care of hospices, then they ought to pay for it. If enough insurance customers complain loudly enough, perhaps insurance companies will hear the message.

Thinking Critically About "Saving Hospices"

1. Compare Sheridan Botts's proposal argument with her exploratory essay on pages 174–77. How did she solve the problems she confronted in the exploratory essay? In your view, how effective are these solutions?
2. One of Sheridan's rhetorical problems is that few audiences are inherently interested in technical issues such as fee-for-service versus per diem payments. Moreover, differences between the two forms of payment are hard to explain succinctly. How does Sheridan try to make her proposal interesting? Does she succeed?
3. Another rhetorical problem is how to make the argument appeal to the values of insurance companies. It is easy to see how this proposal could benefit hospices, patients, and patients' families, but since it would increase the direct costs of hospice care for insurance companies, Sheridan must show how it would benefit insurance companies. Does she do so successfully?
4. How persuasive do you find Sheridan's argument? From your perspective, what are the strengths and weaknesses of her proposal?

The following essay is from *The New Republic*, August 19 and 26, 1996. Its author, Richard Weissbourd, writes extensively about education and has published *The Vulnerable Child: What Really Hurts America's Children and What We Can Do About It* (1996).

RICHARD WEISSBOURD

THE FEEL-GOOD TRAP

In the last twenty-five years, self-esteem has become a watchword in American   1
education. Some schools have set up self-esteem classes and days. Others tack posters
to the walls that exhort and praise: "YOU CAN DO ANYTHING," "YOU ARE BEAUTIFUL." The
manifest risibility of this trend has prompted a sneering backlash; *commentary* pages
and Doonesbury panels alike have lampooned the self-esteem movement as a baleful
confluence of 1960s liberal indulgence and soft psychology that distracts from schools'
central mission of teaching the basics. Even Bob Dole exploited the issue as a 1996
campaign plank. He attacked the demise of old-fashioned pedagogical tools such as
spelling bees, ridiculing the notion that "such competitions can only deal a blow to the
self-esteem of those who don't win."

Plenty of liberals as well as conservatives agree that this attention to self-esteem   2
is not just useless but dangerous. Yet the self-esteem movement has at least tried to
deal with serious problems that its critics have ignored. Indeed, the critics' back-to-
basics call to teach just reading and writing will also fail large numbers of children. Instead, educators need to embark on a third path: developing a wide range of intellectual
and social skills in children and creating more sustained relationships between children
and adults. Such a plan is ambitious, to be sure, but, unlike the current solutions, it at
least stands a chance of helping more children prosper in adult life.

The self-esteem movement arose not only out of a national infatuation, beginning   3
in the late 1960s, with the inner life but also as a way to solve a host of problems plagu-
ing children in schools. Poor and black students lagged behind their non-poor and white
peers, it was argued, because racism and classism eroded their self-worth. The issue
was not their ability to learn but their *confidence* in their ability to learn. Raising their
self-esteem would boost achievement. The notion fast became a panacea in some
quarters, and by 1990, a California state task force enshrined "the promotion of self-
esteem" as a central goal of the curriculum, calling it a "social vaccine" that would
inoculate children against academic failure, drug use, welfare dependence, violence,
and other ills. This task force has since become the whipping boy for the self-esteem
critics.

For good reason. Thousands of studies on self-esteem have shown that the tenets   4
of the movement just don't hold up. While there are different definitions of self-esteem
and problems in measuring it, a multitude of studies reach the same conclusions. Programs to raise self-esteem—defined as a positive, global evaluation of the self—are not
raising it. And the very premise that greater self-esteem will boost academic achievement is simply wrong. Self-esteem has little or no impact on academic achievement or
on drug use, violence, or any other serious problems. Violent criminals, studies show,
often have high self-esteem. And black children *already* have levels of self-esteem similar to white children; they take an equally positive view of themselves, but they're less
likely to have a sense of efficacy: they see the outside world as placing obstacles in
their path.

What's going on? For one thing, self-esteem doesn't lead to greater academic   5
achievement unless a child values such achievement—high-school athletes may have
high self-esteem but no interest in school—and it's no secret that large numbers of children don't. Nor should we expect self-esteem to reduce violence or encourage ethical
self-conduct. Self-esteem comes in part from feeling powerful, and playground bullies,

violent gang leaders, and all sorts of other nonacademic achievers can feel powerful. If children grow up in cultures that condone unethical conduct, they may end up feeling good about such conduct.

6   Further, there's a problem with the concept of self-esteem. Though some violent children have high self-esteem, the self that is being esteemed is immature, incapable of empathy, unaware of itself. Many violent children lash out not because of low self-worth but because they are highly prone to shame (that's why so much violence is triggered by acts of disrespect). Even if schools could jack up children's self-esteem, it might not affect their academic competence, their ability to manage humiliation, or their maturity. These are largely separate problems and require largely separate solutions.

7   Even more troubling, the self-esteem movement has often been harmful. Children know when they have really accomplished something and when they haven't, and too much unconditional praise produces not self-confidence but cynicism about adults and doubts about themselves. Talking about children's selves all the time can also teach them to make how they feel about themselves paramount. As developmental psychologist Robert Karen puts it, too much talk about the value of a child's entire being "trains children to think globally, to make their selves the issue in whatever they do, and thus to be prone to both grandiosity and self-contempt."

8   All this advertises for seriously rethinking the entire self-esteem movement. Some of this rethinking has argued that self-esteem is the *result* of academic achievement, not vice versa; others say academic achievement is important for its own sake, regardless of what it does for self-esteem. Both groups argue that schools should be dedicated to academic achievement—in some cases to rudimentary skills. As John Leo writes in *U.S. News and World Report*, "[U]ntil we grapple with the real agenda of the self-esteem movement—ersatz therapeutic massage instead of learning—there will probably be no reform at all."

9   There's no question schools should focus on academic achievement, both for its own sake and because it builds self-esteem in some (though not all) children. While children should be aware of racism and discrimination, no amount of talking about discrimination can substitute for raising non-white children's achievements. And the focus on self-esteem has sometimes, as critics contend, detracted from academics; teachers dumb down curricula, inflate grades, and avoid discussing real academic problems with parents. A special education teacher who works with almost all poor students told me the last thing she wanted was "for a child to fail," so she spent her time providing "a lot of hugs and kisses." It's hard to imagine a greater threat to poor children's learning than this kind of dismal assessment of their capacities.

10   Nonetheless, to harp on academic achievement is irrelevant and insulting to most educators. It simply doesn't answer the questions they struggle with daily. Most teachers care deeply that children learn basic skills. The problem is how to overcome the hurdles that interfere with that learning. Educators know what self-esteem critics don't: Huge numbers of children suffer from social and emotional problems that both shrink their self-esteem and choke their ability to learn. Some children can't concentrate in class, for instance, because they have been abandoned by a parent, or because their violence-wracked neighborhoods deprive them of an elementary sense of control, or because they live with caregivers who are too depressed to be involved in their lives. For all its failings, the self-esteem movement has at least tried to deal with these problems. To talk of academic achievement without addressing these devastating troubles is fantasy for these children.

Further, academic achievement often doesn't boost self-esteem. Many children, girls especially, achieve at high levels yet have little self-esteem. And anyone who believes academic achievement is a royal road to self-esteem should spend time with first-year law students at Harvard, who are disgusted with themselves because they find themselves ranked not at the top but wallowing somewhere in the middle of their classes. 11

Finally, harping on achievement ignores the evidence that both effectiveness in adult life and self-esteem depend on a wide range of intellectual and social competencies. Harvard education professor Howard Gardner had documented many different types of intelligence, including interpersonal skills, that are crucial to success in adult life. Cultivating capacities such as self-awareness, control of one's impulses, and persistence needn't detract from teaching academics. Good teachers build these competencies in the course of academic instruction. Teaching literature can clearly impart all sorts of social and moral lessons. 12

Schools need to forget about self-esteem altogether as an explicit goal. They should instead set high expectations of children, cultivate in them a wide range of competencies, coping strategies, and ethical sensibilities and show them the value of these abilities. Nonwhite children need to be given tools for understanding and responding to discrimination while still meeting high academic expectations. If schools want children to be less violent and more ethical, they should, among other things, provide them with opportunities to give to others, help them to manage their frustration and shame when they feel disrespected, and enable them to see moral issues from multiple points of view. A teacher might, for example, ask a violent child to host a talk show on gun control or create a classroom city government and ask a scapegoated kid to be mayor. 13

To prepare children for adult life schools also need to focus on something else, which neither self-esteem proponents nor critics talk about. Critical qualities that children need to develop for adulthood—persistence, the capacity to handle shame and disappointment, the ability to recognize the needs of others, and to balance them with one's own—cannot be simply transmitted. They are the ingredients of maturity, and this kind of maturity typically develops when children have a certain kind of relationship with adults. 14

The psychoanalyst Heinz Kohut argues that a child's self matures in two ways: by being mirrored by adults and by being esteemed by consistent, admired adults. By "mirroring," Kohut meant that all children need adults who listen to and understand them and regularly reflect their understanding; such reflections develop children's sense of coherence and rightness in the world. Kohut also recognized that at certain stages of development, every child needs adults whom he or she idealizes. Psychologists have long recognized that in adolescence, children get a second chance to internalize the confident expectations of esteemed adults. That chance should not be squandered. 15

To listen and reflect, adults need first to spend more time with children. The self-esteem movement's constant praising of children is a short cut, a desperate substitute for the inability of teachers and other adults to pay sufficient attention to any one child. But time and attention are real to a child in ways that praise is not. Parents, of course, best provide this time and attention, but when parents cannot or do not do so, other adults should. This doesn't entail "babysitting": It means spending a few (or more) hours a week listening to, challenging, and developing the strengths of a child. 16

Schools need to push beyond the academic achievement versus self-esteem debate and embark on a variety of strategies that involve adults more in children's lives. Class sizes need to come down. Schools need to work harder to involve parents, in- 17 cluding absentee fathers, in their children's education. And schools need to keep trying to bring more adults into children's lives who are worthy of esteem by making teaching and other types of work with children more attractive, including through higher status and better pay. Granted, this all amounts to a tall order. Yet these steps, taken together, would be far more meaningful than focusing simply on a nostrum like returning to basics or on a spurious metasolution like self-esteem.

Thinking Critically About "The Feel-Good Trap"

1. Weissbourd spends considerable time in this essay explaining the problem with the self-esteem movement. What does Weissbourd find objectionable about it? Have you encountered this problem in your own educational experience? Do you agree with Weissbourd?
2. What is Weissbourd's proposed solution?
3. Do you think Weissbourd's proposed solution is practical and workable? How persuasive do you find his argument?
4. What audience is Wiessbourd trying to convince and move to action with his proposal?

Our final reading originally appeared as a "My Turn" column in *Newsweek*. When author Brian A. Courtney wrote the article, he was a student majoring in journalism at the University of Tennessee.

BRIAN A. COURTNEY
FREEDOM FROM CHOICE

1   As my friend Denise and I trudged across the University of Tennessee campus to our 9:05 a.m. class, we delivered countless head nods, "Heys" and "How ya' doin's" to other African-Americans we passed along the way. We spoke to people we knew as well as people we didn't know because it's an unwritten rule that black people speak to one another when they pass. But when I stopped to greet and hug one of my female friends, who happens to be white, Denise seemed a little bothered. We continued our walk to class, and Denise expressed concern that I might be coming down with a "fever." "I don't feel sick," I told her. As it turns out, she was referring to "jungle fever," the condition where a black man or woman is attracted to someone of the opposite race.

2   This encounter has not been an uncommon experience for me. That's why the first 21 years of my life have felt like a never-ending tug of war. And quite honestly, I'm not looking forward to being dragged through the mud for the rest of my life. My white friends want me to act one way—white. My African-American friends want me to act another—black. Pleasing them both is nearly impossible and leaves little room to be just me.

3   The politically correct term for someone with my racial background is "biracial" or "multiracial." My mother is fair-skinned with blond hair and blue eyes. My father is dark-complexioned with prominent African-American features and a head of woolly hair.

When you combine the genetic makeup of the two, you get me—golden-brown skin, semi-course hair and a whole mess of freckles.

Someone once told me I was lucky to be biracial because I have the best of both worlds. In some ways this is true. I have a huge family that's filled with diversity and is as colorful as a box of Crayolas. My family is more open to whomever I choose to date, whether that person is black, white, biracial, Asian or whatever. But looking at the big picture, American society makes being biracial feel less like a blessing than a curse.   4

One reason is the American obsession with labeling. We feel the need to label everyone and everything and group them into neatly defined categories. Are you a Republican, a Democrat or an Independent? Are you pro-life or pro-choice? Are you African-American, Caucasian or Native American? Not everyone fits into such classifications. This presents a problem for me and the many biracial people living in the United States. The rest of the population seems more comfortable when we choose to identify with one group. And it pressures us to do so, forcing us to deny half of who we are.   5

Growing up in the small, predominantly white town of Maryville, Tennessee, I attended William Blount High School. I was one of a handful of minority students—a raisin in a box of cornflakes, so to speak. Almost all of my peers, many of whom I've known since grade school, were white. Over the years, they've commented on how different I am from other black people they know. The implication was that I'm better because I'm only *half* black. Acceptance into their world has meant talking as they talk, dressing as they dress and appreciating the same music. To reduce tension and make everyone feel comfortable, I've reacted by ignoring half of my identity and downplaying my ethnicity.   6

My experience at UT has been very similar. This time it's my African-American peers exerting pressure to choose. Some African-Americans on campus say I "talk too white." I dress like the boys in white fraternities. I have too many white friends. In other words, I'm not black enough. I'm a white "wanna-be." The other day, an African-American acquaintance told me I dress "bourgie." This means I dress very white—a pastel-colored polo, a pair of navy chinos and hiking boots. Before I came to terms with this kind of remark, a comment like this would have angered me, and I must admit that I was a little offended. But instead of showing my frustration, I let it ride, and I simply said, "Thank you." Surprised by this response, she said in disbelief, "You mean you agree?"   7

On more occasions than I care to count, black friends have made sweeping derogatory statements about the white race in general. "White people do this, or white people do that." Every time I hear them, I cringe. These comments refer not just to my white friends but to my mother and maternal grandmother as well. Why should I have to shun or hide my white heritage to enhance my ethnicity? Doesn't the fact that I have suffered the same prejudices as every other African-American—and then some—count for something?   8

I do not blame my African-American or white friends for the problems faced by biracial people in America. I blame society for not acknowledging us as a separate race. I am speaking not only for people who, like myself, are half black and half white, but also for those who are half white and half Asian, half white and half Hispanic, or half white and half whatever. Until American society recognizes us as a distinct group, we will continue to be pressured to choose one side of our heritage over the other.   9

Job applications, survey forms, college-entrance exams and the like ask individuals to check only *one* box for race. For most of my life, I have marked BLACK because my skin color is the first thing people notice. However, I could just as honestly have marked WHITE. Somehow when I fill out these forms, I think the employers, administrators, researchers, teachers or whoever sees them will have a problem looking at my   10 face and then accepting a big x by the word WHITE. In any case, checking BLACK or WHITE does not truly represent me. Only in recent years have some private universities added the category of BIRACIAL or MULTIRACIAL to their applications. I've heard that a few states now include these categories on government forms.

11   One of the greatest things parents of biracial children can do is expose them to *both* of their cultures. But what good does this do when in the end society makes us choose? Having a separate category marked BIRACIAL will not magically put an end to the pressure to choose, but it will help people to stop judging us as just black or just white and see us for what we really are—both.

Thinking Critically About "Freedom from Choice"

1. Brian Courtney's proposal spends 90 percent of its space on the problem. Courtney doesn't propose his solution until the next to the last paragraph, and the justification section is really just one sentence—the last sentence of the essay. Why does Courtney decide to spend so much time on the problem section?
2. Do you find his argument effective? Why or why not?

◢ COMPOSING YOUR ESSAY

Generating and Exploring Ideas

If you are having trouble thinking of a proposal topic, try making an idea map of local problems you would like to see solved. For your spokes, consider some of the following starting points:

Problems at your university: dorm, parking, registration system, grading system, campus appearance, clubs, curriculum, intramural program

Problems in your city or town: dangerous intersections, ugly areas, inadequate lighting, a poorly designed store, a shopping center that needs a specific improvement

Problems at your place of work: office design, flow of customer traffic, merchandise display, company policies, customer relations

Problems related to other aspects of your life: hobbies, recreational time, life as a consumer, and so forth

Another approach is to freewrite your response to these trigger statements:

I would really like to solve the problem of _____.

I believe that X should _____. (Substitute for X words such as *my teacher, the president, the school administration, Congress, my boss,* and so forth.)

Note that the problem you pose for this paper can be personal, but shouldn't be private; that is, others should be able to benefit from a solution to your personal problem. For example, your inability to find child care for your daughter is a private problem. But if you focus your proposal on how zoning laws discourage development of in-home day care—and propose a change in those zoning laws to permit more in-home day-care centers—then your proposal will benefit others.

Using Stock Issues to Explore Your Problem

Once you have decided on a proposal issue, explore it by freewriting your responses to the following questions. These questions are often called *stock issues*, since they represent generic, or stock, questions that apply to almost any kind of proposal.

1. Is there a problem here that has to be solved?
2. Will the proposed solution really solve this problem?
3. Can the problem be solved in a simpler way without disturbing the status quo?
4. Is the proposed solution practical enough that it really stands a chance of being implemented?
5. What will be the positive and negative consequences of the proposal?

You might also try freewriting your responses to number 3 (a–k) in the exploratory exercise on page 391. Although these questions cover much the same territory as the stock issues, their different presentation might stimulate additional thought.

Finally, try thinking of justifications for your solution by using the three approaches strategy described earlier in this chapter.

Avoid Presupposing Your Solution in Your Problem Statement

A common mistake of inexperienced proposal writers is to write problem statements that presuppose their solutions. As a restaurant waitperson, suppose you notice that customers want coffee refills faster than servers can provide them. To solve this problem, you propose placing carafes of hot coffee at each table. When describing your problem, don't presuppose your solution: "The problem is that we don't have carafes of hot coffee at the tables." Rather, describe the problematic situation itself: annoyed customers clamoring for coffee and harassed waitpersons trying to bring around refills. Only by giving presence to the original problem can you interest readers in your proposed solution, which readers will compare to other possible approaches (including doing nothing).

Here are some more examples:

Weak: The problem is that our medical office doesn't have an answering machine during closed hours.

Actual Problem: The problem is that (1) we are overwhelmed with calls from patients canceling appointments during the first few hours every morning; (2) employees can't phone in emergency messages early in the morning (illness, car trouble); and (3) because we are on the West Coast, East Coast insurance companies can't communicate with us until after 12:00 p.m. their time.

Weak: Our supermarket doesn't give new employees a location index for store items.

Actual problem: Customers often ask employees where to find an item and are given a bad first impression when a new employee doesn't know the answer; it wastes valuable time when the new employee walks with the customer to find an experienced employee to actually answer the question.

Weak: The Campus Coffee House doesn't stay open late enough at night.

Actual problem: Late-studying students don't have an attractive, convenient place to socialize or study; off-campus coffee houses are too far to walk to at night; dorm lounges aren't attractive and conducive to study; late nighters make noise in the dorms instead of going to a convenient place.

Shaping and Drafting

The following is a typical organizational plan for a proposal argument you might turn to if you get stuck in composing the first draft of your essay.

1. Presentation of a problem that needs solving
   a. Description of the problem (give it presence)
   b. Additional background, including previous attempts to solve the problem
   c. Argument that the problem is solvable (optional)
2. Presentation of the proposed solution
   a. Succinct statement of the proposed solution
   b. Explanation of specifics for the proposed solution
3. Summary and rebuttal of opposing views (in practical proposals, this section is often a summary and rejection of alternative ways of solving the problem)
4. Justification—persuades reader that proposal should be enacted
   a. Reason 1 presented and developed
   b. Reason 2 presented and developed
   c. and so forth
5. Conclusion—exhorts audience to act (sometimes incorporated into the last sentences of the final supporting reason)

Revising

After you have completed your first draft and begun to clarify your argument for yourself, you are ready to start making your argument clear and persuasive for your readers. Use the strategies for clear closed-form prose outlined in Chapter 18. At this stage, feedback from peer readers can be very helpful. Use the following guidelines for peer reviewers.

g u i d e l i n e s

for Peer Reviewers

Instructions for peer reviews, including use of these guidelines, are provided in Chapter 17, pages 429–35. To write a peer review for a classmate, use your own paper, numbering your responses to correspond to the questions on the guidelines. At the head of your paper place the author's name and your own name, as shown.

Author's Name: _____

Peer Reviewer's Name: _____

I. Read the draft at a normal reading speed from beginning to end. As you read, do the following:
   A. Place a wavy line in the margin next to any passages that you find confusing, that contain something that doesn't seem to fit, or that otherwise slow down your reading.
   B. Place a "Good!" in the margin next to any passages where you think the writing is particularly strong or interesting.
II. Read the draft again slowly and answer the following questions by writing brief explanations of your answers.
   A. Introduction and statement of problem:
      1. Does the title effectively focus the paper and pique the reader's interest? How could the title be improved?
      2. How does the writer convince you that a problem exists and that it is significant (worth solving) and solvable? How does the writer give the problem presence? How could the writer improve the presentation of the problem?
   B. Proposed solution:
      1. Does the writer's thesis clearly propose a solution to the problem? Could the thesis be made clearer or more precise?
      2. Does the writer give you enough details about the solution so that you can understand it and see how it works? How could the writer make the solution clearer?
   C. Justification:
      1. In the justification section, does the writer provide strong reasons for acting on the proposal? Are the reasons supported with details and evidence, and do they appeal to the values and beliefs of the audience?
      2. Can you help the writer think of additional justifying arguments (arguments from principle, from consequences, from precedent or analogy)? How could the writer improve support for the proposal?

3. Where does the writer anticipate and address opposing views or alternative solutions? How does the writer convince you that the proposed solution is superior to alternative solutions?
4. Has the writer persuaded you that the benefits of this proposal will outweigh the costs? Who will pay the costs and who will get the benefits? What do you think the gut reaction of a typical decision maker will be to the writer's proposal?
5. Are there other unforeseen costs that the writer should acknowledge and address? Are there unforeseen benefits that the writer could mention?
6. How might the writer improve the structure and clarity of the argument? Where might the writer better apply the principles of clarity from Chapter 18?

D. Sum up what you see as the chief strengths and problem areas in this draft.
1. Strengths
2. Problem areas

III. Read the draft one more time. Place a check in the margin wherever you notice problems in grammar, spelling, or mechanics (one check per problem).

A Guide to Composing and Revising

part THREE

Writing as a Problem-Solving Process

I rewrite as I write. It is hard to tell what is a first draft because it is not determined by time. In one draft, I might cross out three pages, write two, cross out a fourth, rewrite it, and call it a draft. I am constantly *writing and rewriting*. I can only conceptualize so much in my first draft—only so much information can be held in my head at one time; my rewriting efforts are a reflection of how much information I can encompass at one time. There are levels and agenda which I have to attend to in each draft.

—Description of revision by an experienced writer

I read what I have written and I cross out a word and put another word in; a more decent word or a better word. Then if there is somewhere to use a sentence that I have crossed out, I will put it there.*

—Description of revision by an inexperienced writer

Blot out, correct, insert, refine,
Enlarge, diminish, interline;
Be mindful, when invention fails,
To scratch your head, and bite your nails.

—Jonathan Swift

In Part One of this text we focused on writing as a problem-solving process in which writers pose and solve both subject-matter problems and rhetorical problems. Part Three shows you how to translate these basic principles into effective strategies for composing and revising your writing along the continuum from closed to open forms. The four self-contained chapters, which can be read in whatever sequence best fits your instructor's course plan, will help you compose and revise the essays you write for the assignments in Part Two.

This chapter explains how experienced writers use multiple drafts to manage the complexities of writing and suggests ways for you to improve your own writing

*From Nancy Sommers, "Revision Strategies of Student Writers and Experienced Adult Writers," *College Composition and Communication* 31 (October, 1980): 291–300.

processes. Chapter 18, which takes the form of nine self-contained lessons, focuses on key strategies for composing and revising closed-form prose. Chapter 19 switches from closed to open forms, showing you how, when appropriate, to open your prose by creating surprises of style and structure that engage readers and involve them in the process of completing your text's meaning. Finally, Chapter 20 explains how you can improve your writing processes by working in small groups to solve problems, help each other generate ideas, and provide feedback for revision.

◾ UNDERSTANDING HOW EXPERTS COMPOSE AND REVISE

We begin this chapter with a close look at how experienced writers compose, explaining what they think about when they write and why they often need multiple drafts. In Chapter 3 we quoted Peter Elbow's assertion that "meaning is not what you start out with" but "what you end up with." Thus composing is a discovery process. In the early stages of writing, experienced writers typically discover what they are trying to say, often deepening and complicating their ideas rather than clarifying them. Only in the last drafts will such writers be in sufficient control of their ideas to shape them elegantly for readers.

It's important not to overgeneralize, however, because no two writers compose exactly the same way; moreover, the same writer may use different processes for different kinds of prose. Some writers outline their ideas before they write; others need to write extensively before they can outline. Some write their first drafts very slowly, devoting extensive thought and planning to each emerging paragraph; others write first drafts rapidly, to be sure to get all their ideas on paper, and then rework the material part by part. Some prefer to work independently, without discussing or sharing their ideas; others seek out classmates or colleagues to help them hash out ideas and rehearse their arguments before writing them down. Some seek out the stillness of a library or private room; others do their best writing in noisy cafeterias or coffee shops.

The actual mechanics of composing differ from writer to writer as well. Some writers create first drafts directly at a keyboard, whereas others require the reassuring heft of a pen or pencil. Among writers who begin by planning the structure of their work, some make traditional outlines (perhaps using the flexible outline feature on their word processors), whereas others prefer tree diagrams or flowcharts. Some of those who use word processors revise directly at the computer, whereas others print out a hard copy, revise with pen and ink, and then type the changes into the computer.

Also, writers often vary their composing processes from project to project. A writer might complete one project with a single draft and a quick editing job, but produce a half dozen or more drafts for another project.

What experienced writers do have in common is a willingness to keep revising their work until they feel it is ready to go public. They typically work much harder at drafting and revising than do inexperienced writers, taking more runs at their subject. And experienced writers generally make more substantial alter-ations in their drafts during revision. (Compare the first two quotations that open this chapter—one from an experienced and one from an inexperienced writer.) An experienced writer will sometimes throw away a first draft and start over; a be-ginning writer tends to be more satisfied with early drafts and to think of revision as primarily cleaning up errors. Figure 17.1 (on p. 420) shows the first page of a first draft for a magazine article written by an experienced writer.

◤ WHY EXPERIENCED WRITERS REVISE SO EXTENSIVELY

To help you understand the puzzling difference between beginning and ex-perienced writers, let's consider *why* experienced writers revise. If they are such good writers, why don't they get it right the first time? Why so many drafts? To use the language of Part One, experienced writers need multiple drafts to help them pose, pursue, and solve problems—both subject-matter problems and re-lated rhetorical problems. Faced with many choices, experienced writers use mul-tiple drafts to break a complex task into manageable subtasks. Let's look more closely at some of the functions that revising can perform for writers.

Revising to Overcome Limits of Short-Term Memory

A writer's need for multiple drafts results partly from the limitations of mem-ory. Cognitive psychologists have shown that working memory—often called short-term memory—has remarkably little storage space. People use short-term memory to hold the data on which they are actively focusing at any given moment while solving problems, reading texts, writing a draft, or performing other cogni-tive tasks. People also have long-term memories, which can store an almost infi-nite amount of material. The trouble is that much of the material held temporarily in short-term memory never gets transferred to long-term memory. (Try closing this book for a moment and writing out this paragraph from memory.)

You can conceptualize short-term memory as a small tabletop surrounded by filing cabinets (long-term memory). To use the ideas and data you generate while writing a draft, you have to place them on the tabletop, which can hold only a few items at once.* As you generate ideas for your draft, you pile on your tabletop more data than it can hold. You need some means of holding on to your thoughts in process, lest ideas spill off the table and become permanently lost.

---

*A famous study conducted by psychologist George Miller revealed that the average person's short-term memory can hold "seven plus or minus two" chunks of information at a time. When given, say, a thirty-item list of random words or numbers, the average person can remember between five and nine of them. The items will quickly be lost from short-term memory unless the person actively re-hearses them over and over (as when you repeat a new phone number to yourself so that you won't forget it before you write it down).

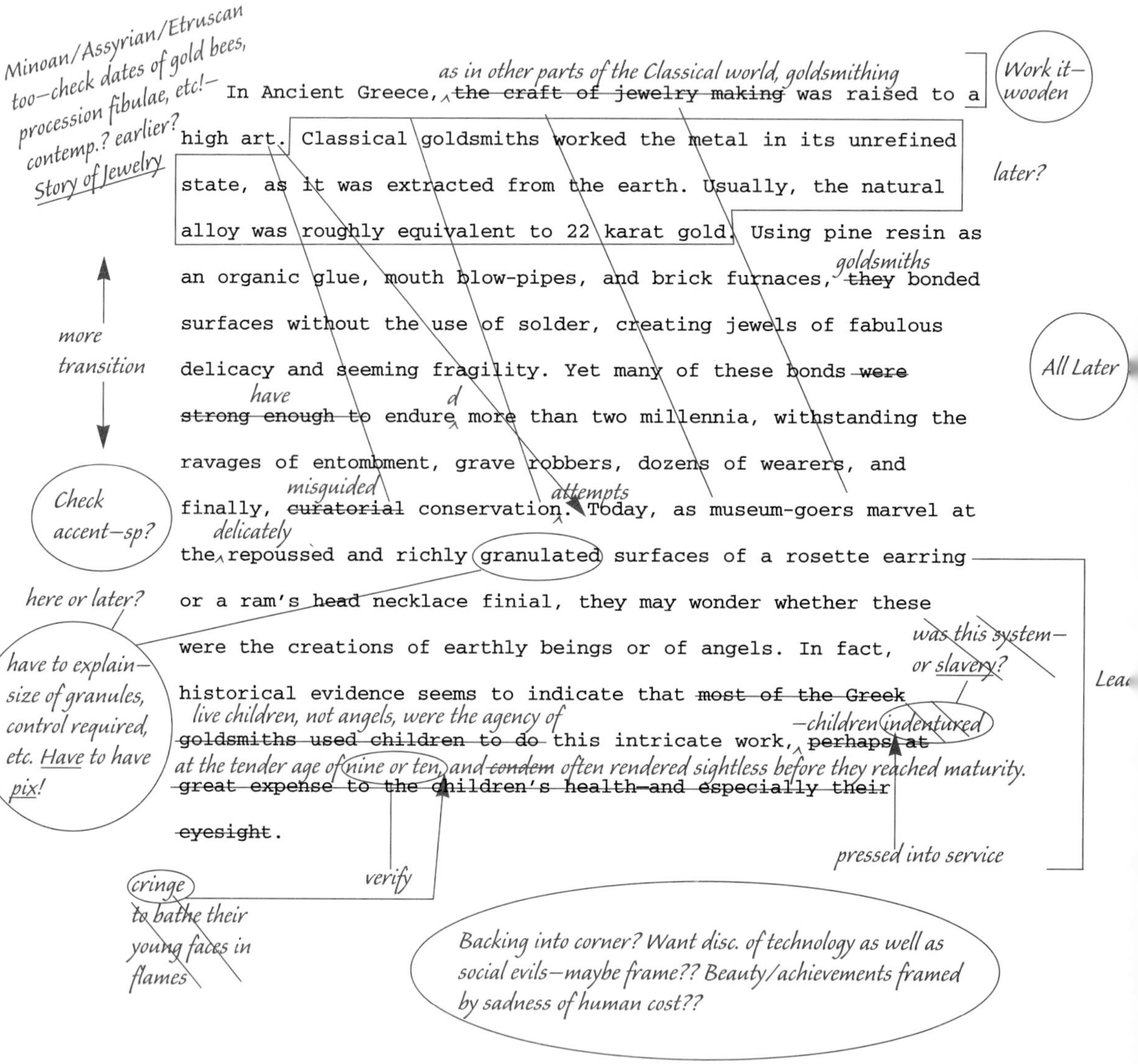

[Handwritten marginal note, top left:] Minoan/Assyrian/Etruscan too—check dates of gold bees, procession fibulae, etc!— contemp.? earlier? Story of Jewelry

[Handwritten marginal note, top right:] Work it— wooden

[Handwritten note:] later?

[Handwritten note, right:] All Later

In Ancient Greece, ^*as in other parts of the Classical world, goldsmithing* ~~the craft of jewelry making~~ was raised to a high art. Classical goldsmiths worked the metal in its unrefined state, as it was extracted from the earth. Usually, the natural alloy was roughly equivalent to 22 karat gold. Using pine resin as an organic glue, mouth blow-pipes, and brick furnaces, *goldsmiths* ~~they~~ bonded surfaces without the use of solder, creating jewels of fabulous delicacy and seeming fragility. Yet many of these bonds ~~were~~ *have* ~~strong enough to~~ endure^*d* more than two millennia, withstanding the ravages of entombment, grave robbers, dozens of wearers, and finally, *misguided* ~~curatorial~~ conservation^*attempts*. Today, as museum-goers marvel at the *delicately* ^repousséd and richly (granulated) surfaces of a rosette earring or a ram's head necklace finial, they may wonder whether these were the creations of earthly beings or of angels. In fact, historical evidence seems to indicate that ~~most of the Greek~~ *live children, not angels, were the agency of* ~~goldsmiths used children to do~~ this intricate work, ~~perhaps at~~ *—children (indentured)* *at the tender age of nine or ten,) and* ~~condem~~ *often rendered sightless before they reached maturity.* ~~great expense to the children's health—and especially their~~ ~~eyesight.~~

[Handwritten marginal notes, left:]
more transition

Check accent—sp?

here or later?

have to explain— size of granules, control required, etc. Have to have pix!

(cringe) to bathe their young faces in flames

verify

[Handwritten notes, right:]
was this system— or slavery?

Lea[...]

pressed into service

[Handwritten note, bottom oval:] Backing into corner? Want disc. of technology as well as social evils—maybe frame?? Beauty/achievements framed by sadness of human cost??

FIGURE 17.1   Draft Page of an Experienced Writer

This analogy illustrates why experienced writers rely on multiple drafts. Because of the limitations of short-term memory, you can actively engage only a few chunks of material at any given moment—a few sentences of a draft or several ideas in an outline. The remaining portions of the evolving essay quickly recede from consciousness without being stored in long-term memory. (Think of your horror when your computer eats your draft or when you accidentally leave your nearly finished term paper on the bus—proof that you can't rely on long-term memory to restore what you wrote.) Writing a draft, however, captures these ideas from short-term memory and stores them on paper. When you reread these stored ideas, you can note problem areas, think of new ideas, see material that doesn't fit, recall additional information, and so forth. You can then begin working on a new draft, focusing on one problem at a time.

What kinds of problems do experienced writers locate in a draft? What triggers further rounds of rewriting? We continue with more reasons why experienced writers revise.

Revising to Accommodate Shifts and Changes in a Writer's Ideas

Early in the writing process, experienced writers often are unsure of what they want to say or where their ideas are leading; they find their ideas shifting and evolving as their drafts progress. Sometimes writing a draft leads the writer to reformulate the initial problem. Just as frequently, the solution that may have seemed exciting at the beginning of the process may seem less satisfactory once it is written out. A writer's ideas deepen or shift under pressure of new insights stimulated by the act of writing. A professional writer's finished product often is radically different from the first draft—not simply in form and style but in actual content.

Revising to Clarify Audience and Purpose

As we noted in Chapter 4, writers need to say something significant to an audience for a purpose. When a writer's sense of audience or purpose shifts, an entire piece may need to be restructured. As they draft, experienced writers pose questions such as these: Who am I picturing as my readers? What is my purpose in writing to them? What effect do I want this piece of writing to have on them? How much background will they need? To which of their values and beliefs should I appeal? What tone and style are appropriate for this audience? What objections will they raise to my argument? In the process of writing, the answers to these questions may evolve so that each new draft reflects a deeper or clearer understanding of audience and purpose.

Revising to Clarify Structure and Create Coherence

Few writers can create detailed outlines before drafting. Those who can, typically set aside their outlines as their drafts take on lives of their own, spilling over the boundaries the writers have laid out. Whereas early drafts usually reflect the order in which writers conceived their ideas, later drafts are often reordered—sometimes radically—in consideration of readers' needs. To help them see their drafts from a reader's perspective, experienced writers regularly put aside those drafts for a time. When they return to a draft, the ideas no longer so familiar, they can more readily see where the material is disjointed, underdeveloped, or irrelevant. Writing teachers sometimes call this transformation a movement from writer-based to reader-based prose.* The lessons in Chapter 18 will help you develop the skills of seeing your drafts from a reader's perspective.

Revising to Improve Gracefulness and Correctness

Finally, writers have to get their grammar right, punctuate effectively, spell correctly, and compose sentences that are concise, clear, graceful, and pleasing to the ear. Late in the revision process, experienced writers focus extensively on these matters. Often this stage of revision involves more than stylistic polishing. Making a single sentence more graceful may entail rewriting surrounding sentences. If an awkward sentence is symptomatic of confused thinking, correcting the sentence may require generating and exploring more ideas.

▨ A WORKING DESCRIPTION OF THE WRITING PROCESS

The writing process we have just described may be considerably different from what you have previously been taught. For many years—before researchers began studying the composing processes of experienced writers—writing teachers typically taught a model something like this:

Old Model of the Writing Process

1. Choose a topic
2. Narrow it
3. Write a thesis
4. Make an outline
5. Write a draft
6. Revise
7. Edit

The major problem with this model is that hardly anyone writes this way. Few experienced writers begin by choosing a topic and then narrowing it—a process that seems passionless, arbitrary, and mechanical. As we explained in Part One, experienced writers begin by looking at the world with a wondering and critical eye; they pose problems and explore ideas; they become dissatisfied with the answers or explanations given by others; they identify questions that impel them to add their own voice to a conversation. Nor is the process neatly linear, as the old model implies. Sometimes writers settle on a thesis early in the writing process. But just as frequently they formulate a thesis during an "Aha!" moment of discovery later in the process, perhaps after several drafts (So *this* is my point! Here is my argument in a nutshell!). Even very late in the process, while checking spelling and

---

*The terms "writer-based" and reader-based" prose come from Linda Flower, "Writer-Based Prose: A Cognitive Basis for Problems in Writing." *College English,* 1979, 41.1, 19–37.

punctuation, experienced writers are apt to think of new ideas, thus triggering more revision.

Rather than dividing the writing process into distinct, sequential steps, let's review the kinds of things experienced writers are likely to do early, midway, and late in the process of writing an essay.

Early in the Process

The activities in which writers engage early in the process are recursive— writing a draft sends the writer back for further exploring, researching, and talking.

Writers Sense a Question or Problem.   Initially, the question or problem may not be well-defined, but the writers sense something unknown about the topic, see it in an unusual way, disagree with someone else's view of it, doubt a theory, note a piece of unexplained data, or otherwise notice something confusing or problematic. In college, the instructor often assigns the problem or question to be addressed. Sometimes, the instructor assigns only a general topic area, leaving writers to find their own questions or problems.

Writers Explore the Problem, Seeking Focus.   The writers gather data from various sources, including readings, laboratory or field research, experience, conversation, and memory. Through exploratory writing and talking, writers analyze, compare, puzzle, and probe, searching for an effective response to the problem. They consider why they are writing, what they want their readers to know about the topic, and how their ideas might surprise the readers, given the readers' background knowledge and point of view. Often writers explore ideas in a journal, research log, Internet chat room, or conversations with colleagues. Writers may also take time off from the problem and do other things, letting ideas cook in the unconscious.

Writers Compose a First Draft.   At some point writers put ideas on paper in a whole or partial draft. Some writers make an informal outline or tree diagram prior to writing. Others discover direction as they write, putting aside concerns about coherence to pursue different branches of ideas. In either case, they don't try to make the draft perfect as they go. One of the major causes of writer's block among less experienced writers is the inability to live with temporary imperfection and confusion. Experienced writers know their first drafts are often times awful, and they lower their expectations accordingly. Writing a first draft often leads writers to discover new ideas, to complicate or refocus the problem, to reimagine audience or purpose, and sometimes to change directions.

Midway Through the Process

Writers Begin to Revise and Reformulate.   Once they have written a first draft, writers are in a better position to view the whole territory and are better able to recognize relationships among the parts. Some writers begin again, selecting insights and perspectives from the first draft and reshaping them into a new draft with a different approach and structure; others keep much of the original draft, but incorporate their newfound perspectives. Writers often find that the conclusion of the first draft is much clearer than its introduction—proof that they discovered and clarified their ideas as they wrote. At this point writers begin a second draft, often by going slowly through the first draft, adding, deleting, reordering, or completely rewriting passages. As writers revise, they ask themselves questions such as, What is my point here? Does this material really fit? What am I really trying to say? To help them see the relationship between the parts and the whole, writers often make new outlines or tree diagrams to clarify the shape of their thinking.

Writers Increasingly Consider the Needs of Readers.   As writers clarify their ideas for themselves, they increasingly focus on their readers' needs. They reorganize material and insert mapping statements, transitions, and cue words to help readers follow their ideas. In particular, they try to write effective introductions to hook readers' attention, explain the problem to be examined, and preview the whole of the essay.

Writers Seek Feedback from Readers.   Midway through the writing process, experienced writers often ask colleagues to read their drafts and offer feedback. They seek readers' responses to such questions as these: Where do you get lost or confused? Where do you disagree with my ideas? Where do I need to put in more evidence or support?

Writers Rewrite in Response to Feedback from Readers.   Readers' responses can often help writers locate confusing spots and better anticipate readers' objections or the need for background. Different readers sometimes respond differently to a draft and offer conflicting advice. Considering the differing responses of multiple readers may allow writers to formulate their own ideas more clearly and may lead to further revisions.

Late in the Process

Writers begin to shift from discovery, shaping, and development to editing. Eventually, the writer's sense of purpose and audience stabilizes and the ideas become increasingly clear, well organized, and developed. At this point writers begin shifting their attention to the craft of writing—getting each word, phrase, sentence, and paragraph just right, so that the prose is clear, graceful, lively, and correct. Even as writers struggle with issues of style and correctness, however, they may discover new meanings and intentions that impel them to rethink parts of the essay.

FOR WRITING AND DISCUSSION

When you write, do you follow a process resembling the one we just described? Have you ever

- had a writing project grow out of your engagement with a problem or question?
- explored ideas by talking with others or by doing exploratory writing?

- made major changes to a draft because you changed your mind or otherwise discovered new ideas?
- revised a draft from a reader's perspective by consciously trying to imagine and respond to a reader's questions, confusions, and other reactions?
- road tested a draft by trying it out on readers and then revising it as a result of what they told you?

Working in groups or as a whole class, share stories about previous writing experiences that match or do not match the description of experienced writers' processes. To the extent that your present process differs, what strategies of experienced writers might you like to try?

▨ IMPROVING YOUR OWN WRITING PROCESSES

The previous section describes the many ways in which experienced writers compose. Although it is difficult for beginning writers simply to duplicate these processes, which evolve from much experience and practice, trial and error, beginning writers can take steps to develop more effective composing habits. Some nuts-and-bolts suggestions for improving your writing processes are given next.

Recognizing Kinds of Changes Typically Made in Drafts

We begin by classifying the kinds of changes writers typically make in drafts and explaining their reasons for making each sort of change.

Kinds of Changes	Reasons for Change
Crossing out whole passage and rewriting from scratch	Original passage was unfocused; ideas have changed.
	New sense of purpose or point meant whole passage needed reshaping.
	Original passage was too confused or jumbled merely to be edited.
Cutting and pasting; moving parts around	Original was disorganized.
	Points weren't connected to particulars.
	Conclusion was clearer than introduction; part of conclusion had to be moved to introduction.
	Rewriting introduction led to discovery of more effective plan of development; new forecasting required different order in body.

Kinds of Changes *(cont.)*	Reasons for Change *(cont.)*
Deletions	Material not needed or irrelevant.
	Deleted material was good but went off on a tangent.
Additions	Supporting particulars needed to be added: examples, facts, illustrations, statistics, evidence (usually added to bodies of paragraphs).
	Points and transitions needed to be supplied (often added to openings of paragraphs).
	New section needed to be added or a brief point expanded.
Recasting of sentences (crossing out and rewriting portions of sentences; combining sentences; rephrasing; starting sentences with a different grammatical structure)	Passage violated old/new contract (see pp. 466–72).
	Passage was wordy or choppy.
	Passage lacked rhythm and voice.
	Grammar was tangled, diction odd, meaning confused.
Editing sentences to correct mistakes	Words were misspelled or mistyped.
	Writer found comma splices, fragments, dangling participles, other grammatical errors.

FOR WRITING AND DISCUSSION

Choose an important paragraph in the body of a draft you are currently working on. Then write out your answers to these questions about that paragraph.

1. Why is this an important paragraph?
2. What is its main point?
3. Where is that main point stated?

Now—as an exercise only—write the main point at the top of a blank sheet of paper, put away your original draft, and, without looking at the original, write a new paragraph with the sole purpose of developing the point you wrote at the top of the page.

When you are finished, compare your new paragraph to the original. What have you learned that might help you revise your original?

Here are some typical responses of writers who have tried this exercise:

I recognized that my original paragraph was unfocused. I couldn't find a main point.

I recognized that my original paragraph was underdeveloped. I had a main point but not enough particulars supporting it.

> I began to see that my draft was scattered and that I had too many short paragraphs.
>
> I recognized that I was making a couple of different points in my original paragraph and that I needed to break it into separate paragraphs.
>
> I recognized that I hadn't stated my main point (or that I buried it in the middle of the paragraph).
>
> I recognized that there was a big difference in style between my two versions and that I had to choose which version I liked best (it's not always the "new" version!).

Practice the Composing Strategies of Experienced Writers

In addition to knowing the kinds of changes writers typically make in drafts, you can improve your composing processes by practicing the strategies used by experienced writers.

Use Expressive Writing for Discovery and Exploration

Use the exploratory strategies described in detail in Chapter 2. Don't let your first draft be the first time you put your ideas into written words. Long before writing a draft, experienced writers typically write extensive notes in the margins of books and articles, explore ideas in journals or research logs, exchange ideas with colleagues on e-mail, and do extensive notetaking, scratch outlining, and idea mapping. Each assignment chapter in Part Two includes exploratory exercises that will help you generate ideas and overcome writer's block.

Talk About Your Ideas; Talk Your Draft

Good writing grows out of good talking. Seek out opportunities to talk about your ideas with classmates or friends. Exchange ideas on topics so that you can appreciate alternative points of view. Whenever possible, talk through your draft with a friend; rehearse your argument in conversation as practice for putting it in writing.

Invent with Research

Depending on your topic, audience, purpose, and genre, you will frequently need to do outside reading and research. In the process of finding new information and exploring the multisided conversation surrounding your subject, you will be deepening your understanding of the topic and reshaping your thinking.

Schedule Your Time

Plan for exploration, drafting, revision, and editing. Don't begin your paper the night before it is due. Talk about your ideas and do exploratory writing before writing a rough draft. Give ideas time to ruminate in your mind. Recognize that your ideas will shift, branch out, even turn around as you write. Allow some time off between writing the first draft and beginning revision. Experienced writers build in time for revision.

Exchange Drafts with Others

Get other people's reactions to your work in exchange for your reactions to theirs. The next section explains procedures for peer review of drafts.

Discover What Methods of Drafting Work Best for You

Some people compose rough drafts directly on a computer; others write longhand. Of those who write longhand, some find that a certain kind of paper or pen best stimulates thought. Different people prefer different surroundings, also. One of the writers of this text works best in a noisy bagel shop or coffeehouse; the other prefers sitting on a sofa with a legal pad in hand. Discover what works best for you.

Revise on Double- or Triple-Spaced Hard Copy

Although some people can revise directly at the computer, research suggests that writers are more apt to make large-scale changes in a draft if they work from hard copy. Double- or triple-space your drafts and write on one side of the page only. Cross out text to be changed and write new text in the blank spaces between the lines. When a draft gets too messy, write revised passages on a separate sheet and tape that sheet to the hard-copy draft. Then, if you are working on a computer, enter your changes into the computer and print out another hard copy for another round of revision.

Save Correctness for Last

To revise productively, concentrate first on the big questions: Do I have good ideas in this draft? Am I responding appropriately to the assignment? Are my ideas adequately organized and developed? Save questions about exact wording, grammar, and mechanics for later. These concerns are important, but they cannot be efficiently attended to until after higher-order concerns are met. Your first goal is to create a thoughtful, richly developed draft.

To Meet Deadlines and Bring the Process to a Close, Learn How to *Satisfice*

Our description of the writing process may seem pretty formidable. Potentially, it seems, you could go on revising forever. How can you ever know when to stop? There's no ready answer to that question, but in our opinion it is much more a psychological than a technical problem. The best advice we can offer is to "satisfice."

Satisficing doesn't require that you be perfectly satisfied with your writing. To *satisfice* is to make it as good as you can under the circumstances—your rhetorical situation, your time constraints, and the pressures of other demands on you. The best advice we can give you for finishing a project is to write a rough draft as early in the process as possible and to allow time for feedback from peers or other readers. Then let the deadline give you the energy for intensive revision. From lawyers preparing briefs for court to engineers developing design proposals, writers have used deadlines to help them put aside doubts and anxieties and to conclude their work, as every writer must. "Okay, it's not perfect, but it's the best I can do" (a good definition of *satisficing*).

◼ USING PEER REVIEWS TO STIMULATE REVISION

One of the best ways to become a better reviser is to see your draft from a *reader's* rather than a writer's perspective. As writer, you know what you mean; you are already inside your own head. But you need to see what your draft is like to someone outside your head.

The best way to learn this skill is to practice reading your classmates' drafts and have them read yours. In this section we offer advice on how to respond candidly to your classmates' drafts and how to participate in peer reviews.

Becoming a Helpful Reader of Classmates' Drafts

When you respond to a writer's draft, learn to make readerly rather than writerly comments; describe your mental experience in trying to understand the draft rather than pointing out problems or errors in the draft. For example, instead of saying, "Your draft is disorganized," say, "I got lost when. . . ." Instead of saying, "This paragraph needs a topic sentence," say, "I had trouble seeing the point of this paragraph."

When you help a writer with a draft, your goal is both to point out where the draft needs more work and to brainstorm with the writer possible ways to improve the draft. Begin by reading the draft all the way through at a normal reading speed. As you read, take mental notes to help focus your feedback. We suggest that you make wavy lines in the margin next to passages that you find confusing; write "Good!" in the margin where you like something; and write "?" in the margin where you want to ask questions.

After you have read the draft, use the following strategies for making helpful responses.

If the ideas in the draft seem thin or undeveloped, or if the draft is too short:

- help the writer brainstorm for more ideas.
- help the writer add more examples, better details, more supporting data or arguments.

If you get confused or lost:

- have the writer talk through ideas to clear up confusing spots.
- help the writer sharpen the thesis: suggest that the writer view the thesis as the answer to a controversial or problematic question; ask the writer to articulate the question that the thesis answers.

- help the writer create an outline, tree diagram, or flow chart (see Chapter 18, pp. 447–49).
- help the writer clarify the focus by asking him or her to complete these statements about purpose:
    My purpose in this paper is _____.
    My purpose in this section (paragraph) is _____.
    Before reading my paper, the reader will have this view of my topic: _____; after reading my paper, my reader will have this different view of my topic: _____.
- show the writer where you get confused or miscued in reading the draft ("I started getting lost here because I couldn't see why you were giving me this information" or "I thought you were going to say X, but then you said Y").

If you can understand the sentences but can't see the point:

- help the writer articulate the meaning by asking "So what?" questions, making the writer bring the point to the surface by stating it directly ("I can understand what you are saying here but I don't quite understand why you are saying it. I read all these facts, and I say 'So what?' What do these facts have to do with your thesis?").

If you disagree with the ideas or think the writer has avoided alternative points of view:

- play devil's advocate to help the writer deepen and complicate ideas.
- show the writer specific places where you had queries or doubts.

FOR WRITING AND DISCUSSION

In the following exercise, we ask you to respond to a student's draft ("Should the University Carpet the Dorm Rooms?," on pp. 431–32). The assignment asked students to take a stand on a local campus issue. Imagine that you have exchanged drafts with this student and that your task is to help this student improve the draft.

Read the draft carefully; make wavy lines in the margins where you get confused, write "Good!" for something you like, and write "?" where you want to ask questions.

On your own, complete the following tasks:

1. Identify one specific place in the draft where you got confused. Freewrite a brief explanation for why you got confused. Make readerly rather than writerly comments.
2. Identify one place in the draft where you think the ideas are thin or need more development.
3. Identify one place where you might write "So what?" in the margins. These are places where you understand the sentences but don't see what the writer is getting at, the point.
4. Identify at least one place where you could play devil's advocate or otherwise object to the writer's ideas. Freewrite your objections.

In groups or as a whole class, share your responses. Then turn to the following tasks:

1. With the instructor serving as a guide, practice explaining to the writer where or how you got confused while reading the draft. Readers often have difficulty explaining their reading experience to a writer. Let several class members role-play being the reader. Practice using language such as "I like the way this draft started because . . ." "I got confused when . . ." "I had to back up and reread when . . ." "I saw your point here, but then I got lost again because . . . ." Writing theorist Peter Elbow calls such language a "movie of your mind."

2. Have several class members role-play being devil's advocates by arguing against the writer's thesis. Where are the ideas thin or weak?

Should the University Carpet the Dorm Rooms?

Tricia, a University student, came home exhausted from her work-study job. She took a blueberry pie from the refrigerator to satisfy her hunger and a tall glass of milk to quench her thirst. While trying to get comfortable on her bed, she tipped her snack over onto the floor. She cleaned the mess, but the blueberry and milk stains on her brand new carpet could not be removed.

Tricia didn't realize how hard it was to clean up stains on a carpet. Luckily this was her own carpet.

A lot of students don't want carpets. Students constantly change rooms. The next person may not want carpet.

Some students say that since they pay to live on campus, the rooms should reflect a comfortable home atmosphere. Carpets will make the dorm more comfortable. The carpet will act as insulation and as a soundproofing system.

Paint stains cannot be removed from carpets. If the university carpets the rooms, the students will lose the privilege they have of painting their rooms any color. This would limit students' self-expression.

The carpets would be an institutional brown or gray. This would be ugly. With tile floors, the students can choose and purchase their own carpets to match their taste. You can't be an individual if you can't decorate your room to fit your personality.

According to Rachel Jones, Assistant Director of Housing Services, the cost will be $300 per room for the carpet and installation. Also the university will have to buy more vacuum cleaners. But will vacuum cleaners be all that is necessary to keep the carpets clean? We'll need shampoo machines too.

What about those stains that won't come off even with a shampoo machine? That's where the student will have to pay damage deposit costs.

There will be many stains on the carpet due to shaving cream fights, food fights, beverage parties, and smoking, all of which can damage the carpets.

Students don't take care of the dorms now. They don't follow the rules of maintaining their rooms. They drill holes into the walls, break mirrors, beds, and closet doors, and leave their food trays all over the floor.

If the university buys carpets our room rates will skyrocket. In conclusion, it is a bad idea for the university to buy carpets.

Conducting a Peer Review Workshop

If you are willing to respond candidly to a classmate's draft—in a readerly rather than a writerly way—you will be a valuable participant in peer review workshops. In a typical workshop, classmates work in groups of two to six to respond to each other's rough drafts and offer suggestions for revisions.* These workshops are most helpful when group members have developed sufficient levels of professionalism and trust to exchange candid responses. A frequent problem in peer review workshops is that classmates try so hard to avoid hurting each other's feelings that they provide vague, meaningless feedback. Saying, "Your paper's great. I really liked it. Maybe you could make it flow a little better" is much less helpful than saying, "Your issue about environmental pollution in the Antarctic is well defined in the first paragraph, but I got lost in the second paragraph when you began discussing penguin coloration."

---

*Chapter 20 discusses additional ways to use groups and strategies to improve the dynamics of groups.

Responsibilities of Peer Reviewers and Writers

Learning to respond conscientiously and carefully to others' work may be the single most important thing you can do to improve your own writing. When you review a classmate's draft, you should prepare as follows:

1. *Understand how experienced writers revise their drafts.*   Prior to reviewing a classmate's draft, review the material in this chapter. Pay particular attention to pages 429–30, which provide general guidelines about what to look for when reading a draft and to pages 425–26, which summarize the kinds of changes writers often make in response to reviews: additions, deletions, reordering, complete refocusing and rewriting, and so forth.

2. *Understand the assignment and the guidelines for peer reviewers.*   For assignments in Part Two of this text, carefully read both the assignment itself and the guidelines for peer reviewers at the end of the chapter in which the assignment appears. These guidelines will help both the writer and you, as peer reviewer, to understand the demands of the assignment and the criteria on which it should be evaluated.

3. *Understand that you are not acting as a teacher.*   A peer reviewer's role is that of a fresh reader. You can help the writer appreciate what it's like to encounter his or her text for the first time. Your primary responsibility is to articulate your understanding of what the writer's words say to you and to identify places where you get confused, where you need more details, where you have doubts or queries, and so on. Although the specific kinds of evaluations called for in the Guidelines for Peer Reviewers will be helpful, you don't need to be an expert who is offering solutions to every problem.

When you play the role of writer during a workshop session, your responsibilities parallel those of your peer reviewers. You need to provide a legible rough draft, preferably typed and double-spaced, which doesn't baffle the reader with illegible handwriting, cross-outs, arrows, and confusing pagination. Your instructor may ask you to bring photocopies of your draft for all group members. During the workshop, your primary responsibility is to *listen*, taking in how others respond to your draft without becoming defensive.

Exchanging Drafts

An excellent method of exchanging drafts is to have each writer read his or her draft aloud while group members follow along in their own photocopies. We value reading drafts aloud when time allows. Reading expressively, with appropriate emphasis, helps writers distance themselves from their work and hear it anew. When you read your work silently to yourself, it's all too easy to patch up bits of broken prose in your head or to slide through confusing passages. But if you stumble over a passage while reading aloud, you can place a check in the margin to indicate where further attention is needed. Another benefit to reading aloud is perhaps more symbolic than pragmatic. Reading your work to others means that you are claiming responsibility for it, displaying your intention to reach a range of readers other than the teacher. And knowing that you will have to read your work aloud will encourage you to have that work in the best possible shape before bringing it to class.

Types of Peer Review Workshops

After you've read your draft aloud, the next stage of your peer review may take one of several forms, depending on your instructor's preference. We describe here three basic strategies: response-centered workshops, advice-centered workshops, and out-of-class reviews. Additional strategies often build on these approaches.

Response-Centered Workshops.   This process-oriented, nonintrusive approach places maximum responsibility on the writer for making decisions about what to change in a draft. After the writer reads the draft aloud, group members follow this procedure.

1. All participants take several minutes to make notes on their copies of the manuscript. We recommend using the "Good!" wavy line, "?" system described in the Guidelines for Peer Reviewers.
2. Group members take turns describing to the writer their responses to the piece—where they agreed or disagreed with the writer's ideas, where they got confused, where they wanted more development, and so forth. Group members do not give advice; they simply describe their own personal response to the draft as written.
3. The writer takes notes during each response but does not enter into a discussion. The writer listens without trying to defend the piece or explain what he or she intended.

No one gives the writer explicit advice. Group members simply describe their reactions to the piece and leave it to the writer to make appropriate changes.

Advice-Centered Workshops.   In this more product-oriented and directive approach, peer reviewers collaborate to give advice to the writer. This method works best if group members use the Guidelines for Peer Reviewers that conclude each chapter in Part Two. For advice-centered reviews, students typically work in pairs, exchanging drafts with each other. But many students prefer the following approach, which allows each class member to collaborate with a partner.

1. The instructor divides the class into groups of four. Each student reads his or her paper aloud to the group. (This step can be omitted if time is limited.)
2. Each group divides into pairs; each pair exchanges drafts with the other pair.
3. The members of each pair collaborate to compose jointly written reviews of the two drafts they have received. These reviews should present the pair's collaborative responses to the questions in the Guidelines for Peer Reviewers in the assignment's chapter.
4. The drafts and the collaboratively written reviews are then returned to the original writers. If time remains, the two pairs meet jointly to discuss their reviews.

Since advice-centered reviews take longer than response-centered reviews, the instructor may ask writers to supply copies of their drafts to their peer reviewers at the class meeting prior to the workshop. The reviewers can read the drafts carefully and come to the review session with critiques already in mind. When two students work together to share observations about a draft, they often produce more useful and insightful reviews than when working alone.

Out-of-Class Peer Reviews

A variation on the advice-centered approach can be used for out-of-class reviews.

1. The instructor divides the class into pairs; each pair exchanges drafts with another pair.
2. Each pair meets outside class to write its collaborative review based on the Guidelines for Peer Reviewers. Then pairs exchange their reviews the next day in class.

This method allows reviewers to spend as long as they need on their reviews without feeling rushed by in-class time constraints.

Responding to Peer Reviews

After you and your classmates have gone over each others' papers and walked each other through the responses, everyone should identify two or three things about his or her draft that particularly need work. Before you leave the session, you should have some notion about how you want to revise your paper.

You may get mixed or contradictory responses from different reviewers. One reviewer may praise a passage that another finds confusing or illogical. Conflicting advice is a frustrating fact of life for all writers, whether students or professionals. Such disagreements reveal how readers cocreate a text with a writer: each brings to the text a different background, set of values, and way of reading.

It is important to remember that you are in charge of your own writing. If several readers offer the same critique of a passage, then no matter how much you love that passage, you probably need to follow their advice. But when readers disagree, you have to make your own best judgment about whom to heed. In our own writing—including the writing of this text—we tend to follow the advice that is presented to us most fully and rationally. We value most a well-explained sense of the reader's difficulty, an explanation of what causes the problem, and a specific suggestion about how to solve it.

Once you have received advice from others, sit down alone and reread your draft again slowly, "re-visioning" it in light of that feedback. Note especially how different readers responded to different sections of the draft. Then, based on your own responses as well as theirs, develop a revision plan, allowing yourself time to make sweeping, global changes if needed. You also need to remember that you can never make your draft perfect. Plan when you will bring the process to a close so that you can turn in a finished product on time and get on with your other classes and your life (see our advice on *satisficing* on pp. 428–29).

◪ CHAPTER SUMMARY

This chapter has focused on the writing processes of experts, showing how experienced writers use multiple drafts to solve subject matter and rhetorical problems. We have also offered advice on how to improve your own writing processes. Particularly, beginning college writers need to understand the kinds of changes writers typically make in drafts, to role-play a reader's perspective when they revise, and to practice the revision strategies of experts. Because peer reviewing is a powerful strategy for learning how to revise, we showed you how to make "readerly" rather than "writerly" comments on a rough draft and how to participate productively in peer review workshops.

Nine Lessons in Composing and Revising Closed-Form Prose

[Form is] an arousing and fulfillment of desires. A work has form insofar as one part of it leads a reader to anticipate another part, to be gratified by the sequence.

—Kenneth Burke, *Rhetorician*

I think the writer ought to help the reader as much as he can without damaging what he wants to say; and I don't think it ever hurts the writer to sort of stand back now and then and look at his stuff as if he were reading it instead of writing it.

—James Jones, *Writer*

Chapter 17 explained the composing processes of experienced writers and suggested ways that you could improve your own writing processes. In this chapter we present nine lessons in composing and revising closed-form prose. This chapter is not intended to be read in one sitting, lest you suffer from information overload. To help you cover the material efficiently, we have made each lesson a self-contained unit that can be read comfortably in a half-hour or less and discussed in class as part of a day's session. You will benefit most from these lessons if you return to them periodically as you progress through the term because their advice becomes increasingly meaningful and relevant as you gain experience as a writer.

The first lesson—on reader expectations—is intended as an overview to the rest of the chapter. The remaining eight lessons can then be assigned and read in any order your instructor desires. You will learn how to think like a reader (Lesson 1); how to convert loose structures into thesis/support structures (Lesson 2); how to use expert strategies for planning and developing your argument (Lessons 3 and 4); how to use point sentences, transitions, and other strategies to guide your readers through the twists and turns of your prose (Lessons 5, 6, and 7); and how to write effective introductions and conclusions (Lessons 8 and 9). Together the lessons will teach you strategies for making your closed-form prose friendly to readers, well structured, clear, and persuasive.

▶ LESSON 1: UNDERSTANDING READER EXPECTATIONS

In this opening lesson, we show you how to think like a reader. Imagine for a moment that your readers have only so much *reader energy*, which they can use either to follow and respond to your ideas (the result you want) or to puzzle over what you are trying to say (the result you don't want).* Skilled readers make predictions about where a text is heading based on clues provided by the writer. When readers get lost, the writer has often failed to give clues about where the text is going or has failed to do what the reader predicted. "Whoa, you lost me on the turn," a reader might say. "How does this passage relate to what you just said?" To write effective closed-form prose, you need to help readers see how each part of your text is related to what came before. (Sometimes with open-form prose, surprise or puzzlement may be the very effect you want to create. But with closed-form prose this kind of puzzlement is fatal.)

In this lesson we explain what readers of closed form prose need in order to predict where a text is heading. Specifically we will show you that readers need three things in a closed-form text:

- They need unity and coherence.
- They need old information before new information.
- They need forecasting and fulfillment.

Let's look at each in turn.

Unity and Coherence

Together the terms *unity* and *coherence* are defining characteristics of closed-form prose. *Unity* refers to the relationship between each part of an essay and the larger whole. *Coherence* refers to the relationship between adjacent sentences, paragraphs, and parts. The following thought exercise will illustrate your own expectations for unity and coherence:

Thought Exercise 1

Read the following two passages and try to explain why each fails to satisfy your expectations as a reader:

A. Recent research has given us much deeper—and more surprising—insights into the father's role in childrearing. My family is typical of the east side in that we never had much money. Their tongues became black and hung out of their

---

*For the useful term *reader energy,* we are indebted to "The Science of Scientific Writing" by George Gopen and Judith Swan, *American Scientist* 78 (1990): 550–559. In addition, much of our discussion of writing in this chapter is indebted to the work of Joseph Williams, George Gopen, and Gregory Colomb. See especially Gregory G. Colomb and Joseph M. Williams, "Perceiving Structure in Professional Prose: A Multiply Determined Experience," in *Writing in Nonacademic Settings,* eds. Lee Odell and Dixie Goswamie (New York: The Guilford Press, 1985), pp. 87–128.

mouths. The back-to-basics movement got a lot of press, fueled as it was by fears of growing illiteracy and cultural demise.

B. Recent research has given us much deeper—and more surprising—insights into the father's role in childrearing. Childrearing is a complex process that is frequently investigated by psychologists. Psychologists have also investigated sleep patterns and dreams. When we are dreaming, psychologists have shown, we are often reviewing recent events in our lives.

If you are like most readers, Passage A comically frustrates your expectations because it is a string of random sentences. Because the sentences don't relate either to each other or to a larger point, Passage A is neither unified nor coherent.

Passage B frustrates expectations in a subtler way. If you aren't paying attention, Passage B may seem to make sense because each sentence is linked to the one before it. But the individual sentences don't develop a larger whole; the topics keep switching from a father's role in childrearing to psychology to sleep patterns to the function of dreams.

To fill a reader's expectations, then, a closed-form passage must be both unified and coherent:

C (Unified and coherent). Recent research has given us much deeper—and more surprising—insights into the father's role in childrearing. It shows that in almost all of their interactions with children, fathers do things a little differently from mothers. What fathers do—their special parenting style—is not only highly complementary to what mothers do but is by all indications important in its own right. [The passage continues by showing the special ways that fathers contribute to childrearing.]

This passage makes a unified point—that fathers have an important role in childrearing. Because all the parts relate to that whole (unity) and because the connections from sentence to sentence are clear (coherence), the passage satisfies our expectations: It makes sense.

Because achieving unity and coherence is a major goal in revising closed-form prose, we'll refer frequently to these concepts in later lessons.

Old Before New

One dominant way that readers process information and register ideas is by moving from already known (old) information to new information. In a nutshell, this concept means that new material is meaningful to a reader only if it is linked to old material that is already meaningful. To illustrate this concept, consider the arrangement of names and numbers in a telephone directory. Because we read from left to right, we want people's names in the left column and the telephone numbers in the right column. A person's name is the old, familiar information we already know and the number is the new, unknown information that we seek. If the numbers were in the left column and the names in the right, we would have to read backwards.

You can see the same old-before-new principle at work in the following thought exercise:

Thought Exercise 2

You are a passenger on an airplane flight into Chicago and need to transfer to Flight 29 to Atlanta. As you descend into Chicago, the flight attendant announces transfer gates. Which of the following formats is easier for you to process? Why?

Option A		Option B	
To Memphis on Flight 16	Gate B20	Gate B20	Flight 16 to Memphis
To Dallas on Flight 35	Gate C25	Gate C25	Flight 35 to Dallas
To Atlanta on Flight 29	Gate C12	Gate C12	Flight 29 to Atlanta

If you are like most readers, you will prefer Option A, which puts old information before new. In this case, the old/known information is our destination and perhaps our flight number (To Atlanta on Flight 29). The new/unknown information is Gate C12. Option B causes us to expend more energy than does Option A because it forces us to hold the number of each gate in memory until we hear its corresponding city and flight number. Whereas Option A allows us to relax until we hear the word "Atlanta," Option B forces us to concentrate intensely on each gate number until we find the meaningful one.

The principle of old before new has great explanatory power for writers. At the level of the whole essay, this principle helps writers establish the main structural frame and ordering principle of their argument. An argument's frame derives from the writer's purpose to change some aspect of the reader's view of the topic (see Chapter 3). The reader's original view of the topic—what we might call the common, expected, or ordinary view—constitutes old/known/familiar material. The writer's surprising view constitutes the new/unknown/unfamiliar material. The writer's hope is to move readers from their original view to the writer's new and different view. By asking what constitutes old/familiar information to readers, the writer can determine how much background to provide, how to anticipate readers' objections, and how to structure material by moving from the old to the new. We discuss these matters in more depth in Lesson 8, on writing effective introductions.

At the sentence level, the principle of old before new also helps writers create coherence between adjacent parts and sentences. Most sentences in an essay should contain both an old element and a new element. To create coherence, the writer begins with the old material, linking back to something earlier, and then puts the new material at the end of the sentence. (See the discussion of the old/new contract in Lesson 7.)

Forecasting and Fulfillment

Finally, readers of closed-form prose expect writers to forecast what is coming and then to fulfill those forecasts. To appreciate what we mean by forecasting and fulfillment, try one more thought exercise:

Thought Exercise 3

Although the following paragraph describes a simple procedure in easy-to-follow sentences, most readers still scratch their heads in bewilderment. Why? What makes the passage difficult to understand?

> The procedure is actually quite simple. First, you arrange things into different groups. Of course, one pile may be sufficient depending on how much there is to do. If you have to go somewhere else due to lack of facilities, that is the next step; otherwise, you are pretty well set. Next you operate the machines according to the instructions. After the procedure is completed, one arranges the materials into different groups again. Then they can be put in their appropriate places. Eventually, they will be used once more and the whole cycle will have to be repeated. However, that is part of life.

Most readers report being puzzled about the paragraph's topic. Because the opening sentence doesn't provide enough context to tell them what to expect, the paragraph makes no forecasts that can be fulfilled. Now try rereading the paragraph, but this time substitute the following opening sentence:

> The procedure for washing clothes is actually quite simple.

With the addition of "for washing clothes," the sentence provides a context that allows you to predict and understand what's coming. In the language of cognitive psychologists, this new opening sentence provides a schema for interpretation. A *schema* is the reader's mental picture of a structure for upcoming material. The new opening sentence allows you as reader to say mentally, "This paragraph will describe a procedure for washing clothes and argue that it is simple." When the schema proves accurate, you experience the pleasure of prediction and fulfillment. In the language of rhetorician Kenneth Burke, the reader's experience of form is "an arousing and fulfillment of desire."

What readers expect from a closed-form text, then, is an ability to predict what is coming and regular fulfillment of those predictions. Writers forecast what is coming in a variety of ways: through titles and thesis statements; through point sentences at the heads of sections and paragraphs; through transitions and mapping passages; and so forth. To meet their readers' needs for predictions and fulfillment, closed-form writers start and end with the big picture. They tell readers where they are going before they start the journey, they refer to this big picture at key transition points, and they refocus on the big picture in their conclusion.

Summary

In this lesson we explained that to think like a reader you need to understand a reader's needs and expectations. The three needs we explained—unity and coherence, old before new, and forecasting and fulfillment—all work together when a reader construes meaning from a text. Your knowledge of these expectations will give you a theoretical basis for understanding the practical advice in the lessons that follow.

◪ LESSON 2: CONVERTING LOOSE STRUCTURES INTO THESIS/SUPPORT STRUCTURES

In Lesson 1 we described readers' expectations for unity and coherence, old information before new, and forecasting and fulfillment. In academic contexts, readers also expect closed-form prose to have a thesis/support structure. As we explained in Chapter 3, closed-form academic writing is governed by a thesis statement, which needs to be contestable and surprising. Because developing and supporting a risky thesis is complex work, requiring much critical thought, writers sometimes retreat into loose structures that are easier to compose than a thesis-based argument with points and particulars.

In this lesson we help you better understand thesis-based writing by contrasting it with prose that looks like thesis-based writing but isn't. We show you three common ways in which inexperienced writers give the appearance of writing thesis-based prose while actually retreating from the rigors of making and developing an argument. Avoiding the pitfalls of these loose structures can go a long way toward improving your performance on most college writing assignments.

And Then Writing, or Chronological Structure

Chronological structure, often called *narrative,* is the most common organizing principle of open-form prose. It may also be used selectively in closed-form prose to support a point. But sometimes the writer begins recounting the details of a story until chronological order takes over, driving out the thesis-based structure of points and particulars.

To a large degree, chronological order is the default mode we fall into when we aren't sure how to organize material. For example, if you were asked to analyze a fictional character, you might slip into a plot summary instead. In much the same way, you might substitute historical chronology ("First A happened, then B happened . . .") for historical analysis ("B happened because A happened . . ."); or you might give a chronological recounting of your research ("First I discovered A, then I discovered B . . .") instead of organizing your material into an argument ("I question A's account of this phenomenon on the grounds of B's recent findings . . .").

The tendency toward loose chronological structure is revealed in the following example from a student's essay on Shakespeare's *The Tempest.* This excerpt is from the introduction of the student's first draft:

Plot Summary—*And Then* Writing

Prospero cares deeply for his daughter. In the middle of the play Prospero acts like a gruff father and makes Ferdinand carry logs in order to test his love for Miranda and Miranda's love for him. In the end, though, Prospero is a loving father who rejoices in his daughter's marriage to a good man.

Here the student seems simply to retell the play's plot without any apparent thesis. (The body of her rough draft primarily retold the same story in more detail.) However, during an office conference, the instructor discovered that the student regarded her sentence about Prospero's being a loving father as her thesis. In fact, the student had gotten in an argument with a classmate over whether Prospero was a good person or an evil one. The instructor helped her convert her draft into a thesis/support structure:

Revised Introduction—Thesis/Support Structure

> Many persons believe that Prospero is an evil person in the play. They claim that Prospero exhibits a harsh, destructive control over Miranda and also, like Faust, seeks superhuman knowledge through his magic. However, I contend that Prospero is a kind and loving father.

This revised version implies a problem (What kind of father is Prospero?), imagines a view that the writer wishes to change (Prospero is harsh and hateful), and asserts a contestable thesis (Prospero is a loving father). The body of her paper can now be converted from plot summary to an argument with reasons and evidence supporting her claim that Prospero is loving.

This student's revision from an *and then* to a thesis/support structure is typical of many writers' experience. Because recounting events chronologically is a natural way to organize, many writers—even very experienced ones—lapse into long stretches of *and then* writing in their rough drafts. In fact, researchers have shown that chronological thinking is a normal strategy for retrieving ideas and details from the writer's long-term memory. But experienced writers have learned to recognize these *and then* sections in their drafts and to rework this material into a closed-form, thesis-based structure.

All About Writing, or Encyclopedic Structure

Whereas *and then* writing turns essays into stories by organizing details chronologically, *all about* writing turns essays into encyclopedia articles by piling up details in heaps. When *all about* writing organizes these heaps into categories, it can appear to be well organized: "Having told you everything I learned about educational opportunities in Cleveland, I will now tell you everything I learned about the Rock and Roll Hall of Fame." But the categories do not function as points and particulars in support of a thesis. Rather, like the shelving system in a library, they are simply ways of arranging information for convenient retrieval, not a means of building a hierarchical structure.

If you've ever paraphrased an encyclopedia for a report on "earthquakes" or "North Dakota," you'll know what we mean by *all about* writing. Because such reports don't require a contestable thesis, they invite you simply to crank out information.

To illustrate the differences between *all about* writing and thesis-based writing, consider the case of two students asked to write term papers on the subject of, for example, female police officers. One student is asked simply to write "all about" the topic; the other is asked to pose and investigate some problem related to female police officers and to support a thesis addressing that problem. In all likelihood, the first student would produce an initial outline with headings such as the following:

I. History of women in police roles
  A. female police or soldiers in ancient times

    B. 19th century (Calamity Jane)
    C. 1900s–1960
    D. 1960–present
  II. How female police officers are selected and trained
 III. A typical day in the life of a female police officer
 IV. Achievements and acts of heroism of female police officers
  V. What the future holds for female police officers

Such a paper is a data dump that places into categories all the information the writer has uncovered. It is riskless, and, except for occasional new information, surpriseless. In contrast, when a student focuses on a significant question—one that grows out of the writer's own interests and demands engagement—the writing can be quite compelling.

Consider the case of a student, Lynnea, who wrote a research paper entitled "Women Police Officers: Should Size and Strength Be Criteria for Patrol Duty?" Her essay begins with a group of male police officers complaining about being assigned to patrol duty with a new female officer, Connie Jones (not her real name), who is four feet ten inches tall and weighs ninety pounds. Here is the rest of the introduction to Lynnea's essay.

> Connie Jones has just completed police academy training and has been assigned to patrol duty in _____. Because she is so small, she has to have a booster seat in her patrol car and has been given a special gun, since she can barely manage to pull the trigger of a standard police-issue .38 revolver. Although she passed the physical requirements at the academy, which involved speed and endurance running, situps, and monkey bar tests, most of the officers in her department doubt her ability to perform competently as a patrol officer. But nevertheless she is on patrol because men and women receive equal assignments in most of today's police forces. But is this a good policy? Can a person who is significantly smaller and weaker than her peers make an effective patrol officer?

Lynnea examined all the evidence she could find—through library and field research (interviewing police officers) and arrived at the following thesis: "Because concern for public safety overrides all other concerns, police departments should set stringent size and strength requirements for patrol officers, even if these criteria exclude many women." This thesis has plenty of tension because it sets limits on equal rights for women. Because Lynnea considers herself a feminist, it caused her considerable distress to advocate setting these limits and placing public safety ahead of gender equity. The resulting essay is engaging precisely because of the tension it creates and the controversy it engenders.

Engfish Writing, or Structure Without Surprise

Unlike the chronological story and the *all about* paper, the *engfish* essay has a thesis.* But the thesis is a riskless truism supported with predictable reasons—

---

*The term *engfish* was coined by the textbook writer Ken Macrorie to describe a fishy kind of canned prose that bright but bored students mechanically produce to please their writing teachers. See *Telling Writing* (Rochelle Park, NJ: Hayden Press, 1970).

often structured as three supports in a traditional five-paragraph theme. It is fill-in-the-blanks writing: "The food service is bad for three reasons. First, it is bad because the food is not tasty. Blah, blah, blah about tasteless food. Second, it is bad because it is too expensive. Blah, blah, blah about the expense." And so on. The writer is on autopilot and is not contributing to a real conversation about a real question. In some situations, writers use engfish intentionally: bureaucrats and politicians may want to avoid saying something risky; students may want to avoid writing about complex matters that they fear they do not fully understand. In the end, using engfish is bad not because what you say is *wrong;* it's because what you say couldn't *possibly be* wrong. To avoid engfish, stay focused on the need to surprise your reader.

Summary

This lesson has explained strategies for converting *and then, all about,* and engfish writing into thesis/support writing. Your goal as a closed-form academic writer is to pose a problematic question about your topic and, in response to it, assert a contestable thesis that you must support with points and particulars.

FOR WRITING AND DISCUSSION

As a class, choose a topic from popular culture such as TV talk shows, tattooing, eating disorders, rock lyrics, or something similar.

1. Working as a whole class or in small groups, give examples of how you might write about this topic in an *and then* way, an *all about* way, and an engfish way.
2. Then develop one or more questions about the topic that could lead to thesis/support writing. What contestable theses can your class create?

▨ LESSON 3: PLANNING AND VISUALIZING YOUR STRUCTURE

We have explained so far how closed-form writing supports a contestable thesis through a hierarchical network of points and particulars. One way to visualize this structure is to outline its skeleton, as we did in Chapter 3 for an argument about a hypothetical college administration that did not care for its students (see p. 48). As the outline makes visually clear, not all points are on equal levels. The highest level point is an essay's thesis statement, which is usually supported by several main points that are in turn supported by subpoints and subsubpoints, all of which are supported by their own particulars. In this lesson we want to show you how to create such a hierarchical structure for your own papers and how to visualize this structure through an outline, tree diagram, or flow chart.

At the outset, we want to highlight two important points. First, think of your structural diagrams as flexible planning devices that evolve as your thinking shifts and changes. The outline of your final draft may be substantially different from your initial and intermediate structural sketches. In fact, we want to show you how to use your outlines or diagrams to help you generate more ideas and reshape your structure.

Second, note that in all our examples of outlines, diagrams, and flowcharts we write *complete sentences* in the high-level slots. We do so because the writer's task is to organize *meanings* rather than topics. Any point—whether a thesis, a main point, or a subpoint—is a contestable assertion that requires its own particulars for support. By using complete sentences rather than topic phrases, the writer is forced to articulate the point of each section of the emerging argument. (We'll have more to say on the value of sentences over phrases later in this lesson.)

With this background, we now proceed to a sequence of stages you can use to plan and visualize a structure.

Articulate the Change You Want to Make in Your Audience's View of Your Subject

Through exploratory writing and talking, you begin to see how your view of a subject differs from that of your imagined audience. You are then ready to plan out the outer frame or "big picture" of your argument. As a planning strategy, we suggest that you write out answers to the following prompts:

1. Before reading my paper, my readers will think this about (my topic):
2. But after reading my paper, my readers will think this about (my topic):
3. The purpose of my paper is: [finish this sentence]
4. The question my paper addresses is:

Here is how one student, Dao (whose Vietnamese heritage will become relevant in later lessons), answered these questions:

1. Before reading my paper my readers will believe that euthanasia is often justified, particularly if someone is elderly and suffering and has no good quality of life.
2. But after reading my paper my readers will believe that euthanasia is wrong.
3. The purpose of my paper is to show that euthanasia cannot be justified.
4. Is euthanasia right or wrong?

Articulate a Working Thesis and Main Points

Once you have articulated your purpose and the kind of change you want to bring about in your audience, you are ready to compose a working thesis statement and develop your main supporting points. This isn't a neatly linear process; often you have to write one or more rough drafts aimed primarily at exploring ideas before you are finally clear about your thesis. But once you have a thesis, you need to visualize a structure of supporting ideas arranged in sections (steps, stages, pieces, paragraphs, parts), each of which is headed by a main point. Try answering these questions:

4. *My working thesis (claim) is:*
5. *My main supporting points are:*

Here are Dao's answers to these questions:

4. Despite my classmate Martha's arguments for legalizing euthanasia, it is wrong.
5. (a) It primarily benefits survivors; (b) it has bad consequences; (c) it doesn't recognize the good aspects of suffering.

Sketch Your Structure Using an Outline, Tree Diagram, or Flowchart

At this point you can make an initial structural sketch of your argument and use the sketch to plan out the subpoints and particulars that will be necessary to support the main points. We offer you three different ways to visualize your argument: outlines, tree diagrams, and flowcharts. Use whichever strategy best fits your way of thinking and perceiving.

Outlines

The most common way of visualizing structure is the traditional outline, which uses letters and numerals to indicate levels of points, subpoints, and particulars. If you prefer outlines, we recommend that you use the outliner feature of a modern word processing program, which allows you to move and insert material and change heading levels with great flexibility. Here is an outline of Dao's argument:

Thesis: Despite Martha's strong argument for legalizing euthanasia, euthanasia is wrong for several reasons.

I. First, I object to euthanasia because it benefits survivors more than the sick person.
   A. Pain can be controlled by modern drugs so sick people don't have to suffer.
   B. Euthanasia most benefits survivors because it saves them worry and money.
II. Second, I oppose euthanasia because of its unfavorable consequences.
   A. Euthanasia would tempt people to murder for inheritance.
   B. Euthanasia would lead to discrimination against those with "unpopular diseases," such as AIDS.
III. Third, I oppose euthanasia because it fails to see the value in suffering (supported by example of my grandmother's caring for my crippled uncle in Vietnam).

Tree Diagrams

A tree diagram displays a hierarchical structure visually, using horizontal and vertical space instead of letters and numbers. Figure 18.1 shows Dao's argument as a tree diagram. Her introduction is at the top of the tree, above the thesis. Her main reasons, written as point sentences, appear as branches beneath her claim. Supporting evidence and arguments are displayed as subbranches beneath each reason.

Unlike outlines, tree diagrams allow us to *see* the hierarchical relationship of points and particulars. When you develop a point with subpoints or particulars, you move down the tree. When you switch to a new point, you move across the tree to make a new branch. Our own teaching experience suggests that for many writers this visual/spatial technique, which engages more areas of the brain than the more purely verbal outline, produces fuller, more detailed, and more logical arguments than does a traditional outline.

Flowcharts

Many writers prefer an informal, hand-sketched flowchart as an alternative to an outline or tree diagram. The flowchart sketches out the sequence of sections as separate boxes, inside which (or next to which) the writer notes the material needed to fill each box. A flowchart of Dao's essay is shown in Figure 18.2.

FIGURE 18.1   Dao's Tree Diagram

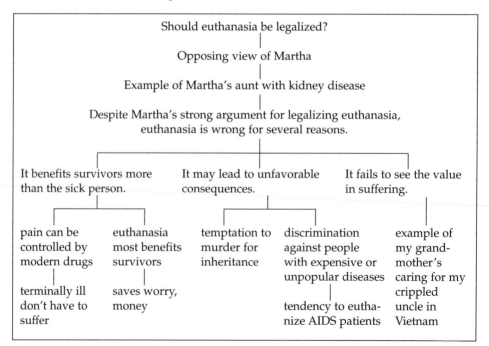

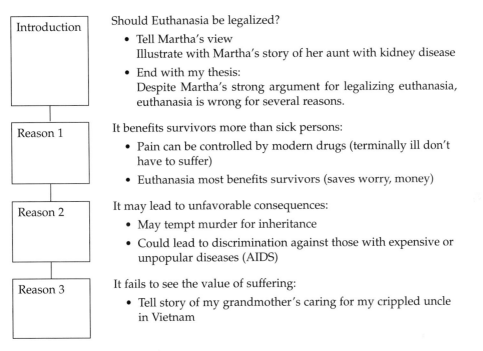

Should Euthanasia be legalized?

- Tell Martha's view
  Illustrate with Martha's story of her aunt with kidney disease
- End with my thesis:
  Despite Martha's strong argument for legalizing euthanasia, euthanasia is wrong for several reasons.

It benefits survivors more than sick persons:

- Pain can be controlled by modern drugs (terminally ill don't have to suffer)
- Euthanasia most benefits survivors (saves worry, money)

It may lead to unfavorable consequences:

- May tempt murder for inheritance
- Could lead to discrimination against those with expensive or unpopular diseases (AIDS)

It fails to see the value of suffering:

- Tell story of my grandmother's caring for my crippled uncle in Vietnam

FIGURE 18.2   Dao's Flowchart

Let the Structure Evolve

Once you have sketched out an initial structural diagram, use it to generate ideas. Tree diagrams are particularly helpful because they invite you to place question marks on branches to "hold open" spots for new points or for supporting particulars. If you have only two main points, for example, you could draw a third main branch and place a question mark under it to encourage you to think of another supporting idea. Likewise, if a branch has few supporting particulars, add question marks beneath it. The trick is to think of your structural diagrams as evolving artist's sketches rather than rigid blueprints. As your ideas grow and change, revise your structural diagram, adding or removing points, consolidating and refocusing sections, moving parts around, or filling in details.

Articulate Points, Not Topics

As we noted at the start of this lesson, we recommend complete sentences rather than topic phrases at the higher levels of a structural diagram. You can see why we make this recommendation if you compare the tree diagram in Figure 18.1 (p. 448) with the phrase-only version in Figure 18.3.

Phrases identify topics, but they don't create meanings. Sentences combine topic-identifying subjects with assertion-making predicates. The *meaning* arises from the assertion-making predicate, as in the following examples:

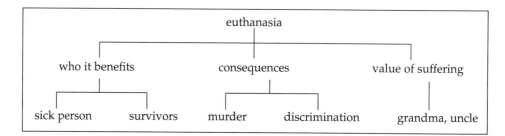

FIGURE 18.3   Dao's Phrase-Only Tree Diagram

Name Something	Make an Assertion About It
Fat	is an essential dietary ingredient without which we would die.
Justice	is hard to get if you are poor or black.
Television	may cause some children to act violently.

Because topic phrases don't have predicates, they don't have clear meanings. If you already know what you intend to say, a phrase-only tree or outline can be useful as a shorthand way to jog your memory. But if you are trying to discover and create meanings, writing out complete sentences for main points and subpoints makes a tree diagram or an outline a far more powerful tool.

Summary

This lesson has shown you the value of framing your argument by articulating the change you are trying to bring about in your reader and then by identifying your purpose, your thesis, and your main supporting points. You can then use outlines, tree diagrams, or flowcharts to help you visualize your structure and use it to develop new ideas.

FOR WRITING AND DISCUSSION

1. Working individually or in small groups, make a traditional outline, a tree diagram, and a flowchart of David Rockwood's argument against wind-generated electricity on pages 12–13. Which method of representing structure works best for you?
2. Working individually or in groups, make a tree diagram with place-holding question marks to guide a next draft for the carpets essay on pages 431–32.

■ LESSON 4: LEARNING FOUR EXPERT MOVES FOR ORGANIZING AND DEVELOPING IDEAS

In this lesson we show you that writers of closed-form prose often employ a conventional set of moves to organize parts of an essay. In using the term *moves,* we are making an analogy with the "set moves" or "set plays" in such sports as basketball, volleyball, and soccer. For example, a common set move in basketball is the "pick," in which an offensive player without the ball stands motionless in order to block the path of a defensive player who is guarding the dribbler. Similarly, certain organizational patterns in writing occur frequently enough to act as set plays for writers. These patterns set up expectations in the reader's mind about the shape of an upcoming stretch of prose, anything from a few sentences to a paragraph to a large block of paragraphs. As you will see, these moves also stimulate the invention of ideas. Next, we describe four of the most powerful set plays.*

The For Example Move

Perhaps the most common set play occurs when a writer makes an assertion and then illustrates it with one or more examples, often signaling the move explicitly with transitions such as *for example, for instance,* or *a case in point is.* . . . Once the move starts, readers can anticipate how it will unfold, just as experienced basketball fans can anticipate a pick as soon as they see a dribbler swerve toward a stationary teammate. You can probably sense this move unfolding now as you wait for us to give an example of the *for example move.* We have aroused an expectation; now we will fulfill it.

A good example of the for example move occurs in the paragraph Dao wrote to support her third reason for opposing euthanasia (see Figure 18.1, p. 448, for the tree diagram of Dao's essay).

For Example Move

My third objection to euthanasia is that it fails to see the value in suffering. ⟵ ——— *Point sentence*
Suffering is a part of life. We only see the value of suffering if we look deeply within our suffering. For example, I never thought my crippled uncle from Vietnam was a blessing to my grandmother until I talked to her. My mother's little — *Transition signaling the move*
brother was born prematurely. As a result of oxygen and nutrition deficiency, he was born crippled. His tiny arms and legs were twisted around his body, preventing him from any normal movements such as walking, picking up things, and lying down. He could only sit. Therefore, his world was very limited, for it consisted of his own room and the garden viewed through his window. Because of his disabilities, my grandmother had to wash him, feed him, and watch him constantly. It was hard, but she managed to care for him for forty-three years. He — *Extended example supporting point*
passed away after the death of my grandfather in 1982. Bringing this situation out of Vietnam and into Western society shows the difference between Vietnamese and Western views. In the West, my uncle might have been euthanized as a baby. Supporters of euthanasia would have said he wouldn't have any quality of life and that he would have been a great burden. But he was not a burden on my grandmother. She enjoyed taking care of him, and he was always her company after her other children got married and moved away. Neither one of them saw his defect as meaningless suffering because it brought them closer together.

*You might find it helpful to follow the set plays we used to write this section. This last sentence is the opening move of a play we call *division into parts.* It sets up the expectation that we will develop four set plays in order. Watch for the way we chunk them and signal transitions between them.

This passage uses a single, extended example to support a point. You could also use several shorter examples or other kinds of illustrating evidence, such as facts or statistics. In all cases the for example move creates a pattern of expectation and fulfillment. This pattern drives the invention of ideas in one of two ways: it urges the writer either to find examples to develop a generalization or to formulate a generalization that shows the point of an example.

FOR WRITING AND DISCUSSION

Working individually or in groups, develop a plan for supporting one or more of the following generalizations using the for example move.

1. Another objection to state sales taxes is that they are so annoying.
2. Although assertiveness training has definite benefits, it can sometimes get you into real trouble.
3. People say large cars are generally safer than small ones, but that is not always the case.
4. Sometimes effective leaders are indecisive.
5. Sometimes writing multiple drafts can make your essay worse rather than better.

The Summary/However Move

This move occurs whenever a writer sums up another person's viewpoint in order to qualify or contradict it or to introduce an opposing view. Typically, writers use transition words such as *but, however, in contrast,* or *on the other hand* between the parts of this move. This move is particularly common in academic writing, which often contrasts the writer's new view with prevailing views. Here is how Dao uses a *summary/however move* in the introduction of her essay opposing euthanasia.

Summary/However Move

Issue over which there is disagreement

Summary of opposing viewpoint

Transition to writer's viewpoint

Statement of writer's view

Should euthanasia be legalized? My classmate Martha and her family think it should be. Martha's aunt was blind from diabetes. For three years she was constantly in and out of the hospital, but then her kidneys shut down and she became a victim of life supports. After three months of suffering, she finally gave up. Martha believes this three-month period was unnecessary, for her aunt didn't have to go through all of that suffering. If euthanasia were legalized, her family would have put her to sleep the minute her condition worsened. Then, she wouldn't have had to feel pain, and she would have died in peace and with dignity. However, despite Martha's strong argument for legalizing euthanasia, I find it wrong.

The first sentence of this introduction poses the question that the essay addresses. The main body of the paragraph summarizes Martha's opposing view on euthanasia, and the final sentence, introduced by the transition "however," presents Dao's thesis.

FOR WRITING AND DISCUSSION

For this exercise, assume that you favor development of wind-generated electricity. Use the summary/however move to acknowledge the view of civil engineer David Rockwood, whose letter opposing wind-generated electricity you read in Chapter 1 (pp. 12–13). Assume that you are writing the opening paragraph of your own essay. Follow the pattern of Dao's introduction: (a) begin with a one-sentence issue or question; (b) summarize Rockwood's view in approximately one hundred words; and (c) state your own view, using *however* or *in contrast* as a transition. Write out your paragraph on your own, or work in groups to write a consensus paragraph. Then share and critique your paragraphs.

The Division-into-Parallel-Parts Move

Among the most frequently encountered and powerful of the set plays is the *division-into-parallel-parts move.* To initiate the move, a writer begins with an umbrella sentence that forecasts the structure and creates a frame. (For example, "Freud's theory differs from Jung's in three essential ways" or "The decline of the U.S. space program can be attributed to several factors.") Typical overview sentences either specify the number of parts that will follow by using phrases such as "two ways," "three differences," "five kinds," or they leave the number unspecified, using words such as *several, a few,* or *many.* Alternatively, the writer may ask a rhetorical question that implies the frame: "What are some main differences, then, between Freud's theory and Jung's? One difference is. . . ."

To signal transitions from one part to the next, writers use two kinds of signposts: transition words or bullets and parallel grammatical structure.* The first kind of signpost can use transition words to introduce each of the parallel parts.

first . . . , second . . . , third . . . , finally. . . .

first . . . , another . . . , still another . . . , finally. . . .

to begin . . . , likewise . . . , in addition . . . , lastly. . . .

either . . . or. . . .

one . . . , in addition . . . , furthermore . . . , also. . . .

Or, instead of transition words, writers can also use a series of bullets followed by indented text.

The Wolf Recovery Program is strictly opposed by a large and vociferous group of ranchers who pose numerous objections to increasing wolf populations.

- They perceive wolves as a threat to livestock.
- They fear the wolves will attack humans.
- etc.

*Note how this sentence itself initiates a division-into-parallel-parts move.

The second kind of signpost uses the same grammatical structure to begin each parallel part, creating a parallel, echolike effect.

> I learned several things from this class. First, *I learned that....* Second, *I learned that....* Finally, *I learned that....*

A typical version of this move is embedded in the following single paragraph taken from a long professional essay. The author is discussing the impact of an article in which psychologist George Miller shows that a person's short-term memory capacity is "seven plus or minus two" pieces of information.* This paragraph uses a rhetorical question as the umbrella sentence that initiates the move.

> Why did this apparently simple point have a decidedly major impact within [cognitive psychology]? First, Miller's essay brought together a large amount of hitherto dispersed data and suggested that they pointed to a common conclusion. Second, it suggested that the number 7 was no mere accident: it designated genuine limitations in human information-processing capacities.... Third, as indicated, the message in the paper was not without hope, for Miller indicated ways by which humans ingeniously transcend this limitation.
>
> —Howard Gardner, *The Mind's New Science: A History of the Cognitive Revolution*

Using the Parallel-Parts Move on a Large Scale

The division-into-parallel-parts move is also frequently used to control larger stretches of text in which a dozen or more paragraphs may work together to complete a parallel series of parts. For example, you are currently in part three of a stretch of text introduced by the mapping sentence on page 451: "Next we describe four of the most powerful set plays." In fact, the division-into-parallel-parts move often forms the major organizational strategy of the whole essay. Here are some examples of common situations in which writers use this move on a large scale.

Classification.   When writers want to divide a concept into various categories—a thinking process often called *classification*—they regularly devote a major piece of the essay to each of the classes or categories.

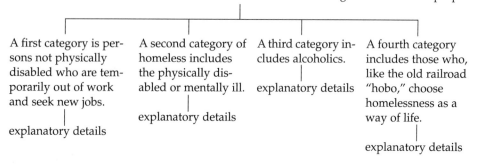

Political solutions to homelessness must take into account four categories of homeless people.

A first category is persons not physically disabled who are temporarily out of work and seek new jobs.

explanatory details

A second category of homeless includes the physically disabled or mentally ill.

explanatory details

A third category includes alcoholics.

explanatory details

A fourth category includes those who, like the old railroad "hobo," choose homelessness as a way of life.

explanatory details

---

*We demonstrated the significance of Miller's article for writers in the discussion of why writers revise in Chapter 17.

Exemplification.   A process sometimes called *exemplification* or *illustration* occurs when a writer illustrates a point with several extended examples.

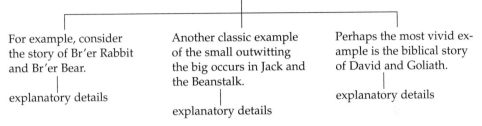

Many of our stories and legends depict cunning little guys outwitting dull-brained big guys.

| For example, consider the story of Br'er Rabbit and Br'er Bear. | Another classic example of the small outwitting the big occurs in Jack and the Beanstalk. | Perhaps the most vivid example is the biblical story of David and Goliath. |
| explanatory details | explanatory details | explanatory details |

Causal Analysis.   Writing that analyzes causes of a phenomenon is also often organized into parallel parts, with each part developing a single cause.

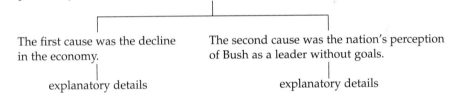

Despite George Bush's enormous popularity following the Gulf War, he nevertheless lost the presidency to Bill Clinton. His decline in popularity can be attributed to two causes.

| The first cause was the decline in the economy. | The second cause was the nation's perception of Bush as a leader without goals. |
| explanatory details | explanatory details |

Process Analysis.   Writers often explain a process by dividing it into a number of separate stages or steps.

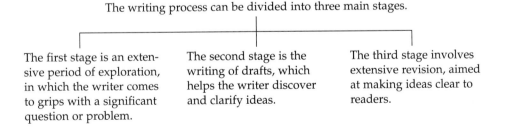

The writing process can be divided into three main stages.

| The first stage is an extensive period of exploration, in which the writer comes to grips with a significant question or problem. | The second stage is the writing of drafts, which helps the writer discover and clarify ideas. | The third stage involves extensive revision, aimed at making ideas clear to readers. |

Argumentation.   When writers of arguments offer two or more parallel reasons for adhering to a particular view or course of action, they typically use the division-into-parallel-parts move. Dao used this large-scale strategy to organize her argument against euthanasia.

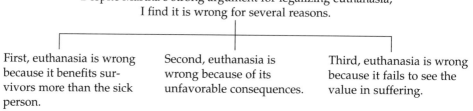

Despite Martha's strong argument for legalizing euthanasia, I find it is wrong for several reasons.

First, euthanasia is wrong because it benefits survivors more than the sick person.

Second, euthanasia is wrong because of its unfavorable consequences.

Third, euthanasia is wrong because it fails to see the value in suffering.

Using the Parallel-Parts Move to Generate Ideas

The division-into-parallel-parts move can serve as a particularly powerful engine for idea generation. When displayed in a tree diagram, the parallel branches created by the move invite you to think of ideas that will fit laterally and vertically into the diagram. For example, in your first draft you might identify two causes of a phenomenon, but in the act of drafting you might think of a third or even a fourth cause. Simultaneously, you might think of more or stronger ways to develop each of the causes. The number of main branches and supporting branches can be expanded or contracted as you think of new ideas or see ways to combine or recombine old ones.

Ordering the Parallel Parts

Whenever you create two or more parallel parts, you must decide which to put first, which to put in the middle, and which to put last. If the parts are of equal weight and interest, or if you are just exploring their significance, the order doesn't much matter. But if the parts are of different importance, significance, or complexity, their order can be rhetorically important. As a general rule, save the best for last. What constitutes "best" depends on the circumstances. In an argument, the best reason is usually the strongest or the one most apt to appeal to the intended audience. In other cases, the best is usually the most unusual, the most surprising, the most thought provoking, or the most complex, in keeping with the general rule that writers proceed from the familiar to the unfamiliar, from the least surprising to the most surprising.

FOR WRITING AND DISCUSSION

Working individually or in small groups, use the division-into-parallel-parts move to create, organize, and develop ideas to support one or more of the following point sentences. Try using a tree diagram to help guide and stimulate your invention.

1. To study for an exam effectively, a student should follow these (specify a number) steps.
2. Why do U.S. schoolchildren lag so far behind European and Asian children on standardized tests of mathematics and science? One possible cause is . . . (continue).

3. There are several ways for an individual to help the homeless without giving money to panhandlers.
4. TV advertisements for male-oriented products, such as beer, razors, and aftershaves, reflect several different kinds of gender stereotypes.
5. Constant dieting is unhealthy for several reasons.

The Comparison/Contrast Move

A common variation on the division-into-parallel-parts move is the *comparison/contrast move*. To compare or contrast two items, you must first decide on the points of comparison (or contrast). If you are contrasting the political views of two presidential candidates, you might choose to focus on four points of comparison: differences in their foreign policy, differences in economic policy, differences in social policy, and differences in judicial philosophy. You then have two choices for organizing the parts: the *side-by-side pattern*, in which you discuss all of candidate A's views and then all of candidate B's views; or the *back-and-forth pattern*, in which you discuss foreign policy, contrasting A's views with B's views, then move on to economic policy, then social policy, and then judicial philosophy. Here is how these two patterns would appear on a tree diagram.

Side-by-side pattern

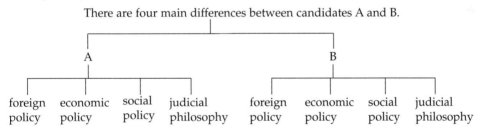

Back-and-forth pattern

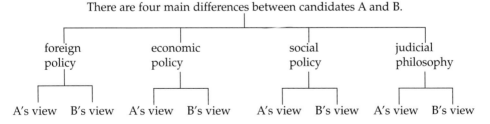

There are no cut-and-dried rules that dictate when to use the side-by-side pattern or the back-and-forth pattern. However, for lengthy comparisons the back-and-forth pattern is often more effective because the reader doesn't have to store great amounts of information in memory. The side-by-side pattern requires readers to remember all the material about A when they come to B, and it is sometimes difficult to keep all the points of comparison clearly in mind.

FOR WRITING AND DISCUSSION

Working individually or in groups, create tree diagrams for possible paragraphs or essays based on one or more of the following point sentences, all of which call for the comparison/contrast move. Make at least one diagram follow the back-and-forth pattern and make at least one diagram follow the side-by-side pattern.

1. There are several significant differences between childbirth as it is practiced by middle-class American women today and childbirth as it was practiced by middle-class American women prior to the women's liberation movement.
2. To understand U.S. politics, an outsider needs to appreciate some basic differences between Republicans and Democrats.
3. Although they are obviously different on the surface, there are many similarities between the Boy Scouts and a street gang.
4. There are several important differences between closed-form and open-form writing.
5. There are significant differences between the classic 1931 film *Frankenstein* and Mary Shelley's original novel by the same title. (You can substitute any other film/novel comparison.)

Summary

In this lesson we have shown you how practicing experts' set moves extends your repertoire of strategies for organizing and developing ideas. In particular, we have explained how to add an example to support a point; how to sum up an alternative view and then switch to your own; how to develop an idea by announcing a series of parallel subparts; and how to compare or contrast two ideas or phenomena. These moves can be used on a large or small scale, wherever appropriate in a paper.

◤ LESSON 5: PLACING POINTS BEFORE PARTICULARS

In our lesson on outlining (Lesson 3), we suggested that you write *point sentences* rather than topic phrases for the high level slots of the outline in order to articulate the *meaning* or *point* of each section of your argument. In this lesson, we show you how to place those point sentences where readers need them: near the front of the sections or paragraphs they govern. When you place points before particulars, you help readers in all three of the important ways we described in Lesson 1. You create unity by relating each new section back to your thesis or next higher point; you forecast what is coming in the section, thereby satisfying your reader's desire for forecasting and fulfillment. And finally, you place old material before new material. The point sentence links back to preceding material but also states the point of what is coming so that keywords in the point sentence can then serve as old information for the rest of the section.

Put Point Sentences at the Beginning of Paragraphs

Although readers expect closed-form paragraphs to open with point sentences (often called *topic sentences*), writers' early drafts often lack them because writers, while drafting, are often unsure of their points and are still searching for them (see Chapter 17 on the writing process). In their rough draft paragraphs, writers often omit point sentences entirely or place them at the end of paragraphs, or they write point sentences that misrepresent what the paragraph actually does or says. In such cases, readers momentarily lose the connection between what they are currently reading and the writer's intended meaning. During revision, then, you should check your body paragraphs carefully to be sure you have placed accurate point sentences near the beginning.

What follows are examples of the kinds of revisions writers typically make. Note how the annotations in the examples that follow identify changes that help the paragraphs become unified and clear to readers. Our first example is from a later draft of the student essay opposing carpeting dorm rooms (Chapter 17, pp. 431–32).

Revision—Point Sentence First

Another reason for the university not to buy carpets is the cost.
According to Rachel Jones, Assistant Director of Housing Services,   *Point sentence placed first*

the initial purchase and installation of carpeting would cost $300 per

room. Considering the number of rooms in the three residence halls,

carpeting amounts to a substantial investment. Additionally, once the

carpets are installed, the university would need to maintain them through

the purchase of more vacuum cleaners and shampoo machines. This money

would be better spent on other dorm improvements that would benefit more

residents, such as expanded kitchen facilities and improved recreational

space. ~~Thus carpets would be too expensive.~~

In the original draft, the writer states the point at the end of the paragraph. In his revision he states the point in an opening topic sentence that links back to the thesis statement, which promises "several reasons" that the university should not buy carpets for the dorms. The words "another reason" thus link the topic sentence to the argument's big picture.

Revise Paragraphs for Unity

In addition to placing topic sentences at the heads of paragraphs, writers often need to revise topic sentences to better match what the paragraph actually says, or revise the paragraph to better match the topic sentence. Paragraphs have unity when all of their sentences develop what is forecast in the topic sentence. Paragraphs in rough drafts are often not unified because they reflect the writer's shifting, evolving, thinking-while-writing process. Consider the following paragraph from an early draft of Dao's argument (see Lessons 3 and 4) against euthanasia. Her peer reviewer labeled it "confusing." What makes it confusing?

```
             Early Draft—Confusing


    First, euthanasia is wrong because no one has the right to take the

life of another person. Some people say that euthanasia or suicide will

end suffering and pain. But what proofs do they have for such a claim?

Death is still mysterious to us; therefore, we do not know whether death

will end suffering and pain or not. What seems to be the real claim is

that death to those with illnesses will end *our* pain. Such pain involves

worrying over them, paying their medical bills, and giving up so much of

our time. Their deaths end our pain rather than theirs. And for that

reason, euthanasia is a selfish act, for the outcome of euthanasia bene-

fits us, the nonsufferers, more. Once the sufferers pass away, we can go

back to our normal lives.
```

The paragraph opens with an apparent topic sentence: "Euthanasia is wrong because no one has the right to take the life of another person." But the rest of the paragraph doesn't focus on that point. Instead, it focuses on how euthanasia benefits the survivors more than the sick person. Dao had two choices: to revise the paragraph to fit the topic sentence or to revise the topic sentence to fit the paragraph. Here is her revision, which includes a different topic sentence and an additional sentence mid-paragraph to keep particulars focused on the opening point.

Revision for Unity

First, euthanasia is wrong because it benefits the survivors more than the sick person. ──────── — Revised point

~~First, euthanasia is wrong because no one has the right to take the~~
    ^

~~life of another person.~~ Some people say that euthanasia or suicide will

the sick person's ←─────────────────────────────
end suffering and pain. But what proofs do they have for such a claim?
    ^

Death is still mysterious to us; therefore, we do not know whether death

                Moreover, modern pain killers can relieve most of the pain a sick person has to endure. ←──
will end suffering and pain. What seems to be the real claim is
                              ^

that death to those with illnesses will end *our* pain. Such pain involves

worrying over them, paying their medical bills, and giving up so much of

our time. Their deaths end our pain rather than theirs. And for that

reason, euthanasia is a selfish act, for the outcome of euthanasia bene-

fits us, the nonsufferers, more. Once the sufferers pass away, we can go

back to our normal lives.

*Revised point
sentence better
forecasts focus
of paragraph*

*Keeps focus on
"sick person"*

*Concludes sub-
point about
sick person*

*Makes subpoint
about how
euthanasia
benefits survivors*

Dao unifies this paragraph by keeping all its parts focused on her main point: "Euthanasia . . . benefits the survivors more than the sick person." You may not be persuaded by her argument, but at least her point is now clear.

A paragraph may lack unity for a variety of reasons. It may shift to a new direction in the middle, or one or two sentences may simply be irrelevant to the point. The key is to make sure that all the sentences in the paragraph fulfill the reader's expectations based on the point sentence.

Add Particulars to Support Points

Just as writers of rough drafts often omit point sentences from paragraphs, they sometimes leave out the particulars needed to support a point. In such cases, the writer needs to make a *for example move* (see Lesson 4) or add other kinds of particulars such as facts, statistics, quotations, research summaries, or further subpoints. Consider how adding additional particulars to the following draft paragraph strengthens the student's argument.

Draft Paragraph: Particulars Missing

One reason that it is not necessary to log old-growth forests is that the timber industry can supply the world's lumber needs without doing so. For example, we have plenty of new-growth forest from which timber can be taken (Sagoff 89). We could also reduce the amount of trees used for paper products by using other materials besides wood for paper pulp. In light of the fact that we have plenty of trees and ways of reducing our wood demands, there is no need to harvest old-growth forests.

Revised Paragraph: Particulars Added

One reason that it is not necessary to log old-growth forests is that the timber industry can supply the world's lumber needs without doing so. For example, we have plenty of new-growth forest from which timber can be taken as a result of major reforestation efforts all over the United States (Sagoff 89). In the Northwest, for instance, Oregon law requires every acre of timber harvested to be replanted. According to Robert Sedjo, a forestry expert, the world's demand for industrial wood could be met by a widely implemented tree farming system (Sagoff 90). We could also reduce the amount of trees used for paper products by using a promising new innovation called Kenaf, a fast growing annual herb which is fifteen feet tall and is native to Africa. It has been used for making rope for many years, but recently it was found to work just as well for paper pulp. In light of the fact that we have plenty of trees and ways of reducing our wood demands, there is no need to harvest old-growth forests.

Added particulars support subpoint that we have plenty of new-growth forest

Added particulars support second subpoint that wood alternatives are available

Summary

Point sentences form the structural core of an argument. In this lesson, we stressed the reader's need to have point sentences placed at the heads of sections and paragraphs. In revising, writers often have to recast point sentences or restructure paragraphs to create unity. We also stressed the reader's need for particulars, which make points vivid and persuasive.

FOR WRITING AND DISCUSSION

Look again at the student draft arguing against university-provided carpets for dorm rooms (Chapter 17, pp. 431–32). Working as individuals or in small groups, write the next draft of this essay, focusing on creating a closed-form piece with unified, coherent, and sufficiently developed body paragraphs headed by topic sentences. You can reshape or combine paragraphs as needed and invent your own plausible particulars to flesh out a point.

■ LESSON 6: SIGNALING RELATIONSHIPS WITH TRANSITIONS

As we have explained in previous lessons, when readers read closed-form prose, they expect each new sentence, paragraph, and section to link clearly to what they have already read. They need a well-marked trail with signposts signaling the twists and turns along the way. They also need resting spots at major junctions where they can review where they've been and survey what's coming. In this lesson, we show you how transition words, summary and forecasting passages, and headings and subheadings can keep your reader securely on the trail.

Use Common Transition Words to Signal Relationships

One of the best ways to keep readers on track is to signal the relationship between sentences and larger parts with transitions. Transitions are like signposts that signal where the road is turning. Without them, a reader can't predict where an argument might be headed. Transitions limit the possible directions that an unfolding argument might take. Consider how the use of "therefore" and "nevertheless" limits the range of possibilities in the following examples:

> While on vacation, Suzie caught the chicken pox. Therefore, _____.
>
> While on vacation, Suzie caught the chicken pox. Nevertheless, _____.

"Therefore" signals to the reader that what follows is a consequence. Most readers will imagine a sentence similar to this one:

> Therefore, she spent her vacation lying in bed itching, feverish, and miserable.

In contrast, "nevertheless" signals an unexpected or denied consequence, so the reader might anticipate a sentence such as this:

> Nevertheless, she enjoyed her two weeks off, thanks to a couple of bottles of calamine lotion, some good books, and a big easy chair overlooking the ocean.

Here is a list of the most common transition words and phrases and what they signal to the reader*:

Words or Phrases	What They Signal
first, second, third, next, finally, earlier, later, meanwhile, afterwards	*sequence*—First we went to dinner; then we went to the movies.
that is, in other words, to put it another way, — (dash) , : (colon)	*restatement*—He's so hypocritical that you can't trust a word he says. To put it another way, he's a complete phony.
rather, instead	*replacement*—We shouldn't use the money to buy opera tickets; rather, we should use it for a nice gift.
for example, for instance, a case in point	*example*—Mr. Carlysle is very generous. For example, he gave the janitors a special holiday gift.
because, since, for	*reason*—Taxes on cigarettes are unfair because they place a higher tax burden on the working class.
therefore, hence, so, consequently, thus, then, as a result, accordingly, as a consequence	*consequences*—I failed to turn in the essay; therefore I flunked the course.
still, nevertheless	*denied consequence*—The teacher always seemed grumpy in class; nevertheless, I really enjoyed the course.

*Although all the words on the list serve as transitions or connectives, grammatically they are not all equivalent; some are coordinating conjunctions, some are subordinating conjunctions, and some are transition adverbs. Each different kind of word requires a different grammatical construction and punctuation.

Words or Phrases *(cont.)*	**What They Signal** *(cont.)*
although, even though, granted that (with still)	*concession*—Even though the teacher was always grumpy, I still enjoyed the course.
in comparison, likewise, similarly	*similarity*—Teaching engineering takes a lot of patience. Likewise, so does teaching accounting.
however, in contrast, conversely, on the other hand, but	*contrast*—I disliked my old backpack immensely; however, I really like this new one.
in addition, also, too, moreover, furthermore	*addition*—Today's cars are much safer than those of ten years ago. In addition, they get better gas mileage.
in brief, in sum, in conclusion, finally, to sum up, to conclude	*conclusion or summary*—In sum, the plan presented by Mary is the best choice.

FOR WRITING AND DISCUSSION

This exercise is designed to show you how transition words govern relationships between ideas. Working in groups or on your own, finish each of the following statements using ideas of your own invention. Make sure what you add fits the logic of the transition word.

1. Writing is difficult; therefore _____.
2. Writing is difficult; however, _____.
3. Writing is difficult because _____.
4. Writing is difficult. For example, _____.
5. Writing is difficult. To put it another way, _____.
6. Writing is difficult. Likewise, _____.
7. Although writing is difficult, _____.
8. _____. In sum, writing is difficult.

In the following paragraph, various kinds of linking devices have been omitted. Fill in the blanks with words or phrases that would make the paragraph coherent. Clues are provided in brackets.

> Writing an essay is a difficult process for most people. _____ [contrast] the process can be made easier if you learn to practice three simple techniques. _____ [sequence] learn the technique of nonstop writing. When you are first trying to think of ideas for an essay, put your pen on your paper and write nonstop for ten or fifteen minutes without ever letting your pen leave the paper. Stay loose and free. Let your pen follow the waves of thought. Don't worry about grammar or spelling. _____ [concession] this technique won't work for everyone, it helps many people get a good cache of ideas to draw on. A _____ [sequence] technique is to write your rough draft rapidly without worrying about being perfect. Too many writers try to get their drafts right the first time. _____ [contrast] by learning to live with imperfection,

you will save yourself headaches and a wastepaper basket full of crumpled paper. Think of your first rough draft as a path hacked out of the jungle—as part of an exploration, not as a completed highway. As a _____ [sequence] technique, try printing out a triple-spaced copy to allow space for revision. Many beginning writers don't leave enough space to revise. _____ [consequence] these writers never get in the habit of crossing out chunks of their rough draft and writing revisions in the blank spaces. After you have revised your rough draft until it is too messy to work from any more, you can _____ [sequence] enter your changes into your word processor and print out a fresh draft, again setting your text on triple space. The resulting blank space invites you to revise.

Write Major Transitions Between Parts

In long closed-form pieces, writers often put *resting places* between major parts—transition passages that allow readers to shift their attention momentarily away from the matter at hand to a sense of where they've been and where they're going. Often such passages sum up the preceding major section, refer back to the essay's thesis statement or opening blueprint plan, and then preview the next major section. The longer the essay, the more readers appreciate such passages. Here are three typical examples.

> So far I have looked at a number of techniques that can help people identify debilitating assumptions that block their self-growth. In the next section, I examine ways to question and overcome these assumptions.

> Now that the difficulty of the problem is fully apparent, our next step is to examine some of the solutions that have been proposed.

> These, then, are the major theories explaining why Hamlet delays. But let's see what happens to Hamlet if we ask the question in a slightly different way. In this next section, we shift our critical focus, looking not at Hamlet's actions, but at his language.

Signal Transitions with Headings and Subheadings

In many genres, particularly scientific and technical reports, government documents, business proposals, textbooks, and other long articles in magazines or scholarly journals, writers conventionally break up long stretches of text with headings and subheadings. Headings are often set in different type sizes and fonts, and mark transition points between major parts and subparts of the argument.

Headings serve some of the same purposes served by the title of the essay or article; they encapsulate the big picture of a part or section and preview its contents. They may also relate back to the thesis statement, but sometimes, especially in scientific and social scientific articles, they are generic section markers, such as "Introduction," "Methods," "Findings," and so forth. Writers are apt to compose their headings late in the writing process, and the act of doing so may lead to further revisions. When you add headings, ask yourself questions such as these: Just where *are* the major transition points in the text? What would be a good title or umbrella that summarizes or previews this part? How clearly do my levels of headings relate to each other?

Writing descriptive headings is almost as demanding as writing a thesis statement. Because composing headings and subheadings is such a powerful exercise, we often ask our students to write headings for their papers, even if headings are not conventionally used for the type of writing they are doing. (For an example of headings in a student paper, see Mary Turla's research paper in Chapter 22, pp. 573–87.)

Summary

In this brief lesson we explained some simple yet effective strategies for keeping your reader on track:

- Mark your trail with appropriate transition words
- Write major transitions between sections
- If the genre allows, use headings and subheadings

Effective use of these strategies will help your reader follow your ideas with ease and confidence.

◪ LESSON 7: BINDING SENTENCES TOGETHER BY FOLLOWING THE OLD/NEW CONTRACT

In the previous lesson we showed you how to mark the reader's trail with transitions. In this lesson we show you how to build a smooth trail without potholes or washed out bridges that force your reader to jump over gaps between sentences.

An Explanation of the Old/New Contract

A powerful way to prevent gaps is to follow the old/new contract—a writing strategy derived from the principle of old before new that we explained and illustrated in Lesson 1. Simply put, the old/new contract asks writers to begin sentences with something old—something that links back to what has gone before—and then to end sentences with new information.

The following examples illustrate how following the old/new contract creates a smooth trail for readers; in contrast, violating the contract creates potholes that the reader must leap over. We'll start with a passage that violates the contract. Note in Passage A how difficult it is to follow the writer's ideas when the writer violates the principle of old-before-new. Each sentence seems unconnected to the one that went before it; the ideas seem disjointed.

Passage A: Violates Old/New Contract

Play is an often overlooked dimension of fathering. From the time a child is born until its adolescence, caretaking is emphasized less by fathers than play. Egalitarian feminists may be troubled by this, and spending more time in care-taking may be wise for fathers. There seems to be unusual significance in the father's style of play. Physical excitement and stimulation are likely to be part of it. With older children more physical games and teamwork that require the competitive testing of physical and mental skills are also what it involves. Re-semblance to an apprenticeship or teaching relationship is also a characteristic of father's play: Come on, let me show you how.

Now note how much easier it is to follow the writer's ideas when each sentence opens with something old:

Passage B: Follows Old/New Contract

An often-overlooked dimension of fathering is play. From their children's birth through adolescence, fathers tend to emphasize play more than caretaking. This may be troubling to egalitarian feminists, and it would indeed be wise for most fathers to spend more time in caretaking. Yet the fathers' style of play seems to have unusual significance. It is likely to be both physically stimulating and exciting. With older children it involves more physical games and teamwork that require the competitive testing of physical and mental skills. It frequently resembles an apprenticeship or teaching relationship: Come on, let me show you how.

If you are like most readers, you have to concentrate much harder to understand Passage A than Passage B because it violates the old-before-new way that our minds normally process information. If a writer doesn't begin a sentence with old material, readers have to hold the new material in suspension until they have figured out how it connects to what has gone before. They can stay on the trail, but they have to keep jumping over the potholes between sentences.

To follow the old/new contract, you place old information near the beginning of sentences in what we call the *topic position* and new information that advances the argument in the predicate or *stress position* at the end of the sentence. We associate topics with the beginnings of sentences simply because in the standard English sentence the topic (or subject) comes before the predicate. Hence the notion of a *contract* by which we agree not to fool or frustrate our readers by breaking with the "normal" order of things. The contract says that the old, backward-linking material comes at the beginning of the sentence and the new argument-advancing material comes at the end.

But what exactly do we mean by "old" or "familiar" information? In the context of sentence-level coherence, we mean everything in the text the reader has read so far. Any upcoming sentence is new information, but once the reader reads it, it becomes old information. For example, when a reader is halfway through a text, everything previously read—the title, the introduction, half the body—is old information to which you can link back to meet your readers' expectations for unity and coherence.

In making these backward links, writers have three targets:

1. They can link back to a key word or concept in the immediately preceding sentence (creating coherence).
2. They can link back to a key word or concept in a preceding point sentence (creating unity).
3. They can link back to a preceding forecasting statement about structure (helping readers map their location in the text).

Writers have a number of textual strategies for making these links. In Figure 18.4 our annotations show how a professional writer links back to old information within the first five or six words of each sentence. What follows is a compendium of these strategies:

- **Repeat a key word.**   The most common way to open with something old is to repeat a key word from the preceding sentence or an earlier point sentence. In our example, note the number of sentences that open with *father, father's,* or *fathering.* Note also the frequent repetitions of *play.*
- **Use a pronoun to substitute for a key word.**   In our example, the second sentence opens with the pronouns *it,* referring to *research* and *their* referring to *fathers.* The last three sentences open with the pronoun *it,* referring to *father's style of play.*

FIGURE 18.4   How a Professional Writer Follows the Old/New Contract

Refers to research in previous sentence

Refers to fathers in previous sentence

Rephrases idea of "childrearing"

Transition tells us new paragraph will be an example of previous concept

Repeats fathers from previous sentence

Refers to fathers

Rephrases concept in previous paragraph

Pronoun sums up previous concept

New information that becomes topic of this paragraph

It refers to fathers' style of play

Repeats words father *and* play *from paragraph point sentence*

Recent research has given us much deeper—and more surprising—insights into the father's role in childrearing. It shows that in almost all of their interactions with children, fathers do things a little differently from mothers. What fathers do—their special parenting style—is not only highly complementary to what mothers do but is by all indications important in its own right.

For example, an often over-looked dimension of fathering is play. From their children's birth through adolescence, fathers tend to emphasize play more than caretaking. This may be troubling to egalitarian feminists, and it would indeed be wise for most fathers to spend more time in caretaking. Yet the fathers' style of play seems to have unusual significance. It is likely to be both physically stimulating and exciting. With older children it involves more physical games and teamwork that require the competitive testing of physical and mental skills. It frequently resembles an apprenticeship or teaching relationship: Come on, let me show you how.

(David Popenoe, "Where's Papa?" from *Life Without Father: Compelling New Evidence that Fatherhood and Marriage Are Indispensable for the Good of Children and Society.*)

■ *Summarize, rephrase, or restate earlier concepts.*   Writers can link back to a preceding sentence by using a word or phrase that summarizes or restates a key concept. In the second sentence, "interactions with children" restates the concept of childrearing. Similarly, the phrase "an often-overlooked dimension" refers to a concept implied in the preceding paragraph—that recent research reveals something significant (rephrased as a *dimension*) and not widely known (rephrased as *overlooked*) about a father's role in childrearing. An "often-overlooked dimension" sums up this idea. Finally, note that the pronoun *this* in the second paragraph sums up the main concept of the previous two sentences. (But see our warning on p. 470 about the overuse of *this* as a pronoun.)

■ *Use a transition word.*   Writers can also use transition words such as *first . . . , second . . . , third . . .* or *therefore* or *however* to cue the reader about the logical relationship between an upcoming sentence and the preceding ones. Note how the second paragraph opens with *For example,* indicating that the upcoming paragraph will illustrate the concept identified in the preceding paragraph.

These strategies give you a powerful way to check and revise your prose. Comb your drafts for gaps between sentences where you have violated the old/new contract. If the opening of a new sentence doesn't refer back to an earlier word, phrase, or concept, your reader could derail, so use what you have learned to repair the tracks.

FOR WRITING AND DISCUSSION

Here is an early draft paragraph from a student's essay in favor of building more nuclear reactors for electricity. This paragraph attempts to refute an argument that building nuclear power plants is prohibitively expensive. Read the draft carefully and then do the exercises that follow.

[1] One argument against nuclear power plants is that they are too expensive to build. [2] But this argument is flawed. [3] On March 28, 1979, Three Mile Island (TMI) Nuclear Station suffered a meltdown. [4] It was the worst accident in commercial nuclear power operation in the United States. [5] During its investigation of TMI the Presidential Commission became highly critical of the U.S. Nuclear Regulatory Commission (NRC), which responded by generating hundreds of new safety regulations. [6] These regulations forced utility companies to modify reactors during construction. [7] Since all the changes had to be made on half-completed plants, the cost of design time, material, and personnel had to be very large. [8] The standards set by the NRC would not be acceptable to a utility company. [9] All reactors now being built had been ordered before 1973. [10] With all the experience gained by research here in the U.S. and overseas, the licensing process can be cut in half without reducing the safety of the plant. [11] A faster approval rate could lower the cost of

the construction of a plant because it eliminates all the delays and cost overruns.

1. Working on your own, place a vertical slash in front of any sentence that doesn't open with some reference back to familiar material.
2. See if your class or small group agrees on the location of these slashes. In each case, how does the writer's violation of the old/new contract create confusion?
3. Working individually or in small groups, try to revise the paragraph by filling in gaps created by violation of the old/new contract.

As we discussed in Lesson 1, the principle of old before new has great explanatory power in helping writers understand their choices when they compose. In this last section, we give you some further insights into the old/new contract.

Avoid Ambiguous Use of "This" to Fulfill the Old/New Contract

Some writers try to fulfill the old/new contract by frequent use of the pronoun *this* to sum up a preceding concept. Occasionally this usage* is effective, as in our example passage on fathers' style of play when the writer says: "*This* may be troubling to egalitarian feminists." But frequent use of *this* as a pronoun creates lazy and often ambiguous prose. Consider how our example passage might read if many of the explicit links were replaced by *this.*

Lazy Use of *This* as Pronoun

Recent research has given us much deeper—and more surprising—insights into **this.** It shows that in doing **this,** fathers do things a little differently from mothers. **This** is not only highly complementary to what mothers do but is by all indications important in its own right.

For example, an often-overlooked dimension of **this** is play.

Perhaps this passage helps you see why we refer to *this* (used by itself as a pronoun) as "the lazy person's all-purpose noun-slot filler."

How the Old/New Contract Modifies the Rule "Avoid Weak Repetition"

Many students have been warned against repetition of the same word (or *weak repetition,* as your teacher may have called it). Consequently, you may not be aware that repetition of key words is a vital aspect of unity and coherence. The repeated words create what linguists call *lexical strings* that keep a passage focused on a particular point. Note in our passage about the importance of fathers' style of play the

---

*It's okay to use *this* as an adjective, as in "this usage"; we refer only to *this* by itself as a pronoun.

frequent repetitions of the words *father* and *play*. What if the writer worried about repeating *father* too much and reached for his thesaurus?

Unnecessary Attempt to Avoid Repetition

Recent research has given us much deeper—and more surprising—insights into the **male parent's** role in childrearing. It shows that in almost all of their interactions with children, **patriarchs** do things a little differently from mothers. What **sires** do . . .

For example, an often-overlooked dimension of **male gender parenting** is . . .

You get the picture. Keep your reader on familiar ground through repetition of key words.

How the Old/New Contract Modifies the Rule "Prefer Active over Passive Voice"

Another rule that you may have learned is to use the active voice rather than the passive voice. In the active voice the doer of the action is in the subject slot of the sentence and the receiver is in the direct object slot, as in the following examples:

The dog caught the Frisbee.

The women wrote letters of complaint to the boss.

The landlord raised the rent.

In the passive voice the receiver of the action becomes the subject and the doer of the action either becomes the object of the preposition *by* or disappears from the sentence.

The Frisbee was caught by the dog.

Letters of complaint were written (by the women) to the boss.

The rent was raised (by the landlord).

Other things being equal, the active voice is indeed preferable to the passive because it is more direct and forceful. But in some cases other things *aren't* equal, and the passive voice is preferable. *What the old/new contract asks you to consider is whether the doer or the receiver represents the old information in a sentence.* Consider the difference between the following passages.

Second Sentence, Active Voice	My great-grandfather was a skilled cabinet-maker. He made this dining-room table near the turn of the century.
Second Sentence, Passive Voice	I am pleased that you stopped to admire our dining-room table. It was made by my great-grandfather near the turn of the century.

In the first passage, the opening sentence is about *my great-grandfather*. To begin the second sentence with old information (*he*, referring to *grandfather*), the writer uses the active voice. The opening sentence of the second passage is about the dining-room table. To begin the second sentence with old information (*it*, referring to *table*), the writer must use the passive voice, since the table is the receiver of the action. In both cases, the sentences are structured to begin with old information.

Summary

This lesson has focused on the power of the old/new contract to bind sentences together and eliminate gaps that the reader must leap over. We have shown various ways that writers can link back to old information by repeating key words, using a pronoun, summarizing or restating an earlier concept, or using a transition word. Additionally, we have advised against the ambiguous use of *this* as a pronoun to link back to old information and have shown how the principle of old before new modifies rules about the avoidance of *weak repetition* and *passive voice*.

FOR WRITING AND DISCUSSION

A helpful technique for understanding how skilled writers keep their readers on track is to reorder a *scrambled* paragraph. The following passage is a paragraph from science writer Carl Sagan's *Broca's Brain*. However, the order of the sentences has been scrambled. Working individually or in small groups, place the sentences in correct order. Try to articulate the thinking processes you used to link the sentences correctly. What cues helped you reconstruct the correct order?

(1) There are also a number of cases where one or two people claim to have been taken aboard an alien spaceship, prodded and probed with unconventional medical instruments, and released. (2) To the best of my knowledge there are no instances out of hundreds of thousands of UFO reports filed since 1947 in which many people independently and reliably report a close encounter with what is clearly an alien spacecraft. (3) Flying saucers, or UFOs, are well known to almost everyone. (4) It might, for example, be an automobile headlight reflected off a high-altitude cloud, or a flight of luminescent insects, or an unconventional aircraft, or a conventional aircraft with unconventional lighting patterns, such as a high-intensity searchlight used for meteorological observations. (5) But seeing a strange light in the sky does not mean that we are being visited by beings from the planet Venus or a distant galaxy named Spectra. (6) But in these cases we have only the unsubstantiated testimony, no matter how heartfelt and seemingly sincere, of one or two people.

▰ LESSON 8: WRITING EFFECTIVE TITLES AND INTRODUCTIONS

In our experience, writers often have trouble writing titles and introductions—so much so that we often advise waiting until late in the writing process to write them (although trying to imagine a title early on can help you nutshell your ideas).

In this lesson, we hope to reduce your anxiety about titles and introductions by explaining some of the principles behind them. Titles and introductions need to include old information that links back to your readers' interests and new information that promises something surprising or challenging. The function of introductions is to hook your readers' interest, tie into their current state of knowledge, orient them to the problem you will investigate, and finally forecast the new surprising material to be presented and supported in the body of your paper. It follows, then, that to write a good introduction you need to know the background knowledge and interests of your readers and the big picture of your own argument.

Writing Effective Titles

A good title has an old-information element that hooks into a reader's existing knowledge and interests and a new-information element that promises something surprising. It is the reader's first indication of an essay's big picture. Typically, readers scan tables of contents, bibliographies, and indexes to select what they want to read by title alone. In a magazine's table of contents, imagine how unhelpful a title such as "My Paper," "Essay 3," or "Democracy" would be. Yet inexperienced writers, forgetting to think about how readers use titles, sometimes select ones such as these.

Your title should provide a brief but detailed overview of what your paper is about. Academic titles are typically longer and more detailed than are titles in popular magazines. They usually follow one of four conventions.

1. Some titles simply state the question that the essay addresses ("Will Patriarchal Management Survive Beyond the Twentieth Century?").
2. Some titles state, often in abbreviated form, the essay's thesis ("The Writer's Audience Is Always a Fiction").
3. Very often the title is a summary of the essay's purpose statement ("The Relationship Between Client Expectation of Improvement and Psychotherapy Outcome").
4. Many titles consist of two parts separated by a colon. To the left of the colon the writer presents key words from the essay's issue or problem or a "mystery phrase" that arouses interest; to the right the author places the essay's question, thesis, or summary of purpose ("Money and Growth: An Alternative Approach"; "Deep Play: Notes on a Balinese Cockfight"; or "Fine Cloth, Cut Carefully: Cooperative Learning in British Columbia").

Although such titles might seem stuffy or overly formal to you, they indicate how much a closed-form writer wishes to preview an article's big picture. Although their titles may be more informal, popular magazines often use these same strategies. Here are some titles from recent issues of *Redbook* and the business magazine *Forbes*.

"Is the Coffee Bar Trend About to Peak?" (question)

"A Man *Can* Take Maternity Leave—And Love It" (abbreviated thesis)

"Why the Department of Education Shouldn't Take Over the Student Loan Program" (summary of purpose statement)

"Feed Your Face: Why Your Complexion Needs Vitamins" (two parts linked by colon)

Composing a title for your essay can help you find your focus when you get bogged down in the middle of a draft. When students come to our offices for help with a draft, we usually begin by asking them their proposed title. Such a question forces them to *nutshell* their ideas—to see their project's big picture. Talking about the title inevitably leads to a discussion of the writer's purpose, the problem to be addressed, and the proposed thesis. Having invested all this conceptual effort, students can appreciate how much information their title provides their readers.

Planning an Introduction

Introductions serve two purposes—to engage the reader's interest and then to pick up where the title leaves off in sketching in the big picture. Closed-form introductions typically describe the problem to be addressed, provide needed background, state the essay's thesis or purpose, and preview the essay's structure, sometimes including a summary of its argument. In a short essay, the introduction may comprise simply the opening paragraph, but in longer essays introductions typically require several paragraphs. Writers often wait until late in the writing process to draft an introduction because, as you saw in Chapter 17, these big-picture features are often in flux during the writer's early drafts.

Whether you do it early in the process as a way to focus your initial plan or late in the process after your ideas have solidified, writing the introduction forces you to focus on your essay's big picture. If you have trouble writing introductions—and many writers do—guide questions can help. Before writing your introduction, take fifteen minutes or so to write out exploratory answers to the following questions.

1. What is your thesis statement?
2. What question does your thesis answer?
3. Why is this a problematic and significant question? What attempts have others made to answer it (include your own previous attempts)? (Freewrite for at least three to four minutes on this one.)
4. Do you imagine that your reader is already interested in this question? If not, how could you make this question interesting for your reader? (Freewrite for several minutes.)
5. How much prior knowledge do you think your reader has about this topic? How much background information will your reader need to understand the problem and appreciate the conversation that your paper is joining?
6. Finish this sentence: My purpose in this paper is

_____.

7. Fill in the blanks: Before reading my paper, I expect my reader to believe this about my topic: _____;

After reading my paper, I want my reader to believe this about my topic:

_____.

8. Finish this sentence: I can describe the structure of my paper as follows:

_____.

These questions will help you get unstuck because they generate all the information you will need to write an initial draft of your introduction.

Typical Features of a Closed-Form Introduction

A typical introduction to an academic article has the following features (for further discussion of academic introductions, see Chapter 2, pages 27–29):

Feature 1: An Opening Lead or Hook Appropriate to Your Rhetorical Context. The lead or hook comprises the opening sentences of the essay and is aimed at capturing the reader's interest in the subject. Academic writers generally assume a reader is already interested in the general topic area and ready to be informed about the specific problem to be addressed. But when you are writing for general audiences, you may need to hook your readers in the opening sentences through a dramatic vignette, a startling fact or statistic, an arresting quotation, or an interesting scene. *Reader's Digest* articles are famous for their interest-grabbing leads. Here is a typical opening from a *Reader's Digest* article.

> The first faint tremor rippled through the city just before ten o'clock that warm summer night. Then came the sound—as if something heavy was rolling along the ground. The tremor intensified into a rapid jerking, sending dishes crashing and tables and chairs dancing. Thousands of frightened people ran out of their houses into the darkness.
>
> *Opening lead used as a hook*
>
> Dawn's light showed the earthquake's horror. At least 60 lay dead, many buried under collapsed buildings. Virtually every home was damaged.
>
> This wasn't just another trembler along one of California's many faults, like the devastating quake that shook the Los Angeles area last January 17. It was one that rocked Charleston, S.C., on August 31, 1886.
>
> While many Americans believe serious earthquakes happen only in California, scientific research confirms that the risk in other states may be higher than anyone thought.
>
> *Thesis*

                    —Lowell Ponte, "Earthquakes: Closer than You Think"

Most academic writing opens less dramatically than does this example. Typically, academic writers begin with old information by describing something familiar about the topic to be investigated and summarizing the current state of knowledge or belief about it—what we might call the ordinary or common view. (This section can be based on your answer to question 7 on p. 474: "Before reading my paper, I expect my reader to believe this about my topic: _____".) The writer then makes a crucial move by raising a problem or question about this common ground. At this point the introduction moves to the next stage—the problem or question to be investigated.

Feature 2: Explanation of the Question to Be Investigated. Readers are intrinsically interested in questions. Once they become engaged with your question, they will look forward to your answer. The question is thus the starting place for your argument; it summarizes the conversation that your essay joins. Academic writers often state the question directly, but sometimes they imply it, letting the reader formulate it from context.

Unless the problem or question is a very familiar one, you will need to show your readers both what makes the question problematic—that is, why it hasn't already been solved—and what makes it significant—that is, why it is a problem worth solving. To demonstrate why a question is problematic, writers often summarize differing views among experts, show why a commonly posed answer to the question is unsatisfactory, or otherwise show what aspects of the problem need more attention, often through a review of the literature. To reveal a problem's significance, writers point either to the benefits that will come from solving it or to the bad consequences of leaving it unsolved. Sometimes these benefits or consequences are measured in practical, real-world terms; at other times they are measured by how much the solution advances knowledge. (See Chapters 1 and 2 for further discussion of academic problems.)

Feature 3: Background Information. Sometimes your readers may need background information before they can appreciate the problem that your paper addresses or the approach you take—perhaps a definition of key terms; a summary of events leading up to the problem at issue; factual details needed for basic understanding of the problem; and so forth. When readers need extensive information, writers sometimes place it in the first main section of the paper *following* the introduction.

Feature 4: A Preview of the Whole. One of the crucial functions of a closed-form introduction is to sketch the big picture by giving readers a sense of the whole. Initially new information, this preview, once read, becomes part of the old information readers will use to locate their position in the journey; simultaneously, by forecasting what's coming, the preview triggers the pleasure of prediction/fulfillment that we discussed in Lesson One. How writers lay out the whole is the subject of the next section.

Laying Out the Whole with a Thesis Statement, Purpose Statement, or Blueprint Statement

The most succinct way to lay out the whole is to state your thesis directly. Think of your thesis statement as your one-sentence answer to the question your paper addresses. In a prototypical short academic paper, your thesis statement is the last sentence of your introduction, in accordance with the principle of old before new. Thus you begin your introduction with the reader's common view (the old) and end with your thesis (the new).

Student writers often ask how detailed their thesis statements should be and whether it is permissible, sometimes, to delay revealing their thesis until the conclusion—an open-form move that gives their paper a more exploratory, mystery novel feel. You have a number of choices for kinds of thesis statements. For an illustration of a writer's options, we will use Dao's essay on euthanasia that we first introduced in Lesson 3:

- *Short thesis:* Your briefest option is simply to state your claim without a summary of your supporting argument or a forecasting of your structure:

  Euthanasia is wrong.

- *Short thesis with structural forecasting:* You can also state your claim but add to it a phrase that predicts structure:

  Euthanasia is wrong for several reasons. [*Or*] Euthanasia is wrong for three reasons.

- *Detailed thesis:* Using this option you not only state your claim but also succinctly summarize your whole argument. Sometimes you begin with an *although* clause that summarizes the view you are trying to change:

  Although my friend Martha argues that euthanasia is justified for terminally ill patients who have lost all quality of life, I am opposed to euthanasia because it benefits the living more than the sick, because it leads to dangerous consequences, and because it fails to appreciate the value of suffering.

- *Purpose statement:* A purpose statement announces a writer's purpose or intention without actually summarizing the argument. A purpose statement typically begins with a phrase such as "My purpose is to . . . " or "In the following paragraphs I wish to . . .":

  My purpose in this essay is to show the flaws in Martha's argument.

- *Blueprint or mapping statement:* A blueprint or mapping statement describes the form of the upcoming essay, usually announcing the number of main parts and describing the function or purpose of each one.

  First I show how euthanasia benefits the living more than the sick; then I discuss the bad consequences of euthanasia; finally I argue that euthanasia fails to acknowledge the value of suffering.

- *Multisentence summary:* In long articles, academic writers often use all three kinds of statements—a purpose statement, thesis statement, and blueprint statement—and also include a detailed summary of the whole argument. This sort of extensive forecasting is common in academic and business writing but occurs less frequently in informal or popular essays. Dao's paper is too short to justify a multisentence summary.

- *Thesis question:* When writers wish to delay their thesis, letting their argument slowly unfold and keeping their final stance a mystery, they often end the introduction with a question. Using this approach, Dao wouldn't tell readers where she stood until late in the paper, treating the body of the paper as an exploration. This powerful open-form strategy invites readers to join the writer in a mutual search for the answer.

  Although I instinctively oppose any sort of mercy killing, I find myself deeply moved by Martha's story about her dying aunt. The question of euthanasia leaves me baffled and troubled. Should euthanasia be legalized or not?

Which of these options should a writer choose? There are no firm rules to help you answer this question. How much you decide to forecast in the introduction and where you reveal your thesis is a function of your purpose, audience, and genre. The more you forecast, the clearer your argument is and the easier it is to read quickly. You minimize your demands on readers' time by giving them the gist of your argument in the introduction, making it easier to skim your essay if they haven't time for a thorough reading. The less you forecast, the more demands you make on readers' time; you invite them, in effect, to accompany you through the twists and turns of your own thinking process, and you risk losing them if they ever get confused, lost, or bored. For these reasons, academic writing is generally closed form and aims at maximum clarity. In many rhetorical contexts, however, more open forms are appropriate (see Chapter 4).

If you choose a closed-form structure, we can offer some advice on how much to forecast. Readers sometimes feel insulted by too much forecasting, so include only what is needed for clarity. For short papers, readers usually don't need the complete supporting argument forecast in the introduction. In longer papers, however, or in especially complex ones, readers appreciate having the whole argument forecast at the outset. Academic writing in particular tends to favor explicit and often detailed forecasting.

Summary

In this lesson we have shown that both titles and introductions must include old information that links back to your readers' interests and background knowledge and new information that predicts what is new, surprising, or challenging in your essay. The key features of a closed-form introduction are the opening lead; explanation of the problem to be investigated; background information (optional); and a forecasting of the whole by means of a thesis statement, purpose statement, blueprint statement, or predictive question.

FOR WRITING AND DISCUSSION

What follows is the introduction to a closed-form essay by paleontologist Stephen Jay Gould. Gould writes for general audiences interested in the philosophy and history of science, especially the field of evolutionary biology. Read the introduction carefully. Then, working in small groups or as a whole class, answer the questions that follow.

The human mind delights in finding pattern—so much so that we often mistake coincidence or forced analogy for profound meaning. No other habit of thought lies so deeply within the soul of a small creature trying to make sense of a complex world not constructed for it. [. . .] No other error of reason stands so doggedly in the way of any forthright attempt to understand some of the world's most essential aspects—the tortuous paths of history, the unpredictability of complex systems, and the lack of causal connection among events superficially similar.

Numerical coincidence is a common path to intellectual perdition in our quest for meaning. We delight in catalogs of disparate items united by the same number, and often feel in our gut that some unity must underlie it all. [Gould then gives numerous examples of people's fascination with certain "mystical" numbers, such as the numbers seven and five.]

In this essay, I shall discuss two taxonomic systems [theories of classification of organisms] popular in the decades just before Darwin published the *Origin of the Species*. Both assumed reasons other than evolution for the ordering of organisms; both proposed a scheme based on the number five for placing organisms into a hierarchy of groups and subgroups. Both argued that such a simple numerical regularity must record an intrinsic pattern in nature, not a false order imposed by human hope upon a more complex reality. I shall describe these systems and then discuss how evolutionary theory undermined their rationale and permanently changed the science of taxonomy by making such simple numerical schemes inconsistent with a new view of nature. This important change in scientific thought embodies a general message about the character of history and the kinds of order that a world built by history, and not by preordained plan, can (and cannot) express.

—Stephen Jay Gould, "The Rule of Five"

1. What question or problem does this article address?
2. What makes this problem both problematic and significant? In Gould's view, why should anyone care that scientists used to interpret the universe as governed by a preordained plan based on the number five?
3. What strategy does Gould use in the opening lead to engage readers' interest?
4. Identify the previewing features in this introduction (thesis statement, purpose statement, blueprint statement, partial summary of what's coming).
5. What is the predicted organization of Gould's article?

The following passage occurred at the end of the introduction for a college research paper on theories of education. Using cues about structure and meaning in this previewing passage, create the top branches of a tree diagram for this essay.

My purpose in the following paragraphs is to reveal the complexity of the arguments surrounding the open curriculum controversy. I will examine first the view of three educators influenced by Rousseau—A. S. Neill, John Holt, and Jerry Farber. Each of these people believes that the goal of education should be the joyful pursuit of self-discovery and that children should be free to explore their own natural interests. I will then turn to two opponents of the open curriculum—Max Rafferty and B. F. Skinner. Rafferty believes that the goal of education is the acquisition of intellectual skills rather than self-discovery. B. F. Skinner believes that the concept of freedom is an illusion and thus opposes the notion that students can "choose" their own curriculum.

◢ LESSON 9: WRITING EFFECTIVE CONCLUSIONS

Conclusions can best be understood as complements to introductions. In both the introduction and the conclusion, writers are concerned with the essay as a whole more than with any given part. In a conclusion, the writer attempts to bring a sense of completeness and closure to the profusion of points and particulars laid out in the body of the essay. The writer is particularly concerned with helping the reader move from the parts back to the big picture and to understand the importance or significance of the essay.

If you are having trouble figuring out how to conclude an essay, consider the following guide questions, which are designed to stimulate thought about how to conclude and to help you determine which model best suits your situation.

1. How long and complex is your essay? Is it long enough or complex enough that readers might benefit from a summary of your main points?
2. What's the most important point (or points) you want your reader to remember about your essay? How long ago in the essay did you state that point? Would it be useful to restate that point as succinctly and powerfully as possible?
3. Do you know of an actual instance, illustration, or example of your main point that would give it added weight?
4. What larger principle stands behind your main point? Or what must your audience accept as true in order to accept your main point? How would you defend that assumption if someone were to call it into question?
5. Why is your main point significant? Why are the ideas in your paper important and worth your audience's consideration? What larger issues does your topic relate to or touch on? Could you show how your topic relates to a larger and more significant topic? What might that topic be?
6. If your audience accepts your thesis, where do you go next? What is the next issue or question to be examined? What further research is needed? Conversely, do you have any major reservations, unexpressed doubts, or "All bets are off if X is the case" provisos you'd like to admit? What do you *not* know about your topic that reduces your certainty in your thesis?
7. How much antagonism or skepticism toward your position do you anticipate? If a great deal, would it be feasible to delay your thesis, solution, or proposal until the very end of the paper?

Because many writers find conclusions challenging to write, we offer the following six possible models.

The Simple Summary Conclusion

The most common, though often not the most effective, kind of conclusion is a simple summary, in which the writer recaps what has just been said. This approach is useful in a long or complex essay or in an instructional text that focuses on concepts to be learned. We use summary conclusions for most of the chapters in this text. In a short, easy-to-follow essay, however, a summary conclusion can be dull and may even annoy readers who are expecting something more significant, but a brief summary followed by a more artful concluding strategy can often be effective.

The Larger Significance Conclusion

A particularly effective concluding strategy is to draw the reader's attention to the *larger significance* of your argument. In our discussion of academic problems (see Chapter 1), we explained that a good academic question needs to be significant (worth pursuing). Although readers need to be convinced from the outset that the problem investigated in your paper is significant, the conclusion is a good place to elaborate on that significance by showing how your argument now leads to additional benefits for the reader. If you started off asking a pure knowledge question, you could show in your conclusion how your thesis leads to potential understanding of a larger, more significant question. If you asked an applied knowledge question, your conclusion could point out the practical benefits of your ideas. If you posed a values question, you could show how your argument clarifies the stance you might take when facing a related problem. Your goal in writing this kind of conclusion is to show how your answer to the question posed in your paper leads to a larger or more significant understanding.

The Proposal Conclusion

Another option, often used in analyses and arguments, is a *proposal conclusion,* which calls for action. A proposal conclusion states the action that the writer believes needs to be taken and briefly demonstrates the advantages of this action over alternative actions or describes its beneficial consequences. If your paper analyzes the consequences of shifting from a graduated to a flat-rate income tax, your conclusion may recommend an action, such as adopting, modifying, or opposing the flat tax. A slight variation is the *call-for-future-study conclusion,* which indicates what else needs to be known or resolved before a proposal can be offered. Such conclusions are especially common in scientific writing.

The Scenic or Anecdotal Conclusion

Popular writers often use a *scenic* or *anecdotal conclusion,* in which a scene or brief story illustrates a theme's significance without stating it explicitly. A paper examining the current trend against involuntary hospitalization of the mentally ill homeless might end by describing a former mental patient, now an itinerant homeless person, collecting bottles in a park. Such scenes can help the reader experience directly the emotional significance of the topic analyzed in the body of the paper.

The Hook and Return Conclusion

A related variety of conclusion is the *hook and return,* in which the ending of the essay returns to something introduced in the opening hook or lead. If the lead of your essay is a vivid illustration of a problem—perhaps a scene or an anecdote—then your conclusion might return to the same scene or story, but with some variation to illustrate the significance of the essay. This sense of return can give your essay a strong feeling of unity.

The Delayed-Thesis Conclusion

This type of conclusion delays the thesis until the end of the essay. Rather than stating the thesis, the introduction merely states the problem, giving the body of the essay an open, exploratory, "let's think through this together" feel. Typically, the body of the paper examines alternative solutions or approaches to the problem and leaves the writer's own answer—the thesis—unstated until the end. This approach is especially effective when writing about highly complex or divisive issues on which you want to avoid taking a stand until all sides have been fairly presented.

> **FOR WRITING AND DISCUSSION**
>
> Choose a paper you have just written and write an alternative conclusion using one of the strategies discussed in this chapter. Then share your original and revised conclusions in groups. Have group members discuss which one they consider most effective and why.

Summary

These six types of conclusion are neither exhaustive nor mutually exclusive. It is possible to imagine a conclusion that mixes several of these types—a few sentences summarizing your essay, a short passage showing the relationship of your topic to some broader issues, a brief call to action, and a final concluding scene. In determining an effective conclusion, you need to assess your audience's attitude toward your thesis, its understanding of your topic, the length and complexity of your essay, and what you want to happen as a result of people's reading your essay. Review the guide questions at the beginning of this section to help determine the most appropriate conclusion for you.

Composing and Revising Open-Form Prose

More and more I think I've entirely lost the knack of identifying issues, making arguments, and joining the debate. I've veered off toward the particular, the peripheral, accelerating so fast in that direction that sometimes I feel myself lost in a kind of aphasia, my left hemisphere almost dormant. All I'm interested in, all I seem to process, are moods and moments, atmosphere, sudden scenes and faces. I'm swept along at the market*, dazed, sometimes elated, and the fish are flying around me and the ferries are coming and going and sometimes the mountain appears from behind the clouds and sometimes it doesn't. . . .

My reading has become purely "literary" in the sense of dwelling in the kind of visceral world only literary detail can re-create, the impulse for meaning and extraction suspended. I sit in the easy chair in the livingroom, in front of the maple tree and the picture window, the trees all around me, and I drink coffee and read and the afternoon fades to evening and I reach up to turn on the light.

—Chris Anderson, *English Teacher and Writer*

Like Chris Anderson in this epigraph, we probably all share the desire at times to do writing that does not meet the requirements of tightly argued, thesis-governed, closed-form prose intended to inform, analyze, or persuade. We understand his longing to let the particulars of his experience—ferries, mountains, flying fish, and the dimming late-afternoon light—into his prose.

Here, we too shift our attention from closed- to open-form writing. In this chapter, we develop some of the concepts introduced in Chapter 7, seeking both to clarify and complicate your understanding of open-form features. This chapter focuses on the main distinctions between the closed and open ends of the form continuum. But we need to acknowledge at the outset that whereas closed-form prose is governed by a few widely accepted conventions, one of the main features of open-form prose is its freedom to play with conventions in a bewildering

---

*Pike Place Market in Seattle, Washington, famous for its fish merchants who throw fish from one station to the next as the fish are being cleaned and iced for sale.

variety of ways. Consequently, our discussion of open-form writing seeks more to introduce you to options rather than to treat open-form writing exhaustively. In this chapter we have two main purposes: (1) to draw your attention to and give you illuminating examples of features and techniques that you can think about as you are composing and revising open-forms; and (2) to make some suggestions about how to enliven your prose when your purpose, audience, and genre call for open-form features. To this end, we begin by reviewing the major differences between closed- and open-form writing.

■ UNDERSTANDING OPEN-FORM FEATURES

Open-form prose differs from closed-form prose in its basic features, in the challenges and options it presents writers, in the demands it places on its readers, and in the mental and emotional pleasures it creates. For our purposes throughout this chapter, when we speak of open-form prose, we are referring to *literary nonfiction*, which is nonfiction writing that uses, in the words of rhetorician Chris Anderson, "the *modes* of fiction for nonfictive *aims*, either the communication of information or the dramatization of a point of view."*

As we discussed in Chapters 4 and 18, closed-form writing seeks to be efficient and reader friendly. By forecasting what's coming, placing points first, using clear transitions, and putting old information before new, closed-form writers place maximum emphasis on delivering clear ideas that readers can grasp quickly. In contrast, open-form writers, by violating or simply stretching those same conventions, set up a different kind of relationship with readers. Open-form writing often demands patience and tolerance for ambiguity from readers. Yet open-form prose yields its own special rewards, for readers and for writers. What follows are some of the main features of open-form writing.

Narrative Base and Reader Involvement

Both the difficulties and the pleasures of open-form writing derive from its narrative base: the tendency to convert explicit themes and conceptual issues into stories with dramatic tensions and implicit themes. This narrative base forces readers to have a different sort of engagement with the text than they have with closed-form writing. Open-form reading affords pleasures akin to solving puzzles, playing games, and making surprising discoveries. The price readers pay for this recreation is the expenditure of considerable intellectual energy. Because ideas are

---

*For the definition of literary nonfiction and the focus on the rhetorical effect of gaps, we are indebted to Chris Anderson, "Teaching Students What Not to Say: Iser, Didion, and the Rhetoric of Gaps," *Journal of Advanced Composition* 7 (1987): 10–22.

embedded in a story's events rather than handed to readers in straightforward statements, readers are asked to become mentally active in a specific way with open-form prose.

The Writer's Role and Reader Involvement

Open-form prose also sets up its own kind of relationship between writer and reader. Thesis-based writers typically discover their ideas offstage. They analyze particulars and test ideas during drafting, delete irrelevant and unsuccessful notions, and then rearrange their remaining ideas and particulars under a hierarchy of points and subpoints in a final draft. Closed-form writers typically begin by telling the audience what conclusion they've reached about the topic, and then use most of the rest of the paper to justify that conclusion.

Open-form writers, in contrast, are just as likely to take readers backstage to share the process that led to their conclusion. They often cast themselves in the role of narrators or characters reporting their quest for understanding and all the coincidences, disappointments, snatches of conversation, puzzling advice, and confusion they experienced along the way. In this process of sharing and in making the readers co-discoverers with the writer, open-form prose may draw more attention than closed-form prose to the writer's persona. In addition, readers become participants in the writer's experiences and reflections.

Artistic Language and Reader Involvement

Open-form prose is also characterized by its emphasis on an aesthetic use of language: that is, language used to please and entertain. Without the benefit of a thesis or a points-first structure to convey meaning, open-form prose depends on the very specificity of words, the ability of words to create mental pictures, to appeal to readers' senses and emotions, and to conjure up memories. Along with the literary features of plot, character, and setting, open-form prose employs language artistically to generate meaning and evoke pleasure. Open-form prose gives prominence to the particulars that writers experience. As Anderson comments, "details make sense. The trivial has meaning." Figurative language—such as metaphors, similes, and personifications—appeals to readers' imaginations, eliciting emotional as well as mental responses.

Of the many kinds of open-form prose, one of the most common and one that you will probably have the most occasion to write is an autobiographical narrative. A personal narrative combines an expressive purpose (writing that emphasizes the writer's experiences and feelings) with a literary purpose (writing that uses strategies of literature for an aesthetic effect.) To help you see the possibilities and demands of open-form writing, we begin with an example of an autobiographical narrative written by a student.

After reading the essay, respond to the questions that follow.

READING

PATRICK KLEIN
BERKELEY BLUES

It was a cold night. That is nothing new in San Francisco, but something made this night particularly frigid. It was early February and the whole city, including the Berkeley section where we were staying, was still held tight in the firm grip of winter. It had also rained that afternoon and the air, having been cleared by the storm, was cold and sharp. It hurt the back of your throat when you inhaled and turned into mist when you exhaled. As the six of us hurriedly walked in a huddled mass, the water that was lying in puddles on the dimly lit sidewalk jumped out of our way as we slammed our dress shoes down into its dregs. We silently decided on our destination and slipped into the grungy, closet-like pizza joint. We took the only seats the place had and as we pulled them into a circle, we all breathed a sigh of relief. 1

This was our first night at Berkeley. We were there for a debate tournament to be held the next day at the university. On this night, however, we were six high school sophomores in search of food. So, dressed in our suits and ties (we were required to wear them) and heavy coats, we ventured out of the university and entered the city of Berkeley. 2

Berkeley is an interesting place. Many might have romantic notions of a bunch of shaggy intellectuals discussing French existentialism while sipping cappuccino, but while this might have been the case a few decades ago, the reality is that Berkeley is a ghetto. The place is filled with grungy closet shops while newspapers cover the sidewalks and the people lying on them. The university is divided from this ghetto by a two-lane street. 3

As the six of us crossed the two-lane street that fateful night, my thoughts drifted to my own neighborhood, which up until that moment had been the extent of my world. 4

McCormick Ranch, Arizona, is a sheltered place. To a certain extent it's mostly white, with little crime and few domestic problems. Everybody has a pool, at least two cars, and a beautiful desert sunset every night. I had everything I ever wanted. It seemed very gentle and dreamlike compared to the harsh slum we found ourselves in. 5

When we made it into the pizza place and moved the chairs into a protective circle around a square table, anxiety about our "hostile" environment was quickly swept away with hot, greasy pizza. We ate until we were content and were trying to decide how to divide the few remaining pieces among ourselves when it happened. 6

The pizza place was separated from the rest of humanity by a large window. Our table was directly in front of that window and two feet from the door. People had been passing the window and probably remarking on the six well-dressed kids inside, but we paid them no mind and they all walked by without incident. Still, our hearts were seized with terror every time a human being would pass that window, and we hoped with all that we could muster that every one of them would continue on. We were almost right. 7

On this night, when six young yuppie kids from an upper middle-class world decided to risk it and go eat pizza in a ghetto, he walked by. He didn't look any different from others we'd seen that night. Black. Dirty. Tired. Cold. His clothes consisted of a 8 grimy, newspaper-stained jacket, a T-shirt with who-knows-how-old dirt on it, flimsy pants with holes at the knees, and tattered excuses for shoes. He was not quite up to par with our Gucci loafers and Armani jackets.

9   He shuffled past the window and glanced in. We didn't notice. He stopped. We noticed. Twelve eyes glanced up as casually as they could and six hearts stopped beating for a second. Yep, still there. All eyes went back to the floor, except for two. Those eyes belonged to Chad, and in some act of defiance, his eyes met the poor man's eyes and glared.

10   The man opened the door. "We're all going to die," I thought. "All my hopes and dreams are going to end here, in a stupid pizza place, at the hands of a crazy black bum."

11   He took something out of his pocket.

12   It was shiny.

13   I couldn't look.

14   A knife.

15   No. It was a flask. He took a swig from it, and, still propping the door open with his sagging frame, spoke the most jolting, burning words I've ever heard.

16   "I love you," he said. "All of you." He glanced at Chad, "Even you." He stepped back and said, "I know what you think of me, but I still love you." I will probably never forget those words or how he said them with a steady, steely voice.

17   Then he left. That was it. Gone. It took about five minutes for anyone to talk. When the talking started, we exchanged jokes and responded with empty, devastating laughter.

18   We soon left the shop. It had grown colder outside and we quickly returned to our climate-controlled hotel room. We had just eaten a filling meal and paid for it with our own money. We were all about fifteen. The man we had encountered was probably in his fifties. He had no roof, no money, or food. It seemed strange that I owned more than an adult, but in truth, he had more than I. He was able to love us when we ostracized him and thought stereotypically about him.

19   I remember later trying to rationalize my sickening behavior by thinking that there is nothing wrong with being and acting afraid in a strange environment. I tried to use my age as an excuse. Nothing worked. I was guilty of fearing a fellow human being because of his color and my preset notions of bums.

20   To this day I still think about what difference, if any, it would have made if we had given him our leftover pizza. It might have eased my conscience. It was a very cold night and we had made it colder.

FOR WRITING AND DISCUSSION

1. A piece of advice often given to open-form writers is "Above all else, be interesting." How does student writer Patrick Klein hook and sustain readers' interest?

2. This essay does not assert a thesis statement in the introduction, yet the narrative has a focus and a theme that becomes increasingly clear near the end. What do you see as the theme of significance of this essay?

3. According to his instructor, Patrick was at first unable to think of a topic to write about. (The assignment was to write an autobiographical

narrative about an event that made a difference in your life.) "But I can't think of anything that made a big difference in my life!" he commented. Then his teacher asked him to write a journal entry in which he looked at some event, situation, or behavior, however minor, that he now regretted. This journal entry led him to remember the incident in the pizza joint, which he still thought was no big deal and too minor to write about. What Patrick came to understand is the point that Chris Anderson made about open-form writing: "Details make sense. The trivial has meaning." How has Patrick invested a seemingly trivial event with meaning?

IDENTIFYING AND CREATING A MINIMAL STORY

In open-form prose, where you do not have a thesis upon which to build a hierarchy of points and subpoints, you need to use other structures to convey meaning. Open-form writing relies heavily on narrative for its substance and form. Another word for the term *narrative* is story. As we show in this section, what distinguishes a story from *and then* writing, which also follows chronological order, is *significance* conveyed through and embodied in a writer's conscious shaping of events and meaning. *And then* writing becomes a story when it has certain features: depicted events, connectedness, tension, and resolution. We say that to be a *minimal story*—a narrative must depict connected events that create a sense of tension or conflict that is resolved through insight, understanding, or action.

Depiction of Events

The depiction of events is the defining feature of narrative. Whereas thesis-based writing descends from problem to thesis to supporting reasons and evidence, stories unfold linearly, temporally, from event to event over time. Consider the sequence of events in the following fable.

Minimal Story: Depiction of Events

A crow stole a large chunk of cheese off a windowsill and flew away to a high tree to eat it. A fox witnessed the theft and trotted over beneath the tree. As the crow prepared to eat the cheese, the fox watched quietly. Finally, the fox cleared his throat and caught the crow's attention.

"Excuse me, sir. I couldn't help but notice the lovely black sheen of your feathers. Really quite striking. And the graceful lines of your body, the perfect proportions. One just doesn't see that sort of beauty around here everyday."

The crow listened closely, puffing himself up with each of the fox's compliments.

"I also can't help wondering if your voice is as beautiful as your body. If it is, you are, to be sure, the king of birds in these woods."

The crow, eager to affirm the fox's high opinion of him, broke out in a raucous, cawing serenade. The moment he opened his beak, the cheese fell to the ground at the fox's feet. The fox promptly ate the morsel and trotted away, calling out over his shoulder as he left:

"So much for your beauty; next time we meet, let's discuss your brains."

Moral: "It is a maxim in the schools,
 That Flattery's the food of fools;"
And whoso likes such airy meat
Will soon have nothing else to eat.

—Oliver Goldsmith, "The Crow and the Fox," *Aesop's Fables*

This story recounts the events of a crow stealing a piece of cheese and a wily fox cajoling the crow into forfeiting the cheese.

In addition to the temporal unfolding of events in a story, the events should convey a sense of "onceness." Things that happen at a point in time happen only once, as the classic fairytale opening, "Once upon a time," suggests. To be sure, many people enter college or get married every day, but no one else's account of that experience can be substituted for your account of your own experience of universal events. Composing and revising your narrative involves the challenge of depicting your experience as a series of events that capture the "onceness" of that experience.

Connectedness

To be a minimal story, the events of a narrative must also be connected—not merely spatially or sequentially connected, but causally or thematically related as well. They must affect one another. Stories are more than just chronicles of events. Novelist E. M. Forster offered the simplest definition of a true narrative when he rejected "The King dies and then the queen died," but accepted "The king died and then the queen died . . . of grief." The last two words in the second version connect the two events to each other in a causal relationship, converting a series of events into a patterned, meaningfully related sequence of events. Now examine the following passage to see the kinds of connections the writer establishes between the scenes he describes.

Minimal Story: Thematic and Causal Connectedness

I have been so totally erased from nature lately, like a blackboard before school starts, that yesterday when I was in the Japanese section of San Francisco, Japantown, I saw the sidewalk littered with chocolate wrappers.

There were hundreds of them. Who in the hell has been eating all these chocolates? I thought. A convention of Japanese chocolate eaters must have passed this way.

Then I noticed some plum trees on the street. Then I noticed that it was autumn. Then I noticed that the leaves were falling as they will and as they must every year. Where had I gone wrong?

—Richard Brautigan, "Leaves"

Brautigan's narrative becomes a story only when you realize that the "chocolate wrappers" are really plum leaves; the two images are connected by the writer's changed perception, which illuminates the thematic question raised at the beginning and the end: Why has the writer become "so totally erased from nature"? As you write, make the elements of your narrative connect causally and thematically.

Tension or Conflict

The third criterion for a minimal story—tension or conflict—creates the anticipation and potential significance that keeps the reader reading. In whodunit stories, the tension follows from attempts to identify the murderer or to prevent the murderer from doing in yet another victim. In many comic works, the tension is generated by confusion or misunderstanding that drives a wedge between people who would normally be close. Tension always involves contraries, such as those between one belief and another, between opposing values, between the individual and the environment or the social order, between where I am now and where I want to be or used to be. In the following passage, see how the contraries create dramatic tension that engages readers.

Minimal Story: Dramatic Tensions

Straddling the top of the world, one foot in China and the other in Nepal, I cleared the ice from my oxygen mask, hunched a shoulder against the wind, and stared absently down at the vastness of Tibet. I understood on some dim, detached level that the sweep of earth beneath my feet was a spectacular sight. I'd been fantasizing about this moment, and the release of emotion that would accompany it, for many months. But now that I was finally here, actually standing on the summit of Mount Everest, I just couldn't summon the energy to care.

It was early in the afternoon of May 10, 1996. I hadn't slept in fifty-seven hours. The only food I'd been able to force down over the preceding three days was a bowl of ramen soup and a handful of peanut M&Ms. Weeks of violent coughing had left me with two separated ribs that made ordinary breathing an excruciating trial. At 29,028 feet up in the troposphere, so little oxygen was reaching my brain that my mental capacity was that of a slow child. Under the circumstances, I was incapable of feeling much of anything except cold and tired.

—Jon Krakauer, *Into Thin Air*

Notice how this passage presents several contraries or conflicts: the opposition between the narrator's expectation of what it would be like to stand on the top of Mount Everest and the actuality once he's there; and the opposition between the physical strength and stamina of the climber and the extreme danger of climbing this mountain. The reader wonders how Krakauer reached the summit with no sleep, almost no food, and a violent and agonizing cough; more important, the reader wonders why he kept on climbing. We can ask this important query of any narrative: What conflicts and tensions are prompting readers' ongoing questions and holding their interest?

Resolution, Recognition, or Retrospective Interpretation

The final criterion for a minimal story is the resolution or retrospective interpretation of events. The resolution may be stated explicitly or implied. Fables typically sum up the story's significance with an explicit moral at the end. In contrast, the interpretation of events in poetry is almost always implicit. Note how the following haiku collapses events and resolution.

A strange old man
stops me,
Looking out of my deep mirror.

—Hitomaro, *One Hundred Poems from the Japanese*

In this minimal story, two things happen simultaneously. The narrator is stopped by a "strange old man" and the narrator looks into a mirror. The narrator's *recognition* is that he is that same old man. This recognition—"That's I in the mirror; when I wasn't looking, I grew old!"—in turn ties the singular event of the story back to more universal concerns and the reader's world.

The typical direction of a story, from singular event(s) to general conclusion, reverses the usual points-first direction of closed-form essays. Stories force readers to read inductively, gathering information and looking for a pattern that's confirmed or disconfirmed by the story's resolution. This resolution is the point *toward* which readers read. It often drives home the significance of the narrative. Typically, a reader's satisfaction or dissatisfaction with a story hinges on how well the resolution manages to explain or justify the events that precede it. Writers need to ask: How does my resolution grow out of my narrative and fit with the resolution the reader has been forming?

FOR WRITING AND DISCUSSION

1. Working as a whole class or in groups, explain how the student essay "Berkeley Blues" (pp. 486–87) qualifies as a minimal story. How does it meet the four basic criteria for a minimal story: depiction of events, connectedness, tension, and resolution?
2. In contrast, how does the following *and then* narrative fail to meet the criteria for a minimal story? How does your experience as a reader differ as you ponder "Berkeley Blues" versus "The Stolen Watch?"

```
                  The Stolen Watch


      Last fall and winter I was living in Spokane with my brother, who

during this time had a Platonic girlfriend come over from Seattle

and stay for a weekend. Her name was Karen, and we became interested

in each other and I went over to see her at the first of the year.
```

She then invited me to, supposedly, the biggest party of the year, called the Aristocrats' Ball. I said sure and made my way back to Seattle in February. It started out bad on Friday, the day my brother and I left Spokane. We left town an hour late, but what's new. Then my brother had to stop along the way and pick up some parts; we stayed there for an hour trying to find this guy. It all started out bad because we arrived in Seattle and I forgot to call Karen. We were staying at her brother's house and after we brought all our things in, we decided to go to a few bars. Later that night we ran into Karen in one of the bars, and needless to say she was not happy with me. When I got up the next morning I knew I should have stayed in Spokane, because I felt bad vibes. Karen made it over about an hour before the party. By the time we reached the party, which drove me crazy, she wound up with another guy, so her friends and I decided to go to a few bars. The next morning when I was packing, I could not find my watch and decided that someone had to have taken it. We decided that it had to have been the goon that Karen had wound up with the night before, because she was at her brother's house with him before she went home. So how was I going to get my watch back?

We decided the direct and honest approach to the problem would work out the best. We got in contact and confronted him. This turned out to be quite a chore. It turned out that he was visiting some of his family during that weekend and lived in Little Harbor, California. It turned out that Karen knew his half brother and got some information on him, which was not pretty. He had just been released by the army and was trained in a special forces unit, in the fields of Martial Arts. He was a trained killer! This information did not help matters at all, but the next bit of information was just as bad if

not worse. Believe it or not, he was up on charges of attempted murder and breaking and entering. In a way, it turned out lucky for me,
because he was in enough trouble with the police and did not need
any more. Karen got in contact with him and threatened him that I
would bring him up on charges, if he did not return the watch. His
mother decided that he was in enough trouble and sent me the watch.
I was astounded, it was still working and looked fine. The moral of
the story is don't drive 400 miles to see a girl you hardly know,
and whatever you do, don't leave your valuables out in the open.

▧ CONSIDERING STRUCTURAL OPTIONS FOR OPEN-FORM WRITING

The epigraph to Chapter 18 by the philosopher Kenneth Burke speaks about form as "an arousing and fulfillment of desires." In closed-form prose, we can easily see this process at work: The writer previews what he or she is going to say, arousing the reader's desire to see the general statement translated into specifics, and then fulfills that desire speedily through a presentation of pertinent points and particulars.

In more open-form prose, the fulfillment of desire follows a less straightforward path. Writers offer fewer overviews and clues, leaving readers less sure of where they're headed; or writers mention an idea and then put it aside for a while as they pursue some other point, whose relevance may seem tenuous. Rather than establish the direction or point of their prose, writers suspend that direction, waiting until later in the prose to show how the ideas are meaningfully related. In other words, the period of arousal is longer and more drawn out; the fulfillment of desire is delayed until the end, when the reader finally sees how the pieces fit together.

Open-form prose gives you the opportunity to overlay your narrative core with other patterns of ideas—to move associatively from idea to idea, to weave a complex pattern of meaning in which the complete picture emerges later. Often the way you achieve these surprising twists and turns of structure and meaning is by playing with the conventions of closed-form prose. For example, in the auto-biographical narrative "Berkeley Blues," Patrick Klein breaks the cardinal closed-form rule that pronouns should refer only to previously stated antecedents; he introduces the stranger only as *he* and gradually reveals that person's identity. This violation creates an aura of mystery and suspense. Here we describe some of your open-form options to surprise your readers and delay their fulfillment of desires.

Suspending and Disrupting Readers' Desire for Direction

Open-form writers frequently violate the principle of forecasting and mapping that we stressed in Chapter 18. Consider the following introduction to an essay.

Passage with Suspended Direction

Whose bones?
What feathers?
Birds? What
birds?

I suppose their little bones have years ago been lost among the stones and winds of those high glacial pastures. I suppose their feathers blew eventually into the piles of tumbleweed beneath the straggling cattle fences and rotted there in the mountain snows, along with dead steers and all the other things that drift to an end in the corners of the wire. I do not quite know why I should be thinking of birds over the *New York Times* at breakfast, particularly the birds of my youth half a continent away. It is a funny thing what the brain will do with memories and how it will treasure them and finally bring them into odd juxtapositions with other things, as though it wanted to make a design, or get some meaning out of them, whether you want it or not, or even see it.

What do birds
have to do with
the working of the
brain? Where is
this writer going?

—Loren Eisley, "The Bird and the Machine"

Note the sequence of ideas from bones to birds to breakfast over the *New York Times* to comments about the workings of the brain. In fact, in this essay it takes Eisley six full paragraphs in which he discusses mechanical inventions to return to the birds with the line: ". . . or those birds, I'll never forget those birds. . . ."

Throughout these paragraphs, what drives the reader forward is curiosity to discover the connections between the parts and to understand the meaning of the essay's title "The Bird and the Machine." Actually, Eisley's comment about the brain's "odd juxtaposition" of memories with "other things, as though it wanted to make a design, or get meaning out of them" could be a description of this open-form technique we've called *suspending direction*. Open-form writers can choose when "odd juxtapositions" are an appropriate strategy for inviting the reader to accompany the discovering, reflecting writer on a journey toward meaning.

Leaving Gaps

An important convention of closed-form prose is the old/new contract, which specifies that the opening of every sentence should link back in some way to what has gone before. Open-form prose often violates this convention, leaving *gaps* in the text, forcing the reader to puzzle over the connection between one part and the next.

The following passage clearly violates the old/new contract. This example recounts the writer's thoughts after startling a weasel in the woods and exchanging glances with it.

Passage with Intentional Gaps

What goes on in [a weasel's brain] the rest of the time? What does a weasel think about? He won't say. His journal is tracks in clay, a spray of feathers, mouse blood and bone: uncollected, unconnnected, loose-leaf, and blown.

I would like to learn, or remember, how to live. I come to Hollins Pond not so much to learn how to live as, frankly, to forget about it.

—Annie Dillard, "Living like Weasels"

Gap caused by unexplained or unpredicted shift from weasel to philosophic musing

Dillard suddenly switches, without transition, from musing about the mental life of a weasel to asserting that she would like to learn how to live. What is the connection between her encounter with the weasel and her own search for how to live? Dillard's open-form prose leaves these gaps for readers to ponder and fill in, inviting us to participate in the process of arriving at meaning. Just as open-form writers can deliberately avoid predicting or mapping statements, they also have the liberty to leave gaps in a text when it suits their purpose.

Employing Unstable or Ironic Points of View

Whereas the closed-form style encourages a single sort of viewpoint—rational, trustworthy, thoughtful—the open-form style tolerates a variety of viewpoints, including some that are more perplexing than reassuring. In open-form prose, writers are free to don masks and play around with different personae, including some that the writer may question or even loathe. A particular favorite of open-form writers is the ironic point of view. In this context, *irony* means saying one thing while intending other things, one of which may be the exact opposite of what's being said.

Consider the following bit of irony from eighteenth-century writer Jonathan Swift:

I have been assured by a very knowing American of my acquaintance in London, that a young healthy child well nursed is at a year old a most delicious, nourishing, and wholesome food, whether stewed, roasted, baked, or boiled; and I make no doubt that it will equally serve in a fricassee or a ragout.

The shock of this passage comes in part from the narrator's sudden change of direction. The opening seemingly points toward some elevating discussion of child wellness. Then, without warning, the reader is plunged into a grotesque treatise on the tastiness of cooked children.

Clearly the narrator's values are not shared by Swift, a religious Irishman who spent much of his life protesting the very sort of inhumanity he presents in this passage. What does Swift gain by adopting the persona of a moral monster and proposing that poor Irish people sell their children to English gentry for food in order to reduce Ireland's population and make some money? For one thing, he gains immediacy.

By stepping inside the persona that he reviles, Swift dramatizes what he sees as the snobbish, self-assured, and predatory English "gentleman." He doesn't talk about his enemy; he *becomes* that enemy so that the reader can see him as Swift sees him. Swift could have written an essay condemning the callous attitudes that were causing the Irish people so much suffering. But consider what would happen to the passage if Swift were to speak for himself.

> The landed English gentry who control Ireland treat the Irish people like consumer goods to be bought, sold, and used up in the service of their self-interests. For all the English care, we Irish could be chunks of mutton to be tossed into their nightly stew.

That's still pretty strong, but it leaves the reader outside the evil that Swift describes. The audience hears about "landed English gentry" but doesn't experience their attitudes, values, and language directly, as in the original passage. The difference in the two passages is the difference between being told that someone is really hideous and spending half an hour trapped in a phone booth with that person.

Unstable viewpoints aren't always this dramatic. But they always offer writers the freedom to present directly, through dialogue and perspective, points of view that they might otherwise have to re-present via summary and argument. Such viewpoints also require readers to be more attentive in order to distinguish the author's point of view from that of the narrator.

■ USING LANGUAGE ARTISTICALLY FOR MEANING AND PLEASURE

Perhaps the first thing you notice about open-form prose is its great range of styles. In many cases, you can read a paragraph of open-form prose and identify the writer solely by the style. The primacy of style in open-form prose results from the writer's desire to use language artistically for meaning and pleasure. In open-form writing, you may well be arrested by a writer's peculiar use of language—an evocative word, a striking phrase, an unexpected metaphor, or an unusual construction.

Let us consider more closely some of the ways that open-form writers play with the medium of language.

Using Specific Words

According to the poet William Blake, "To Generalize is to be an Idiot." Open-form writers don't usually go that far, but they do tend to stay at a fairly low level of abstraction, typically eschewing a hierarchy of points and subpoints in favor of an artful array of particulars.

To illustrate what might constitute "an artful array of particulars," consider the case of writer John McPhee. When asked why he wrote the sentence "Old white oaks are rare because they had a tendency to become bowsprits, barrel staves, and queen-post trusses" instead of a more generic sentence, such as "Old white oaks are rare because they used to be so valuable as lumber," he responded in a way that reveals his love of the particular.

> There isn't much life in [the alternative version of the sentence]. If you can find a specific, firm, and correct image, it's always going to be better than a generality, and hence I tend, for example, to put in trade names and company names and, in an instance like this, the names of wood products instead of a general term like "lumber." You'd say "Sony" instead of "tape recorder" if the context made it clear you meant to say tape recorder. It's not because you're on the take from Sony, it's because the image, at least to this writer or reader, strikes a clearer note.

Some readers might complain that the particulars "bowsprits, barrel staves, and queen-post trusses" aren't helpful in the way that particulars in closed-form prose are. In closed-form prose, examples clarify and support points. McPhee, on the other hand, uses three unusual examples that will give most readers a moment's pause. Today most barrel staves and bowsprits are made of metal, not oak, and few contemporary readers encounter them on a regular basis no matter what they're made of. Furthermore, few readers at any time could readily identify "queen-post trusses," a technical term from the building trade. Instead of smoothly completing the reader's understanding of a point, McPhee's particulars tend to arrest and even sidetrack, sending the reader in pursuit of a dictionary.

But if McPhee's examples momentarily puzzle, it's the sort of puzzlement that can lead to greater understanding. Precisely because they are exotic terms, these words arouse the reader's curiosity and imagination. "Exotic language is of value," says McPhee. "A queen-post truss is great just because of the sound of the words and what they call to mind. The 'queen,' the 'truss'—the ramifications in everything."

For McPhee, the fact that these words trip up the reader is a point in their favor. If McPhee had said that old white oaks are rare these days because they became parts of "floors, buckets, and fences" no one would blink or notice. If you were to visualize the items, you'd probably call up some ready-made pictures that leave little trace in your mind. You also wouldn't hear the sounds of the words. (In this regard, notice McPhee's emphasis on images sounding "a clearer note.") Your forward progress toward the point would be unimpeded, but what would be lost? A new glimpse into a lost time when oak trees were used to make exotic items that today exist mostly in old books and memories.

Another quality also recommends words that readers trip over, words such as *bowsprit*, *barrel stave*, and *queen-post truss*: their power to persuade the reader to believe in the world being described. Tripping over things, whether they're made of steel or words, forces the reader to acknowledge their independence, the reality of a world outside the reader's own head. For this reason, writers of formula fiction—thrillers, westerns, romances, and the like—will load their texts with lots of little details and bits of technical information from the time and place they describe. Because their stories are otherwise implausible (e.g., the description of the Evil Empire's doomsday machine) they need all the help they can get from their details (the size of the toggle bolts used to keep the machine in place while it's blasting out intergalactic death rays) to convince readers that the story is real.

Using Revelatory Words

We use the term *revelatory words* for specific details that reveal the social status, lifestyle, beliefs, and values of people. According to writer Tom Wolfe, carefully chosen details can reveal a person's *status life*—"the entire pattern of behavior and possessions through which people express their position in the world or what they think it is or hope it to be."

Wolfe favors writing that records "everyday gestures, habits, manners, customs, styles of furniture, clothing, decoration, styles of traveling, eating, keeping house, modes of behaving toward children, servants, superiors, inferiors, peers, plus the various looks, glances, poses, styles of walking and other symbolic details that might exist within a scene." For example, Patrick Klein and his classmates are economically revealed as middle class by their attire—"Armani jackets" and "Gucci loafers."

FOR WRITING AND DISCUSSION

Try your own hand at using descriptive details that reveal status life. Working in small groups or as a whole class, create a list of specific details that you might associate with each of the following: junior-high boys standing on a street corner; college professor's office; the kitchen of an upscale apartment of a two-professional couple; the kitchen of a lower-middle-class blue-collar family; the kitchen of an apartment shared by college students.

Example: Junior high boys standing on a street corner might be associated with baggy pants with crotch at the knee level and exposed boxer shorts; Nike Air Jordans with the top laces loose; Marlboro cigarettes; Chicago Bulls cap on backwards.

Using Memory-Soaked Words

Wolfe offers a psychological explanation for the pleasure people take in exotic or revelatory language: "Print (as opposed to film or theater) is an indirect medium that does not so much 'create' images or emotions as jog the reader's memories." The best way to jog that memory and evoke sensations, according to Wolfe, is through careful selection of very specific words and images that evoke complex responses in the brain; the "human memory seems to be made up of *sets of meaningful data*" (emphasis ours) as opposed to separate bits of data that people consciously combine. In the following passage, Wolfe describes the complex interplay between writers' words and readers' responses.

> These memory sets often combine a complete image and an emotion. The power of a single image in a story or song to evoke a complex feeling is well known. I have always enjoyed the opening lines of a country and western song by Roger Miller called "King of the Road." "Trailers for Sale or Rent," it begins, "Room to Let Fifty Cents." It is not the part about trailers that I enjoy so much as the "Room to Let." This is the sort of archaic wording that, in my experience, is found only in windows or on door frames in the oldest and most run-down section of a city. It immediately triggers in my memory a particular view of a particular street near Worcester Square in New Haven, Connecticut. The emotion it calls up is one of loneliness and deprivation but of a rather romantic sort (bohemia). One's memory is apparently made up of millions of such sets, which work together. . . . The most gifted writers are those who manipulate the memory sets of the reader in such a rich fashion that they create within the mind of the reader an entire world that resonates with the reader's own real emotions.
>
> —Tom Wolfe, *New Journalism*

Had Miller opened his song with "Room *for Rent* Fifty Cents," there would have been no loss of clarity; if anything, most people would process the more familiar "rent" more rapidly than "let." The loss would have been associational and emotional. "For Rent" signs are too common to evoke any particular set of associations for most people. "To Let" signs, however, are rare enough that they are much more likely to evoke particular times and places for those who've encountered them. People who have never heard the phrase "to let" will either puzzle over it and eventually experience the pleasure of making sense of it or not notice the substitution and pass over it.

FOR WRITING AND DISCUSSION

Make a list of specific words and names associated with your childhood that you now rarely hear or use. Share your list with others in your group and identify the items that provoke the strongest associations. Examples include *Flexible Flyer* for those who remember those old sleds; *tetherball,* for those who have played that game on a playground; *Cookie Monster* from *Sesame Street; Pez guns; Mister Bill;* or *8-track tapes.* The idea is to think of specific words that are soaked with memories. Identify the emotions you associate with these words.

Using Figurative Words

Open-form writers often use figurative language in situations in which closed-form writers would use literal language. When journalist Nicholas Tomalin describes a captured Vietnamese prisoner as young and slight, the reader understands him in a literal way, but when he compares the prisoner to "a tiny, fine-boned wild animal," the reader understands him in a different way; the reader understands not only what the subject looks like—his general physical attributes—but how that particular boy appears in that moment to those around him—fierce, frightened, trapped.

Metaphors abound when literal words fail. When writers encounter eccentric people or are overwhelmed by the strangeness of their experiences, they use *figurative language*—imaginative comparisons—to explain their situation and their reactions to it. Figurative language—similes, metaphors, and personifications—enables the writer to describe an unfamiliar thing in terms of different, more familiar things. The surprise of yoking two very unlike things evokes from the reader a perception, insight, or emotional experience that could not otherwise be communicated. The originality and vividness of the imaginative comparison frequently resonates with meaning for readers and sticks in their minds long afterwards.

In the following passage, Isak Dinesen describes an experience that most of us have not had—seeing iguanas in the jungle and shooting one. After reading this passage, however, we have a striking picture in our minds of what she saw and a strong understanding of what she felt and realized.

Passage Using Figurative Language

In the Reserve I have sometimes come upon the Iguana, the big lizards, as they were sunning themselves upon a flat stone in a river-bed. They are not pretty in shape, but nothing can be imagined more beautiful than their coloring.

Similes heaped up   They shine like a heap of precious stones or like a pane cut out of an old church window. When, as you approach, they swish away, there is a flash of azure,

Simile   green and purple over the stones, the color seems to be standing behind them in the air, like a comet's luminous tail.

Once I shot an Iguana. I thought that I should be able to make some pretty things from his skin. A strange thing happened then, that I have never afterwards forgotten. As I went up to him, where he was lying dead upon his stone,

Metaphor of   and actually while I was walking a few steps, he faded and grew pale, all color
dying applied   died out of him as in one long sigh, and by the time that I touched him he was
to color simile   gray and dull like a lump of concrete. It was the live impetuous blood pulsating
Metaphor   within the animal, which had radiated out all that glow and splendor. Now that
Simile   the flame was put out, and the soul had flown, the Iguana was as dead as a sandbag.

—Isak Dinesen, "The Iguana"

The figurative language in this passage enables readers to share Dinesen's experience. It also compacts a large amount of information into sharp, memorable images.

To see how structural and stylistic options contribute to the effectiveness of a piece of literary nonfiction, read the following essay, "Living like Weasels," by nature writer and essayist Annie Dillard from her book *Teaching a Stone to Talk: Expeditions and Encounters*. After you have read the essay, address the questions that follow.

READING

ANNIE DILLARD
LIVING LIKE WEASELS

1   A weasel is wild. Who knows what he thinks? He sleeps in his underground den, his tail draped over his nose. Sometimes he lives in his den for two days without leaving. Outside, he stalks rabbits, mice, muskrats, and birds, killing more bodies than he can eat warm, and often dragging the carcasses home. Obedient to instinct, he bites his prey at the neck, either splitting the jugular vein at the throat or crunching the brain at the base of the skull, and he does not let go. One naturalist refused to kill a weasel who was socketed into his hand deeply as a rattlesnake. The man could in no way pry the tiny weasel off, and he had to walk half a mile to water, the weasel dangling from his palm, and soak him off like a stubborn label.

2   And once, says Ernest Thompson Seton—once, a man shot an eagle out of the sky. He examined the eagle and found the dry skull of a weasel fixed by the jaws to his throat. The supposition is that the eagle had pounced on the weasel and the weasel swiveled and bit as instinct taught him, tooth to neck, and nearly won. I would like to have seen that eagle from the air a few weeks or months before he was shot: was the whole weasel still attached to his feathered throat, a fur pendant? or did the eagle eat what he could reach, gutting the living weasel with his talons before his breast, bending his beak, cleaning the beautiful airborne bones?

3   I have been reading about weasels because I saw one last week. I startled a weasel who startled me, and we exchanged a long glance.

4   Twenty minutes from my house, through the woods by the quarry and across the highway, is Hollins Pond, a remarkable piece of shallowness, where I like to go at sunset and sit on a tree trunk. Hollins Pond is also called Murray's Pond; it covers two acres of bottomland near Tinker Creek with six inches of water and six thousand lily pads. In winter, brown-and-white steers stand in the middle of it, merely dampening their hooves; from the distant shore they look like miracle itself, complete with miracle's nonchalance. Now, in summer, the steers are gone. The water lilies have blossomed and spread to a green horizontal plane that is terra firma to plodding blackbirds, and tremulous ceiling to black leeches, crayfish, and carp.

5   This is, mind you, suburbia. It is a five-minute walk in three directions to rows of houses, though none is visible here. There's a 55 mph highway at one end of the pond, and a nesting pair of wood ducks at the other. Under every bush is a muskrat hole or a beer can. The far end is an alternating series of fields and woods, fields and woods, threaded everywhere with motorcycle tracks—in whose bare clay wild turtles lay eggs.

6   So. I had crossed the highway, stepped over two low barbed-wire fences, and traced the motorcycle path in all gratitude through the wild rose and poison ivy of the pond's shoreline up into high grassy fields. Then I cut down through the woods to the mossy fallen tree where I sit. This tree is excellent. It makes a dry, upholstered bench at the

upper, marshy end of the pond, a plush jetty raised from the thorny shore between a shallow blue body of water and a deep blue body of sky.

The sun had just set. I was relaxed on the tree trunk, ensconced in the lap of lichen, watching the lily pads at my feet tremble and part dreamily over the thrusting path of a carp. A yellow bird appeared to my right and flew behind me. It caught my eye. I swiveled around—and the next instant, inexplicably, I was looking down at a weasel, who was looking up at me.

Weasel! I'd never seen one wild before. He was ten inches long, thin as a curve, a muscled ribbon, brown as fruitwood, soft-furred, alert. His face was fierce, small and pointed as a lizard's; he would have made a good arrowhead. There was just a dot of chin, maybe two brown hairs' worth, and then the pure white fur began that spread down his underside. He had two black eyes I didn't see, any more than you see a window.

The weasel was stunned into stillness as he was emerging from beneath an enormous shaggy wild rose bush four feet away. I was stunned into stillness twisted backward on the tree trunk. Our eyes locked, and someone threw away the key.

Our look was as if two lovers, or deadly enemies, met unexpectedly on an overgrown path when each had been thinking of something else: a clearing blow to the gut. It was also a bright blow to the brain, or a sudden beating of brains, with all the charge and intimate grate of rubbed balloons. It emptied our lungs. It felled the forest, moved the fields, and drained the pond; the world dismantled and tumbled into that black hole of eyes. If you and I looked at each other that way, our skulls would split and drop to our shoulders. But we don't. We keep our skulls. So.

He disappeared. This was only last week, and already I don't remember what shattered the enchantment. I think I blinked, I think I retrieved my brain from the weasel's brain, and tried to memorize what I was seeing, and the weasel felt the yank of separation, the careening splashdown into real life and the urgent current of instinct. He vanished under the wild rose. I waited motionless, my mind suddenly full of data and my spirit with pleadings, but he didn't return.

Please do not tell me about "approach-avoidance conflicts." I tell you I've been in that weasel's brain for sixty seconds, and he was in mine. Brains are private places, muttering through unique and secret tapes—but the weasel and I both plugged into another tape simultaneously, for a sweet and shocking time. Can I help it if it was a blank?

What goes on in his brain the rest of the time? What does a weasel think about? He won't say. His journal is tracks in clay, a spray of feathers, mouse blood and bone: uncollected, unconnected, loose-leaf, and blown.

I would like to learn, or remember, how to live. I come to Hollins Pond not so much to learn how to live as, frankly, to forget about it. That is, I don't think I can learn from a wild animal how to live in particular—shall I suck warm blood, hold my tail high, walk with my footprints precisely over the prints of my hands?—but I might learn something of mindlessness, something of the purity of living in the physical senses and the dignity of living without bias or motive. The weasel lives in necessity and we live in choice, hating necessity and dying at the last ignobly in its talons. I would like to live as I should, as the weasel lives as he should. And I suspect that for me the way is like the weasel's: open to time and death painlessly, noticing everything, remembering nothing, choosing the given with a fierce and pointed will.

I missed my chance. I should have gone for the throat. I should have lunged for that streak of white under the weasel's chin and held on, held on through mud and into the wild rose, held on for a dearer life. We could live under the wild rose wild as weasels, mute and uncomprehending. I could very calmly go wild. I could live two days in the den, curled, leaning on mouse fur, sniffing bird bones, blinking, licking, breathing musk, my hair tangled in the roots of grasses. Down is a good place to go, where the mind is single. Down is out, out of your ever-loving mind and back to your careless senses. I remember muteness as a prolonged and giddy fast, where every moment is a feast of utterance received. Time and events are merely poured, unremarked, and ingested directly, like blood pulsed into my gut through a jugular vein. Could two live that way? Could two live under the wild rose, and explore by the pond, so that the smooth mind of each is as everywhere present to the other, and as received and as unchallenged, as falling snow?

15   We could, you know. We can live any way we want. People take vows of poverty, chastity, and obedience—even of silence—by choice. The thing is to stalk your calling in a certain skilled and supple way, to locate the most tender and live spot and plug into that pulse. This is yielding, not fighting. A weasel doesn't "attack" anything; a weasel lives as he's meant to, yielding at every moment to the perfect freedom of single necessity.

16   I think it would be well, and proper, and obedient, and pure, to grasp your one necessity and not let it go, to dangle from it limp wherever it takes you. Then even death, where you're going no matter how you live, cannot you part. Seize it and let it seize you up aloft even, till your eyes burn out and drop; let your musky flesh fall off in shreds, and let your very bones unhinge and scatter, loosened over fields, over fields and woods, lightly, thoughtless, from any height at all, from as high as eagles.

FOR WRITING AND DISCUSSION

Working in small groups or as a whole class, use the questions that follow to guide your close examination of Dillard's structural and stylistic choices.

1. How does Dillard's essay meet the requirements for a minimal story? What are the events depicted in this piece? How are they connected? What are the contraries that give the story tension and conflict? What resolution or interpretation does Dillard offer?
2. To what extent do the opening paragraphs of this essay predict its focus and meaning? How does she create a design of ideas through juxtapositions? What would you say is the theme or meaning of this piece? What is it about?
3. Choose *three* consecutive paragraphs in this essay and examine how Dillard employs gaps between sentences to stimulate readers to think actively with her about the questions she is raising. Try tracking her ideas from sentence to sentence in these paragraphs. Where are the biggest gaps?
4. How does Dillard experiment with viewpoint, and how is this shifting of perspective part of the significance of her narrative?
5. Find *ten* examples of Dillard's use of specific words and *ten* examples of figurative language and explain how these are particularly effective

in holding the reader's interest and in portraying the intensity of her experience. Can you find examples of memory-soaked words? What possible memories does Dillard appeal to?

COMBINING CLOSED AND OPEN ELEMENTS

So far we have been talking about features of open-form prose in its purer forms. Sometimes, however, writers wish simply to loosen basically closed-form prose by combining it with some features of open-form prose. If, for example, an academic wanted to share new developments in a field with a popular audience, he or she would be well advised to leaven his or her prose with some elements of open-form writing. In this final section, we offer several pieces of advice for loosening up closed-form prose.

Introducing Some Humor

Humor is rare in tightly closed prose because humor is nonfunctional—it doesn't *have* to be there for a writer to make a point—and closed-form prose values efficiency, getting what you have to say said in the most economical fashion. Also, closed-form writers are concerned with being taken seriously, and for some readers, serious writing and humorous writing are incompatible. Writers who make people laugh may find themselves being taken less seriously, no matter how unfair that may be.

Humor is closely related to one of the mainsprings of open-form style, surprise. Humor typically depends on sudden twists and abrupt changes in direction. In physical comedy, pratfalls are funny in direct proportion to the audience's inability to see them coming. In verbal humor, the less clearly the audience sees the punch line coming, the more it makes the audience laugh.

Humor is particularly valuable in that it can make imposing subjects more manageable for readers. Just as humor can deflate pretensions and bring down the high and the mighty in an instant, it can make difficult and foreign subjects less anxiety producing. Formal, abstract language can put readers off, estranging them from the subject; humor has the power to "de-strange" a subject, to allow the audience to look at it long enough to understand it. Many popular books on science and many of the best instructional books on car repair, cooking, money management, and other of life's drearier necessities use a humorous style to help their phobic readers get on with life.

To appreciate the effect of humor, consider the following passages from two different instructional books on how to operate the database program Paradox. The first passage, from *Windows in 21 Days*, uses a clear, humor-free, closed-form style.

In this book, you learn by following detailed step-by-step exercises based on real-world problems in database application design. Every exercise leads you further into the power of "Paradox for Windows" as you develop the components of an automated application. This section does the following: explains the assumptions and conventions used in this book; lists the hardware and software requirements and setup needed to run Paradox for Windows and use this book efficiently; and offers some suggestions for strategies to get the most from this book. The step-by-step exercises make it easy.

Now note the different effect produced by the following passage from one of the hugely popular *Dummies* books:

> Welcome to *Paradox for Windows for Dummies,* a book that's not afraid to ask the tough questions like "When's lunch?" and "Who finished the cookie dough ice cream?" If you're more interested in food (or Australian Wombats, for that matter) than you are in Paradox for Windows, this book is for you. If you're more interested in Paradox for Windows, please get some professional help before going out into society again.
>
> My goal is to help you get things done despite the fact that you're using Paradox. Whether you're at home, in your office, or at home in your office (or even if you just *feel* like you live at work) *Paradox for Windows for Dummies* is your all-in-one guidebook through the treacherous, frustrating, and appallingly technical world of the relational database.

FOR WRITING AND DISCUSSION

1. Which of these two instructional books would you prefer to read?
2. The second passage says that the world of relational databases is "treacherous, frustrating, and appallingly technical," whereas the first stresses that the "step-by-step exercises [in the book] make it easy." Why do you suppose the humorous passage stresses the difficulty of databases whereas the humorless passage stresses the ease of a step-by-step approach? Is it good strategy for the humorous writer to stress the difficulty of Paradox?
3. Under what rhetorical circumstances are humorous instructions better than strictly serious instructions? When is a strictly serious approach better?

Using Techniques from Popular Magazines

Writers who publish regularly for popular audiences develop a vigorous, easy-reading style that differs from the style of much academic writing. The effect of this difference is illustrated by the results of a famous research study conducted by Michael Graves and Wayne Slater at the University of Michigan. For this study, teams of writers revised passages from a high school history textbook.* One team consisted of linguists and technical writers trained in producing closed-form texts using the strategies discussed in Chapter 18 (forecasting structure, putting points

---

*The study involved three teams, but for purposes of simplification we limit our discussion to two.

first, following the old/new contract, using transitions). A second team consisted of two *Time-Life* book editors.

Whereas the linguists aimed at making the passages clearer, the *Time-Life* writers were more concerned with making them livelier. The result? One hundred eleventh grade students found the *Time-Life* editors' version both more comprehensible and more memorable. Lack of clarity wasn't the problem with the original textbook; unbearable dryness was the problem. According to the researchers, the *Time-Life* editors did not limit themselves

> to making the passages lucid, well-organized, coherent, and easy to read. Their revisions went beyond such matters and were intended to make the texts interesting, exciting, vivid, rich in human drama, and filled with colorful language.

To see how they achieved this effect, let's look at their revision. Here is a passage about the Vietnam War taken from the original history text.

Original History Text

The most serious threat to world peace developed in Southeast Asia. Communist guerrillas threatened the independence of the countries carved out of French Indo-China by the Geneva conference of 1954. In South Vietnam, Communist guerrillas (the Viet Cong) were aided by forces from Communist North Vietnam in a struggle to overthrow the American-supported government. . . .

Shortly after the election of 1964, Communist gains prompted President Johnson to alter his policy concerning Vietnam. American military forces in Vietnam were increased from about 20,000 men in 1964 to more than 500,000 by 1968. Even so, North Vietnamese troops and supplies continued to pour into South Vietnam.

Here is the *Time-Life* editors' revision.

History Presented in Popular Magazine Style

In the early 1960's the greatest threat to world peace was just a small splotch of color on Kennedy's map, one of the fledgling nations sculpted out of French Indo-China by the Geneva peacemakers of 1954. It was a country so tiny and remote that most Americans had never uttered its name: South Vietnam. . . .

Aided by Communist North Vietnam, the Viet Cong guerrillas were eroding the ground beneath South Vietnam's American-backed government. Village by village, road by road, these jungle-wise rebels were waging a war of ambush and mining: They darted out of tunnels to head off patrols, buried exploding booby traps beneath the mud floors of huts, and hid razor-sharp bamboo sticks in holes. . . .

No sooner had Johnson won the election than Communist gains prompted Johnson to go back on his campaign promise. The number of American soldiers in Vietnam skyrocketed from 20,000 in 1964 to more than 500,000 by 1968. But in spite of GI patrols, leech-infested jungles, swarms of buzzing insects, and flash floods that made men cling to trees to escape being washed away—North Vietnamese troops streamed southward without letup along the Ho Chi Minh Trail.

What can this revision teach you about loosening up prose? What specifically are the editors doing here?

First, notice how far the level of abstraction drops in the revision. The original is barren of sensory words; the revision is alive with them ("South Vietnam" becomes a "small splotch of color on Kennedy's map"; "a struggle to overthrow the American-supported government" becomes "[They] buried exploding booby traps beneath the mud floors of huts and hid razor-sharp bamboo sticks in holes").

Second, notice how much more dramatic the revision is. Actual scenes, including a vision of men clinging to trees to escape being washed away by flash floods, replace a chronological account of the war's general progress. According to the editors, such scenes, or "nuggets"—vivid events that encapsulate complex processes or principles—are the lifeblood of *Time-Life* prose.

Finally, notice how the revision tends to delay critical information for dramatic effect, moving information you would normally expect to find early on into a later position. In the first paragraph, the *Time-Life* writers talk about "the greatest threat to world peace" in the early 1960s for five lines before revealing the identity of that threat—South Vietnam.

FOR WRITING AND DISCUSSION

Here is a passage from a student argument opposing women's serving on submarines. Working individually or in small groups, enliven this passage by using some of the techniques of the *Time-Life* writers.

> Not only would it be very expensive to refit submarines for women personnel, but having women on submarines would hurt the morale of the sailors. In order for a crew to work effectively, they must have good morale or their discontent begins to show through in their performance. This is especially crucial on submarines, where if any problem occurs, it affects the safety of the whole ship. Women would hurt morale by creating sexual tension. Sexual tension can take many forms. One form is couples' working and living in a close space with all of the crew. When a problem occurs within the relationship, it could affect the morale of those directly involved and in the workplace. This would create an environment that is not conducive to good productivity. Tension would also occur if one of the women became pregnant or if there were complaints of sexual harassment. It would be easier to deal with these problems on a surface ship, but in the small confines of a submarine these problems would cause more trouble.

Delaying Your Thesis

In Chapter 8, we described a strategy for taking your reader on an exploratory journey toward a thesis rather than stating the thesis explicitly in the introduction. The effect is twofold. First, the *problem*, not the writer's solution, is put in the foreground. Second, readers are invited to co-investigate the mystery, which increases their delight in discovering a resolution. When making an argument, the writer might propose several opposing theses or review several other people's theses without committing to one until late in the essay. Or, the writer might simply reject all the arguments and choose to end in a quandary. In either case, the writer enlists the reader in a hunt for closure. Although such essays still have theses at their hearts, they follow the pattern of quest narratives and can possess all the compelling readability of a mystery tale.

FOR WRITING AND DISCUSSION

In the quotation that follows, Chris Anderson argues the need for forest engineers to write essays (what we would call open-form writing) as well as articles (closed-form writing) because the two ways of writing entail two different ways of seeing.

> It may even be that the essay is the only form that can honestly and accurately reflect the complexities and the dynamics that the New Forestry [forestry with a strong ecological/environmental bent] is trying to understand. It may be that only the structure of the essay can communicate the larger ecologies, natural and personal. It may be that scientists should be writing essays in addition to articles because in writing them they would be forced into a stance of wonder, humility, tentativeness, attention.

Put into your own words what you think Chris Anderson is getting at when he says that foresters should write essays as well as articles. What would it be like for an article writer, such as civil engineer David Rockwood (whose letter opposing wind power you read in Chapter 1, pp. 12–13), to turn from the closed-form article mode to the open-form essay mode? How might such a person's thinking be changed?

◪ CHAPTER SUMMARY

Open-form writing tries to do more with language than state a thesis and support it. We have shown how open-form writing uses a narrative base. When narrative is effective, it meets the criteria for a minimal story—depiction of events, connectedness, tension, and resolution. Typically, open-form writers create surprising structural twists by suspending and disrupting the direction of their ideas, by leaving intentional gaps in the text, and by adopting various points of view, including, on occasion, unstable viewpoints, such as irony. Open-form writers also have a penchant for concrete, sensory language—specific details, revelatory words, memory-soaked words and figurative words. We suggested several ways of loosening up closed-form prose by writing midway along the continuum: using humor, trying out some of the strategies of popular writers (using concrete language and dramatic construction), or delaying the thesis.

c h a p t e r   **20**

Working in Groups to Pose and Solve Problems

The consensual process of truth seeking is based on the simple assumption that all of us thinking together are smarter than any one of us thinking alone.

—Parker Palmer, Educator

For excellence, the presence of others is always required.

—Hannah Arrendt, Philosopher

There are many reasons why writers benefit from working in groups. As we have stressed throughout this book, thinking and writing are social acts. At first, this notion may contradict certain widely accepted stereotypes of writers and thinkers as solitary souls who retreat to cork-lined studies where they conjure great thoughts and works. But in most cases the works they produce have grown out of intense conversations with others. For this reason, writers tend to belong to communities of peers with whom they test and share ideas, theories, and work.

Writing communities are especially important in academic, business, and professional settings. The vast majority of scientific and technical articles are team written, often by three or more authors. And few major reports or proposals in the business or academic world are the product of a single author. Increasingly, legal briefs, ad campaigns, professional proposals, research reports, brochures to stockholders, and so forth are team-produced efforts.

The reasons for this trend are not hard to trace. First, much contemporary work is so complex and technical that no single person has enough expertise to compose a nonroutine document. Second, many large businesses now use self-directed teams, as opposed to middle managers overseeing a hierarchically organized staff, to accomplish tasks, most of which require the production of documents. And perhaps most important, much professional writing is now produced on networked computers. Writers on a network can easily transfer files to multiple team members, each of whom can enter changes electronically without converting the file to paper or redoing the entire draft.

Clearly, the ability to write effectively as part of a team is an increasingly critical skill for career advancement. Many businesses now regard group skills as one of the three or four most important determinants of employee success. But the ability to form writing communities is important for reasons that transcend economics and career ambitions.

Humans construct knowledge through interaction with others. Throughout this text we have said that to write an essay is to join a conversation about a topic; the back-and-forth dialogue involved in group work is a real time version of the conversations embodied in printed texts. Through discourse with others, you gather multiple perspectives on phenomena, which you synthesize through the filter of your own perspective. In other words, you construct your knowledge by exposing yourself to alternative views. Moreover, purposeful, thoughtful group interaction is a source not only for knowledge of the world around you, but also for self-knowledge. It allows you to stand outside yourself—to see the products of your mind the way that others see them. The kind of thinking that you practice in groups, therefore, is the kind you must exhibit in writing.

In the rest of this chapter, we offer advice on how to work effectively in groups and to become more adept at critical thinking, composing, and revising. We examine some basic principles of group interaction, explore typical problems small groups encounter, and then provide several strategies for thinking in groups. Perhaps the most common kind of group activity in a writing classroom—conducting peer reviews of drafts—we have covered earlier in Chapter 17 on revision (pp. 429–35).

BASIC PRINCIPLES OF SUCCESSFUL GROUP INTERACTION

If the thought of group work makes you uncomfortable, you are not alone. Most people have had unpleasant or unproductive experiences working in groups. Jokes about committees ("Committees keep minutes and waste hours," or "A zebra is a horse designed by a committee") attest to the innate distrust of groups felt by most born in the United States. Middle-class popular literature, film, and media all lionize the exploits of the single individual working apart from the herd.

Keep in mind, however, that small groups in writing classrooms are less like unwieldy, bureaucratic committees than they are like problem-solving design teams analogous to the engineering teams that design cars or the marketing teams that plan new sales strategies. And recall that one of the world's most influential documents—the Declaration of Independence—was written as a small-group project.

To help you form efficient and productive teams, we recommend that you and your teammates practice the following principles.

Avoid Clone-Think and Ego-Think

Many group tasks ask you to propose and justify a solution to a problem by consensus. As we will show later in this chapter, a group consensus is not the same as a majority view. Although a consensus is a form of agreement, a good one grows out of respectful and productive *disagreement*. The best small groups build solutions thoughtfully, beginning with different points of view and encouraging dissent along the way. Weak groups either reach closure too early or bicker endlessly, never building on disagreement to reach consensus.

To steer a middle ground between early closure and endless bickering, you need to avoid two common problems of group interaction: clone-think and ego-think. When groups lapse into *clone-think*, discussions degenerate into "feel-good sessions" guaranteed to produce safe, superficial solutions. Everyone agrees with the first opinion expressed to avoid conflict and difficult work. At the other extreme is the *ego-think* group, in which group members go their own way, producing a collection of minority views. Whereas clone-thinkers view their task as conformity to a norm, ego-thinkers see their goal as safeguarding the autonomy of individual group members. At both extremes, group members fail to take one another's ideas seriously.

When we talk about taking other people's ideas seriously or about reaching consensus, we don't mean that group discussions should transform people's fundamental values and attitudes. But we do mean that they should bring about realistic changes: softening a position, complicating an understanding, or simply acknowledging an alternative possibility. These sorts of changes in understanding happen only when people learn how to present and consider alternative views in a constructive, nonthreatening manner. One approach to avoiding both clone-thinking and ego-thinking is to practice our next principle, empathic listening.

Listen Empathically

Sometimes called Rogerian listening, after the psychologist Carl Rogers, who popularized the technique, empathic listening is a powerful strategy for helping people resolve conflicts. To be *empathic* is to try to stand in the other person's shoes—to understand the values, beliefs, and fears underlying that person's position. Empathic listeners are *active*, not passive; they interpret not only the speaker's words, but also the speaker's tone of voice, body language, and even silences. Empathic listeners invite speech from others by maintaining eye contact, avoiding disapproving frowns or gestures, asking clarifying questions, and nodding or taking notes.

The rules of empathic listening are simple. Before you respond to someone else's position on an issue, summarize that person's viewpoint fairly in your own words. Carl Rogers discovered that when negotiating parties in a dispute (or couples in marital therapy) were required to summarize each other's views, the experience often defused their anger and encouraged them toward compromise or synthesis. In small groups, empathic listening can deepen conversation. If there is a dispute, the acting group leader might ask one disputant to summarize the other's position. For example: "Irwin, what do you understand Beth's position to be here and how do you see your position differing from hers?" Once Irwin and Beth understand their differences, they will be better able to reconcile them.

When a group becomes skilled at listening, here's what happens.

1. *There are fewer interruptions.*   Group members have more "space" in which to complete their thoughts. They take turns speaking. To get the floor, one person doesn't have to interrupt another.
2. *Participation is more equitable.*   Group discussions are less apt to be dominated by one or two group members. The group draws out shy or quiet group members and values their contributions.
3. *Discussions are more connected.*   Speakers are apt to begin their contributions by referring to what previous speakers have said. "I really liked Pam's point about . . ." or "I see what Paul was saying when . . . , but. . . ."

FOR WRITING AND DISCUSSION

Freewrite your response to the following questions:

1. In the group work we have done so far in this class, how well do I think the group members have listened to and understood my views?
2. How good a listener have I been?
3. What might our group do differently to promote better listening?

Then share your freewrites in groups and take turns summarizing each other's views. Reach consensus on several ways in which the group might improve its listening skills.

Play Assigned Roles

Writing groups accomplish tasks more efficiently when members take turns playing two distinct roles.

1. *Leader/Coordinator.*   This person's job is to ensure that the assigned task is clearly understood by all, to set clear goals for the session, to monitor the time, to keep the group on task, and to make sure that the group has its assigned product completed in the time allocated by the instructor. To prevent early closure or endless bickering, the leader/coordinator must draw out divergent views, promote good listening, and help the group achieve a consensus, without ever being dictatorial.
2. *Recorder/reporter.*   The recorder keeps notes on the group's decision-making process, constantly asking group members for clarification, and reads back what he or she understands group members to have said and decided. The recorder also synthesizes the group's deliberations and reports the results to the class.

In writing classrooms, we have found that groups work best when each student takes a rotation in each of these roles. Some instructors prefer to combine the two roles so that a group recorder serves as both leader and note taker.

Be Sensitive to Body Language

Groups can often learn to function more effectively by reading body language. Groups that draw their chairs close together are more effective than groups that maintain distance from each other or marginalize some members through irregular placement of chairs. Group members should note potential problems signaled by body language. A person who sits with arms folded across the chest staring out a window is signaling alienation. Other signs of dysfunction include side conversations, division of the group into subgroups, and domination of the discussion by one or two people who ignore others.

Invest Time in Group Maintenance

Group members periodically need to reflect on and think critically about their performance, a process called *group maintenance.* Group maintenance may be as simple as taking several minutes at the completion of a task to discuss the things the group did well or not so well and to identify steps for improvement.

Occasionally a more extensive and formal sort of group-maintenance task is required. One such task calls for each member to do a self-assessment by freewriting responses to questions such as the following:

Our group performs best when _____.

Our group's effectiveness could be improved if _____.

My greatest strength as a group member is _____.

Another thing I could contribute is _____.

The members then share these self-assessments with the whole group.

An even more ambitious group-maintenance project involves an ethnographer, a student from another group who observes the group in action and writes up a report on his or her observations. Figure 20.1 is a list of items we ask ethnographers to look for when observing a group.

FIGURE 20.1   Ethnographer's Questionnaire

1. How much time did the group spend reviewing the instructions before plunging into discussion?
2. How were the coordinator and recorder chosen? Had they fulfilled these responsibilities previously?
3. Describe how the group undertook its task. How did it begin the actual work?
4. On average, how long did each group member speak? What was the total amount of time that each group member spoke during the entire session?
5. How many times did group members interrupt each other?
6. How often did group members refer to what others had said before presenting their own contributions?
7. How were disagreements resolved or not resolved?
8. How well did the coordinator and recorder perform their functions?

After responding to these questions, the ethnographers should present the observations to the group and answer any questions the group may have about them. Later, the group should discuss the report on its own. Finally, the group should present to the whole class a brief summary of what it learned from being observed and how it intends to improve its processes.

▨ SOME SPECIAL PROBLEMS IN MAKING GROUPS WORK

How groups handle problem situations is crucial to their success. In this section we suggest how an understanding of the effects of learning style and cultural background on group behavior can alleviate potential problems. We also discuss ways of handling an "impossible" group member.

Recognizing How Personality and Culture Affect Group Participation

Group interaction can often be improved if group members understand the influence of personality and culture on a person's behavior in a group. Psychologists have discovered that people with different personality types have different reactions to working in groups. According to interpreters of the Myers-Briggs Type Indicator,* one of the most highly regarded personality assessment tests, people who test as *extroverts* like to think through an issue by talking out their ideas with others; they tend to be vocal and highly engaged during group discussions. People who test as *introverts* prefer thinking privately about an issue before talking about it and are often uncomfortable discussing their ideas in groups, although they listen carefully and take in what everyone is saying. Often, quiet group members are listening more carefully and thinking more deeply than more vocal people realize. Until the group gently encourages them to contribute, however, they may be silent.

Judgers like to reach decisions rapidly, and they often grow impatient if the group wants to extend discussion of an issue. In contrast, *perceivers* resist early closure and want to talk through all possible points of view on an issue before reaching a decision. If you understand such personality differences, then you might better tolerate classmates' behaviors that are different from your own.

Other important differences are related to culture. Most U.S.-born students are used to talking in class, holding class debates, and even disagreeing with the teacher. In many cultures, however, it is disrespectful to argue with the teacher or to speak in class unless called on. Students are socialized to listen and not to talk. They can find group work in a North American college extremely painful.

---

*The Myers-Briggs Type Indicator locates persons along four different continuums: introversion/extroversion, thinking/feeling, sensing/intuition, perceiving/judging. Composition researchers have used the Myers-Briggs inventory to reveal fascinating differences among writers that throw valuable light on students' behavior in groups. See G. H. Jensen, and J. K. DiTiberio, *Personality and the Teaching of Composition* (Norwood, NJ: Ablex, 1989).

Speech habits also vary widely. Typically, North Americans state their desires bluntly and assertively in ways that would seem rude to people from Asian cultures, who are taught to mask their statements of desire in roundabout conversation. Some cultures have a strong oral tradition of storytelling or speech making, whereas others have a tradition of silence. If your institution has a diverse student body that includes members of ethnic minority groups and international students, then group work can be a fascinating laboratory for the study of cultural differences.

FOR WRITING AND DISCUSSION

Your instructor or institution might arrange for your class to take the Myers-Briggs Type Indicator or the Kolb Learning Style Inventory. If so, then you can share what these tests reveal about you with other members of your group. If not, then you can take your own mini-inventory by checking off the description in Table 20.1 that best represents you for each of the pairs listed. After you have made your choices, share your self-assessment with other members of your group. How do the differences in your responses account for the different ways in which you behave in the group?

Dealing with an "Impossible Group Member"

Occasionally groups face a critical test of their ability to manage conflict: the Impossible Group Member, or IGM. IGMs may dominate group discussions; they may be rude or intimidating, trying to turn every discussion into a conflict; they may

TABLE 20.1   Mini–Personality Inventory

Do you like to:

_____ Organize the discussion	_____ Go with the flow
_____ Assert your own views and rights	_____ Compromise
_____ Stick to the central issue	_____ Examine all facets of a problem
_____ Reach a firm decision	_____ See merit in all sides of an issue
_____ Think out your own position before talking	_____ Think by talking now
_____ Reason problems out logically	_____ Trust your instincts and feelings
_____ Get serious	_____ Lighten up
_____ Show passion	_____ Stay calm
_____ Reach a resolution	_____ Talk for talk's sake
_____ Follow teacher's instructions carefully	_____ Value spontaneity
_____ Apply rules rigorously	_____ Allow exceptions to rules
_____ Stay on the assigned task	_____ Digress; engage in off-topic talk

sit sullenly, draining off group enthusiasm; or they may be generally unprepared or fail to do the work assigned to them outside class.

Although it's not easy to deal with an IGM (sometimes the instructor has to intervene), most impossible group members are really possible group members who need encouragement and direction. The root of most IGMs' problems is their difficulty in recognizing the effects they're having on other people. Direct criticism of their behaviors will likely surprise them—they won't see it coming—and cause them to react defensively. IGMs need to see the consequences of their actions and they need to see positive behaviors modeled for them. If IGMs dominate discussions, they need to learn to listen. If they are sullenly silent, they need to have their input actively solicited and their responses taken seriously. They have to take their turns in leadership positions and learn to appreciate the difficulties of consensus building and decision making. And they must be made aware that their actions are bothering the other group members.

The best way to deal with IGMs is to discuss the problem candidly, perhaps during a group-maintenance session (see pp. 513–14). If group members reflect on and evaluate *how* the group did its task, focusing on group shortcomings ("What could we do better next time?") rather than on individuals' failures ("Martine, you drive me crazy!"), then it becomes easier for errant group members to accept responsibility for their actions. In explaining a problem to an IGM, try using what communication experts call *I statements* rather than *you statements*. Keep the focus on your own feelings and avoid launching accusations. Note the different tones in the following examples:

You **Statement**	Martine, you're always insulting us by looking out the window.
I **Statement**	Martine, when you look out the window, it makes me feel like I'm a boring person.
You **Statement**	Pete and Valencia are always dominating the discussion.
I **Statement**	On some days I want to say something in the group but there is never a break in the conversation where I can join.

Using *I* statements helps defuse defensiveness by calling attention to the consequences of behaviors without attaching blame or censure.

We are now ready to turn to productive group strategies for addressing three kinds of tasks: consensus-seeking, brainstorming, and orally rehearsing drafts.

◪ THINKING IN GROUPS

Group work is one of the most effective ways to practice critical thinking. This section examines three ways that groups can think together.

Seeking Consensus

Most of the problems posed in the For Writing and Discussion exercises in this text have alternative solutions—there is no single "right" answer. Seeking a consensus answer—especially when group members have different views—can lead to highly productive critical thought. When different group members propose different answers to the same problem, how does a group reach a consensus?*

First, don't assume that every group member has to be completely satisfied with the group's final solution. Instead, everyone should agree that the proposed solution is feasible and rationally supportable. Your solution must be achieved through *consensus* rather than through majority vote, coin flip, or turn taking. This approach means that each group member has veto power over the final solution. But this option should be used sparingly, and only if a person truly cannot live with the proposed solution. After an initial discussion to be sure that everyone understands the task, you can use the following guidelines to embark on a problem-solving procedure that encourages consensus:

1. *Ask every group member to propose at least one tentative solution for discussion.* Members should present justifying arguments as well, so that group members can appreciate the reasoning behind each approach.

2. *Once you have presented a possible solution, avoid arguing for it a second time.* Your goal is now to be flexible and listen to other viewpoints rather than to press for adoption of your own position. Remember, however, not to give up your viewpoint quickly just to avoid conflict. Yield only if you see legitimate strengths in other approaches.

3. *If none of the proposed solutions wins everyone's approval, begin brainstorming for alternatives that synthesize good features from various proposals.* Sometimes you can formulate a lowest-common-denominator solution—one that everyone grudgingly accepts but that no one really likes—and brainstorm ways to improve it.

4. *Don't think in terms of winners and losers* ("If Lenore's solution wins, then Pete's must lose"). Rather, try to negotiate win/win solutions in which all parties give up something but also retain something.

5. *Accept disagreement and conflict as a strength rather than a weakness.* Chances are that the disagreements in your group mirror disagreements in the larger community to which your solution must appeal. From these disagreements you can forge a synthesis that is much stronger than any individual's private solution. As Parker Palmer says in the epigraph to this chapter, "The consensual process of truth seeking is based on the simple assumption that all of us thinking together are smarter than any one of us thinking alone."

Brainstorming

Group brainstorming uses intuitive, unstructured thinking. During a brainstorming session, everyone is encouraged to suggest ideas, however outlandish they may seem on the surface, and to build on, without criticizing or questioning,

---

*The discussion of consensus making is adapted from Parker Palmer, *To Know as We Are Known: Education as a Spiritual Journey* (San Francisco: Harper & Row, 1983), pp. 94–96.

all other suggestions generated by group members. Groups often begin brainstorming by asking individual members to take turns offering ideas. Frequently, a high-energy, almost frantic atmosphere develops. In its zanier moments, brainstorming crosses over into free association.

For a writer exploring topic ideas, brainstorming sessions can provide a variety of options to consider as well as clues about an audience's potential reaction to a topic and ideas about how the writer might change those views. Brainstorming can also generate arguments in support of a thesis. When the class is assigned a persuasive paper, playing the believing and doubting game with each group member's proposed thesis can help writers anticipate alternative possibilities and counter-evidence as well as new support for a position (see Chapter 2, pp. 37–39).

Oral Rehearsal of Drafts

Rehearsing a draft orally is an excellent way to generate and clarify ideas. A good procedure for doing so is to interview one another in pairs or in groups of three early in the writing process. One-on-one or one-on-two interviews that enable writers to talk through their ideas can help clarify their sense of direction and stimulate new ideas. When you are the interviewer, use the set of generic questions in Figure 20.2, modifying them to fit each assignment.

When you conduct your interview, get the writer to do most of the talking. Respond by offering suggestions, bringing up additional ideas, playing devil's advocate, and so forth. The goal is for the writer to rehearse the whole paper orally. Whenever the writer gets stuck for ideas, arguments, or supporting details, help to brainstorm possibilities.

During these sessions, it is best for writers not to look at notes or drafts. They should try to reformulate their ideas conversationally. We recommend that each student talk actively for fifteen to twenty minutes as the interviewer asks probing questions, plays devil's advocate, or helps the writer think of ideas.

FIGURE 20.2   Guide Questions for Interviewers

- What problem or question is your paper going to address?
- Why is this an interesting question? What makes it problematic and significant?
- How is your paper going to surprise your readers?
- What is your thesis statement? (If the writer doesn't have a good thesis statement yet, go on to the next question and then come back to this one. Perhaps you can help the writer figure out a thesis.)
- Talk me (us) through your whole argument or through your ideas so far.

◼ CHAPTER SUMMARY

This chapter has focused on the value of small groups for writers, both student and professional. Because to write is to join a conversation, working in groups teaches us to appreciate the dialectic nature of knowledge and to practice the kind of dialectic thinking that writers need. Specifically, we looked at basic principles of group interaction, special problems in making groups work, and ways that groups can think together to vary perspectives and build consensus, to brainstorm, and to conduct interviews that help classmates rehearse their drafts orally. An additional use of groups—providing peer reviews of drafts—is covered in Chapter 17, pages 429–35.

Chapter 21 Focusing a Problem
and Finding Sources
Chapter 22 Using and Citing
Sources
Chapter 23 Electronic Writing
and Research

A Guide to
Research

part **F O U R**

Focusing a Problem
and Finding Sources

College writers regularly use research information in their work, whether it is a short analytical or persuasive piece that cites one or two sources or a longer research paper that cites dozens of sources. A research paper, although longer than many other kinds of papers, follows the same principles of writing discussed throughout this text. In a research paper, the writer poses an interesting and significant problem and responds to it with a surprising thesis. However, in a formal research paper, the writer is expected to use extensive research data for support and to cite and document all sources in a formal academic style.

Much popular writing takes on the characteristics of a research paper, but without the documentation. Consider the following excerpt from an article in *Glamour*.

> Subliminal self-help tapes—which promise everything from instant relaxation to higher earning power—are a big business: Industry watchers estimate they generate about $60 million in sales annually. But a number of recent studies show no evidence that they work.
> . . . Philip Merkle, Ph.D., of the University of Waterloo, analyzed commercially available tapes using a spectrograph that reveals patterns of auditory signals. He found no evidence of speech-associated patterns on the tapes. The messages embedded in the tapes are so completely masked by the other sounds that they cannot be heard *even subliminally.*
> —Pamela Erens, "Are Subliminal Self-Help Tapes a Hoax?"

As does a good research paper, this article has a thesis (subliminal self-help tapes are not effective) and uses research data for development and support (a statistic about the size of the subliminal self-help tape industry and a summary of the research by Philip Merkle). But if you doubt the figure of $60 million, you have no way to check the author's accuracy. Nor can you find Merkle's work to read it for yourself. You might be able to contact the researcher at the University of Waterloo, but that would be an inefficient approach to tracking down his work.

The purpose of citing sources and giving complete bibliographic information in academic research papers is to enable readers to follow the trail of the author's research. Although the conventions for documentation seem cumbersome at first, they are designed to give readers essential information about a source quickly and efficiently.

The three chapters in Part Four give you the information you need to produce an effective research paper. This chapter guides you through the process of posing and focusing a good research problem and shows you how to find sources by unlocking the resources of your library and community. Chapter 22 takes you through the process of writing a research paper, teaching you skills for summarizing, paraphrasing, and quoting sources (and for avoiding plagiarism). Chapter 22 also explains how to cite and document your sources according to the conventions of two primary academic systems—those of the Modern Language Association (MLA) and of the American Psychological Association (APA). Chapter 23 discusses how to make active use of computers and networking technology to find and retrieve sources and to manage the research process and explains specifically how to conduct electronic searches and how to use the Internet to converse with others interested in your research area.

▨ WHAT DO WE MEAN BY SOURCES?

Before starting a research project, you need to know what researchers mean by the word *sources*. There are two kinds of sources. *Primary sources* include newspaper articles, letters, diaries, eyewitness accounts, laboratory notes, interviews, court records, government data, historical documents, and the like, and *secondary sources* are articles and books written by investigators who have themselves analyzed and evaluated the primary sources. For Mary Turla's research project on mail-order brides (pp. 573–87), for example, a catalog distributed by a mail-order bride service would be a primary source, whereas a book on culture in the Philippines would be a secondary source.

Understanding how secondary sources get published may also be helpful to you. When scholars undertake a research project, they generally record their findings first as field notes, exploratory entries in research logs, write-ups of interviews, computer spreadsheets of statistics, and so forth. Other scholars can occasionally access these immediate data if the researcher is willing to share it informally in personal letters, e-mail postings, interviews, or casual discussions. The first formal sharing of research data often takes place at academic conferences, when scholars with similar interests get together to present papers orally and to participate in discussions. A paper presented orally often becomes a first draft, which the researcher will revise as an article for a scholarly journal. Sometimes conferences publish their proceedings in a microfilm format or in an electronic forum, such as a World Wide Web site. Conference presentations usually occur within six months to a year following completion of the research.

Research results deemed important by the scholar's research community are often published as articles in specialized scholarly journals, usually one to three years after completion of the research. Most academic research is published in scholarly journals rather than in books. Scholarly journals are usually refereed—

an editorial board evaluates submissions and accepts or rejects them on the basis of their scholarly merit. Because prestigious journals have a high rejection rate, acceptance of an article by an important journal marks a high point in a scholar's academic career.

Later—three to six years after completion of the research—a fraction of the research published in journals finds its way into books. Many scholarly books are reworkings of material originally published as articles in scholarly journals. These books are typically aimed at more general audiences than are scholarly articles and usually integrate more material, giving readers a more complete view of a topic and a much richer sense of context. The bibliographies in the back of scholarly books are often an excellent resource for further research.

Finally, when ideas and information have been established as central to a discipline, they are published in reference sources, such as encyclopedias. Later in this chapter we list a variety of specialized encyclopedias that will enable you to get a quick overview of any topic.

In summary, you will find the newest information on a topic in the papers presented at recent scholarly conferences. The next most recent sources are articles in academic journals, and then information and ideas in recent scholarly books. The currently accepted ideas of a field—its established and less controversial tenets—can be found in reference books, such as encyclopedias. In addition, much of the research generated by academic institutions is picked up by the popular media and reported in newspapers or integrated into feature articles in popular magazines, such as *Scientific American*, *Psychology Today*, or *The Atlantic Monthly*.

FOR WRITING AND DISCUSSION

Prior to class, go to your college's library and ask the reference librarian for a recently acquired scholarly book in a field you find interesting. (Many libraries have special shelves for new acquisitions.) Look at the copyright date of the book. Then look at the bibliography in the back of the book. What is the most recent date of the sources cited in the bibliography? What can you surmise about the lag time between the last research the writer was able to do and the time the book was actually published? Peruse the book's preface to see if the writer gives any overview of his or her research process. Whom does the writer thank in the acknowledgments section, usually placed near the end of the preface? Does the writer mention debts to previous researchers? What can you surmise about how this book came to be published?

In class, share your findings with your classmates.

◼ BEGINNING A RESEARCH PAPER

Your first goal in writing a research paper is to convert a general topic area into a research question. The research question focuses your investigation, and later, when your answer to that question emerges as a thesis, it focuses your writing.

Developing Your Research Question

How do you choose a topic and develop it into a significant research question? First, you need to choose something that interests you. Your initial interest in a subject is likely to be broad and unfocused. For instance, you may be interested in eating disorders, say, or homelessness, but you may not be ready or able to pose specific research questions. To formulate questions, you need to do some preliminary reading. We recommend the following strategy:

- Read an overview of your topic in an encyclopedia.
- Skim a recent book related to your topic, looking carefully at its table of contents and examining the titles in its bibliography.
- Locate and read a recent scholarly article related to your topic (later in this chapter we show you how to find articles in academic journals). Note carefully the problem that the article addresses, and peruse the titles in its bibliography.
- Find and read a popular article related to your topic from the kinds of magazines indexed in *The Reader's Guide to Periodical Literature* or INFOTRAC.

This preliminary reading should give you some initial insights into the kinds of questions or controversies that writers are investigating or debating. The bibliographies in your sources may lead you to other books or articles that spark your interest. After doing this preliminary reading, try freewriting your answers to probe questions.

- What problems, questions, or issues about my topic are examined in the material I have read?
- What problems or questions does this material raise for me?
- When people discuss my topic, what questions do they ask or what do they argue about?

Another way to develop a research question is to discuss your topic with friends, trying to discover issues that particularly interest you. You don't need to know the answer to your question right away; your research will help you find a response. But until you settle on a research question, you won't know what part of your reading will be useful in your paper. Once you develop a research question—for example, "What is the current thinking about in-patient versus out-patient treatment of anorexia nervosa?" or "Should eating disorders be covered by insurance policies?" or "What role did the deinstitutionalization of the mentally ill play in the increase in homelessness?"—your research efforts can become focused and efficient.

In Chapter 1 we illustrated the development of a research question by following the exploratory process of student writer Mary Turla, who had selected the topic "mail-order brides." As we explained, Mary was attracted to this topic by a notorious murder case in Seattle in which an American husband gunned down his Filipina mail-order bride outside the courtroom where she was filing for divorce. Mary's initial abhorrence of the mail-order bride industry was later tempered when her mother commented that becoming a mail-order bride might be the only way for many young Filipina woman to escape abject poverty in the Philippines.

Mary then posed her research problem this way: Should the mail-order bride industry be made illegal? (See Chapter 1, pp. 9–10.) We return to Mary's story later.

Evaluating Your Research Question

Once you have posed an initial research question (remember that your question may evolve considerably as your research progresses), test it for feasibility by considering the following questions:

- Are you personally interested in this question?
- Is the question both problematic and significant?
- Is the question limited enough for the intended length of your paper?
- Is there a reasonable possibility of finding information on this question?

This last question is particularly crucial. Good research writers depend on their skill at sleuthing out sources from a wide variety of places—college library, specialized libraries in the community, government and industry reports, nonprint media such as radio and television, the Internet, personal correspondence and interviews, or your own field research using observation and questionnaires. The rest of this chapter shows you how to unlock the resources of your library and your community. (For advice on using the Internet, see Chapter 23.)

FOR WRITING AND DISCUSSION

Review the criteria for evaluating research questions. Working as a whole class or in small groups, discuss each of the following research questions, evaluating them against the criteria. Does the question seem interesting? Is it problematic and significant? Is it limited enough for a short research project? Will there be information available on the topic? Is the question clear and precise? If a question doesn't meet the criteria, try revising it.

1. Do students work better if they don't work for grades?
2. Should pregnant women receive prenatal care?
3. Are helmet laws for motorcyclists effective in preventing injuries?
4. Is education good for children?
5. Why are there so many wars?
6. Why don't we do something about the welfare system?
7. Does a low-fat diet increase life expectancy?
8. Is Western medicine superior to traditional nonwestern medicine?
9. Should the United States limit immigration?
10. Does birth order affect children's development?

◪ FINDING LIBRARY SOURCES

To be a good researcher, you need to know how to find materials in your college's or university's library. Because most people think "books" when they enter a library, they tend to focus on the bookshelves and neglect the wealth of other resources available. Much of the valuable—and the most up-to-date—information in a library resides in articles in newspapers and periodicals (magazines and academic journals). Libraries also contain a wealth of special reference tools, ranging from specialized encyclopedias to vital statistics.

Searching for Books

Until recently, a library's holdings were listed in a card catalog. Today, most libraries use online catalogs. A library's catalog, whether accessed by cards or by computer, is the guidepost to its books as well as to its magazines, journals, newspapers, dissertations, major government documents, and multimedia (videos, cassettes, and microform collections).

The basic logic of card catalogs—author cards, title cards, and subject cards—is retained in online systems. In both systems, books are listed by author, title, and subject. Our discussion of card catalogs highlights the logic of this approach. We provide brief additional information about card catalogs here, and additional information about online catalogs in Chapter 23.

In a card catalog, the author card (the main entry card) displays the author's name in the top left just under the call number. Other cards for the same work are identical to the author card but have a line added above for the title or subject. Because many famous authors not only write books but also have books written about them, their names may be on cards both as authors and as subjects. On a subject card the subject heading—in this case, a proper name—is written in capital letters or typed in red above the author of the work. Author cards—books by a person—are filed in front of subject cards—books about a person. In a library with a large collection, remembering how to navigate around these similar-looking cards can help you avoid becoming confused. Sometimes files include cards for editors, coauthors, illustrators, or translators as well. Individual essays, stories, or plays in an anthology may also have separate cards.

Making Shrewd Use of Subject Headings

At the start of a research project, when you have only a topic area in mind, the subject cards (or subject entries in an online catalog) are probably your most important resource. Subject headings used for the subject entries are logical, uniform, and consistent. Most libraries use the headings established by the Library of Congress, which you can find listed in a four-volume reference book entitled *Library of Congress Subject Headings* (ask your librarian where this source is located in your library). This book can be especially helpful if you have trouble finding a subject heading that fits your topic.

Suppose that you are researching the effectiveness of state-run alcohol-treatment programs for street people. What subject heading do you start with? Alcoholism? Treatment programs? Homeless? Let's say you decide to begin with "alcoholism." You discover in the *Library of Congress Subject Headings* that "alcoholism" is a mammoth topic, with more than a page of subheadings. You then try "street people." Under that heading you find the instruction "USE Homeless persons." So you look up "homeless persons," where you find the following listing:

Homeless persons *(May Subd Geog)*

　UF Homeless adults

　　Homeless people

　　Street people

　BT Persons

　RT Homelessness

　NT Church work with the homeless

　　Homeless aged

　　Homeless children

　　Homeless students

　　Homeless veterans

　　Homeless women

　　Homeless youth

　　Libraries and the homeless

　　Police services for the homeless

　　Rogues and vagabonds

　　Shelters for the homeless

　　Social work with the homeless

　　Tramps

　　Underground homeless persons

Mental health services *(May Subd Geog)*

Law and legislation *(May Subd Geog)*

Means that the subject heading "homeless persons" is used for (UF) these other three terms.

Means that "persons" is a broader term (BT).

Means that "homelessness" is a related term (RT).

Means that all these headings are narrower terms (NT).

Indicates subheadings under "homeless persons."

These listings use several abbreviations. *(May Subd Geog)* stands for "may be subdivided geographically" and indicates that listings under this category may be further subdivided by state or region. UF means "used for." The remaining abbreviations classify other subject headings that you might want to call up in your search: BT = "broader term"; RT = "related term"; and NT = "narrower term." In this case, because you are interested in treatment programs for homeless alcoholics, you might decide to try the subject headings "Social work with the homeless" and "Homeless mental health services."

　In traditional card catalogs, subject headings place the most important or general word first and list specific qualities or subdivisions next. For example, the topic "the government of France" is listed under "France—Politics and government." Be creative as you look for subject headings, and use the helpful hints provided by the card or online catalog. A "See" or "Use" reference will lead you from an unused heading to a used heading. A "See also" reference suggests other related subject headings. Finally, when you find a book on your topic, look at the bottom of the card, which lists all the subject headings under which your book is filed. An online catalog usually provides the same information, but its location on the screen may vary from library to library. These other subject headings may lead you to other books.

In an online catalog, you don't need to worry about alphabetizing. With a card catalog, however, the following alphabetizing rules will be helpful.

- Headings are alphabetized word by word rather than letter by letter. For example, *New Zealand* comes before *Newark.* Remember the rule "Nothing before something."
- Articles (*a, an,* and *the*) at the beginning of headings or titles are ignored.
- Abbreviations are alphabetized as if they were spelled out. For example, *St.* is filed under *Saint.*
- Names beginning with *Mc* and *M'* are grouped with names beginning with *Mac.*
- Chronological order is used for historical subheadings. "Great Britain— Literature—Sixteenth Century" precedes "Great Britain—Literature— Eighteenth Century."

The Logic of Shelving Systems

Once you have found a book in your library's catalog, you use the call number to locate the book in the library. Most libraries have open stacks, allowing you to go to the shelf and pick up a book yourself. Take advantage of your trip to the shelf to browse through the nearby volumes because other books on the same subject will be housed in the same area. Often your best sources turn up through casual browsing.

The call number will be either a Dewey Decimal number, generally used in elementary, high school, and local public libraries, or a Library of Congress (LC) number, generally used in academic libraries. Some older libraries have books shelved under both systems. Following is an overview of each system.

Dewey Decimal System

000	General Works
100	Philosophy and Related Disciplines
200	Religion
300	Social Sciences
400	Language
500	Pure Science
600	Technology and Applied Science
700	The Arts
800	Literature and Rhetoric
900	General Geography and History

Library of Congress System

A	General Works
B	Philosophy, Psychology, and Religion

C	Auxiliary Sciences of History
D	General and Old World History (except America)
E–F	American History
G	Geography, Anthropology, Manners and Customs, Folklore, Recreation
H	Social Science, Statistics, Economics, Sociology
J	Political Science
K	Law
L	Education
M	Music
N	Fine Arts
P	Language and Literature
Q	Science
R	Medicine
S	Agriculture, Plant and Animal Industry, Fish Culture, Fisheries, Hunting, Game Protection
T	Technology
U	Military Science
V	Naval Science
Z	Bibliography and Library Science

These numbers and letters represent general categories that are further subdivided as other letters and numerals are added. A book titled *Familiar Trees of America*, by William C. Grimm, for instance, has the Library of Congress call number QK481 (Q = science; K = botany; 481 = North American trees). If you are aware of the system's logic, you can browse more productively.

Searching for Articles in Periodicals

Most of the information in periodicals (magazines and academic journals) and newspapers never finds its way into books. You can find articles in these important sources either through computerized indexes or through traditional printed indexes. (For information on computerized searches, see Chapter 23, pp. 602–6.) This section explains traditional indexes, which remain an important resource even if your library offers online searching of periodicals.

Before discussing how to use the indexes, let's review some of the most useful ones. We have divided them into two categories. The indexes listed under Current Affairs cover a variety of subjects and lead the researcher to current controversies and issues in numerous fields. The specialized indexes focus on individual areas of study.

Current Affairs

Readers' Guide to Periodical Literature.   The best-known index, the *Readers' Guide*, covers popular magazines for a general audience including such topics as current events, famous people, movie reviews, and hobbies. It focuses primarily on nonscholarly publications, such as *Time, Newsweek, Popular*

Mechanics, and *People,* but it also indexes many highly respected intellectual sources such as *Foreign Affairs* and *Scientific American.*

New York Times Index.   The subject index to the *New York Times* includes brief synopses of articles and gives exact references to date, page, and column. Its wide circulation, comprehensive coverage, and extensive indexing make this publication especially useful. Once you have found the date of an event through this index, you can search the back issues of other papers for their coverage of the same event.

Wall Street Journal Index.   A monthly and annual guide to the *Wall Street Journal,* this index is organized in two parts: (1) corporate news indexed by name of company and (2) general news indexed by subject.

Business Periodical Index.   This index leads you to articles on marketing, management, public relations, advertising, and economics.

Biography Index.   This quarterly and annual index lists biographical material in current books and periodicals.

Public Affairs Information Service (P.A.I.S.) Bulletin.   Serving as a guide to articles, pamphlets, and books on economic and social issues, public administration, politics, and international relations, this index is useful for finding information on current public policy, both domestic and international.

General Science Index.   This index to general science periodicals covers topics such as biology, botany, chemistry, environment and conservation, medicine and health, physics, and zoology.

Education

Education Index.   This index includes more than 300 periodicals, proceedings, and yearbooks covering all phases of education, organized by author and subject. It also has good coverage of sources related to children and child development.

Current Index to Journals in Education.   This index lists more than seven hundred education and education-related journals, organized by author and subject.

History and Literature

MLA (Modern Language Association) International Bibliography of Books and Articles in Modern Language and Literature.   This comprehensive index of scholarly articles on languages and literature of various countries is arranged by national literatures with subdivisions by literary periods.

Annual Bibliography of English Language and Literature.   A subject index of scholarly articles on English language and literature, this index covers major writers and is arranged chronologically.

Humanities Index.   This subject index covers topics in archeology, classics, folklore, history, language and literature, politics, performing arts, philosophy, and religion. It was called the *Social Sciences and Humanities Index* until 1974.

Historical Abstracts.   This work includes abstracts of scholarly articles on world history, excluding the United States and Canada, covering the period from 1775 to 1945.

America: History and Life.   This work comprises abstracts of scholarly articles on the history of the United States and Canada.

Nursing and Medical Sciences

Cumulative Index to Nursing and Allied Health Literature.   This major index covers topics on nursing and public health.

Index Medicus.   This monthly subject index includes periodical literature on medicine and related topics published in all principal languages.

Philosophy and Religion

Philosophers' Index.   Scholarly articles in books and periodicals are indexed by author and subject. The subject section includes abstracts.

Religion Index One: Periodicals.   This index has a Protestant viewpoint but includes Catholic and Jewish periodicals as well. It provides a subject and author index of scholarly articles on topics in religion.

Physical and Social Sciences

Social Sciences Index.   This index covers all subjects and disciplines in the social sciences, including anthropology, area studies, psychology, political science, and sociology. It concentrates on scholarly journals, but includes some popular magazines. The title was *Social Sciences and Humanities Index* until 1974.

Psychological Abstracts.   This subject and author index covers books, journals, technical reports, and scientific documents and includes an abstract of each item.

Applied Science and Technology Index.   This work is a subject index to periodicals in the fields of aeronautics and space sciences, automation, earth sciences, engineering, physics, telecommunications, transportation, and related topics.

Biological and Agricultural Index.   This subject index covers English-language periodicals in agricultural and biological sciences.

General Science Index.   See under Current Affairs.

Using Periodical Indexes

Although there are many periodical indexes, they are all organized similarly and include clear directions for use in the front of each volume. The key to using these indexes efficiently is thinking of good subject headings. Be creative and persistent. Most indexes have extensive cross-references that will eventually lead you to the heading you need. Keeping a list of the subject headings you use can save you time if you return to the indexes a second time or if you use more than one index for the same topic.

Once you have found appropriate articles listed under a subject heading, copy the bibliographic information you will need to find the articles. The library will have a list of its periodicals; check that list to see whether the journal or magazine you need is in the library. If it is, note its call number. Periodicals are often shelved by call number in the stacks just as books are shelved, although some libraries have a separate periodicals section arranged alphabetically.

Your library may also store some periodicals on microfiche (a small card containing page-by-page photographic negatives of a journal or magazine) or microfilm (a roll of film, similar to a traditional filmstrip). Your librarian will help you use machines that allow you easily to read the text and even copy pages that you will need for further reference. If your library does not have the article you need in any form, ask your librarian about getting the article through an interlibrary loan—an increasingly quick and common practice.

Finding Information in Special Reference Materials

Reference works are usually kept in a special section for use in the library only. They offer excellent help, ranging from background information as you begin your reading to statistics that provide hard evidence related to your thesis. The following list gives you some examples of reference works. Be sure to ask your librarian for other suggestions.

> *Encyclopedias.*   Encyclopedias are extremely helpful for background reading in the initial stages of research. By giving you the big picture, encyclopedias provide a context for better understanding articles and books. In addition to general encyclopedias, you will find many specialized encyclopedias, among them the *Dictionary of American History, The International Encyclopedia of the Social Sciences,* the *McGraw-Hill Encyclopedia of Science and Technology,* and the *Encyclopedia of World Art.*
>
> *Book Review Digest.*   This reference work provides a summary of the reviewed book and excerpts from a variety of reviews so that you can gain an understanding of controversies and issues in a given field. To use the *Book Review Digest* efficiently, you need to know the publication date of the book in question, as reviews are published the year the book is published and in the two to three succeeding years.
>
> *Congressional Record.*   The *Congressional Record* contains the transcript of what is said on the floors of the Senate and the House of Representatives. It also contains an appendix of materials that members have asked to be included as part of the permanent record. Its index allows you to trace every reference to a given subject and to find out who discussed or acted on a bill. Many reference libraries carry this useful tool for people interested in history, politics, biography, and current events.
>
> *Statistical Abstract of the United States.*   This publication dates back to 1879 and contains statistical tables on birthrates, abortion, marriage, divorce, health care, employment, nutrition, and so forth. It is a good primary source on life in the United States.

Facts on File.   Summaries of news stories in this publication show the development of events so that you see how they played out over the space of a year. Stories are arranged by subject, person, and country.

At each step of your library search, remember that your best aid is your librarian. Librarians are experienced in helping you find the right subject headings, pointing out nonbook holdings in the library, leading you through the interlibrary loan process, and introducing you to less-known resources in the library. Librarians will also steer you to the most helpful of the various reference tools designed for research projects such as yours.

FOR WRITING AND DISCUSSION

Working in groups, choose a current issue about public affairs (for example, global warming, gangs, or the federal deficit) that will allow you to use a wide range of library resources, including the *New York Times Index* and *Congressional Record.* With your group, go to your college library and use indexes to find titles of articles on the issue you selected; also locate relevant information from specialized references, such as encyclopedias, *Facts on File*, and *Statistical Abstracts of the United States.* You will probably want to divide up the work, having each group member become familiar with several sources in order to teach them to the rest of the group. When the group has finished, everyone should have a good idea of how to use these sources.

◼ SPECIALIZED LIBRARIES AND LOCAL ORGANIZATIONS

Sometimes a search of your college library doesn't give you the information you need. In these cases, don't give up too quickly. Mary Turla, whose freewriting on mail-order brides we have been following, found little information in two academic libraries, even though one of them is the largest academic library in her part of the country. Instead, she was able to find the material she needed at a small specialized library devoted to Filipino culture and history. The public libraries in many cities house directories of specialized libraries.

Businesses and organizations also have libraries and information services. Public relations departments can provide brochures and pamphlets. For example, if you were writing about diabetes, you could ask the American Diabetes Association for books and articles available to the public. Check the Yellow Pages of your telephone directory for businesses or organizations that might be good sources of information. Student writer Sheridan Botts, who wrote an exploratory paper (pp. 174–77) and a research paper (pp. 401–3) on the funding of hospices, obtained much of her information from materials provided by local hospices and insurance companies.

Be aware, however, that businesses and organizations that provide information to the public do so for a reason. Often the reasons are benign. The American

Diabetes Association, for example, wants to provide helpful information to persons afflicted with diabetes. But it is wise to keep in mind the bias of any organization whose information you use. Bias does not mean that the information is wrong, but bias will affect the slant of writing and the choice of aspects of a question that will be discussed. A good researcher looks at many points of view with an open and questioning mind. If you are researching whether to cut old-growth timber, you will want to read publications of both the environmentalists and the timber industry, keeping in mind the goals and values of each group. If the "facts" of either group seem hazy, you will need to seek more reliable data from a disinterested source. In one respect, you have an advantage when working with data provided by organizations because their biases are readily visible.

◢ FINDING INFORMATION THROUGH INTERVIEWS AND PERSONAL CORRESPONDENCE

Interviews and personal correspondence can often provide special perspectives as well as the most current look at what is happening in an area.

Interviews

An interview is often a highly effective way to gather specialized information. Although asking a busy professional for an interview can be intimidating, many experts are generous with their time when they encounter a student who is truly interested in their work. Depending on circumstances, your interview can be formal or informal; you may even conduct an interview over the telephone, without a face-to-face meeting. No matter what the format, all interviews benefit from the following practices:

1. *Be prepared for the interview.*   Be professional as well as friendly. Explain what you are working on and why you are asking for an interview. Know in advance what you hope to learn from the interview.
2. *Be sure you have done background reading before the interview.*   Ideally, interviews should give you knowledge or perspectives unavailable in books or articles. The interview should supplement what you have learned from your reading, not take the place of your reading. Although you needn't be an expert at the time of the interview, you should be conversant about your subject.
3. *Have well-thought-out questions ready.*   Be as thorough with your questions as possible. Most likely you will have only one chance to interview this person. Although you may include some short-answer questions, such as "How long have you been working in this field?" the heart of your interview should focus on open-ended questions, such as "What changes have

you seen in this field?" "What solutions have you found to be most success-ful in dealing with . . . ? or "What do you see as the causes of . . . ?" Ques-tions framed in this way will elicit the information you need but still allow the interviewee to range freely. Avoid yes-or-no questions that can stall con-versation with a one-word answer. Also try to avoid leading questions. For example, instead of asking a social worker, "What do you think about in-fringing on the rights of the homeless by making some of them take antipsy-chotic medication?" ask instead, "What are your views on requiring the mentally ill homeless to take antipsychotic medications as a condition for welfare assistance?" The more you lead the interviewee to the answers you want, the less valid your research becomes.

4. *If the interviewee rambles away from the question, don't jump in too fast.* You may learn something valuable from the seeming digression. You may even want to ask unanticipated questions once you have delved into new ideas. In short, be prepared, but also be flexible.

Before you conduct an interview, consider how you plan to record the infor-mation. Many people like to use a portable tape recorder, but be sure to ask your interviewee's permission if you plan to do so. You may still want to take notes, but taping allows you to focus all your attention on the interaction, following the speaker's train of thought and asking yourself what else you need to know. If you do not tape-record the interview, try to get all the main ideas down on paper and to be accurate with quotable material. Don't hesitate to ask if you are unsure about a fact or statement or if you need to double check what the person intended to say.

You will probably leave the interview feeling immersed in what you heard. No matter how vivid the words are in your mind, take time *very* soon after the in-terview to go over your notes or to transcribe your tape. What may seem unfor-gettable at the moment is all too easy to forget later. If you do your checking soon, you can usually fill in gaps in your notes or explain unclear passages on the tape. Do not trust your memory alone.

FOR WRITING AND DISCUSSION

You can practice interview techniques by interviewing fellow students. Imagine that your class is conducting field research to answer the following question: What are the chief problems that students encounter in producing college-level research papers? Working in small groups, develop a short se-quence of interview questions that will elicit the information you seek. Out-side class, each class member should interview a fellow student, preferably one not in your current writing class. The next day, you should all report the results of your interviews to the class, discussing any difficulties in conduct-ing the interviews and sharing insights into how to improve interviewing techniques.

Personal Correspondence

Occasionally, it is appropriate to write a letter requesting information from an individual or organization. In the letter, state who you are and explain the purpose of your request. Make your request clear and concise. Enclose a stamped, self-addressed envelope for the reply.

◪ GATHERING INFORMATION THROUGH QUESTIONNAIRES

The results of a questionnaire can often add weight to your argument. Although questionnaires always raise problems of bias and statistical validity, careful planning, decision making, and accurate reporting can alleviate most of the problems. You must first decide whether to make your questionnaire anonymous. Although respondents are likely to answer more honestly when the questionnaire is anonymous (for instance, a person is not likely to admit having plagiarized a paper if you are watching him or her fill out the questionnaire), anonymous questionnaires often have a low rate of return. Typically, those who feel strongly on an issue are most likely to fill out and return an anonymous questionnaire, so the returned questionnaires may not accurately reflect a random sampling of opinions. Choose carefully what group of people receive your questionnaire. In your paper, you have an obligation to describe your sample accurately and to state your rate of return.

Finally, the construction of the questionnaire is crucial to its success. Experts work days or weeks perfecting survey questions to avoid bias in answers. Including your questionnaire as an appendix to your paper will lend credibility to your evidence because readers will then be able to check the quality of your questions. Keep your questionnaire clear and easy to complete. Proofread it carefully, and try it out on a guinea pig respondent before you make your final version. Once your questionnaire is complete, type it neatly and write an introduction that explains its purpose. If possible, encourage response by explaining why the knowledge gained from the questionnaire will be beneficial to others.

◪ CONCLUDING YOUR INFORMATION GATHERING

Once you have posed an interesting research question, your search for sources can take on the fascination of a detective puzzle. For many students it is difficult to bring the process of information gathering to a close and to begin the process of reading, note taking, exploratory writing, and drafting. But it is important to do some actual writing early in the process because only by producing a preliminary draft will you detect gaps in your knowledge that require additional research. Exploratory writing and drafting help you focus and increase the efficiency of your information gathering.

◪ CHAPTER SUMMARY

This chapter has discussed the purpose of citing sources and introduced the terms *primary source* and *secondary source*. We presented strategies for converting a general topic into a research question, including preliminary reading and discussions with friends. Once a research question has been chosen, we suggested testing it by posing a series of questions, considering especially the availability of sources. We also described library sources and suggested ways to use them effectively. We pointed out additional sources of information, such as specialized libraries and local organizations. Finally, we addressed strategies for information gathering through interviewing, correspondence, and questionnaires.

The next chapter guides you through the process of reading, note taking, reflecting, and drafting, showing you how to incorporate research information into your own prose.

Using and Citing Sources

The previous chapter helped you pose a good research question and begin unlocking the resources of your library and community. This chapter helps you continue the research process, focusing on the purposeful use of sources. First we look at ways to read source material and to take notes that alternate between recording and reflecting. Then we examine strategies for integrating research information gracefully into your paper, using quotations, paraphrases, and summaries. Finally, we discuss conventions for crediting sources through citations and documentation.

■ FOCUSING AND REFINING YOUR RESEARCH QUESTION

In the last chapter, we reviewed Mary Turla's thinking as she settled on her research question: Should the mail-order bride industry be made illegal? In this section we follow her process through the next stages as she works to focus and refine the question.

Mary began researching her question by looking for newspaper and magazine articles, but she found only occasional references to the subject of mail-order brides. Nor did she find many direct references to the subject in her college library's catalog or periodical indexes. Apparently, this topic had rarely been addressed by academic writers.

Mary turned to creative searching in special libraries and was finally able to locate some articles on mail-order brides as well as some books on Filipino culture that helped her understand the psychology of Filipina women. (See Mary's exploratory essay, pp. 171–74.) Soon she had amassed a considerable amount of information about the mail-order bride industry. The more she read, the more Mary decided that she was totally opposed to it. Despite her mother's argument in its favor (that it helped Filipina women escape poverty), Mary planned to oppose the industry. She felt that the information she had gathered would serve as condemning evidence.

At this point, Mary was following two lines of thought for her paper, both supporting her view that the mail-order bride industry was harmful. First, she believed that the industry posed dangers both for the would-be husband and, especially, for the would-be wife, whose immigrant status and isolation from family made her extremely vulnerable. Second, Mary felt that the industry had a detrimental effect on the image of all Asian women. She planned to use both lines of reasoning to support her initial thesis that the industry should be abolished.

As Mary began to draft her paper, however, she found that she could not cover both areas adequately within the page limit set by her instructor. In addition, the volume of information on the two lines of reasoning was skewed; Mary found more articles on the fate of mail-order brides than on the image of Asian women. Most important, she began to appreciate more fully the potentially positive benefits of the industry. So, she altered her thinking and her thesis—perhaps the mail-order bride business should remain legal but should be strictly regulated.

Mary's case is instructive to all research writers. Often when you begin to write—or even before that, while you are doing research—you discover that you must change your focus, by narrowing it, expanding it, or shifting it in some other way. Sometimes you must alter your purpose as well and adopt a different approach to your problem. Mary started out thinking that she would be an advocate in a public controversy; her thesis was that the mail-order bride business should be made illegal. But when she began searching for materials she discovered that the controversy had not yet made it into the public consciousness. So, she had to amplify her purpose. Her first task became to bring the controversy to people's attention; *then* she could advocate a position. However, as her research progressed, Mary became less certain of her stance and began to see both sides of the controversy more fully. Hence she changed her thesis to "The mail-order bride industry should be regulated." We discuss the relationship between research and purpose more fully later.

What Mary's example shows is that, as a researcher, you must walk a fine line. You must not be so fickle as to shift direction each time you gather information from a new source, but you must be flexible enough to deviate from your original plans when substantial information urges you to go in a new direction.

▨ READING, THINKING, AND NOTETAKING

As you read through your sources, you should engage in two intertwined tasks. First, you need to take effective notes so that you can retrieve information efficiently when you begin drafting. Second, you need to reflect on your reading, imagining how each particular source might be used in your paper and how it influences your thinking about your topic.

There is no one right way to conduct these two activities, but we can offer two techniques that have worked for other writers. First, you can try using a dialectic, or double-entry, journal. Divide a page in half, entering notes on one side and writing reflections about what you've read on the other; for an example, see Chapter 8, pp. 188–89. Or you can take notes on index cards and then do your reflective thinking in a separate research journal. We suggest that you try both techniques and perhaps experiment with a method of your own to discover what works best for you.

One common practice that does *not* work for most writers is *not* to take notes as you read and *not* to do any exploratory writing. We've seen students check out numerous books from the library and photocopy a dozen or more articles, but then write nothing as they read (sometimes they highlight passages with a marker), hoping to rely on memory to navigate through the sources later. This practice can lead to severe writer's block and often results in a cut-and-paste, "all about" report rather than in a focused, well-developed paper.

In this section we want to show you how to take purposeful notes on your readings and how to use exploratory writing to discover your purpose. Because the value of any source depends on your purpose for using it, and because your purpose evolves as your research progresses, taking notes on your readings requires looping back and forth between recording and reflecting.

The Logic of Notetaking

What kind of notes should you take? You can answer this question only in the context of your own research question, purpose, and thesis. To help you appreciate the logic of notetaking, we begin by describing some typical roles that you might adopt when writing an academic research paper.

Synthesizer of current best thinking on a problem.   In this role, you research the current thinking of experts on some important problem and report what the experts currently think. Your paper has primarily an informative purpose. Examples of research questions: What is the current thinking on the value of insulin pumps in managing Type I diabetes? What is the current view of experts on the causes of homosexuality?

Problem-solving detective or critical analyst.   You seek a satisfactory answer that resolves the research question. You may find information that answers the question directly (informative purpose), or you may need to analyze primary sources or other data (analytical purpose). Examples of questions that require you to take this role: What were orphanages like in the nineteenth-century United States? To what extent has the North American Free Trade Agreement (NAFTA) caused U.S. jobs to go to Mexico?

Original field researcher.   You pose an original research problem and conduct field research through observation, interviews, or questionnaires to gather data. You may also do library research to review what others have said about the problem. Such papers generally combine an informative and an analytical purpose and often take the form of a five-section scientific report. Examples of field research questions: What effect has the new Student Union building had on commuter students' bonding with the university? What is our campus environment like for gay and lesbian students?

Analytical thinker who must position himself or herself in a critical conversation.   In this case much of your paper depends on your original analysis of a phenomenon, but you must relate your views to others who have addressed the same or similar questions. Examples: What is the function of violence in fairy tales for children? What effect do beauty and fashion magazines have on the identity and values of teenage girls?

Reviewer of a controversy.   In this role, you report the arguments on various sides of a controversy (informative purpose). For example: What are the current arguments for and against the single-payer health-care system? What are the arguments for and against creating a five-year undergraduate engineering curriculum?

Advocate in a controversy.   You shift from an informative to a persuasive purpose—your paper becomes a researched argument. Examples: Should the United States permit managed harvesting of old-growth forests? Should the United States adopt a single-payer health-care system?

Once you understand the typical roles that academic researchers play, it is easy to see the logic of notetaking, which is a function of your purpose in using a source. As a writer, you read sources for two main reasons.

1. ***To gather data and information.***   Often you read sources to find data and information relevant to your research question—facts, statistics, examples, anecdotes, testimony, and so forth. If your purpose is informative, you will select and organize this information for readers; if your purpose is analytic, you will use the data in more complex ways, seeking to find meaningful patterns that lead to a surprising answer to your research question; if your purpose is persuasive, the data will become supporting evidence for your argument or counterevidence that complicates the issue and may support opposing views.

2. ***To understand other voices in the conversation.***   You also read sources to find out what others have said about your research question, to learn who the experts are, to discover various perspectives and points of view, to find out what is accepted and what is controversial, and so forth. Often your notes in this category will be summaries or paraphrases of a writer's argument, sometimes including brief quotations. As you learn about different points of view, you also try to determine how each writer's perspective on an event, analysis of a phenomenon, or position on an issue may be similar to or different from your own.

Taking Purposeful Notes

To make your notes purposeful and hence efficient, rather than randomly selective or needlessly exhaustive, you need to imagine how a given source might be used in your research paper. Table 22.1 shows how research notes are a function of your purpose.

TABLE 22.1   Notetaking According to Purpose

Informative/Analytical Purpose	
How Source Might Be Used in Your Paper	Notes to Take
For background information about your topic or for new information used in the body of your paper	Summarize the information; record specific data.
As part of a section reviewing previous research on your question	Summarize the problem addressed, the findings, and the conclusions (review of literature for experimental report).
As part of a section describing differing analyses or perspectives related to your research question	Summarize the writer's perspective, analysis, or point of view; in your reflection notes, explore how and why the sources disagree.
Persuasive Purpose	
For background information about your issue	Summarize the information; record specific data.
As data, information, or testimony to be used as supporting evidence for your position	Record the data or information; summarize or paraphrase supporting argument with occasional quotes of key phrases; directly quote short passages for supporting testimony; note the credentials of writer or person quoted.
As data, information, or testimony that counters your position and supports opposing views	Take notes on counterevidence; in your reflection notes, speculate on how you might respond to counterevidence.
As an opposing or alternative position on your issue	Summarize the argument fully and fairly; in your reflection notes, explore causes of disagreement (disagreements about facts, values, beliefs, assumptions) and speculate whether you can refute argument, concede to it, or compromise with it.

Purposeful notetaking entails looping back and forth between recording and exploratory reflection. Exploratory writing lets you imagine how a given source might be used in your paper and thus guides your notetaking. In turn, reading and notetaking might cause you to discover new ideas that lead to further exploratory reflection.

Strategies for Taking Notes

When you take notes, keep a few general principles in mind. First, take notes that are complete. Going back to the library to check for accuracy or to get a fact that you have forgotten wastes time. Also, make sure that when you have used a source's exact words you mark the quoted passage with prominent quotation marks. If you don't intend to quote from the source, be sure that you record the information you need, restating it completely in your own words (we discuss summarizing and quoting later in this chapter).

If you are fairly certain that you plan to use a source extensively in your paper, you might want to photocopy it to facilitate quoting and citing later. As we have explained, however, it is both expensive and inefficient to substitute photocopying for notetaking. The time you save early on by not taking notes will be eaten up later by your confusion over what to use and by your insufficient tilling of the soil through exploratory writing.

In many cases, particularly early in the research process, you might not know whether a source will be useful or how you might want to use it. In these cases, you could include a brief summary of the source's contents in your notes, indicating what kinds of data it offers. Later, when you are more sure of your purpose, you can make an informed decision about whether to use the source.

Next, check that you have all the bibliographic information needed for a citation, including the page numbers for each entry in your notes. It's a good habit to write down the author, title, and other bibliographic data before you begin to take notes. Whether you quote or summarize, you will need to cite the source if you use the writer's ideas (we discuss how to cite sources and avoid plagiarism later in this chapter).

You can record your notes in a journal-style notebook, on cards, or on a computer disk. Many students find that a spiral notebook is efficient for note taking; it keeps everything together and offers the option of putting exploratory writing next to reading notes. When you use a notebook, place bibliographic information at the top of the first page of notes from a particular book or article; then include page references in parentheses after each quotation or paraphrase.

Some students prefer to use note cards. Some writers put bibliographic information on 3-by-5-inch cards and the actual notes on 5-by-8-inch cards. The advantage to this system is that you can use subject headings on the cards and arrange them in various categories when you are planning and writing your paper. The disadvantage is that you might mix up or lose cards; also, some students feel that the cards are cumbersome to carry.

You can also use a computer for recording notes. Depending on the capabilities of your software and your own facility with computer technology, you can take advantage of the speedy data-entry-and-retrieval systems that computers offer.

Reflecting on Your Notes

You should use the strategies for active reading and response discussed in Chapter 6 to reflect on your notes. Exploratory writing will not only help you imagine how a given source might be used in your argument, but it will also help you deepen and complicate your thinking and begin formulating a thesis and a plan for support.

For each set of notes you take on a source, consider doing exploratory writing to answer one or more of the following questions:

- How might I use this source in my own paper?
- How does this source affect my thinking about my subject?
- How reliable and credible is this source? What are its limitations and biases? (See next section.)
- What new questions does this source raise?

Analyzing Bias in Sources

When you read sources for your research project, you always need to consider their trustworthiness, limitations, and biases. Follow our advice in Chapter 6 on reading with and against the grain. When you read against the grain, consider the following issues:

- How up to date is this source? Recent sources are usually better than older ones, so check the publication date. However, many older sources are highly respected and influential. Generally, you can gauge an older source's credibility by seeing how often it is referred to by recent writers in the field.
- What is the writer's point of view? Most closed-form writers attempt to change a reader's view in some way. As you read a source, identify the writer's thesis and ask questions about the writer's use of evidence to support it. What is omitted? What differing viewpoints have other writers taken?
- How credible is this writer? What are the writer's political views? What are the writer's credentials and affiliations? Is the writer affiliated with an organization known for its advocacy of certain positions or viewpoints? For example, scientists and engineers employed by the nuclear power industry are apt to have different views about nuclear energy from those of scientists affiliated with sun- or wind-power research. Knowing a writer's organizational affiliation doesn't mean you can discount the writer's arguments and data; it just means that you need to raise appropriate questions.
- What is the reputation and editorial slant of the publication in which the source appears? Editorial slants can range from liberal (*Utne Reader, Mother Jones, The Nation*) to conservative (*National Review, Reader's Digest*). Likewise, publications affiliated with advocacy organizations (the Sierra Club, the American Association of Retired People, the National Rifle Association) will have a clear editorial bias. If you are uncertain about the editorial bias of a particular magazine or newspaper, consult the *Gale Directory of Publications and Broadcast Media* or *Magazines for Libraries,* which, among other things, identifies the intended audience and political biases of a wide range of magazines and newspapers.

The value of our advice on purposeful notetaking will become clearer in the following section, as we show you how writers can use the same source in different ways for different purposes.

◼ CONTEXT AND PURPOSE IN THE USE OF SOURCES

One of the most useful skills you can learn as a research writer is how to incorporate sources smoothly into your own prose. Your decisions about what to borrow from another writer will be shaped by your own context and purpose. To begin our examination of how writers incorporate sources into their prose, let's look at how three hypothetical writers might use the following article about violence in the old West.

READINGS

▼

ROGER D. MCGRATH
THE MYTH OF VIOLENCE IN THE OLD WEST

1   It is commonly assumed that violence is part of our frontier heritage. But the historical record shows that frontier violence was very different from violence today. Robbery and burglary, two of our most common crimes, were of no great significance in the frontier towns of the Old West, and rape was seemingly nonexistent.

2   Bodie, one of the principal towns on the trans-Sierra frontier, illustrates the point. Nestled high in the mountains of eastern California, Bodie, which boomed in the late 1870s and early 1880s, ranked among the most notorious frontier towns of the Old West. It was, as one prospector put it, the last of the old-time mining camps.

3   Like the trans-Sierra frontier in general, Bodie was indisputably violent and lawless, yet most people were not affected. Fistfights and gunfights among willing combatants—gamblers, miners, and the like—were regular events, and stagecoach holdups were not unusual. But the old, the young, the weak, and the female—so often the victims of crime today—were generally not harmed.

4   Robbery was more often aimed at stagecoaches than at individuals. Highwaymen usually took only the express box and left the passengers alone. There were eleven stagecoach robberies in Bodie between 1878 and 1882, and in only two instances were passengers robbed. (In one instance, the highwaymen later apologized for their conduct.)

5   There were only ten robberies and three attempted robberies of individuals in Bodie during its boom years, and in nearly every case the circumstances were the same: the victim had spent the evening in a gambling den, saloon, or brothel; he had revealed that he had on his person a significant sum of money; and he was staggering home drunk when the attack occurred.

6   Bodie's total of twenty-one robberies—eleven of stages and ten of individuals—over a five-year period converts to a rate of eighty-four robberies per 100,000 inhabitants per year. On this scale—the same scale used by the FBI to index crime—New York

City's robbery rate in 1980 was 1,140, Miami's was 995, and Los Angeles's was 628. The rate for the United States as a whole was 243. Thus Bodie's robbery rate was significantly below the national average in 1980.

Perhaps the greatest deterrent to crime in Bodie was the fact that so many people were armed. Armed guards prevented bank robberies and holdups of stagecoaches carrying shipments of bullion, and armed homeowners and merchants discouraged burglary. Between 1878 and 1882, there were only thirty-two burglaries—seventeen of homes and fifteen of businesses—in Bodie. At least a half-dozen burglaries were thwarted by the presence of armed citizens. The newspapers regularly advocated shooting burglars on sight, and several burglars were, in fact, shot at.   7

Using the FBI scale, Bodie's burglary rate for those five years was 128. Miami's rate in 1980 was 3,282, New York's was 2,661, and Los Angeles's was 2,602. The rate of the United States as a whole was 1,668, thirteen times that of Bodie.   8

Bodie's law enforcement institutions were certainly not responsible for these low rates. Rarely were robbers or burglars arrested, and even less often were they convicted. Moreover, many law enforcement officers operated on both sides of the law.   9

It was the armed citizens themselves who were the most potent—though not the only—deterrent to larcenous crime. Another was the threat of vigilantism. Highwaymen, for example, understood that while they could take the express box from a stagecoach without arousing the citizens, they risked inciting the entire populace to action if they robbed the passengers.   10

There is considerable evidence that women in Bodie were rarely the victims of crime. Between 1878 and 1882 only one woman, a prostitute, was robbed, and there were no reported cases of rape. (There is no evidence that rapes occurred but were not reported.)   11

Finally, juvenile crime, which accounts for a significant portion of the violent crime in the United States today, was limited in Bodie to pranks and malicious mischief.   12

If robbery, burglary, crimes against women, and juvenile crime were relatively rare on the trans-Sierra frontier, homicide was not: thirty-one Bodieites were shot, stabbed, or beaten to death during the boom years, for a homicide rate of 116. No U.S. city today comes close to this rate. In 1980, Miami led the nation with a homicide rate of 32.7; Las Vegas was a distant second at 23.4. A half-dozen cities had rates of zero. The rate for the United States as a whole in that year was a mere 10.2.   13

Several factors contributed to Bodie's high homicide rate. A majority of the town's residents were young, adventurous, single males who adhered to a code of conduct that frequently required them to fight even if, or perhaps especially if, it could mean death. Courage was admired above all else. Alcohol also played a major role in fostering the settlement of disputes by violence.   14

If the men's code of conduct and their consumption of alcohol made fighting inevitable, their sidearms often made it fatal. While the carrying of guns probably reduced the incidence of robbery and burglary, it undoubtedly increased the number of homicides.   15

For the most part, the citizens of Bodie were not troubled by the great number of killings; nor were they troubled that only one man was ever convicted of murder. They accepted the killings and the lack of convictions because most of those killed had been willing combatants.   16

Thus the violence and lawlessness of the trans-Sierra frontier bear little relation to the violence and lawlessness that pervade American society today. If Bodie is at all representative of frontier towns, there is little justification for blaming contemporary American violence on our frontier heritage.   17

18   What we want to show in this section is how there is no one right way to use this article in your own research paper. What you use depends on your own research question and your own purpose in using the source. Sometimes you will summarize a source's whole argument; sometimes you will summarize only a part; at still other times you will use an isolated fact or statistic from the source or quote a sentence or two as testimonial evidence. In what follows we show how three hypothetical writers, addressing three different research questions, use this source in different ways.

Writer 1: Summary for an Analytical Paper

Our first hypothetical writer is analyzing the causes of violence in contemporary U.S. society. She wants to reject one possible cause—that contemporary violence grows out of our violent past. To make this part of her argument, she summarizes McGrath's article.

> Many people believe that violence is part of our Wild West heritage. But Roger McGrath, in his article "The Myth of Violence in the Old West," shows that frontier violence was very different from contemporary violence. He explains that in a typical frontier town, violence involved gunslingers who were "willing combatants," whereas today's typical victims—"the old, the young, the weak, and the female"—were unaffected by crime. Because the presence of an armed populace deterred robbery and burglary, theft was much less common in the old West than today. On the other hand, McGrath explains, killings were fueled by guns, alcohol, and a code of conduct that invited fighting, so murders were much more frequent than in any U.S. city today (6). Thus, according to McGrath, there is little resemblance between violence on the frontier and violence in today's cities, so we cannot blame current violence on our tumultuous frontier past.

In this passage the author summarizes McGrath's argument in order to refute the violent frontier theory about the causes of contemporary violence. Presumably, this author will proceed to other causes of violence and will not return again to McGrath.

Writer 2: Partial Summary for a Persuasive Paper

In our next case, our hypothetical writer uses McGrath's article in an argument supporting gun control. He wants to refute the popular anti-gun-control argument that law-abiding citizens need to be armed to protect themselves against crime.

> Opponents of gun control often argue that guns benefit society by providing protection against intruders. But such protection is deadly, as Roger McGrath shows in his study of violence in the frontier town of Bodie, California. Although guns reduced theft, as seen in the low rate of theft in the well-armed town of Bodie, the presence of guns also led to a homicide rate far above that of the most violent city in the U.S. today. The homicide rate in the frontier town of Bodie, California, for example, was 116 per 100,000, compared to the current national average of 10.2 per 100,000 (McGrath 20). True, Bodie citizens reduced

the theft rate by being heavily armed, but at a cost of a homicide rate more than ten times the current national average. To protect our consumer goods at the cost of so much human life is counter to the values of most Americans.

McGrath's article contains data that could be used on either side of the gun control debate. This writer acknowledges the evidence showing that gun possession reduces theft and then works that potentially damaging information into an argument for gun control. How might you use the McGrath article to oppose gun control?

Writer 3: Partial Summary for an Analytical Paper

Looking at another facet of McGrath's article, our last hypothetical writer summarizes part of McGrath's article to support her thesis that a community's definition of crime is constantly shifting.

> Our notion of criminal activity shifts over time. For example, only a short time ago on the American frontier, murder was often ignored by law enforcement. Roger McGrath, in his discussion of violence in the frontier town of Bodie, California, during the 1870's and 1880's, showed that the townspeople accepted homicides as long as both the murderer and the victim were "willing combatants" who freely participated in gunfights (McGrath 20). These young males who were the "willing combatants" in Bodie share many characteristics with modern gang members in that they were encouraged to fight by a "code of conduct": "A majority of the town's residents were young, adventurous, single males who adhered to a code of conduct that frequently required them to fight even if . . . it could mean death" (20). Today's gang members also follow a code of conduct that requires violence—often in the form of vengeance. Although joining a gang certainly makes a youth a "willing combatant," that status doesn't prevent prosecution in court. Today's "willing combatant" is a criminal, but yesterday's "willing combatant" was not.

This writer uses McGrath's article to make a point completely different from McGrath's. But by extending and applying information from McGrath's article to a new context, the writer gathers fuel for her own argument about shifting definitions of the word *criminal.*

FOR WRITING AND DISCUSSION

Each of our hypothetical writers uses McGrath's article for a different purpose. Working individually or in groups, answer the following questions. Be ready to elaborate on and defend your answers.

1. What are the differences in the ways the writers use the original article? How are these differences related to differences in each writer's purpose?
2. What differences would you expect to find in the research notes each writer took on the McGrath article?

3. What makes each writer's passage different from a purposeless listing of random information?

Next, read Edward Abbey's article, "The Damnation of a Canyon," in Chapter 6 (pp. 130–33). Imagine that you are going to use Abbey's article in an essay of your own. Working individually or in small groups, write an appropriate passage for each of the following scenarios. (*Note:* For more help in writing your passages, read the next section on summarizing, paraphrasing, and quoting.)

Scenario 1	You are a supporter of dams and wish to write an article supporting the Glen Canyon Dam and opposing Abbey's article. Write a one-paragraph summary of Abbey's views to include in your own essay.
Scenario 2	You are doing research on the ecological effects of dams and want to use Abbey's article as one source. For your essay, write a paragraph, citing Abbey's article, on how building the Glen Canyon Dam changed the river's ecology.
Scenario 3	You are investigating the socioeconomic status of people who use Lake Powell for recreation. You particularly want to investigate Abbey's claim that the lake is used only by the wealthy. For your essay, write a short passage that reports Abbey's view of the socioeconomic status of the lake's recreational users.

◾ SUMMARIZING, PARAPHRASING, AND QUOTING

In this section we examine some of the techniques our three hypothetical writers used to adapt the McGrath article to their own purposes: summarizing, paraphrasing, and quoting.

Summarizing and Paraphrasing Sources

A common way to work a source into your own prose is to summarize its thesis or argument. This is an especially useful strategy when the source's argument can directly support your own or when the source represents an opposing or alternative view. You may summarize only a portion of the source's argument if only that portion is relevant. Summaries can be as short as a single sentence or as long as a paragraph. The passage by Writer 1 is a good example of how to use a summary gracefully. (See Chapter 6, pp. 110–15, for detailed advice on summary writing.)

Another effective way to use sources is to paraphrase. *Paraphrasing* means "restating in your own words." Unlike a summary, which condenses the original, a paraphrase is approximately the same length as the original. The writer of a paraphrase keeps the source's original ideas and information but changes the wording.

Because it is about the same length as the original, a paraphrase usually covers only a small section of the original source. You paraphrase when you want to include the actual details of the source's argument. To avoid plagiarism, you must transform the writer's original words entirely into your own language as well as acknowledge the source in a citation. (See the discussion of plagiarism later in this chapter.)

Attributive Tags and Citations

Whenever you summarize or paraphrase, you will need to use *attributive tags*, phrases that indicate that material is from another source; "according to McGrath," "McGrath contends," and "in McGrath's view" all serve this purpose. In most documentation systems the source of the quoted or paraphrased material is cited in parentheses at the end of the borrowed material. (We discuss citation of sources later.) The attributive tag, together with the parenthetical citation, helps the reader distinguish between the writer's own ideas and those borrowed from sources. In the following excerpt from Mary Turla's paper, note how she uses attributive tags and parenthetical citations to acknowledge her sources. Attributive tags and citations are underlined in color.

> Based on ancient Malay tradition, Filipina women, compared to Chinese or Japanese women, have historically enjoyed full equality with the Filipino male. Guthrie and Jacobs describe this equality, relating several aspects of the culture that indicate equal status of men and women. They note that in the Philippines daughters and sons traditionally share equally in inheritance. Within the family, children owe some respect and obedience to all older family members; age, not necessarily sex, is what commands respect in the culture. Guthrie and Jacobs also point to the important position of numerous women in business and government in the Philippines (42). . . . Stanley Karnow also stresses the powerful position of women both in past and present. He states that. . . .

Quoting a Source

A good rule of thumb for research writers is to use quotations sparingly. Inexperienced writers usually quote too often, filling their paper with so many others' voices that their writing loses its own voice and sense of purpose. Quotations are important when you use another author as testimony; they are also useful for imparting the flavor and tone of an original source; and they can enhance your credibility. Often a quotation of just a few words, worked smoothly into the syntax of your own prose, is as effective as a longer quotation. We demonstrate how to work quotations into your own prose after we discuss plagiarism in more detail.

◢ AVOIDING PLAGIARISM

Before we proceed to the nuts and bolts of quoting and citing sources, we will take a brief excursion into the realm of ethics to explain plagiarism. As you know from writing your own papers, developing ideas and putting them into words is hard work. *Plagiarism* occurs whenever you take someone else's work and pass it off as your own. Plagiarism has two forms: borrowing another person's ideas without giving credit through proper citation and borrowing another writer's language without giving credit through quotation marks or block indentation.

The second kind of plagiarism is far more common than the first, perhaps because inexperienced writers don't appreciate how much they need to change the wording of a source to make the writing their own. It is not enough just to change the order of phrases in a sentence or to replace a few words with synonyms. In the following example, compare the satisfactory paraphrase of a passage from McGrath's piece with a plagiarized version.

Original	There is considerable evidence that women in Bodie were rarely the victims of crime. Between 1878 and 1882 only one woman, a prostitute, was robbed, and there were no reported cases of rape. (There is no evidence that rapes occurred but were not reported.)
Acceptable Paraphrase	According to McGrath, women in Bodie rarely suffered at the hands of criminals. Between 1878 and 1882, the only female robbery victim in Bodie was a prostitute. Also, rape seemed nonexistent, with no reported cases and no evidence that unreported cases occurred (McGrath 20).
Plagiarism	According to McGrath (20), there is much evidence that women in Bodie were seldom crime victims. Between 1878 and 1882 only one woman, a prostitute, was robbed, and there were no reported rapes. There is no evidence that unreported cases of rape occurred (McGrath 20).

FOR WRITING AND DISCUSSION

This writer of the plagiarized passage perhaps assumes that the accurate citation of McGrath is all that is needed to avoid plagiarism. Yet this writer is guilty of plagiarism. Why? How has the writer attempted to change the wording of the original? Why aren't these changes enough?

The best way to avoid plagiarism is to be especially careful at the notetaking stage. If you copy from your source, copy exactly, word for word, and put quotation marks around the copied material or otherwise indicate that it is not your own wording. If you paraphrase or summarize material, be sure that you don't borrow any of the original wording. Also be sure to change the grammatical structure of the original. Lazy notetaking, in which you follow the arrangement and grammatical structure of the original passage and merely substitute occasional synonyms, leads directly to plagiarism.

Also remember that you cannot borrow another writer's ideas without citing them. If you summarize or paraphrase another writer's thinking about a subject, you should indicate in your notes that the ideas are not your own and be sure to record all the information you need for a citation. If you do exploratory reflection to accompany your notes, then the distinctions between other writers' ideas and your own should be easy to recognize when it's time to incorporate the source material into your paper.

CONVENTIONS FOR QUOTING AND CITING SOURCES

We discuss next conventions for using source material in your research paper. These rules are specified by two organizations whose style manuals are followed by academic writers everywhere: the MLA, or Modern Language Association, for papers in the arts and humanities, and the APA, or American Psychological Association, for papers in the social sciences and education. Other disciplines may use their own conventions, so before you begin drafting a research paper, check to see which system your instructor recommends.

Long Quotations

Writers typically distinguish long quotations from the rest of the text by using block indentation. If a quoted passage is more than four lines long (MLA system) or more than forty words (APA system), use block indentation rather than quotation marks. The quoted material should be indented one inch (or ten spaces if you are using a typewriter) from the left margin for the MLA system and one-half inch (or five spaces) from the left margin for the APA system. For quotations of only one paragraph or less, do not add an additional indentation to mark the start of a paragraph. For a quotation of two or more paragraphs, indent an additional one-half inch (or five spaces if you are using a typewriter) more for the first line of each paragraph. List the citation in parentheses two spaces after the punctuation at the end of the quotation. Do not use quotation marks at the beginning and end of the passage because the block format itself indicates a quotation. Here is an example of a block quotation indented ten spaces per the MLA system.

> McGrath describes the people most affected by violence in the frontier town of Bodie:
>
> > Fistfights and gunfights among willing combatants—gamblers, miners, and the like—were regular events, and stagecoach holdups were not unusual. But the old, the young, the weak, and the female—so often the victims of crime today—were generally not harmed. (18)

Short Quotations

When a quotation is too short for the block method, it should be inserted directly into your own sentences and set off with quotation marks. The attributive tag may be put at the beginning, middle, or end of your sentence.

Beginning	McGrath claims, "It was the armed citizens themselves who were the most potent—though not the only—deterrent to larcenous crime" (19).
Middle	"Rarely were robbers or burglars arrested," says McGrath, "and even less often were they convicted" (19).
End	"Robbery was more often aimed at stagecoaches than at individuals," McGrath asserts (18).

Note that the parenthetical citation follows the closing quotation mark and precedes the period ending the sentence.

In these examples, the quotations are complete sentences. The opening word of the sentence is capitalized, and a comma separates the attributive tag from the quotation. Often, however, you'll choose not to quote a complete sentence but to weave a quoted phrase or clause directly into your own sentence.

> McGrath contrasts frontier violence to crime today, pointing out that today's typical crime victims are "the old, the young, the weak, and the female" (19) and showing that these groups were not molested in Bodie.

Here no comma precedes the quotation; the writer is not quoting a complete sentence introduced by an attributive tag. Rather, the quotation becomes part of the grammar of the writer's own sentence.

Modifying Quotations to Fit Your Grammatical Structure

Occasionally the grammar of a desired quotation won't match the grammatical structure of your sentence or a word, such as a pronoun, will not be clear if it is taken out of its original context. In these cases, you change the quotation or add a clarifying word, placing brackets around the changes to indicate that the material is not part of the original wording. You also use brackets to show a change in capitalization.

Original Passage	The newspapers regularly advocated shooting burglars on sight, and several burglars were, in fact, shot at.

Quotation Modified to Fit Grammar of Writer's Sentence

In Bodie, an armed citizenry successfully eliminated burglaries, with "newspapers regularly advocat[ing] shooting burglars on sight" (McGrath 206).

Original	Highwaymen, for example, understood that while they could take the express box from a stagecoach without arousing the citizens, they risked inciting the entire populace to action if they robbed the passengers.

Use of Brackets to Change Capitalization and to Explain Missing Referents

Public sentiment influenced what laws were likely to be broken. "[W]hile they [highwaymen] could take the express box from a stagecoach without arousing the citizens, they risked inciting the entire populace to action if they robbed the passengers" (McGrath 19).

Perhaps the most frequent modification writers make is to omit portions of a quotation. To indicate an omission in a quotation, use three spaced periods, called an *ellipsis*, enclosed in a pair of brackets.

Original	Finally, juvenile crime, which accounts for a significant portion of the violent crime in the United States today, was limited in Bodie to pranks and malicious mischief.
Ellipses Used to Indicate Omission	"Finally, juvenile crime [. . .] was limited in Bodie to pranks and malicious mischief" (McGrath 20).

When your ellipsis comes at the boundary between sentences, use an additional period to mark the end of the sentence. Do not place this period inside the brackets. Placement of the ellipsis depends on where the omitted material occurs.

Original	Bodie's law enforcement institutions were certainly not responsible for these low rates. Rarely were robbers or burglars arrested, and even less often were they convicted. Moreover, many law enforcement officers operated on both sides of the law.
Ellipses Following Period	According to McGrath, "Bodie's law enforcement institutions were certainly not responsible for these low rates. [. . .] Moreover, many law enforcement officers operated on both sides of the law" (20).
Ellipses Preceding Period	According to McGrath, "Bodie's law enforcement institutions were certainly not responsible for these low rates. Rarely were robbers or burglars arrested [. . .]. Moreover, many law enforcement officers operated on both sides of the law" (20).

Quotations Within Quotations

Occasionally a passage that you wish to quote will already contain quotation marks. If you use block indentation, keep the quotation marks exactly as they are in the original. If you set the passage within your own quotation marks, however, change the original double marks (") into single marks (') to indicate the quotation within the quotation. The same procedure works whether the quotation marks are used for quoted words or for a title.

Original Passage: Robert Heilbroner Quoting William James

And finally, we tend to stereotype because it helps us make sense out of a highly confusing world, a world which William James once described as "one great, blooming, buzzing confusion."

Quoted Passage: Writer Quoting Heilbroner

Robert Heilbroner explains why people tend to create stereotypes: "And finally, we tend to stereotype because it helps us make sense out of a highly confusing world, a world which William James once described as 'one great, blooming, buzzing confusion' " (22).

■ CONVENTIONS FOR DOCUMENTING SOURCES

Documentation often seems like a thankless chore after the long effort of thinking, researching, and writing, but it is a valuable service for readers; it also gets easier with time and practice. In general, you should cite any information that you have taken from others with the exception of commonly known or commonly available knowledge (the birthdate of John F. Kennedy, the boiling point of water).

In the recent past, writers documented their work with footnotes or endnotes. Academic writers now use new conventions that greatly simplify documentation. They place citations in parentheses in the text just after the material requiring documentation, and they place the complete source information in a bibliography at the end of the paper.

The MLA and APA specify different forms for citation that emphasize or highlight information in useful ways for people who read and write in different disciplines. For instance, APA style foregrounds the date of publication because some scientific studies become outdated more rapidly than research in the humanities, which uses the MLA style. While the differences and details of citation may seem arbitrary in the beginning, you will discover as you become more experienced that they serve useful purposes. For an example of MLA documentation, see Mary Turla's paper on pages 573–87; for APA documentation, see Susan Meyers's paper on pages 303–10.

Next, we illustrate how to use both systems.

In-Text Citations

To cite sources in your text using the *MLA system*, place the author's name and the page references in parentheses immediately after the material being cited. If an attributive tag already identifies the author, give only the page number in parentheses. Once you have cited the author and it is clear that the same author's material is being used, you need cite only the page references in parentheses. The following examples show parenthetical documentation with and without an attributive tag. Note that the citation precedes the period. If you are citing a quotation, the parenthetical citation follows the quotation mark but precedes the final period.

> The Spanish tried to reduce the status of Filipina women who had been able to do business, get divorced, and sometimes become village chiefs (Karnow 41).

> According to Karnow, the Spanish tried to reduce the status of Filipina women who had been able to do business, get divorced, and sometimes become village chiefs (41).

> "And, to this day," Karnow continues, "women play a decisive role in Filipino families" (41).

A reader who wishes to check up on the source will find the bibliographic information in the Works Cited section by checking the entry under Karnow. If more than one work by Karnow was used for the paper, the writer would include in the in-text citation an abbreviated title of the book or article following Karnow's name.

> (Karnow, "In Our Image" 41)

In the *APA system*, the parenthetical reference includes the author's name and the date of the source as well as the page number if a particular passage or table is cited. The elements in the citation are separated by commas and a *p.* or *pp.* precedes the page number. If a source has more than one author, you use an ampersand (&) to join their names. When the author is mentioned in an attributive tag, you include only the date and page. The following examples show parenthetical documentation with and without attributive tags according to APA style.

> The Spanish tried to reduce the status of women who had been able to do business, get divorced, and sometimes become village chiefs (Karnow, 1989, p. 41).

> According to Karnow, the Spanish tried to reduce the status of women who had been able to do business, get divorced, and sometimes become village chiefs (1989, p. 41).

> "And, to this day," Karnow continues, "women play a decisive role in Filipino families" (1989, p. 41).

Just as with MLA style, with APA style readers will look for sources in the list of references at the end of the paper if they wish to find full bibliographic information. In the APA system, this bibliographic list is titled "References" and, as in the MLA Works Cited list, only includes sources cited in the body of your paper. If your sources include two works by the same author published in the same year, you place an *a* after the date for the first work and a *b* after the date for the second, ordering the works alphabetically by title. If Karnow had published two different works in 1989, your in-text citation would look like this:

> (Karnow, 1989b, p. 41)

Citing a Quotation or Other Data from an Indirect Source

Occasionally you may wish to use a quotation or data that appears as a citation in another text (called an *indirect source* in MLA style, and a *secondary source* in APA style). If possible, find the quotation in its original source and cite the quotation or data from that source. If the original source is not available, you should cite the indirect source by using "qtd. in" (MLA) or "as cited in" (APA). List only the indirect source in your Works Cited or References section. In the following example, the writer wishes to use a quote from a book entitled *Living Buddha, Living Christ*, written by a Buddhist monk, Thich Nhat Hanh. The writer is unable to locate the book and instead has to quote from a book review by Lee Moriwaki. Here is how the in-text citations will look.

> **MLA**   A Buddhist monk, Thich Nhat Hanh, stresses the importance of inner peace: "If we can learn ways to touch the peace, joy, and happiness that are already there, we will become healthy and strong, and a resource for others" (qtd. in Moriwaki: C4).

> **APA**   A Buddhist monk, Thich Nhat Hanh, stresses the importance of inner peace: "If we can learn ways to touch the peace, joy, and happiness that are already there, we will become healthy and strong, and a resource for others" (as cited in Moriwaki, 1995, p. C4).

In the next section we describe the format for the bibliographic entries under Works Cited in the MLA system and under References in the APA system.

Bibliographic Listings at the End of Your Paper

Both the MLA and APA systems specify a complete list of all items cited, placed at the end of the paper. The list should comprise all sources from which you gathered information, including articles, books, videos, letters, and electronic sources. The list should not include works you read but did not cite. In both systems, all works are listed alphabetically by author, or by title if there is no author.

In the MLA system, the words *Works Cited,* in uppercase and lowercase letters, are centered one inch from the top of the page. Sources are listed alphabetically, the first line flush with the left margin and succeeding lines indented one-half inch (or five spaces if you are using a typewriter). Here is a typical example of a work cited in MLA form.

> Karnow, Stanley. In Our Image: America's Empire in the Philippines. New York:
> Random, 1989.

The same information with a slightly different arrangement is used in the APA system. The word *References* is typed in uppercase and lowercase letters at the top of the page. Entries for sources are listed alphabetically. After the first line, which is flush at the left margin, succeeding lines are indented three spaces.

> Karnow, S. (1989). In our image: America's empire in the Philippines. New York:
> Random House.

The remaining pages in this section show examples of MLA and APA formats for different kinds of sources, including the electronic sources described in Chapter 23. Following these examples is a typical page from a Works Cited or References list that features formats for the most commonly encountered kinds of sources.

General Format for Books

MLA   Author. Title. Edition. City of Publication: Publisher, year of publication.

APA   Author. (Year of Publication). Title. City of Publication: Publisher.

Note these important differences between the two systems:

- In MLA style, author entries include first names and middle initials; in APA style, only the initials of the first and middle names are given, unless full names are needed to distinguish persons with the same initials.
- In MLA style, the first word and all nouns are capitalized in the title; in APA style, only the first word, proper nouns, and the first word after a dash or a colon are capitalized in the title.
- In MLA style, the year of publication comes last, after the publisher; in APA style, the year of publication follows immediately after the author's name.
- In MLA style, names of publishers have standardized abbreviations, listed in section 8.5 of the *MLA Style Manual,* 2nd ed.; in APA style, names of publishers are not usually abbreviated except for the elimination of unnecessary words such as *Inc., Co.,* and *Publishers.*
- In MLA style, punctuation following the underlined title is not underlined; in APA style, punctuation following the underlined title *is* underlined.

One Author

MLA   Coles, Robert. The Youngest Parents: Teenage Pregnancy as It Shapes Lives. New York: Norton, 1997.

APA   Coles, R. (1997). The youngest parents: Teenage pregnancy as it shapes lives. New York: W. W. Norton.

Two or More Listings for One Author

MLA   Hass, Robert. Human Wishes. New York: Ecco, 1989.

---, ed. Rock and Hawk: A Selection of Shorter Poems by Robinson Jeffers. New York: Random, 1987.

---. Sun Under Wood. New York: Ecco, 1996.

---, ed. Thomas Transtromer: Selected Poems 1954–1986. New York: Ecco, 1987.

In the MLA style, when two or more works by one author are cited, the works are listed in alphabetical order by title. For the second and all additional entries, type three hyphens and a period in place of the author's name. Then skip two spaces and type the title. If the person named edited, translated, or compiled the book, place a comma (not a period) after the three hyphens and write the appropriate abbreviation (*ed., trans.,* or *comp.*) before giving the title.

APA   Hass, R. (Ed.). (1987a). Rock and hawk: A selection of shorter poems by Robinson Jeffers. New York: Random House.

Hass, R. (Ed.). (1987b). Tomas Transtromer: Selected poems 1954–1986. New York: Ecco Press.

Hass, R. (1989). Human wishes. New York: Ecco Press.

Hass, R. (1996). Sun under wood. New York: Ecco Press.

In APA style, when an author has more than one entry in "References," the author's name is repeated and the entries are listed chronologically (oldest to newest) rather than alphabetically. When two entries by the same author have the same date, they are then listed in alphabetical order. Lowercase letters are added after the year of publication to distinguish them from each other when cited by date in the text.

Two or More Authors of a Single Work

MLA   Ciochon, Russell, John Olsen, and Jamie James. The Search for the Giant Ape in Human Prehistory. New York: Bantam, 1990.

APA   Ciochon, R., Olsen, J., & James, J. (1990). The search for the giant ape in human prehistory. New York: Bantam Books.

Note that the APA style uses the ampersand (&) to join the names of multiple authors.

Using et al. for Works with Several Authors

MLA   Maimon, Elaine P., et al. Writing in the Arts and Sciences. Cambridge, MA: Winthrop, 1981.

In the MLA system, if there are four or more authors, you have the option of using the form *et al.* (meaning "and others") after the name of the first author listed on the title page.

APA   Maimon, E. P., Belcher, G. L., Hearn, G. W., Nodine, B. F., & O'Connor, F. W. (1981). Writing in the arts and sciences. Cambridge, MA: Winthrop.

APA style calls for you to write out the names of all authors, no matter how many, for one work.

Edited Anthology

MLA	Gates, Henry Louis, Jr., and Nellie Y. McKay, eds. <u>The Norton Anthology of African American Literature</u>. New York: Norton, 1997.
APA	Gates, H. L., & McKay, N. Y. (Eds.). (1997). <u>The Norton anthology of African American literature</u>. New York: W. W. Norton.

Essay in an Anthology or Other Collection

MLA	Thomson, Peter. "Playhouses and Players in the Time of Shakespeare." <u>The Cambridge Companion to Shakespeare Studies</u>. Ed. Stanley Wells. Cambridge, Eng.: Cambridge UP, 1986. 67–83.

In the MLA system, the words *University Press* are always abbreviated as *UP*. If several cities are listed in the book as the place of publication, list only the first. For cities outside the United States, add an abbreviation of the country (or province in Canada) if the name of the city is ambiguous or unfamiliar.

APA	Thomson, P. (1986). Playhouses and players in the time of Shakespeare. In S. Wells (Ed.), <u>The Cambridge companion to Shakespeare studies</u> (pp. 67–83). Cambridge, England: Cambridge University Press.

Book in a Later Edition or Revised Edition

MLA	Burns, E. Bradford. <u>Latin America: A Concise Interpretive History</u>. 6th ed. Englewood Cliffs: Prentice, 1994.
	Schmidt, Rick. <u>Feature Filmmaking at Used-Car Prices: How to Write, Produce, Direct, Film, Edit, and Promote a Feature-Length Film for Less than $10,000</u>. Rev. ed. New York: Penguin, 1995.
APA	Burns, E. B. (1994). <u>Latin America: A concise interpretive history</u> (6th ed.). Englewood Cliffs, NJ: Prentice Hall.
	Schmidt, R. (1995). <u>Feature filmmaking at used-car prices: How to write, produce, direct, film, edit, and promote a feature-length film for less than $10,000</u> (Rev. ed.). New York: Penguin.

Multivolume Work

Cite the whole work when you have used more than one volume of the work.

MLA	Churchill, Winston S. <u>A History of the English-Speaking Peoples</u>. 4 vols. New York: Dodd, 1956–58.
APA	Churchill, W. S. (1956–1958). <u>A history of the English-speaking peoples</u> (Vols. 1–4). New York: Dodd, Mead.

Include the volume number when you have used only one volume of a multivolume work.

MLA	Churchill, Winston S. <u>The Great Democracies</u>. New York: Dodd, 1957. Vol. 4 of <u>A History of the English-Speaking Peoples</u>. 4 vols. 1956–58.
APA	Churchill, W. S. (1957). <u>A history of the English-speaking peoples: Vol. 4. The great democracies</u>. New York: Dodd, Mead.

Reference Work with Frequent Editions

MLA	Pei, Mario. "Language." <u>World Book Encyclopedia</u>. 1976 ed.

In citing familiar reference works under the MLA system, you don't need to include all the normal publication information.

> **APA**   Pei, M. (1976). Language. In World book encyclopedia (Vol. 12, pp. 62–67). Chicago: Field Enterprises.

Less Familiar Reference Work Without Frequent Editions

> **MLA**   Ling, Trevor O. "Buddhism in Burma." Dictionary of Comparative Religion. Ed. S. G. F. Brandon. New York: Scribner's, 1970.
>
> **APA**   Ling, T. O. (1970). Buddhism in Burma. In S. G. F. Brandon (Ed.), Dictionary of comparative religion. New York: Scribner's.

Edition in Which Original Author's Work Is Prepared by an Editor

> **MLA**   Brontë, Emily. Wuthering Heights. 1847. Ed. V. S. Pritchett. Boston: Houghton, 1956.
>
> **APA**   Brontë, E. (1956). Wuthering Heights (V. S. Pritchett, Ed.). Boston: Houghton, Mifflin. (Original work published 1847)

Translation

> **MLA**   Camus, Albert. The Plague. Trans. Stuart Gilbert. New York: Modern Library, 1948. Trans. of La Peste. Paris: Gallimard, 1947.

In MLA style, some or all of the original publication information may be added at the end of the entry. Though it is not required, adding the date avoids the suggestion that the original work was written in the same year that it was translated.

> **APA**   Camus, A. (1948). The plague (S. Gilbert, Trans.). New York: Modern Library. (Original work published 1947)

In APA style, the date of the translation is placed after the author's name; the date of original publication of the work is placed in parentheses at the end of the reference. In text, this book would be cited as follows:

> (Camus, 1947/1948)

Corporate Author (a Commission, Committee, or Other Group)

> **MLA**   American Red Cross. Standard First Aid. St. Louis: Mosby Lifeline, 1993.
>
> **APA**   American Red Cross. (1993). Standard first aid. St. Louis: Mosby Lifeline.

Anonymous Work

> **MLA**   The New Yorker Cartoon Album: 1975–1985. New York: Penguin, 1987.
>
> **APA**   The New Yorker cartoon album: 1975–1985. (1987). New York: Penguin Books.

Republished Work (For Example, a Newer Paperback Published After the Original Edition)

> **MLA**   Wollstonecraft, Mary. The Vindication of the Rights of Woman, with Strictures on Politican and Moral Subjects. 1792. Rutland, VT: Tuttle, 1995.
>
> **APA**   Wollstonecraft, M. The vindication of the rights of woman, with strictures on politican and moral subjects. Rutland, VT: Tuttle and Company. (Original work published in 1792)

General Format for Articles

MLA (Scholarly Journals)

> Author. "Article Title." <u>Journal Title</u> volume number (year): inclusive pages.

MLA (Magazines and Newspapers)

> Author. "Article Title." <u>Magazine or Newspaper Title</u> day month year: inclusive pages.

> **APA**   Author. (year, month day). Article title. <u>Magazine, Newspaper, or Scholarly Journal title, volume number,</u> inclusive pages.

Note these important details about the two systems:

- MLA style changes slightly between scholarly and popular media sources. Scholarly journals are cited by volume number with the year given in parentheses, while citations for popular media sources do not use the volume number and give all details of the date without parentheses.
- Titles of articles in MLA style are placed in quotation marks (with the period *inside* the closing quotation mark), while APA style does not place quotation marks around titles.
- In MLA style, the date is followed by a colon, followed by the inclusive page numbers, while the APA system uses a comma to separate the title and volume number from the inclusive pages.
- As in book citations, the two styles differ in underlining. MLA style underlines only the title (not the punctuation or volume) while APA style calls for the title, volume (if there is one) and comma to be underlined, unless there is an issue. In that case, neither the issue nor the comma is underlined (see the example that follows).

Scholarly Journal with Continuous Annual Pagination

> **MLA**   Barton, Ellen L. "Evidentials, Argumentation, and Epistemological Stance." <u>College English</u> 55 (1993): 745–69.

> **APA**   Barton, E. L. (1993). Evidentials, argumentation, and epistemological stance. <u>College English, 55,</u> 745–769.

Scholarly Journal with Each Issue Paged Separately

> **MLA**   Pollay, Richard W., Jung S. Lee, and David Carter-Whitney. "Separate, but Not Equal: Racial Segmentation in Cigarette Advertising." <u>Journal of Advertising</u> 21.1 (1992): 45–57.

> **APA**   Pollay, R. W., Lee, J. S., & Carter-Whitney, D. (1992). Separate but equal: Racial segmentation in cigarette advertising. <u>Journal of Advertising,</u> <u>21</u>(1), 45–57.

Note that in both systems when each issue is paged separately, both the volume (in this case, 21) and the issue number (in this case, 1) are given.

Magazine Article

> **MLA**   Fallows, James. "Vietnam: Low-Class Conclusions." <u>Atlantic Monthly</u> Apr. 1993: 38–44.

APA   Fallows, J. (1993, April). Vietnam: Low-class conclusions. <u>Atlantic Monthly,</u> 38–44.

Note that this form is for a magazine published each month. The next entry shows the form for a magazine published each week.

Anonymous Article

MLA   "The Rebellious Archbishop." <u>Newsweek</u> 11 July 1988: 38.

APA   The rebellious archbishop. (1988, July 11). <u>Newsweek,</u> 38.

Review

MLA   Lakey, Jennifer. "Exploring Native American Traditions with Children." Rev. of <u>She Who Watches</u>, by Willa Holmes. <u>Writers NW</u> Winter 1997: 7.

For both movie and book reviews, if the reviewer's name is not given, begin with the title of the reviewed work, preceded by "Rev. of" in the MLA system or "[Review of *title*]" in the APA system. Begin with the title of the review if the review is titled but not signed.

APA   Lakey, J. (1997, Winter). Exploring Native American traditions with children [Review of the book <u>She Who Watches</u>]. <u>Writers NW</u>, 7.

Newspaper Article

MLA   Henriques, Diana B. "Hero's Fall Teaches Wall Street a Lesson." <u>Seattle Times</u> 27 Sept. 1998: A1+.

The *A1+* indicates that the article begins on page 1 but continues later in the newspaper on a later page or pages.

APA   Henriques, D. B. (1998, September 27). Hero's fall teaches Wall Street a lesson. <u>The Seattle Times,</u> pp. A1, A24.

The pp. A1, A24 indicates that the article begins on page 1 and ends on page 24. Note that for both systems, the newspaper section is indicated if each section is paged separately.

Newspaper Editorial

MLA   Dowd, Maureen. "Legacy of Lust." Editorial. <u>New York Times</u> 23 Sept. 1998: A31.

APA   Dowd, M. (1998, September 23). Legacy of lust [Editorial]. <u>The New York Times,</u> p. A31.

Letter to the Editor of a Magazine or Newspaper

MLA   Tomsovic, Kevin. "Culture Clash." Letter. <u>New Yorker</u> 13 July 1998: 7.

APA   Tomsovic, K. (1998, July 13). Culture clash [Letter to the editor]. <u>The New Yorker,</u> p. 7.

Include a title if one is given to the letter in the publication.

Information Service such as ERIC (Educational Resources Information Center) or NTIS (National Technical Information Service)

MLA   Eddy, P. A. <u>The Effects of Foreign Language Study in High School on Verbal Ability as Measured by the Scholastic Aptitude Test—Verbal.</u> Washington: Center for Applied Linguistics, 1981. ERIC ED 196 312.

APA   Eddy, P. A. (1981). <u>The effects of foreign language study in high school</u>
<u>on verbal ability as measured by the Scholastic Aptitude Test—Verbal.</u>
Washington, DC: Center for Applied Linguistics. (ERIC Document
Reproduction Service No. ED 196 312)

Chapter 23 introduces you to many research sources on the Internet: electronic
mail, Listservs and Listserv discussion groups, Usenet newsgroups, World Wide
Web sites, links, and online texts. Everyone who uses the Internet for research
needs to develop some discernment about the quality of the information offered.
For instance, data or texts offered at the Library of Congress or the U.S. Geological Survey, which can be corroborated with material from print sources, is more
likely to be reliable than the material an individual may put on a personal
homepage—material that may be difficult or impossible to corroborate.

Since there are few national or international regulations governing access or
use of the Internet, anyone can design a homepage and include whatever "information" he or she pleases. For instance, some homepages promote racism, anti-
Semitism, and pornography. Other homepages offer misinformation for political
or ideological reasons. Yet advanced Web design tools, like PageMill, enable anyone to make a site look as official as the Library of Congress or the U.S. Geological Survey. The problem is clear: material taken from the Internet has to be
carefully analyzed to determine its claim to authority; otherwise you could be basing your research on faulty or biased information. (See Chapter 15, pp. 370–77, for
a discussion of how to evaluate websites.)

While it's true that print sources can also be faulty and biased, it's more difficult to get a book or an article published than to design a website. Editors hold authors to standards of accuracy and importance before they will publish a work,
while there are no requirements at all for placing material on a website. Even a text
that would appear to be "foolproof," such as a famous book or an article originally
printed in a journal, may have been accidentally altered in the process of scanning
or typing it onto the electronic source. The best rule of thumb is to remember that
checking the facts is an essential step in all forms of research—especially on the
Internet.

Formats for Electronic Sources

While rules for formatting electronic sources are still being developed, the
principle that governs electronic citations is the same as for print sources: *give*
enough information so that the reader can find the source you used. If the reader cannot
relocate the Web page, Listserv, or other electronic source from your citation, then
you haven't given enough details. It is also important to give the date that you accessed the material as part of your citation, since websites are fluid—frequently
updated, altered, or dropped. The reader will know from the date of your citation
whether a cite may be inaccessible because it has not been updated, or whether
the information on the page is different from your data because it has been
updated.

The MLA and APA have developed general guidelines for citing electronic
sources, which are applied here to specific examples. Nevertheless, you have more

freedom of judgment in this area than in the area of print media citations, because electronic sources are in constant development and flux. When in doubt, always make entries as clear and informative as possible. Also, when you write an electronic citation, use your own citation to relocate the data just to make sure your address is accurate. If you cannot duplicate your own path to the material, give a simpler citation to the site's homepage directory that will lead the reader to the original source. (See the example that follows.)

Books, Pamphlets, or Texts in Online Databases or CD-ROMs that Are Also Available in Print

MLA   Melville, Herman. Moby-Dick, or The White Whale. 1851. Eds. Luther S. Mansfield and Howard P. Vincent. New York: Hendricks, 1952. 27 Sept. 1998 <http://etext.lib.virginia.edu/modeng/modeng0.browse.html>.

MLA style uses the book citation format followed by the date of access and the URL (Uniform Resource Locator) enclosed in angle brackets. In this case, the URL is so long that the reader is directed to the browser at the University of Virginia Electronic Text Center. The reader can easily access *Moby-Dick* from there. If you must divide the URL to go to another line, break at the clear end of a section, such as a period or a backslash.

APA   Melville, H. (1851). Moby-Dick, or the white whale [Online]. University of Virginia Electronic Text Center. Retrieved September 27, 1998 from the World Wide Web: http://etext.lib.virginia.edu/modeng/modeng0.browse.html

APA style calls for a definition of the medium, the website that provides the text, the word *Retrieved* followed by the access date and the phrase *from the World Wide Web,* and the URL.

Journals or Periodicals in Databases or CD-ROMs that Are Also Available in Print

MLA   Kowaleski-Wallace, Beth. "Women, China, and Consumer Culture in Eighteenth Century England." Eighteenth Century Studies 29.2 (1995–96): 153–67. 1 Feb. 1999 <http://direct.press.jhu.edu/journals/eighteenth-century_studies/toc/ecsv029.html#v029.2>.

APA   Kowaleski-Wallace, B. (1995–96). Women, China, and consumer culture in eighteenth century England. Eighteenth Century Studies [Online], 29(2), 153–167. Retrieved February 1, 1999 from the World Wide Web: http://direct.press.jhu.edu/journals/eighteenth-century_studies/toc/ecsv029.html#v029.2

Books, Journals, or Periodicals in Online Databases or CD-ROMs that Are Not Available in Print

MLA   Lal, Vinay. "Indians and The Guinness Book of World Records: The Political and Cultural Contours of a National Obsession." Suitcase: A Journal of Transcriptural Traffic 3 (1998). 2 Oct. 1998 <http://www.suitcase.net/lai.html>.

APA   Lal, V. (1998). Indians and The Guinness book of world records: The political and cultural contours of a national obsession. Suitcase: A journal of

transcriptural traffic, 3, [Online]. Retrieved October 2, 1999 from the
World Wide Web: http://www.suitcase.net/lai.html

Computer Disks that Are Not Available in Print

MLA Microsoft Age of Empires. CD-ROM. Redmond, WA: Microsoft, 1998.

APA Microsoft age of empires [Computer software]. (1998). Redmond, WA:
Microsoft Software.

Include the medium, city of issue, vendor name, and date of issue.

The APA style follows the specifications for online books available in print.

Information Service Data Bank

MLA Starr, Kenneth W. "Report of the Independent Counsel." Thomas: Legislative Information on the Internet. 9 Sept. 1998. Lib. of Congress, Washington. 2 Oct. 1998 <http://icreport.loc.gov/icreport/1cover.htm>.

Include the title of project or database (underlined), the name of the editor of the
project if there is one, and the electronic publication information, including date
of last update, date of access, and URL.

APA Starr, K. W. (1998, September 9). Report of the Independent Counsel.
Thomas: Legislative information on the internet [Online]. Library of
Congress. Retrieved October 2, 1998 from the World Wide Web: http://
icreport.loc.gov/icreport/1cover.htm

The access date and URL follow the same format as in an entry for an online book
or article.

E-mail, Listservs, and Other Nonretrievable Sources

MLA Rushdie, Salman. "My Concern about the Fatwa." E-mail to the author.
1 May 1995.

Note that this format specifies that the document is an e-mail letter, to whom it
was addressed, and the date of transmission.

In APA style, this material is not listed in "References." You should, however,
acknowledge it in in-text citations.

The novelist has repeated this idea recently (Salman Rushdie, personal communication, May 1, 1995).

Bulletin Board or Newsgroup Posting

MLA MacDonald, James C. "Suggestions for Promoting Collaborative Writing in
College Composition." Online posting. 10 Nov. 1994. NCTE Forum/
current topics/bulletin posting. 12 Mar. 1995. America Online.

Include the date of transmission or posting, the medium, network name, location
information, an address or path for electronic access, and date of access.

In APA style, this material is acknowledged in in-text citations only. See the
specifications for e-mail, listservs, and other nonretrievable sources.

Miscellaneous Materials

Films, Filmstrips, Slide Programs, and Videotapes

MLA Chagall. Dir. Kim Evans. Ed. Melvyn Bragg. Videocassette. London Weekend Television, 1985.

APA   Evans, K. (Director), & Bragg, M. (Editor). (1985). <u>Chagall</u> [Videocassette]. London: London Weekend Television.

Television and Radio Programs
MLA   <u>Korea: The Forgotten War</u>. Narr. Robert Stack. KCPQ, Seattle. 27 June 1988.

APA   Stack, R. (Narrator). (1988, June 27). <u>Korea: The forgotten war.</u> Seattle: KCPQ.

Interview
MLA   Deltete, Robert. Personal interview. 27 Feb. 1994.

APA   Deltete, R. (1994, February 27). [Personal interview].

The APA publication manual says to omit nonrecoverable material—such as personal correspondence, personal interviews, lectures, and so forth—from "References" at the end. However, in college research papers, professors usually like to have such information included.

Lecture, Address, or Speech
MLA   North, Oliver. Speech. Washington Policy Council. Seattle. 20 July 1988.

APA   North, O. (1988, July 20). Speech presented to Washington Policy Council, Seattle, WA.

In the MLA system, if the title of the speech is known, give the title in quotation marks in place of "Speech." The *Publication Manual of the American Psychological Association* has no provisions for citing lectures, addresses, or speeches because these are nonrecoverable items. However, the manual gives authors leeway to design citations for instances not covered explicitly in the manual. This format is suitable for college research papers.

For more complicated entries, consult the *MLA Handbook for Writers of Research Papers,* fourth edition, or the *Publication Manual of the American Psychological Association,* fourth edition. Both books should be available in your library or bookstore.

Quick Check Reference: MLA and APA Bibliographic Entries

As a handy reference to the most commonly encountered kinds of entries in college research papers, see pages 569–70. These two pages illustrate a Works Cited list (MLA format) and a References list (APA format). These lists give you a quick summary of the formats for the most commonly used sources.

▟ FORMATTING A RESEARCH PAPER

College instructors usually ask students to follow standard academic conventions for formatting research papers. Although conventions vary from discipline to discipline, the most common formatting styles are the MLA or the APA. The MLA formatting style is illustrated in Mary Turla's paper on pages 573–87. The APA formatting style is illustrated in Susan Meyers's paper on pages 303–10.

Works Cited: MLA Style Sheet for the Most Commonly Used Sources

Ross 27

Works Cited

Adler, Freda. <u>Sisters in Crime</u>. New York: McGraw, 1975.

Andersen, Margaret L. <u>Thinking about Women: Socio-</u>
<u>logical Perspectives on Sex and Gender</u>. 3rd ed.
New York: Macmillan, 1993.

Bart, Pauline, and Patricia O'Brien. <u>Stopping Rape:</u>
<u>Successful Survival Strategies</u>. New York:
Pergamon, 1985.

Durkin, Kevin. "Social Cognition and Social Context in
the Construction of Sex Differences." <u>Sex</u>
<u>Differences in Human Performances</u>. Ed. Mary Anne
Baker. New York: Wiley, 1987. 45-60.

Fairburn, Christopher G., et al. "Predictors of 12-
month Outcome in Bulimia Nervosa and the Influence
of Attitudes to Shape and Weight." <u>Journal of Con-</u>
<u>sulting and Clinical Psychology</u> 61 (1993): 696-98.

Kantrowitz, Barbara. "Sexism in the Schoolhouse."
<u>Newsweek</u> 24 Feb. 1992: 62.

Langewiesche, William. "The World in Its Extreme."
<u>Atlantic Monthly</u> Nov. 1991: 105-40.

"Selected Rights of Homeless Persons." <u>National Law</u>
<u>Center on Homelessness and Poverty</u> 19 Apr. 1998
<http://www.nlchp.org/rights2.htm>.

Taylor, Chuck. "After Cobain's Death: Here Come the
Media Ready to Buy Stories." <u>Seattle Times</u>
10 Apr. 1994: A1+.

Author's last name and page number in upper right corner.

Book entry, one author. Use standard abbreviations for common publishers.

Book entry in a revised edition.

Book with two or three authors. With four or more authors use "et al.," as in Jones, Peter, et al.

Article in anthology; author heads the entry; editor cited after the title. Inclusive page numbers come two spaces after the period following year.

Article in scholarly journal paginated consecutively throughout year. This article has four or more authors.

Weekly or biweekly popular magazine; abbreviate all months except May, June, and July.

Monthly, bimonthly, or quarterly magazine.

Unauthored document online; title in quotations; website underlined; date of access; web address in angle brackets.

Newspaper article with identified author; if no author, begin with title.

References: APA Style Sheet for the Most Commonly Used Sources

Running head with page number double-spaced below.

Book entry, one author. Don't abbreviate publisher but omit unnecessary words.

Book entry in a revised edition.

Book with multiple authors; uses ampersand instead of and *before last name. Authors' names listed last name first.*

Article in anthology; no quotes around article. Name of editor comes before book title.

Article in scholarly journal paginated consecutively throughout year. APA lists all authors rather than using et al. *(except when there are six or more authors).*

Weekly or biweekly popular magazine; abbreviate all months except May, June, and July

Monthly, bimonthly, or quarterly magazine.

Unauthored document online; roman title; type of medium in square brackets; website; access date; no period after Web address.

Newspaper article with identified author; if no author, begin with title.

Women, Health, and Crime

27

References

Adler, F. (1975). Sisters in crime. New York: McGraw-Hill.

Andersen, M. L. (1993). Thinking about women: Sociological perspectives on sex and gender (3rd ed.). New York: Macmillan.

Bart, P., & O'Brien, P. (1985). Stopping rape: Successful survival strategies. New York: Pergamon Press.

Durkin, K. (1987). Social cognition and social context in the construction of sex differences. In M. A. Baker (Ed.), Sex differences in human performances (pp. 45–60). New York: Wiley & Sons.

Fairburn, C. G., Pevaler, R. C., Jones, R., & Hope, R. A. (1993). Predictors of 12-month outcome in bulimia nervosa and the influence of attitudes to shape and weight. Journal of Consulting and Clinical Psychology, 61, 696–98.

Kantrowitz, B. (1992, February 24). Sexism in the schoolhouse. Newsweek, p. 62.

Langewiesche, W. (1991, November). The world in its extreme. The Atlantic Monthly, pp. 105–40.

Selected rights of homeless persons [Online]. National Law Center on Homelessness and Poverty. Retrieved April 19, 1998 from the World Wide Web: http://www.nlchp.org./rights2.htm

Taylor, C. (1993, April 10). After Cobain's death: Here come the media ready to buy stories. The Seattle Times, pp. A1+.

Formatting Features Common to Both MLA and APA

- Double-space the text throughout, including quotations and notes.
- Use one-inch margins top and bottom, left and right.
- Indent five spaces at the beginning of every paragraph.
- Number pages consecutively throughout the manuscript including the bibliographic section at the end.
- Begin the bibliographic section (called Works Cited in MLA and References in APA) on a separate page.

Distinctive Formatting Features for MLA

- Do not include a cover page. Type your name, professor's name, course number, and date in the upper left-hand corner of your paper (all double-spaced) beginning one inch from the top of the page; then double-space and type your title, centered, without underlines, boldface, or all caps (capitalize first word and important words only); then double-space and begin your text (see page 573 for an example).
- Page numbers go in the upper right-hand corner flush with the right margin and one-half inch from the top of the page. The page number should be preceded by your last name (see pp. 573–87). The text begins one inch from the top of the page.
- Start a new page for your bibliography, which is titled "Works Cited" (centered, one inch from top of page, without underlining, quotation marks, bold face, or all caps). Format each entry according to the instructions on pages 558–68 (see p. 569 for an example; also see pp. 586–87).

Distinctive Formatting Features for APA

- Has a separate title page, numbered page 1, and a 100–150 word Abstract, numbered page 2 (the main body of your text begins with page 3). Papers for undergraduate courses often omit the abstract. Approximately one-third from the top of the page, type your title centered and double-spaced, without underlines or all caps (capitalize first word and important words only). Two spaces below the title type your name (centered). Two spaces below your name, type your course number (centered), and two spaces below that type the date (for an example of an APA title page, see page 303).
- Page numbers go in upper right-hand corner, flush with right margin. Five spaces to the left of your page number, type your running head (a short version of your title), capitalizing only the first letters. Note that the first page of the main text is numbered either 2 or 3 depending on whether the paper includes an abstract (see pp. 303–10).
- Start a new page for your bibliography, which is titled "References" (centered, one inch from top of page, without underlining, quotation marks, bold face, or all caps). Format each entry according to the instructions on pages 558–68 (see p. 310 for an example; also see p. 570).

◪ CHAPTER SUMMARY

This chapter has shown that research writing is a variation on the thesis-governed writing with which you are already familiar. We have discussed how to focus and refine your research question, suggesting that you remain flexible throughout your research process so that your purpose and thesis can evolve as you discover new information. The chapter has explained purposeful strategies for reading, thinking, and notetaking to help you avoid random inclusion of data and keep all research information focused on your own thesis. The chapter has also discussed methods of summarizing, paraphrasing, and quoting through the effective use of attributive tags, quotation marks, and block indentation. These methods enable you to work research sources smoothly into your own writing, distinguish your ideas from those of your sources, and avoid plagiarism. Finally, the chapter has explained how to use the MLA and the APA systems to cite and document your sources.

Student Example

We conclude with a sample of a successful effort: Mary Turla's research paper on mail-order brides. She uses the MLA system for citing and documenting her sources.

1"

½"

Turla 1

Mary Turla

Professor Nichols

English 125

30 May 1995

Mail-Order Bride Romances: The Need for Regulation

1   On March 2, 1995, an angry and outraged Timothy Blackwell took the law into his own hands. Packing a 9mm Tau-
rus semiautomatic handgun, he walked into a Seattle
courthouse and gunned down his wife, Susanna Remarata
1" Blackwell, a mail-order bride. According to the Seattle 1"
Times, the couple were nearing the end of a year-long annulment case when the murder took place. Timothy wanted
the marriage annulled, claiming that his wife, a native of
the Philippines, had used him to get money and to gain
U.S. citizenship. Susanna, however, filed for divorce, al-
leging physical and emotional abuse. She was also seeking
residency under a battered-wife exception to deportation
law. Seated outside the Seattle courtroom with two supportive friends, Susanna was awaiting the final proceedings in the legal dispute when Timothy shot all three
(Haines and Sevens A1, A8).

2   The Blackwell case highlights the complex issues
surrounding the controversial mail-order bride industry.
Their tragic marriage illustrates the potential frustration and turmoil for both partners in a mail-order
match. They were victims of an industry that exploits

1"

Turla 2

the poverty of third-world women and the romantic fantasies of American men. To build clientele and profits,
the agencies employ marketing techniques that promote
inaccurate and harmful stereotypes of both men and
women, particularly Asian women. Therefore, regulations
and controls must be implemented to control the problems
and abuses that result.

Background: How Mail-Order Bride Agencies Work

   Despite bad press, the mail-order bride business has   3
grown into a thriving multi-million-dollar industry
(Henderson A8). Over a thousand organizations in the
United States, Canada, Western Europe, and Australia
peddle mail-order introductions (Krich 36). Most of the
agencies are "struggling, small-time operations, run out
of a post-office box," some started by couples who had
met through another pen-pal service (Krich 36). However,
there are other agencies that are long-established
and more successful. One of the largest and most successful agencies is California-based Rainbow Ridge
Consultants, owned by Harvard Ph.D. John Broussard and
his wife, Kelly Pomeroy. Begun in 1974, Rainbow Ridge
Consultants publishes three separate bimonthly directories. The catalogs, running up to 48 pages, feature
Philippine "Island Blossoms," Asian women in general,
and random brides-to-be from Peru to Yugoslavia
(Krich 36).

Turla 3

4   Most agencies follow the operating pattern established by Rainbow Ridge Consultants. At the supply end, agencies place ads in local papers to lure women into sending pictures with pertinent biographies and personal information to the mail-order service--usually at no charge (Krich 44). This information is then placed in catalogs with names like "Jewel of the Orient," "Asian Sweethearts," and "East Meets West Club." The agencies then advertise their catalogs to men in magazines such as Psychology Today, Playboy, and Rolling Stone (Mochizuki 1). In 1984 alone about 7,000 Filipino women married Australians, Europeans, and Americans through this system (Agbayani-Siewert and Revilla 158). Despite their claim that the only service their agencies offer is a "pen-pal service," their wide variety of fees and services indicates deliberate efforts to arrange marriages.

How the Agencies Justify Their Services

5   The proliferation of agencies demonstrates what is perhaps the strongest argument for the existence of mail-order bride agencies--that there is at present a strong demand for their services. Villipando cites a 1983 study that surveyed 265 men actively seeking brides from Asia. According to this study, the typical men who use the service were middle aged, had a good income, and were often professionals or managers, but they were burnt out by this society's high-pressure singles' scene

Turla 4

and were in search of a woman who was traditional and family oriented rather than feminist and career oriented (6). As another researcher puts it, men seeking mail-order brides are tired of American women, whom they find "too aggressive, too demanding, and too career-oriented" (Valdez 5).

While the men approach the agencies in search of emotional fulfillment, poverty appears to be the major reason that potential brides enter the market. For many, any option is better than the economic desperation found in much of the third world. For example, although the Philippine government has outlawed agencies from openly advertising catalog services and recruiting women, the practice remains and flourishes (Henderson 48). Poverty and improvement of the bride's and her family's economic status are the main reasons why Filipinas join mail-order clubs (Yuchengco 28). "These women are likely to turn to a correspondence marriage as a way to escape the poverty and lack of economic opportunity in the Philippines" (Agbayani-Siewert and Revilla 158).

Moreover, in some cases the mail-order bride system leads to satisfactory marriages. If a couple views their mail-order marriage as a practical partnership rather than as an "emotional cure-all" (Krich 46), it can sometimes succeed. Filipina Juliet Manalo Boxall is the

6

7

Turla 5

director of the Filipino Friendship Club, the same mail-order service through which she met her English husband, Geoff Boxall. Their marriage has, thus far, lived up to their expectations. Boxall argues for the advantages of a "long-distance romance." (She feels that the use of the terms "mail-order bride" or "mail-order marriage" is a damaging mis-labeling of the service.) She believes that time, distance, and shared values help ensure a couple's compatibility. Because they write and phone for months before they meet, she says, the couple often "knows each other" better than couples whose courtship is "ordinary." She adds that without the constant pressures of sex or "instant gratification" from the ordinary dating scene or services, "a couple can get to know each other without the distractions of sex and how to handle it" (Boxall 27).

Rebuttal: "Fantasy Catalogs," Not a Pen-Pal Service

Although the agencies claim to be just a pen-pal service, the agencies use the catalogs to attract and entice would-be suitors by playing up the advantages of marrying a third-world bride. The language and imagery found in most of the bride catalogs not only demonstrate the white man's fantasy of a submissive and erotic Oriental woman, but it also promotes the image that the women featured are sexual and economic commodities.

"The bride catalogs are frank: virginity, subservience, powerlessness," writes Filipina activist Ninotchka Rosca (48). American Asian Worldwide Service perpetuates the stereotypes when it says in its brochure: "Asian ladies are faithful and devoted to their husbands" (Villipando 13). "Like the Filipina, Malaysian and Indonesian women are raised to respect and defer to the male. [. . .] The young Oriental woman [. . .] derives her basic satisfaction from serving and pleasing her husband," states a Broussard catalog (Villipando 13). Agencies use such marketing techniques because they work. The earlier mentioned 1983 study cited by Villipando showed that 80 percent of the active foreign-bride seekers accept this false image as true (13).

On the other side of the world, the prospective brides initially seem ideally prepared for life in the West, especially if the bride is Filipina. (According to Agbayani-Siewert and Revilla, 75 percent of mail-order brides come from the Philippines.) The Pinay (or Filipina), compared with many of her third-world counterparts, is westernized, educated, and conservative as well as Roman Catholic. Many speak English reasonably well. Some women may also possess the "colonial mentality" so that for them "anything or anyone that comes from the West is good" (Yuchengco 28). They also believe strongly in marriage and family.

Turla 7

10

However, the man expecting a docile "Island Blossom" may be in for quite a surprise if he chooses a Filipina to fulfill his dreams. So warns David Watkins:

> Yet the writer would caution any Australian
> male who is seeking "a meek, obedient slave"
> that he may well be in for a rude awakening
> if he sees a Filipino bride as the answer to
> his dreams. [. . .] [M]any of the girls are
> well educated professionals. [. . .] More
> importantly, every Filipina is used to being
> treated with respect and is very capable
> of making life very uncomfortable for a
> husband who treats her as a (sexy) domestic
> helper. (82)

Based on ancient Malay tradition, Filipino women, compared with Chinese or Japanese women, have historically enjoyed full equality with the Filipino male. Guthrie and Jacobs describe this equality, noting several aspects of the culture that indicate equal status of men and women. In the Philippines, daughters and sons traditionally share equally in inheritance. Within the family, children owe respect and obedience to all family members who are older; age, not gender, is what commands respect in the culture. Guthrie and Jacobs also point to the important position of numerous women in business and government in the Philippines. And even the language

carries a sense of gender equality. In Tagalog, the most
important Filipino language, the words he and she are
both expressed by the one word siya so that, unlike many
languages, Tagalog makes it unlikely for one sex to be
considered superior to the other (Guthrie and Jacobs
42). Stanley Karnow also stresses the powerful position
of women both in the past and present. He states that
the Spanish tried to reduce the status of women who
could do business, get divorced, and sometimes become
village chiefs, but that the image of the Virgin Mary
upheld the force of women though limiting their power
more to the family (41). In addition to having women in
strong economic and political roles, the Philippines
provides similar educational opportunities for males and
females. This egalitarian tradition doesn't create a
spineless, weak wife.

Echoing the words of Watkins, Filipina activist
Ellen Ayaberra argues that mail-order catalogs' misrepresentation of the Filipina may lead not only to
a grossly distorted image of the Filipina, but also
to a disastrous marriage. As she told me in a private
interview:

> The mail-order bride industry should be
> abolished, one reason being that it mis-
> represents Asian women as being stupid and
> dumb. [. . .] The truth is that many Filipinas

11

Turla 9

are hardworking, degree-holding professionals
who want to excel in both the workplace and
the home.

As the warnings above suggest, both the men and women
involved would do well to be critical of advertisements
and catalogs that attempt to reduce the lives and
personalities of real people into two-dimensional
fantasies.

The Dark Side of Mail-Order Romance: The Wife's
Helplessness and the Man's Power

12   Although mail-order agencies claim that they build
lasting friendships, the truth is that they exploit
fantasies. When reality sets in, what happens to the
marriage? Whether the man turns violent, as did Timothy
Blackwell, or simply uses other forms of power, the inherent inequality in the mail-order marriage places the
bride in a vulnerable position. Even before addresses
are exchanged, the men have a significant advantage. In
most cases, only the woman is subjected to a lengthy investigation before she can be featured in a catalog. One
catalog, for example, requires that a woman submit proof
of single status, vital statistics, and other information about her education, career interests, and hobbies
(Yuchengco 25). On the other hand, the interested male
customer is not required to undergo an inquisition. Some
companies even discourage men from "revealing certain

types of information in their letters, including such
negative characteristics as being black or physically
disabled" (Krich 36). Krich concludes, "The inequity of
power is heightened by the inequity of knowledge" (36).

The bride's vulnerability is intensified when she
marries her American husband, moves to the United
States, and assumes immigrant status. Marriage to an
American enables the bride to apply for permanent resident status, commonly known as "the green card," in
three years. Because the husband can deport her, he
holds tremendous power in their relationship. "If becoming an American is their main aim, they are at the complete mercy of their spouse for the three years until
citizenship is granted--and the husband holds the
power to deport her if she doesn't play by his rules"
(Krich 45).

Although it is difficult to document that domestic
violence is a direct result of the mail-order marriage,
victims, social workers, and women's rights' activists
around the world have voiced their outrage, concerns,
and fears. Donna Lewen, an advocate for the Northwest
Immigration Rights Project and the woman who also handled Susanna Blackwell's case, claims that the connection between abuse and the fear of being deported is a
familiar pattern in mail-order marriages. "In every case
I've handled in which the immigrant woman is being

13

14

Turla 11

abused, the threat of deportation is part of the cycle,"
she commented (qtd. in Haines and Sevens A1). Ignorance
of immigration laws, little or no access to resources,
and little or no community support are among the other
forces that keep these immigrant women vulnerable to and
dependent on their husbands. Asian victims of abuse are
also reluctant to seek help because their failed marriage is often a source of shame (Mochizuki 25).

15

It should also be noted that males, as well as
females, suffer from mail-order romance. "Challenged
with evidence of abuse, the mail-order husbands like to
cite rumors they've heard of brides who take their American men for all the money they're worth, then disappear
once they've got their citizenship papers" (Krich 46).
Timothy Blackwell felt justified in his anger at his wife.
He wanted the marriage annulled on the basis that she
had used him only to gain citizenship. During the proceedings, he "complained bitterly throughout his testimony
about the money he had sent to her" (Haines and
Sevens A8).

The Need for Regulation

16

Unfortunately, because there is such a great demand
for mail-order bride services and because some mail-
order marriages are successful, total prohibition of
the mail-order bride industry seems unlikely. However,

Turla 12

governmental regulation may prevent some of the
abuses.

The industry thrives on desperate circumstances and
false expectations. Yet with most agencies unregulated,
the potential for abuse and exploitation is great, so
measures must be taken to protect the interests of the
men and women whose futures are at stake. For example,
agencies should be required to provide education concerning the realistic consequences of pursuing a mail-
order marriage. Brides should be supplied with realistic
explanations of what life is like in America and
understand thoroughly how American immigration and
citizenship laws work. Grooms should have detailed
information about the cultural backgrounds of the women
they see in the catalogs. Brides should be aware of programs and support services available to immigrant wives.
Another safeguard for potential abuse would be to require a background check on the male clients before they
begin to correspond. Furthermore, the agencies should
perform a follow-up service to see how the mail-order
marriages work out. Most important, however, is that
both the men and women are fully aware of the issues
involved. Before correspondence begins, the couples
must be educated enough to have formed realistic
expectations concerning people, cultures, and
relationships.

17

Turla 13

18

 The horrible ending of the Blackwell marriage demonstrates the potentially tragic outcome of mail-order
dating and marriages. Blackwell was a lifelong bachelor
when he met and married Susanna. He was drawn in by the
fantasy of the Asian woman as the ideal mate who would
satisfy his every wish. During the annulment proceedings, he testified, "I had heard so much that these
women were very sincere, very loving, very faithful. And
I always admired Polynesian-type women, with very long,
straight, black hair and very light brown skin" (Haines
and Sevens A8). Both Timothy and Susanna Blackwell
bought into the fantasy portrayed through the catalogs.
For the Blackwells, pain and frustration resulted when
fantasy and reality collided. Their dream world eventually turned into a nightmare.

Turla 14

Works Cited

Agbayani-Siewert, Pauline, and Linda Revilla. "Filipino
Americans." <u>Asian Americans</u>. Ed. Pyong Gap Min.
Thousand Oaks: Sage, 1995. 135-65.

Ayaberra, Ellen. Personal interview. 26 Apr. 1995.

Boxall, Juliet. "The Filipino Friendship Club and the
Courtship of a Filipino Bride" <u>Filipinas</u> Oct. 1992:
27-29.

Guthrie, George M., and Pepita Jimenez Jacobs. <u>Child Rear-
ing and Personality Development in the Philippines</u>.
Philadelphia: Pennsylvania State UP, 1967.

Haines, Thomas W., and Richard Sevens. "Gunman Felt
Duped by Bride from the Start." <u>Seattle Times</u>
4 Mar. 1995: A1+.

Henderson, Diane. "Mail-Order Bride Industry Thrives."
<u>Seattle Times</u> 4 Mar. 1995: A1.

Karnow, Stanley. <u>In Our Image: America's Empire in the
Philippines</u>. New York: Random, 1989.

Krich, John. "The Blooming Business of Imported Love."
<u>Mother Jones</u> Feb.-Mar. 1986: 34-46.

Mochizuki, Ken. "I Think Oriental Women Are Just Great."
<u>International Examiner</u> 7 May 1986: 25.

Rosca, Ninotchka. "Skin Trade Adventures." <u>Special Edition Press</u> Spring 1984: 46-49.

Valdez, Marybeth. "Return to Sender: The Mail-Order
Bride Business in the Philippines." <u>The Philippine
Review</u> May 1995: 5.

Turla 15

Villipando, Venny. "The Business of Selling Mail-Order

Brides." <u>San Diego Asian Journal</u> 1 Feb. 1990: 6-16.

Watkins, David. "Filipino Brides: Slaves or Marriage

Partners?" <u>Australian Journal of Social Issues</u> 17.1

(1982): 73-84.

Yuchengco, Mona Lisa. "The Changing Face of the Filipino

Woman." <u>Filipinas</u> Oct. 1992: 24+.

chapter 23

Electronic Writing and Research

When most people think about writing with a computer, the first thing that comes to mind is a word processor, equipped with a spell checker and a thesaurus. However, today's computer technology offers writing students countless options for exploring ideas, writing collaboratively, and conducting research. Online interest groups exchange information about topics ranging from aliens to zygotes. Writers can create hypertext compositions on the Web and instantaneously distribute them to coauthors around the world. Online archives offer resources from the world's greatest libraries at the touch of a finger. In this chapter we introduce you to some of these new options. Given the rapid pace of technological change, more resources will probably be available by the time you are reading this book, but the information here should serve as a guide to potential uses for these new resources.

OPPORTUNITIES FOR EXPLORING IDEAS WITH OTHERS

Many colleges and universities provide students with some form of access to the global network of computers called the Internet, either in the writing classroom or through a computer center or lab. Some institutions use independent personal computers (PCs), whereas others rely on workstations connected to a central computer. In either case, you need instructions from an experienced user on how to access the Internet from your system.

In this section, we look closely at some of the resources available to you via the Internet and discuss strategies for accessing these resources in ways that will be useful to you as a writer. We focus first on e-mail, Usenet newsgroups, and local and global chat, and then we turn to electronic collaboration possibilities and new forms of writing that use hypermedia, such as the World Wide Web.

E-mail and Listservs

You may already be using electronic mail (e-mail) at school, at work, or at home. E-mail sends messages from one network user to another around the globe in a matter of seconds. Many college instructors use e-mail as a way to enable student-to-student and student-to-instructor contact. For people with access to the Internet, e-mail has largely replaced traditional letters. This medium differs from traditional correspondence in that it is less formal; e-mail correspondents abbreviate more and labor less over grammar and spelling. However, in e-mail as in traditional correspondence, the appropriate level of formality is a function of the rhetorical situation. A quickly written response to a suggested meeting can consist of a simple "yes, OK at 10," whereas a job inquiry should be crafted more carefully.

Some people have likened e-mail to a written phone call. But unlike phone or face-to-face conversations, e-mail conversations can't rely on tone of voice or gesture to convey meaning. To compensate, e-mail users employ "emoticons"—symbols constructed from keyboard characters—to express emotion or sarcasm. Figure 23.1 provides a sampling of these symbols; mentally rotate each symbol a quarter turn to the right to get the picture right side up.

To use e-mail, you need an address and you need to know the addresses of people whom you want to contact. E-mail addresses have three components: the individual account, or mailbox name; the @ sign; and the name of a mail server or domain. The mail server gathers messages sent to a network and then delivers them to individual users. Figure 23.2 shows a sample e-mail address.

You may choose your own account or mailbox name, but you must use the preassigned name for your server. Check with your instructor or computer center about setting up your Internet account and e-mail address.

Once your account is set up, you can send messages to anyone who has an Internet account. Your computation center may offer you a choice of mail-reading programs, which transfer messages back and forth from the campus mail server to your own PC or terminal. Some programs require you to type or enter textual commands to read your mail; others provide a point-and-click interface. To send e-mail, you need to know (a) the command for opening new messages; (b) the

FIGURE 23.1   Sampling of E-mail "Emoticons"

:-)	basic smiley—indicates a joke or playfulness
;-)	winking smiley—indicates irony or sarcasm
:-O	surprised smiley
:-<>	angry smiley
:-(	sad smiley
:-/	smirking smiley
:-[	pouting smiley

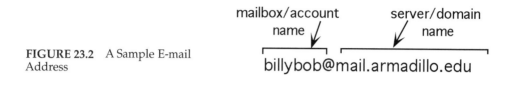

FIGURE 23.2   A Sample E-mail Address

procedures for configuring recipients' addresses in the header of your message; and (c) the "send" command for transferring your messages.

Messages you receive will likely be stored in an in-box. To read e-mail, you open the in-box or mailbox in which it is stored and select the messages you want to read. To respond to a message, you use a "Respond" or "Reply" command. When you choose to "reply" to a message, a new message format is set up for you, usually with the original author's address and the text of the original message quoted in a response window. Most mail-reading programs have online help for these basic commands. After you have mastered the logistics of e-mail, you can incorporate it into your writing process. We describe two means of doing so here, but you may find other possibilities as well.

Exploring Ideas on E-mail

If you're just beginning to explore a topic for a paper or if you're wrestling with a major supporting point, try doing an e-mail freewrite and sending it to one or more friends or classmates. E-mail's spontaneity will encourage them to respond quickly and informally, and you can begin an easygoing exchange that you may choose to sustain until you've finished your essay.

Since most mail programs quote the original message (signified by > on the screen) in a response, your partners can easily comment on thought letters. Here is an example of a freewrite about Internet media and the responses received.

Part of your original message

>From my limited experience online, it seems as if websites are much

>more poorly written than essays. On student websites I see lots of

>typos and poor grammar.

Friend's response

I see your point. One reason that things seem so unpolished on the

Web, however, might be that you are looking at student work that

otherwise might not be placed in the public eye. There are probably

typos and errors on essays, we just don't see them as often.

Another section from your original message

>Also, there are many sites that consist of mostly glitz. It seems as

>if the authors are more concerned with grabbing the reader's eye than

>carefully arguing or explaining anything.

```
Still, I think you may be overlooking the fact that Web pages and
```
Friend's response
```
essays are usually aimed at different audiences. Yes, there are often

flashy elements, but the purpose of the website may be to grab the

reader, so these elements make sense. If you went to a Web essay,

you would probably see more carefully constructed arguments.
```

The original quoted message is indicated by the greater than signs (>) in front of each line. With e-mail, you can write freely in a message and your peers can easily refer to specific points or ideas as they respond.

Listserv Discussions

Another potentially productive way to use e-mail is to join a Listserv interest group. A Listserv compiles any number of e-mail accounts into a mailing list and forwards copies of messages to all people on the list. There are thousands of well-established Listservs about a wide variety of topics. You need to know the address of a list in order to join. Specific information about joining various Listservs and an index of active lists can be found by entering either the Uniform Resource Locator (URL) address "http://tile.net/lists/" or "http://www.liszt.com" once you are on the World Wide Web in a browser.* Once you have subscribed to a Listserv, you receive all messages sent to the list and any message you send to the list address will be forwarded to the other members.

A message sent to a Listserv interest group is sure to find a responsive audience because all members on the list have chosen to take part in an ongoing discussion on the list's specific topic. Often lists archive and periodically post important messages or frequently asked questions (FAQs) for you to study. Most lists are for serious students of the list's topic, so to avoid offending any list members, learn the conventions for posting a message before you jump in.

Although you might find all kinds of interactions on a Listserv, many users expect thoughtful, well-organized statements. If you are posting a message that introduces a new thread of discussion, you should clearly state your position (or question) and summarize those of others. Here is a sample posting to a Listserv on the environment.

```
To: environL@brahms.usdg.org

From: alanw@armadillo.edu (Alan Whigum)

Subject: Acid Rain and Action

I've been doing research on acid rain and am troubled by some of the

things I've found. For instance, I've learned that washing coal gases
```

---

*Each file on the World Wide Web has a unique address, or URL, which allows writers to link to information on the Web and lets users move to specific sites.

```
with limestone before they are released could reduce sulfur emissions.

I know that the government has the power to mandate such devices,

but the real problem seems to be lack of public pressure on the

government. Why don't people push for better legislation to help

end acid rain? I suppose it's an economic issue.
```

In turn, you can expect cogent, thoughtful responses from the list members. Here's a possible reply to the preceding message.

```
To: environL@brahms.usdg.org

From: bboston@armadillo.edu

Subject: Re Acid Rain and Action

I think you are right in pointing out that it is ultimately public

pressure that will need to be applied to reduce acid rain. I've heard

the argument that it is cost that prevents steps from being taken;

people will pay more for goods and services if these measures are

taken, so they resist. However, judging from the people I've talked to

about the subject, I would say that a bigger problem may be knowledge.

Most of them said they would be willing to pay a little bit more for

their electricity if it meant a safer environment. People aren't aware

that action needs to be taken now, because the problem seems remote.
```

When you join a Listserv, you are granted instant access to a discourse community that is committed and knowledgeable about its topic. You can join one of the discussions already taking place on the list or post a request to get information and clarification about your own interests.

Listservs can take your ideas through a productive dialectic process as your message is seconded, refuted, complicated, and reclarified by the various list members. They also afford valuable opportunities to practice your summarizing skills as you respond to messages or provide additional information in a second posting. For example, suppose you take issue with a long message that placed the blame for youth violence on the music industry. Rather than reproducing that entire message, you might provide a brief summary of the main points. The summary would not only give the readers enough background information to appreciate fully your response, it would also help you determine the main points of the original message and pinpoint the issues on which you disagree.

Usenet Newsgroups

Among the most useful sections of the Internet for writers are the bulletin-board-like forums of Usenet newsgroups. Newsgroups are electronic forums that allow you to post or respond to messages about virtually any topic imaginable. Newsgroups can be powerful tools for exploring problems and considering alternative viewpoints. The news server at your school determines the organization and number of groups available to you. Some schools carry groups that provide articles from professional news services, such as AP, Reuters, and UPI. Others provide topic-centered discussion groups. Your campus system may also offer class newsgroups for exchanging messages and drafts with others at your school.

The majority of newsgroups are used by members of the larger Internet community. Although some groups are devoted to subjects that don't lend themselves directly to the work you are probably undertaking in the composition class, many are frequented by regulars who are professionals in their fields or individuals deeply interested in the topic of the newsgroup. One key to successfully interacting on newsgroups, then, is finding a group that is appropriate to your work. Most of the newsreading programs that are built into Web browsers have a search function that can help you select appropriate groups. Another strategy is to spend some time searching through the archives of newsgroup postings at the DejaNews site (http://www.dejanews.com). Using keywords, you can comb through postings either to tap into preexisting conversations or to pinpoint newsgroups that seem to take up the issues that you are interested in.

Once you find an appropriate group, you will need to work through the logistics of accessing the newsgroup, reading messages and, perhaps, posting messages of your own. Check with your instructor or computer center to find out how to access and interact with the groups available to you.

Although you may be tempted to begin participating in a group immediately, you should familiarize yourself with some of the style conventions and the audience for that particular newsgroup before jumping in. Take time to read and listen in (lurk) to the group's postings. Debate on Usenet can become fairly heated, and a message that ignores previous postings can elicit angry responses ("flames"). In addition, a message that doesn't consider the newsgroup's audience or its favored style will likely be challenged. For example, if you want to post something in the "alt.fan.rush-limbaugh" group, you should be cautious about composing a message that openly contradicts Rush Limbaugh's brand of politics. If you send a message to the newsgroup "soc.history," you might be able to tread less carefully—this list is more politically diverse—however, members of this group might take offense if asked an obvious factual question.

Regardless of their makeup, most groups resent being asked questions that have already been answered. Some groups provide an archive of frequently asked questions (FAQs). If your interest is in something practical that is likely to be covered in the FAQ files, refer to them before posting a query. You should use the expertise of the group to find information that you might not be able to uncover otherwise.

When you are ready to post a message, use of some of the strategies outlined for composing a message to a Listserv: try to summarize and synthesize your own position as well as those of others; highlight what you see as the most problematic or murky aspects of the topic. Carefully constructed messages are more likely to receive useful responses.

When you do receive feedback, evaluate it with special care. The unfiltered nature of all Internet media makes critical reading an essential skill. Because anyone with an Internet connection can take part in a discussion or post a message or article, you need to evaluate this information differently than you would articles from national newsmagazines, which are professionally written, edited for clarity, and checked for accuracy.

Although most postings are thoughtful, you will also find carelessly written messages that misconstrue an argument, personal rants that offer few, if any, stated reasons for their claims, and propaganda and offensive speech of many kinds in certain newsgroups. It is your responsibility, and unique opportunity, to read newsgroup messages critically, looking for their various biases and making decisions about their relative authority.

Of course, printed sources are marked by their own biases. Deadlines and space constraints may limit the depth and accuracy of printed coverage, and first-hand insights may be screened by authors and editors. If you were studying attitudes toward the Middle East peace process, a newsgroup exchange between a conservative Jew in Israel and a Palestinian student in the United States might provide better insight than a news article for your work. As you read through newsgroup messages, take time to evaluate the users' personal investments in the issue. Compare their comments to those in traditional sources, check for accuracy, and look for differing perspectives. Work these perspectives into your own thinking and writing about the topic. Treat information and points of view gathered from the Internet as primary rather than as secondary material; many of the people who contribute such material care passionately about an issue. It is up to you to place this material in context and edit it for your own audience.

Real-Time Discussion or Chat

Real-time discussions, or "chat," are synchronous exchanges that take place on a network—meaning that messages are transferred instantly back and forth among members taking part in the discussion. We focus on real-time interactions that take place on the Internet, but you can apply many of the strategies outlined here to local chat programs in your writing class. One of the most popular forms of real-time interaction takes place in the various channels of Internet Relay Chat (IRC). Additionally, many course websites now incorporate a chat function. As with newsgroup and Listserv communications, in chat you compose messages on your own computer and send them through the chat program to other users on the network. Since the specifics for connecting and issuing the various commands vary, you will need to check with your instructor or an experienced user for information about using chat resources at your school.

Like other Internet forums, chat groups are organized around common interests; but real-time sessions are more spontaneous and informal than is communication through newsgroups or Listservs, because they consist of exchanges from people who are logged on at the same time. In these conversations, typographical and spelling errors are mostly overlooked, and abbreviations are an acceptable part of real-time style. The pace can be extremely fast, so users generally focus on getting their thoughts out rather than on producing highly polished messages.

Chat sessions and many other real-time exchanges also allow users to act as characters and to include scripted actions in the conversations. Imagine three users discussing flag burning.

```
William: I'm studying the constitutionality of flag-burning amendments.

Does anybody have any opinions?


Pat Buchanan: I think that if you are an American, you should respect

the country enough not to deface her symbols.


*Thomas Jefferson takes out a match and sets fire to the corner of

an old thirteen star flag. It's probably more important to respect

the underlying principles of our country than its symbols.
```

The asterisk denotes that the user Thomas Jefferson has issued an "Action" or "Emote" command. By putting his name at the beginning of the message, other users see whatever follows as an action performed by that character. Users can construct a third-person narrative by mixing speech with the actions of their characters. You may use this feature in role-playing exercises or to explore some open-ended thinking about your topic.

Often, when you join a chat session, you will be asked to choose a nickname. As you ponder your choice, think about some of the issues of persona that we discussed in Chapter 4. How do you want others to perceive you? How will your persona affect what you write? As you work in these sessions, you will refine your ability to weave various personae into your writing.

Perhaps even more than newsgroup or Listserv discussions, chat sessions tend to heat up easily. Many real-time forums on the Internet allow users to take on pseudonyms, and some people use the opportunity to become irresponsible in what they say and write.

Real-time interactions give rise to several ethical issues. In these uncensored forums, you will at times encounter discussions and materials that aren't appropriate for your assignments and classwork. You may be challenged to assess your own feelings about censorship, pornography, hate speech, and free speech. And you will need to consider the impact of your persona and words on others as you take on a character or act out an idea.

Perhaps the most useful function of chat sessions is that they promote brain-storming and freewriting. When you are writing in a real-time environment, treat the activity as an exploratory one. Expect the message that you send to be challenged, seconded, or modified by the other writers in the session. Keep an open mind about the various messages that fly back and forth and be sure to respond to points that you find particularly useful or problematic. If you are interacting with classmates, you will be talking to people you know, so the conversation will be more predictable. When it's over, you might ask your instructor for a transcript of a chat session; reading it later will help solidify the free thinking that goes into a real-time discussion.

▨ OPPORTUNITIES FOR COLLABORATIVE DISCUSSION AND WRITING

In many ways, all of the Internet is a medium for collaboration. Whether you use e-mail, postings to a newsgroup, or online chat, working with the Internet involves interaction with others. There are some specific approaches to using forums such as e-mail and chat for productive collaborative work; and there are other electronic forums specially designed for collaborative efforts.

E-mail and Newsgroups

If you are undertaking a group project, you can use e-mail to facilitate discussion. You should familiarize yourself with the "nickname" function of your mail reader. After converting members' e-mail addresses into nicknames, you can send messages directly to the nickname without having to write out the entire address. E-mail is also an excellent vehicle for conducting peer reviews. Not only can reviewers easily react to a paragraph or essay, but they can also work at their convenience and take as much time as they need to write their response. If a piece is long or contains special formatting, you will probably want to send it as an attached file that will be downloaded along with your message. Check the documentation for your mail program or see your instructor or computer center if you need help with nicknames and attachments.

It can be difficult to comment on a draft sent via e-mail. Some people insert comments in parentheses or use boldface or capital letters within the text of an assignment. But sentence-level changes are generally difficult to note. E-mail draft exchanges are probably more beneficial in the development stage than in the final stages of polishing a paper. You can focus on larger issues of organization, style, readability, and coherence by writing a paragraph or two at the end of the draft.

Newsgroups provide an excellent space for posting drafts, collaborating, and sharing classwork. You may also be able to share work with other classes through a designated newsgroup. If you are working with other classes on a newsgroup, you might be tempted to respond mostly to members of your own class, but you'll get more out of the experience if you treat the members of the other courses as equal partners. There is value for writers in communicating with people who don't share all their assumptions, values, and language. In this regard, international newsgroups can be especially worthwhile. But you should take care not to flood your international partners with your assignments. Instead, perhaps working in smaller groups, brainstorm about an interpretation or stance on an issue and share your thoughts with your foreign partners.

Web Message Forums

Many classes now use websites to help students join discussion forums where they can exchange messages with one another. One of the biggest benefits of Web message forums is their ease of use. By simply entering an Internet address in a Web browser or following a link from the class website, you can quickly and easily begin participating in a Web-based conversation. More important than learning the logistics of interacting in Web forums, then, is developing skills at conversing with classmates in productive ways.

Web message forums are like newsgroups and e-mail in that messages are exchanged asynchronously rather than in real time. Participants can take as much time as they need to read and respond to the postings of others. Unlike an essay, however, message forums are usually devoted to exploring different facets of an issue or topic in a conversational way. For instance, an instructor or student might pose a question to the class in the form of an initial message. Other participants will then respond to the original posting and to each other, developing a discussion *thread* in the process (see Figure 23.3).

FIGURE 23.3   A Thread of Discussion in a Web Message Forum

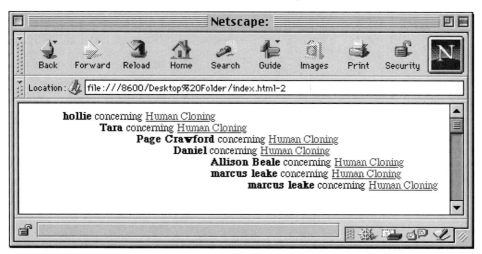

Figure 23.3 shows a series of messages that have been posted by students debating the ethics of human cloning. Figure 23.4 shows two of those messages, the initial message posted by Holly Woods and a subsequent message posted by Marcus Leake. Woods begins the conversation by arguing that cloning is "unacceptable," noting that scientists might use cloning to create a master race of humans. Leake points out that even in the light of that possibility, we should consider the role of the environment in human development. As you participate in these conversations, you may find that the debates range back and forth, with some partic-

FIGURE 23.4   Two Messages from a Web Forum Discussion Thread

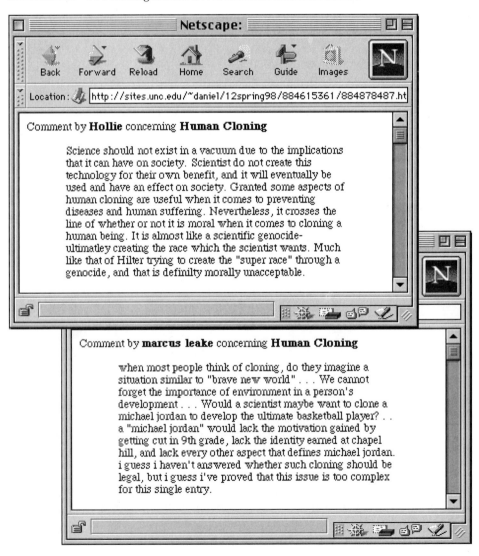

ipants agreeing with one another, others disagreeing entirely, and still others offering perspectives in the middle.

As you interact in these forums, keep in mind that often your goal will be to expose the different facets of a topic. If a message seems plausible initially, interrogate it with an eye toward counterarguments. Survey the range of responses in a discussion thread to get a sense of the viewpoints toward the subject. Consider opposing perspectives as you craft your own messages and be prepared to see some healthy debate. Note how the participants in the cloning conversation are careful to focus on the issues involved rather than personalizing the debate and attacking one another.

Your instructor will most likely outline expectations for your interactions within the Web message forums. You may need to post a minimum number of messages each week, or be asked to moderate the class conversations. You may also be required to use Web forums or similar tools for turning in assignments or reviewing the work of your peers. Some instructors may ask you to use Web forums for your smaller group work. As you participate in these various activities using Web tools, focus on the goals that your instructor has in mind. Be sure to return to the resources that you have created while interacting as you work through your more formal assignments at a later time.

Writing for the Web

In the early years of the World Wide Web, composing websites required writers to learn the intricacies of the *markup* language that controls the appearance and functionality of pages on the Web.* Recently, however, editing programs have greatly simplified the process of creating Web pages and the Web has become a central resource for communication. Consequently, more instructors are asking their students to compose Web-based projects in their writing courses.

The tools for creating Web pages will differ depending on your school, but a few essential concepts will help you understand the process. Suppose that student writer Sheridan Botts wished to create a website based on her investigation of hospice care (see her exploratory paper, pp. 174–77, and her proposal argument, pp. 401–3). Figure 23.5 shows how one might go about composing the opening page of the hospice project. In the figure, Netscape's Composer Web editing program is shown in the lower screen, while the website itself is shown on the upper screen.

Whatever Web editing program you use, you will find that the process of creating and formatting elements on the page is surprisingly easy, much like composing in a word processor. You should understand, however, the relationship between a Web document that you compose and the displaying of that document

---

*Some instructors will ask their students to learn the codes that comprise hypertext markup language (HTML). HTML tags tell Web browsers how to display and link to information on the Web. An HTML editor takes on the task of inserting these tags into the Web document that you compose. For more information about HTML tags, see http://www.abacon.com/connections/resources/webauthoring.html.

FIGURE 23.5 Composing with a Web Editing Program

in the Web browser. You will compose and save files using the Web editor. These files will then be displayed by the Web browser. There are more complexities that you will need to work through using the resources and information at your school, but the most important skill is learning to compose and save Web pages using your editing application and viewing those pages with a Web browser.

Chances are that with a little guidance and some hands-on time, you will find yourself becoming adept at Web composing in no time. There are still, however, a number of rhetorical issues related to writing for the Web that you will want to consider. For instance, whereas traditional essays are linear (a reader starts at the beginning and reads through a document to the end), a Web composition can be seen as a network of different paths that lead a reader through a landscape of information.

To illustrate, consider the more developed version of Botts's hypothetical Web project shown in Figure 23.6. Contrast the opening screen of the Web project with Sheridan Botts's proposal argument on pages 401–3. Whereas Botts's paper takes the reader linearly through the introduction, the problem, the solution, and the justification, the Web project offers several potential entries into the information space in the form of the menu of links on the initial page. A Web reader who is already familiar with the financial issues related to hospice care may elect to begin the project with information about the human impacts of various kinds of hospice care. Another reader might begin by looking for information in the Cost Issues section, and still another reader might begin by combing through the collection of resources.

FIGURE 23.6 Initial Page of a Web Project

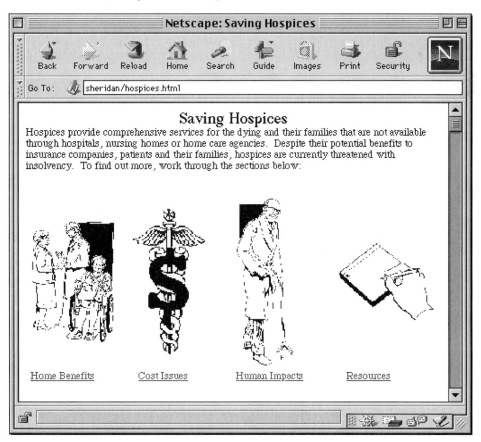

Also, notice the limited amount of introductory text in the Web project and the use of graphics. While the conventions of print lend themselves to extended development of topics and ideas using long blocks of text, the audience expectations for Web pages are slightly different. Note how the Web page takes Botts's introduction, distills it into an introductory hook, and then incorporates images (gathered from public domain clip art sites) to represent the subsequent sections of the project.

Obviously the fluid nature of Web reading and the emerging conventions of the Web raise some concerns for writers. Imagine how difficult composing a print essay would be if you knew that your audience might begin reading on any page. Imagine using a graphic to refute the argument that paying hospices on a per diem basis would cost insurance companies money. At some point, you will need to balance the conventions of the Web with your own goals as a writer as you make decisions about your compositions. For instance, you might forego covering every aspect of hospice cost issues on the opening page of the project but decide to include all of the arguments and evidence on a subsequent page. This way, Web readers can quickly navigate through your introductory screens, but those who are concerned about financial matters can choose to spend time working through the more detailed information.

You and your instructor will no doubt grapple with many other considerations as you work together to create Web compositions. Keep in mind that the best strategies will involve the concepts that we have been discussing throughout this book. Envision Web writing as a decision-making process; as you build your pages, assess the needs of your readers and your goals as a writer. Also, think of Web writing as a problem-solving activity. Determine how your understanding of an issue or topic might be represented in print or on the Web, and then make choices accordingly. For more information about composing for the Web, see Allyn & Bacon's CompSite (http://www.abacon.com/compsite).

OPPORTUNITIES FOR CONDUCTING RESEARCH

We've been talking so far about ways in which networked computers can change how you interact and write. Next we discuss how computers can alter your approach to research. You have instant access to a vast array of information through electronic catalogs, archives, and Internet resources. We provide here an introduction to electronic research capabilities, although many more resources will undoubtedly be available by the time this book is in your hands. (For information on citing sources described here, see Chapter 22, pp. 565–68.)

Online Catalogs and Electronic Databases

Most libraries today offer online catalogs. In years past, researchers had to flip through rows and rows of card-catalog drawers to find a source; today you can type in a few words on a computer keyboard and produce a comprehensive listing of the library's resources on your topic. Most online catalogs will tell you which items are available and where they can be found.

To use an online catalog—or most other electronic research technology—effectively, you need to be adept at keyword searching. As we suggested in Chapter 21, you may want to begin by checking the *Library of Congress Subject Headings* for your initial keyword entry. You will need to be persistent and flexible. For example, if you are trying to find information on the economic influence of the timber industry in South America, you might enter the keywords "timber and economics." If these keywords produce numerous entries on the spotted owl controversy in the Pacific Northwest, you might alter your keywords to "timber and economics not owl" and free your screen of owl references. Most online catalogs allow you to refine keyword searches in a similar way, but you should check the options available before you begin working with an unfamiliar system.

Many libraries also provide computerized indexes that tap into international databases of articles and information or that are built around specific subject areas, and most of these indexes offer the option of keyword searching. The Lexis Nexis catalog, which provides information about, and access to, news and legal publications, is particularly useful for writers. Many schools charge a fee to use these resources, but the breadth of information they offer makes the fee worthwhile. Other subject-area indexes useful to writers include the Modern Language Association's bibliographic listings (see Chapter 21 for a brief description), the ERIC abstracts of articles on education, the General Science Index (see Chapter 21), and the Academic Periodical index. Check with the reference desk in your library to learn how to make the best use of the indexes available. Many of these indexes are moving to the Internet via the World Wide Web.

Listservs, Newsgroups, and Chat as Resources

One of the most important steps in the research process is to convert your topic into a workable research question. Internet forums offer an opportunity for you to place your question before an interested and knowledgeable audience and to receive feedback. By posting your question to a newsgroup, for example, you can test your thinking about the issue through dialogue and also get suggestions for resources from subject-area experts in the group.

Interactions on the Internet can provide valuable source material, and you should use the same sort of care you use with traditional sources when you incorporate these into your projects. Treat conversational resources as interviews. If you are involved in a chat session, let the participants know what you are working on and request their permission if you think you might cite any of the discussion. For material from a Listserv or newsgroup, try to contact personally (via e-mail) any individuals whose comments or postings you might later incorporate into your work. In general, items posted to the Internet are considered in the public domain and available for your use, but as a responsible writer you should make every effort to obtain permission before using online materials. (See the discussion of intellectual property and copyright later in this chapter.)

If you are using an Internet forum for research, it is crucial for you to save and document any items you might use because information comes and goes on the Internet. When you save material on a diskette or drive, jot down or append information about when and where you found it so that you can document the item properly later on; note the name of the chat session, Listserv, or newsgroup, the identity of the poster, and the date.

The World Wide Web

In addition to the many conversational resources that we've mentioned, the Internet offers an unsurpassed collection of government documents, online articles, and other useful files. In the past, researchers had to use several different programs to find these files and to wade through the information; today, technologies such as the World Wide Web offer far more efficient options for searching the Internet.

Some institutions still have limited access to the Internet. You may have to confine your searching to technologies like Gopher. If so, see your instructor or computer center for more information.

If you have access to the World Wide Web, we recommend that you do most of your searching there. The Web has powerful search engines that have collected and categorized a large number of Internet files and will perform keyword searches. Most of these search engines will find not only text files but also graphical, audio, and video files. Some look through the titles of files, whereas others scan the entire text of documents. Different search engines can scan different resources, so it is important that you try a variety of searches when you look for information. Although the web is evolving rapidly, some of the best search engines are fairly stable. For starters, you might try the following:

Yahoo (http://www.yahoo.com)

Lycos (http://www.lycos.com)

Webcrawler (http://www.webcrawler.com)

AltaVista (http://www.alta-vista.net)

HotBot (http://www.hotbot.com)

These search engines will also let you browse through large subject categories, or trees. The most important thing to keep in mind as you move through these trees (or do any browsing on the web) is that it is easy to lose track of where various resources are located. Most Internet software allows you to compile lists of locations that you've visited. These lists—usually referred to as *Bookmarks* or *Favorites*—allow you to return quickly to previously visited sites. We recommend that you save on a diskette or drive any items that you think are particularly valuable. Websites can disappear over time; the only way to ensure that an item will be available for you to use later is to save a copy.

Browsing the Web is an excellent way to help focus your thinking about an issue or topic. For example, suppose that you were searching for information about mining and its impact on Third World countries. As you browsed through some subject trees related to the environment, you might discover an item listing a protest over human rights abuses at Third World mining sites. If you followed the thread of information in the protest listing, you might find out that American students were upset because they felt that an international mining corporation was using their university as part of a public relations effort. This information might prompt you to reconsider your topic; you might decide to broaden your focus to include ways in which mining firms try to shape perceptions at home of their activities abroad.

As you search the Internet for resources, you will be exposed to new information and perspectives. You will want to remain flexible in the early stages of your research effort so that you can reap the benefits of the wealth of information available online. You will also want to play both the explorer and the investigator as you move through the research process. Your initial searches on the Web can help you scout for resources. Some of the links that you follow will be dead ends; others will lead to new discoveries and useful collections of subject-related resources.

Once you've arrived at a topic and gathered some resources, you'll need to investigate them with care. Just as anyone with a connection can post thoughts to a newsgroup or chat forum, anyone can put up a Web page that furthers his or her own agenda. Flashy graphics and other design elements on Web pages can sometimes overwhelm the information that is being presented or lend an air of authority to an otherwise suspect argument or position. Judge these sites critically, with an eye on both the presentation and the reliability of the information. (For further discussion of how to evaluate websites, see Chapter 15, pp. 370–77.)

Sample Research Session

The best way to get a feel for how to use the Internet for research is to try a search yourself. To get you started, we describe what we found when we experimented with the international mining operations topic. Let's review your hypothetical interest in international mining and its impact on the Third World. After a brief search on the Web, you broadened your focus to include how public perception of mining operations is shaped in the United States. Then you decided to work on a specific controversy involving a protest at a U.S. university. The protest was staged by students at the University of Texas at Austin against Freeport McMoRan, Incorporated. With your focus in mind, we began a search of the net.

Using a combination of search engines on the World Wide Web and the keywords "Freeport and protest," "mining and protest," and "McMoRan," we were able to locate hundreds of files with potential information. One search for "McMoRan" alone produced ninety-eight items. By following some of these links we found United Nations documents, company statements, articles by professors at the university, articles from newspapers and magazines, firsthand accounts of the impact of mining on indigenous people, and websites devoted entirely to the controversy.

The large number of items in this search highlights a potential problem for researchers working on the Internet—too much information. You would need to narrow this search to make the resources more manageable. Using the refined keywords "McMoRan and UT," we found only two items, both related directly to the controversy. Since two files aren't likely to provide enough information to fully understand a topic, you would probably want to wade through some of the longer lists of results to get a wider angle on the controversy and to read critically the most likely sources. You would look for biases in the files distributed by Freeport McMoRan, Inc. and those written by students and professors. You might compare files originating in the mainstream press with firsthand items found on the net. Critically reading through the resources would sharpen your thinking and help you determine what items to use in your research project.

■ INTELLECTUAL PROPERTY AND COPYRIGHT

If you've spent even a small amount of time on the Net, you've probably come across sites where articles, papers even images from popular movies and TV shows are freely shared. It is easy to get the impression that all of the information that you find online is available for you to use in any way you choose. Nothing could be further from the truth. As you work with items that have been posted on the Internet, you will need to pay special attention to issues of ownership and copyright.

Some items (an online article, for example) can be treated much as you would a resource found in the library. You would cite the article anytime you used it to collect significant evidence, paraphrased it, or quoted from it. Other kinds of online information, however, are more problematic. For instance, imagine that you discovered an image of your favorite cartoon character on someone's website. You could easily download it and insert it into a paper or website, but you would most likely be in violation of copyright law. Just because someone else initially overlooked the owner's copyright protection for the image by placing it on the Web doesn't mean that you can freely do so.

There are, however, some instances when using online resources is acceptable. Many items on the Net are classified as belonging in the public domain. Resources are said to be in the public domain when their copyright has expired or when creators or owners have relinquished their rights to the items. You are free to use these items for your own purposes. Also, you may find that you have good success in attaining permission to use materials that you find online. Since electronic resources are usually associated with an individual who can be quickly contacted via e-mail, you can send a permission request concerning materials that you wish to use. Sending the request does not, however, mean that you may freely use the materials. You must wait for a response and respect the wishes of the copyright owner.

Finally, you can often use some materials in your work by relying on the Fair Use clause of copyright law. The Fair Use clause stipulates that copyrighted materials may be used for certain purposes, including education. However, Fair Use does not allow you to insert materials into your work in any way you please. In general, you may use only the minimum amount necessary for the purposes of your argument or project. Additionally, the materials must be relevant to your project. For instance, arbitrarily inserting an image of Homer Simpson into your work would not qualify as fair use; however, if you were writing about the representation of middle-aged men in popular culture and you used the image to further your argument, it might.

Obviously, these issues are complex. Many of the standards for using electronic information are still being determined. When you are uncertain about using online materials, check with your instructor. For more information, you can also visit the Stanford University Fair Use site (http://www.fairuse.stanford.edu).

◪ CHAPTER SUMMARY

In this chapter, we discussed uses for networked computers beyond word processing for writers. Computer networks can provide entry into important discourse communities, offering a unique opportunity to examine various rhetorical situations and explore ideas through ongoing electronic conversations. Each of the forums for exploration—e-mail, listservs, newsgroups, and online chat—provides opportunities to hone such rhetorical skills as synthesizing, problem posing, and critical reading. Because each of these forums also has particular conventions and unique memberships, you need to study the rhetorical situation carefully before you join the conversation. We also discussed using the Internet for collaboration. We suggested how you can use e-mail, newsgroups, and collaboration programs to work with your peers. We showed how hypertextual media, such as the World Wide Web, can be used to create writing projects. Finally, we examined the research potential of electronic resources both as repositories for online texts and documents and as rich sources of dialogue. We looked at intellectual property issues and considered how using electronic resources can help to stimulate and refine ideas and also serve as primary sources for a paper.

A Guide to Special Writing Occasions

part FIVE

Essay Examinations
Writing Polished Prose in a Hurry

I'm pretty good at writing term papers, but when I have to write under pressure, I freeze. Last time I took an essay test, I wrote two pages before I realized that I'd left out an important piece of my argument. By the time I had scratched out, made additions, and drawn arrows all over the page, my paper was such a mess that I couldn't decipher it. Needless to say, the instructor couldn't either.

—Student A

For me, the worst thing about exams is trying to figure out what the professor wants. The final in my European literature course was a perfect example: There was only one question. It started with a difficult-to-follow quotation from an author we hadn't studied, which we were supposed to apply to a whole slew of questions about novels we had read during the semester. The question went on for half a page (single spaced!) and had at least five or six subsections. By the time I finished reading it, I didn't have a clue about where to start or how to cover so much ground in a single essay.

—Student B (Anonymous undergraduate students at the University of Oklahoma, paraphrased from responses written when asked to comment on their experiences with essay examinations)

We have focused thus far on writing assignments that you complete outside class over a period of days or weeks. This amount of time allows you to plan, explore, draft, and revise through a process that is something like the following:

- You receive an open-ended assignment well in advance of its due date and mull it over until you find an interesting angle to pursue
- You explore the ongoing arguments about your issue, immersing yourself in reading, research, coffeehouse conversations with your classmates, and exploratory writing—perhaps changing your view along the way
- As the deadline approaches, you revise through several drafts until you arrive at a satisfactory final product

However, much of the writing you do in college doesn't allow for the luxury of extended exploration and revision. According to researcher Mary Meiser, as

611

much as 50 percent of academic writing in college consists of timed essay examinations. For such writing, your composing scenario will probably be something like the following:

- You arrive in a classroom with your brain crammed full with facts, theories, and arguments
- Your instructor asks a narrowly focused question that you've never seen before and may not have much interest in addressing
- Working in a relatively uncomfortable, stressful classroom setting, you have an hour or so to shape your knowledge into a polished single draft that convinces your professor you've mastered the material

The writing you do during this hour may count for as much as half your course grade. No doubt this kind of writing is challenging. It can be rewarding if you have prepared appropriately and have mastered some specific writing skills.

WRITING UNDER PRESSURE

When instructors give essay exams, they want to see how well students can restate, apply, and assess course material. Just as important, they want to see whether students can discuss in their own words what they have studied—whether they can participate in that discipline's discourse community. These twin demands make essay exams doubly challenging. Not only must you master course material, but you must also write about it quickly and confidently. Some students have trouble streamlining their writing process to fit a strict time limit (see the first epigraph for this chapter). Others students have problems understanding complicated essay prompts or shaping their knowledge to fit the assignment (see the second epigraph for this chapter). Still others find it difficult to study effectively, recall information, or organize their essay responses.

Even students who perform adequately on essay tests often dislike them. They see essay exams as rigid exercises that stifle intellectual exploration or as artificial busywork unrelated to the real writing they will do outside school. Although you will rarely take exams once you leave college (unless you plan to attend graduate school—and both the LSAT and the MCAT exams have essay components), writing essay tests can help you develop skills relevant to many real-world situations. In such fields as journalism, advertising, marketing, publishing, engineering, teaching, you will need to compose documents on tight deadlines. In the following excerpt, journalist Linda Ellerbee describes her audition for a job as anchor of the NBC weekend news. She was required to write a feature story under pressure.

> I spent hours . . . running the film back and forth, stopping and starting, trying to figure out what to say in this 15.5-second gap, that 6-second pause, how to arrange the information I had so that it wove smoothly in and out of interviews, music, and background noise. . . . The whole time, I felt like a cowboy heading for the shootout at high noon.

Ellerbee argues that her college training in English helped her handle the stress; she ultimately won the job.

Although you probably accept that it's important to learn how to write essay exams, you may still ask, "Aren't some people simply bad test takers?" or "Professors and courses are so diverse—can any approach work for all of them?" No single method can guarantee a high grade in every subject. You will always have to adapt your exam response to the course, the instructor, and the test question. But this chapter shows you how to plan and draft an exam essay and how to adapt to the unique requirements of in-class essay writing. Practice exercises will also help you identify features of successful essay responses and let you try your hand at writing under pressure.

First, though, take a few minutes to think about your past experiences with writing under pressure.

FOR WRITING AND DISCUSSION

Freewrite for five or ten minutes in response to the following questions, then share your responses with classmates.

1. Think of a timed writing assignment that you wrote particularly well or one that ended in disaster. What happened? Which parts of the task caused you particular trouble, and which seemed easy? How might you approach future assignments differently?
2. Which do you think is more difficult, writing an essay exam or writing a research paper? Explain why, focusing on the different thinking, writing, and revision skills each requires.

HOW ARE EXAMS DIFFERENT FROM OTHER ESSAYS?

Essay exams do share similarities to other assignments. Most of the instruction in this book applies to exam writing. For instance, you already know how to respond to rhetorical context—audience, purpose, genre, and style—as you write a paper. You can transfer this ability to a test situation by analyzing your instructor's expectations. Does your instructor stress analysis of material or application of roles? Does your instructor encourage individual interpretations and opinions? In the movie *Dead Poets Society*, Robin Williams plays an English literature teacher who, in the very first class, tells students to tear out and destroy the introductory section of their poetry textbooks. His students learn quickly that they need to develop independent insights about the material in order to pass the course. Although most professors don't communicate their preferences so dramatically, knowing what your professor expects can help you focus exam responses much as analyzing an audience can help you focus an out-of-class paper.

You also know the importance of knowing what you're talking about. Even the most brilliant writers will stumble on a test if they haven't bothered to attend class regularly, take notes, participate in class discussions, and keep up with the reading. Familiarity with the material lays the groundwork for a successful exam performance, just as thorough research and exploratory writing grounds a good paper.

However, not all the writing strategies you use for papers will serve you well in a test situation. Writing researcher Randall Popken, after reviewing more than two hundred sample exams in various disciplines, identified three skills unique to essay exam writing.

1. The ability to store, access, and translate appropriate knowledge into an organized essay
2. The ability to analyze quickly the specific requirements of an exam question and formulate a response to fit them
3. The ability to deal with time pressure, test anxiety, and other logistical constraints of the exam situation

We examine each of these skills in the next section.

▨ PREPARING FOR AN EXAM: LEARNING AND REMEMBERING SUBJECT MATTER

One of the biggest differences between writing a paper and writing an exam essay involves how you access subject matter. Think about the last time you wrote a paper outside class. You may have used your memory to search for ideas or to explore personal knowledge about the topic, but you also had access to other sources—the library, course readings, your classmates' and instructor's input. In an exam, you're on your own. You won't know beforehand which of the many pages of material you'll be asked to synthesize and comment on. Although you may have studied hard and learned a great deal, you may not know how to display your knowledge in writing. Many inexperienced undergraduates fail exams either because they scribble down everything they can remember, however remotely related to the topic, or because they agonize so much over what to include that they write very little. Preparing for an exam involves finding efficient ways to organize and recall your knowledge so that you can easily construct an intelligent argument on paper.

Identifying and Learning Main Ideas

No instructor will expect you to remember every single piece of information covered in class. Most instructors are happy if you can remember main ideas and theories, key terminology, and a few supporting examples. The best strategy when you study for an essay exam is to figure out what is most important and learn it first.

How do you determine the main ideas and key concepts? Sometimes they're obvious. Many professors outline their lectures on the board or distribute review sheets before each exam. If your professor does not provide explicit instructions, listen for a thesis statement, main points, and transitions in each lecture to determine the key ideas and relationships among them. For example,

> The *most important critics* of the welfare state are . . .
>
> *Four developments* contributed to the re-emergence of the English after the Norman invasion . . .
>
> Hegel's dialectic was *most influenced by* Kant . . .
>
> *Three major interpretations* of Grant Wood's *American Gothic* are . . .

Look for similar signals in your textbook and pay special attention to chapter summaries, subheadings, and highlighted terms. If the course involves a lot of discussion or if your professor prefers informal remarks to highly structured lectures, you may have to work harder to identify major points. But streamlining and organizing your knowledge in this way will keep you from feeling overwhelmed when you sit down to study.

Most instructors expect you to master more than the information they cover in class. Essay exams in humanities, social science, and fine arts courses often ask for an individual interpretation, argument, or critique. To prepare for such questions, practice talking back to course readings by developing your own positions on the viewpoints they express. If the professor has lectured on factors involved in mainstreaming schoolchildren with physical disabilities, look at your notes and try to define your own position on mainstreaming. If the textbook identifies salient features of Caravaggio's art, decide how you think his paintings compare to and differ from his contemporaries' work. Questioning texts and lectures in this way will help personalize the material and expand your understanding. In feminist scholar Adrienne Rich's words, it will allow you to "claim your education" rather than to passively accept what's taught. Remember, though, that professors won't be impressed by purely subjective opinions; as you explore your views, search for evidence and arguments, not just from your own experience, but from the course as well, that you can use to support your ideas in the exam. For specific strategies to help you understand and respond to reading material, review Chapter 6.

Applying Your Knowledge

In business, science, social science, and education courses, professors may ask you to apply a theory or method to a new situation; for example, they might ask you to show how first in, last out accounting might work in bookkeeping for a washing machine factory or how you might use Freudian concepts to analyze a hypothetical psychiatric case. If you suspect that such a question might appear, use some study time to practice this kind of thinking. Brainstorm two or three current situations to which you could apply the theories or concepts you've been learning. Check local newspapers or browse the World Wide Web for ideas. Then freewrite for a few minutes on how you might organize an essay that puts the theory to work. For instance, if you've studied federal affirmative action law in a public administration course you might ask the following questions: How does the law apply to the recent decision by the California regents to abolish race as a factor in college admissions? How might it apply to a local controversy over hiring female firefighters? You won't be able to predict exactly what will appear on the exam, but you can become skilled at transferring ideas into new settings.

Making a Study Plan

Once you've identified crucial subject matter, you need to develop a study plan. If you're a novice at studying for a major exam, try following some tried-and-true approaches. Review your instructor's previous exams. Don't be afraid to ask your instructor for general guidelines about the type, length, and format of questions he or she normally includes on tests. Then generate your own practice questions and compose responses. If you can, organize group study sessions with two to four classmates. Meet regularly to discuss readings, exchange practice questions, test each other informally, and critique each other's essays.

Avoid study techniques that are almost universally ineffective. Don't waste time trying to reread all the material or memorize passages word for word (unless the exam will require you to produce specific formulas or quotations). Don't set an unreasonable schedule. You can seldom learn the material adequately in one or two nights, and the anxiety produced by cramming can hurt your performance even more. Most important, don't stay up all night studying. Doing so can be worse than not studying at all, since sleep deprivation impairs your ability to recall and process information.

No matter how you decide to study, remember that the point of developing exam-preparation strategies isn't simply to do well on a single test, but to become comfortable with learning difficult, complex material and to acquire a level of intellectual confidence that will help you grow as a writer.

■ ANALYZING EXAM QUESTIONS

Whereas paper assignments typically ask you to address broad problems that can be solved in numerous possible ways, essay exams usually require much more narrowly focused responses. Think about some of your paper assignments. They might have read, "Write a persuasive research paper in which you propose a solution to a current local controversy" or "Write a ten-page essay exploring an ethical issue in the field of vertebrate biology"; they might have called for either closed- or open-form prose; but in virtually all cases you were free to choose from among several possible approaches to your topic. Essay exams, in contrast, feature well-defined problems with a very narrow range of right answers. They require you to recall a particular body of information and present it in a highly specific way. However, what your instructors are asking you to recall and how they want it presented will not always be clear to you. Exam questions often require interpretation.

Although the language of essay exams varies considerably across disciplines, professors typically draw on a set of conventional moves when they write exam prompts. Consider the following question from an undergraduate course in the history of the English language:

> Walt Whitman once wrote that English was not "an abstract construction of dictionary makers" but a language that had "its basis broad and low, close to the ground." Whitman reminds us that English is a richly expressive language because it comes from a variety of cultural sources. One of these is African-American culture. Write an essay discussing the major ways in which African-American culture and dialect have influenced the English language in the United States. Identify and illustrate at least three important influences: What were the historical circumstances? What important events and people were involved? What were the specific linguistic contributions?

This question presents an intimidating array of instructions, but it becomes manageable if you recognize some standard organizational features.

Outside Quotations.   First, like many exam questions, this sample opens with a quotation from an author or work not covered in the course. Many students panic when they encounter such questions. "Whitman?! We didn't even study Whitman. What am I supposed to do now?" Don't worry. The primary function of such quotations is to encapsulate a general issue that the instructor wants you to address in your response. When you encounter an unfamiliar quotation, look carefully at the rest of the question for clues about what role it should play in your essay. The point of the Whitman quotation is restated in the very next sentence—English is shaped by numerous cultural influences—and the function of the quotation is simply to reinforce that point. Because the rest of the question tells you specifically what kinds of cultural influences your response should address (African-American culture, three major linguistic contributions), you don't need to consider this quotation when you write your essay.

Sometimes professors will ask you to take a position on an unfamiliar quotation and support your argument with material covered in the course. Suppose that the question was, What is your position on Whitman's view? Do you believe that English is enriched or corrupted by multicultural influences? In this case the quotation is presented as the basis for a thesis statement, which you would then explain and support. A successful response might begin, "Whitman believes that multicultural influences make our language better, but this view is hopelessly naive for the following reasons. . . ." or "Whitman correctly argues that the contributions of different cultures enrich our language. Take these three examples. . . ."

Organizational Cues.   The question itself can show you the best way to organize your response. Questions tend to begin with general themes, which often suggest a thesis statement. Subsequent divisions tell you how to organize the essay into sections and in what order to introduce supporting points. For example, a successful response that follows the organization of our sample might be arranged as follows:

- A thesis stating that several contributions from African-American language and culture have enriched English
- Three supporting paragraphs, each discussing a different area of influence by
  1. summarizing historical circumstances
  2. noting important people and events
  3. providing one or two examples of linguistic contributions

Key Terms.   As do all exam questions, this one asks you to write about a specific body of information in a specific way. When you encounter a lengthy question such as this, first pick out the *noun phrases* that direct you to specific areas of knowledge: "African-American culture," "major influences on the English language in the United States," "historical circumstances," "important events and people," "linguistic contributions." Pay careful attention to words that modify these noun phrases. Does the question tell you how many influences to discuss? What kinds of examples to cite? Does the instructor include conjunctions, such as *or,* to give you a choice of topics, or does he or she use words such as *and* or *as well as* that require you to address all areas mentioned? Words, such as *who, what, where,* and *why,* also point to particular kinds of information.

After you've determined the specific areas you will need to address, look for *directive verbs* that will tell you what to do: *discuss, identify,* or *illustrate,* for example. These verbs define the horizons of your response: some mandate detailed responses, others don't; some ask for personal insights, others don't; some, such as *list* and *construct,* even suggest the form your answer should take. Table 24.1 defines some key directives that frequently appear in essay exams and provides sample questions for each.* Meanings vary somewhat according to the course, the context of the question, and the professor's expectations, but you'll feel more confident if you have basic working definitions.

In some questions, directives are implied rather than stated directly. If a question asks, "Discuss the effects of Ronald Reagan's tax policies on the U.S. economy during the 1980s," you'll need to summarize what those policies were before you can assess their effects. Before you can take a position on an issue, you have to define what the controversy is about. In general, when you answer any question, you should include sufficient background information about the topic to convince your instructor that you're making an informed argument, whether or not the question specifically asks for background information.

*Our thanks to Michael C. Flanigan, who suggested the format and some of the terms for this table.

TABLE 24.1   Some Common Question Verbs

Analyze—asks you to break an argument, concept, or approach into parts and examine the relations among them; discuss causes and effects; evaluate; or explain your interpretation or judgment. Look carefully at the rest of the question to determine which of these strategies to pursue in your response. Example: *Analyze the various technical, acoustic, and aesthetic factors that might lead a musician to choose analogue over digital recording for a live performance. Be sure to include the strengths and weaknesses of both methods in your discussion.*

Apply—asks you to take a concept, formula, theory, or approach and adapt it to another situation. Example: *Imagine that you've been hired to reengineer the management structure of a major U.S. automaker. How might you apply the principles of Total Quality Management in your recommendations?*

Argue—asks you to take a position for or against an issue and give reasons and evidence to support that position. Example: *Argue whether you believe that cloning should be pursued as a method of human reproduction. Be sure to account for the relationship between cloning and mitosis in your discussion.*

Compare—asks you to note similarities between two (or more) objects or ideas. Example: *Compare the leadership styles of Franklin Delano Roosevelt, John F. Kennedy, and Ronald Reagan, focusing particularly on their uses of popular media and political rhetoric.*

Construct—asks you to assemble a model, diagram, or other organized presentation of your knowledge about a concept. Example: *Construct a model of the writing process that illustrates the major stages writers go through in developing an idea into a finished text.*

Contrast—asks you to point out differences between two or more objects or ideas. Example: *Contrast the use of religious imagery in Edward Taylor's "Upon Wedlock, and Death of Children" and Anne Bradstreet's "Before the Birth of One of Her Children." Then identify and discuss some possible sources of these differences.*

Critique—asks you to analyze and evaluate an argument or idea, pointing out and explaining both strengths and weaknesses. Example: *Dinesh D'Souza's "Illiberal Education" sparked widespread controversy when it was published in 1991. Write an essay critiquing D'Souza's arguments against affirmative action, identifying both the strengths and the weaknesses of his position. Use examples from the text, class discussion, and other class readings to illustrate your points.*

Define—asks you to provide a clear, concise, authoritative meaning for an object or idea. Your response may include describing the object or idea, distinguishing it clearly from similar objects or ideas, and providing one or more supporting examples. Example: *How was "equality" defined by the Supreme Court in* Plessy v. Ferguson *(1896)? How did that definition influence subsequent educational policy in the United States?*

Discuss—asks you to provide a comprehensive presentation and analysis of important concepts, supported by examples or evidence. These questions generally require detailed responses, so be sure to cover several key points or to examine the topic from several perspectives. Refer to the rest of the essay question for more detailed guidelines about what information to include in your response. Example: *Discuss the controversy that surrounded Stanley Milgram's studies of authority and state your own position on the relevance and validity of the experiments.*

Enumerate—asks you to list steps, components, or events pertaining to a larger phenomenon, perhaps briefly explaining and commenting on each item. Example: *A two-year-old child falls from a swing on the playground and lies unconscious. As the head preschool teacher, enumerate the steps you would take from the time of the accident until the ambulance arrives.*

continued

TABLE 24.1   Some Common Question Verbs *continued*

Evaluate—asks you to make a judgment about the worth of an object or idea, examining both strengths and weaknesses. Example: *Evaluate William Whyte's "Street Corner Society" as an ethnographic study. What are its methodological strengths and weaknesses? Do you believe the weaknesses make Whyte's research obsolete?*

Explain—asks you to clarify and state reasons to show how some object or idea relates to a more general topic. Example: *Explain the relationship of centripetal force to mass and velocity and give an example to illustrate this relationship.*

Identify—asks you to describe some object or idea and explain its significance to a larger topic. Example: *Identify the major phonetic characteristics of each of the following language groups of southern Africa, and provide illustrative examples of each: Koisan, Niger-Kordofanian, and Nilo-Saharan.*

Illustrate—asks you to give one or more examples, cases, or other concrete instances to clarify a general concept. Example: *Define monopoly, public utility, and competition, and give specific illustrations of each.*

List—asks you to name a series of related objects or concepts one by one, perhaps briefly explaining each. Example: *List the major sampling designs used in communications research and briefly identify their advantages and disadvantages. Which of these designs would you use to conduct a market test of a new children's television program for Nickelodeon? Why?*

Prove—asks you to produce reasons and evidence to establish that a position is logical, supportable, or factual. Example: *Use your knowledge about the findings of the 1991 National Assessment of Educational Progress to prove either that (1) public schools are doing an adequate job of educating children to become productive U.S. citizens, or (2) public schools are doing an inadequate job of educating children to become productive U.S. citizens.*

Review—asks for a quick survey or summary of something. Example: *Review the major differences between Socrates' conception of ethics and the ethical theories of his contemporaries in the fifth century* B.C.E.

Summarize—asks you to lay out the main points of a theory, argument, or event in a concise and organized manner. Example: *Summarize Mill's definition of justice and explain how it differs from Kant's. Which definition comes closest to your own, and why?*

Trace—asks you to explain chronologically a series of events or the development of an idea. Example: *Write an essay that traces the pathway of a nerve impulse through the nervous system, being sure to explain neuron structure, action potential, and the production and reception of neurotransmitters in your discussion.*

FOR WRITING AND DISCUSSION

Bring in an exam question from another class or choose one of the sample questions from Table 24.1. In collaboration with one or two classmates, analyze the question, then construct a potential thesis and scratch outline for a successful response. Be prepared to share your work with the class.

This next exercise will hone your ability to analyze essay questions. Each of the following student essays received an A as a response to one of the four closely related questions that follow it. Each essay may address issues raised in two or more questions, but each is an A response to only one. Your task is to figure out which question the essay answers best. Although you have not read the specific material on which each essay draws, you should nonetheless be able to match the responses based on the kinds of information included and how the information is used.

Decide on your answer independently, then compare answers in small groups. Try to come to a group consensus, referring to Table 24.1 to help resolve disagreements. As you discuss your responses, note any successful strategies that you may be able to adapt to your own writing.

From a Library Science Course

Bandura's social learning theory breaks from the behaviorist learning theory developed by B. F. Skinner. Behaviorists believe that humans learn only those behaviors which are positively reinforced; behaviors which are not reinforced become "extinct." Bandura, however, argued that some learning happens vicariously, as a child models the behaviors of people around him or her. Such learning does not depend on direct reinforcement, but on observation and imitation. For example, a child from a violent family may behave aggressively toward his or her friends, not because there is a reward for behaving that way, but because he has seen the behavior continually at home.

Many variables affect whether a child will learn from a model, according to Bandura. These include the type of behavior, whether the model is someone the child admired, and whether the behavior is punished or reinforced. For example, if a movie villain slapped a woman, a child might not imitate the behavior, since the model is not someone he or she wants to identify with. But if the hero of the movie did the same thing, especially if the woman responded by passionately kissing him (a reward), the child would be more likely to repeat the behavior.

Bandura's theory has clear implications for library staff in selecting children's books. It is important that children have available a variety of positive role models to identify with and imitate—especially to provide a balance to the violent, sexist role models often presented in television and movies. School-age boys who survive on a TV diet of Arnold Schwarzenegger and Power Rangers need to also read about males who are admirable without being violent. Biographies of men like Abraham Lincoln and Mahatma Gandhi, and novels like *Johnny Tremain* and *Encyclopedia Brown* that show characters who succeed by helping others, give boys some positive behaviors to imitate. Stories about strong, independent girl characters, such as *Caddie Woodlawn* and *The Summer of the Swans,* give young girls whose ideas are shaped by Barbie and *Beverly Hills 90210* more admirable role models.

These are just a few examples. Many books give both boy and girl readers characters to look up to. Bandura's theory shows us just how important that is to children's social learning.

Which question does this response address most successfully?

1. Summarize the learning theories of Skinner and Bandura, and explain how each might inform book selections at a children's library.

2. Review the major components of Bandura's theory of social learning. Then discuss the following: How might these principles apply if you were responsible for selecting children's books for a public library system? What kinds of books might Bandura's theory lead you to choose?

3. Bandura's social learning theory proposes that children learn partly from imitating the behavior of role models. Based on what you know about children's reading preferences, do you believe this is the case? Support your position with examples of particular books, characters, and themes.

4. Compare and contrast Skinner's learning theory, Bandura's theory of social learning, and current theories on children's book selection.

From a British Literature Course

Gulliver's Travels and *Frankenstein* portray characters whose adventures bring them face to face with the innate weaknesses and limitations of humankind. Victor Frankenstein and Lemuel Gulliver find out during their travels that humans are limited in reasoning capacity and easily corruptible, traits that cause even their best intentioned projects to go awry. These characters reflect the critical view that Swift and Shelley take of human nature. Both believe that humans have a "dark side" that leads to disastrous effects.

In *Gulliver's Travels*, Gulliver's sea voyages expose him to the best and worst aspects of human civilization. Through Gulliver's eyes, readers come to share Swift's perception that no matter how good people's original intentions, their innate selfishness corrupts everything they attempt. All the societies Gulliver visits give evidence of this. For example, Lilliput has a system of laws once grounded on justice and morality, but which slowly were perverted by greedy politicians into petty applications. Even the most advanced society, Brobdingnag, has to maintain a militia even though the country is currently peaceful—because they acknowledge that because humans are basically warlike, peace can't last forever. By showing examples of varied cultures with common faults, Swift demonstrates what he believes to be innate human weaknesses. He seems to believe that no matter how much progress we make, human societies will eventually fall back into the same old traps.

Victor Frankenstein also experiences human limitations, this time in his own personality, as he pushes to gain knowledge beyond what any human has ever possessed. When he first begins his experiments to manufacture life in the laboratory, his goals are noble—to expand scientific knowledge and to help people. As he continues, he becomes more concerned with the power that his discovery will bring him. He desires to be a "god to a new race of men." Later, when the creature he creates wreaks havoc, Frankenstein's pride and selfishness keep him from confessing and preventing further deaths. Like the societies Gulliver observed, Frankenstein is a clear example of how human frailties corrupt potentially good projects.

Even though Swift and Shelley wrote during two different historical periods, they share a critical view of human nature. However, several unambiguously good characters in *Frankenstein*—including the old man and his daughter—suggest that Shelley feels more optimism that people are capable of overcoming their weaknesses, while Swift seems adamant that humans will eternally backslide into greed and violence. Basically, however, both works demonstrate vividly to readers the ever present flaws that prevent people and their societies from ever attaining perfection.

Which question does this essay address most successfully?

1. Contrast Swift's and Shelley's views of human nature, illustrating your points with specific examples from *Gulliver's Travels* and *Frankenstein*.
2. Analyze the use Swift and Shelley make of scientific knowledge to show the limits of human progress in *Gulliver's Travels* and *Frankenstein*, citing specific illustrations from each work.
3. Discuss the characters of Lemuel Gulliver in *Gulliver's Travels* and Victor Frankenstein in *Frankenstein:* What purpose does each serve in the text? How does each author use the character to illustrate important traits or concepts?
4. Many of the writers we've studied this semester explored the limitations of human potential in their work. Write an essay showing how any two of the following works deal with this idea: William Blake's *Songs of Innocence and Experience,* Jonathan Swift's *Gulliver's Travels,* Mary Shelley's *Frankenstein,* Percy Shelley's "Prometheus Unbound." Does each writer suggest a pessimistic or optimistic view of human nature? Be sure to support your argument with specific illustrations from each text.

◢ DEALING WITH CONSTRAINTS: TAKING AN ESSAY EXAM

Suppose that you've organized the course material, studied faithfully, analyzed the exam questions, and know generally how you'll respond. You still need one more skill to succeed: the ability to thrive within the limits of a test situation. You will be confined in a classroom with no computer and given an extremely short amount of time in which to write, with little opportunity to correct mistakes or revise. How can you overcome these logistical hurdles?

First, you need to minimize test anxiety. Many students feel anxious if a test question looks unfamiliar or difficult. Others freeze up if they lose their train of thought midway through an essay. Still others panic when time begins to run out. You can't control the level of difficulty of test questions; you will lose your train of thought occasionally; and time will run out. But you don't have to respond by collapsing. You can learn to anticipate potential disasters and brainstorm ways to handle them. If you tend to panic when a test question looks impossible on first reading, make a deal with yourself to close your eyes and count to ten, then read it again and try to screen off the parts that you don't have to consider. If you usually run out of time, set a time limit for writing some practice questions so that you can get used to performing under pressure. Finally, make sure that you're in top form to take the exam: organize your supplies, including extra exam booklets and scratch paper, pens, and any testing aids your instructor allows, the night before; get plenty of sleep; eat breakfast; arrive at class a few minutes early; give yourself a pep talk. These measures will increase your confidence and head off debilitating nerves.

Lack of time when writing an essay exam is perhaps the hardest constraint for most people to deal with. Most writers produce their best work only after writing several drafts. You won't be able to compose a perfectly polished essay in an exam—there simply isn't time—so you will need to streamline your writing process through planning. After you have analyzed the exam question carefully, take a few minutes to jot down a quick outline or a list of key concepts you want to discuss. Exploratory writing techniques, such as tree diagrams and freewriting, can help you generate and arrange ideas. Prewriting gives you a sense of direction and helps you remember where the essay is going as you write.

For example, one undergraduate student jotted down this five-minute scratch outline in response to the following exam question in a Texas government course:

> What are the relative advantages and disadvantages of the district method versus the at-large method in municipal elections? Analyze the strengths and weaknesses of each and then either argue in favor of one method over the other or propose a different plan that avoids the limitations of both.

> *Thesis*
> *District method*
> *Advantages--history of discrimination and underrepresentation of minorities (examples)*
> *   --race consciousness important for overcoming injustice*
> *Disadvantages--encourages racial divisions*
> *   --not necessary because much racism has been overcome; minorities may now be freely elected (ex. Sen. Barrientos, Ann Richards) BUT*
> *At-large*
> *Advantages--all citizens can work together for common good, not just concerned with narrow group interests*
> *Disadvantages--majority rule may ignore important minority needs (ex. East Austin)*
> *THESIS--B/c minorities have been and are still underrepresented in local government, the district method of local elections, while flawed, offers the best chance for these communities' voices to be heard.*

Once you have a plan, you need to determine how much time to give to each answer. Many students' grades suffer because they blow all their time on the first question and then race through the rest of the exam. To determine how much time to allot each response, you need to solve a quick ratio problem. Divide the points assigned to a given question by the points for the whole exam; the result equals the percentage of time you should spend on that question. When you write your answer, follow the example of journalists and load critical information in your lead. Write a first paragraph that nutshells your whole answer (the second student response in the For Writing and Discussion exercise on pages 620–23 does this beautifully). Add examples and details to the extent that you have time, moving from more important to less important. If you can't finish a response in time, stop, but don't panic. You may have time to return to it later. If not, write a brief note directing the professor to your original notes or outline; let your professor know that you intended to write more but ran out of time. Many instructors will award partial credit for outlined responses.

You can save time by focusing only on elements important to your grade. Instructors don't expect dramatic, polished introductions and conclusions or artistically constructed sentences in an exam. They would rather you provide a clear thesis statement and explain your main points fully. Most instructors also value organization, although some grade almost entirely on content.

Instructors differ in how they treat errors in grammar, spelling, and punctuation. Some believe it's unfair to expect students to edit their work thoroughly in a short time and don't penalize such errors unless they interfere with the argument (as do garbled or fragmented sentences, for example). Other instructors deduct points for grammatical errors on the grounds that correct usage is always important. You should know your instructor's position on this issue. If your instructor is a stickler for these details, you may want to save the last five or ten minutes of the exam period for proofreading. Even the strictest professor, however, is unlikely to penalize you heavily for minor errors (such as writing *to* for *too,* minor comma errors, misplaced modifiers).

Even if you know a lot about a question, avoid writing more than it asks—unless, perhaps, you know absolutely nothing about one question and want to demonstrate extreme depth of understanding about the others to compensate. It may be intellectually rewarding to showcase additional insights, examples, or arguments, but you'll squander time that you need for other questions. Also, remember that your instructor has lots of exams to read. Extraneous material may make it difficult for your instructor to find the core of your argument.

Producing a quality first draft is a reasonable goal for you to have when you write an exam essay. A disorganized, poorly thought-out, or scratched-up response is likely to land you in trouble, but a clear, reasonably organized, readable response will fare well in virtually any course.

Guidelines for Producing Successful Responses

No matter how committed you are to studying, planning, analyzing exam questions, and managing time constraints, your worries about essay tests probably come down to a single, inevitable question: What does an A response look like?

Research suggests that most professors want closed-form, thesis-based prose that develops key ideas fully, drawing on supporting facts and examples. Although your essay's shape will be influenced by your individual writing style and the particular rhetorical context, the following summary of the points covered in this chapter can serve as a template for a successful essay.

Clear thesis statement.   Show your professor that you understand the big picture the question addresses by including a thesis statement early on. Many professors recommend that you state your thesis clearly, though not necessarily stylishly, in the very first sentence.

Coherent organization.   Although a few instructors will read your essay only to see whether you've included important facts and concepts, most expect a logical presentation. Each paragraph should develop and illustrate one main point. Use transition words and phrases to connect each paragraph clearly to the thesis of the essay ("Another factor that led to the economic decline of the South was . . . "; "In contrast to Hegel, Mill believed . . ."). Show your instructor that you know where the essay's going, that you're proving your thesis.

Support and evidence.   When the question calls for supporting facts and examples, be specific. Don't assert or generalize unless you present names, dates, studies, examples, diagrams, or quotations from your reading as support.

Independent analysis and argument.   Your response should not be a pedestrian rehash of the textbook. When the question allows, present your own insights, criticisms, or proposals, making sure to support these statements with course material and relate them clearly to your thesis.

Conclusion.   Even if you're running short of time, don't leave the instructor wondering at the end of your essay, "What does all this mean?" Write a sentence or two to tie together main points and restate your thesis. Your conclusion, even if brief, serves an important rhetorical function. It confirms that you've dealt adequately with the question and proved your point.

Clearly we can't teach you everything you need to know about exam writing in one chapter. Becoming comfortable with any genre of writing requires patience and experience. Practicing the suggestions in this chapter for preparing for essay exams, comprehending exam questions, and organizing your answers will help you build your mastery of this kind of writing.

FOR WRITING AND DISCUSSION

To gain some practical experience, your instructor may ask you to write an essay exam on one of the following topics. Use the preparation and prewriting strategies you've practiced in this chapter and any other strategies you find useful to prepare for the exam. Review the guidelines for writing a successful response presented on pages 625–26 and, if possible, organize and conduct group study sessions with your classmates.

Exam Option 1   Imagine that you've been appointed to a campus committee charged with developing minimum requirements for writing assignments in undergraduate courses. Specifically, the committee is trying to decide whether to require professors to assign a final essay exam or a major research paper in core-curriculum courses. Write an essay in which you argue in favor of mandatory essay exams or mandatory research papers, using examples from your own experience and material from Chapters 1 through 4 and this chapter to support your position. You may want to consider some or all of the following questions in your discussion: Which kind of writing helps students learn the most? Which kind of writing most accurately gauges how well students know course material? Which kind of writing develops skills students are most likely to need in the future?

Exam Option 2   Explain the difference between closed-form and open-form prose as presented in Chapter 1 and Chapters 18–19. Illustrate your answer with examples taken from Richard Weissbourd's "The Feel-Good Trap" (pp. 404–7) and Annie Dillard's "Living like Weasels" (pp. 501–3). Why does Weissbourd choose to write near the closed end of the closed-to-open continuum, whereas Dillard chooses to write near the open end?

Exam Option 3   Write an essay on a topic of your instructor's choice.

▨ CHAPTER SUMMARY

This chapter has discussed strategies for writing effective examination essays under time pressure. We have shown how exam essays differ from essays written outside class and have suggested strategies for learning and remembering subject matter, for analyzing exam questions, and for dealing with the constraints of an exam situation. We have also provided guidelines for producing successful examination essays: a clear thesis statement, coherent organization, support and evidence, independent analysis and argument, and an effective conclusion.

Writing a Reflective Self-Evaluation

> Reflection becomes a habit of mind, one that transforms.
>
> —Kathleen Blake Yancey, Writing and Composition Theorist

> Being an adult student, returning after a twelve-year layoff, working full-time and taking a twelve-credit load, I found that I really had to make time to reinvent my writing. These were times of incredible discovery and frustration. Odd as it seems, frustration breeds discovery.
>
> —William Jensen, Student

Before we explain in detail what we mean by a reflective self-evaluation, let's begin with some examples. Consider the following scenarios:

Scenario 1: Your boss sends you to a one-week professional development seminar in Chicago. Upon your return, she asks you to write a memo reflecting on what you learned from the seminar, how you might apply it to your current job, and how it has helped you grow professionally.

Scenario 2: Your history professor has assigned a major term paper and is willing to read and comment on a rough draft. When you submit your draft, the professor asks you to write out your answers to three questions: What do you like best about this draft? What has been your greatest difficulty in composing this draft? If you were on your own, how would you revise this current draft?

Scenario 3: The composition program at your college requires students to submit a portfolio of their work at the end of the term. You have been given the following assignment:

> Write a reflective letter, addressed to other instructors of this course, that will introduce you and your portfolio. It may describe and compare the process used in creating the out-of-class essays contained in your portfolio, explain why you chose these pieces as your best work for the semester, assess the strengths and weaknesses of your writing, discuss how the writ-

ing for this course fits in with previous or future writing, or combine these approaches. Your letter should provide readers with a clearer understanding of who you are as a writer. It should be approximately 500 to 750 words.

All these assignments ask you to look back over a recently completed process; to think reflectively about that process; and to evaluate critically what went well, what didn't go well, what you might have done differently, and how you might change in the future. Our aim in this chapter is to explain in more detail this kind of reflective, self-evaluative writing. We begin by explaining what we mean by reflective writing, how reflective writing is assigned in writing courses, and why reflective writing is important. We then give examples of different kinds of reflective assignments and describe strategies for composing good reflections.

◢ UNDERSTANDING REFLECTIVE WRITING

What Is Reflective Writing?

Broadly defined, reflective writing is writing that describes, explains, interprets, and evaluates any past performance, action, belief, feeling, or experience. To *reflect* is to turn or look back, to reconsider something thought or done in the past from the perspective of the present.

Whether or not you record your thinking on paper, you think reflectively all the time. Suppose you ask your boss for a raise and get turned down. An hour later, as you cool your anger over coffee and a doughnut, you think of a particular point you could have made more effectively. On a larger scale, this kind of informal reflective thinking can be made more formal, systematic, and purposeful. Consider, for example, a football team that systematically reviews game tapes to evaluate their own and their opponents' strategies and patterns of play. The camera's eye offers players and coaches new perspectives on their performance; it enables them to isolate, analyze, and evaluate specific moves that were unconsciously performed in the heat of the game.

Similar ways of thinking can be applied to any past performance. Writing reflectively encourages you to train your own camera's eye, metaphorically speaking, on the past. Reflective writing is now required in many jobs where employees are asked to write an annual self-reflective review of their job performance. The following example comes from the performance review of a student who worked for a health maintenance organization. In this excerpt, she describes how she plans to make herself more productive in her job and then considers how this improvement will help the company's efficiency generally:

Excerpt from a Self-Evaluation of Job Performance

To improve my claims processing knowledge, I signed up to take a CPT4 coding class. This will allow me to answer coding questions quickly without having to contact our Cost Containment Department. The Cost Containment Department will have more time to work on their projects if our department does not have to continually call to get answers to simple coding questions.

Similarly, a writer can look back reflectively on a writing performance. The following example is from an e-mail message sent by student writer Susan Meyers to her writing instructor concerning his comments on a draft she had submitted. (The topic is the causes of anorexia; you can read Meyers's final version of the paper on pp. 303–10.) On the draft, the instructor had puzzled over a confusing sentence and suggested a revised version. Here is her e-mail response.

Excerpt from a Student Reflection on a Draft

I think that your suggested revision changes what I intended. I'd like that sentence to read: "Perhaps anorexics don't pursue desirability but are rather avoiding it." I am arguing not that anorexics want to be "undesirable" (as your sentence suggests) but rather that they want to avoid the whole issue; they want to be neutral. Sexuality and desire can be tremendously scary if you're in a position that places the value of your body over the value of your self/personage; one can feel that, by entering the sexual world of mature adults, one will lose hold of one's essential self. This is the idea I'm trying to express. Perhaps I should try to draft it some more. [. . .] At any rate, thank you for pointing out the inadequacies of the topic sentence of this paragraph. I struggled with it, and I think your impulse is right: it needs to encompass more of a transition.

As these examples suggest, reflection involves multiple angles of vision. Just as light waves are thrown or bent back from the surface of a mirror, so, too, reflective writing throws our experience, action, or performance back to us, allowing us to see differently. We view the past from the angle of the present, the unconscious from the angle of consciousness, *what was* from the angle of *what could have been or might be.*

This process resembles the kind of dialectical thinking introduced in Chapter 8 on exploratory writing, where we explain how juxtaposing one thesis against its opposite can lead to synthesis that incorporates some aspects of each of the opposing views. Similarly, the process of doubling or multiplying one's angle of vision through reflection yields new insights and a more complicated understanding of a particular action, question, problem, or choice.

FOR WRITING AND DISCUSSION

Working individually, think of a past experience that you can evaluate reflectively. This experience could be your performance in a job; participation in a sport, play, music recital, or other activity; development of a skill (learning to play the piano, juggle a soccer ball, perform a complex dance movement); or problem with an institution (a coach, your dorm Resident

Assistant, job supervisor). To encourage you to think about the past from the perspective of the present, try the formula "How do I see the experience differently now from the way I saw it then?" Imagine you are doing a debriefing of your participation in the experience. Working on your own for ten minutes, freewrite reflectively about your performance. What did you do well? What wasn't working for you? What could you have done better?

Then in groups or as a whole class, share what you learned through your reflective freewrites. How did the process of looking back give you a new angle of vision on your experience? How might reflective writing help you bring about changes and improvements in future performances?

Reflective Writing in the Writing Classroom

Reflective writing in college writing courses can take several forms. One common type of reflective assignment asks you to write a brief, informal reflection on a particular draft in progress or a recently completed essay. Susan Meyers's e-mail reflection on her anorexia draft is an example of this type of reflective writing.

Perhaps the type most frequently assigned is the reflective letter or essay that accompanies a writing portfolio handed in at the end of a term. This final portfolio is a collection of representative work produced for a particular course. Sometimes this work includes rough drafts and informal writing such as freewrites and journal entries as well as polished final drafts; at other times, it includes just the polished final products. Almost always, however, writers have some or complete say in what goes into the final portfolio. Just as architects select their best designs or photographers their best photographs to put into a portfolio to show a potential employer, so, too, student writers assemble their best writing to demonstrate to the instructor or portfolio readers what they have learned and accomplished during the term. The role of the accompanying reflective letter or essay is to offer the author's perspective on the writing in the portfolio, to give a behind-the-scenes account of the thinking and writing that went into the work, and to assess the writer's struggles and achievements during the term.

To distinguish the two types of reflective writing, we use the terms *single reflection* and *comprehensive reflection*. When you write a single reflection, you focus on one piece of writing, either recently completed or in process; you formulate your ideas primarily for yourself and perhaps for a friendly, nonjudgmental audience. When you write a comprehensive reflection, you offer your perspective on a series of completed writing projects for presentation to an outside audience, either your instructor or a portfolio reader. The aim of a single reflection is to learn about a particular piece of writing in order to understand and often to revise it in the present or near future. The aim of a comprehensive reflection is to demonstrate what you have learned from your writing over the course of the term in order to transfer that learning to future writing situations.

Why Is Reflective Writing Important?

According to learning theorists, reflective writing can substantially enhance both your learning and your performance.* Reflective writing helps you gain the insights needed to transfer current knowledge to new situations. For example, one of our students recently reported that the most important thing she had learned in her first-year writing course was that research could be used in the service of her own argument. In high school, she had thought of research as merely assembling and reporting information she had found in various sources. Now she realized that writers must make their own arguments, and she saw how research could help her do so. Clearly, this new understanding of the relationship between argument and research will help this student to do the kind of research writing expected in upper-level college courses.

Learning theorists call this kind of thinking *metacognition:* the ability to monitor consciously one's intellectual processes or, in other words, to be aware of how one "does" intellectual work. Reflection enables you to control more consciously the thinking processes that go into your writing, and it enables you to gain the critical distance you need to evaluate and revise your writing successfully.

◢ REFLECTIVE WRITING ASSIGNMENTS

In this section we describe the kinds of reflective writing that your instructors across the disciplines may ask of you.

Single Reflection Assignments

Single reflection assignments are usually informal exploratory pieces, similar to other kinds of informal writing you have done. Like the exploratory writing described in Chapter 2, single reflections are conversational in tone, open in form, and written mainly for yourself and, perhaps, a friendly, nonjudgmental audience. However, single reflections differ from most other kinds of exploratory writing in timing, focus, and purpose.

Whereas exploratory writing helps you generate ideas early in the writing process, reflective writing is usually assigned between drafts or after you have completed an essay. Its focus is your writing itself, both the draft and the processes that produced it. Its aim is critical understanding, usually for the purpose of revi-

*Learning theorists who have made this general claim include J. H. Flavel, "Metacognitive Aspects of Problem-Solving," in L. B. Resnick (Ed), *The Nature of Intelligence* (Hillsdale, NJ: Erlbaum, 1976); Donald Schon, *Educating the Reflective Practitioner* (San Francisco: Jossey-Bass, 1987); and Stephen Brookfield, *Becoming a Critically Reflective Teacher* (San Francisco: Jossey-Bass, 1995). Throughout this chapter we are indebted to Kathleen Blake Yancey, *Reflection in the Writing Classroom* (Logan, UT: Utah State UP, 1998), who has translated and extended this work on reflection for writing instructors. We are also indebted to Donna Qualley, *Turns of Thought: Teaching Composition as Reflexive Inquiry* (Portsmouth, NH: Boynton/Cook, Heinemann, 1997), who draws on feminist and other critical theorists to argue for the value of reflexive approaches to writing instruction.

sion. In it, you think about what's working or not working in the draft, what thinking and writing processes went into producing it, and what possibilities you see for revising it.

Instructors use a variety of assignments to prompt single reflections. Some examples of assignments are the following:

- *Process log:* Your instructor asks you to keep a process log in which you describe the writing processes and decisions made for each essay you write throughout the term. In particular, you should offer a detailed and specific account of the problems you encountered (your "wallowing in complexity") and the rhetorical and subject-related alternatives considered and choices made.

- *Writer's memo:* Your instructor asks you to write a memorandum to turn in with your draft. In it, you answer a series of questions: How did you go about composing this draft? What problems did you encounter? What do you see as this draft's greatest strengths? What are its greatest weaknesses? What questions about your draft would you like the instructor to address?

- *Companion piece:* Less structured than a formal memorandum, a companion piece asks you to reflect briefly on one or two questions. A typical assignment might be this: "Please turn over your draft and on the back tell me what you would do with this draft if you had more time."

- *Talk-To:* In this type of companion piece, your instructor asks you to do four things: (1) believe this is the best paper you've ever written and explain why; (2) doubt that this paper is any good at all and explain why; (3) predict your instructor's response to this paper; and (4) agree or disagree with what you expect your instructor's response to be.

- *Talk-Back:* In another type of companion piece, the instructor asks you to respond to his or her comments after you get the paper back: (1) What did I value in this text as a reader? (2) Do you agree with my reading? and (3) What else would you like for me to know?*

Guidelines for Single Reflection Assignments

If you are inexperienced with reflective writing, your tendency at first may be to generalize about your writing. That is, you may be tempted to narrate your writing process in generic, blow-by-blow procedural terms ("First I took some notes. Then I wrote a first draft and showed it to my roommate, who gave me some suggestions. Then I revised.") or to describe your rhetorical choices in general, prescriptive terms ("I started with a catchy introduction because it's important to grab your reader's attention.").

---

*We are indebted to Kathleen Blake Yancey and Donna Qualley for a number of the definitions, specific assignments, and suggestions for single and comprehensive reflection tasks that are discussed in the rest of this chapter. Yancey explains the "Talk-To" and "Talk-Back" assignments in her book *Reflection on the Writing Classroom.* Donna Qualley draws on feminist and other critical theorists to argue for the value of reflexive approaches to writing instruction. See her book *Turns of Thought: Teaching Composition as Reflexive Inquiry.* Portsmouth, NH: Boyton/Cook, Heinemann, 1997.

To write an effective single reflection, select only a few ideas to focus on, look at specific aspects of a specific paper, explore dialectically your past thinking against your present thinking, and support your analysis with adequate details. We suggest the following questions as a guide to producing such reflections. But don't answer them all. Rather, pick out the two or three questions that best apply to your performance and text. (Try to select your questions from at least two different categories.) Your goal should be depth not a broad survey. The key criteria are these: be *selective*, be *specific*, show *dialectic thinking*, and include *adequate details*.

Process questions: What specific writing strategies did I use to complete this paper?

- Which strategies were the most or least productive?
- Did this writing project require new strategies or did I rely on past strategies?
- What was the biggest problem I faced in writing this paper, and how successful was I in solving that problem?
- What was my major content-level revision so far?
- What were my favorite sentence or word-level revisions?
- What did I learn about myself as a writer or about writing generally by writing this paper?

Subject-related questions: How did the subject of my paper cause me to "wallow in complexity"?

- What tensions did I encounter between my ideas/experiences and those of others? Between the competing ideas about the subject in my own mind?
- Did I change my mind or come to see something differently as a result of writing this paper?
- What passages in the paper show my independent thinking about the subject? My unresolved problems or mixed feelings about it?
- What were the major content problems I had with this paper, and how successful was I in solving them?
- What did writing about this subject teach me?

Rhetoric-related questions: How did the audience I imagined influence me in writing this paper?

- What do I want readers to take away from reading my paper?
- What rhetorical strategies please me most (my use of evidence, my examples, my delayed thesis, etc.)? What effect do I hope these strategies have on my audience?
- How would I describe my voice in this paper? Is this voice appropriate? Similar to my everyday voice or to the voices I have used in other kinds of writing?
- Did I take any risks in writing this paper?
- What do readers expect from this kind of paper, and did I fulfill those expectations?

Self-assessment questions: What are the most significant strengths and weaknesses in this essay?

- Do I think others will also see these as important strengths or weaknesses? Why or why not?
- What specific ideas and plans do I have for revision?

Student Example of a Single Reflection

In the following companion piece, a student, Jaime, writes about what she sees as the strengths and weaknesses of an exploratory essay in which she was asked to pose a question raised but not clearly answered in a collection of essays on issues of race and class. (She posed the question: "What motivates people to behave as they do?") She was then asked to investigate various perspectives on the question offered by the readings, consider other perspectives drawn from her own knowledge and experience, and assess the strengths and weaknesses of differing points of view.

Jaime's Single Reflection

Although this paper was harder than the first one, I believe I have a good opening question. I like how I divided her [the author of the essays] ideas about motivation into two parts—individual and social. I also like how I used examples from many different essays (this proves I really read the whole book!). Another thing I like about this essay is how I include some examples of my own, like the Michael Jordan example of how he did not make the basketball team in his freshman year and that motivated him to practice every day for a year before making the team his sophomore year. I wonder if he ever would have been as good as he is if he had made the team his freshman year? I wish I could or would have added more of my own examples like this one.

What I'm not sure about is if I later ask too many other questions, like when I ask, "If someone is doing something because of society's pressures, is he responsible for that behavior?" and "How much are we responsible to other people like the homeless?" I felt that I piled up questions, and also felt I drifted from my original questions. The paper was confusing for me to write, and I feel that it jumps around. Maybe it doesn't, but I don't know.

Since *Alchemy* [the title of the essay collection] was such a hard book, I'm kind of happy with my paper (although after hearing some of the others in my peer group, I don't know if it's up to par!!).

FOR WRITING AND DISCUSSION

Working as a whole class or in small groups, consider the following questions:

1. To what extent does this reflection show that Jaime has deepened her thinking about the question "What motivates people to behave as they do?"

2. Where does Jaime show an awareness of audience and purpose in her self-evaluation of her essay?
3. To what extent does Jaime show us that she can identify strengths and weaknesses of her essay?
4. What are Jaime's most important insights about her essay?
5. How would you characterize Jaime's voice in this reflection? Does this voice seem appropriate for this kind of reflective writing? Why or why not?
6. What are the greatest strengths and weaknesses in Jaime's single reflection?

Comprehensive Reflection Writing Assignments

You may also be asked to write a final, comprehensive reflection on your development as a writer over a whole term. Although end-of-the term reflective essays differ in scope and audience from single reflections, similar qualities are valued in both: selectivity, specificity, dialectical thinking, and adequate detail.

In some cases, the reflective essay will introduce the contents of a final portfolio; in other cases, this will be a stand-alone assignment. Either way, your goal is to help your readers understand more knowledgeably how you developed as a writer. Most important, in explaining what you have learned from this review of your work, you also make new self-discoveries.

Guidelines for Comprehensive Reflection Assignments

Instructors look for four kinds of knowledge in comprehensive reflections: self-knowledge, content knowledge, rhetorical knowledge, and critical knowledge or judgment. Here we suggest questions which you can use to generate ideas for your comprehensive reflective letter or essay. Choose only a few of the questions to respond to, questions that allow you to explain and demonstrate your most important learning of the course. Also, choose experiences to narrate and passages to cite that illustrate more than one kind of knowledge.

Self-Knowledge

By *self-knowledge*, we mean your understanding of how you are developing as a writer. Think about the writer you were, are, or hope to be. You can also contemplate how the subjects you have chosen to write about (or the way you have approached your subjects) relate to you personally beyond the scope of your papers. Self-knowledge questions you might ask are the following:

- What knowledge of myself as a writer have I gained from the writing I did in this course?
- What changes, if any, have occurred in my writing practices or my sense of myself as a writer?

- What patterns or discontinuities can I identify between the way I approached one writing project versus another?
- How can I best illustrate and explain the self-knowledge I have gained through reference to specific writing projects?

Content Knowledge

Content knowledge refers to what you have learned by writing about various subjects. It also includes the intellectual work that has gone into the writing and the insights gained from considering multiple points of view and from grappling with your own conflicting ideas. Perhaps you have grasped ideas about your subjects that you have not shown in your papers. These questions about content knowledge can prod your thinking:

- What kinds of content complexities did I grapple with this semester?
- What *earned insights** (a term from theorist Donna Qualley) did I arrive at through confronting clashing ideas?
- What new perspectives did I gain about particular subjects from my considerations of multiple or alternate viewpoints?
- What new ideas or perspectives did I gain that may not be evident in the essays themselves?
- What passages from various essays best illustrate the critical thinking I did in my writing projects for this course?

Rhetorical Knowledge

Our third category, *rhetorical knowledge,* focuses on your awareness of your rhetorical decisions—how your contemplation of purpose, audience, and genre affected your choices about content, structure, and style. The following questions about rhetorical choices can help you assess this area of your knowledge:

- What important rhetorical choices did I make in various essays to accomplish my purpose or to appeal to my audience? What passages from my various essays best illustrate these choices? Which of these choices are particularly effective and why? About which choices am I uncertain and why?
- What have I learned about the rhetorical demands of audience, purpose, and genre, and how has that knowledge affected my writing and reading practices?
- How do I expect to use this learning in the future?

Critical Knowledge or Judgment

A fourth area of knowledge, *critical knowledge* or *judgment*, concerns your awareness of significant strengths and weaknesses in your writing. This area also encompasses your ability to identify what you like or value in various pieces of

---

*Thomas Newkirk, in *Critical Thinking and Writing: Reclaiming the Essay* (Urbana, IL: NCTE, 1989), coined the phrase "earned insights," a phrase that Donna Qualley also refers to in *Turns of Thought,* pp. 35–37.

writing and to explain why. You could ask yourself these questions about your critical knowledge:

- Of the papers in my portfolio, which is best and why? Which is the weakest paper and why?
- How has my ability to identify strengths and weaknesses changed during this course?
- What role has peer, instructor, or other reader feedback had on my assessments of my work?
- What improvements would I make in the enclosed papers if I had more time?
- How has my writing changed over the term? What new abilities will I take away from this course?
- What are the most important things I still have to work on as a writer?
- What is the most important thing I have learned in this course?
- How do I expect to use what I've learned from this course in the future?

Student Example of a Comprehensive Reflection

Now let's look at the draft of a reflective letter written by a student, Bruce, for a second-semester composition course that involved large-scale portfolio assessment. Bruce's portfolio as a whole will be read and scored (Pass or Fail) by two outside readers (and a third if the first two disagree). The contents of Bruce's portfolio include two essays written out of class and revised extensively and one essay written in class under test conditions. As his letter suggests, his two out-of-class essays were classical arguments (see Chapter 14) written in response to the nonfiction texts which his class read during the semester. The assignment he was given for this comprehensive reflection is similar to the one on pages 628–29.

> Dear Portfolio Reader:
>
> This is my first college course in five years. I left school for financial reasons and a career opportunity that I couldn't pass up. I thought of contesting the requirement of this course because I had completed its equivalent back in 1993. But, as I reflected on the past few years, the only books I have read have been manuals for production machinery. My writing consists of shorthand, abbreviated notes that summarize a shift's events. Someday, after I finish my degree and move up in my company, I'm going to have to write a presentation to the directors on why we should spend millions of dollars on new machinery to improve productivity. I need this course if I expect to make a persuasive case.
>
> I was very intimidated after I read the first book in the course, *No Contest: The Case Against Competition* by Alfie Kohn. The author used what seemed to me a million outside sources to hammer home his thesis that competition is unhealthy in our society and that cooperation is the correct route. I felt very frustrated with Kohn and found myself disagreeing with him although I wasn't always sure why. I actually liked many of his ideas, but he seemed so detached from his argument. Kohn's sources did all the arguing for him. I tried to take a fresh perspective by writing about my own personal experience. I also used evidence from an interview I conducted with a school psychologist to back up my argument about the validity of my own experiences with cooperative education. The weakness of this paper is my lack of opposing opinions.

For my second essay, on Terry Tempest Williams's *Refuge: An Unnatural History of Family and Place,* I certainly could not use any personal experience. Williams, a Mormon woman, writes about the deaths of her mother, grandmother, and other female relatives from breast cancer, believed to be caused by the atomic testing in Utah. I argued that the author, Williams, unfairly blamed men and the role women play in the Mormon religion for the tragic death of her mother and other relatives. She thinks that if the Mormon Church had not discouraged women from questioning authority, maybe some of them would have protested the nuclear testing. But I think this reasoning ignores the military and government pressures at the time and the fact that women in general didn't have much power back in the 50s. Since I didn't know anything about the subject, I asked a Mormon woman that I know to comment on these ideas. Also, my critique group in class was comprised of myself and three women. I received quite a bit of verbal feedback from them on this essay. I deal with men at work all day. This change, both for this essay and the entire semester, was welcome.

In-class, timed essay writing was my biggest downfall. I have not been trained to develop an idea and present support for it on the fly. Thoughts would race through my head as I tried to put them on paper. I thought I was getting better, but the in-class essay in this portfolio is just awful. I really wish I could have had more practice in this area. I'm just not comfortable with my writing unless I've had lots of time to reflect on it.

A few weeks ago, I found a disk that had some of my old papers from years ago stored on it. After reading some of them, I feel that the content of my writing has improved since then. I know my writing has leaped huge steps since my first draft back in September. As a student not far from graduation, I know I will value the skills practiced in this course.

FOR WRITING AND DISCUSSION

Working individually or in groups, discuss your responses to the following questions:

1. What kinds of self-knowledge does Bruce display in his reflective letter?
2. Does Bruce demonstrate dialectical thinking about himself as a writer? If so, where? What multiple writing selves does Bruce identify in his letter?
3. What has Bruce learned from writing about *No Contest* and *Refuge*? What specific examples does he give of "earned insights" or dialectical thinking regarding his subject?
4. Does Bruce demonstrate his ability to make judgments about his essays' strengths and weaknesses?
5. What learning from this course do you think Bruce is likely to use in the future?
6. Which of the four kinds of writer's knowledge would you like Bruce to address more closely in revising this reflective letter? What kinds of questions does he overlook? Which points could he build up more? Where could his comments be more text specific and adequately detailed?

◢ CHAPTER SUMMARY

In this chapter, we have introduced you to the value of reflective thinking as a path to self-discovery and improvement as a writer. We have shown how single reflections enable you to reexamine your writing processes, subject-matter choices, and rhetorical choices for individual pieces of writing, often with the goal of targeting problems to resolve in your revision of that writing. In contrast, comprehensive reflections sum up and give you more of a long-range, wide-angle view of your writing over the course of a term. They encourage you to consider your growth as a writer, your intellectual and personal discoveries as you wrestled with subjects, your understanding of the effectiveness of rhetorical choices, and the development of your critical reading and writing skills. This chapter has emphasized how you can benefit the most from the reflective process by making all your reflective writing selective, specific, dialectical, and adequately detailed.

*A Guide
to Editing*

part **S** **I** **X**

h a n d b ☐ o o k   1

Improving Your Editing Skills

◢ WHY EDITING IS IMPORTANT

In our discussion of the writing process in Chapter 17, we recommend saving editing for last. We do so not because editing is unimportant, but because fine-tuning a manuscript requires that the main features of the text—its ideas and organization—be relatively stable. There is no point in correcting mistakes in a passage that is going to be deleted or completely rewritten.

Of course, no text is completely stable. During the late stages of editing you may well make some revisions by moving sentences, by rewriting passages to improve clarity or coherence, or even by reformulating an entire section. Eventually, however, you will reach a stage at which you focus primarily on finding and eliminating errors—catching a nonparallel construction, untangling a garbled sentence, deciding between a comma and a semicolon, repairing sentence fragments, or double-checking the spelling of an author's name.

This late-stage concern for clarity and correctness is a crucial part of the writing process because editing and proofreading errors reflect directly on your *ethos,* that is, on the reader's image of you as a writer. The problem with sentence-level errors is that they inevitably show up to embarrass us whenever we let our guard down. They are like the grinning tricks of an Idiot Twin Sibling in Algonquin mythology. This character is a screwup, an oaf, a goofmeister who can take over when you're not alert. Remember when you stood in front of your eighth-grade class to deliver that stirring science report on fish parasites? After a few minutes you noticed that a lot of your classmates were inexplicably snickering. When you returned to your desk, Velda Sleeth, whom you've worshiped from afar for six months, said in a stage whisper, "You might want to pick that big hunk of lettuce outta your teeth, John." Well, that lettuce was the work of your Idiot Twin Sibling.

Think of editing and proofreading as a way to foil this jokester's attempts at undermining your successes. If you're writing something with real-world consequences—a job-application letter, a grant proposal, a letter to a client, a field report for your boss—then typos, misspellings, sentence fragments, and dangling participles are like a piece of lettuce between your teeth. Instead of focusing on your message, your readers may not even take you seriously enough to finish reading what you have written.

Another reason to edit is more existential than rhetorical. It has to do with the care we devote to the details of something that matters to us. In Robert Pirsig's philosophical novel about writing, *Zen and the Art of Motorcycle Maintenance,* editing and proofreading belong to the "motorcycle maintenance" side of writing, not to the Zen side. For Pirsig, motorcycle maintenance is a metaphor for the unglamorous but essential aspect of any thoughtful enterprise. It requires discipline; you must give yourself up to the object before you, whether it is a motorcycle, a philosophical system, or the draft of an essay. Editing and proofreading, like motorcycle maintenance, require us to focus painstakingly on the parts. It can seem unrelentingly, oppressively nitpicky, but in a complex engine or complex essay misfires and mistakes among the parts keep the whole from realizing its full potential. Even if you are the only one aware of these failures, you gain an innate satisfaction in making the parts function perfectly—the sort of satisfaction that carries over into larger pursuits.

■ OVERVIEW OF THIS GUIDE TO EDITING

We are not about to call this guide "The Joy of Grammar" or "Zen and the Art of Punctuation." But we do believe that you will find satisfaction in gaining control over the details of sentence structure and punctuation. The six handbook chapters of this guide are intended to help you master various aspects of editing.

In the rest of this chapter, Handbook 1, we suggest ways to improve your editing processes. The chapter concludes with a series of short microthemes, which your instructor might use for writing assignments, group miniprojects, or in-class problem-solving tasks.

Handbook 2, "Understanding Sentence Structure," provides a brief review of grammar, including a discussion of sentence patterns, parts of speech, and various kinds of phrases and clauses. Knowledge of these primary sentence elements will help you better apply the principles of punctuation and usage presented throughout this editing guide.

Handbook 3, "Punctuating Boundaries of Sentences, Clauses, and Phrases," describes the main punctuation system for signaling readers where sentences begin and end and for guiding them through the internal structure of sentences. We focus on three common sentence-boundary problems—fragments, run-ons, and comma splices. We also describe how writers use internal punctuation to signal the boundaries of clauses and phrases.

Handbook 4, "Editing for Standard English Usage," focuses on the most common kinds of sentence-level errors: grammatical tangles, errors in agreement and consistency, lack of parallel structure, dangling or misplaced modifiers, and other errors in the use of pronouns, verbs, adjectives, and adverbs.

Handbook 5, "Editing for Style," explains how to make your prose more lively and readable. We offer suggestions for pruning your prose (by eliminating wordiness), enlivening it (by avoiding nominalizations and clichés and adding sentence variety and details), and making it more coherent (by putting old information before new). In this chapter we also review the active and passive voice and provide guidelines for using inclusive language.

Finally, Handbook 6, "Editing for Punctuation and Mechanics," presents a comprehensive overview of the rules governing the use of terminal punctuation or endmarks, commas, semicolons, colons, dashes, and other punctuation marks. The chapter concludes with a brief discussion of manuscript form.

◢ IMPROVING YOUR EDITING AND PROOFREADING PROCESSES

You can become a more attentive editor and proofreader of your own prose if you practice the kinds of editing strategies we suggest in this section.

Keep a List of Your Own Characteristic Errors

When one of your papers is returned, look carefully at the kinds of sentence-level errors noted by your instructor. A paper with numerous errors might actually contain only two or three *kinds* of errors repeated several times. For example, some writers consistently omit apostrophes from possessives or add them to plurals; others regularly create comma splices when they use such words as *therefore* or *however* at the beginning of an independent clause. Try to classify the kinds of errors you made on the paper, and then try to avoid these errors on your next paper.

Do a Self-Assessment of Your Editing Knowledge

Look over the detailed table of contents for this editing guide and note the various topics covered. Which of these topics are familiar to you from previous instruction? In which areas are you most confident? In which areas are you most shaky? We generally recommend that students study the topics in Handbook 3 early in a course because this chapter explains the main punctuation codes that let you avoid fragments and comma splices and that help you make decisions about comma placement within a sentence. The remaining handbook chapters can function as handy references when specific questions arise. Become familiar with the organization of this guide so that you can find information rapidly.

Read Your Draft Aloud

A key to good editing is noting every word. An especially helpful strategy is to read your paper aloud—really aloud, not half aloud, mumbling to yourself, but at full volume, as if you were reading to a room full of people. When you stumble over a sentence or have to go back to fit sound to sense, mark the spot. Something is probably wrong there and you will want to return to it later. Make sure that the words you read aloud are actually on the page. When reading aloud, people often unconsciously fill in missing words or glide over mispunctuated passages, so check carefully to see that what you say matches what you wrote. Some writers like to read aloud into a tape recorder and then reread their draft silently while playing back the recording. If you haven't tried the tape-recorder technique, consider doing so at least once; it is a surprisingly powerful way to improve your editing skills.

Read Your Draft Backwards

Another powerful editing technique—strange as it might seem—is to read your paper backwards, word by word, from end to beginning. When you read forward, you tend to focus on meaning and often read right past mistakes. Reading backwards estranges you from the paper's message and allows you to focus on the details of the essay—the words and sentences. As you read backwards, keep a dictionary and this handbook close by. Focus on each word, looking for typos, spelling errors, misused apostrophes, pronoun case errors, and so forth, and attend to each sentence unit, making sure that it is a complete sentence and that its boundaries have been properly marked with punctuation (see Handbook 3).

Use a Spell Checker and (Perhaps) Other Editing Programs

The advent of powerful spell checkers means that if you have access to a computer, you have almost no excuse for including misspelled words or typos in a formal paper. Become a skilled operator of your computer's spell checker, and always allow yourself time to run the program before printing out your final draft.

Be aware, however, that a spell checker isn't foolproof. These programs match strings of letters in a document against strings stored in memory. A spell checker may not contain some of the specialized words you use (authors' names or special course terms), nor can it tell whether a correctly spelled word is used correctly in context (*it's, its; their, there,* or *they're; to, too,* or *two*).

Many writers use "grammar" checkers, also called style or usage checkers. We place "grammar" in quotation marks because these programs do not really check grammar. They can perform only countable or matchable functions, such as identifying *be* verbs and passive constructions, noting extremely long sentences, identifying clichés and wordy expressions, and so forth. Although these programs can be useful by drawing your attention to some areas where you may be able to tighten or enliven your prose, they have to be used with caution. So-called grammar checkers can't catch most of the most common errors in usage and grammar that writers make, and they often flag nonexistent problems.

Summary

We have explained that careful editing and proofreading are important not only to improve the clarity of your writing but also to ensure that you project an ethos of professionalism and responsibility. We have suggested several ways to improve your editing processes: keep track of your own characteristic errors; do a self-assessment of your editing knowledge; read your draft aloud; read your draft backwards; and run your draft through a spell-checking program (and perhaps a grammar-checking program as well).

■ MICROTHEME PROJECTS ON EDITING

The following microtheme assignments focus on selected problems of editing and style. Since you never know a concept so well as when you have to teach it to someone else, these assignments place you in a teaching role. They ask you to solve an editing problem and to explain your solution in your own words to a hypothetical audience that has turned to you for instruction.

Your instructor can use these microtheme assignments as individual or group writing projects or as prompts for classroom discussion.

MICROTHEME 1: APOSTROPHE MADNESS

Your friend Elmer Fuddnick has decided to switch majors from engineering to creative writing. Poor Elmer has a great imagination, but he forgot to study basic punctuation when he was in high school. He's just sent you the first draft of his latest short story, "The Revenge of the Hedgehogs." Here are his opening sentences.

> The hedgehogs' scrambled from behind the rock's at the deserts edge, emitted what sounded like a series of cats scream's and then rolled themselve's into spiny balls. One of the hedgehogs hunched it's back and crept slowly toward a cactus' shadow.

Although you can't wait to finish Elmer's story, you are a bit annoyed by his misuse of apostrophes. Your job is to explain to Elmer how to use apostrophes correctly. Begin by correcting Elmer's sentences; then explain to Elmer the principles you used to make your corrections. Your explanation of apostrophes should be clear enough so that Elmer can learn their use from your explanation. In other words, you are the teacher. Use your own language and make up your own examples.

MICROTHEME 2: STUMPED BY *HOWEVER*

You are putting yourself through college by operating a grammar hot line and charging people a hefty sum for your advice. One day you receive the following fax:

Dear Grammarperson:

I get really confused on how to punctuate words like "however" and "on the other hand." Sometimes these words have commas on both sides of them, but at other times they have a comma in back and a semicolon in front. What's the deal here? How can I know whether to use a comma or a semicolon in front of a "however"?

Bewildered in Boston

Write a fax response to Bewildered explaining why such words as *however* are sometimes preceded by a comma and sometimes by a semicolon (or a period, in which case *however* starts with a capital letter). Use your own language and invent your own examples.

MICROTHEME 3: THE COMIC DANGLER

Here is another letter received at the grammar hot line (see Microtheme 2).

Dear Grammarperson:

My history teacher was telling us the other day that editing our papers before we submitted them was really important. And then she mentioned in passing that some editing mistakes often create comic effects. She said that the dangling participle was her favorite because it often produced really funny sentences. Well, maybe so, but I didn't know what she was talking about. What are dangling participles and why are they funny?

Not Laughing in Louisville

Explain to Not Laughing what dangling participles are and why they are often funny. Illustrate with some examples of your own and then show Not Laughing how to correct them.

MICROTHEME 4: HOW'S THAT AGAIN?

The grammar hot line is doing a great business (see Microtheme 2). Here is another letter.

Dear Grammarperson:

It has often been said by some instructors that I have had in the various educational institutions that I have attended that a deadening effect is achievable in the prose produced by writers through the transformation of verbs into nouns and through the overuse of words that are considered empty in content or otherwise produce a redundant effect by the restating of the same idea in more words than are necessary for the reader's understanding of the aforementioned ideas. Could these teachers' allegations against the sentence structure of many writers be considered to be at least partially true in the minds of those persons who read these writers' prose?

Verbose in Vermont

Help Verbose out by rewriting this question in a crisper style. Then explain briefly, using your own language and examples, the concepts of wordiness and nominalization.

MICROTHEME 5: THE INTENTIONAL FRAGMENT

Advertisers frequently use sentence fragments on purpose. Find an advertisement that makes extensive use of fragments in its copy. Rewrite the copy to eliminate all sentence fragments. Then write a one-paragraph microtheme in which you speculate why the advertisers used fragments rather than complete sentences. Try to suggest at least two possible reasons.

MICROTHEME 6: CREATE YOUR OWN

Following the model of the five preceding assignments, create your own microtheme assignment on an editing problem related to any section of this handbook (or to a section assigned by your instructor). Then exchange assignments with a classmate and write a microtheme in response to your classmate's assignment. Be prepared to write a microtheme in response to your own assignment also.

Understanding Sentence Structure

This chapter provides a basic review of English grammar. Throughout we emphasize that you already have an innate understanding of grammar, based on your ability to speak and understand English. In this chapter we want to give you a more conscious understanding of the structures you use all the time subconsciously. We also introduce some useful terms and labels that will facilitate your learning rules for usage and punctuation. Handbook 2 covers the following elements:

- An explanation of your innate knowledge of grammar
- The concept of the sentence
- Basic sentence patterns
- Parts of speech
- Types of phrases
- Types of clauses
- Types of sentences

▨ WHAT YOU ALREADY KNOW ABOUT GRAMMAR

By *grammar* we mean the set of rules in any language for combining words into patterns that can convey meanings. In English, these rules govern both the order of words and the endings added to words. Students often complain that they don't understand grammar. The truth is that you learned grammar when you learned to talk. If you didn't know grammar, neither of the following groups of words would make sense:

1. Complain don't that grammar often they understand all at students.
2. Students often complain that they don't understand grammar at all.

If 2 makes more sense to you than 1, you understand English grammar; that is, you understand the required order of English words ("The dog chased the cat" has a different meaning from "The cat chased the dog"), and you understand the meaning of endings placed on words (*cats* is different from *cat, chased* from *chase*). What people mean when they say they don't understand grammar is that they don't understand the terms that language teachers use to describe grammatical structures, even though they internalized those structures when they first learned to talk. Be aware that you know English grammar at a much deeper level than you may appreciate—far deeper than any computer has yet been programmed to understand it. You can rely on that innate knowledge of grammar to help you understand the terms and concepts covered in the rest of this chapter.

◪ THE CONCEPT OF THE SENTENCE

The *sentence* is perhaps the most crucial grammatical concept for writers to understand. A sentence is a group of related words with a complete subject and a complete predicate. The subject names something, and the predicate makes an assertion about the thing named.

Name Something	Make an Assertion About It
Cheese	tastes good on crackers.
Lizards and snakes	are both kinds of reptiles.
Capital punishment	has been outlawed in many countries.

Every sentence must include at least one subject and one predicate. These components answer two different questions: (1) Who or what is the sentence about? (subject); and (2) What assertion does the sentence make about the subject? (predicate). Consider the following example:

Tree ants in Southeast Asia construct nests by sewing leaves together.

What is this sentence about? *Tree ants in Southeast Asia* (subject). What assertion is made about tree ants? (They) *construct nests by sewing leaves together* (predicate).

Grammarians sometimes distinguish between simple and complete subjects and between simple and complete predicates. A simple subject is the single word or phrase that the sentence is about. In our example, *ants* is the simple subject and *tree ants in Southeast Asia* is the complete subject (the simple subject plus all its modifiers). A simple predicate is the main verb (along with its helping or auxiliary verbs) that makes the assertion about the subject. In our example, *construct* is the simple predicate (the verb) and *construct nests by sewing leaves together* is the complete predicate (the main verb plus modifiers and nouns needed to complete its meaning).

Ordinarily a sentence begins with the subject, followed by the verb. Sometimes, however, word order can be changed. In the following examples, the subjects are underscored once and the verbs are underscored twice.

Normal Word Order The most terrifying <u>insects</u> <u>wander</u> through the countryside seeking prey.

Question	What <u>are</u> the most terrifying <u>insects</u>?
Imperative	<u>Watch</u> for the driver ants. ("You" is understood as the subject.)
"There" Opening	There <u>are</u> various <u>kinds</u> of terrifying insects.
Inverted Order	Across the jungles of Africa <u>marched</u> the driver <u>ants</u>.

Sentences can also have more than one subject or predicate.

Compound Subject	The army <u>ants</u> of South America and the driver <u>ants</u> of Africa <u>march</u> in long columns.
Compound Predicate	The <u>hunters</u> at the head of a column <u>discover</u> prey, <u>swarm</u> all over it, and eventually <u>cut</u> it apart.

◣ BASIC SENTENCE PATTERNS

All sentences must have a complete subject and a complete predicate. However, the predicates of sentences can take several different shapes, depending on whether the verb needs a following noun, pronoun, or adjective to complete its meaning. These words are called *complements.* The four kinds of complements are *direct objects, indirect objects, subject complements,* and *object complements.*

Pattern One: Subject + Verb (+ Optional Adverb Modifiers)

adverb modifiers

The <u>eagle</u> <u>soared</u> gracefully across the summer sky.

In this pattern, the predicate contains only a verb and optional adverbial modifiers. Because the verb in this pattern does not transfer any action from a doer to a receiver, it is called *intransitive.*

Pattern Two: Subject + Verb + Direct Object (DO)

DO

<u>Peter</u> <u>was fixing</u> a flat tire over in Bronco County at the very moment of the crime.

Direct objects occur with *transitive verbs,* which transfer action from a doer (the subject) to a receiver (the direct object). Transitive verbs don't seem complete in themselves; they need a noun or pronoun following the verb to answer the question What? or Whom? Peter was fixing *what*? *The flat tire.*

Pattern Three: Subject + Verb + Subject Complement (SC)

SC

My <u>mother</u> <u>is</u> a professor.

SC

The <u>engine</u> in this car <u>seems</u> sluggish.

In this pattern, verbs are *linking verbs,* which are followed by subject complements rather than direct objects. Unlike direct objects, which receive the action of the verb, subject complements either rename the subject (a noun) or describe the subject (an adjective). You can best understand a subject complement if you think of the linking verb as an equals sign (=).

Pattern Four: Subject + Verb + Direct Object + Object Complement (OC)

That woman called me an idiot.

DO = me, *OC* = an idiot

Whereas a subject complement describes the subject of the sentence, an object complement describes the direct object, either by modifying it or by renaming it. Compare the patterns.

Pattern Three   I am an idiot.   *SC* = an idiot

Pattern Four   The woman called me an idiot.   *DO* = me, *OC* = an idiot

Pattern Five: Subject + Verb + Indirect Object (IDO) + Direct Object

My mother sent the professor an angry letter.   *IDO* = the professor, *DO* = an angry letter

My father baked me a cake on Valentine's Day.   *IDO* = me, *DO* = a cake

Sometimes transitive verbs take an *indirect object* as well as a direct object. Whereas the direct object answers the question What? or Whom? following the verb, the indirect object answers the question To what or whom? or For what or whom? My mother sent *what*? *A letter* (direct object). She sent a letter *to whom*? *The professor* (indirect object). My father baked what? *A cake* (direct object). My father baked a cake for whom? *For me* (indirect object).

PARTS OF SPEECH

Although linguists argue about the best way of classifying the functions of words in a sentence, the traditional eight parts of speech listed here are most often used in dictionaries and basic introductions to grammar.

Parts of Speech

nouns (N)	adverbs (Adv)
pronouns (PN)	prepositions (P)
verbs (V)	conjunctions (C)
adjectives (Adj)	interjections (I)

Each part of speech serves a different function in a sentence and also possesses structural features that distinguish it from the other parts of speech. Because many words can serve as different parts of speech in different circumstances, you can determine what part of speech a word plays only within the context of the sentence you are examining.

Nouns

Nouns are the names we give to persons (Samuel, mechanic), places (Yellowstone, the forest), things (a rock, two potatoes), and abstract concepts (love, happiness). Nouns can be identified by structure as words that follow the articles *a, an,* or *the;* as words that change their form to indicate number; and as words that change their form to indicate possession.

  a rock   several rocks   the rock's hardness

But not: *a* from; several froms; the from's coat.

Pronouns

Pronouns take the place of nouns in sentences. The noun that a pronoun replaces is called the pronoun's *antecedent.* English has the following types of pronouns:

Type of Pronoun	Examples
Personal	I, me, you, he, him, she, her, it, we, us, they, them
Possessive (with Noun)	my, your, his, her, its, our, their
Possessive (No Noun)	mine, yours, his, hers, ours, theirs
Demonstrative	this, that, these, those
Indefinite	any, anybody, someone, everyone, each, nobody
Reflexive/Intensive	myself, yourself, himself, herself, itself, ourselves, yourselves, themselves
Interrogative	who, what, whom, whose, which, whoever, whomever
Relative	who, whom, whose, which, that

Verbs

Verbs are words that express action (*run, laugh*) or state of being (*is, seem*). Structurally, they change form to indicate tense and sometimes to indicate person and number. A word can function as a verb if it can fit the following frames:

  I want to _____.   I will _____.
  I want to *throw.*   I will *throw.*

But not: I want to *from*; I will *from*.

Verbs are used as complete verbs or as incomplete verbs, often called *verbals.* When used as complete verbs, they fill the predicate slot in a sentence. When used as incomplete verbs, they fill a noun, adjective, or adverb slot in a sentence. Verbs often require helping verbs, also called auxiliary verbs, to fulfill their function.

Person and Number

In many instances, verbs change form to agree with the person or number of the subject.

Person	Singular	Plural
First person	I give. I am giving.	We give. We are giving.
Second person	You give. You are giving.	You give. You are giving.
Third person	He (she, it) gives. He (she, it) is giving.	They give. They are giving.

Principal Parts

Verbs have five principal parts, which vary depending on whether the verb is *regular* or *irregular*.

Principal Part	Regular Verb Examples	Irregular Verb Examples
Infinitive or Present Stem (infinitives begin with *to*; the word following the *to* is the *present stem*)	to love to borrow	to begin to get
Present Stem + s (used for third-person singular, present tense)	loves borrows	begins gets
Past Stem (regular verbs add *-ed* to present stem; irregular verbs have different form)	loved borrowed	began got
Past Participle (same as past stem for regular verbs; usually a different form for irregular verbs)	loved borrowed	begun gotten
Present Participle (add *-ing* to present stem)	loving borrowing	beginning getting

The irregular verb *to be* has more forms than do other verbs.

Infinitive	to be
Present Forms	am, is, are
Past Forms	was, were
Past Participle	been
Present Participle	being

Tenses

Verbs change their forms to reflect differences in time. A verb's time is called its tense. There are six main tenses, each with three forms, sometimes called *aspects*—simple, progressive, and emphatic. For two of the tenses—the simple present and simple past—a complete verb is formed by using one word only. For all other tenses, two or more words are needed to form a complete verb. The additional words are called *helping,* or *auxiliary,* verbs. In some tenses the main verb or one of the helping verbs changes form to agree with its subject in person and number (see pp. 676–79 on subject-verb agreement).

Simple Form.   Here are regular and irregular examples of the simple form for the six main tenses.

Simple Present	She *enjoys* the pizza. They *begin* the race.
Simple Past	She *enjoyed* the pizza. They *began* the race.
Simple Future	She *will enjoy* the pizza. They *will begin* the race.
Present Perfect	She *has enjoyed* the pizza. They *have begun* the race.
Past Perfect	She *had enjoyed* the pizza. They *had begun* the race.
Future Perfect	She *will have enjoyed* the pizza. They *will have begun* the race.

Progressive Form.   Each tense also has a progressive form to indicate actions that are ongoing or in process.

Present Progressive	Sally *is eating* her sandwich.
Past Progressive	Sally *was eating* her sandwich.
Future Progressive	Sally *will be eating* her sandwich.
Present Perfect Progressive	Sally *has been eating* her sandwich.
Past Perfect Progressive	Sally *had been eating* her sandwich.
Future Perfect Progressive	Sally *will have been eating* her sandwich.

Emphatic Form.   Several tenses have an emphatic form, which uses the helping verb *to do* combined with the present stem. The emphatic form is used for giving special stress, for asking questions, and for making negations.

I *do go.* I *did go.*

Did the dog *bark*?

Do you *like* peanuts?

The child *does* not *sit* still.

Modal Forms.   Additionally, a variety of other helping verbs, often called *modals,* can be used to form complete verbs with different senses of time and attitude (see the section on subjunctive mood, p. 657).

will, would	may, might
can, could	must
shall, should	

Mood

Verbs have three moods: indicative (by far the most common), subjunctive, and imperative. These three moods indicate the attitude of the writer toward the statement the verb makes.

Indicative Mood.   The indicative mood is so common that you might call it the default mood. It is used for both statements or questions.

> The dog *rode* in the back of the pickup. Where *is* Sally?

Subjunctive Mood.   The subjunctive mood is used to indicate that a condition is contrary to fact and, in certain cases, to express desire, hope, or demand. The subjunctive is formed in the present tense by using the infinitive stem.

> I request that Joe *pay* the bill.
>
> Compare with the indicative: Joe *pays* the bill.

In the past tense, only the verb *to be* has a distinctive subjective form, which is always *were*.

> If I *were* the teacher, I would give you an A for that project.
>
> Here the subjunctive *were* means that "I am *not* the teacher"; it expresses a condition contrary to fact.

The subjunctive frequently causes problems for writers in sentences with if-clauses. If an if-clause uses the indicative mood, then the independent clause uses the simple present or the simple future. However, if an if-clause uses the subjunctive mood, then the independent clause uses a modal auxiliary, such as *would, could, might,* or *should.*

Indicative in If-clause	If he *takes* chemistry from Dr. Jones, he *will learn* a great deal.
Subjunctive in If-clause	If he *were* a good science student, he *would have taken* chemistry long ago.

> The subjunctive in the second sentence implies the following meaning: "He is not a good science student, so he didn't take chemistry."

Imperative Mood.   Finally, the imperative mood conveys a command or request. For most verbs the imperative form is the same as the second-person present tense. An exception is the verb *to be,* which uses *be.*

> *Be* here by noon. *Pay* the bill immediately.

Voice

The voice of a verb indicates whether the subject of the verb acts or is acted on. The concept of voice applies only to *transitive* verbs, which transfer action from a doer to a receiver. In the active voice, the subject is the doer of the action and the direct object is the receiver.

Active Voice	The professor graded the paper.

In the passive voice, the subject is the receiver of the action; the actor is either omitted from the sentence or made the object of the preposition *by.* The passive voice is formed with the past participle and some form of the helping verb *to be.*

Passive Voice	The paper was graded (by the professor).

(For advice on when to use active and passive voice see pp. 696–97.)

Adjectives and Adverbs

Adjectives and adverbs describe or *modify* other words.

Adjectives

Adjectives modify nouns by answering such questions as Which one? (*those* rabbits), What kind? (*gentle* rabbits), How many? (*four* rabbits), What size? (*tiny* rabbits), What color? (*white* rabbits), What condition? (*contented* rabbits), and Whose? (*Jim's* rabbits).

Articles (*a, an, the*) form a special class of adjectives. *A* and *an* are indefinite and singular, referring to any representative member of a general class of objects.

I would like *an* apple and *a* sandwich.

The is definite and can be singular or plural. It always specifies that a particular object is meant.

I want *the* apple and *the* sandwich that were sitting on my desk a few minutes ago.

Adverbs

Adverbs modify verbs, adjectives, or other adverbs. They answer the questions How? (he petted the rabbit *gently*), How often? (he petted the rabbit *frequently*), Where? (he petted the rabbit *there* in the corner of the room), When? (he petted the rabbit *early*), and To what degree? (he petted the rabbit *very* gently).

Conjunctive adverbs, such as *therefore, however,* and *moreover,* modify whole clauses by showing logical relationships between clauses or sentences.

Positive, Comparative, and Superlative Forms

A distinctive structural feature of adjectives and adverbs is that they take positive, comparative, and superlative forms.

Positive	This is a *quick* turtle. It moves *quickly.*
Comparative	My turtle is *quicker* than yours. It moves *more quickly* than yours.
Superlative	Of the three turtles, mine is the *quickest.* Of all the turtles in the race, mine moves *most quickly.*

Conjunctions

Conjunctions join elements within a sentence. *Coordinating* conjunctions (*and, or, nor, but, for, yet,* and *so*) join elements of equal importance.

John *and* Mary went to town.

The city rejoiced, *for* the rats had finally been exterminated.

Subordinating conjunctions (such as *when, unless, if, because, after, while, although*) turn an independent sentence into a subordinate clause and then join it to an independent clause.

After I get off work, I will buy you a soda.

She won't show him how to use the Internet *unless* he apologizes.

If you are going to the city, please get me a new album at Caesar's.

(See pp. 664–73 for additional discussion of coordinating and subordinating conjunctions.)

Prepositions

Prepositions show the relationship between a noun or pronoun (the object of the preposition) and the rest of the sentence. The preposition and its object together are called a *prepositional phrase*. Common prepositions include *about, above, across, among, behind, between, from, in, into, of, on, toward,* and *with*.

The cat walked *under* the table.

The vase was *on* the table.

The table is a mixture *of* cherry and walnut woods.

Interjections

Interjections (*Yippee! Baloney! Ouch!*) are forceful expressions, usually followed by exclamation marks, that express emotion. They can be removed from a sentence without affecting the sentence grammatically.

Hooray, school's out! *Ah, shucks,* I'm sorry!

◤ TYPES OF PHRASES

A phrase is a group of related words that does not contain a complete subject and a complete verb. There are four main kinds of phrases:

1. prepositional
2. appositive
3. verbal (participial, gerund, and infinitive)
4. absolute

Prepositional Phrases

A preposition connects a noun, pronoun, or group of words acting as a noun to the rest of the sentence, thereby creating a prepositional phrase that serves as a modifying element within the sentence. Prepositional phrases usually begin with the preposition and end with the noun or noun substitute, called the object of the preposition.

We watched the baby crawl *under the table.*

The man *in the gray suit* is my father.

Appositive Phrases

Appositive phrases give additional information about a preceding noun or pronoun. They sometimes consist of only one word.

Jill saw her friend *Susan* in the café.

We stopped for a mocha latte at Adolpho's, *the most famous espresso bar in the city.*

Verbal Phrases

Verbals are incomplete forms of verbs that can't function as predicates in a sentence. They function instead as other parts of speech—nouns, adjectives, and adverbs. Verbals are somewhat similar to verbs in that they can show tense and can take complements, but they also function as other parts of speech in that they fill noun, adjective, or adverb slots in a sentence. When a verbal is accompanied by modifiers or complements, the word group is called a *verbal phrase.* There are three kinds of verbals and verbal phrases:

1. participial
2. gerund
3. infinitive

Participial Phrases

Participles have two forms: the present participle and the past participle. The present participle is the *-ing* form (*swimming, laughing*); the past participle is the *-ed* form for regular verbs (*laughed*) and an irregular form for irregular verbs (*swum*). Participles and participial phrases always act as adjectives in a sentence. In the following examples, the noun modified by the participle is indicated with an arrow.

I saw some ducks *swimming in the lake.*

Laughing happily, Molly squeezed Jake's arm.

The 100-meter freestyle, a race *swum by more than twenty competitors last year,* was won by a thirteen-year-old boy.

Gerund Phrases

Gerunds are always the *-ing* form of the verb, and they always serve as nouns in a sentence.

Swimming is my favorite sport.   *[serves as subject]*

I love *swimming in the lake.*   *[serves as direct object]*

I am not happy about *losing my chemistry notebook over in the student union.*   *[serves as object of preposition]*

Infinitive Phrases

An infinitive is the dictionary form of a verb preceded by the word *to* (*to run, to swim, to laugh*). Infinitives or infinitive phrases can serve as nouns, adjectives, or adverbs in a sentence.

To complete college with a major in electrical engineering is my primary goal at the moment.

The person *to help you with that math* is Molly Malone.

Absolute Phrases

An absolute phrase comprises a noun or noun substitute, followed by a participle. It is *absolute* because it doesn't act as a noun, adverb, or adjective; rather, it modifies the whole clause or sentence to which it is attached.

Her face flushed with sweat, the runner headed down Grant Street.

The secretary hunched over the keyboard, *his fingers typing madly.*

■ TYPES OF CLAUSES

Clauses have complete subjects and complete predicates. Some clauses can stand alone as sentences (*independent,* or *main,* clauses), whereas others (*dependent,* or *subordinate,* clauses) cannot stand alone as sentences because they are introduced with a *subordinating conjunction* or a *relative pronoun.*

Here are two independent sentences that could serve as independent clauses.

Sam broke the window.

Lucy studied the violin for thirteen years.

Now here are the same two sentences converted to subordinate clauses.

because Sam broke the window

who studied the violin for thirteen years

In the first example, the subordinating conjunction *because* reduces the independent clause to a subordinate clause. In the second example, the relative pronoun *who,* which replaces *Lucy,* also reduces the independent clause to a subordinate clause.

Finally, here are these subordinated clauses attached to independent clauses to form complete sentences.

Because Sam broke the window, he had to pay for it out of his allowance.

Lucy, who studied the violin for thirteen years, won a music scholarship to a prestigious college.

Subordinate clauses always act as nouns, adjectives, or adverbs in another clause.

Noun Clauses

A noun clause is a subordinate clause that functions as a noun in a sentence. Noun clauses act as subjects, objects, or complements.

He promised *that he would study harder.*   [serves as direct object]

Why he came here is a mystery.   [serves as subject]

He lied about *what he did last summer.*   [serves as object of preposition]

Adjective Clauses

An adjective clause is a subordinate clause that modifies a noun or a pronoun. Adjective clauses are formed with the relative pronouns *who, whom, whose, which,* and *that.* For this reason they are sometimes called *relative clauses.*

Peter, *who is a star athlete,* has trouble with reading.

The future threat *that I most fear* is a stock market collapse.

Adverb Clauses

An adverb clause is a subordinate clause that modifies a verb, an adjective, or another adverb. Adverb clauses begin with subordinating conjunctions, such as *although, because, if,* and *when* (see pp. 658–59 for a list of subordinating conjunctions).

Because he had broken his leg, he danced all night using crutches.

When he got home, he noticed unusual blisters.

◪ TYPES OF SENTENCES

Sentences are often classified by the number and kinds of clauses they contain. There are four kinds of sentences:

1. simple
2. compound
3. complex
4. compound-complex

Simple Sentences

A sentence is *simple* if it consists of a single independent clause. The clause may contain modifying phrases and have a compound subject and a compound predicate.

John laughed.

John and Mary laughed and sang.

modifying phrase

Laughing happily and holding hands in the moonlight, John and Mary walked

independent clause (with compound subject and predicate)

along the beach, wrote their names in the sand, and threw pebbles into the crashing

waves.

Compound Sentences

A sentence is *compound* if it consists of two independent clauses, linked either by a semicolon or by a comma and a coordinating conjunction. (See the discussion of comma splices and run-ons on pp. 669–72) Each clause may contain modifying phrases as well as compound subjects and predicates.

independent clause   independent clause

John laughed, and Mary sang.

modifying phrase   independent clause (with compound subject)

Laughing happily, John and Mary walked hand in hand toward the kitchen, but they

independent clause

weren't prepared for the surprise on the countertop.

Complex Sentences

A sentence is *complex* if it contains one independent clause and one or more subordinate clauses.

independent clause   subordinate clause

John smiled to himself while Mary sang.

subordinate clause   independent clause

When John and Mary saw the surprise on the countertop, they screamed uncontrol-

subordinate clause

lably until John fainted.

Compound-Complex Sentences

A *compound-complex sentence* has at least one subordinate clause and two or more independent clauses joined by a semicolon or by a comma and a coordinating conjunction.

independent clause   subordinate clause   independent clause

John smiled to himself while Mary sang, for he was happy.

subordinate clause   independent clause

When John and Mary saw the surprise on the countertop, they screamed uncontrol-

independent clause

lably; soon John collapsed on the floor in a dead faint.

h a n d b o o k   3

Punctuating Boundaries of Sentences, Clauses, and Phrases

Readers can quickly get lost if writers fail to signal sentence boundaries accurately. Readers also rely on internal punctuation, primarily commas, to help them recognize the boundaries of clauses and phrases within a sentence. Periods, capital letters, commas, and, occasionally, semicolons are to readers what stop signs and yield signs are to drivers: They guide the reader through the twists and turns of prose.

This chapter focuses on punctuation rules that help readers recognize the boundaries of sentences and of clauses and phrases within sentences. Here's what you'll find.

- A demonstration of why readers need punctuation
- Four basic punctuation rules for signaling internal sentence elements
- Guidelines for identifying and correcting sentence fragments
- Guidelines for identifying and correcting comma splices and run-on sentences
- A reference chart summarizing the rules for joining clauses within a sentence

Additional punctuation rules are covered in detail in Handbook 6.

You will have mastered the skills of this chapter if you can create sentences of your own that follow these patterns.

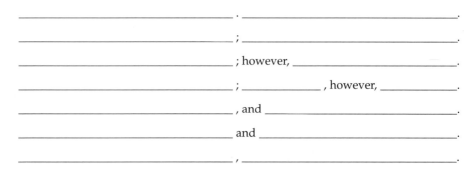

Because_____ , _____ .

_____ because _____ .

WHY READERS NEED PUNCTUATION

To understand why it is important to punctuate sentence and clause boundaries, try to read the following passage:

> RECENTLY A GROWING NUMBER OF COMMENTATORS HAVE BEEN
> FOCUSING ON THE MENTALLY ILL HOMELESS IN RESPONSE TO THE
> VIOLENT MURDER OF AN ELDERLY PERSON BY A HOMELESS MENTALLY
> ILL MAN NEW YORK CITY RECENTLY INCREASED ITS EFFORTS TO
> LOCATE AND HOSPITALIZE DANGEROUS HOMELESS MENTALLY ILL
> INDIVIDUALS THEIR PLAN WILL INCLUDE AGGRESSIVE OUTREACH
> SUCH AS ACTIVELY GOING OUT INTO THE STREETS AND SHELTERS
> TO LOCATE MENTALLY ILL INDIVIDUALS AND THEN INVOLUNTARILY
> HOSPITALIZING THOSE DEEMED DANGEROUS ALTHOUGH MANY
> CRITICS OBJECT TO THIS APPROACH MANY APPLAUD THE CITY'S
> ACTION.

In this passage the use of all capital letters and the deletion of punctuation eliminates all visual clues for sentence boundaries. How many complete sentences do you find in this passage? Where do they begin and end?

RULES FOR PUNCTUATING CLAUSES AND PHRASES WITHIN A SENTENCE

If writers used nothing but short simple sentences, a capital letter and a period would suffice to signal sentence structure. But when writers combine clauses to form compound, complex, or compound-complex sentences, they must use internal punctuation to help readers perceive the boundaries of these elements. This section explains four main punctuation rules for marking the boundaries of clauses and phrases within a sentence. Once you understand these rules, you will find it easier to mark the boundaries of complete sentences and thus to avoid fragments, run-ons, and comma splices.

Rule 1: Join two independent sentences with a semicolon or with a comma and a coordinating conjunction

You can join two complete sentences to form a compound sentence in two ways: (1) with a semicolon, or (2) with a comma and a coordinating conjunction. You should learn the seven coordinating conjunctions.

and   but   or   nor   for   yet   so

When you join two sentences using either of these methods, each sentence becomes an independent clause in the compound sentence; the punctuation signals the joining point.

Two sentences	Melissa hasn't changed the oil in her car. However, she is still willing to take it to the game.
Joined with Semicolon	Melissa hasn't changed the oil in her car; however, she is still willing to take it to the game.
Joined with Comma and Coordinating Conjunction	Melissa hasn't changed the oil in her car, but she is still willing to take it to the game.

Rule 2: Use a single comma to set off an introductory adverb clause

Another common way to join sentences is to use a subordinating conjunction to convert one sentence to an adverb clause. Subordinating conjunctions are words such as *because, when, if, although,* and *until.* (See pp. 658–59 for a longer list.) If the resulting adverb clause opens the sentence, set it off from the independent clause with a comma. If it follows the independent clause, don't set it off.

Adverb Clause Preceding Independent Clause	If the sun is shining in the morning, we'll go for the hike.
Adverb Clause Following Independent Clause	We'll go for the hike if the sun is shining in the morning.

Note that no comma is used in the latter example because the adverb clause follows, rather than precedes, the independent clause.

An exception to this rule occurs with the subordinating conjunction *although.* You should use a comma to set off a clause introduced by *although* even if it comes at the end of a sentence.

The police officer still gave me a ticket, although I explained to her that my speedometer was broken.

Rule 3: Inside a sentence core use pairs of commas to set off interrupting elements

The core of a sentence consists of the subject, verb, and direct object or subject complement. Within the core of a sentence, never use a single comma; either omit commas or use commas *in pairs* to set off interrupting elements.

Sentence Core	My dog chased the cat around the room.
Interrupting Element Inside the Core	My dog, barking loudly and snapping his teeth, chased the cat around the room.

Note that *a pair* of commas—a comma preceding the element and a comma following the element—marks the boundaries of the interrupting element.

Sentence Core	The police officer still gave me a ticket.
Interrupting Element Inside the Core	The police officer, however, still gave me a ticket.

Rule 4: Use a single comma to set off some introductory or concluding phrases

An introductory phrase often precedes the core of a sentence. Set off an introductory phrase if it is long or if your voice pauses noticeably between the phrase (or single word such as *however*) and the start of the sentence core. Similarly, use a single comma to set off long concluding elements if your voice pauses noticeably after the core. In either case, the comma signals the boundary between the sentence core and the introductory or concluding element.

Introductory Element

Barking loudly and snapping his teeth, my dog chased the cat around the room.

According to many authorities, this author's treatment of women is historically inaccurate.

However, I disagree.

Concluding Element

My dog chased the cat around the room, his jaws snapping angrily.

The scholar's claim bothered Jensen, leaving him bewildered and possibly angry.

Your familiarity with these four rules will help you understand the logic for punctuating sentences that combine two or more clauses or that include introductory, interrupting, or concluding phrases. Knowing these rules, in turn, will help you learn to signal sentence boundaries to readers.

EXERCISE

Return to the sentence templates on pages 664–65 that show blank lines punctuated with commas and semicolons and using the words *and, however,* and *because.* On a separate sheet of paper, create sentences of your own to fill these templates. Share your sentences with class members.

Next we turn to three common sentence-boundary errors:

1. *Sentence fragment:* a nonsentence is punctuated as a sentence or an independent clause.
2. *Run-on:* two sentences are fused together without punctuation.
3. *Comma splice:* a sentence boundary is marked with a comma.

IDENTIFYING AND CORRECTING SENTENCE FRAGMENTS

FRAG

A sentence fragment is a nonsentence (any structure lacking a complete subject or a complete predicate) that is punctuated either as a sentence or as an independent clause.

Types of Fragments

There are two kinds of sentence fragments.

1. *Phrase fragments* may lack either a subject or a complete predicate or both. In the following passage, the phrase fragments are italicized.

   Paul and Sarah love their mountain home. *Going fishing in the morning. Watching the deer graze in the meadows.* Outside their cabin, a pair of majestic eagles nest in the top of a lone pine; *with only the starry sky as a night roof.*

   The first two fragments are participial phrases punctuated as complete sentences. The last fragment is a prepositional phrase punctuated as an independent clause. The semicolon signals to readers that two independent clauses are joined together.

2. *Subordinate clause fragments* have a subject and a complete predicate, but they begin with either a subordinating conjunction or a relative pronoun, which prevents them from standing alone as a sentence. In the following examples, the subordinate clause fragments are italicized.

   Sarah and Paul often go for a hike. *As soon as the sun comes up.* At night they love to watch the eyes of owls. *Which blink at them from the branches of nearby trees.*

   The first fragment is created by the subordinating conjunction *as soon as*; the second is created by the relative pronoun *which.*

Methods for Correcting Sentence Fragments

There are various ways to correct a fragment; each method produces a slightly different variation in meaning and emphasis.

Method 1: Change a phrase fragment to a complete sentence by converting an incomplete verb into a complete verb or by adding a verb.

This method emphasizes the material in the fragment by giving it the weight of a full sentence.

Fragment	The buffalo began to stampede. Their heads flailing wildly.
Revised	The buffalo began to stampede. Their heads flailed wildly.

The fragment has been converted to a complete sentence by changing the participle *flailing* to the complete verb *flailed.*

Method 2: Change a clause fragment to a complete sentence by removing the subordinator.

This method also emphasizes the ideas in the original fragment.

Fragment	For Native Americans, killing buffalo was very dangerous. Because the stampeding buffalo herd had to be guided toward the cliff by braves shaking wolf skins.
Revised	For Native Americans, killing buffalo was very dangerous. The stampeding buffalo herd had to be guided toward the cliff by braves shaking wolf skins.

Removing the subordinating conjunction *because* converts the fragment into a complete sentence.

Method 3: Correct the fragment by joining it to the sentence that precedes or follows it, whichever makes more sense.

This method subordinates the material in the fragment and can work for either phrase or clause fragments. With this method, you may need to use a comma to signal the joining point.

Fragment   The buffalo crashed to their deaths. Although the braves killed the animals that were still alive. The squaws did most of the work in preparing the hides and meat.

Revised   The buffalo crashed to their deaths. Although the braves killed the animals that were still alive, the squaws did most of the work in preparing the hides and meat.

The original passage contains a subordinate clause fragment beginning with *although*. The revised passage attaches the *although* clause to the second sentence.

EXERCISE

Proofread the following passage adapted from a student paper. Underline all of the sentence fragments. Then, on a separate sheet of paper, revise the fragments using one of the main correction methods—turn the fragment into a complete sentence or connect the fragment to a neighboring sentence. Choose the correction method that seems most appropriate for the context of the passage.

Another difference between a taxi driver and other occupations being the way that taxi drivers interact with people. Driving a taxi is one of the few jobs where you really get to "know the customer." In other service jobs, you rarely get to know the customer's name. Such as waiter or bartender. In those jobs you can wait on one hundred people in a night or mix drinks for two hundred. Without personally talking to five of them. In a taxi, however, each customer spends at least ten to fifteen minutes in a quiet car. Having nothing else to do but talk with the driver.

◼ IDENTIFYING AND CORRECTING RUN-ONS AND COMMA SPLICES

RO

CS

Writers make run-on errors or comma splices whenever they fail to show where one sentence ends and the next begins.

A *run-on error* occurs when two sentences are fused together without any punctuation.

I explained to the police officer that my speedometer was broken she still gave me a ticket.

Two sentences come together between *broken* and *she*, but no period or capital letter marks the boundary.

A *comma splice* occurs when a writer marks the end of a sentence with a comma instead of with a period and a capital letter.

> I explained to the police officer that my speedometer was broken, she still gave me a ticket.

A comma by itself cannot mark the boundary between two sentences.

Methods for Correcting Run-Ons and Comma Splices

Run-ons and comma splices can be corrected in a variety of ways, depending on the meaning you wish to convey. You may choose to separate the ideas by placing them in two separate sentences, or you may wish to join the ideas into a single sentence. To choose the most appropriate method, consider the rhetorical context of the passage you are writing.

Method 1: Separate the sentences with a period and a capital letter.

This method gives equal emphasis to both sentences. If you wish to indicate a logical relationship between the two sentences, you can add a conjunctive adverb (such as *therefore* or *nevertheless*) somewhere in the second sentence.

> **Revised**   I explained to the police officer that my speedometer was broken. She still gave me a ticket.
>
> **Revised**   I explained to the police officer that my speedometer was broken. However, she still gave me a ticket.

Method 2: Join the sentences with a semicolon.

This method creates a compound sentence with two equally strong independent clauses.

> **Revised**   I explained to the police officer that my speedometer was broken; however, she still gave me a ticket.

Method 3: Join the sentences with a comma and a coordinating conjunction.

This method also creates a compound sentence with two equally strong independent clauses.

> **Revised**   I explained to the police officer that my speedometer was broken, but she still gave me a ticket.

Method 4: Join the sentences with a subordinating conjunction or a relative pronoun.

This method creates a complex sentence with an independent clause and a subordinate clause. The material in the independent clause receives more emphasis than does the subordinated material.

> **Revised**   Although I explained to the police officer that my speedometer was broken, she still gave me a ticket.

Method 5: Convert one of the sentences into a phrase.

This method creates a simple sentence with an added or embedded phrase. The phrase has less importance than the rest of the sentence.

Revised   Despite my explanation of the broken speedometer, the police officer gave me a ticket.

Choosing the Most Appropriate Method for Correction

Although each of these methods of correcting run-ons and comma splices will produce a grammatically correct solution, the method used in a given situation depends on the meaning and emphasis you intend. Consider the following example:

Comma Splice   The weather is beautiful, my neighbor is washing her car.

To determine the best way to correct this comma splice, you need to consider the passage in which it occurs. Different correction methods create different effects.

Revised   It is a great day. The weather is beautiful. My neighbor is washing her car. Kids are playing in the street. The dog is sleeping in the sun.

Here the focus is on the writer's sense of a great day. The beautiful weather and the neighbor washing her car are only two of four separate pieces of evidence the writer uses to support the feeling. By putting them all in separate sentences the writer emphasizes each one.

But consider how the comma splice might be corrected in a different context.

Revised   I was hoping to invite my neighbor over to watch the football game with me this afternoon. But because the weather is beautiful, she is washing her car.

In this version, the main point is the writer's disappointment that the neighbor isn't coming over to watch football. The beautiful weather is the cause of her washing the car, but the subordinating conjunction *because* makes that information secondary. The writer isn't interested in the beautiful weather for its own sake, so a separate sentence such as that in the first example would be inappropriate.

These differences illustrate that punctuation is a way of controlling and signaling meaning for readers. As you learn ways of correcting comma splices and run-ons, you will also become aware of the wide variety of options available to convey subtleties of thought and feeling.

EXERCISE

In the following sentences, underline the comma splices or run-ons (some sentences may be correct). Then, on a separate sheet of paper, revise the underlined sentences.

1. I love to hear coffee perking in the pot on lazy Saturday mornings another of my favorite sounds is rain on a tin roof.

2. When the ice cream wagon begins playing its song in our neighbor-hood, the children run to greet it, clasping their dimes and quarters in grubby little hands.
3. Freud assumed that the unconscious was the basis for human behavior, therefore, he believed that the pleasure audiences receive from art comes from art's embodiment of unconscious material.
4. Because St. Augustine's conception of God was Neoplatonic, Augus-tine believed that existence in itself is good.
5. Although scientists don't know for sure how much dinosaurs actually ate, they know that the food intake of the great reptiles must have been enormous, a question they ask themselves, therefore, is what the dino-saurs actually ate.
6. The doctor told me that my X ray revealed nothing to be alarmed about, nevertheless, she wants me to come back in six months for another checkup.
7. Juan and Alicia began taking the engine apart they worked diligently for four hours and then discovered that they didn't have the right tools to continue.
8. I should apologize for the snide letter I wrote you last week, although I must admit that I am still angry.
9. In a home aquarium fish will sometimes die from overeating the in-structions on fish-food boxes, therefore, stress that you feed fish a specified amount on a strict schedule.
10. The upgrade on Manuel's word-processing program seems more trou-ble than it's worth, so he has decided to return it.

■ OVERVIEW OF METHODS FOR JOINING CLAUSES

Figure HB3.1 (on p. 673) summarizes the methods used in standard written English to join two sentences.

Methods for Joining Two Sentences

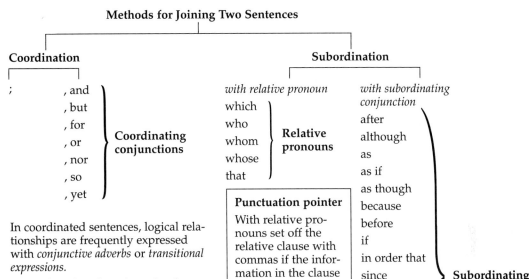

Coordination

;

, and
, but
, for
, or
, nor
, so
, yet

} **Coordinating conjunctions**

In coordinated sentences, logical relationships are frequently expressed with *conjunctive adverbs* or *transitional expressions*.

Examples of conjunctive adverbs

accordingly	instead
also	likewise
anyhow	meanwhile
besides	moreover
consequently	nevertheless
furthermore	otherwise
hence	still
henceforth	then
however	therefore
indeed	thus

Examples of transitional expressions

after all	in addition
after a while	in fact
as a result	in other words
at any rate	in particular
at the same time	in the first place
for example	on the contrary
for instance	on the other hand

Punctuation pointer

In coordinated sentences, a semicolon or a coordinating conjunction with a comma must be used where the two independent clauses come together.

Set off conjunctive adverbs or expressions with commas if your voice pauses around them.

Subordination

with relative pronoun

which
who
whom
whose
that

} **Relative pronouns**

Punctuation pointer

With relative pronouns set off the relative clause with commas if the information in the clause is not needed to identify the noun the clause modifies.

Do not set off the relative clause if the information is needed to identify the noun being modified (see pp. 670–71).

with subordinating conjunction

after
although
as
as if
as though
because
before
if
in order that
since
so that
that
though
unless
until
when
whenever
where
wherever
while

} **Subordinating conjunctions**

Punctuation pointer

Set off adverb clauses with commas if the adverb clause comes before the independent clause.

Do not set off adverb clauses at the end of a sentence unless they reverse the direction of thought (for example, *although*).

FIGURE HB3.1   Methods for Joining Sentences

Editing for Standard English Usage

In this chapter we address common errors in sentence structure or usage. This chapter will help you recognize and correct the following kinds of errors:

- Grammatical tangles such as mixed constructions or faulty predication
- Consistency errors (unnecessary shifts in verb tense or pronoun person)
- Agreement errors (lack of subject-verb agreement or pronoun-antecedent agreement)
- Nonparallel constructions
- Dangling or misplaced modifiers
- Pronoun case errors
- Verb-form errors
- Adjective/adverb errors

▨ FIXING GRAMMATICAL TANGLES

Among the most frequent errors in rough drafts are grammatically tangled sentences that result in *mixed constructions* or *faulty predication.*

MC

Mixed Constructions

In the heat of composing a first draft, a writer sometimes starts a sentence with one kind of construction and shifts midway to another construction.

Faulty   By buying a year's supply of laundry soap at one time saves lots of money.

This sentence opens with a prepositional phrase that cannot serve as a sentence subject. The writer can correct the error by eliminating the preposition or by supplying a subject.

Revised   Buying a year's supply of laundry soap at one time saves lots of money.

             or

             By buying a year's supply of laundry soap at one time, the average consumer can save lots of money.

Faulty Predication

Another kind of grammatical tangle, called faulty predication, occurs when the action specified by the verb can't logically be performed by the subject.

FP

Faulty   Throughout *The Scarlet Letter,* Hester Prynne's "A" is imbibed with symbolic significance.

Imbibe means "to drink," so its use makes no sense in this sentence.

Revised   Throughout *The Scarlet Letter,* Hester Prynne's "A" is invested with symbolic significance.

◾ Maintaining consistency

Consistency errors occur whenever a writer illogically shifts verb tenses or shifts the person or number of pronouns.

Shifts in Tense

SHIFT

Readers can become confused when writers change tenses without explanation. You should avoid shifting verb tenses in a passage unless you mean to signal a shift in time.

Faulty   The display cases of the little bakery were filled with cakes, pies, doughnuts, and special pastries. From the heated ovens against the back wall *drifts* the aroma of buttery croissants.

The verbs in the first sentence are all in the past tense. The verb in the second sentence shifts to the present without an explanation.

Revised   The display cases of the little bakery were filled with cakes, pies, doughnuts, and special pastries. From the heated ovens against the back wall *drifted* the aroma of buttery croissants.

Shifts in the Person and Number of Pronouns

Pronouns have three persons: first (*I, we*); second (*you*); and third (*he, she, it, one, they*). Keep your point of view consistent by avoiding confusing shifts from one person to another or from singular to plural.

Confusing   As readers, we are not prepared for Hamlet's change in the last act. When one sees Hamlet joking with the grave diggers, you forget momentarily about his earlier despair.

The pronouns shift from first to third to second person.

Revised   As readers, we are not prepared for Hamlet's change in the last act. When we see Hamlet joking with the grave diggers, we forget momentarily about his earlier despair.

(*Note:* For advice on avoiding sexist language when using third person pronouns, see pages 697–99.)

◪ MAINTAINING AGREEMENT

Writers often have to choose between singular and plural forms of verbs and pronouns to ensure that verbs match their subjects and pronouns their antecedents. In some cases, special rules determine whether a subject or an antecedent is singular or plural.

AGR-SV Subject-Verb Agreement

In many tenses a verb changes its form to agree in number with its subject.

Singular	This violin *is* beautiful.
Plural	These violins *are* beautiful.

In most cases, it is easy to determine whether the subject is singular or plural, but some cases are tricky. The following rules cover most cases.

Plural Words Between Subject and Verb

It may be difficult to find the subject when it is separated from the verb by intervening words, phrases, or embedded clauses or when an indefinite word such as *one*, *each*, or *kind* is followed by a prepositional phrase beginning with *of.* In the latter case the object of the preposition is often mistaken for the subject.

Faulty	One of the recent shipment of boxes containing computers, printers, and modems *were* delayed.
Revised	One of the recent shipment of boxes containing computers, printers, and modems *was* delayed.

In this sentence, *one* is the subject, not any of the intervening plural words.

Similarly, prepositional phrases beginning with *as well as*, *in addition to*, *along with*, and *including* can trick writers into thinking that a singular subject is plural.

Faulty	My mother, along with several of her coworkers, *are* getting a special award for excellence in customer relations.
Revised	My mother, along with several of her coworkers, *is* getting a special award for excellence in customer relations.

In this sentence the subject is *mother;* the intervening prepositional phrase must be ignored.

Compound Subjects Joined by *and*

Use a plural verb for singular or plural subjects joined by *and* unless the nouns joined by *and* are thought of as one unit, in which case the verb is singular. Notice the different meanings of the following sentences:

My brother and my best friend *is* with me now.

This sentence means that my brother is with me now and that my brother is my best friend.

My brother and my best friend *are* with me now.

This sentence means that two people are with me—my brother and my best friend.

Compound Subjects Joined by *or, nor, either . . . or, neither . . . nor*

The coordinating conjunctions *or, nor, either . . . or,* and *neither . . . nor* take singular verbs if they join singular subjects and plural verbs if they join plural subjects. If they join a singular subject to a plural subject, the verb agrees with the nearer subject.

Either a coyote or a dog *is* getting into the chicken coop.

Both subjects are singular, so the verb is singular.

Either coyotes or dogs *are* getting into the chicken coop.

Both subjects are plural, so the verb is plural.

Either some coyotes or a dog *is* getting into the chicken coop.

The subject closest to the verb is singular, so the verb is singular.

Indefinite Pronoun as Subject

Some indefinite pronouns are always singular; others can be singular or plural depending on context.

Always Singular		**Singular or Plural**
anybody	none	all
anyone	each	any
anything	everybody	some
either	neither	
nobody		

The indefinite pronouns in the left-hand column are always singular.

Faulty	Each of the dogs *are* thirsty.
Revised	Each of the dogs *is* thirsty.

The indefinite pronouns in the right-hand column can be singular or plural. These words are generally followed by a prepositional phrase beginning with *of.* The number of the pronoun depends on whether the object of the preposition is singular or plural.

Some of the table *is* sanded.

The object of the preposition (*table*) is singular, so the verb is singular.

Some of the tables *are* sanded.

The object of the preposition (*tables*) is plural, so the verb is plural.

Inversion of Subject and Verb

Locating the subject may be tricky in inverted sentences, in which the subject comes after the verb.

Just beyond the fence line on the other side of the road are some pheasants.

The subject is *pheasants,* so the verb is plural.

Be especially careful with inverted sentences that begin with *here, there,* or *where.* Errors occur most frequently when a writer uses these words in contractions or in questions.

> **Faulty**   Where's my belt and sweater?
>
> The subject is *belt and sweater,* so the verb should be plural.
>
> **Revised**   Where are my belt and sweater?

Relative Pronoun as Subject

Relative pronouns used as subjects (*who, that, which*) are singular or plural depending on their antecedents.

> A person who *builds* glass houses shouldn't throw stones.
>
> *Who* is singular because its antecedent, *person,* is singular; hence the verb should be singular.
>
> People who *build* glass houses shouldn't throw stones.
>
> *Who* is plural because its antecedent, *people,* is plural; hence the verb should be plural.

Be especially careful when the antecedent is the object of the preposition *of.*

> One of the reasons that *are* frequently given is inflation.
>
> The verb of the main clause (*is*) is singular because its subject is the singular pronoun *one*. But the verb of the relative clause (*are*) is plural because its subject (*that*) has a plural antecedent (*reasons*).

Subject Followed by Linking Verb and Subject Complement

Linking verbs should agree with the subject of the sentence, not with the subject complement.

> Sleeping, eating, and drinking *are* his whole life.
>
> The verb *are* agrees with the plural subject, not with the singular subject complement.
>
> His whole life *is* sleeping, eating, and drinking.
>
> In this case, the verb agrees with the singular subject, not with the plural subjective complement.

Collective Noun as Subject

With collective nouns, such as *group, committee, crew, crowd, faculty, majority,* and *audience,* use a singular verb if the collective group acts as one unit; use a plural verb if the members of the group act individually.

> The faculty at Hogwash College *is* delighted with the new president.
>
> Here the faculty functions as a single unit.

The faculty at Hogwash College *are* arguing at this very moment.

Here *faculty* refers to individuals who act independently.

Some collective nouns present special problems or follow special rules, for instance, *a number* versus *the number*. *A number* refers to a collection of individual items and takes a plural verb. *The number* refers to a unit and takes a singular verb.

A number of students *are* studying grammar this semester.

The number of students studying grammar *is* declining every year.

Titles or words referred to as words use singular verbs.

Snow White and the Seven Dwarfs is a famous Disney movie.

The italics indicates a title, which takes a singular verb. If you were referring to the characters rather than the title, the verb would be plural: "Snow White and the seven dwarfs are my favorite Disney characters."

EXERCISE

In the following sentences, underline the true subject or subjects of the verb in parentheses. Then underline the correct verb form twice.

1. Under a pile of old rags in the corner of the basement (is/are) a mother mouse and a squirming family of baby mice.
2. Hard work, together with intelligence, initiative, and a bit of good luck, (explains/explain) the success of many wealthy businesspeople.
3. The first thing she emphasized (was/were) the differences between Pacific and Atlantic breeding patterns of these fish.
4. The myth, legend, prayer, and ritual of primitive religions (contains/contain) many common themes.
5. Unfortunately, neither of the interviewers for the local TV station (has/have) read any of her works.
6. There (is/are) a number of students who (is/are) waiting to see the teacher.
7. (Does/Do) one of the students still have my notebook?
8. One of the students who (is/are) trying out for the play (wants/want) to become a professional actor.
9. He is the only one of all the students in the theater arts class who really (has/have) professional ambitions.
10. The committee (is/are) writing individual letters to the judge.

Pronoun-Antecedent Agreement

AGR-PN

Just as a subject must agree in number with its verb, so must a pronoun agree in number with its antecedent (the noun that the pronoun stands for). To apply this rule, you must first determine the antecedent of the pronoun and then decide whether the antecedent is singular or plural, following rules presented in the previous section. Pronoun-antecedent agreement occasionally presents some difficulties. The following rules cover most cases.

Compound Construction as Antecedent

If a compound antecedent is joined by *and,* choose a plural pronoun; if a compound antecedent is joined by *or,* the pronoun should agree in number with the closest antecedent.

Rebecca and Paul invited us to their party.

Either Jim or Pete will bring his volleyball to the party.

Either Jim or his sisters will bring their volleyball.

Collective Noun as Antecedent

Use a singular pronoun to refer to a collective noun that acts as one unit; use a plural pronoun if members of the group act individually.

The committee reported its opinion.

The committee began arguing among themselves.

Indefinite Pronoun as Antecedent

Generally, if the antecedent is an indefinite pronoun, such as *either, neither, everyone, everybody, someone, somebody, anyone, anybody,* you use a singular pronoun.

Everybody coming to the party should bring his or her own drinks.

Note: Sentence constructions such as this one can lead to the use of noninclusive language. See pages 697–99 for suggestions on alternative constructions.

▨ MAINTAINING PARALLEL STRUCTURE

When joining items in series or lists, make sure that each item has the same grammatical structure: nouns should be joined to nouns, verbs to verbs, prepositional phrases to prepositional phrases, clauses to clauses, and so forth. Parallelism greatly increases the clarity and force of your sentences.

A nonparallel construction occurs whenever a writer fails to maintain the same grammatical structure for each item in a series.

Faulty   Joan likes playing soccer and to roller-skate.

Here the writer has joined a gerund phrase (*playing soccer*) to an infinitive (*to roller-skate*). The problem can be solved by making both items gerunds or both infinitives.

Revised   Joan likes playing soccer and roller-skating.

or

Joan likes to play soccer and to roller-skate.

Faulty   As a teacher, he was a courteous listener, helpful during office hours, and he lectured in an exciting way.

Revised   As a teacher, he was a courteous listener, a good helper during office hours, and an exciting lecturer.

In this revision the writer converts all items in the series to nouns.

Faulty   This term paper is illogical, poorly documented, and should have been typed.

Here the first two items are parallel (the adjectives *illogical* and *poorly documented*), but the last item is a verb phrase (*should have been typed*).

Revised   This term paper is illogical, poorly documented, and illegible.

    or

    This term paper, which should have been typed, is illogical and poorly documented.

To increase clarity, writers often repeat function words such as articles, prepositions, conjunctions, or the infinitive sign (*to*) at the beginning of each item in a parallel series.

Confusing   The drill sergeant told the recruits that there would be no weekend passes and they would be on KP instead.

Revised   The drill sergeant told the recruits that there would be no weekend passes and that they would be on KP instead.

The repetition of *that* clarifies the writer's intention: to report two things the drill sergeant told the recruits.

Placement of Correlative Conjunctions

When using correlative conjunctions (such as *either . . . or, neither . . . nor, both . . . and,* and *not only . . . but also*), make sure that each unit of the correlative precedes the same grammatical structure.

Faulty   I not only like ice cream but also root beer.

Here the writer places *not only* in front of a verb (*like*), but places *but also* in front of a noun (*root beer*).

Revised   I like not only ice cream but also root beer.

Use of *and which/that* or *and who/whom*

Be sure that a clause beginning with *and which, and that, and who,* or *and whom* is preceded by a parallel clause beginning with *which, that, who,* or *whom.*

Faulty   Of all my friends, Paul is the one with the greatest sense of courage and who most believes in honesty.

The writer links a pronoun (*one*) to a relative clause (*who most believes . . .*), creating a nonparallel structure.

Revised   Of all my friends, Paul is the one who has the greatest sense of courage and who most believes in honesty.

EXERCISE

In the following sentences, underline the nonparallel constructions. Then, on a separate sheet of paper, revise the sentences to create parallel structures.

1. We improved our car's acceleration by resetting the spark-plug caps and also we boiled out the carburetor.
2. Race-car driving requires much practical experience, and your reactions must be quick.
3. After reading the events calendar, we decided to go to a festival of Japanese art and on attending the symphony afterward.
4. I want to read a biography of a flamboyant figure living in the twentieth century and who has altered history.
5. Carol not only does volunteer work in the school, but also coaching soccer every fall.
6. Either you must leave early or leave after the major rush hour.
7. The harvest moon shone brightly, pouring its light over the surrounding water, and which made the evening a special moment in their lives.
8. You can avoid a comma splice by joining main clauses with a comma and a coordinating conjunction, with a semicolon, or by changing one of the main clauses to a subordinate clause.
9. Again and again psychologists explore the same questions: Are we shaped by our heredity, by our environment, or do we have free will?
10. To make friends you must first be a friend and then listening carefully.

◪ AVOIDING DANGLING OR MISPLACED MODIFIERS

DANG

Dangling Modifiers

When a sentence opens with a modifying phrase, the phrase must be followed immediately by the noun it modifies, which is usually the grammatical subject of the sentence; otherwise, the phrase is said to dangle. You can correct a dangling modifier by (a) recasting the sentence so that the subject is the word modified by the opening modifier; or (b) expanding the modifying phrase into a clause that has its own subject.

modifier	subject

Faulty   Walking down the street, a flower pot fell on my head.

This sentence brings to mind a walking flower pot.

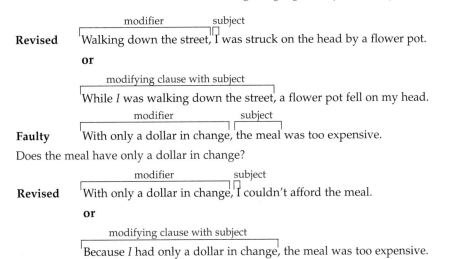

Revised   Walking down the street, I was struck on the head by a flower pot.

or

While *I* was walking down the street, a flower pot fell on my head.

Faulty   With only a dollar in change, the meal was too expensive.

Does the meal have only a dollar in change?

Revised   With only a dollar in change, I couldn't afford the meal.

or

Because *I* had only a dollar in change, the meal was too expensive.

Misplaced Modifiers

MM

A misplaced modifier occurs when a modifying word or phrase is separated from the element it modifies. To correct this type of error, change the location of the modifier so that it is next to the word or phrase it modifies.

Faulty   The students gave a present to their teacher in a big box.

This sentence suggests that the teacher is in a big box.

Revised   The students gave their teacher a present in a big box.

(**Note:** Be careful to place limiting adverbs, such as *only, just,* and *merely,* next to the words they limit. As the following example shows, changing the location of *only* can often change the meaning of a sentence.)

Only I baked the cake. (I am the person solely responsible for baking the cake.)

I only baked the cake. (I baked it, but I didn't put the frosting on it.)

I baked only the cake. (Someone else baked the cookies.)

Place limiting adverbs *directly in front of* the words they modify.

Faulty   I should get a higher grade because I only failed one exam.

The writer intends to modify *one exam* rather than *failed* and thus needs to move *only.*

Revised   I should get a higher grade because I failed only one exam.

EXERCISE

In the following sentences, underline the dangling or misplaced modifiers (some sentences may be correct). Then, on a separate sheet of paper, revise the faulty sentences.

1. Feeling cold, tired, and depressed, tears streamed from my friend's eyes.
2. Their heads tilted back in awe, the children on this summer's night began trying to count the stars.
3. Seen through a telescope that magnifies things sixty times, Jupiter appears as big as the moon.
4. By studying the light reflected by Jupiter, its clouds are a poisonous mixture of ammonia floating in hydrogen.
5. Having long expected to return to Harlem after graduation, the young accountant was not prepared for the changes he saw on Lennox Avenue.
6. While cruising at 10,000 feet 45 miles east of Albuquerque, New Mexico, on July 16, 1945, at approximately 5:30 a.m., a brilliant flash of light, brighter than the sun, blazed across the horizon.
7. We were absolutely startled, unable to explain the sunlike flash or to grasp the meaning of the huge mushroom cloud that soon appeared above the desert floor.
8. Reporting what we had seen by radio to ground authorities, no satisfactory explanation could be found.
9. The following morning, still plagued by the event, the newspapers only reported that an ammunition dump had exploded in the approximate area where we had seen the flash.
10. Listening to the radio on August 6, 1945, a similar flash of light occurred over Hiroshima, Japan; then we realized what we had seen several weeks earlier—the first explosion of an atomic bomb.

CASE ▨ CHOOSING CORRECT PRONOUN CASES

Many pronouns change their form according to the grammatical slot they fill in a sentence.

Case Name	Used for These Slots	Personal Pronouns	Relative Pronouns
subjective	subject, subject complement	I, we, he, she, they	who, whoever
objective	direct object, indirect object, object of preposition, subject of infinitive	me, us, him, her, them	whom, whomever
possessive	adjective showing possession	my, our, his, her, their	whose

The case of a pronoun is determined by its slot in the sentence.

She and *I* are good friends. *[subjects]*

Paul likes *her* and *me*.   *[direct objects]*

Give *her* and *me* the present.   *[indirect objects]*

Paul did it for *her* and *me*.   *[objects of preposition]*

The winners were *she* and *I*.   *[subject complements]*

Patricia asked *her* and *me* to write the final report.   *[subjects of infinitive]*

Although writers generally handle pronoun cases accurately, the following instances give special trouble.

Cases of Relative Pronouns

In relative or noun clauses, the pronouns *who, whom, whoever,* or *whomever* take their case from their function in their own clause, not from the function of that clause in the rest of the sentence.

Faulty   Give the prize to *whomever* says the secret word.

Although *whomever* at first seems to be the object of the preposition *to,* it is actually the subject of the verb *says* and should be in the subjective case. The object of the preposition *to* is actually the whole noun clause.

Revised   Give the prize to *whoever* says the secret word.

Faulty   I voted against Ralph Winkley, *who* big business especially supports.

In this case the relative pronoun fills a direct object slot in its own clause. Compare: Big business especially supports *him*. The writer should choose *whom*.

Revised   I voted against Ralph Winkley, *whom* big business especially supports.

Intervening Parenthetical Clauses

When choosing the case of relative pronouns, don't let such words as *I think* or *he supposes* influence your choice. These are parenthetical expressions that can be discarded from the sentence.

Faulty   I voted for Marion Fudge, *whom* I think is the most honest candidate.

Here the relative pronoun is the subject of the verb *is,* not the direct object of *I think,* and hence it should be subjective.

Revised   I voted for Marion Fudge, *who* I think is the most honest candidate.

Pronouns as Parts of Compound Constructions

Case errors are especially frequent in compound constructions. Many people who were reprimanded as children for saying "Him and me are going outside" overcorrect by using "he and I" even when "him and me" is warranted. Pronouns that fill object slots (or subjects of infinitives) must be in the objective case. You can usually avoid case errors in compound constructions by choosing the same case you would select if you were using the pronoun alone.

Faulty   Martha appointed Ralph and *I* to the committee.

The pronoun is a direct object and should be in the objective case. Compare: Martha appointed *me* to the committee.

Revised   Martha appointed Ralph and *me* to the committee.

Note that subjects of infinitives are in the objective case.

Faulty   The dean of students wants *she* and *I* to represent the student council at the convention.

Compare: The dean of students wants *me* to represent the student council. . . ."

Revised   The dean of students wants *her* and *me* to represent the student council at the convention.

Be especially careful with pronouns in front of occasional infinitives that omit the *to*.

Faulty   Let's you and *I* go to the show this evening.

The pronoun is the subject of the infinitive *(to) go* and should be in the objective case. Compare: Let *me* go to the show.

Revised   Let's you and *me* go to the show this evening.

Pronouns in Appositive Constructions

In appositive constructions, in which the pronoun is followed by an identifying noun, use the pronoun case that would be correct if the noun were not there:

The principal told *us* boys to go home.

Compare: The principal told us to go home.

We boys hid around the corner until the principal went back to her office.

Compare: We hid around the corner.

Pronouns as Parts of Implied Clauses

When a pronoun occurs after *than* introducing an implied clause, choose the pronoun's case according to the pronoun's use in the implied clause. Both of the following sentences are correct, but their meanings are different.

I like Paul better than he.

This sentence means "I like Paul better than he likes Paul."

I like Paul better than him.

This sentence means "I like Paul better than I like him."

Pronouns Preceding Gerunds or Participles

Use the possessive case before gerunds (*-ing* verbals used as nouns) and the subjective or objective case before present participles (*-ing* verbals used as adjectives).

I saw *him* running away from the police.

In this sentence, *running* is a participle modifying the direct object *him*.

I think *his* running away from the police was his biggest mistake.

Here *running* is a gerund, the subject of *was*.

EXERCISE

In the following sentences, underline the correct pronoun from the choices given in parentheses.

1. (We/Us) girls want to bike to the store.
2. Natalie, (who/whom) received the scholarship, will study microbiology.
3. If you and (he/him) can visit Tim and (I/me) next month, we will tour the national park.
4. Jessica and Lin-Ju will bring (her/their) skis.
5. (His/Him) playing loud music annoyed the neighbors.
6. He is the racer (who/whom) I believe fell at the finish line.
7. This vacation was necessary for you and (I/me).
8. A burglar stole our computer, but no one saw (his/him) entering the house.
9. Stephen or Tom will do (his/her/their) practicing before school.
10. Emily and Amy do (his/her/their) practicing faithfully every day.

◼ CHOOSING CORRECT VERB FORMS

VF

As we explained in Handbook 2 (pp. 654–56), English verbs change structure to form different tenses. *Regular* verbs add *ed* to the base form to create the past and past participle; *irregular* verbs form the past and past participle through internal spelling changes.

Verb-form errors occur when the writer uses a nonstandard form, often with irregular verbs.

Faulty   I *seen* Bill in the back room at 8:00.

The past form of *to see* is *saw*.

Revised   I *saw* Bill in the back room at 8:00.

Another verb-form error arises when the preposition *of* is substituted for the auxiliary verb *have*. In spoken English, *have* often sounds like *of*, especially in contractions: "I should've finished my paper earlier." In written English, be sure not to confuse the two words.

Faulty   I should *of* finished my paper earlier.
Revised   I should *have* finished my paper earlier.

◪ CHOOSING CORRECT ADJECTIVE AND ADVERB FORMS

Although adjectives and adverbs are both modifiers, they cannot be used interchangeably because adjectives modify nouns or pronouns whereas adverbs modify verbs, adjectives, other adverbs, and sometimes whole phrases, clauses, or sentences. (See p. 658 for a fuller discussion of adjectives and adverbs.)

Problems with adjectives and adverbs can occur in the following cases.

Confusion of Adjective and Adverb Forms

Do not use adjectives when adverbs are warranted.

Faulty   I did *real good* on that test.

The adverb form is *well*, not *good*. Similarly, *real* is an adjective, which cannot modify an adverb.

Revised   I did *really well* on that test.

Be careful to use the appropriate modifier after verbs that can be either linking verbs or action verbs. Linking verbs (such as *is, are,* and *seem*) take subject complements (pp. 654–57), which are either nouns or adjectives. Certain linking verbs, especially the sense verbs *feel, look, taste, smell,* and *sound,* as well as a few others, can also be action verbs. After such verbs choose an adjective if the word modifies the subject and an adverb if it modifies the verb.

The captain looked *angry.*

Here *angry* is an adjective modifying *captain.* Compare: The angry captain . . .

The captain looked *angrily* at the crew.

Here, *angrily* is an adverb telling how the captain did the looking.

Problems with Comparative and Superlative Forms

Short adjectives (with one syllable or two syllables ending in *-y* or *-le*) form their comparative and superlative degrees by adding *-er* and *-est* to the simple form. Other adjectives and most adverbs generally use *more* (*less*) for the comparative and *most* (*least*) for the superlative. A few modifiers are irregular.

Choosing Comparatives Versus Superlatives

Use the comparative degree for two persons or things and the superlative for three or more.

Of the two players, Mary is the *better.*

Of the whole team, Mary is the *best.*

Misuse of Comparatives with Absolute Adjectives

Do not use comparative and superlative degrees with absolute adjectives, such as *unique* or *impossible.*

Faulty   Her dress was the *most unique* one I had ever seen.

Unique already means "one of a kind" and can't be further modified.

Revised   Her dress was *unique.*

      or

      Her dress was the *most unusual* one I had ever seen.

Double Comparatives

Avoid double comparatives or superlatives.

Faulty   Raphael is *more smarter* than George.
Revised   Raphael is *smarter* than George.

Illogical Comparisons

Avoid making illogical comparisons between items that are not actually comparable. Sometimes illogical comparisons result from a missing word such as *other.*

Faulty   Our Volvo is better than any car on the road.

This sentence inadvertently implies that this Volvo isn't on the road.

Revised   Our Volvo is better than any *other* car on the road.

At other times an illogical comparison arises when the grammar of the sentence mixes apples and oranges.

Faulty   Handwritten papers are harder to read than typing.

Papers cannot be compared with typing.

Revised   Handwritten papers are harder to read than typed papers.

Ambiguous Adverbs

Problems rarely occur with adverbs except when they are used ambiguously to modify whole sentences. Normally an adverb modifies a single word or a group of words in a sentence. Sometimes, however, writers use an adverb to modify an entire sentence. Sometimes such sentences are ambiguous.

Ambiguous   Unluckily, the wide receiver dropped the pass.

Who has the bad luck here? The wide receiver? Or the speaker of the sentence who hopes her team will win? The ambiguity can be eliminated by clarifying what *unluckily* modifies.

Revised   The wide receiver unluckily dropped the pass.

      or

      Unluckily for us, the wide receiver dropped the pass.

Editing for Style

In Handbook 4 we focused on sentence-level errors. In this chapter we consider stylistic concerns, with the goal of making your prose more lively, interesting, and clear. The problems we address in this chapter are not errors. Rather, they are more like noise or interference in a radio broadcast; they annoy your reader and can sometimes distort your message.

This chapter will teach you to do the following:

- Prune your prose to cut out deadwood
- Enliven your prose by eliminating nominalizations, noun pileups, pretentious diction, and clichés and by varying sentence structure and using specific details
- Avoid broad or unclear pronoun references
- Put old information before new
- Make informed decisions about the use of the active or passive voice
- Use inclusive language

WDY

▨ PRUNING YOUR PROSE

In most rhetorical contexts, conciseness is a virtue. Readers like efficient prose that makes its point without padding. Avoiding wordiness does not mean eliminating details or cutting into the muscle of an essay; it means eliminating inefficient words and bulky phrases that take up space without adding meaning.

Cutting Out Deadwood

Good writers typically write first drafts that are much longer than their final versions. Eliminating unneeded words and phrases is an essential part of revision.

Wordy   At the present time it can be considered a truism that families with incomes neither too far above nor too far below the median income can send their children to expensive colleges with no more out-of-pocket charges and expenses than it would cost to send these same children to colleges whose tuition and related expenses are much lower.

Revised   The truth is that for average-income families an expensive college costs no more than a cheap one.

When eliminating deadwood, watch out for common wordy phrases such as the following:

at the present time (use *now*)

because of the fact that (use *because*)

are of the opinion that (use *believe*)

have the ability to (use *can*)

in spite of the fact that (use *although*)

You can easily delete these expressions—and dozens more like them—without sacrificing meaning.

Combining Sentences

Another cause of wordiness is the inefficient use of short, choppy sentences. Try to recast a choppy passage by combining sentences, thus saving words while creating more complex and graceful structures.

Wordy   Jim Maxwell took two years to build his solar building. Building his solar building included nearly one year of planning. His solar building was intended mainly as a grain drier. But it also provided a warm winter shop. Additionally he had the advantage of a machinery shed. This shed kept his machinery dry. His new solar building would pay dividends for years to come.

Revised   It took two years to build, including nearly one year of planning, but when Jim Maxwell finished his solar building, he had a grain drier, a warm winter shop, and a dry machinery shed that would pay dividends for years to come.

EXERCISE

On a separate sheet of paper, improve the style of the following sentences by cutting out deadwood, recasting the words, or combining elements to eliminate wordiness.

1. It appears to me that he seems to be an unusually quiet person but also that he is the kind of person who really cares a lot about other people.
2. If a person is the kind of person who hurries rapidly when that person tries to do things, then that person is apt to find that he or she has wasted a lot of valuable time and material by trying to do the events too rapidly.
3. Molly was interested in finding out the answer to a question that she had recently been puzzling about. The question was this: What is the

important and essential difference between a disease that most people would call "mental illness" and a disease that is simply a disease of the brain?

4. It is unfortunate that the mayor acted in this manner. The mayor settled the issue. But before he settled the issue he made a mistake. He fostered a public debate that was very bitter. The debate pitted some of his subordinates against each other (and these were key subordinates, too). It also caused many other people to feel inflamed passions and fears as a result of the way the mayor handled the whole affair.

LANG/ STYLE

▨ ENLIVENING YOUR PROSE

You can often revise your prose to make the tone livelier and more interesting.

Avoiding Nominalizations

Lively writers express actions with verbs. Lifeless writers often *nominalize* their sentences by converting actions into nouns (for example, by writing, "arrive at a conclusion" rather than "conclude"). A highly nominalized style characterizes much bureaucratic and administrative prose, making it sound stilted, impersonal, and dead.

Nominalized	For the production of effective writing, the expression of an action through the use of a verb is the method most highly preferred.
Revised	Effective writers express actions with verbs.

A nominalized sentence is not only long and dull, but also confusing. Nominalized sentences often include two additional problems: overuse of the verb *to be* and a pileup of prepositional phrases. To revise a nominalized sentence, ask yourself who is doing what; then make the doer of the action the subject and make the action a verb.

Nominalized	Jim's receiving of this low grade was the result of his reading of the material too quickly.
Revised	Jim received a low grade because he read the material too quickly.

By putting *Jim* in the subject slot, the writer eliminates the weak verb *was* as well as three prepositional phrases.

EXERCISE

On a separate sheet of paper, revise the following sentences to eliminate nominalizations.

1. The person who received the rewards is the person who was the victor.

2. The killing of a goose from which the laying of golden eggs is frequent is usually seen to be a mistake.
3. The socialization of children in the avoidance of risky behaviors often results in their timidity as adults.
4. Juanita came to the realization that her preference of major was changing from history to mathematics.
5. The teacher's examination of the student's locker was caused by the teacher's suspicion of the possibility of the hiding of drugs by the student.

Avoiding Noun Pileups

Noun pileups result from the tendency, again common in bureaucratic prose, to use nouns as adjectives.

Noun Pileup	Consideration of an applicant physical disability access plan by the student services reform committee will occur forthwith.
Revised	The committee to reform student services will soon consider a plan for improving access to buildings for physically disabled applicants.

Avoiding Pretentious Language

Unless you are intentionally imitating a longwinded style, strive for language that sounds natural and clear rather than pretentious (or developed through overuse of a thesaurus).

Stilted	The tyro in the field of artistic endeavors commenced to ascertain the suitability of different constituencies of pigment.
Revised	The student artist began wondering which color paint would be most suitable.

Avoiding Clichés, Jargon, and Slang

Clichés are tired, frequently repeated phrases, such as "last but not least," "easier said than done," or "a chill ran up my spine." Replace them with fresh language.

Deciding when to avoid jargon and slang is more problematic because their use may be appropriate depending on your audience, purpose, and genre. Technical jargon is acceptable if you are writing for an audience that understands it within a genre that uses it; slang is also fine if it suits your purpose, audience, and genre. In general, you should avoid jargon that may not be understood by your audience and you should avoid slang in most formal contexts.

Inappropriate Jargon for a Teacher's Letter to Parents

	Your child displays maladaptive socialization behaviors.
Revised	Your child is sometimes rude to classmates.

Inappropriate Slang for a College Essay

	The gods are all bent out of shape because Oedipus killed his dad.
Revised	The gods are angry because Oedipus killed his father.

Creating Sentence Variety

Prose can feel wooden or choppy if each sentence has the same construction and length. Skilled writers combine sentences in various ways for emphasis and grace.

Monotonous   Martin watched carefully for loose rocks. He picked his way along the edge of the cliff. Martin didn't hear the rattles at first. Then he suddenly froze with fear when he heard them. A timber rattler was about two feet away. It was coiled like a garden hose. The rattler's neck was arched. Its fangs looked like twin needles of death.

In this passage, each sentence starts with the subject, and all the sentences are about the same length.

Revised   Watching carefully for loose rocks as he picked his way along the edge of the cliff, Martin suddenly froze with fear. At first he didn't hear the rattles. Then he heard them for sure. About two feet away, coiled like a garden hose, was a timber rattler, its neck arched, its fangs looking like twin needles of death.

Here the longest sentence is twenty-four words and the shortest is six words. The two short sentences emphasize dramatically important moments.

Using Specific Details

Except in philosophical or theoretical writing, which uses abstract language precisely, abstract prose can be dull. You can enliven abstract prose by replacing abstract terms with concrete words or by adding specific, colorful details for support.

Abstract   The poor are often stereotyped as beggars, drunks, or people with uncared-for children. We think of them as being without spirit or hope.

Revised   We often stereotype poor people as panhandlers demanding our spare change, as scruffy drunks holding a bottle in a paper bag, or as barefoot children with matted hair, filthy clothes, and tears streaking down their dirty faces as they tug on their mother's arm. We picture the poor as spiritless or hopeless, isolated in their own world, eyes glazed with despair.

Note that in this example, adding concrete language makes the passage *longer*, whereas pruning deadwood makes a passage shorter. What is the difference between deadwood and detail?

◪ AVOIDING BROAD OR UNCLEAR PRONOUN REFERENCE

Each time you use a pronoun, make sure that the noun to which it refers, its *antecedent*, is clearly apparent. Unclear use of pronouns can confuse readers.

Avoiding Broad Reference

A broad reference occurs whenever a pronoun—usually *this, that,* or *it*—stands for an idea or a whole group of words rather than for a single noun. Although this usage is sometimes acceptable, it is often ambiguous or vague. (See p. 470 for further discussion of *this* as a pronoun.)

Broad   Harold Krebs in Hemingway's "Soldier's Home" rebels against his
Reference   parents. He does *this* by refusing to accept their values, and *this* is why his parents are so upset by *it.*

In this sentence the italicized pronouns refer not to specific nouns but to ideas, which shift with each pronoun, confusing the reader.

Revised   Harold Krebs in Hemingway's "Soldier's Home" rebels against his parents by refusing to accept their way of life. His rejection of their values explains why his parents are so upset by his later actions.

Do not make broad references with the pronoun *which*, which must have a single noun for its antecedent.

Faulty   He drinks a lot, which is something I disapprove of.
Revised   I disapprove of his heavy drinking.

In the original sentence, *which* has no noun antecedent.

Avoiding Unclear Antecedents

To avoid confusing your readers, make sure that every pronoun has a clear antecedent. Avoid using pronouns that seem to stand for two different antecedents.

Unclear   Jim explained to his son the reasons he couldn't go to the meeting.
Antecedent
Revised   Jim explained the reasons why his son couldn't go to the meeting.

In the original sentence, *he* could stand for either *Jim* or *son,* making it unclear whether Jim or his son couldn't go to the meeting.

▇ PUTTING OLD INFORMATION BEFORE NEW INFORMATION

O/N

In closed-form prose, clear writers begin sentences with old information—a key word or concept from the previous sentence, from the paragraph's topic sentence, or from the essay's thesis, purpose, or thesis statement—to keep their readers on track. Revise the structure of sentences that violate this rule. (Chapter 18, pp. 466–72, describes this rule in detail as one of the chief principles of clarity in closed-form prose.)

| New Information Before Old | When the experts disagree, therefore, what advice can be given? Ferreting out the facts that all sides agree on is a first step that we can take. |
| Revised | What advice can we give, therefore, when the experts disagree? First, we try to ferret out the facts that all sides agree on. |

▨ DECIDING BETWEEN ACTIVE AND PASSIVE VOICE

You must choose active or passive voice whenever you use a transitive verb—an action verb that has a receiver of the action as well as a doer (see p. 657). The active voice makes the doer of the action the subject and the receiver of the action the direct object; the passive voice makes the receiver of the action the subject and either omits the doer or makes the doer the object of the preposition *by.*

| Active Voice | Our cat just caught a mouse. |
| Passive Voice | A mouse was just caught by our cat. |

Strength of the Active Voice

Experienced writers usually prefer the active voice because it is stronger and more economical. The passive voice requires *to be* helping verbs and prepositional phrases for the doer of the action.

| Weak | The cake and ice cream were eaten, and then games were played. |
| Revised | The children ate the cake and ice cream and then played games. |

However, the passive voice isn't always wrong. The choice of voice depends on the context of your sentence.

When to Use the Passive Voice

Writers sometimes choose the passive voice to create appropriate emphasis or to evade responsibility.

Passive Voice When Doer Is Unimportant

The passive voice is appropriate whenever the receiver of the action is more important than the doer. It is often used in scientific writing, which tends to emphasize the material acted on rather than the doer of the action.

The distillate is then removed from the liquid.

Passive Voice to Place Old Information Before New

The passive voice is also appropriate when the old information in a sentence is the receiver of the action rather than the doer.

Graphs are essential tools for economic analysis. They *are* commonly *used* by economists to display both concrete economic data and abstract economic concepts.

In the second sentence, the passive voice allows the writer to begin with old information. The pronoun *they* refers to *graphs* in the previous sentence.

(See pp. 471–72 for a more detailed discussion of this use of the passive voice.)

Passive Voice to Evade Responsibility

Sometimes writers use the passive voice intentionally to avoid naming a responsible party. This practice is ethically questionable. Avoid it when you can.

Evasive	The decision has been made to raise the dues.
Forthright	The president and the treasurer have decided to raise the dues.

EXERCISE

On a separate sheet of paper, convert the transitive passive sentences to transitive active, and convert the transitive active sentences to transitive passive. Leave the intransitive sentences unchanged. In converting some transitive passive sentences to transitive active, you may have to add an actor or agent. For each sentence, explain in which rhetorical situations the active-voice version would be better and in which the passive would be better.

1. The wrong carpets were installed by the carpet layers while the owners were away.
2. Smoke rose in thick billows above the burning house.
3. Beth ladled hot liquid blackberry jelly into sterilized jars.
4. The little girl in the green sunsuit slowly covered her sleeping father with piles of sand.
5. Some of the most important scientific principles have been discovered accidentally.
6. The motor was probably ruined by the turbine bearing's being rusted out.

▨ USING INCLUSIVE LANGUAGE   BIAS?

For much of the history of the English language, grammarians accepted the use of masculine pronouns ("Everyone should bring *his* own lunch") and the use of *man* ("Peace and good will to *men* everywhere") as generic references for both men and women. Many contemporary writers believe that these usages reflect pro-male bias. Many writers are also now aware of other ways in which language subtly reflects attitudes toward gender, culture, and ethnicity. In this section, we offer suggestions that will help you construct sentences free of biased language.

Avoiding Sexist Labels and Stereotypes

Avoid language that labels or stereotypes women. Referring to women as "the weaker sex," "the ladies," "the girls," or "the distaff side" implies that women are not equal to men. Similarly, it is inappropriate to identify women as wives or mothers in a context where their professional or work status is more relevant or to refer to a woman's appearance unless the context demands it. Let the same considerations guide you whether you are describing a man or a woman.

> **Sexist**   Janet Peterson, stunning in her new, blue-sequined evening gown, gave the keynote address at the annual mayors' conference.

> Would you say, "Robert Peterson, stunning in his new tuxedo, ruffled shirtfront, and cumberbund, gave the keynote address at the annual mayors' conference"?

> **Revised**   Janet Peterson, newly elected mayor of the state's third largest city, gave the keynote address at the annual mayors' conference.

Avoiding Use of Masculine Pronouns to Refer to Both Sexes

Whenever possible, revise sentences to avoid using the masculine pronouns *he, him, his,* and *himself* to refer to people of both sexes. Often you can use plural pronouns (*they, them, their,* and *themselves*), which do not indicate gender.

> **Problematic**   If a person wants to bring his text to the exam, he may.
> **Revised**   If persons want to bring their texts to the exam, they may.

In informal writing, you can also use *you* and *your* to avoid sexist language; in formal prose you can use *one* and *one's,* although this usage sometimes sounds stilted.

> **Revised**   If you want to bring your texts to the exam, you may.
> **Revised**   If one wants to bring one's text to the exam, one may.

Another strategy is to alternate between masculine and feminine forms.

> At the revising stage, the writer should go over *his* draft carefully, making sure that the central idea of each paragraph is clear. At the editing stage a writer's focus shifts. Now *she* should check for sentence-level problems, paying particular attention to spelling, punctuation, and problems of usage.

(*Note:* This practice, although common in some academic journals, is not yet widely accepted in the popular media.)

Avoid bureaucratic constructions, such as *him/her* or *s/he,* which are cumbersome and inelegant. Occasional use of the combined forms *he or she* or *him or her* is acceptable, but overuse of this construction is tiresome.

Avoiding Inappropriate Use of the Suffix *-man*

Use of *-man* as a suffix in such words as *repairman, mailman, policeman,* or *mankind* seems to ignore the presence of women in the workforce and in the human race. The suffix *-person* may be an acceptable substitute; *chairperson* and *salesperson* are becoming increasingly common in formal usage. However, *weatherperson* still sounds odd, as does "Joan is a new *freshperson* at state college." Look for alternative expressions.

Avoid	Prefer
chairman	chairperson
coed	student
congressman	representative, member of congress
forefathers	ancestors
mailman	mail carrier
man (generic)	person, people, humans, human beings
wives, husbands	spouses
manmade	synthetic
policeman	police officer
salesman	sales representative, salesclerk
waiter, waitress	waitperson, server
newsman	reporter, journalist
fireman	firefighter
weatherman	weather announcer, meteorologist
sportsman	sports enthusiast, athlete
stewardess	flight attendant

Avoiding Language Biased Against Ethnic or Other Minorities

Avoid language that reflects stereotypes against ethnic or other minorities. Language referring to minorities evolves rapidly. In the 1980s *black* and *Afro-American* were preferred terms, but in the 1990s these have largely given way to *African American.* Similarly, the terms *Latino* and *Latina* are replacing *Hispanic.* Homosexual people now prefer the terms *gay* and *lesbian* and in some contexts are reviving the word *queer.* Today the term *people of color* is in favor, but the term *colored person* is an intense insult.

As a writer, you need to be sensitive to the subtle ways in which language can make people feel included and welcomed or excluded and insulted. Nowhere is the evolving and charged nature of language more evident than in the connotations of words referring to cultural minorities.

Editing for Punctuation and Mechanics

This chapter provides a handy compendium of rules and guidelines for using punctuation marks, underlining (italics), and capital letters. It also includes a section on manuscript form. The following main topics are covered:

- Periods, question marks, and exclamation points
- Commas
- Semicolons
- Colons, dashes, and parentheses
- Apostrophes
- Quotation marks
- Underlining (italics)
- Brackets, slashes, and ellipses
- Capital letters
- Numbers
- Abbreviations
- Manuscript form

PERIODS, QUESTION MARKS, AND EXCLAMATION POINTS

Periods, question marks, and exclamation points, sometimes called *terminal punctuation* or *end marks,* signal the end of a sentence. These marks generally raise few problems for writers except in the case of sentence fragments (when an end mark follows a nonsentence), comma splices (when a comma is substituted for an end mark), and run-ons (when two sentences are fused together without an end mark). For a full discussion of sentence boundaries, including advice for avoiding fragments, comma splices, and run-ons, see Handbook 3.

A few other situations that sometimes pose problems for writers are discussed next.

Courtesy Questions

Courtesy questions—mild commands phrased politely as questions—normally end with a period.

Would you please return the form in the enclosed envelope.

The absence of a question mark makes this a mild command, not a real question.

Indirect Questions

Although direct questions require a question mark, indirect questions end with a period.

Direct Question   He asked me, "Where are you going?"

Indirect Question   He asked me where I was going.

Placement of Question Marks with Quotations

When quotation marks and a question mark appear together, the question mark goes inside the quotation marks if only the quotation is a question and outside if the whole sentence is a question.

Quotation Is Question

The professor asked, "Can you solve the fox and chicken puzzle?"

Entire Sentence Is Question

Did you hear the professor talk about the "fox and chicken puzzle"?

Note: When the question mark goes inside the quotation marks, do not follow the question mark with a comma or period.

Faulty   "Can we go with you?," she asked. She asked, "Can we go with you?,"

Revised   "Can we go with you?" she asked. She asked, "Can we go with you?"

Exclamation Points

An exclamation point is used after a sentence or word group to express strong emotion. Exclamation points are used primarily in dialogue to indicate shouting or an especially strong feeling. Avoid using exclamation points in most other instances—especially academic prose—because they rarely have the effect on a reader that the writer intends. Expressing emotion through word choice, sentence structure, and tone is more effective. When an exclamation mark goes inside a quotation, do not follow the exclamation mark with a comma or period.

COMMAS

The comma is the most frequently used mark of internal punctuation. A comma mistakenly used as an end mark creates a comma splice (see Handbook 3, pp. 669–72). The main rules for use of commas to mark the boundaries of phrases, clauses, and sentences are covered in depth in Handbook 3. These rules are reviewed in this section, along with additional guidelines.

Using Commas

Using Commas with Coordinating Conjunctions

Use a comma and a coordinating conjunction (*and, or, nor, for, but, yet,* and *so*) to join two independent clauses.

> I released the dog's leash, and the dog trotted off across the field.

If the main clauses are very short, it is acceptable to omit the comma before the coordinating conjunction, but it is never acceptable to omit the coordinating conjunction; doing so will create a comma splice.

Comma Splice	We crossed the meadow, then we headed toward the mountain.
Revised	We crossed the meadow, and then we headed toward the mountain.

Comma after Introductory Adverb Clauses and Long Introductory Phrases

Use a comma to set off introductory adverb clauses and long introductory phrases from the rest of the sentence.

Introductory Adverb Clause	When I get home from work, I always fix myself a big sardine sandwich.
Introductory Phrase	Having lost my balance, I began waving my arms frantically.

Note: Initial gerund phrases or infinitive phrases used as sentence subjects must not be set off because they are part of the sentence core.

Faulty	To know him, is to love him. Playing her guitar every evening, is Sally's way of relaxing.

These introductory phrases serve as the subject of their sentences and should not be set off.

Revised	To know him is to love him. Playing her guitar every evening is Sally's way of relaxing.

Comma After Introductory Transitional Words and Expressions

Set off most introductory transitional words and phrases, such as *on the other hand, in sum, however, moreover,* and *for example,* with a comma. (See p. 673 for a list of these expressions.)

> On the other hand, bicycle racing involves an astonishing amount of strategy.

Writers often do not use a comma to set off *thus* and *therefore* and some other transitional expressions that do not noticeably interrupt the flow of the sentence. In such cases let your voice be your guide. If you pause noticeably after the transitional expression, set it off with a comma.

Commas to Set Off Absolute Phrases

An absolute phrase comprises a noun followed by a participle or participial phrase. These phrases are *absolute* because they are complete in themselves; they modify the entire sentence rather than an individual word within the sentence (see p. 661). Absolute phrases are always set off with commas.

His hand wrapped in a blanket, Harvey hobbled toward the ambulance.

The bear reared on its hind legs, *its teeth looking razor sharp in the glaring sun.*

Comma Before Concluding Participial Phrases

Use commas to set off participial phrases at the end of a sentence if they modify the subject.

The doctor rushed quickly toward the accident victim, fumbling to open his black bag.

In this example, it is the doctor who fumbles to open his bag. The comma indicates that *fumbling* modifies *doctor* (the sentence subject) and not *victim* (the noun immediately preceding the participle).

Do not use a comma to set off a participial phrase at the end of the sentence if it modifies the immediately preceding noun.

The doctor rushed quickly toward the accident victim lying face forward on the soft shoulder of the road.

Here the participial phrase modifies the preceding noun, *victim,* instead of the sentence subject. It is not set off with commas.

Commas to Avoid Confusion

Use commas to separate sentence elements if failure to separate them would create confusion.

Confusing	Every time John ate his dog wanted to be fed too.
Revised	Every time John ate, his dog wanted to be fed too.

Commas to Set Off Nonrestrictive Clauses and Phrases

Adjective modifiers following a noun are either *restrictive* or *nonrestrictive,* depending on whether they are needed to identify the noun they modify. Use commas to set off nonrestrictive clauses and phrases.

Restrictive and Nonrestrictive Clauses.   An adjective clause is *nonrestrictive* if it is not needed to identify the noun it modifies. In such cases, set off the clause or phrase with commas.

Nonrestrictive Clause   My father dislikes Bill Jones, who rides a noisy motorcycle.

In this case, you know whom father dislikes: Bill Jones. The fact that Bill rides a noisy motorcycle is additional information about him.

If the modifying clause is needed to identify the noun it is modifying, then it is *restrictive* and is not set off with commas.

Restrictive Clause   My father dislikes people who ride noisy motorcycles.

Here the meaning is "My father doesn't dislike all people, just those people who ride noisy motorcycles." The adjective clause restricts the meaning of *people*; that is, it narrows down the class "people" to the subclass of "people who ride motorcycles." Because the phrase is needed to identify which people father dislikes, it is a restrictive clause used *without* commas.

To help you remember this rule, think of this saying: Extra information, extra commas; necessary information, no commas.

Nonrestrictive Clause   My grandmother, who graduated from college when she was eighty-two years old, deserves a special award.

You know who deserves a special award: my grandmother. The adjective clause provides extra information, so the sentence needs extra commas.

Restrictive Clause   Any woman who graduates from college at age eighty-two deserves a special award.

Here *who graduates from college* is needed information. Otherwise the sentence would mean that "any woman" deserves a special award, rather than only those women who graduate from college at age eighty-two. This sentence follows the rule "needed information, no commas."

Restrictive and Nonrestrictive Phrases.   The same extra information/needed information rule holds for adjective phrases.

Restrictive Phrase   The man wearing the double-breasted suit is an accountant.

Here the phrase *wearing a double-breasted suit* identifies which man is an accountant. The sentence implies that there are two or more men. (Which man is the accountant? The one wearing the double-breasted suit.) Because the phrase is needed to identify which man is meant, it is not set off with commas.

Nonrestrictive Phrase   Elvis Dweezle, wearing a double-breasted suit, looked at himself briefly in the mirror before knocking on his boss's door.

Here the phrase *wearing a double-breasted suit* merely adds extra information about the already identified Elvis Dweezle.

Commas to Set Off Nonrestrictive Appositives

An *appositive* is a noun or noun phrase that immediately follows another noun, renaming it or otherwise referring to it. Appositives also follow the extra information/needed information rule. An appositive is restrictive (needed information) if it serves to identify the preceding noun; it is nonrestrictive (extra information) if it simply contributes additional information to an already identified noun. As with nonrestrictive adjective clauses and phrases, set off nonrestrictive appositives with commas.

Nonrestrictive Appositive	Angela, a good friend of mine, has just been promoted to chief accountant.

In this example you know who has just been promoted: Angela. The appositive *a good friend of mine* adds extra information about Angela.

Restrictive Appositive	My friend Angela offered to do my income taxes for me.

Here the appositive *Angela* is needed to identify which friend offered to do the taxes. No commas are used.

Commas to Separate Items in a Series

Use commas to separate items in a series of three or more words, phrases, or clauses. The first comma leads readers to anticipate a list, with the last two elements joined by *and* or *or.* Place commas after each item in the series except the last.

He especially likes golf, jogging, and swimming.

We went to the movies, had dinner downtown, and then went bowling.

(*Note:* Although British writers and some American writers omit the comma before the coordinating conjunction in a series, sentences are generally clearer if the comma is included.)

Confusing	I like three kinds of pizza: pepperoni, Canadian bacon and pineapple and Italian sausage.
Clearer	I like three kinds of pizza: pepperoni, Canadian bacon and pineapple, and Italian sausage.

In the first version, the reader initially thinks that the first *and* marks the end of the series when it simply joins one of the elements (*Canadian bacon and pineapple*). Placing a comma before the final *and* in the series clarifies the sentence.

Commas to Separate Coordinate Adjectives Preceding a Noun

Coordinate adjectives in series are separated by commas. Adjectives are coordinate if they can be separated by *and* or if they can be placed in a different order.

Coordinate Adjectives	A nearsighted, tall, thin, grumpy-looking man walked slowly down the street.

In this case you could say a "thin and grumpy-looking and nearsighted and tall man," thus separating the elements with *and* and placing them in a different order. These are coordinate adjectives separated with commas.

Noncoordinate Adjectives	Three aluminum-plated frying pans sat on the shelf.

These adjectives are not coordinate because you cannot say "frying and aluminum-plated and three pans." Hence these adjectives are not separated by commas.

Note: Do not place a comma after the last coordinate adjective in a series.

Faulty	A lightweight, sleekly designed, ten-speed, bicycle was my summer's dream.
Revised	A lightweight, sleekly designed, ten-speed bicycle was my summer's dream.

Commas to Set Off Parenthetical or Interrupting Elements

Use commas to set off parenthetical words, phrases, or clauses and other similar elements that interrupt the flow of the sentence. By reading your sentences aloud in a natural voice, you can generally identify parenthetical material that interrupts the flow of a sentence. Such material should be set off by pairs of commas. The following are common examples of interrupting material:

Contrasting Elements Introduced by *but, not,* or *although*

The man at the front desk, not the mechanic, was the one who quoted me the price.

Words of Direct Address, *yes* and *no,* and Mild Interjections

I tell you, Jim, your plan won't work.

Transition Words and Expressions

She will, however, demand more money.

Tag Phrases Citing Sources

This new car, according to the latest government reports, gets below-average mileage.

Attributive Tags Identifying Speakers

"To be a successful student," my adviser told me, "you have to enjoy learning."

Commas to Set Off Elements of Places, Addresses, and Dates

Use commas to set off each separate element in a date, place, or address.

He drove to Grand Forks, North Dakota, on July 5, 1971, in an old, blue Ford.

Do not place a comma in front of zip codes in addresses.

I live on 23 Elm Street, Seattle, WA 98115.

Omitting Commas

Many beginning writers tend to use too many commas rather than too few. Do not use a comma unless a specific rule calls for one. "When in doubt, leave commas out" is a good rule of thumb. Learn to recognize the following situations that do *not* require commas. These are sources of frequent error in student papers.

Do Not Use a Comma to Separate a Subject from Its Verb or a Verb from Its Complements

Faulty   The man in the apartment next to mine, swallowed a goldfish.

Here a comma mistakenly separates the subject from the verb.

Revised   The man in the apartment next to mine swallowed a goldfish.

Do Not Use a Single Comma Within a Sentence Core

Faulty   My brother, who recently won a pole-sitting contest swallowed a goldfish.

Here a comma occurs on one side of a nonrestrictive clause but not on the other side.

Revised	My brother, who recently won a pole-sitting contest, swallowed a goldfish.

Do Not Use a Comma Before *and* If It Joins Only Two Words or Phrases

Faulty	She pedaled uphill for twenty minutes, and won the race by several lengths.

The *and* joins two verbs rather than two main clauses.

Revised	She pedaled uphill for twenty minutes straight and won the race by several lengths.

Do Not Use a Comma After *such as*

Faulty	They forgot some key supplies such as, candles, matches, and trail mix.
Revised	They forgot some key supplies such as candles, matches, and trail mix.

EXERCISE

Insert commas where needed in the following sentences.

1. Whenever I go home to Bismarck North Dakota for Christmas vacation the dinner conversation turns to cross-country skiing.
2. On my last visit during dessert my dad who is an expert skier asked me if I wanted to try dogsled racing.
3. "I've wanted to try dogsledding for years" Dad said "but we've never had the equipment or the dogs. Now however my friend Jake Jackson the new agent for Smith Insurance has just bought a team and wants his friend to give it a try."
4. Rock shrimp unlike some other species have hard shells that make them difficult to peel.
5. Hiking or biking through southern Germany you will discover a rich mosaic of towns regional foods colors sounds and smells of the rural countryside and historic Black Forest region.
6. Instead of riding on busy boulevards you can pedal on a network of narrow paved roads built for farm vehicles or on graveled paths through lush green forests.
7. According to historian Daniel T. Rodgers a central question that divided workers and employers in the nineteenth and early twentieth centuries was how many hours a day the average worker should work.
8. Believing strongly in tradition the early factory owners thought their workers should follow the old sunrise to sunset work schedule of agricultural laborers.
9. This schedule which meant fourteen-hour workdays during the summer could also be maintained during the winter thanks to the invention of artificial light which owners rapidly installed in their factories.

> 10. Spurred on by their desire to create a shorter working day laborers began to organize into forerunners of today's labor unions and used their collective powers to strive for change.

◪ SEMICOLONS

A semicolon is stronger than a comma. It can be used to join two independent clauses into a single sentence or to separate the main items in a list that already contains commas.

Semicolon to Join Main Clauses

When a semicolon is used to join main clauses it signals a close relationship between the meanings in the two main clauses and creates a sentence with two balanced, equal parts.

> I asked the professor for an extension on my essay; she told me I was out of luck.

Semicolons are frequently used to connect main clauses when the second clause contains a conjunctive adverb or transitional phrase such as *however, therefore, nevertheless,* and *on the other hand.*

> The new airport won't be finished until June; therefore we'll have to land at Fitzsimmons Field.

Note: Joining two main clauses with only a comma creates a comma splice (see pp. 669–72).

Comma Splice	He spent all morning baking the pie, however, nobody seemed to appreciate his efforts.
Revised	He spent all morning baking the pie; however, nobody seemed to appreciate his efforts.

Semicolon in a Series Containing Commas

Use a semicolon to separate elements in a series when some of those elements already contain commas.

> On vacation we went to Laramie, Wyoming; Denver, Colorado; Salt Lake City, Utah; and Boise, Idaho.

> Since commas are used to separate the cities from the states, the semicolons are needed to separate the elements of the series.

EXERCISE

In the following sentences, insert semicolons and commas as needed. Some sentences may need no additional punctuation. Make sure that your marks of punctuation can be easily read.

1. The two men defended themselves before the justice of the peace in Bilford across the river a similar case was being tried with attorneys and a full jury.
2. She claimed that most teenage shoplifters are never caught moreover those that are caught are seldom punished.
3. I admit that I went to the party I did not however enjoy it.
4. I admit that I went to the party but I did not enjoy it.
5. Although I went to the party I did not enjoy it.
6. When the party ended our apartment was in chaos from one end of the living room to the other end of the bedroom a fine layer of confetti blanketed everything like snow.
7. Within twenty minutes of leaving the trail we saw an antelope two elk one of which had begun to shed the velvet on its antlers an assortment of squirrels gophers and chipmunks and most startling of all a large black bear with two cubs.
8. An effective education does not consist of passive rote learning rather it consists of active problem solving.
9. Failure to introduce and to use calculators and computers in school creates needless barriers for teachers and learners furthermore computer literacy is rapidly becoming a basic skill for the new millennium.
10. We watched the slides of their vacation for what seemed like an eternity—Toledo Ohio Columbus Missouri Topeka Kansas Omaha Nebraska and on and on across the continent.

◼ COLONS, DASHES, AND PARENTHESES

Colons

The most frequent uses of a colon are to introduce a list; to announce a word, clause, or phrase predicted in a preceding main clause; or to introduce a block quotation. Colons are generally preceded by main clauses and are not used as internal punctuation within a clause.

Colon to Introduce a List

Use a colon to introduce a list when the list follows a grammatically complete independent clause.

We can win in two ways: changing our defense or adding Jones to the offensive lineup.

Do not use a colon in the middle of a clause or after the words *such as, for example,* or *including.*

Faulty	The things you should bring to the party are: chips, salsa, and your own drinks.
Revised	The things you should bring to the party are chips, salsa, and your own drinks.
	or
	Please bring to the party the following: chips, salsa, and your own drinks.

In the first example the offending colon is removed. In the second, the structure preceding the colon has been expanded to a main clause by adding *the following,* which serves as the direct object of *bring.*

Faulty	We have many opportunities to improve our score, such as: retaking the exam, doing an extra credit project, or doing a longer paper.
Revised	We have many opportunities to improve our score, such as retaking the exam, doing an extra credit project, or doing a longer paper.

Colon to Introduce a Predicted Element Following an Independent Clause

Following an independent clause, use a colon to introduce a predicted element, which can be a word, a phrase, or a clause.

The professor agreed to something remarkable: grading contracts for all students.

The professor agreed to something remarkable: He allowed Jack to submit a late paper.

Note on capitalization: If what follows the colon is a main clause, you have the option of beginning the clause with a capital letter; if what follows the colon is not a complete sentence, use a lowercase letter.

Colon to Introduce Block Quotations or Quotations Receiving Special Emphasis

A colon is used to introduce a block quotation (see p. 715 for further explanation of block quotations). You can also use a colon to introduce a short quotation that you want to emphasize.

His father replied slowly, carefully, thoughtfully: "Buying the tractor now, when we are already too deeply in debt, is not a good idea."

A comma could also be used to introduce this quotation; a colon is more formal and emphatic.

Colon in Salutations, Time Notations, Titles, and Biblical Citations

Colons are sometimes used in letter salutations and within titles. They are also used in time expressions and biblical notations.

Salutation	Dear Sarah:
Time notation	4:30 a.m.
Titles	*Teaching Critical Thinking Skills: Theory and Practice*
Biblical citations	John 3:16

Dashes

P--

Think of the dash as a strong comma that gives special emphasis to the material being set off. (To make a dash using a typewriter or most word-processing programs, type two hyphens; leave no space before, after, or between the hyphens.)

> Sir Walter Raleigh brought the potato--as well as tobacco--to Queen Elizabeth I on his return from Virginia.

> In this example a pair of commas could replace the pair of dashes. The dashes emphasize the material between them by calling for a greater pause when reading.

Sometimes a dash is used to set off nouns placed for special emphasis at the beginning of a sentence. The nouns are then summarized by a pronoun following the dash.

> Joy, happiness, prosperity--all this is promised to investors in the new Whackoburger fast-food chain.

Parentheses

P( )

Parentheses are used to enclose nonessential, supplemental information or to enclose citations or list numbers.

Supplemental Information

The most common use of parentheses is to enclose supplemental information.

> He took one look at my computer (an old Kaypro from the early 1980s) and started to laugh.

Citations and Numbered Items in a List

Parentheses are also used to enclose citations in many documentation systems or to enclose numbers or letters identifying parts of a list. (See pp. 556–68 for an explanation of the MLA and APA documentation systems.)

> To graduate, a student must fill out three forms: (1) the transcript summary, (2) the request form, and (3) the adviser's sign-off sheet (*Junebug State Bulletin,* 32).

> Parentheses enclose the list numbers and the citation to the *Junebug State Bulletin,* page 32, where this information is found.

Punctuating Sentences that Include Parentheses

When you place a complete sentence within parentheses, the concluding end mark goes inside the parentheses. When you end a sentence with parenthetical elements, the end mark goes outside the parentheses.

When visiting England, we watched a lot of cricket (a British game somewhat similar to American baseball).

When visiting England, we watched a lot of cricket. (Cricket is a British game something like American baseball.)

P′   ◼ APOSTROPHES

The apostrophe is used mainly for showing possession, but it is also used to indicate missing letters in contractions and to form special plurals.

Apostrophe to Show Possession

Use the apostrophe to indicate possession of nouns and indefinite pronouns. Possessive constructions show both a possessor and a thing possessed: the thing possessed occurs last in the construction; the person or thing that possesses (the possessor) comes first and contains an apostrophe.

Possessor	Thing Possessed	Alternative Construction
Sally's	car	car belonging to Sally
men's	coats	coats for men
cats'	fur	fur of cats
three minutes'	work	work lasting three minutes

Because plurals and possessives both add an *s* sound to words, they are identical to the ear. To the eye, however, they are easily distinguished by use of the apostrophe in the possessive. Be sure that you don't confuse your reader by mixing possessives and plurals.

Faulty   Our neighbor's have two horse's and ten cat's on their grandfathers old farm.

Revised   Our neighbors have two horses and ten cats on their grandfather's old farm.

Neighbors, horses, and *cats* are plurals, not possessives; *grandfather's* is a possessive, not a plural.

Forming the Possessive

To make a noun possessive, you must first determine whether it is singular or plural. Add an apostrophe and an *s* ('s) to singular nouns and to plural nouns that do not end in *s*; add an apostrophe only (') to plural nouns that end in *s*.

The man's car   *[the car belonging to the man]*

The men's cars   *[the cars belonging to the men]*

The cats' food dish   *[the food dish belonging to the cats]*

The cat's food dish   *[the food dish belonging to the cat]*

To form the possessive of hyphenated words, compound words, and word groups, add an apostrophe and an *s* (*'s*) to the last word only.

> her mother-in-law's lawnmower

> the ladies-in-waiting's formal gowns

Do Not Use Apostrophes for Possessives of Personal Pronouns

Do not use apostrophes with the possessive forms of personal and relative pronouns (*yours, his, hers, ours, theirs, its, whose*). When an apostrophe is used with personal or relative pronouns, it indicates a contraction. Be especially careful to distinguish between *it's* ("it is") and *its* (possessive).

Possessive	Contraction
The dog chases its tail.	It's (it is) a funny dog.
Your tie is crooked.	You're (you are) a sloppy dresser.
Whose dog is that?	Who's (who is) at the door?

Apostrophes with Contractions

Use an apostrophe (') to indicate omitted letters in contractions.

> you're (you are)
> it's (it is)
> isn't (is not)
> spring of '34 (spring of 1934)

Note: Be sure to insert the apostrophe exactly where the missing letters would be.

Faulty	is'nt
Revised	isn't

Apostrophes to Form Plurals

Use an apostrophe and an *s* (*'s*) to form the plural of letters and words used as words. Underline (italicize) the letter or word but not the plural ending (see pp. 716–17 on underlining).

> On your test I can't distinguish between your <u>t</u>'s and your <u>E</u>'s. You also use too many *very*'s and *extremely*'s.

QUOTATION MARKS

Use quotation marks to enclose words, phrases, and sentences that are someone's spoken words or that you have copied from a source. Also use quotation marks to set off titles of short works and to indicate words used in a special sense. Quotation marks always occur in pairs, one marking the beginning and the other the ending of the quoted material. (See Chapter 22, pp. 552–68, for a detailed discussion of how to quote sources and avoid plagiarism.)

Punctuating the Start of a Quotation

When a quotation is introduced with an attributive tag (such as "my instructor says" or "Sharon Smith acknowledges"), the tag can be followed by a comma, a colon, or *that*. If you use a comma or a colon, begin the quotation with a capital letter. If you introduce a quotation with *that*, you do not capitalize the first letter of the quotation even if it is capitalized in the original. In this case, you do not precede the quotation with a comma.

My instructor always says, "You should never leave an essay exam early."

My instructor always says: "You should never leave an essay exam early."

My instructor always says that "you should never leave an essay exam early."

If you work a short quotation into the structure of your own sentence, use no punctuation other than quotation marks to introduce the quoted passage.

My instructor advises us never to "leave an essay exam early."

Placement of Attributive Tags

Attributive tags can be placed before, inside, or after the quotation. When an attributive tag is placed inside a quotation, the second half of the quotation is not capitalized unless it begins a new sentence.

Michael Karnok says, "To be a father is to know the meaning of failure."

"To be a father," says Michael Karnok, "is to know the meaning of failure."

"To be a father is to know the meaning of failure," says Michael Karnok.

Punctuating the End of a Quotation

Put commas and periods inside quotation marks.

He told me to "buzz off," and then he went about his business.

He told me to "buzz off." Then he went about his business.

Note that both the comma (first sentence) and the period (second sentence) go inside the quotation mark.

In documented papers that place citations inside parentheses at the end of the quotation, put the comma or period after the parenthetical citation.

According to Immunex Chief Executive Edward Fritzky, "Genetic Institute is doing very, very well" (Lim C5).

Note the order: quotation mark, parenthetical citation, final period.

Place colons and semicolons outside the ending quotation mark.

> He told me to "buzz off"; then he went about his business.

> My sexist husband wants his "privileges": Monday night football and no household chores.

> Note that the semicolon (first sentence) and the colon (second sentence) go outside the quotation mark.

Place question marks and exclamation marks inside quotation marks if they belong to the quotation; place them outside the ending quotation mark if they belong to the whole sentence. (See p. 701 for an example.)

Indirect Quotations

Use quotation marks for *direct* quotations—the actual words spoken by someone—but not for *indirect* quotations, which report what someone said without using the exact words.

Direct Quotation	"Do you want to go to the library?" Sally asked Harry.
Indirect Quotation	Sally asked Harry whether he wanted to go to the library.

Indented Block Method for Long Quotations

When quoting more than four typed lines (MLA style) or forty words (APA style), use the indented block method rather than quotation marks to indicate direct quotations. Double-space the quotation for both styles. For the MLA style, indent each line ten spaces from the left margin. Indent five spaces for the APA style. Do *not* put quotation marks around the blocked passage. (For an example, see p. 554.)

Single Quotation Marks

In American practice, use a single quotation mark, made with an apostrophe on most keyboards, to enclose a quotation within a quotation.

> Molly angrily told her discussion group, "Every time I ask my husband to help me with the ironing, he says that 'men don't iron clothes' and stalks out of the room in a huff."

> Inside Molly's directly quoted words is a direct quotation from Molly's husband: *men don't iron clothes.* The husband's words in this case are enclosed in single quotation marks.

With the block indentation method, use regular quotation marks to enclose a quotation within a quotation.

Quotation Marks for Titles of Short Works

Use quotation marks for titles of essays, short stories, short poems, songs, book chapters, and other sections that occur within books or periodicals.

I liked Spenser's sonnet "Most Glorious Lord of Lyfe" better than *The Faerie Queene.*

In this sentence, both the sonnet and *The Faerie Queene* are poems, but the former is in quotation marks because it is short, and the latter is underlined (italicized) because it is long.

Quotation Marks for Words Used in a Special Sense

Use quotation marks to call attention to a word or phrase used in a special sense. Often your intention is to show that you disagree with how someone else uses the word or phrase.

My husband refuses to do what he considers "woman's work."

In this example, the quotation marks indicate that the writer would not use the phrase *woman's work* and that she and her husband have different ideas about what the phrase means.

Although you may set off words used in a special sense with quotation marks, avoid using quotation marks for slang and clichés as an attempt to apologize for them. Rephrase your sentence to eliminate the triteness.

Weak   I've been "busy as a bee" all week, so I'm exhausted.

Revised   I've been so busy this week that I'm exhausted.

EXERCISE

In the following sentences, insert apostrophes and single or double quotation marks as needed.

1. My mother told me that she didn't want me to buy a car until I had a permanent part-time job.
2. Jake has his little quirks, as Molly calls them, but he is still lovable.
3. My adviser recently remarked: The nervous student who encounters a professor who states, Twenty percent of this class usually fails, must learn to say, Not I, instead of giving up.
4. Did your friends teacher really say Attendance is necessary in this class?
5. We are guilty of gross misuse of language, continued the speaker, whenever we use disinterested to mean uninterested.
6. I spent two hours worth of good homework time, complained Thomas friend Karen, trying to invent a tongue twister that would make people stand up and shout Thats a masterpiece.

ITAL

▨ UNDERLINING (ITALICS)

In handwritten or typed papers, indicate italics with underlining. Although most word-processing programs support italic script, it is usually acceptable (and easier) to underline rather than shift fonts. Check with your instructor.

Underlines for Titles of Long Complete Works

Use underlines for titles of books, magazines, journals, newspapers, plays, films, works of art, long poems, pamphlets, and musical works. Capitalize and underline *a, an,* and *the* only if they are part of the title.

Moby Dick   Michaelangelo's David

Newsweek   the Encyclopaedia Britannica

Star Wars   The Sound and the Fury

Note: Books of the Bible and the Bible itself are not underlined.

Exodus   Revelations   Luke   the Bible

Underlines for Foreign Words and Phrases

Use underlines for foreign words and phrases.

You should avoid the post hoc ergo propter hoc fallacy.

Underlines for Letters, Numbers, and Words Used as Words

Use underlines for letters, for numbers, and for words when they are referred to as words and phrases and not as what they represent.

To spell the word separate correctly, remember there is a rat in separate.

▨ BRACKETS, ELLIPSES, AND SLASHES

Brackets and ellipses (three spaced dots) indicate changes within quotations and have occasional other uses. Slashes are used primarily to indicate line breaks in quoted poetry or, in informal or bureaucratic prose, to indicate an option of alternative words or phrases.

Brackets

Brackets [] are made with straight lines and should not be confused with parentheses (), which use curved lines.

Brackets to Set Off Explanatory Material Inserted into Quotations

Use brackets to set off explanatory material inserted into a quotation.

According to Joseph Menosky, "Courses offered to teach these skills [computer literacy] have popped up everywhere."

The original source of this quotation did not contain the words *computer literacy,* since the context of the original source explained what *these skills* meant. In this example,

P[ ]

computer literacy is inserted in brackets to make up for the missing context. The brackets indicate that the material they enclose did not occur in the original version.

Brackets to Indicate the Writer's Alteration of the Grammar of a Quotation

Use brackets when you need to change the grammar of a quotation to make it fit the grammar of your own sentence.

Original Source	I see electric cars as our best hope for reducing air pollution.
	—Jean Haricot
Correct Use of Brackets	Jean Haricot says that "electric cars [are] our best hope for reducing air pollution."

In this example the writer has to change the original *as* to *are* to make the quotation fit the grammar of his or her own sentence. This change is placed in brackets.

Brackets to Enclose *Sic* to Indicate a Mistake in a Quotation

If you quote a source that contains an obvious mistake, you can insert *sic* in brackets to indicate that the mistake is in the original source and is not your own.

According to Vernon Tweeble, not your greatest sportswriter, the home-run king is still "Baby [*sic*] Ruth."

Here the *sic* indicates that Tweeble said "Baby Ruth," not "Babe Ruth." The mistake belongs to Tweeble, not to the writer.

Brackets to Enclose the Spaced Periods of an Ellipsis

Whenever you use an ellipsis to indicate omitted material in a quotation, enclose the three spaced periods in a pair of brackets. See the next section on ellipses.

Ellipses

P . . .

An ellipsis is made with three spaced periods enclosed in a pair of brackets. It is used to indicate an omission within a quotation. When an ellipsis occurs at the end of a sentence, a fourth period is used to mark the sentence boundary. Place this period outside the brackets. (For more extensive discussion of the use of ellipses in quotations, see pages 555–56).

Original	Before the dam, a float trip down the river through Glen Canyon would cost you a minimum of seven days' time, well within anyone's vacation allotment, and a capital outlay of about forty dollars—the prevailing price of a two-man rubber boat with oars, available at any army-navy surplus store. A life jacket might be useful but not required, for there were no dangerous rapids in the 150 miles of Glen Canyon.
	—Edward Abbey, "The Damnation of a Canyon"
Correct Use of Ellipses	According to Edward Abbey, before the dam was built "a float trip trip down the river through Glen Canyon would cost you a minimum of seven days' time [. . .] and a capital outlay of about forty dollars [. . .]. A life jacket might be useful but not required [. . .]" (351).

Here the first ellipsis indicates words omitted in the middle of a sentence. The second ellipsis shows words omitted at the end of a sentence and hence includes a fourth period to mark the sentence boundary. In the last example, the period marking the sentence boundary occurs after the parenthetical citation indicating the page number of the source.

When quoting poetry, use a line of dots to indicate that one or more full lines of the poem have been omitted, as in this example using Ben Jonson's "Come, My Celia":

> Come, my Celia, let us prove,
> While we can, the sports of love;
> ....
> Why should we defer our joys?
> Fame and rumor are but toys.

Slashes

The main use of the slash is to divide lines of poetry written as a quotation within a sentence.

> Ben Jonson evokes the *carpe diem* tradition when he says: "Come, my Celia, let us prove, / While we can, the sports of love."

If you quote more than four lines of poetry, use the indented block method (see p. 554) rather than quotation marks with slashes.

Slashes are sometimes used to indicate options, but these uses are too informal for most essays.

Informal	He told me to take algebra and/or trigonometry.
Formal	He told me to take either algebra or trigonometry or both.

◢ CAPITAL LETTERS

Most writers agree on the conventions for using capital letters, but on occasion usage varies. When in doubt about whether to capitalize a particular word, consult a good dictionary.

Capitals for First Letters of Sentences and Intentional Fragments

Capitalize the first letter of the first word in every sentence and also in sentence fragments used intentionally for effect. In fragmentary questions in a series, initial capital letters are optional.

> That man is a liar and a scoundrel. What do you want me to do? Like him? Invite him to dinner? Offer him my money?

or

> What do you want me to do? like him? invite him to dinner? offer him my money?

Capitals for Proper Nouns

Use capitals for all proper nouns. The following rules cover most cases you will encounter.

Capitalize the names of people, places, and things.	Pete Rose; Washington; Coke
Capitalize titles of people when the title precedes the name or when the title follows the name without an article.	Doctor Sarah Smith; John Jones, Professor of Mathematics
Do not capitalize titles of people that include an article (*a* or *an*).	Sarah Smith, a medical doctor; John Jones, a mathematics professor
Capitalize family relationship names (Mother, Uncle) when used with a name. When used in place of a name, capitalization is optional.	Please, Aunt Eloise, tell Grandfather (or, grandfather) that dinner is ready.
Do not capitalize relationship words when not used with a name or as a name.	I hear that my uncle and your father are going to visit Tony's grandfather.
Capitalize the names of specific geographic locations, areas, and regions, including compass directions if they are part of a name.	Mount Everest; the Pacific Northwest; Idaho; Main Street; the Salmon River; the South
Do not capitalize geographic locations indicated by compass directions but not considered actual names.	the northwest part of the United States; a mountain south of here
Capitalize historical events, names, movements, and writings.	the Korean War; the Oregon Territory; Articles of Confederation; the Renaissance; the Impressionist Period
Capitalize the names of ships and buildings and capitalize brand names.	USS *Missouri;* the Empire State Building; Sanka
Capitalize specific academic courses but not academic subject areas, except English and foreign languages.	This term I am taking Chemistry 101, Integral Calculus, and French. But: This term I am taking chemistry, calculus, and French. (In the first sentence, the writer names specific courses; in the second sentence, the writer names subject areas only.)
Capitalize specific times, days, months, and holidays, but not names of seasons.	Monday; the Fourth of July; Halloween; last year; autumn; winter
Capitalize abbreviations derived from proper names.	NFL U.S.A. RCA NAFTA U. of W.

Capitals for Important Words in Titles

In titles of books, articles, plays, musical works, and so forth, capitalize the first and last words, any word following a colon or a semicolon, and all other words except articles, prepositions, and conjunctions of fewer than five letters.

"Ain't No Such Thing as a Montana Cowboy"

Famous Myths and Legends of the World: Stories of Gods and Heroes

Capitals in Quotations and Spoken Dialogue

Capitalize the first words of spoken dialogue but do not capitalize the first word in the second half of a broken quotation following an attributive tag.

She said, "Because it is raining, we won't go."

"Because it is raining," she said, "we won't go."

Do not capitalize indirect quotations.

She said that we wouldn't go because it is raining.

Consistency in Use of Capitals

Use capitals consistently and avoid unnecessary capitals. Contemporary writers generally use capitals sparingly. Once you make a decision in optional or ambiguous cases, stick with it throughout your essay.

NUMBERS

NUM

Writers often have to decide whether to write numbers as words (ten) or as numerals (10). Follow the conventions of the genre in which you are writing.

Numbers in Scientific and Technical Writing

Scientific and technical writers generally use numerals for all numbers. Check with your instructor about how to handle numbers in lab reports and other formal papers in science, mathematics, or engineering.

Numbers in Formal Writing for Nontechnical Fields

In the humanities and other nontechnical fields and in most business and professional writing, writers usually adhere to the following conventions:

Use Words Instead of Numerals

For single-word numbers	eight dogs; a hundred doughnuts
For common fractions	one-third of a cup; half a pie
In the humanities, for two-word numbers	twenty-three students (however, business and professional writers prefer numerals for two-word numbers—23 students)
For numbers greater than a million, use a combination of words and numerals	72 billion dollars

Use Numerals Instead of Words

For addresses	1420 Heron Street
For times and dates	I'll be there at 10:00 a.m. on November 5th.
For percentages and statistics	At least 30 percent of the students scored above 15 on the standardized test.
With decimals	The average score was 29.63.
For amounts of money that include cents	That notebook cost around $3.95.
With symbols	20° C; 5'4"
For scores	The Yankees beat the Indians 5 to 3.
To refer to chapters, pages, and lines	You'll find that statistic in Chapter 12 on page 100 at line 8.

Numbers at the Beginning of a Sentence

Spell out in words any number that begins a sentence. If the result is awkward, rewrite the sentence.

Faulty	375 students showed up for the exam.
Revised	Three hundred seventy-five students showed up for the exam.
	or
	We counted 375 students at the exam.

Plurals of Numbers

Do not use an apostrophe for the plural form of numbers.

Faulty	Most of my golf scores are in the low 90's.
Revised	Most of my golf scores are in the low 90s.

Numbers in a Series for Comparison

Use numerals instead of words to express numbers in a series when easy comparison is important.

There were 700 persons at the professor's first public lecture, 270 at the second, and 40 at the third.

▨ ABBREVIATIONS

Whenever it is necessary to save space, such as in tables, indexes, and footnotes, you may use abbreviations. In the main text of formal writing, however, you should generally spell out rather than abbreviate words. Abbreviations are acceptable in the following cases.

Abbreviations for Academic Degrees and Titles

Use abbreviations for academic degrees and for the following common titles when used with a person's name: Mr., Ms., Mrs., Dr., Jr., Sr., St. (Saint). Other titles, such as governor, colonel, professor, and reverend, are spelled out.

> The doctor asked Colonel Jones, Ms. Hemmings, and Professor Pruitt to present the portrait of St. Thomas to Judge Hogkins on the occasion of her receiving a Ph.D. in religious studies.

Abbreviations for Agencies, Institutions, and Other Entities

Use abbreviations for agencies, groups, people, places, or objects that are commonly known by capitalized initials.

FBI	UCLA
IOOF	DNA molecules
Washington, D.C.	CD-ROM

If you wish to use a specialized abbreviation that may be unclear to your audience, write out the term in full the first time it occurs and place in parentheses the abbreviation that you will use subsequently.

> The Modern Language Association (MLA) recently issued new guidelines for citing electronic sources.
>
> This example indicates that the writer will henceforth use the abbreviation *MLA*.

Abbreviations for Terms Used with Numbers

Use abbreviations for terms commonly used with numbers, especially times, dates,* amounts, and other units of measure.

1200 C.E.	$15.05
500 B.C.E.	no. 12 in a series
2:45 p.m.	

---

*If used, A.D. always precedes the date while B.C. follows it. The abbreviations B.C. ("before Christ") and A.D. (*anno domini* "in the year of the Lord") are now often replaced with B.C.E. ("before the common era") and C.E. ("common era"). In both cases the abbreviation appears after the date. Thus A.D. 500 would be rewritten 500 C.E.

Note that you should use abbreviations for units of measure only when they appear with numbers; never use abbreviations by themselves.

Faulty	I will meet you sometime in the p.m.
Revised	I will meet you sometime in the afternoon.

There is no clear rule about when to use a period with abbreviations (*U.S.A.* or *USA*; *kg.* or *kg*). Most publishing houses establish their own guidelines, which they follow consistently.

Abbreviations for Common Latin Terms

Use abbreviations for common Latin terms used for footnotes, bibliographies, or parenthetical comments. In the main text, spell out the English equivalents.

e.g.	for example
i.e.	that is
c.f.	compare

This rule applies also to *etc.* (*et cetera,* meaning "and so forth"). Avoid using *etc.* in formal writing. Instead, use the English *and so forth* or *and so on,* or rewrite your sentence to make it more inclusive, thus eliminating the need for *and so forth.* Never write *and etc.,* because *et* is the Latin for "and."

Weak	During my year in London I went to ballets, the opera, Shakespeare plays, etc.
Revised	During my year in London I saw many cultural events, including two ballets, one opera, and four Shakespeare plays.

Plurals of Abbreviations

Do not use an apostrophe when forming the plural of an abbreviation.

Faulty	I've misplaced two of my CD's.
Revised	I've misplaced two of my CDs.

MF   ▪ MANUSCRIPT FORM

An attractive manuscript contributes to your *ethos* as a writer (see Chapter 4, pp. 70–71). A sloppily prepared, visually unattractive manuscript, or one that violates standard conventions or your instructor's special instructions, creates a negative first impression and weakens the rhetorical effectiveness of your writing.

Unless told otherwise by your instructor, use the following format for all your college papers:

1. Use white, twenty-pound, 8½-by-11-inch paper.
2. Use a dark ribbon and letter-quality type. Check with your instructor before using a dot matrix printer.

3. Avoid fancy typefaces and icons. Make the text look like a typed manuscript rather than a published document unless the assignment calls for such appearance.
4. Double-space the text throughout, including quotations and notes.
5. Use one-inch margins at the top and bottom, and left and right sides.
6. Indent five spaces for paragraphs. Leave two spaces after periods and other terminal punctuation; leave one space after commas and other marks of punctuation.
7. Make a dash with two unspaced hyphens so that it looks like this--a proper dash.
8. Distinguish between brackets [] and parentheses () and make ellipses correctly with spaced periods (see pp. 717–19).
9. Proofread carefully. Make final corrections *neatly* in ink by crossing out typographical errors and writing corrections above the cross-out. Retype if there are more than one or two corrections per page.
10. Do *not* make a separate title page unless you are using the APA style or have been give special directions by your instructor. Rather, follow the MLA style which places "cover page" information on the first page of the paper itself (see pp. 568 and 571 for instructions on how to format a paper following the MLA style; an example of an opening page is shown on p. 573; for an example of a cover page using the APA style, see p. 303).
11. Staple your pages in the upper left-hand corner. Do *not* place your essay in a binder unless your instructor requests you to do so.

Acknowledgments *(continued from copyright page)*

Page 6.   Excerpts from a workshop for new faculty members, Jeffrey R. Stephens (Department of Chemistry, Seattle University), Bridget Carney (School of Nursing, Seattle University), and Tomas Guillen (Department of Speech Communication and Journalism, Seattle University).

Page 8.   Paulo Freire, *Pedagogy of the Oppressed* (New York: Continuum, 1989).

Page 9.   Pauline Agbayani-Siewert and Linda Revilla, "Filipino Americans," *Asian Americans,* ed. Pyong Gap Min (Thousand Oaks: Sage, 1995): 135–165.

Page 9.   Mary Turla, 2 journal entries, student writing. Reprinted with the permission of the author.

Page 12.   David M. Rockwood, letter to editor, *The Oregonian* (January 1, 1993): E4. Reprinted with the permission of David M. Rockwood.

Page 13.   Minnie Bruce Pratt, excerpt from "Identity: Skin, Blood, Heart," in *Yours In Struggle: Three Perspectives on Anti-Semitism and Racism* by Elly Bulkin, Minnie Bruce Pratt, and Barbara Smith. Copyright © 1984 by Elly Bulkin, Minnie Bruce Pratt, and Barbara Smith. Reprinted with the permission of Firebrand Books, Ithaca, New York.

Page 18.   Melissa Davis, "Why Do Some Dogs Like Cats While Others Hate Them?", student essay. Reprinted with the permission of the author.

Page 22.   David Wallechinsky, "This Land of Ours," *Parade Magazine* (July 5, 1992): 4.

Page 23.   A. Kimbrough Sherman, in *Thinking and Writing in College: A Naturalistic Study of Students in Four Disciplines* by Barbara E. Walvoord and Lucille P. McCarthy (Urbana, IL: NCTE, 1990): 51.

Page 23.   William G. Perry, *Forms of Intellectual and Ethical Development in the College Years* (Troy, MO: Holt, Rinehart & Winston, 1970).

Page 27.   Evelyn Fox Keller, "Women in Science: An Analysis of a Social Problem," *Harvard Magazine* (1974).

Page 30.   Stephen Bean, student writing.

Page 33.   "Proposed Law Calls for Fines, Arrests," *Seattle Times* (October 1, 1993). Copyright © 1993 Seattle Times Company. Used by permission.

Page 37.   Peter Elbow, *Writing Without Teachers* (New York: Oxford University Press, 1973): 147–190.

Page 38.   Paul Theroux, *Sunrise with Seamonsters* (Boston: Houghton Mifflin, 1985).

Pages 40 and 42.   Peter Elbow, *Writing Without Teachers* (New York: Oxford University Press, 1973): 14–15.

Page 54.   James Moffett, *Active Voice: A Writing Program Across the Curriculum* (Montclair, NJ: Boynton/Cook Publishers, 1981).

Page 72.   Victoria Register-Freeman, "My Turn: Hunks and Handmaidens," *Newsweek* (November 4, 1996): 16. Copyright © 1996 by Newsweek, Inc. Reprinted with the permission of *Newsweek.* All rights reserved.

Page 72.   Louise Erdrich, "A Woman's Work: Too Many Demands, and Not Enough Selves," *Harper's Magazine* (May 1993): 35–46.

Page 73.   Beryl Markham, "Flying Elsewhere," *West with the Night* (San Francisco: North Point Press, 1983).

Page 73.   Garrison Keillor, "State Fair," *Leaving Home* (Penguin Books, 1987).

Page 74.   Barbara Tuchman, "This Is the End of the World," *A Distant Mirror* (New York: Knopf, 1978).

Page 75.   Penny Parker, "For Teeth, Say Cheese," from *New Scientist* (April 6, 1991). Copyright © 1991. Reprinted with the permission of *New Scientist.*

Page 75.   Carlo Patrono, "Aspirin as an Antiplatelet Drug," *The New England Journal of Medicine* 330, (May 5, 1994): 1287–1294. Copyright © 1994 by the Massachusetts Medical Society. Reprinted by permission of *The New England Journal of Medicine.*

Page 82.   Randal Rubini, "A Vicious Cycle," *Seattle Times* (August 27, 1992): G1+.

Page 84.   Lorna Marshal, *The !Kung of Nyae Nyae* (Cambridge: Harvard University Press, 1976): 177–178.

Page 84.   P. Draper, "!Kung Women: Contrasts in Sexual Egalitarianism in Foraging and Sedentary Contexts," in *Toward an Anthropology of Women,* ed. R. Reiter (New York: Monthly Review Press, 1975): 82–83.

Page 87.   Sarah Bean, "Contrasting Descriptions," student essay. Reprinted with the permission of the author.

Page 90.   Mike Royko, *Chicago Tribune,* reprinted in *Seattle Times* (April 7, 1995): B11.

Page 90.   Mark Twain, "Two Ways of Seeing a River," in *Life on the Mississippi* (New York: Harper & Row, 1899).

Page 92.   Henry Morton Stanley, "Henry Morton Stanley's Account" from "A Classroom Laboratory for Writing History" from *Social Studies Review* 31, no. 1 (1991). Copyright © 1991. Reprinted with permission.

Page 92.   Donald C. Holsinger, "A Classroom Laboratory for Writing History," *Social Studies Review* 31, no. 1 (1991): 59–64.

Pages 101 and 120.   Andrés Martin, M.D., "On Teenagers and Tattoos," *Journal of the American Academy of Child and Adolescent Psychiatry* 36, no. 6 (June 1997): 860–861. Reprinted with the permission of Williams & Wilkins.

Page 106.   Robert B. Cullen with Sullivan, "Dangers of Disarming," *Newsweek* (October 27, 1986). Copyright © 1986 by Newsweek Inc. All rights reserved. Reprinted with the permission of *Newsweek.*

Page 115.   Carl Rogers, *On Becoming a Person: A Therapist's View of Psychotherapy,* 3rd ed. (Boston: Houghton Mifflin, 1961).

Page 122.   Jane Tompkins, " 'Indians': Textualism, Morality, and the Problem of History," *Critical Inquiry* 13, no. 1 (Autumn 1986). Copyright © 1986 by The University of Chicago. Reprinted with the permission of the author and The University of Chicago Press.

Page 124.   Richard Lynn, "Why Johnny Can't Read, but Yoshio Can," *National Review* (October 1988): 41–43. Copyright © 1988 by National Review, Inc. Reprinted with the permission of the publishers, 215 Lexington Avenue, New York, NY 10016.

Page 128.   Victoria Register-Freeman, "My Turn: Hunks and Handmaidens," *Newsweek* (November 4, 1996): 16. Copyright © 1996 by Newsweek, Inc. Reprinted with the permission of *Newsweek.* All rights reserved.

Page 130.   Edward Abbey, "The Damnation of a Canyon," from *Beyond the Wall: Essays from the Outside* by Edward Abbey. Copyright © 1971, 1977, 1979, 1984 by Edward Abbey. Reprinted by permission of Henry Holt and Company, Inc.

Page 133.   Patricia J. Williams, "The Death of the Profane: A Commentary on the Genre of Legal Writing," from *The Alchemy of Race and Rights* by Patricia J. Williams (Cambridge, Mass.: Harvard University Press): 44–51. Copyright © 1991 by the President and Fellows of Harvard College. Reprinted by permission of Harvard University Press.

Page 147.   Richard Wright, *Black Boy* (New York: Harper & Row, 1966): 216–217.

Page 150.   Bill Russell, excerpt from *Second Wind: The Memoirs of an Opinionated Man* by Bill Russell with Taylor Branch (New York: Random House, 1979). Copyright © 1979 by William F. Russell. Reprinted with the permission of The Robbins Office.

Page 152.   William Least Heat-Moon, "West by Northwest" from *Blue Highways: A Journey into America.* Copyright © 1982 by William Least Heat Moon. Reprinted with the permission of Little, Brown and Company, Inc.

Page 156.   Chris Kordash, "Making My Mark," student essay. Reprinted with the permission of the author.

Page 159.   Sheila Madden, "Letting Go of Bart," *Santa Clara Magazine* (Summer 1994). Copyright © 1994 by Sheila Madden. Reprinted with the permission of the author.

Pages 166 and 168.   Anonymous, "Essay A/Essay B" from "Inventing the University," in *When A Writer Can't Write* by David Bartholomae. Reprinted with the permission of The Guilford Press.

Page 171.   Mary Turla, "Mail-Order Bride Romances: Fairy Tale, Nightmare, or Somewhere in Between?", student essay. Reprinted with the permission of the author.

Page 174.   Sheridan Hopper Botts, "Exploring Problems About Hospices," student essay. Reprinted with the permission of the author.

Page 177.   Jane Tompkins, " 'Indians': Textualism, Morality, and the Problem of History," *Critical Inquiry* 13, no. 1, (Autumn 1986). Copyright © 1986 by The University of Chicago. Reprinted with the permission of the author and The University of Chicago Press.

Pages 188 and 190.   Stephen Bean, "Sam" journal entries and "Should Women Be Allowed to Serve In Combat Units?", student writing. Reprinted with the permission of the author.

Page 197.   Article abstract of "Reefer Madness" by Eric Schlosser (August 1994). Abstract reprinted with the permission of *The Atlantic Monthly.*

Page 197.   Article abstract of "The Sex-Bias Myth in Medicine" by Andrew G. Kadar, M.D. (August 1994). Abstract reprinted with the permission of *The Atlantic Monthly.*

Page 197.   Article abstract of "It's Not the Economy, Stupid" by Charles R. Morris (July 1993). Abstract reprinted with the permission of *The Atlantic Monthly.*

Page 197.   Article abstract of "Midlife Myths" by Winifred Gallagher (May 1993). Abstract reprinted with the permission of *The Atlantic Monthly.*

Page 198.   Leo W. Banks, "Not Guilty: Despite Its Fearsome Image, the Tarantula Is a Benign Beast," *America West Airlines Magazine* (February 1988). Copyright © 1988 by Leo Banks. Reprinted with the permission of the author.

Page 200.   Elaine Robbins, "The New Eco *Moooovement,*" *Utne Reader* (September/October 1998): 20. Reprinted with the permission of the author.

Page 201.   Cheryl Carp, "Behind Stone Walls," student essay. Reprinted with the permission of the author.

Page 204.   David Quammen, "The Face of a Spider: Eyeball to Eyeball with the Good, the Bad, and the Ugly," *Outside Magazine* (March 1987). Copyright © 1987 by David Quammen. Reprinted by permission of the author, c/o Reneé Wayne Golden. All rights reserved.

Page 216.   Sut Jhally, *The Codes of Advertising: Fetishism and Political Economy of Meaning in the Consumer Society* (New York: St. Martins, 1987): 2.

Page 217.   "Attention Advertisers: Real Men Do Laundry," *American Demographics* (March 1994): 13–14.

Page 222.   Coors advertisement: "Sam and Me." Courtesy Coors Brewing Co.

Page 224.   Erving Goffman, *Gender Advertisements* (New York: Harper & Row, 1979).

Page 225.   Zenith advertisement: "Of Sound Body." Courtesy Zenith Audio Products, a Division of S.D.I. Technologies.

Page 226.   Hennessy advertisement: "The World's Most Civilized Spirit." Courtesy Schieffelin & Somerset Co., 2 Park Avenue, New York, NY 10016.

Page 228.   Vance Packard, excerpt from *The Hidden Persuaders.* Copyright © 1957 and renewed 1985 by Vance Packard. Reprinted with the permission of the author.

Page 229.   Gillian Dyer, "On Manner and Activity," excerpt from *Advertising as Communication.* Copyright © 1982 by Gillian Dyer. Reprinted with the permission of Methuen & Co., International Thomson Publishing Services, Andover, UK.

Page 232.   Stephen Bean, "How Cigarette Advertisers Address the Stigma Against Smoking: A Tale of Two Ads," student essay. Reprinted with the permission of the author.

Page 238.   "Help Troubled Teens—Don't Forget Them," *USA Today* (November 8, 1985). Copyright © 1985 by the Society for the Advancement of Education. Reprinted with the permission of *USA Today.*

Pages 243 and 244.   "Family Finances in the U.S.: Recent Evidence from the Survey of Consumer Finances," *Federal Reserve Bulletin* 83, no. 1 (January 1997): 3.

Page 252.   Bryant Stamford, "Understand Calories, Fat Content in Food," *Seattle Times* (July 27, 1995). Copyright © 1995. Reprinted with the permission of Gannett News Service.

Page 256.   John Burbank, "The Minimum Wage: Making Work Pay," *The Seattle Times* (October 29, 1998): B9. Copyright © 1998 by the Seattle Times Company. Reprinted with the permission of *The Seattle Times* and the author.

Page 257.   David R. Henderson, "Minimum Wage + $1 = More Poverty," *Fortune* 138, no. 7 (October 12, 1998). Copyright © 1998 by Time, Inc. Reprinted by special permission of *Fortune.*

Page 261.   Evelyn Dahl Reed, "Medicine Man," from *Coyote Tales from the Indian Pueblos* by Evelyn Dahl Reed. Copyright © 1988 by Evelyn Dahl Reed. Reprinted with the permission of Sunstone Press, P.O. Box 2321, Sante Fe, NM 87504-2321.

Page 270.   Alice Walker, "Everyday Use (for your grandmama)," in *In Love & Trouble: Stories of Black Women.* Copyright © 1973 by Alice Walker. Reprinted by permission of Harcourt Brace & Company.

Page 276.   Gabriel García Márquez, "A Very Old Man with Enormous Wings," from *Leaf Storm and Other Stories* by Gabriel García Márquez, trans. Gregory Rabassa. Copyright © 1971 by Gabriel García Márquez. Reprinted by permission of HarperCollins Publishers, Inc.

Page 281. Elizabeth M. Weiler, "Who Do You Want to Be?", student essay. Reprinted with the permission of the author.

Page 291. Monica Yant, "Many Female Athletes at Risk of 'Triad' of Health Problems," *Seattle Tribune* (June 18, 1992): B14.

Page 294. "Where Have All the Boys Gone?" *Scientific American* (July 1998): 22–23.

Page 296. David H. Levy, "How to Make Sense Out of Science," *Parade* (September 20, 1998). Copyright © 1998 by David H. Levy. Reprinted with the permission of the Scott Meredith Literary Agency.

Page 298. Michael Castleman, "The .02 Percent Solution," *Mother Jones* (September/October 1998): 40–42. Copyright © 1998 by Foundation for National Progress. Reprinted with the permission of the publishers.

Page 301. Walter S. Minot, "Students Who Push Burgers," *Christian Science Monitor* (November 22, 1988). Copyright © 1988 by Walter S. Minot. Reprinted with the permission of the author.

Page 303. Susan Meyers, "Denying Desire: The Anorexic Struggle with Image, Self, and Sexuality," student essay. Reprinted with the permission of the author.

Page 325. Stephen Toulmin, *The Uses of Argument* (Cambridge: Cambridge University Press, 1958).

Page 326. Walter Wink, "Biting the Bullet: The Case for Legalizing Drugs," *The Christian Century* (August 8–15, 1990).

Page 327. Michael Levin, "The Case for Torture," *Newsweek* (June 7, 1982).

Page 339. Edward I. Koch, "Death and Justice: How Capital Punishment Affirms Life," *The New Republic* (April 15, 1985). Copyright © 1985 by the New Republic, Inc. Reprinted with the permission of *The New Republic.*

Page 344. David Bruck, "The Death Penalty," *The New Republic* (May 20, 1985). Copyright © 1985 by the New Republic, Inc. Reprinted with the permission of *The New Republic.*

Page 347. Diane Hunsaker, "My Turn: Ditch the Calculators," *Newsweek* (November 3, 1997). Copyright © 1997 by Newsweek, Inc. Reprinted with the permission of *Newsweek.* All rights reserved.

Page 349. Walt Spady, "A Misguided Ban on Personal Watercraft," *Seattle Times* (February 1996), written by John Wood, edited by Walt Spady. Reprinted with the permission of Walt Spady.

Page 351. Tiffany D. Linder, "Salvaging Our Old-Growth Forests," student essay. Reprinted with the permission of the author.

Page 360. Barbara E. Walvoord and Lucille P. McCarthy, *Thinking and Writing in College: A Naturalistic Study of Students in Four Disciplines* (Urbana, IL: National Council of Teachers of English, 1990): 7.

Page 363. Copyright © 1982, 1990 by Jessie Levine. "Turnabout Map"™ Dist. by Laguna Sales, 7040 Via Valverde, San Jose, CA 95135.

Page 373. *U.S. English Home Page,* U.S. English, Inc., <http://www.us-english.org/index.html>. Reprinted with the permission of U.S. English.

Page 375. Glenn Moen, Nicki Rayburn, and Yohei Kaga, *English as the Official Language,* Dakota State University, <http://www.homepages.dsu.edu/turnerm//mainpage.htm>.

Page 376. *English For the Children,* Proposition 227, The 1998 California "English for the Children" Initiative, <http://www.onenation.org>.

Page 377. Diane Helman and Phyllis Bookspan, "Sesame Street: Brought to You by the Letters M-A-L-E," *The Seattle Times* (July 28, 1992). Reprinted with permission.

Page 379. Elayne Rapping, "In Praise of Roseanne," *The Progressive.* Reprinted with the permission of the author and *The Progressive,* 409 East Main Street, Madison, WI 53703.

Page 383. Sarah Erickson, "*Picnic at Hanging Rock* as an Art Film," student essay. Reprinted with the permission of the author.

Pages 373, 375, and 376. Microsoft Internet Explorer screens courtesy of Microsoft Corporation, Inc. Copyright © 1999 Microsoft Corporation, Inc.

Page 397. Theresa LaPorte, "A Proposal to Create a Quiet Study Lounge," student essay. Reprinted with the permission of the author.

Page 401. Sheridan Hopper Botts, "Saving Hospices: A Plea to the Insurance Industry," student essay. Reprinted with the permission of the author.

Page 404. Richard Weissbourd, "The Feel-Good Trap," *The New Republic* (August 19 and 26, 1996). Copyright © 1996 by The New Republic, Inc. Reprinted with the permission of *The New Republic.*

Page 407. Brian A. Courtney, "My Turn: Freedom from Choice," *Newsweek* (February 13, 1995). Copyright © 1995 by Newsweek, Inc. Reprinted with the permission of *Newsweek*. All rights reserved.

Page 417. Nancy Sommers, "Revision Strategies of Student Writers and Experienced Adult Writers," *College Composition and Communication* 31 (October, 1980): 291–300.

Page 417. Jonathan Swift, quoted in Jon Winokur (Ed.), *Writers on Writing* (Philadelphia: Running Press, 1986).

Page 437. Kenneth Burke, *The Grammar of Motives* (Berkeley: University of California Press, 1969).

Page 437. James Jones, quoted in Jon Winokur (Ed.), *Writers on Writing* (Philadelphia: Running Press, 1986).

Page 441. Adapted from J. D. Bransford and M. K. Johnson, "Conceptual Prerequisites for Understanding," *Journal of Learning Behavior* 11 (1972): 717–726.

Page 444. Lynnea Clark, excerpt and outline from "Women Police Officers: Should Size and Strength Be Criteria for Patrol Duty?", student essay.

Pages 451, 452, 460, and 461. Dao Do, "Choose Life," student essay. Reprinted with the permission of the author.

Page 454. Howard Gardner, *The Mind's New Science: A History of the Cognitive Revolution* (New York: Basic Books, 1985): 90.

Page 461. Tiffany D. Linder, "Salvaging Our Old-Growth Forests," student essay. Reprinted with the permission of the author.

Page 468. David Popenoe, "Where's Papa?" from *Life Without Father: Compelling New Evidence that Fatherhood and Marriage Are Indispensable for the Good of Children and Society.* As published in "The Decline of Fatherhood," *Wilson Quarterly* (September/October 1996).

Page 472. Carl Sagan, *Broca's Brain: Reflections on the Romance of Science* (New York: Ballantine Books, 1974).

Page 475. Lowell Ponte, "Earthquakes: Closer Than You Think," *Reader's Digest* (April 1994).

Page 478. Stephen Jay Gould, "The Rule of Five," in *The Flamingo's Smile: Reflections in Natural History* (New York: Norton, 1985).

Page 483. Chris Anderson, excerpt from *Edge Effects: Notes from an Oregon Forest.* Copyright © 1993 by University of Iowa Press. Reprinted with the permission of the publisher.

Page 486. Patrick Klein, "Berkeley Blues," in *University of Arizona First Year Composition Guide.* Copyright © 1995 by University of Arizona First Year Composition Program. Reprinted with the permission of Burgess Publishing Company.

Page 488. Oliver Goldsmith, "The Crow and the Fox," *Aesop's Fables.*

Page 489. Richard Brautigan, "Leaves," in *The Tokyo-Montana Express* by Richard Brautigan (New York: Delacourt Press, 1980). Copyright © 1980 by Richard Brautigan. Reprinted with the permission of Ianthe Brautigan Swenson.

Page 490. Jon Krakauer, excerpt from *Into Thin Air.* Copyright © 1997 by Jon Krakauer. Reprinted with the permission of Villard Books, a division of Random House, Inc.

Page 491. Hitamaro, "A strange old man," haiku translated by Kenneth Rexroth, in *One Hundred Poems from the Japanese.* Copyright © 1956 by Kenneth Rexroth. All rights reserved. Reprinted by permission of New Directions Publishing Corp.

Page 495. Annie Dillard, "Living Like Weasels," in *Teaching a Stone to Talk: Expeditons and Encounters.* Copyright © 1982 by Annie Dillard. Reprinted with the permission of HarperCollins Publishers, Inc.

Page 495. Jonathan Swift, "A Modest Proposal," in *The Prose Works of Jonathan Swift* (London: Bell, 1914).

Page 497. *College Composition and Communication*, Viponid Interview with John McPhee (May 1991): 203–204.

Page 498. Tom Wolfe, "New Journalism," introduction to *New Journalism*, ed. Tom Wolfe and E. W. Johnson (New York: Harper & Row, 1973): 32.

Page 499. Nicolas Tomalin, in *New Journalism*, ed. Wolfe and Johnson: 201.

Page 500. Isak Dinesen, "The Iguana," *Out of Africa* (New York: Modern Library, 1952).

Page 501.   Dillard, "Living Like Weasels," from *Teaching a Stone to Talk: Expeditions and Encounters*. Copyright © 1982 by Annie Dillard. Reprinted with the permission of HarperCollins Publishers, Inc.

Page 504.   *Windows in 21 Days*.

Page 505.   John Kaufeld, *Paradox 5 for Windows for Dummies* (San Mateo, CA: IDG Books Worldwide, Inc., 1994).

Page 506.   Michael F. Graves and Wayne H. Slater, "Could Textbooks Be Better Written and Would It Make a Difference?" *American Educator* (Spring 1986): 36–42.

Page 509.   Parker Palmer, *To Know as We Are Known: Education as a Spiritual Journey* (San Francisco: Harper & Row, 1983).

Page 509.   Hannah Arendt, *The Human Condition* (Chicago: University of Chicago Press, 1958).

Page 511.   Carl Rogers, *On Becoming a Person: A Therapist's View of Psychotherapy*, 3rd ed. (Boston: Houghton Mifflin, 1961).

Page 517.   Parker Palmer, *To Know as We Are Known: Education as a Spiritual Journey* (San Francisco: Harper & Row, 1983): 94–96.

Page 523.   Pamela Erens, "Are Subliminal Self-Help Tapes a Hoax?" *Glamour* (October 1994): 62.

Page 547.   Roger D. McGrath, "The Myth of Violence in the Old West," in *Gunfighters, Highwaymen, and Vigilantes*. Copyright © 1984 by The Regents of the University of California. Reprinted with the permission of University of California Press.

Page 552.   Mary Turla, "Mail-Order Bride Romances: The Need for Regulation," student essay. Reprinted with the permission of the author.

Page 573.   Mary Turla, "Mail-Order Bride Romances: The Need for Regulation," student essay. Reprinted with the permission of the author.

Page 591.   Alan Whigum, posting to a Listserv.

Pages 597, 598, 600, and 601.   Netscape screens. Copyright © 1998 Netscape Communications Corporation. All rights reserved. Protected by the copyright laws of the United States and international treaties.

Page 611.   Mary Meiser, "Survival Skill: Learning to Write the Essay Exam," *Wisconsin English Journal* 21 (1982): 20–23.

Page 612.   Linda Ellerbee, *"And So It Goes": Adventures in Television* (New York: Putnam, 1986).

Page 614.   Randall Popken, "Essay Exams and Papers: A Contextual Comparison," *Journal of Teaching Writing* 8 (1989): 51–65.

Page 614.   Michael C. Flanigan, "Processes of Essay Exams," manuscript. University of Oklahoma, 1991.

Page 630.   Susan Meyers, excerpt from an e-mail message, student writing. Reprinted with the permission of the author.

Page 635.   Jaime Finger, "Jaime's Single Reflection," student essay. Reprinted with the permission of the author.

Page 638.   Bruce Urbanik, "Reflective Letter." Reprinted with the permission of the author.

Index